Reading Heidegger
from the Start

SUNY Series in Contemporary Continental Philosophy

Dennis J. Schmidt, Editor

Reading Heidegger
from the Start

Essays in His
Earliest Thought

EDITED BY

Theodore Kisiel
and
John van Buren

State University of New York Press

Published by
State University of New York Press, Albany

© 1994 State University of New York

For information, address State University of New York
Press, State University Plaza, Albany, N.Y., 12246

Production by Diane Ganeles
Marketing by Fran Keneston

Library of Congress Cataloging-in-Publication Data

Reading Heidegger from the start : essays in his earliest thought /
    edited by Theodore Kisiel and John van Buren.
        p.   cm. — (SUNY series in contemporary continental
    philosophy)
    Includes bibliographical references and index.
    ISBN 0-7914-2067-1 (CH : alk. paper). — ISBN 0-7914-2068-X (PB :
    alk. paper)
    1. Heidegger, Martin, 1889–1976. I. Kisiel, Theodore J.
    1930–   . II. Van Buren, John, 1956–   . III. Series.
    B3279.H49R365   1994
    193—dc20   93-38957
                                                                    CIP

10 9 8 7 6 5 4 3 2 1

Contents

Acknowledgments

We gratefully acknowledge the permission of J.C.B. Mohr (Paul Siebeck) to publish a translation of Hans-Georg Gadamer's "Der eine Weg Martin Heideggers" from the third volume of his *Gesammelte Werke* (Tübingen: J.C.B. Mohr [Paul Siebeck], 1987), pp. 417–30. We would also like to thank Wolfe Mays, editor of the *Journal of the British Society for Phenomenology*, for permission to publish a revised version of George Kovacs' "Philosophy as Primordial Science (Urwissenschaft) in the Early Heidegger," which appeared in the 1990 issue, volume 21, pp. 121–35.

It was in 1990 that we first proposed this anthology to Dennis Schmidt, editor of the SUNY series in Contemporary Continental Philosophy. To him and to William Eastman, Director of SUNY Press, we are grateful for their support of both the present volume and a related anthology of Heidegger's shorter writings from his student years to the early thirties.

Finally, we wish to express our deep appreciation to our contributors and translators for their participation in this project.

Introduction

*Denkwege, für die Vergangenes zwar vergangen, Gewesendes jedoch
im Kommen bleibt, warten, bis irgendwann Denkende sie gehen.*

"Paths of thought, past and gone, yet in having been still in advent,
await a time for thinkers to ply them."
(Foreword to *Vorträge und Aufsätze*, 1954)

"For as you began, so will you remain" (US 93/7). This citation from
Hölderlin's hymn to "The Rhine" is about as close as the old Heidegger
comes to giving justification to the kinds of investigation embodied in the
following group of "essais," which "venture" to read Heidegger's vast opus
from the very start. The same "Dialogue on/from Language between a Japanese and an Inquirer" at once deprecates the texts transmitted from
those earliest beginnings, since the courses under discussion belong to his
"juvenilia" and so are "quite imperfect," and the student transcripts made
of them are "muddy sources" (US 91/6). Nevertheless, just as the old Husserl had "generously tolerated" the young Heidegger's penchant for the
Logical Investigations twenty years after their first appearance, at a time
when Husserl himself no longer held this early work "in very high es-
teem," so the old Heidegger was prone to "generously tolerate" the interest
in his own "youthful starts [*Sprünge*]" expressed by "the gentlemen from
Japan," by Otto Pöggeler, and even earlier by Karl Löwith, even though
one can "easily do injustice by them" (US 90f./5f., 128/35).[1] Nevertheless,
in the end, the old Heidegger hesitated to include his earliest Freiburg
courses (1915–1923) in the posthumously published *Gesamtausgabe* (Collected Edition), leaving the decision to his literary heirs. Yet it is these
texts in particular that warrant the maxim that the old Heidegger affixed
to his *Gesamtausgabe* shortly before his death, "Ways—not Works." Thus,
of the "quite imperfect" early course under discussion in the Dialogue,
Heidegger adds: "And yet stirring within it was the attempt to walk a path
of which I did not know where it would lead" (US 91/6). "The entire course
remained a suggestion. I never did more than follow a faint trace of a trail
[*Wegspur*], but follow I did. The trace was a barely perceptible promise
announcing a liberating release into the open, now dark and confusing,
now lightning-sharp like a sudden insight, which then again long eluded

1

every attempt to say it" (US 137/41). The following "ventures" to retrace these fleeting initial trails from one start to another (*anderer Anfang*)² thus themselves serve to turn the extant early works into ways.

The problem that the old Heidegger discovers in retrospect to be faintly stirring in the "startling [*erregenden*] years" (FS X) of his first ways, in the guise of early terms like "hermeneutics," is the topic (*Sache*) that dominated the last decades of his career, namely, that of the relation of language and being, or the question of the language *of* being. Indeed, he can point to the Scotus habilitation of 1915 as the place where the two poles were already thematized as separate questions, the question of being in the guise of the problem of the categories of being, the question of language in the doctrine of signification, or what Scotus called his speculative grammar. What was obscured, however, was the profound interrelation of the two questions (US 91f./6), whose very obscurity was itself left in the dark by the dominant authority of the doctrine of judgment then prevalent in every "onto-logic" (FS IX).

The same cluster of questions was already operative in the background of an even earlier start made by the young Heidegger, namely, his theological studies, through which he first became familiar with the term "hermeneutics." "Without this theological start, I would never have come onto the path of thought. But antecedents [*Herkunft*] always come to meet us out of the future [*Zukunft*], provenance always remains adventure" (US 96/10). It is this unique combination of starts, theological and philosophical, that spawned the unique line of questioning that the later Heidegger opted to pursue. "Not that I already knew then all that I am still asking today" (US 93/7). "In the meantime I have learned a bit more, so that I can ask questions better than I did several decades ago" (US 94/8). Nevertheless, operative in the background from the start "was the same relationship, namely, that between language and being, only veiled and inaccessible to me, so that I sought in vain for a guiding thread through many a detour and false start" (US 96/10). One such detour or dead end is *Being and Time* itself, Heidegger's major work of 1927, in which, in his later judgment, "I ventured forward too far too soon" (US 93/7). This master work, published as a fragment, was doomed to remain incomplete because of a "failure of language." According to the old Heidegger's own assessment, the path to the problem of language and being first struck in 1915 did not find its true bearings until his third academic course entitled simply "Logic," the one in SS 1934, in which his first public interpretations of Hölderlin developed into a deliberation on the sense of *logos*, which itself is still not the fitting word for the larger problem (US 93/8).

So much for the old Heidegger's sense of the relationship of his beginnings to his later thought. Suffice it to say that his own assessment of already published works, like the 1915 habilitation and *Being and Time*, varied according to the station at which he had newly arrived in the course of his own thought. "At every stop, the indicated way in retrospect and prospect appears in another light and another tone and evokes other interpretations" (FS IX). Thus, with the completion of the published version of *Being and Time*, the habilitation itself was understood as the start of the effort "to go all out after the fac*tic* in order to make fac*ticity* into a problem at all."[3] The dominant problem of this effort toward a hermeneutics of facticity becomes the "formal indication" of that facticity of our already "being here" willy nilly, already caught up in life and underway in existence. And this still very Scotian problem of "formal indication" is precisely the form that the problem of "language and being" took in the period in which the early Heidegger was under way toward his magnum opus, as a number of the essays below will point out. So there is more to the exploration of his first stops and starts than the old Heidegger's hesitant invitation warrants us to do. First of all, it is not at all clear whether the old Heidegger ever took more than a cursory look at the accumulated mass of unpublished papers from these beginnings, which are now gradually being edited and published by way of the posthumous decision recently made by his literary heirs. His very hesitation may perhaps reflect a clear sense on his part of how archivally imperfect the literary "remains" (*Nachlass*) of his juvenilia have been found to be: incomplete and missing autographs of the lecture courses, such that they have had to be supplemented from the start by sketchy notes and even "muddy" student transcripts; a complex note structure within the autographs themselves, whose assembly was perhaps no longer transparent even to Heidegger himself; incomplete records of sometimes pivotal seminar exercises; shards and scraps of loose notes out of chronological order scattered throughout his papers, likewise in need of clarifying supplementation, say, from his voluminous correspondence. It is this archival material, some of which may never be published, that some of the essays below have already applied in their venture to follow Heidegger from the very start.

We of course are in a very different position than Heidegger himself when it comes to appreciating his earliest starts. Witness the marvelling reaction in our lead essay by Heidegger's oldest living student, Hans-Georg Gadamer, in the first startling encounter with a side of Heidegger hitherto unknown to him, with the 1985 publication of the lecture course of WS 1921–22, the very first of the early Freiburg courses to appear in print. Against Heidegger's low estimation of his "juvenilia," Gadamer counters: "One must have the courage to admit that even a great man himself can underestimate his own brilliance and, above all, the rich promise of his beginnings. . . . I can imagine that Martin Heidegger himself might have found many new things in this text of his juvenilia had he been able to read it with someone else's eyes." It is therefore left to us to read these startling "new" texts from Heidegger's youthful opus in the new situation for the study of Heidegger created by their very exposition, starting all over again by finding new resonances in them appropriate for our time, traversing paths suggested by them left unexplored by Heidegger himself, retracing how Heidegger himself developed "the rich promise of his beginnings" in his more mature works, at times reading Heidegger destructively against himself, against his own express wishes, hesitations, and the depreciative, forgetful, and thus factually incorrect self-interpretation of his very first ways. This is the variegated task of reading Heidegger from the start and toward a new start to which the following essays are dedicated. They represent some of the first responses to a growing new opus that exposes hitherto unknown sides to Heidegger, and are driven not only by the ongoing publication of the *Gesamtausgabe* but also by new archival discoveries by independent researchers. The collection thus represents a cross-section of sometimes "differing" responses to the newly found texts and fragments by leading scholars in Europe and America. The gathering of these essays as chapters, organized into nine separate parts, is roughly chronological and topical to suggest both the progression of emergence of the topics and the sometimes conflicting interpretations and styles of interpretation of those topics in the present "hermeneutic situation" of the reception of Heidegger's work. The following schematic summary of these contributions seeks to further this sense of progression and regression in the twists, turns, and new starts of Heidegger's vaunted way(s), with the conviction that the conflict of interpretations will find its best resolution through a more intensive explication of Heidegger's start(s). Especially the old Heidegger, waxing autobiographical and not above self-romanticization, has given us a partial record of this plurality of early starts: the excitement over his reading list during the student years of 1910–14 (FS X), a religious conversion in 1917, the breakthrough to a hermeneutics of facticity in 1919 (GA56/57 73–75, 115–7), the sudden self-recognition in which "the scales fell from my eyes" in rereading Kant in late 1925 (GA25 431), and especially the startling "flash of genius" (*Geistesblitz*) in 1923, in the midst of a period of intense exegesis of Aristotle, when he first recognized that *ousia* for the Greeks means constant presence. The old Heidegger came to regard this "start" as the real beginning of his life's work, such that 1923 became the watershed year serving to divide his authentic opus from his juvenilia, which in part also accounts for his reluctance to publish the latter.[4]

I. Topic Indication Way

Needless to say, many an old interpretation of Heidegger's thought falls by the wayside with the revelations contained in the newly published texts from the early years. In our lead essay, "Martin Heidegger's Single Way," Gadamer goes so far as to find the "turning" in Heidegger's thought long before the usual "turning" that has been used to divide Heidegger into two Heideggers, an early and a later Heidegger. Ontological formulations of the single topic of thought like "It's worlding" and "It's happening by properizing" (*Es er-eignet sich*),[5] which already occur in the breakthrough "war emergency" semester of 1919, anticipate by at least a decade the official turning in Heidegger's thought, which should then be understood as a turning back or re-turn to incipient traces of the topic already present in Heidegger's first beginnings. There is therefore no radical break among the plurality of ways traversed by Heidegger's long career of thought. Even the detours, false starts, and deadends (*Holzwege*) are all but a continuation of a single path from the very beginning of his first ways. In turn, a central formulation like "formal indication" that is found only in his early thought, in which we find Heidegger already "wrestling" with the language of being, "formulates something that holds for the whole of his thought." This is precisely the invitation to concretize the indicated topic in our own way, demanding of each individual to carry out one's own fulfillment of the indicated topic (way).

Wooter Oudemans, in an essay that outspokenly differs with the usual "Heidegger literature," seeks to highlight the paradoxical extremities of this hortatory demand for individual self-enactment already operative in subtle ways in the very unpoetic texts of the early Heidegger. The essay is accordingly not about "Heidegger" (content sense) since what Heidegger himself is about is to point individuals toward the individualized philosophical asking (enactment sense) that arises from and turns back upon the full ownness of one's concrete facticity in its concrete world. The issue (topic, matter) is accordingly not what is declaratively said by Heidegger but rather whether the I here and now responds to Heidegger's protreptic indication to address its solitary "that" and to give this facticity its own and full "say." Oudemans explores all of the cryptically subtle nuances of these formally indicative strategies broached especially at the "totally mobilized" extremities of everyday representation (ruinance) and of everyday boredom.

II. The First Years of Breakthrough

Steven Crowell takes us back to Heidegger's earliest concerns, not just with logic but in fact with a "logic of logic," a "transcendental" (philosophical, ontological, phenomenological, hermeneutical) logic, by summarizing the nexus of questions that revolve around categories in their truth and meaning in the very Neo-Kantian period that culminates with the 1916 Conclusion of Heidegger's published habilitation. As Crowell shows, the phenomenological backtrack from truth as judicative correspondence to truth as demonstrative meaning, from category to world, from scientific theory to the "living spirit," from metaphysics to fundamental ontology, aided and abetted by the pivotal work of Emil Lask, is already underway in the 1915 habilitation. Heidegger's earliest logical works thus anticipate later developments, like the "ontological difference" (first in the guise of the Neo-Kantian impersonal *es gilt*, "it holds") and the ordering of the world according to human relevance (*Bewandtnis*). Logic is already assuming the form that Heidegger's more mature courses entitled simply "Logic" will fully develop, namely, that of an "original logic" or a "logic of origins" of fundamental concepts (categories) from the pretheoretical pragmatic life or "matter" of the historical world. But in late 1916, despite the initial release provided by Husserl's doctrine of intentionality, the hampering influence of the old "doctrine of judgment" (e.g., Lask's second book) upon Heidegger is still very much in evidence.

István Fehér also begins with the issues of the early logical writings in order to fully trace the complex "proto-hermeneutic situation" out of which Heidegger carries out his hermeneutic-ontological transformation of Husserl's transcendental phenomenology, with the help of elements assimilated from the life-philosophies of Dilthey and Jaspers. Thus, from early on, an anti-psychologistic "psychology" centered on the sense of intentional acts gradually transforms logic as the doctrine of *logos* into a concern for the being possessed by *logos* in all of its acts, namely, the human being, a concern that results in embedding logic first in a "hermeneutics of facticity" and then in an "existential analysis of Dasein." For example, Fehér finds a "hermeneutic logic of question and answer" already anticipated as early as the 1914 dissertation against psychologism. The postwar turns toward a radicalized sense of pretheoretical experience is tentatively explored in its two methodological phases, namely, Heidegger's halting transformation (1919–21) of received phenomenology into one more sensitive to a non-theoretical language growing out of life-experience at its origins (an account based in part on unpublished course transcripts), and his explicit deconstructive critique of Husserl (SS 1925) for still being too theoretical in his overly naturalistic description of the natural attitude of life. But since the primacy of the theoretical that still prejudices Husserl is not a modern development but rather goes back to the Greeks, the phenomenological quest for a more natural language also calls for the destruction of the conceptuality inherited from the entire history of philosophy, the study of which the ahistorical Husserl wished to eschew.

As Fehér indicates, the early Heidegger identifies philosophy with phenomenology and phenomenology with hermeneutical ontology. The essay by George Kovacs roots this lifelong question, "What is Philosophy?," in the definition it first receives in the breakthrough courses of 1919, namely, philosophy (phenomenology) as the pretheoretical originary science of life's origins. On the one hand radically separating philosophy from any concern whatsoever for worldviews, on the other, the full paradox of seeking to make it over into a wholly non-theoretical "science": both already signal the end of philosophy as it has been millenially understood. Kovacs at first characterizes this radical reconceiving of philosophy as the "search for a method" apropos of this wholly pretheoretical "matter" of philosophy. But, ultimately, matter and method become one as Way, so that the problem then becomes how to understand a matter that is always under way, in short, how to understand its being and our inescapable relation to this being, our incessant being under way in It and toward It. Thus, at the end of Heidegger's own Way, "philo-sophy" is no longer the original science, strictly speaking not scientific at all, not even philosophy, but "simply (poetic) thinking."

III. Destruction

Several of the essays point out how "destructive" Heidegger virtually from the start was in hammering out his own unique niche among the leading philosophical movements of the day, typically criticizing them for not following their most radical impulses, noting that historicism was not historical enough, that scientism was not scientific enough, that phenomenology was still too unphenomenological, etc. (cf. Fehér). By the opening day of SS 1919, therefore, Heidegger is explicitly defining the character of such an originary "Kritik" of all "standpoint" philosophies, a critique that is always positive by being attuned to the "genuine motives" of their problems, and making this positive critique an indispensable part of his phenomenological method (GA56/57 125–128). By the end of WS 1919–20, he clearly identifies "critical-phenomenological destruction" as the method of returning any and all presuppositions back to their origins in factic life experience, a procedure which in SS 1920 is also called "systematic deconstruction [Abbau]." We accordingly bring together three essays that especially thematize this staple of Heidegger's method both early and late.

Jeffrey Barash brings his unique perspective of intellectual historian to bear on the thoroughgoing destruction of Western humanism that the ontologically minded early Heidegger is already mapping out. The postwar cynicism over "Western culture" and its progressivist assumptions, popularized especially by Spengler's The Decline of the West (1918), receives its ontological expression in Heidegger's deconstruction of the metaphysical residue of Greek permanence and constant presence in modern "historical consciousness," insofar as it still clings to "the comforting illusion of the timeless presence of the past in the continuous development of an over-arching cultural and world historical context." The anti-continuity or anti-contextualist thrust of this destruction receives its more positive note in Heidegger's proposal to situate authentic historicity instead in the "repeti-tion" of the authentic meaning still implicit in the past in the light of the future possibilities of any interpreter of the past. But the mere continuity of repetition in the finite context of the singular Dasein oriented toward its singular future, based as it is on the discontinuity of an eschatological time borrowed from otherworldly Christianity, is too constraining for Barash in his historian's craft. The only "overarching" continuity that Hei-degger seems to allow, in what he later calls the history of Being, is the inauthentic forgetfulness which harbors the unthought human finitude from which future thinkers draw their own great thought. What Barash the historian especially misses, and what Heidegger's currently influential idea of the essential historicity of interpretation seems to disallow, is ac-cessibility to the past intentions of an author or historical actor within the linguistic horizon of a past sociopolitical context, and a contextual analysis of the circumstances that mark the reception and influence of such thoughts and actions. Such a critique clearly has immediate ramifications, for example, in the present historian's endeavor to understand Heidegger's Nazism in its incipience, influence, and consequences.

Beginning in 1922 (PIA), Heidegger repeatedly stressed that the cri-tique of history is always but a critique of the present. This critique of a tradition rigidified into "self-evident" public fashions of the present, like the ethnological rage for exotic cultures, is the only negative facet that Robert Bernasconi will allow in the otherwise thoroughly positive move-ment of destructuration to appropriate one's own past through repetition. He exemplifies the liberation from a constraining present and the expan-sive breakthrough to the future of the past by way of Heidegger's "phe-nomenological critique" (so still in SS 1927) of some of the traditional theses of being. Destructuring is here more a re-constructive genealogy that decides whether the "birth certificate" of our prevalent ontological concepts is genuine or illegitimate within the unity of a Western tradition that Heidegger tends to read in reverse order in tracking it back to its Greek sources. But only with the later Heidegger's rethinking of the his-tory of Being does it become clear that destructuring is more than geneal-ogy, since the tradition, once cleared, delivers us over to the unthought yet to be thought from it. This granting of access to the unthought is the ultimate positivity of destructuring.

Destruction and construction, the historical and the systematic, thus belong together in philosophy; they are the same. Philosophy is temporal interpretation through and through. Otto Pöggeler develops its positive thrust by emphasizing that destruction is always oriented toward the eschatological moment that is not at our disposal, that it appropriates its unique tradition in order to construct the site of the unique historical moment that would illuminate our time for those rare few who are ready to make the inaugurating leap (*Ur-sprung*). Destruction is to uncover "an orientation towards the moment, which alone makes destruction possible," inasmuch as the originating moment is "the most proper essence of time." Pöggeler's destructive analysis accordingly recites the litany of traditional forms of the moment: the Greek dialectical moment of sudden transformation of concepts, the Christian moment of decision, the Judaic crisis of discrimination within a temporal whole still accented by the ancient "passing," the forerunning retrieve schematized by the existential Heidegger, Nietzsche's moment of eternal return, Hölderlin's moment of divine hinting, the desacralized moments of the postmodern novel. This new philosophy pointing to the fitting moment is however not just an exhortation to existentiell decision, but likewise calls for a new formally indicative logic that not only formalizes the moment itself but also, by way of situating that inaugural moment in its fulness, schematizes the structures of all of the other temporal spheres in which the human being has to lead its life.

IV. The Retrieval of Primal Christianity

The young theologian Heidegger became a Catholic phenomenologist of religion and mysticism as early as 1915 and inclined toward the Protestant retrieval of primal Christianity by 1917. The archival record, still largely unpublished, suggests that his youthful interest in the atheoretical dimension of religious life not only became a proving ground for shaping his unique brand of the phenomenological method, but also provided direct parallels for that method which would get back "to the things themselves," such as the "reduction" implied in Eckhart's ascetic-mystical concept of "detachment." Thus, John van Buren points to biblical texts glossed by Luther as a source of Heidegger's own sense of *destruere* of the "wisdom" of the Greeks by way of the more factic life experience found in original Christianity. Probing deeply into Luther's texts and subsequent Luther scholarship, van Buren even finds the positive thrust of a destruction of ontology already exemplified in Luther's developing attitude toward Aristotle, who is at first vilified in his patristic-scholastic garb for cloaking Christian realities over the centuries with categories alien to them, but whose practical writings are then acknowledged for their telling penetration into the kinetic unfinished character of life experience. Much of the early Heidegger's own positive interpretation of Aristotle, as well as the vocabulary of his early courses leading up to *Being and Time*, like the strikingly idiosyncratic terminology in which the *ruina* (fall) of ruinance is couched in WS 1921–22, is in great detail traced back to the same Lutheran-biblical sources.

The power to schematize structures and formally order concepts contained in the formal indication, say, of intentionality, is graphically illustrated by the two diagrams on "becoming a Christian" that the teacher Heidegger sketched on the blackboard in the two religion courses of 1920–21. Such visual concretizations of the formally indicative method serve to highlight the degree to which the early Heidegger is already pondering the structural possibilities (and limits) of Indo-European grammars to express the experientially tensed character of being itself, in what Theodore Kisiel calls Heidegger's "grammaontology."

V. Aristotle

Heidegger gave his first postwar seminar on Aristotle in SS 1921, and did not miss a semester until the end of 1924 to submit various aspects of the Aristotelian opus to an unrelenting exegesis that was driven by the concurrent all-out effort to prepare a treatise on Aristotle for publication. It is out of this academic exigency that the plan and first draft of *Being and Time* came into being. We should therefore not be surprised to find that its two extant Divisions draw their manifestly pretheoretical paradigms of human disclosure from *Nicomachean Ethics* 6, the art of making things and using tools in the First and the prudential insight into self-referential human action in the Second.

Franco Volpi pursues this deconstructive retrieve of Aristotle's practical philosophy into *Being and Time* by developing Heidegger's ontologizing of praxis into the basic way of being human, such that "theorizing," traditionally the highest of human vocations, is reordered with "making" into a mode of concern, and both are made derivative to the praxis that Dasein itself is, structured as "care." This refiguration accounts in *Being and Time* for the shift in temporal priority from the present to the future, the prudential emphasis on "mineness," the radical distinction between Dasein and all other beings, and the shift from lucid self-reflection to perspicuous self-recovery down to the opaque levels of moods. The transformation is outlined by a series of correspondences of the specific concepts, like *phronesis* (prudential insight) "violently" understood as conscience, that Heidegger "translates" from Aristotle into his own temporally ontological frame.

Utilizing Derridean strategies of interpretation, Walter Brogan follows the same trajectory, with particular concern for the truth problem, by leaping from the very first Aristotelian "staging area" for the book *Being and Time*, the Aristotle Introduction of October 1922, to the very last, the course of WS 1925–26 on the logic of truth. In view of Heidegger's intensive development at this time, the last is virtually three "light years" removed from the first. Indeed, the Aristotle *Einleitung* embodies the very first intensive treatment of *aletheia* as unconcealment that we have from Heidegger. But in WS 1925–26, Aristotle's most fundamental form of truth, that of *nous*, is deconstructed to its very end, exposing the need to understand truth in all of its forms, the theoretical as well as the practical dia-noetic virtues, out of the phenomenon of time. Thus, in *Being and Time* itself, the eternal *nous* of the Greeks is for the first time re-placed by the "lighted clearing" (*Lichtung*) of original temporality, a novel term destined to play a pivotal role in the later Heidegger.

VI. Husserl

As Fehér points out, Heidegger's transformation of Husserl's phenomenology into his own brand of hermeneutic phenomenology, by way of the method of formal indication, is virtually complete by 1921. The first "ex post facto" overt critique (deconstruction) of the Cartesian Husserl's "concern for known knowledge" occurs in Heidegger's first Marburg course in WS 1923–24, "Introduction to Phenomenological Research." The second direct critique, following the same pattern by way of a detailed deconstruction of the Sixth Logical Investigation, and especially significant inasmuch as it is made to preface the penultimate draft of *Being and Time*, occurs in SS 1925. The following three essays pick up the story at that point. Their divergence suggests the need to examine all of the earlier archival documents in order to truly comprehend the complex phenomenological transition from Husserl to Heidegger from the start.

Daniel Dahlstrom traces Husserl's significant shift in the locus of truth from the valid proposition to the intentional relation between intention in absence and intuition in presence, where truth thus becomes their identification across time. Already utilizing word-play, Heidegger accuses Husserl of obscuring his insight by regarding this truth-relation (*Wahrverhalt*) as a fact-relation (*Sachverhalt*). Further methodological infidelity crops up in Husserl's unconscious reliance on the traditional concept of being as presence in regarding the natural attitude in a prejudicially naturalistic way. Yet this reproach is belied by the feature of empty intending in truth and being, which prevents Husserl's analyses of the preobjective

flow of internal time-consciousness from lapsing into the "prejudice of the
now." Heidegger's silence about such stark similarities with his sense of
time is in part excused by his fundamentally different ecstatic-horizonal
sense of time with its primacy placed upon a finite future.

Working out of the recent French discussion of the phenomenological
reduction, Rudolf Bernet compares the surprisingly similar structure of
manifestation yet distinctly different mode of accessibility of the "double
life" found, by way of the reduction, in both Husserl's transcendental subject and Heidegger's Dasein. Just as the reduction extracts the constituting
subject from its blind involvement in constituting the world, by way of the
intervention of the phenomenologizing "impartial spectator," thereby disclosing both constituting agent and its new-found observer, so the anxiety-
ridden Dasein is brought out of lostness in the Anyone and back to itself in
all of its solitude by the call of conscience, dividing the self into its present
inauthentic existence and its endlessly possible modification into authentic
existence. But Husserl's leap of reduction occurs by way of the overt will to
scientific evidence, while Heidegger's follows an unwilled "reduction" occurring by way of an unexpected event subjugating Dasein to a sudden
illumination in passage across a forced absence. Controlled methodological
artifice yields to more spontaneous "leaps and splits," like the malfunctioning of a tool and the crisis of the self. Finally, the anxiety-ridden Dasein
does not first offer itself as an object of a self-reflective gaze, but experiences its individualization in a self-affection that instead offers an inelucta-
bly prereflective phenomenon of enigmatic depth to endless exploration.
The impartial gaze of the spectator, by contrast, does not rest until the
manifesting object is given to it fully and in person.

Starting from the old Heidegger's own admission that Husserl's doctrine of categorial intuition first enabled him to reawaken the question of
being in *Being and Time*, Jacques Taminiaux energetically defends the
stark thesis that Heidegger's ontologizing of this Husserlian heritage,
whereby categorial intuition becomes the understanding of being, remains
intuitionist through and through. One has only to highlight the recurrent
references to understanding's "sight"—its transparent perspicuity of the
whole of existence, its attestation by the intimate cognitive insight of conscience, the eye's glance (*Augen-blick*) in the resolute clarity of the moment of vision—to measure the potential sweep of this thesis. The closer
we approach the full ipseity (its *solus ipse*) of the matter "itself," which
marks phenomenology's move of return to ontology, the more evident it
becomes that this must ultimately be an intuitionist and not a hermeneutic ontology. After the pattern of Husserl's First Logical Investigation,
Heidegger still reduces the everyday order of expression, indication, indeed
the entire symbolic order ever infected by absence, covertness, and impli-

cation, in order to return to the fully concentrated vigilance of the authentic self's simply seeing "itself," in a pure philosophical act of meaningfulness divested of any sign and mediating expression. The *logos* of phenomenology is ultimately not linguistic or hermeneutic, but purely and simply the self-visibility of self-showing.

VII. Back to Kant

The most seminal individual influences on the student Heidegger's initial development are Aristotle and Husserl, in that order. But when was Heidegger not also a Kantian by Teutonic osmosis, imbibing the very air (*Geist*) of the university that he attended as a student of the "Southwest German school of Neo-Kantianism"? Yet this atmospheric influence endures a period of relative latency as well as revolt during Heidegger's early teaching career, only to materialize unexpectedly in mid-course just before Christmas 1925, in a startling jolt of discovery and self-recognition that waxed enthusiastically through to the composition of the Kant-book of 1929. The nature of this revelation, its timing and duration, its motivation and tendency as reflected in its impact upon the final draft of *Being and Time* and upon the works that follow, are traced in the following two essays.

Daniel Dahlstrom distills the essence of Heidegger's phenomenological interpretation and critique (destruction) of the *Critique of Pure Reason*, during this period of two Kant-courses ripening into the Kant-book, into five central theses from Kant himself, unified in their anticipation, albeit timid and hesitant, of the themes of *Being and Time*. Counterpoint to Heidegger's "violent" reading is provided by the then current Neo-Kantian interpretation of the strange ordering of the first parts of the Critique, and of the original sense of the "manifold." For Heidegger, Kant's original "manifold" of "thick" time is a horizon-constituting succession that is preconceptual, unthematic, and given in intuition, not produced in a synthesis and confined to the inner sense, nor a mere series of nows or something empirically on hand.

Frank Schalow summarizes the same period of retrieval of transcendental philosophy around the dominant theme of finite transcendence, the new formal indication of Being *and* Time that now "makes possible" and grounds the earlier indications of intentionality and ex-sistence. He then wonders whether this new destructive retrieval truly supplements the earlier phenomenological retrieval of the experience of factic life or instead breaks and departs from it, whether, for example, the horizonal schemata of original time that objectify being itself for a new temporal science in fact lose touch with the old "It's worlding" of life in and for itself. Finite transcendence is explicated in its usual middle-voiced Kantian facultative manifestations of the self-affection of intuition, the receptive spontaneity of imagination and its schematizing of sensitized concepts that demarcates the horizon and leeway of manifestation of objects. But Schalow in the end also wishes to return to a metontology of the practical issues of "being here" by refracting the essence of freedom through the lens of Kant's account of moral respect.

VIII. The Question of Ethics

Heidegger's remarkable reticence toward this question over a long career eventually prompted Jean Beaufret's question, after the cataclysms of the Second World War, on the relationship of his ontology to a possible ethics. Even the young Heidegger was clearly interested more in "the true" and "the one" among the transcendentals of being and the Neo-Kantian scheme of values than in "the good." A repeated promise to pursue the latter was repeatedly put aside for more pressing aletheiological issues. The absence of an outspoken ethics is made all the more acute for us now, as we learn more and more about both the "ontic" and "ontological" career of this prominent native son of a Germany caught up in the thick of the world-historical events of our century.

John Caputo examines the early Heidegger's retrieval of primal Christianity and finds his reading of the biblical narratives woefully one-sided in favor of a tough-minded Pauline-Lutheran machismo, of taking up one's cross and resolutely putting one's shoulder to the heavy weight of life. What Heidegger misses in the biblical message is the tender-hearted dimension of *kardia*, mercy, lifting the burden of the enfeebled other who is afflicted and downtrodden, solicitude (*Fürsorge*) for the flesh of the suffering and disabled other, and the facticity of the pain of the other exercising its claim over me. For us earth-dwellers the remote essentialist ethics in the later Heidegger, for whom the staggeringly incomprehensible megadeaths of annihilation camps and nuclear holocausts are but grim spinoffs of the technological efficiency of global agricultural/industrial complexes, where the new global plague of AIDS meets its match in the global mobilization of medical demographics, clearly becomes even more insensitive to the concrete suffering subjects of actual history.

Inverting the implications of Emmanuel Levinas's critique of the absence of an ethics in a Heideggerian ontology thus subject to totalitarianism like all ontologies, Jean Grondin demonstrates instead that a presuppositionally attuned ontology of Dasein is in fact the overt rehabilitation of the radically ethical and practical from the start, in reaction to the overly theoretized epistemological and methodological bent of philosophies then current. The futurally conative "to-be" of care is ethically even more formal than Kant's *Sollen* (ought), and the tendency to fall from self-determination is akin to the young Hegelian "self-alienation." The latter adoption by Heidegger suggests that a formalization of the critique of ideology, its unmasking of the obstacles of false consciousness to the exercise of human freedom, is at work here. But the ultimate ethical thrust of all of Heidegger's formal indications is in their indexical exhortation to individual appropriation and self-actualization in accord with our differing situations. This ethical exhortation to our own occasionality, both individual and collective, is itself ontologically formalized in the existential of the call of conscience. The absence of a specific ethics is a reaction against the traditionally sharp division and fragmentation of disciplines in a philosophy that always must re-turn such divisions to the whole of experience. Thus the ethical motive in the later Heidegger expresses itself in the even larger concern of preparing a transformed dwelling (*ethos*) on this earth for the human being subject to the epochal destiny of technological nihilism. The utopian magnifications of such a messianic orientation, also reminiscent of the young Hegelians, may account for Heidegger's own political errancy, and indeed that of any philosophical ethics.

IX. Toward the Later Heidegger and Back

That "life," like being, "is said in many ways" was regarded by the early Heidegger not as a disadvantage but rather as a sign of its proximity to the "matter itself" of philosophy, and thus as a fitting and proper focus for phenomenology. In this spirit, in the breakthrough years of 1919–1923, Heidegger variously identifies his lifetime topic in terms like "life in and for itself," "factic life," and "factic life experience," while deconstructing its plurivocity in both the Greek and the Christian traditions as well as in current disciplines like *psych*ology and *bio*graphy. David Krell picks up the story at the juncture where "factical life" is terminologically re-placed by the ontological neuter, "Dasein" (SS 1923), while both looking forward to the bracketing of 'life' in the scare-quotes of *Being and Time* and glancing backward to its thoroughgoing phenomenological-grammatological exegesis in WS 1921–22. This frame provides a genetic perspective for examining the direction of the renewed deconstruction of 'life' in a more biological context in WS 1929–30 and during the Nietzsche years of the late thirties, as well as for Krell's own disseminative critique of Heidegger's critique of 'life."

John Sallis frames the tautological bond between truth and knowledge, and the related nousiological bond between knowledge and intuition (ergo presence), that are still intact in the Logic course of WS 1925–26, between the two final drafts (SS 1925 and March 1926) of *Being and Time*. Both drafts undo these traditional bonds by way of displacement toward a more radical truth that is not of knowledge but of praxis, not of oriented consciousness but of situated Dasein, not of insight but of the more circumspective sight of understanding. The regress is more specifically from truth to its condition of possibility in disclosedness, which Heidegger, by way of a peculiar doubling, also calls truth, originary truth. This doubling virtually writes the story of the later Heidegger, in the truth of art, in the history of being from Plato to Nietzsche, until the old Heidegger retracts the very name of truth for this unconcealment in 1964. But the double remains decisive as the granting of truth, and still calls upon us to *think* how this unconcealment "itself" (also a doubling?) is not of knowledge.

Will McNeill's deliberation on the ultimately "precursory" movement of hermeneutics and essential thinking provides a fitting climax to this series of essays that attempt to read Heidegger from the start, as well as to learn how and to understand why. For his reading of a late text by Heidegger at "the end of philosophy" compels McNeill to circle back and return to the very "onset" (*Ansatz*) of the question in *Being and Time*, inasmuch as all of the later Heidegger is but an attempt to recast that precursory question "more incipiently" (*anfänglicher*). Working Heidegger's *Denkweg* from one end to the other, from end to beginning and back, McNeill finds it driven by the same regressing forerunning movement back to a fore-structure of presuppositions and a preunderstanding governed by the ambiguous prefix "Vor" (pre-, fore), which is at once "before" and "ahead," precedented and anticipatory, such that one advances forward by stepping back, and one steps back in order to advance forward, back to the future. Since our heritage of "antecedents always comes to meet us only out of the future," McNeill finds that Heidegger's later thought is governed by a "futuricity" more radical and "earlier" than the future inscribed in originary temporality. Earlier than the "point of departure" provided by any of the series of formal indications demarcating the *Denkweg* is the initial "onset," the start, of questioning marked by the existentiell engagement of a Dasein that is in each case mine. This is the final message behind those peculiar philosophical concepts that the early Heidegger calls formal indications. And since all philosophical concepts are merely formally indicative, what where when exactly in this endless circling is the end of philosophy?[6]

THEODORE KISIEL

Part I

Topic Indication Way

1

Martin Heidegger's One Path

Hans-Georg Gadamer
Translated by P. Christopher Smith

This moment in my life moves me deeply, for only now that I have grown old am I able to be here—for the first time in my life. I was not at Heidegger's funeral because, as one with strong personal ties to him, I knew that he would have wanted to be laid to rest in the closest circle of his family. And there are other occasions, too, on which I might have come here but did not yet come. Thus I was delighted to accept the kind invitation of the Heidegger-Society. It is also an honor for me to speak in a circle of Heidegger's old friends whose lives bear witness to their loyalty to him and to their genuine intimacy with him: his sons, but also, for example, Medard Boss, whose medical wisdom surely had a part in the path of Heidegger's life, or Hermann Mörchen, who was one of the students who came to hear Heidegger in Marburg and whom I remember from a very long time ago. And I could continue—along the lines of the kindly greeting you have already heard from the acting mayor—and name still others among us, knowledge of whose attendance here presents me with a very special task.[1]

What I have to do in commemoration of the tenth anniversary of Heidegger's death is, it seems to me, clearly indicated by our new circumstances. And to that extent, the choice of my theme [the unity of Martin Heidegger's path] was not in any way arbitrary. To show this unity is, after all, the task that we, once again and now more than ever, must set for ourselves, now that the possibilities for bringing younger generations to the entirety of Heidegger's path of thought have been so enormously expanded by the new edition of his works. There is much to criticize in this edition, and I, who am, of course, a classical philologian, would be the last one not to know how many mistakes such an edition contains. Still it was, I think, a very wise decision on Martin Heidegger's part to make his contributions to philosophy, especially his lecture courses, available quickly to today's generation. Thus I must say that if this edition turns out as badly as the Hegel edition by "the friends of the eternal one," it will be excellent.

Indeed, the worldwide reputation of Hegel was not the result of his *Phenomenology* or his *Logic* but of the publication of his lecture courses, and it might well be the same with Heidegger. However this turns out, we should be aware that the publication of his lecture courses presents us with a genuine task.

For in the last decades we have passed through a peculiar period of latency or waiting, which, I might add, has cast its shadow not only over such a thinker as Martin Heidegger. No, the same thing has happened to such a poet as Rainer Maria Rilke, for instance, who is perhaps better known in the whole world than in Germany—or to such a poet as Friedrich Hölderlin. He, of course, will always be assured of a certain Schwabian loyalty, but nonetheless he stirred the feelings of German youth in much greater measure thirty, forty, fifty, sixty years ago than he does today. The all-revealing light of publicity has its concealing effects too.

In the context of a "sobriety movement"—what else should I call it?—in which one essays to surrender oneself completely to the spirit of technology that suffuses our contemporary and most recent past, any further thinking along Martin Heidegger's path of thought is a tall order, and one given to all of us in all generations. It is precisely the younger ones among us who will have to carry on with this assignment and raise Heidegger's work to the level of a living possession. In short, I believe that the situation now is a new one. A thinker like Heidegger always finds new resonances as the consciousness of an era shifts, and the chance of this is especially enhanced when new, if not unknown, works of his reach the public eye. In this regard I have in mind two recent changes in our circumstances.

First, there is the publication of Volume 61 [in 1985] in the new edition of Heidegger's works, prepared by Walter Bröcker and Käte Oltmanns-Bröcker [GA61]. I am most grateful to Hermann Heidegger and the others responsible that they so promptly decided the question left open by Heidegger, namely whether his courses prior to his Marburg period should be published. One must have the courage to admit that even a great man himself can underestimate his own brilliance and, above all, the rich promise of his beginnings. This Volume 61 of the new edition was my first encounter with this text and poses a task for me that as of now I have not even begun to complete. The text forms the first bridge between the developing Heidegger and his mature works. He himself would not yet have counted this text among his works, evidently because he believed that only in Marburg did he find the ultimate direction his path of thought was to take. Nevertheless, for us precisely this early lecture course is one of the most important preparatory paths in Heidegger's experience of thinking. I must confess that I felt almost miniscule when, a year ago, I read these lectures of a thirty four year old for the first time, and when, afterwards, I thought them through anew. I can imagine that Martin Heidegger himself might have found many new things in this text of his juvenilia had he been able to read it with someone else's eyes. After all, one of the great mysteries of human life is that one must make choices and, in choosing some things, must relinquish others. Not all paths that one is shown can be traversed if one wants to move ahead. Heidegger, too, had to choose when he moved ahead.

The second change in our circumstances is, of course, that this grand edition is bringing out the lecture courses after Marburg, which I myself did not hear personally, and that it thereby puts the path to his later work in a brighter light than has heretofore existed.

If I may say a few words about my own hermeneutical approach, so to speak, I am indeed the oldest of those students of Heidegger's who can bear witness to him today. And this constitutes an obligation to the extent that I can speak from living experience about things that virtually anyone might know. I am closer than all others to the intellectual situation in which Heidegger began philosophizing because I— be it my good fortune or misfortune—am somewhat older.

What was this situation? When my decisive encounter with Heidegger occurred, I was a young man and had just completed by doctorate in philosophy with Paul Natorp of the "Marburg School." For the entire time of my study with Natorp and with Nicolai Hartmann, the feeling had accompanied me that something was missing, a feeling whose ultimate sources very likely lay in my own nature and what I had experienced in my intellectual and cultural development, and a feeling about which I was somehow reassured when I met Heidegger. All at once I knew. This was what I had missed and what I had been seeking, namely the insight that philosophical thought should not consider history and the historicity of our existence to be a constraint, but rather that it should raise this, our very ownmost impulse in our lives, up into thinking. Later, on still another occasion in my ongoing encounter with Heidegger, I experienced similar reassurance. That was in 1936 when, having left Heidegger and taken up my own teaching responsibilities in Marburg, I travelled to Frankfurt to hear the three lectures on the work of art. This was a kind of second reassurance, for from early in my youth it had been one of my guiding convictions that the value of philosophical thought—and its lack of value—was to be measured against the nature of art.

This much, then, should be said of the personal experience that I take as my starting point when I attempt to describe the situation in which Heidegger began. Neo-Kantianism, which at that time dominated the philosophical scene in Germany, was characterized, on the one hand, in Marburg, by its ahistorical attitude and, on the other, in Southwest Germany, by its epistemological reductiveness in regard to historical experience. One must view the young Heidegger, and in particular the Heidegger of the course in 1921–22, in the light of this situation.

As an illustration of how the young Heidegger viewed the matter, I would like to quote the motto from the volume of these lectures edited by Bröcker. It is a sentence from Kierkegaard's *Training in Christianity* that Heidegger himself singled out for the book he had planned. Above it is written, "motto and at the same time grateful indication of the source." Then the text follows: "Modern philosophy in its entirety is based, both in regard to what is ethical and to what is Christian, on a mere bit of frivolousness. Instead of jolting human beings and calling them to order by talking of the radical doubt of despair [*Verzweifeln*] and by getting angry with them, philosophy has quietly beckoned to them and invited them to indulge the fantasy that they are doubting [*zweifeln*] and have doubted. The rest of philosophy floats, abstract, in the indeterminacy of the metaphysical."[2] This is the quotation that Heidegger himself felt had pointed him in the direction in which all his efforts were to go. We can see in it two things to which Heidegger wants to draw our attention. On the one side is the view that opens out upon the religious and ethical disquietude in which Kierkegaard articulated his own situation, in opposition to speculative idealism and its Cartesian foundations in "universal doubt" and the methodological ideal of certainty. On the other side, we see, as if it were said for today, that "the rest of philosophy" of that time floated in the abstract indeterminacy of the metaphysical.

When we attempt to make clear to ourselves what the first impulses were for the Heidegger of that time, it turns out that this expression of thanks to Kierkegaard fits logically into the path on which Heidegger then found himself, a path which, as the one path he took, lasted until the end of both his path of thought and his path of life. At the conclusion of his *Habilitationsschrift* we find the sentence, "This is what matters: as such, living mind and spirit is by nature historical mind and spirit" [GA1 407]. This sounds, of course, like a profession of allegiance to Hegel, and also like a quotation from Dilthey.

As far as Dilthey is concerned, we all know today what I have known for a long time: namely that it is a mistake to conclude on the basis of the citation in *Being and Time* that Dilthey was especially influential in the development of Heidegger's thinking in the mid-1920s. This dating of his influence is much too late. That it is, is ultimately made clear beyond a doubt precisely by the sympathetic evaluation of Dilthey's work that we find in *Being and Time*. Nor was Dilthey's influence any longer at its height when Misch's important introduction—praised by Heidegger—to Volume V of the edition of Dilthey's collected works, then nearing completion, appeared in 1924. No, it was no longer at its height even at that moment, epoch-making in its own way, when the correspondence between Count Yorck von Wartenburg and his friend Wilhelm Dilthey was published (1923), the correspondence that moved Dilthey once again into Heidegger's field of vision.

This moment I experienced in the closest proximity to Heidegger when I was a guest at his cabin during the stormy weeks of inflation in the fall of 1923. It was plain at that time that Heidegger, with deep inner satisfaction, indeed with an almost perverse delight, saw displayed in these letters the clear superiority of Count Yorck over the famous scholar, Dilthey. Now in order to feel this way, a precise familiarity with Dilthey's later work would have been prerequisite, a familiarity which obviously existed in Heidegger's case. As a matter of fact, Heidegger himself had recounted to me how burdensome it had been to lug home the heavy volumes of the Berlin Academy publications that contained Dilthey's late works, only to have to lug them back because somebody or other at the Freiburg University Library had ordered, not Dilthey's treatises, but some other piece in the fat Berlin Academy tomes. This has to have been sometime before 1920.

What Heidegger sensed when he read their correspondence, namely the superiority of Count Yorck, evidently Dilthey himself sensed, and this is truly to his credit. In Volume VIII of Dilthey's works we can now read notes that he wrote down after a nighttime discussion with Count Yorck. This was very likely the last time the two friends were together. There Dilthey finds the superiority of his friend so overwhelming that in comparison he himself seemed quite insignificant. The superiority, of course, was not superiority in the academic, but in the "existentiell," sense. Here was a genuine Lutheran. The Count had evidently confided to his friend that he was suffering from a terminal illness. The composure and steadfastness with which Yorck, then in possession of the fullest intellectual and spiritual life energy, foresaw his end, a relatively early end, had plainly moved Dilthey most deeply. Heidegger, too, recognized in the Count a genuine Lutheran by his rootedness in the soil and his committed involvement in a circle of life apportioned him. Anyone who did his thinking in this way, out of the context of his historical destiny, could easily rebuff the insanity of some new epistemological founding of the human sciences or of philosophy, and reject it for what it was.

None of this, of course, changes the fact that Dilthey's rich and stimulating life's work, despite its conceptual weakness, provided essential help to Heidegger in distancing himself from the systematic ideal of Neo-Kantianism, as Heidegger acknowledges in *Being and Time*. In starting from Dilthey, and in line with his own phenomenologico-hermeneutical turn, Heidegger could justify his doubts about the transcendental reduction and transcendental ego in Husserl's *Ideas*. Thus on the one hand, the philosophical significance Dilthey had for Heidegger at that time as a mediator between Hegel and the historical school does become clear. On the other hand, however, the impulses of which Kierkegaard speaks with such rigor and intensity in the motto quotation point up the critical distance that Heidegger was seeking from Hegel, and from Dilthey and Husserl as well.

The first lecture course of Heidegger's that I had heard, precisely in Freiburg in the Southwest of Germany, was listed as "Ontology," significantly enough, but it bore the subtitle, "Hermeneutics of Facticity." What this hermeneutics of facticity actually was could be guessed from the Kierkegaardian motto cited above. Certainly it went beyond even what Heidegger himself had taken to be the task of phenomenology, and beyond the things that had become paradigmatic for him not only in Husserl but in Aristotle too. This is not to say that the influences of Husserl, the founder of phenomenology, or of Aristotle—a very different Aristotle from the one Heidegger had learned in those years as a student of Catholic theology—were not of the very greatest importance for him. Heidegger had learned from both and had, of course, not only absorbed something from them but had also sought throughout to keep to a task of his very own. And these are indeed just the influences that are worth worrying about for anyone who is compelled to find himself in an encounter with someone else. Doubtless it was this way with Heidegger: the analyses of time in Husserl, for instance, but also his renewed encounter with Aristotle, put him on the path of his own thinking.

"Hermeneutics of Facticity"—the word 'facticity' is quite readily understandable for anyone with an ear for the German language (and he who has no ear for words does not know the concepts at which they aim). There is no doubt but that the concept 'facticity' was formulated in the dispute over faith in the Resurrection. This is how the word 'facticity' figures in Rothe and other theologians of the Hegelian and post-Hegelian generation. Of course when Heidegger uses the word, it had been given the quite different stamp which at that time the concept of 'life' and the irreducibility of 'life' had imposed on the word. Facticity refers, after all, to the fact in its being a fact, i.e., precisely the thing back of which and behind which one cannot go. In Dilthey (as early as Volume XIX of the new edition of his works) we find life characterized as such an irreducible fact. And surely something like this was the case with Bergson, with Nietzsche, with Natorp.

What, then, does the new program of a "hermeneutics of facticity" mean? Here explication and interpretation, which are, after all, the business of hermeneutics, plainly are not concerned with something that becomes an object by being interpreted. The "hermeneutics *of* facticity" is thus a possessive and not objective genitive, meaning "facticity's hermeneutics." Facticity lays itself into its own interpretive explication or laying things out [*Auslegung*]. Facticity, which lays itself out, which interprets itself, does not bring interpretive concepts to bear on itself, rather it is a kind of conceptual speaking that wants to hold onto its origin and, thus, onto its own life's breath, once it is translated into the form of a theoretical statement. In our lecture course we find a sentence that runs, "living = being-there [*Dasein*], being in and through living" [GA61 85]. If we think this sentence through, we have before us the unity of Heidegger's entire path of thought. Yes, there are indeed astonishing things in this early text. It is said there that life is worrying [*Sorgen*], that in its own agitatedness and being moved it is concerned with the world, and that it thereby follows a pattern of decadence [*Verfall*] all its own, and that in opposing itself it shuts itself off from itself. (The word 'Verfall' is not yet terminological, hence it is called 'ruination' here.) All this already sounds very much like the transcendental analytics of being-there in *Being and Time*. Life is inclination, tendency, eradication of the distance it has from what it worries about and procures. And in so living, it shuts itself off from itself in opposition to itself, so that it does not encounter itself. Plainly, in the facticity of worry [*Sorge*], the facticity of the eradication of distance, yes, in the facticity of the "haziness" of life, the task is posed of carrying out this thinking oneself, of becoming keenly aware of one's being-there and making it one's own.

I call to mind these well known points of departure in *Being and Time* that we already come across here in 1921, in order to raise a question that has almost been officially sanctioned as dogma, in particular by Richardson's meritorious book and his distinction between Heidegger I and Heidegger II: who is Heidegger before the turning [*die Kehre*], and who is Heidegger after the turning? The answer can best be clarified by what Heidegger himself says about "the ontological difference." I am reminded here of a scene in Marburg in 1924. After the lecture I joined my fellow student Gerhard Kruger in accompanying Heidegger on his way home. This has to have been still during the first year at Marburg, for the way did not yet lead through the south of the city to the Schwanallee, that is to say, not yet to his later apartment. We asked Heidegger what the "ontological difference" was actually about, for we had no clear conception of how one came to make such a distinction. At that time, 1924, Heidegger answered, "*We* do not make the distinction. That's not what we are talking about. On the contrary, the 'difference' is something into which we enter."

Thus, in 1924, the "turning" was there in a conversation. It was there too, I am convinced, in the first expression of Heidegger's that I ever heard in my life. A young student, who had just come back to Marburg from Freiburg, related with great enthusiasm that there a young professor had said from the lectern, "It's worlding" ["Es weltet" in KNS 1919]. This too was the turning before the turning. In this statement no "I" occurs and no subject and no consciousness. Rather, we experience expressed in it a fundamental structure of being, and expressed in such a way, moreover, that, like a seed, the world "comes up" [*aufgeht*].

Thus we must ask ourselves: taken as the fundamental experience of facticity, is not the tendency toward decadence in worrying life already *eo ipso* something like a turning away from oneself? In any case Heidegger already says here that, as living in the world, factual life itself does not really generate its own movement. Only by starting from its absorption [*Aufgehen*] *in* the world is the "coming up" [*Aufgehen*] *of* the world, the event [*Ereignis*] of the "there," encounterable, albeit, in the words of this course, as "relucent" to the ". . . plunge heading toward the world itself. That amounts to such an intensification of the plunge that it is carried out in the plunge itself in its own opposite direction." This is what we find on p. 154 of Volume 61.

With these references as a basis we might come to see more clearly why Heidegger says later, "For the thinking that represents, puts things in front of itself [*das vorstellende Denken*], being is encountered as ontological difference." That was the way Heidegger expressed it in the 1930s. We, certainly, should not merely repeat what he says, but know what is meant: namely that when we raise the question about being [*das Sein*] and when our concern is understanding being, then, to begin with, we have to take being in distinction from things that are [*das Seiende*]. The question about being can only be described within this distinction. Only late in his life did Heidegger dare to distance himself decisively from what he called the "language of metaphysics," and did he then speak of the "Ereignis" or "event" of "beon," and say that this event is not the being of things that are.[3]

Whenever I spoke of the later Heidegger I always emphasized that for him the "*Kehre*" or "turning" was a continuation along the same path. In support of this contention I believed that I could appeal to the Alemannic sense of "*Kehre*": when climbing onto a height-of-land the path is said to turn, *sich kehren* or switch back. I do not know to what extent this meaning of "*Kehre*" was really in the foreground of Heidegger's thinking, and perhaps whether it was is not so very important. Does one ever find negotiable paths in one's own thinking? Heidegger would indeed have been the last to describe his paths as paths always leading to a destination. Still, we find in the notes in the *Contributions to Philosophy*, which I was able to read in the meantime thanks to the kindness of Hermann Heidegger, that Heidegger himself linked quite diverse structural analogies to the concept of "*Kehre*," as well as the hermeneutical circle and all forms of circularity. Thus it seems to me that basically I was tending in the right direction: one moves on, and this, even when in truth one switches back, or is in a circle, or goes in a circle in which one always comes back to oneself again. Probably our tendency to go "back" is the actual schema that Heidegger started with when he began to speak of "*Kehre*."

But what is *vorstellendes Denken*, this representative thinking that places things in front of itself? Is thinking ever something other than placing something in front of us? Could we ever see differently the *deloun* or making plain that Aristotle, in the famous passage from the *Politics* [1253a 14–15], calls the accomplishment of speech? Does it not create presence, suddenly "there," near enough to touch, manifest now? Is there supposed to be any other kind of thinking at all? No, I believe, not strictly speaking. However, there can be another way of thinking besides the thinking in which *something* is thought of as present and grasped conceptually. It is necessary, I think, that we be clear about what is at issue here: namely that a particular way of thinking, thinking of what is as what is, has been tied together with the primal human capacity of thinking and speech to generate presence. And as a matter of fact this was the way Heidegger saw the Greek beginning. He saw that contained in it was putting-in-front, pro-duction [*Her-stellen*].

It was only quite late that I understood this. I remember that once I resisted Heidegger, and as a philologist I was not altogether wrong. (Besides, we always think we are right.) I objected that in truth *poiēsis*, making something, only came to be singled out as such in a particular circumstance of Greek thinking, namely once *physis* and *technē* were seen in opposition to each other. To which Heidegger replied, "Yes, but *Poiēsis* with a capital." As I now better understand, with the help of his later lecture courses and the *Contributions to Philosophy*, he meant by this that experiences of producing something had become firmly fixed in the conceptual words in which thinking had crystallized, so to speak. Among these, for example, are *logos* or collecting and gathering, and *hypokeimenon* or that upon which one can lay something. These basic concepts then found their most radically pointed formulation in the *logos apophantikos*, the statement, and in logic, and thus they provided the foundation for thought's total "placement" of the world [*Weltstellung*] a "placement" that was to become the historical destiny of the West.[4]

It is not excessive, it seems to me, to claim that here we find prefigured, as it were, the predestined path of Western civilization. That Heidegger recognized these, the very first beginnings, indeed distinguishes him,

in my opinion, from the grand succession of those thinkers who have
defined, who have taken the measure of, what it was that we human beings
in the West were destined to think. And he did this without hastening, in
the Neo-Kantian manner, to reconcile and equate the Greek beginnings
with Kant and transcendental philosophy—in the way, for instance, that
Natorp had turned Plato into a Kantian before Kant—and without believ-
ing himself, as Hegel did, to have found historical mind and spirit per-
fected in Aristotle's absolute presence of *nous* to itself. Heidegger saw that
the character of the West had been definitively prefigured for it in just
these decisive steps that were taken in the classical philosophy of Plato and
Aristotle, steps that also forced even the *kērygma* of Christianity into the
train of a scholastic logic. It is the language of conceptual logic that has
made the West what it is. Today, when the world seems to be approaching
a global unity, we might see how different horizons of the experience of
being, and different horizons of the interpretation of this experience, connect different horizons of thinking with our own. May we be so fortunate.
Heidegger himself noted something of this possibility in his "Conversation
with a Japanese" [GA12].

Here we should be aware of what first paths are like. When the young
Heidegger was seeking his path on which to think of being on the basis of
life, "in life, and all the way through it," he tried a lot of paths. As one
might expect, he took a hard look at Neoplatonism. He gave lecture
courses on Augustine. Courses on Plotinus were at least announced. And I
myself experienced the enthusiasm with which he greeted the 1923 publication of Meister Eckhart's *Opus tripartitum*. Thus the line of Platonism,
too, runs through the first of Martin Heidegger's paths of thought, until
he then chose his own path, or, better, until his own path drew him away
from these other paths. His later work shows that along this path lay
Leibniz and Kant and that ultimately Schelling played a decisive role and,
at the very end, Nietzsche. But by that time, out of the very Neo-Kantianism in whose circles the early Heidegger had moved, Hegel's thought had
begun to rise anew as the grand counterpart of Heidegger's own new
paths. Thus it came about that the figure of Hegel, always present for him,
loomed up before him obstructing his path and confronting him with the
singularly intensive challenge of trying to demarcate his own thought
from Hegel's. Plainly, on all these paths of the early Heidegger there stood
the question of the *Wesen* or nature of the divine. From early on *Wesen* no
longer meant *essentia* in the sense of the Scholastic concept, but rather
had that sense which Heidegger brought to life for us, and of which he
made us aware, according to which *Wesen*, in exceeding any limited presence, is a presenc*ing* or "*Anwesen.*"

One can go this far, I think, in describing the basic directions in which Heidegger I, the Heidegger before the turning, was tending, and then one cannot help but see what significance Nietzsche had for him and, at the end, what a challenge Nietzsche represented. To be sure, I mean only the Nietzsche who had arrived at his radical demands, i.e., not the thinker of the Dionysian *and* Apollonian but the thinker of the Dionysius who also contains even Apollo within himself in the movement of creation and destruction that ends at the self-dissolution of all knowledge in the "will to power." At the same time, Heidegger felt the new "push" of being, as he himself liked to call it, and out of this followed the reception of Hölderlin into his thinking and the motto of "another beginning."

The most direct knowledge of this "other beginning" is to be obtained from study of the *Contributions to Philosophy* whenever it is published.[5] For there one finds the formulations of the "first beginning" and of "another beginning" as a leitmotif. The manuscript is actually not the awaited magnum opus of Heidegger's that one thinks it is. Rather, it is a provisional anticipation [*Vorgriff*], conceived at a particular moment, of the life's work Heidegger planned but never completed. It is a giant programmatic projection in which early things, and the very latest things which we got to read only in the 1970s, and things from the early Heidegger which we are getting to read for the first time now in the 1980s, join with Heidegger's own publications to make a unified whole. But even if still at an entirely preliminary stage, this manuscript from the years 1936–38 is precious enough.

Now what is the story with this first and second beginning? I remember clearly how in Marburg Heidegger liked to speak of "what is on the whole."[6] Like the "ontological difference," this expression has a breath of near-mystical presence surrounding it. Expressed in this particular form, even the very turn of speech, "what is on the whole," already forbade combining any sort of conceptual formulations with the question about being it raises. Plainly, with this formula, "what is on the whole," Heidegger was seeking to avoid any and all thinking of "totality" or "absoluteness," any thinking of a universal, comprehensive concept of being. In this turn of speech, "being-in" very likely played a part too, an expression which was later to acquire its particular meaning in the expression *In-der-Welt-sein* or being-in-the-world. Surely Heidegger consciously and carefully chose this locution instead of following the normal German usage, "*auf der Welt sein*," or being on [*auf*] earth. He wanted to emphasize our being within something, our finding ourselves in a certain mood or condition, or at a certain place. For all of this makes it impossible for us to think of the entirety of what is, as an object. Plainly with this "what is on the whole" Heidegger wanted to characterize the *thaumazein*, the astonishment of the first beginning as it occurred in Greek thinking. It is "what is on the whole" that displayed itself like the appearance, in the twilight of the dawn, of an island in the Aegean. Nothing but appearance, nothing but presence.

Alongside this "first beginning" now comes the great task of "another beginning." This task is posed at a time in which the path of the West has led past the "correctness" of what is said, and led to the self-certainty of knowledge and of science, has led, that is to say, from *veritas* to *certitudo*. Heidegger called the modern way of thinking that has spread out from here into the last centuries, "abandonment of being" and "forgottenness of being," a thinker's way of preliminarily sketching in what the signals of technology in our epoch proclaim to us. How are we supposed to learn to think of "being" again when we have forgotten it? To be sure, this cannot mean that there is another thinking that no longer representationally places something in front of us, as if it were tangible, corporeal. On the other hand, the expectations with which we think and the intentions on which we act can indeed be different from the currently prevailing ones. We can doubt whether it is allowed us to aim only at taking possession of what is, in its being, to aim only at grasping it conceptually. Heidegger never spoke in any other way of the "transition" in which we find ourselves, i.e., of our being in the midst of our task of preparing for another way of thinking.

Certainly, if this remembering or commemoration is not just to be by single individuals, if it is to become a real way of thinking for all of us, it cannot come about again with some mere "astonishment" about "what is on the whole." Rather, as Heidegger proposes in juxtaposition to this, it must come about with what he calls *"Entsetzen."* And, as is characteristic of him, Heidegger means *"Entsetzen"* here in a double sense. (It is his manner, after all, to make words so articulate that they state both themselves and their opposites.) Thus in the *Contributions* he uses *"Entsetzen"* not only in the usual emotional sense of "horror" and "disgust" that we generally associate with the word, but, at the same time, in the military sense of "relieving" those under siege, of "liberating" them. The siege that holds us encircled is our ability to do and make anything, and the fascination this ability has for us. "Relief" from this siege must at the same time be the "horror" and "disgust" brought on by our technology having run amok, horror and disgust at this abandonment of being. Taking this seriously could be the first step in our liberation from the siege of our untrammeled ability to do and make anything at all, a siege pressing in on us from all sides.

Perhaps the most graphic thing of all that I have found in Heidegger's thinking is what he says about the abyss or *Abgrund*. This word surfaces now and then in the later writings where Heidegger is seeking deeper comprehension of the nature [*Wesen*] of the reason or ground [*Grund*], of the abyss [*Abgrund*], and of the underground [*Untergrund*]. The nature of the abyss can, I think, be quite easily portrayed. Let me appeal again here to all those who would administer Heidegger's heritage. Certainly, on the basis of any given expression of Heidegger's, one may and one should try to think for oneself. But one ought never to use Heidegger's words as if they were the kind of words we had thought of already. And it is that way with the abyss or *Abgrund*. What is an abyss? Plainly it is something whose depths one can never completely plumb, or better something that one can *only* plumb and never get to the bottom of. This, however, implies something else: at the bottom of the abyss there is ground, but of such nature that as we penetrate to it, this ground always recedes again, away from us and into the depths, depths at the bottom of which there is nevertheless ground.

When we bring this intrinsic self-explication of the abyss more sharply into focus, we see the outlines emerging of the real thinking the later Heidegger was destined to think. Again and again he leaned over the abyss and sought to get to the ground at the bottom of it. In his search for the other beginning, or better, in preparing for a thinking that could make another beginning, he tried to get back behind Aristotle's metaphysics and back behind Plato. In the earliest thinking of the Presocratics he believed he had reached the bottom and ground of *alētheia*, that he had reached the thinking of *alētheia*. For my part, I found the supposition quite unconvincing that it was Plato who had covered up this ground with his doctrine of the ideas, insofar as he substituted the thinking of correctness [*orthotēs*] for thinking of truth [*alētheia*]. Heidegger himself later revised this hypothesis. He saw that it was not first Plato but the primal Greek experience of being that understood itself in this way. In the search for this other beginning, he tried calling up Anaximander and Parmenides and Heraclitus, in that order, only to be forced in the end to admit to himself that this beginning constantly receded, just as the ground at the bottom of an abyss constantly recedes when one tries to plumb it. This was the way Heidegger's experience of getting back to the first beginning looked, and so too, consequently, the search for another beginning, any attempt at which presupposes getting back to the first beginning. This seems to be the lesson or, better, the vision that emerges here: namely that there is no such thing possible as getting back to a first beginning. On the contrary, any getting back is rather more a ball played back and forth [*Zuspiel*, a soccer term] between the search for another beginning and the search for the first beginning. In the end, something like a space of time becomes clear and visible in which the temporal destiny of the West articulates itself in a single, grand "epoch," as it were, as that *Schickung des "Seyns"* or the destiny that *"beon"* has sent us. Heidegger lets us divine something of this in his late treatises.

I would not want to close, however, without emphasizing two things more. When Freiburg University celebrated its jubilee, Heidegger gave a lecture, which received a great deal of attention, on "Identity and Difference." I remember how on the evening before, as we took leave of each other, he said to me, "I am eager to know what will happen tomorrow." This did not mean, of course, that he believed that through his lectures or talks he could achieve some sort of widespread effect that would, so to speak, open the path into a transformed thinking. Heidegger was not like that. I have often asked myself since then what he really meant—when reading this lecture even more than when hearing it for the first time. The conclusion I came to was that in this lecture Heidegger was trying to think the nature of technology and the technical anew, which is to say, not only as being's abandonment, but also as being's final presence. This seems to me to follow, first, from the fact that in this lecture Heidegger speaks of humankind's and being's reciprocal challenging of each other and that he sees the actual event [*Ereignis*] here in just this reciprocal challenging. And, he continues, ". . . the path would then be open on which humankind will experience more inceptively what is, more from at the beginning: namely the whole of the modern technological-technical world, nature, and history, and above all, their being."[7] In other words, if I may risk a play on words of my own, the path will be open once we have placed the entirety of what we have placed in front of us, *das Ge-stell*, back where it serves to open the path and not where it shuts it off. This possibility, it seems to me, is inherent in the nature of the technological-technical *per se*. And this would be a transformation of our way of thinking that is not merely postulated in private by a Professor Martin Heidegger, but that grows out of global civilization's confrontation with its future.

I do not wish to go into more detail at this point, rather to say only this: for some centuries now an ever-greater disproportion between our knowledge and capabilities, on the one hand, and our *praxis* in that deeper sense of being-in-the-world, on the other, has, like a cloud, been coming in over us. Our survival will depend upon whether we find the time and the will to diminish this disproportion and to tie our capabilities back to the limitations on our being that destiny has assigned us, and thus to rein them in. This, I think, Heidegger saw with the vision of a native son and citizen of Messkirch, one who took note of the world only selectively but who penetrated everything with such power of thought that he anticipated the things we, perhaps more passively than actively, are slowly experiencing.

Finally, let me say a word bearing directly on this Society and our tasks. All of us should ever be relearning that when Heidegger spoke in his early works of "formal indication" [*formale Anzeige*], he already formulated something that holds for the whole of his thought. At issue here is something decisive for the entire enterprise of his thinking. The inheritance of phenomenology's concepts of "seeing" or, respectively, of "evidence," and the "fulfillment" towards which phenomenology, working the way it does, is under way, takes a new turn here into the "existentiell" as well as the historical. Plainly, the expression 'indication' tells us that here no claim is being made to have found a concept, to have grasped something conceptually. The concern, then, is not eidetic universality in Husserl's sense. An indication [*Anzeige*] always stays at the distance necessary for pointing something out [*Zeigen*], and this, in turn, means that the other person to whom something is pointed out must see for himself. Here the "problem of concretization," which even in the 1920s was basic to the critique of idealism, receives a new formulation. Heidegger uses a word for this that at first I could not get a handle on. He spoke of "savoring something to the full" and "fulfilling," and expatiated on "savoring to the full" with a thing's taking on contours in "being set off from its background" [*aus ihm herausheben*] (see vol. 61, p. 33).

First, in starting from Heidegger's later talk of the abyss and the ground, I tried substituting "to plumb to its depths" [*Ausloten*] for "to savor to the full" [*Auskosten*], but this was mistaken, given the level of conceptualization in this course. The semantic fields that Heidegger brings to bear here, on the initiatory character of the indication and on its fulfillment, are plainly "foretaste" and "savoring to the full," on the one side, and, on the other, something's "not yet being set off" [*Unabgehobenheit*] and its "being set off" [*Heraushebung*]. In both these fields of meaning, "empty," in the sense of "formal," is juxtaposed to being filled. But the point is that what is initially "empty" leads directly into the "concrete."

Here we detect traces of the basic attitude in phenomenology which Heidegger amplified with his concept "destruction." Taking down whatever covers something up, whatever has rigidified, whatever has become abstract—this was the great passionate appeal in Heidegger's beginnings and his defense against that "ruination" of life which he was later to call the proclivity to decadence and fallenness [*Verfallenheit*] in our being-there. The task is to resist the tendency to turn something into dogma. Instead, we are called upon to grasp in our own words, to put into words, that which we are shown when we are given an indication of something. The "formal indication" points us in the direction in which we are to look. *We* must learn to say what shows up there and learn to say it in our own words. For only our own words, not repetitions of someone else's, awaken in us the vision of the thing that we ourselves were trying to say.

The young Heidegger, and not only the later, makes enormous demands on us. In the text of 1921 we find, "'Formal' renders the initiatory character of carrying out the temporal fruition of the original fulfillment of the thing we are given an indication of" [GA61 33]. Younger readers might take the measure of how little the audience at those lectures understood! Such is the way one who sees something wrestles with language. But when we have immersed ourselves in these things and taken to heart that what formal indication is describing in this way is itself a formal indication, then what was important to Heidegger comes into view: namely, that it remains for each and every one of us to carry out individually our own fulfillment of the thing of which we are given an indication.

2

Heidegger: Reading against the Grain

Th.C.W. Oudemans

Reading Heidegger's work is im-possible. This work is a challenge to interpretation, assimilation, mimetic reproduction. At the same time it resists every rapprochement, not however for being mysterious or profound. This resistance has its own formal nature, as it in no way obstructs the literary and philosophical assimilation of Heidegger's thought. No passages in Heidegger's work can be pointed out that oppose the literature on Heidegger, or that are overlooked by this literature. Yet the entire Heidegger-literature bypasses Heidegger in a specific way. When this happens, this literature is *against* Heidegger. No matter how multifaceted and correct the interpretations of Heidegger may be, they still leave "something" untouched through their way of asking. This "something" cannot be indicated in any specific regard. A curious indifference encircling the Heidegger-literature manifests itself.

In his early Freiburg lecture courses, Heidegger warns his readers against any philosophical and therefore literary reception of his work. *"Man ignoriere lieber das Buch, als daß man darüber das heute übliche fade Geschreibe und Gerede mache, das seit langer Zeit bei uns blüht"* ("It is better to ignore the book than to produce the usual insipid scribbling and chatter that has been flourishing in our midst for so long.") All of this is literature (GA61 193, cf. 70). This does not mean that my intention now will be to write about Heidegger in a way that is interesting or fascinating. In all writing about lies hidden the nature of literature. All literature about Heidegger reproduces Heidegger, argues something, divides his work into periods, places his work in time, criticizes it—and is therein surrounded by indifference.

What remarkable phenomenon is this, that a cloud of oblivion, the dying breath of *Vorhandenheit* (presence-at-hand), has shrouded all secondary literature about Heidegger? In order to answer this question, we must first of all obtain clarity about the formal resistance that Heidegger himself presents to interpreting his work. At the outset of his thinking he points out that his work is in no way a continuation of the philosophical

35

discourse of western tradition. For in this discourse something general and definite is established.[1] In Heidegger's work nothing is established. It therefore has neither objectivity not subjectivity. No discussion is possible about the "findings" of this thinking, since it does not argue for or against any proposition.[2] In recognizing the finitude of knowledge, fundamental-philosophical thinking has abandoned the pretence to absolute knowledge and the construction of philosophical systems. It does not follow, however, that fundamental-philosophical thinking is relative or perspectival. This thinking assumes no standpoints.[3]

If Heidegger's thinking is not thinking about but, as will be pointed out, shifts within the movement that is inherent to any thinking about, then any interpretation of Heidegger that speaks about his work has already moved away from it, has vaulted over it. That also applies to any division of this work into historical periods, as can be seen, for instance, in the title of the collection in which this essay appears. As soon as mention is made of the "early" Heidegger—whether he is opposed to the "later" Heidegger or placed in a continuum with him—Heidegger is positioned; in other words, he is an object of comparison: a re-presented subject.

If Heidegger's work has no object of conversation and cannot be an object of conversation, this thinking can have no significance in any traditional-philosophical sense whatsoever: it leaves the history of philosophy to itself, and from beginning to end it is detached from any worldview (*Weltanschauung*), from any contribution to humanity, to values, and to culture.[4] As a contribution to academic discourse understood as a value of western culture, the Heidegger-literature has already moved away from the horizon encompassing his thinking.

Not only can no object of this thinking be found, it is equally impossible to speak of a subject of this thinking, or of its addressee. The "author" of this work is not "somebody," a "person" called Heidegger. The only sense in which we can speak of an "I"—and this appears from the beginning of Heidegger's way (*Weg*) of thinking—is by pointing in the direction of "somebody" who is not yet there, who only becomes what he is in the concrete enactment of fundamental-philosophical questioning.[5] It is impossible to call Heidegger a philosophical author. As for the copyright and biographical side, "Heidegger" is of no significance, for this name is nothing but a sign along a way of thinking, a sign that is erected in treading the road and only then points the way. And who is being addressed? The "we" in which every philosophical discourse is necessarily embedded, does this indifferent "we" belong to the horizon that Heidegger points to? (See GA65 48.) Heidegger addresses neither humanity in general, nor a specific humanity (*Menschentum*), no philosophical or academic community nor even a human being as "we" know it.[6] "We" read in the *Beiträge*, "No one understands what 'I' am thinking, because every one understands '*my*' attempt by tying it to what has gone before [*Vergangenes*] (and in so doing, leaving it to indifference). And whoever will understand '*my*' attempt does not need it" (GA65 8). The essential question is, what do these inverted commas mean?

Only a metamorphosis (*Verwandlung*) of author and reader, a breaking-through to the supposedly necessary solidarity of the "we" of philosophical discourse, makes the writing of Heidegger possible as well as "our" answering to this possibility. This metamorphosis breaks through every communality and generality of philosophical discourse. Listening to this thinking takes place in the utmost loneliness (*Vereinzelung*), which admits of no communication and hence no mimetic reproduction whatsoever (GA45 199).[7] The question is how this metamorphosis of writer and reader can occur. In short: how is it possible to answer Heidegger when he refers to himself in inverted commas, when he speaks of *Sein und Zeit* as "*dieses 'Buch*'" in inverted commas (GA65 284)? How to read written words that do not constitute a book? And: how am I going to be the reader of this "book"?

The aporia of not knowing where and how to begin with Heidegger is needed in order to get into his way of thinking at all, which is to experience and articulate its im–possibility. The place where this aporia arises can be found in a fundamental "against." In a way Heidegger is against philosophical literature, the Heidegger-literature is against Heidegger, this article is both against this literature and against Heidegger. But this "against" will also have to contain the possibility of the exponentially expanding literary philosophy in such a way that the formal character of this "against" becomes clear. Since this "against" cannot be pinned down, cannot be followed back to an inaccuracy, an exchange of perspectives or a philosophical controversy, it is not to be understood as an *anti*.

Thinking against the Heidegger-literature and against Heidegger is not academic-philosophical "disproof" or "criticism"; it is taking seriously the datum that Heidegger does not speak about whatever it may be, and that therefore talking about Heidegger is im-possible, when nonetheless writing "about" as a mimetic reproduction of indifference belongs essentially to Heidegger's thinking. Writing against Heidegger is a continuous and tenacious repulsion of the possibility—never to be ruled out and by its nature lying in this work itself—of reading this work as a contribution to philosophical literature.[8]

If this article concerns the "early" Heidegger from the early Freiburg lecture courses (§ 1) through *Sein und Zeit* to *Die Grundbegriffe der Metaphysik* (§ 2), then this is not to point to a development in Heidegger's thinking, or to state that he stands his "ground"; nor is it to "solve" "problems" in the interpretation of his work. The choice of texts has been determined only by the formal enquiry about the possibility of access to Heidegger's thinking, a thinking that itself exists in no other sense than in finding access to "that which is." In a fundamental sense, the texts chosen here are of a methodical nature, and therefore steer away from the unavoidable thought that *Sein und Zeit*, as a transitional work, should be a philosophical book with philosophical standpoints. What the *Beiträge* says must be adhered to *against Sein und Zeit*: *"Alle 'Inhalte' und 'Meinungen' und 'Wege' im Besonderen des ersten Versuchs von 'Sein und Zeit' sind zufällig und können verschwinden."* ("All 'contents' and 'opinions' and 'ways', particularly of the initial attempt of *Being and Time*, are accidental and can disappear") (GA65 242). The question whether I here and now really answer Heidegger's indication of what constitutes proper understanding can only be sharpened in the actual writing of this article: *"Wirkliches Verstehen bewährt sich nie im Nachsagen, sondern in der Kraft der Überleitung des Verstehens in ein wirkliches Handeln, in objektive Leistung, die keineswegs und gar nicht in erster Linie in der Vermehrung der philosophischen Literatur besteht."* ("Real understanding never proves itself in rote-saying, but rather in the force of carrying understanding over into real action, into objective performance, which never and in no way consists in the first place in adding to the philosophical literature") (GA29/30 434).

1. "against"

The question that must become concrete and thereby more sharply pointed is: how to respond to the *factum* that Heidegger's thinking merely concerns thinking itself, but is not meta-philosophical self-reflection in any sense? In their emptiness, self-reflections are pervaded by the indifference of *Vorhandenheit*. How to find the way to the thought that the *Gegenstand*, the ob-ject, of fundamental philosophy is nothing but "having" this *Gegenstand*? The *Fragwürdigkeit* (question-worthiness) of philosophy consists of this having itself (GA61 19). The *Gegenstand* of philosophy is a *Gehalt*, but *Gehalt* is not content; rather it is being gripped by the asking itself, i.e., a hold. It consists of getting involved in the asking as a having-to-do-with (*Bezug*). In a provisional formal sense, it can be seen that the asking must become bound up with "that" for which it is asking. It must become held fast by it, *gehalten*: *"das Etwas, wozu das Verhalten ist, ist das, was der Bezug bei sich hält, was von ihm und in ihm gehalten ist.*" ("The something, towards which comportment is, is that which the having-to-do-with holds to itself, that which is held by it and in it") (GA61 53). For the time being, these indications are void, they "do not say anything." They indicate that the subject of philosophical asking is not ready to be discussed, but "becomes" only in and through the asking. The asking will have to become concrete, i.e., will have to become bound up with its "subject." This bond begins to reign in the articulation of asking, i.e., in reading and in writing.

How to get involved in Heidegger's thinking? Where to begin? It seems as if a beginning can be made anywhere and nowhere. An enigmatic *factum* is here: that this aporia reigns, that there is something like the impossibility of asking. This *factum* is enigmatic, because there is no situation for this asking. It cannot be understood why describing and explaining the world as the totality of re-presented entities should stop anywhere, could meet with resistance at any point whatsoever. Re-presenting as describing, clarifying, interpreting, changing, experiencing, securing is limitless in principle. In re-presentation as the way of being of all deeds, knowledge, and experience, there is an "and so on" that can move from one entity to another without any notable transition or delay. We board the train, talk to other people, call the dog, watch the sunset; we attend a lecture on philosophy, after which we go to a pub. In this extreme variety of possibilities for encounters there is a steady public openness: there is no resistance in the transitory character of the re-presented. The limitlessness of presence indicates the everydayness of all life, those things that concern "us" people every day, that indicate the day-side of presence: the absence of basic darkness or resistance in the "and so on."

The movement of everydayness is the easy transition from one entity to another. This ease is further enhanced when it is understood that in this transience there is an augmentation (*Steigerung*): the transitions fan out and accelerate. The explanation, control, and experience of present objects progress, extend over ever new areas, enlarge, branch off. The entities, people included, are taken along in the movement of total mobilization.[9] The mobilization has not been manufactured and cannot be stopped. The objects and subjects re-presented are taken along in it, are involved in this movement beyond their control. That is why the mobilization is called "fall" (*Sturz*) in the early Freiburg courses, while the sense of it, which contains the possibility of understanding it (*Verstehen*), is called *Ruinanz* (ruinance). When being swept along in the mobilization is called "fall," there is then the question of where the fall comes from and where it is broken, in short, where it meets with resistance. The answer is: nowhere. ". . . *der Sturz ist lediglich und nur Sturz. Es gibt für diese Bewegtheit als*

*solche keine Aufhaltbarkeit von etwas her, das von anderem Gegenstands-
und Seinscharakter wäre als es selbst.* The fall is simply and only the fall.
For this movedness as such there is no haltability from out of something
that would have a character of an object and being other than its own"
(GA61 145). This implies that the fall does not move in the direction of
something else. No limit has been set to the progress, not even in the
sense that interpreting inseparably belongs to the movement of falling.
Everything present already belongs to presence (GA61 134; GA63 53).
Presence means already having been interpreted: an indication of *Ruinanz*,
in which literature, as well as the Heidegger-literature, is included.

     Now it cannot be seen how there can be questions about this move-
ment; there is no position to be taken outside this movement. It is utterly
unclear how an "against" could ever appear in regard to this all-embracing
movement. *And yet there is the factum of the possibility of philosophically
asking about this movement.* There is something like *"das interpretative
Nachgehen und Verfolgen des Richtungscharakters der Ruinanz"* ("the interpretive follow-up and pursuit of the directional character of the *ruinance.*"). But interpreting is already involved in this *Ruinanz*, which is a
"moment of the movedness" (*Bewegtheitsmoment*) of the asking itself.
With that, however, asking is not simply ruinant, it is *sturzbildend*, it
develops, articulates, accentuates the fall (GA61 149). Asking is not outside
the movement of falling, but furthers its movement, is an augmentation of
it. But if asking augments the movement of falling, then it is "something"
within that movement which is even stronger than that movement. Then
the *factum* of asking is a formal breach made in the well-rounded nature
of re-presentation (GA61 151).

     The question is, what is this breach? The philosophical asking does
not detract one iota from the limitlessness of re-presentation—it is a
"Steigerung" of it (GA61 136, 139, 154). Philosophical asking takes the
progress of re-presentation to the extreme limit [ἔσχατον].[10] The "breach"
in the limitlessness of re-presentation is not a restriction of it, but the
possibility that the limitlessness of re-presentation is increased to the utmost. This "utmost" is a formal emptiness that pervades and embraces the
limitless re-presentation.

     The formal emptiness appears in nothing other than the *factum* of
the possibility of asking, more specifically in the confrontation of asking
with the absence of its own necessity.[11] There is no grip to be found for
this asking, it gropes around in emptiness, since there is no place outside
re-presentation. *And yet the asking is there.* The only thing that asking
can do is to hold on to its own emptiness, to move within it. This seems to
indicate that formal emptiness itself includes the possibility of philosophical asking, but this possibility is and remains empty—it is an im-possi-

bility.* In a formal manner the emptiness keeps the asking away, whereas the possibility of asking lies only in this staying away. Only in abiding by this staying away can asking take place. Thus formal emptiness binds asking to itself. Only by holding onto this bond, by allowing the formal emptiness of asking to be directional for asking, can there be asking at all. The formal emptiness is directional, signalling; it is binding for the asking (GA61 33).

The formal emptiness is empty and yet it binds, because it allows for a movement to be experienced—the movement of the necessity of asking being kept away. This staying away of the necessity of asking is the nebulosity enveloping the limitlessness of re-presentation. The staying away of asking ensures that re-presentation can go on limitlessly. When asking enters into this staying away, it serves to bring *Ruinanz* to its extreme limit, the extreme limit that shows that re-presentation is well-rounded, is a whole in a singular way. This well-rounded nature appears in the philosophical thought that there is nothing but re-presentation. Outside re-presentation there is "nothing," there is "emptiness." But the thought that there is nothing but re-presentation is not itself re-presentative. This is a sign that the well-rounded nature of re-presentation can only emerge in an emptiness that stays away. When the well-rounded nature of re-presentation is mentioned, then thinking has lifted itself above [*herausheben*] the limitlessness of re-presentation, without getting outside it. It is here that formal emptiness speaks, the formal emptiness in which re-presentation as a whole rests. But re-presentation vaults over this staying away in which it rests. Only in this way can it be limitless and measureless. But then formal emptiness is the absent limit and measure of re-presentation, that to which it is bound.[12]

Here the following datum appears: re-presentation cannot reach itself—it can only relate to itself in a re-presenting way. Any reflection about present objects, any self-reflection of the subject, is already pervaded

---

*An editorial word of caution is warranted at this point to avoid confusion between the frequently hyphenated "im-possibility" and straightforward "impossibility." Im-possibility refers to the intertwining inner conflict and sameness between possibility and impossibility that Heidegger has uncovered in originary temporality (cf. SZ), the possible impossibility "and" impossible possibility that can never be fulfilled in a presence. This paradox of originary temporality points to the hidden dimension in this essay that is never mentioned therein, which is concerned with a formally indicative ex-hortatory discourse that seeks to say the traditionally unsayable [*individuum est ineffabile*] found at the extremity of solitude. For Heidegger, such an indexical discourse becomes possible because solitude (*Einsam-keit*) is at once a gathering (*Sammeln*: US 61), the very con-cretion of the taut extremes of originary temporality. (T. K.)

by *Vorhandenheit*. Thus re-presentation is interposed between itself and the access to itself. Re-presentation cannot reach its limit. Re-presentation keeps something away. This means that, according to its very own nature, it is against itself, namely, there where it derives its measure from itself, its measure being that in which it rests as re-presentation. Formal emptiness as measure stays away. The limitless nature of re-presentation is against its own limit; but there is no shortage or want in this "against."

In the 1921–22 course, this is explained as follows: life is inside *Ruinanz* in the sense of being taken along from one meaning to another. It is bound to the movement of this tendency, which scatters itself everywhere and fortifies itself limitlessly. Thanks to this total mobilization of everydayness, of living *"in den Tag hinein,"* from day to day (GA61 101–102), re-presentation can absorb everything. Life is settlement of distance in a hyperbolic increase (GA61 104). But in this movement of settling distance, life shuts itself off from the possibility of coming towards itself. The limitlessness of re-presentation and or re-presenting oneself is a mask, a formal blindness.

The limitlessness of re-presentation masks the extreme line in it, the de-limiting measure. Consequently the hyperbole (excess) of progress is at once an ellipsis (defect), a staying away. Strangely enough, the limit within limitlessness is not a restriction. If this were so, the "and-so-on" would certainly experience resistance from something else—which is incompatible with the phenomenon of the limitlessness of re-presentation itself. As delimitation, formal emptiness cannot stop re-presentation. It can only show that re-presentation's being un-bound is in fact a keeping away of bounds. Despite its being un-bound, human life is fixed, not to one or another entity, but to the formal emptiness that binds by staying away. Thus, strictly speaking, re-presentation is against itself, in the sense that it stays away from its own measure. "Im Sorgen riegelt sich das Leben gegen sich selbst ab und wird sich in der Abriegelung gerade nicht lost." ("In caring, life cordons itself off against itself and in this cordoning-off is precisely not rid of itself") (GA61 107).

The "against" is not an anti-, it does not oppose anything. It indicates the meaning of -less (-*los*) in the limit-less and the end-less, as the pushing away of formal emptiness—its own measure. The nature of the against lies in "away from." The 1921–22 course states "daß sich in diesem Vonsich-weg des Lebens es selbst ein 'Gegen-es' ausbildet und durch und durch in dieser Ausbildung 'ist'," "that in this being-away-from-itself belonging to life, it itself cultivates an 'against it' and 'is' in this cultivation through and through" (GA61 123). The strange thing is that this against is simply not visible and interpretable.[13] Its being away cannot be cancelled;

it keeps itself away, and any interpretation that wants to put this staying-away aside is already part of its against, although it cannot truly get involved in it. The question is: how can this against be held fast?

For the time being, the against is formal emptiness. It is a pre-supposition that has yet to gain weight, as the interpretation enters into emptiness as its own presupposition (GA61 132). The possibility of a true concretion of asking lies only within *Ruinanz*, where the against is not ready and waiting to be interpreted. The against only truly becomes against in its interpretation, and its interpretation only truly becomes interpretation by entering into the against. This enigmatic growing together of interpretation and interpretandum, its *Zusammenwachsen*, the con-cretion, is the movement of fundamental-philosophical thinking. Not until thinking gets permeated with the movement of *Ruinanz*, and takes it to its extreme, does that against which *Ruinanz* is appear—and only then does the against become proper (*eigentlich*): "*das (ruinante) Gegen, bzw. (formal)* Wo-gegen *als ein* faktisch Eigentliches *des Lebens*," "the (ruinous) against or the (formal) against-which as something factically proper belonging to life" (GA61 132–33).

Proper asking is against the im-proper-ty of *Ruinanz*: this does not mean that it is outside *Ruinanz* or is anti-*Ruinanz*.[14] Being against the im-proper (*Un-eigentlichkeit*) means being against the staying away of the against in *Ruinanz*. This is an augmentation of the against, actually letting it reign. Proper-ty (*Eigentlichkeit*) is allowing the against of "proper" and "im-proper" to reign. Interpretation must not detach itself from the against, but must enter into it in such a way that the hiddenness against which interpretive clarity turns begins to reign over the interpretation. Interpreting is letting being-away be *da* (there) in its character of being-against.

To begin with, the "world" is the re-presented totality of re-presented entities: a cosmos or environment. But the progress of representation is being-in-the-world, where "in" indicates the familiarity in which re-presentation as a whole lives. The world as re-presented totality conceals the world in a more fundamental sense, as familiarity (*Vertrautheit*). This familiarity itself permeates the totality of re-presentation; it is all-embracing. Now the question is whether this familiarity itself does not rest in *Ruinanz*—is there not something that stays away in the familiarity of the world, viz., that this familiarity itself is without measure? Re-presentation is fully entering into the world, a being absorbed that cannot and need not ask any more questions about this. Then the familiar world is as it should be, an absorbing emptiness, an enclosing that stays away. The world is the formal emptiness by which life as re-presentation "is held fast, to which it holds itself" (*gehalten ist, woran es sich hält*: GA61 86). Then the following applies: being in the world as being familiar with all things re-presented keeps its own emptiness away, and is thereby against itself.

Now the interpretation gains in concreteness. Being in the world as being familiar with everything is being confined by this formal emptiness. The world as totality of entities, and the world as familiarity with this totality, is a mask for the world in the proper sense, as that which encircles re-presentation as a heaviness—a heaviness that stays away and thereby drags re-presentation along. In being confining and entangling, the world lures the movement of *Ruinanz* towards itself. For the world, it is essential to be *Umwelt*, en-vironment, a heaviness that has coiled itself around re-presentation as an encompassing ring: the measure of re-presentation (GA61 129).

The world is called "*Gehaltssinn*," the very sense of *Gehalt*, not for being the significance of the contents within the world, like a framework of rules, but because the world is the possibility of understanding, the openness in which re-presentation is bound. Fundamental philosophy has no content, but is driven by its *Gehalt*, The *Gehalt* is that which keeps to itself its way of having-to-do-with-it (*Bezug*). Philosophy can only venture to leap into its own "*Gehaltensein*," being held, which is interpretation being held inside that by which it is enclosed (GA61 53). Philosophy is "*Verhalten*," in the double sense of "behaving" and "having-to-do-with" (*Bezogensein*). Philosophy is the movement in the direction of that to which it is bound (*gehalten*) and by which it is surrounded. That means philosophy moves in the direction of the world that already encircles it. Philosophical interpretation is after that in which it is already confined. So the world is at once the *Woraufhin*, the upon-and-towards-which (the direction the interpretation takes) and the *Worin*, the wherein (that which already surrounds it) of interpretation.[15]

The heaviness of this being bound in the world, which hides itself in the lightness of re-presenting transience, is called *facticity*, as asking's belonging and being bound in that in which asking rests. This "concept" must above all be kept away from any connection with the weight, the definiteness, the limitation, the passivity, or the fatality of human life; these are all present properties of present humanity as a subject. Facticity is a heaviness that can only become evident in a factical manner—in an asking that gets permeated with facticity. Facticity is concreteness keeping itself away, the weight of formal emptiness, the against-which of *Ruinanz*. The asking of philosophy becomes concrete by turning in upon facticity. This asking finds its source in facticity and goes back into it (GA61 115). In this source, there reigns the "against" of facticity itself, the fundamental

"against" in which facticity gives re-presentation the possibility to be measureless, even in the Heidegger-literature.

The entire way of thinking of *Sein und Zeit* is nothing but the way of
thinking that returns to its own source, where that very source remains
against this thinking. Already on p. 8/28 "we" can read the fundamental
indication on how to understand this "book." It cannot be understood as a
book; it can only be understood as the very language of facticity: *"Die
wesenhafte Betroffenheit des Fragens von seinem Gefragten gehört zum
eigensten Sinn der Seinsfrage."* ("How the the questioning is essentially
affected by what is asked about belongs to the ownmost sense of the question of being.") There is in the word *Betroffenheit* not only the sense of
asking being struck (*getroffen*) by facticity, but also, especially, the sense
of remaining ensnared: asking remains confined in that which it is after.

Only when asking lets itself be bound by facticity does it become concrete. Not until the moment of that concretion does the one who asks
"come into existence." Only in the leap away from the subjectivity of authorship, from the subjectivity that has always vaulted over its facticity,
only in the leap toward facticity, which has always reigned, can the questioner's own-ness (*das Eigene*) arise, can it be indicated "who" is asking.
Here author and readers do not matter anymore, the questioner's own "I"
is a movement of "Hinzeigen auf mein konkretes faktisches Leben in
seiner konkreten Welt," "pointing towards my concrete factical life in its
concrete world" (GA61 174). As the heaviness that surrounds the world of
present entities and thus keeps asking away, facticity is as such the only
possibility of asking. Entering into this possibility is the utmost loneliness:
"die Wurzeln der eigenen Faktizität des eigenen konkreten Lebens," "the
roots of one's own facticity belonging to one's own life" (GA61 169). This
im-possible source of asking has only one possibility: the "against" of being
there (*da*) and being away (*weg*), of the proper and the im-proper. Then
facticity becomes what it already was: asking's own possibility. That only
happens when facticity unexpectedly gives the possibility of asking in a
genuine sense.

Rational and empirical insights about present objects are essentially
non-rational and non-empirical, inasmuch as they have vaulted over their
own possibility, facticity.[16] Truly empirical thinking will have to go back
along the way into facticity. In asking's being bound to facticity lies the
only possibility of a bond, a measure for philosophical speaking: *"die in der
ergriffenen Faktizität entspringende Bindung der faktisch vollzogenen
Verbindlichkeit,"* "the binding (originating in the grip of facticity) of factically actualized bindingness" (GA61 170). If being bound in facticity became a bond, so that facticity would set the measure for asking, then

asking could take place in the name of facticity: "*Der Gegenstand, wozu ich mich verhalte, bestimmt mit seinem eigensten Namen das Verhalten selbst,*" "the object to which I comport and hold myself defines the comportment, the holding, with its own proper name" (GA61 60).

In going its own way, asking builds itself into its own source (*Einbildung*). It turns back to its own ground and roots. While asking becomes factical, facticity grows together with it (*con-crescere*), and calls upon asking to speak. In this growing together of asking and facticity, the existing indifferent meanings of the words belonging to everyday language as "conceptual tools" can leap toward their own source: a supporting word. Thus it may happen "*daß den in der spezifisch nivellierten Rede des faktischen Lebens gebrauchten Bedeutungen aus der Explikation ein bestimmter Sinn zuspringt,*" "that a particularly tuned sense springs out of the explication into the meanings used in the specifically levelled discourse of factical life" (GA61 126). The moment when the utmost loneliness of asking grows together with facticity, facticity finds its own word. This is the moment when facticity casts a glance (*Blick*) at the eye (*Auge*) of the interpreter: the *Augenblick* (the eye-opening moment).[17]

In an essential phrase from *Sein und Zeit* concerning language, there is the indication how this "book" has been written and how it should be read. On p. 161/204 it reads: "*Den Bedeutungen wachsen Worte zu. Nicht aber werden Wörterdinge mit Bedeutungen versehen*" ("Words grow towards meanings. It is not the case that word-things get supplied with meanings").[18] The existent, equalized meanings of words in the traffic of language contain the possibility that they be no longer *Wörter* (isolated words), but *Worte* (supportive words). That is not a matter of concocting a philosophical terminology. There are no word-things to which meanings are being clipped. The genesis of a supporting word is a *zu-wachsen*, a growth towards a word that occurs only when facticity, thanks to philosophical asking, is asked to speak, and when facticity genuinely speaks.

This leap toward one another of facticity and its factical interpretation will not erase the essential "against" of facticity, but will reinforce it. The sense of being (*Seinssinn*) of factical life remains broken (*gebrochen*) (GA61 155), in the sense that it at once makes impossible the interpretation that it makes possible as sense. Philosophical interpretation is impossible. But facticity and interpretation belong together in this "against." The question is how a sense of belonging together, an "and," can be hidden in the "against." On the basis of a fundamental repetition (*Wiederholung*) of the lectures of 1921–22, viz., those of 1929–30, I shall below pursue the "and" as an indication of "finitude." It is not a question of balancing one course against another by measuring out similarities and differences. Any comparison belongs in the indifference of *Vorhandenheit*.

Considering the courses as different perspectives of the same thing, or as variations on a theme, is out of the question. Only in their diversity, their utter uniqueness as separate rock formations, are the courses echoes of one another, namely, in such a way that in this echo there appears what remains unsaid, which is what Heidegger writes against: the facticity in which they belong together.

2. "and"

In the 1929–30 lecture course entitled *Die Grundbegriffe der Metaphysik* the fundamental mood of profound indifference (*Langeweile*) is evoked, namely, the profound indifference or boredom that is characteristic of *us* in *our* time; there is no appearance of an essential need, of an essential "Bedrängnis," distress, with relation to being as a whole (*das Seiende im Ganzen*) and to ourselves within it (GA29/30 244). This fundamental mood is evoked by pursuing the ambiguity that characterizes each mode of boredom in its own way, namely, that of being left behind empty (*Leergelassenheit*) and of remaining bound (*Hingehaltenheit*—note the reference to *Halten* and *Gehalt* in *Hingehaltenheit*). When we have missed a train at the station and are bored in the interim before the next train arrives, we are left behind empty, in the sense that our usual busi-ness in our contact with the surrounding entities can no longer engage us. But anyone who is left behind empty like this, as a result of the fact that the relevance of things has withdrawn, is at the same time bound in that boredom, bound not by the surrounding entities, but by the slowness of time unwilling to pass. The essence of the question is how being left empty, on the one hand, and being bound, on the other, are concerned with one another, how they are not just randomly coupled, but rather belong together in boredom, in the sense that they are joined (*bezogen*) together (GA29/30 162).

This question finds its sharpest intensification in the fundamental mood of *profound* boredom. The issue here is not being left behind empty by this or that entity, by this or that situation; it is being left behind empty by all entities, including our situation, including ourselves. In this state of profound boredom the indifference of all things, and of ourselves in their midst, is revealed. This indifference is not the outcome of a sum of assessments, but overwhelms "us" all at once (GA29/30 208). It is essential that this being left empty permeates everydayness as the levelled openness (*Offenbarkeit*) of present objects in the widest sense.[19]

What emerges all at once in profound boredom is the emptiness that like a mist shrouds the totality of entities as the whole of present objects.

While expanding planetary needs are all taken care of, a needlessness with relation to the whole manifests itself; a *Bedrängnis im Ganzen* fails to come. For example, amidst the diversity of philosophical problems and their solutions is hidden a fundamental sense-lessness of these problems and their solutions. Philosophy masks this emptiness by throwing itself into the accelerating mimetic reproduction of philosophical literature. In this literature, philosophy passes by without touching being as a whole and without being affected by it. Philosophy is part of human life as a pastime, as the battle against time, in which fundamental boredom is vaulted over, and thereby reigns.

Essential in profound boredom is that, in being left empty, there emerges the indication of that which is masked by emptiness, that which embraces the whole of re-presented entities, the world—being as a whole (*das Seiende im Ganzen*). This whole is not a totality, but the dimension, the openness (*Offenheit*) reigning over the totality of present objects and their representation. Where re-presentation progresses ever more in the acceleration of itself, the world, the openness in which this happens, stays away.[20] This staying away of the world manifests itself as emptiness when profound boredom emerges. But this emptiness is itself an indication that in the emptiness something stays away: the weight of being encompassed by the world as the openness surrounding re-presentation. The world reigns over the re-presentation; it takes re-presentation along and therein stays away: "*Alles je gerade zugängliche Seiende, uns selbst mit ein-begriffen, ist von diesem Ganzen umgriffen. Wir selbst sind mit ein-begriffen in diesem 'im Ganzen'...*" ("Every immediately accessible being, ourselves included, is encompassed by this whole. We ourselves are also included in this 'as a whole'...") (GA29/30 513). Only from the heaviness of this being encompassed by the world can the indifference, the fundamental boredom, of all representation be understood (GA29/30 515, cf. 208, 221).

When the emptiness of deep indifference is taken to its utmost limit, the world is revealed. This revelation only takes place when the emptiness of indifference gives an indication of its own nature: indifference is a denial. In boredom every possibility of doing and acting is denied us. But—and here we are confronted with the crux of Heidegger's interpretation—denial is a mode of speaking. In denial something is said. In German: all *Versagen* (nay-saying) is still a mode of *Sagen* (saying).[21]

The profound indifference of all beings is a denial, and every denial is a mode of speaking, a paradoxical speaking that points to its own impossibility. When denial is an impossible mode of speaking, then there is also an im-possible answer to it: what is said by indifference is the impossibility of answering. When *Dasein* is confronted with this impossibility, it is confronted with the world. It is confined by a weight that denies it every possibility of acting or leaving alone. Here the emptiness (*Leergelassen-heit*) is revealed as being bound by the weight of the world (*Hingehalten-heit*).

With this, a first indication has been found for the "and" as the juncture of leaving empty and keeping bound as the constituents of profound boredom. In profound boredom, emptiness first of all appears as the passing away of all entities in indifference. But in this emptiness what is concealed is the *factum* that the emptiness is a heaviness that keeps itself away, *abziehende Schwere*. Suddenly the emptiness of indifference turns out to be that which encloses every possibility: ". . .*mit einem Mal ist alles von dieser Gleichgültigkeit umfangen und umhalten. . .[wir] finden uns inmitten des Seienden im Ganzen, d.h. im Ganzen dieser Gleichgültig-keit.*" ("All at once everything is enveloped and constrained by this indifference. . .[we] find ourselves in the midst of being as a whole, in the whole of this indifference") (GA29/30 208). Then emptiness and being bound are the same; emptiness is the hiding of being bound.

The question is: how can the weight of *Hingehaltenheit* be put into concepts? When Heidegger calls the fundamental-philosophical "concepts" *In-begriffe*, incepts, and in doing so indicates that they include (*begreifen in sich*) the whole of being, the point is that these "concepts" by their nature show how they belong in the midst of being as a whole, how they are enclosed by it. This can only happen when being as a whole itself becomes the measure of comprehending, becomes "*die umfangende Grenze des Seienden im Ganzen*," "the enveloping limit of being as a whole" (GA29/30 217). Speaking must become the saying of being-enclosed itself.

When at this moment I try to point from and to *Hingehaltenheit*, this pointing itself is still pervaded with emptiness, the nebulosity of indifference. How can interpretation become concrete in tearing open this nebulosity? Only by an examination, which does not belong in a philosophical treatise in any sense, of the other side of philosophy's inclusiveness, the side pointing to *Hingehaltenheit* in its proper sense, that *Dasein* is also included in these "concepts."[22]

In profound boredom everything that is characteristic of "us" is sucked away into indifference: name, status, profession, role, age and fate, mine and yours—all this ceases to have a grip upon us. We become an indifferent nobody (GA29/30 203); we are "we" no more. Then even the "somebody" is lacking who is left behind empty in boredom; "nobody" is bored. This nobody whom indifference bypasses is called *Dasein*.

In the mood of profound indifference every possibility of existence is denied "somebody." In this denial somebody is spoken to, somebody is summoned to exert "his/her" possibilities, but in the mode of denial. This denial as im-possibility points to Dasein in the proper sense: Dasein is this impossible possibility, the possibility that is denied.[23] In the proper sense, Dasein is living up to this impossibility, i.e., to being bound in the weight of the surrounding world. Here it appears how the two senses of *In-begriff* belong together. *In-begriffe* point to the inclusion of Dasein itself in the world that includes Dasein's "concepts."

Dasein becomes concrete, becomes its own self in utter loneliness, when it properly enters into the surrounding world as *Hingehaltenheit*. Dasein recognizes being enclosed in the world as its own possibility; it allows itself to be invited by this possibility of entering into the enclosure of the world.[24] The world as enclosure is the source from which Dasein in the dispersion of representation has sprung away, and which conceals the invitation to spring back into it. The enclosure is what gives Dasein its possibility, *das Ermöglichende*, that which enables, possibilizes. *Das Ermöglichende* is not the possibility for Dasein to become this or that; rather the enclosure is Dasein's *own* possibility: the possibility to return into its own confinement, its im-possibility.[25]

This source of Dasein is a denial, and what Dasein is about is to let this denial speak, to let the enclosure of the world reign in the words that are used. Only then does it become clear what is meant by the analytic of Dasein, in contrast to analysis, which is always bound to representation.[26] Analytic means comprehension (*begreifen*) as inclusion (*einbegriffen*) in the world, in the openness that is the enclosure of Dasein.

Hingehaltenheit in its proper sense consists in the return into the world as Dasein's own possibility. Heidegger names *Hingehaltenheit* proper: the extreme point at which the eye is opened (*die Spitze des Augenblicks*). This extreme point is not a "moment" at which Dasein can elevate itself above its facticity, at which it can finally be fully present. This extreme point is a reinforcement of the enclosure of the world—otherwise it would be impossible to understand that this extremity is still called *Hingehaltenheit*.[27] What happens in this intensification of *Hingehaltenheit* is that it itself gets into the possibility of speaking, namely, to *Dasein* as its own im-possibility.

Here it becomes clear what the "and" that pervades the analysis of indifference consists of. This "and" is the indication of a fundamental sameness. In the end, re-presentation is boredom that keeps itself away as pastime, boredom as emptiness is the weight of the world keeping itself away, the world is the extreme point that opens the eyes. How is this identity to be understood? How is it possible that representation in the proper sense is pastime and therefore boredom, that boredom in the proper sense is world, that world in the proper sense is the eye-opener? This possibility is there because each time there is an "aspect" that stays away, but in this staying away it still holds sway and cannot be removed.

This is the structure of the spell. A spell holds something or somebody and hides itself in that hold. All traffic with represented entities (both in technique and in experience) is under the spell of boredom, as a pastime, the boredom that in turn is under the spell of the world.[28]

When Dasein becomes proper, the same-ness of representation, pastime, world, and eye-opener is revealed. How does this revelation take place? How does this sameness come into being? Here it appears that this "identity" itself is a fundamental brokenness. Only when the spell is broken do representation, boredom, world, and eye-opener turn out to be the same.[29] Dasein becomes proper when it breaks the spell that holds it; only then does the fundamental sameness manifest itself. Profound boredom breaks the spell of representation, the world breaks the spell of emptiness, the opening of the eye of Dasein breaks the spell of the world. Thanks simply to this break, the reign of "against," is it possible for "and" to arise as "the same." Dasein's being proper lies in this broken sameness:

> *Warum muß am Ende jene Weite des bannenden Horizontes gebrochen werden durch den Augenblick, und warum kann sie nur durch diesen gebrochen werden, so daß das Dasein gerade in dieser Gebrochenheit zur eigentlichen Existenz kommt? Ist am Ende das Wesen der Einheit und Fügung beider ein* Bruch? *Was meint diese* Gebrochenheit des Daseins in sich selbst? (Why must that breadth of the spellbinding horizon be broken in the end through the eye-opening moment, and why can it be broken only through this such that precisely in this brokenness, Dasein comes to proper existence? Is the essence of the unity and juncture of both ultimately a *breach*? What does this *brokenness of Dasein in itself* mean?) (GA29/30 252)

In the course *Grundbegriffe der Metaphysik* we are confronted with three fundamental "concepts": world (*Welt*), finitude (*Endlichkeit*), and individualization (*Vereinzelung*). The question is: why just these three *Grundbegriffe*, and how are they bound together? Thanks to the analytic of the "and" as broken identity, it is possible to reveal the interconnectedness of these "concepts." The world is the openness surrounding *Dasein,* the openness that gives all representation its boundary. The world as openness becomes proper openness when *Dasein* recognizes and accepts the weight of the world surrounding it as its own possibility. Then the world opens the eye of *Dasein,* and *Dasein* returns to this possibility. This return is only possible when every support from entities, from other people, and from the self has fallen away, when Dasein is thrown back upon itself, plunged into its extreme loneliness.

World and loneliness are revealed as being the same, but that revelation only takes place when the spell of the world is broken, at the moment when the eye of Dasein is opened. This brokenness of the same is what the most fundamental "concept" points to: finitude.[30]

With this, however, the final word has not been said. Even as broken identity, finitude remains pervaded with the *abziehende Schwere* of being away; brokenness and identity remain hidden, cannot truly reign.[31] With respect to its own finitude Dasein is finite as well; it is always turned away from its broken identity—this concealment itself belongs to the character of finitude. The leap back to Dasein's fundamental possibility is cut off, and even this concealment cannot be genuinely experienced. Dasein is an elevation that is at the same time carried away, concealed; it is *fortnehmende Zukehr*, a turning-to that takes away. The moment when Dasein's eye is opened is also the moment when this "insight" disappears, and the spell is reinstated.[32]

There is the suspicion that Dasein's enabling (*das Ermöglichende*) is an inexhaustible source, an overflow.[33] Dasein's attempt to answer this overflow is not equal to it; finite Dasein remains bound in its *abziehende Schwere*. Dasein's spring back to its own source (*Ursprung*) always vaults over the impossibility of reaching it. Thus Dasein's answer to this overflow is always excess, ὕβρις. As excess, Dasein is again and again thrown back upon its finitude. But *now*, in the epoch of fundamental boredom, even this problem of finitude and excess is indifferent.[34] The indifference of Dasein's finitude in the contemporary situation points to the fact that we, today, know of no enigma, of no secret (GA29/30 244). In this denial of the secret of finitude today lies the only indication of the nature of Dasein. In the never-ending progress of representation, as exemplified in philosophical literature, Dasein has to answer this denial, which is its only possibility.

Part II

The First Years of Breakthrough

3

Making Logic Philosophical Again (1912–1916)

Steven Galt Crowell

1. Toward a Philosophical Logic

Between 1912 and 1916 Heidegger published a series of writings in which he confronts the major current theories of logic, including the metaphysical grounding of logic in Neo-Scholasticism, Neo-Kantian "critical idealism" (transcendental logic or epistemology as first philosophy), O. Külpe's "critical realism," and Husserl's phenomenology.[1] In each of these positions, a central issue is the theory of categories. Whether inspired by Aristotle or Kant, logical theory sought to account for concepts which make empirical scientific knowledge possible, the ground of the "objective validity" of knowledge. Thus logic did not merely elaborate formal properties of argument; as transcendental logic or "logic of truth" it embraced fundamental questions of the theory of knowledge and science. Even Neo-Scholastic positions subordinating logic to metaphysics were formulated in terms of the transcendental question of the conditions of possibility for knowledge, though they would restore to the term "transcendental" the pre-Kantian connotation of the medieval *transcendentia* to recover the ontological sense of categories as determinations of being.[2] Heidegger's most original contribution to this debate, his 1915 *Habilitationsschrift* and its 1916 *Schluss*, shows the strain of trying to find an independent path between Neo-Kantian and Neo-Scholastic logics.

The main text revisits an issue left hanging in Heidegger's Dissertation—roughly, determining the relation between logic and grammar. Heidegger had argued that "the true preparatory work for logic . . . is not accomplished by psychological investigations into the genesis and composition of representations, but by unambiguous definition and clarification of the significations of words" (GA1 186).[3] But what *are* significations? Philosophical incorporation of this preparatory work requires that significations be distinguished categorially from the spoken, written, or mental sign token, which in turn requires a general theory of categories. Heidegger's reconstruction of *Duns Scotus's Theory of Categories and Significa-*

tion, guided explicitly by "the perspective of modern [logical] research," (GA1 202)—aims to address both issues.[4] Scotus's theory of categories allows Heidegger to argue that "the guiding value for the investigation of significations is . . . *truth* as valid meaning" (GA1 307). Since the orientation toward truth "unavoidably requires a decision on the relation between the region of significations and the being of object" (GA1 307), Heidegger manages to retain the ontological character of Scotus's categories. But the reconstruction in the main text is informed far less by ontological perspectives than by Neo-Kantian critical idealism. Because (as Heidegger puts it in 1912) logic is a "theory of theory" (GA1 23), it has (as he says in 1915) "absolute hegemony over all cognizable or cognized object worlds" (GA1 279). Logic is first philosophy.

But another note is struck in *Das Kategorienproblem*, a short conclusion appended to the Scotus book upon its publication in 1916. Here Heidegger offers a limited, "preliminary look at the *systematic* structure of the category problem" which draws out "the essential *Potenzen* of the problem and its context" (GA1 300). The account in the main text has been "strictly conceptual" and "to a certain extent one-sided"; it has "self-consciously excluded deeper-reaching sets of metaphysical problems" (GA1 400). There is need for a "metaphysical resolution to the problem of knowledge" (GA1 403). "In the long run" philosophy, including logic, cannot "avoid its genuine optic, metaphysics" (GA1 406). The "absolute hegemony" of logic thus appears compromised here by the need for "metaphysical" resolution; transcendental logic must be seen within a "translogical context" (GA1 405). Hence *Das Kategorienproblem* identifies three problem areas that adumbrate a metaphysics which Heidegger, having dispatched psychologism and grammaticism, believes can restore philosophical significance to logic, make logic philosophical again.

The project of making logic philosophical again is not limited to Heidegger's student years. In his 1912 review of logical theory Heidegger asked "What is logic?" and answered that "here we already stand before a problem whose solution is reserved for the future" (GA1 18). Fifteen years later, in his lecture course on the *Grundprobleme der Phänomenologie*, Heidegger still calls for a "radical conception of the problems of logic as such" (GA24 252). Alluding to two dominant influences on his early work, Heidegger argues that neither Husserl's phenomenology nor Lask's theory of categories does justice to the "ontological problems" which emerge, under pressure of the "things themselves," in a philosophical inquiry into logic (GA24 253). If one is ever to succeed in "making logic again into philosophy," one must first overcome Hegel's "reduction of ontology to logic" and ask what logic, the being of the *logos*, *is* (GA24 254).

This problem had been suggested two years earlier, when Heidegger

opened his lecture course on *Logik: die Frage nach der Wahrheit* by criticizing contemporary "school logic" for leaving "all philosophy, i.e., all
questioning and investigating, behind" (GA21 12). A cozy discipline within
the philosophical *Fach*, the "science" of logic is in fact rootless, confused
about its own object, its scientific domain. Defining it as the science of
logos—as argument, discourse, sentence, proposition—does not distinguish it from other sciences investigating these things, unless one adds
that logic is specifically concerned with *logos* "in respect to truth." Other
sciences seek "what is true" by inquiring methodically into their objects;
logic alone, "strictly speaking," is the science of "truth" as such (GA21 7).
Thus, if logic "wants to be a form of scientific research, a philosophizing
logic," then what "should most concern it" is not further technical development, but the question of "the primary being of truth," what it means to
be true (GA21 12). To make logic philosophical again is to re-establish the
connection, posited by Aristotle and renewed by Kant, between logic and
the question of being, by determining the being of truth.

The concept of truth already governs Heidegger's perspective when, in
1916, he identifies the *Potenzen* of the category problem. But his call for a
"metaphysics of the truth problem" (GA1 402) only gives a name to the
basic tension between the *Habilitation* thesis and its *Schluss*. On the one
hand, Heidegger's appeal to metaphysics signals his proximity to the Neo-
Scholastic project, but the argument in the main text rules out a metaphysical solution in the Neo-Scholastic sense. And on the other, focussing
metaphysics on the problem of *truth* preserves the main text's critical insistence on the priority of truth as "logically valid meaning," but without
the Neo-Kantian willingness to subordinate metaphysics wholly to logic.[5]
The transcendental logical theory of truth thus sets the terms for Heidegger's projected move into metaphysics, but the uneasy compromise he
suggests cannot hold. Making logic philosophical again ultimately calls for
something other than metaphysics, viz., the "ontology" of *Sein und Zeit*.
In this Chapter I will suggest some of the reasons for this which lie immanent in the issues Heidegger identifies as horizons of the category problem. This requires that one first recover their origin in the transcendental
logical approach to truth.

2. The Problem of Truth

Kant had distinguished formal from transcendental logic by arguing
that while the former provides a "negative condition" of truth (without
which our thinking could not be consistent with itself), the latter is a
"logic of truth" since it provides the conditions without which our think-

ing could have no "relation to any object."[6] If the former concerns the apriori syntax of thought, the latter concerns its apriori semantics. Granting "the nominal definition of truth, that it is the agreement of knowledge with its object,"[7] Kantian categories become conditions of possibility for truth as agreement or correspondence. Within this framework, the issue between Neo-Kantians and Neo-Scholastics turned on whether or not the logic of truth needed to be grounded in "ontological truth" (*ens tanquam verum*), viz., in a metaphysical concept of the object as the measure of judgment. Can a purely logical account of correspondence be given? Both sides agree that merely analyzing the structure of truth is not enough; it is further necessary to show how a cognitive grasp of truth, the *knowing* of the known, is possible. But if to know is to grasp the correspondence between thought and thing, judgment and object, a problem arises, cited by Heidegger in his 1914 review of Sentroul's *Kant und Aristoteles* as the "antinomy in the problem of truth" (GA1 51): "Either one has both elements of the comparison requisite for truth, namely, the thought and the thing, yet without the possibility of comparing them, or else one has an actual comparison, but not between the desired elements" (GA1 51). The first case takes judgment or thought as a real existent, a certain subjective act, and the object as an equally real existent, independent of the process of knowing. But then, since comparison itself is simply another subjective act, even where truth as correspondence obtains, it is impossible to *know* that it does. The second case assumes that a comparison obtains, for example between the judgment and the thing as given to perception, but since what is given cannot apriori be identified with the real thing, the comparison is not "between the desired elements."

The Neo-Scholastic solution advocated by Sentroul invokes the idea of ontological truth, viz., the metaphysical "relation of identity between the 'thing which is' and 'what it is'" (GA1 52). Here the judgment is supposed to correspond to an "objective counterpart" which "in some sort of way is necessarily the thing itself." For Heidegger this is no solution: "What is this objective counterpart? Wherein consists its objectivity?" (GA1 52). Heidegger thus poses the classic Neo-Kantian question. Though he too will move toward a theory of ontological truth, he finds pre-critical Neo-Aristotelian realism epistemologically inadequate. Its concept of the "object of knowledge" remains "metaphysically encumbered" (GA1 50), nor can it do justice to actual science: "the orientation toward the theory of science is lacking even now in Aristotelian-Scholastic philosophy" (GA1 53). Heidegger will not try to resolve the antinomy by a return to Aristotelian realism.

There remain, then, two possibilities: scepticism, or else a purely "logical" account of correspondence that preserves the real transcendence of the object while showing how it can possibly be known. In his Dissertation Heidegger suggests such an account: "Insofar as the significative content [of a judgment] is valid as a determination of the object of judgment, the judgment is true or false. The old concept of truth—*adaequatio rei et intellectus*—can thus be rendered purely logically, if *res* is conceived as object and *intellectus* as determining significative content" (GA1 176). How does this avoid the antinomy? Clearly, the main question is how one is to understand "object." If it is conceived metaphysically, dogmatism results; and if it is conceived as subjective representation, scepticism. If knowledge is possible, the logical object must be the thing itself, though with an essential (apriori) relation to knowing.

The logical character of the object becomes a dominant theme in Heidegger's *Habilitationsschrift*. The theory of categories is a theory of the objecthood of the object (GA1 216); it thus assumes such importance because, in the context of the truth problem, it must provide the principles for understanding what objects *are*, such that they can serve to measure knowledge. Anticipating later discussion, two aspects of Heidegger's view should be noted early on.

First, part of the solution to the antinomy involves replacing the misleading metaphor of "comparison" with the phenomenological notion of *Erfüllung*, as when, in 1912, Heidegger suggests that truth is a matter of whether or not "the 'intentional thought' [is] fulfilled by the object" (GA1 35–36). But this says nothing about what the object must be in order to fulfill the judgment. What is the cognitive relation? Heidegger starts with the anti-psychologistic thesis that the judgment is "significative content," neither the psychical act nor the grammatical structure but "valid meaning" (GA1 31). Significative content can be true or false. By 1915 Heidegger argues that what determines it to be one or the other, the object, is "the significative content of what is given, the intuited state of affairs *simpliciter*" (GA1 273).

The second point thus concerns this significative content of the given. Appeal to givenness distinguishes Heidegger's position from dogmatic metaphysical realism, but it also invites the opposite charge, scepticism, if the given is merely "subjective." The logical object cannot be the mere thing, but neither can it be a subjective, psychically real representation. For Heidegger, it is the meaning of the thing as given. The antinomy of truth demands a transcendental theory of that meaning-full object presupposed in both metaphysical and physical-psychologistic theories of knowledge. The "metaphysics of the truth problem" projected in the *Schluss*, then, will be a metaphysics of meaning. But how can a metaphysics of meaning resolve the problem of knowledge (truth) if metaphysics already presupposes the transcendental logical concept of the object? This is an aporia in Heidegger's early work itself; its parameters are reflected in the three issues Heidegger identifies as horizons of the category problem.

3. The Object and Object Domains

The first—"the basic requirement of the theory of categories"—is the "delimitation of the various object domains into categorially irreducible regions" (GA1 400). An object domain is roughly that set over which a scientific theory quantifies, an "interpretation" in the sense of contemporary logic. Heidegger's transcendental logical interest lies above all in determining the categorial relations in and among such domains, in locating objects within "regional ontologies" (Husserl) or "realms of reality" whose "particular structure and constitution" is governed by the "category" (GA1 210–11).[8]

Categories provide the "logical place" of any object. "Place" makes sense only in terms of a certain "order," and thus "whatever has its logical place fits in a particular way into a particular totality of relations" (GA1 212). Any phenomenon "within the realm of the thinkable" occupies a place in logical space. A particular event is cognized in chemistry, e.g., as an instance of an alkali-base reaction. It thus becomes part of the object domain of chemistry by being given—being shown to have—a place in the logical space (or realm of reality) governed by the categories of nature.[9] Categories belong to the rational structure of science and provide the object-constituting principles which make science a "theoretical elaboration of what is objective" (GA1 208). Given this view, why does Heidegger find it so important to delimit logical space into irreducible categorial regions?

In part this is a function of his relation to a debate within Neo-Kantianism. Focussing upon mathematical natural science, Natorp's Marburg school developed a theory of categories roughly adhering to Kant's own, in which to be an object of a science is to be capable of being brought under categories that have formal validity irrespective of the kind of object.[10] But Rickert's Southwest German school, with whom Heidegger sides here, proposed a more pluralistic approach to categories, which recognizes, e.g., that concepts grounding knowledge in history are not identical to those holding for physics. Dilthey's call for a critique of historical reason and Husserl's demand for non-naturalistic categories in psychology also reflect this trend. For Heidegger, logic as a theory of science must recognize that "the Aristotelian categories" (and so also the Kantian) "appear as merely a particular class of a particular region and not *the* categories *simpliciter*" (GA1 211). Categories can neither be "deduced" from thought in abstraction from the sort of object considered, nor established "analogically" by reference to an ultimate metaphysical instance; they can only be uncovered phenomenologically. In reflection upon the ground of the various sciences, the "irreducible" regions of reality *show themselves* and so are "demonstrated" (GA1 213).[11]

But beyond this internal debate, there is a more pressing reason to delimit categorial regions. If logic is a science, a "theoretical elaboration of the object," to which realm of reality does the object of logic belong? The problem of truth requires a logical theory of the object, and if that theory is to be a true theory, its principles must apply to itself: "Logic itself therefore requires its own categories" (GA1 288); "there must be a logic of logic" if logic is to clarify how knowledge of objects, including its own, is possible. This issue informs the first problem horizon as well as Heidegger's early thinking generally.

What is the "object" of logic? Immediate background for this question is the critique of psychologism which purported to show the absurdity of identifying the logical judgment, where we "most easily and immediately encounter the object peculiar to logic" (GA1 166), with the psychical act of judging.[12] In his Dissertation Heidegger had further argued against identifying it with the sentence ("grammatical form"), and for the same reason: act and word belong to the categorial region of changing, sensibly existing being, while the judgment shows itself to involve something "identical" that "makes itself felt with an insistence and irrevocability" in contrast to which "psychical reality can be termed merely fleeting and insubstantial" (GA1 170). Heidegger terms this object of logic, the identical factor in the judgment, "meaning" (*Sinn*). But to what realm of reality does meaning belong? What are the categories of meaning (GA1 171)?

The question of meaning "has, in the entire course of the history of philosophy, never been given its due in a fully conscious and consequential way" (GA1 24). If Heidegger will later address it within the ontological framework of *Sein und Zeit*, here he does not ask about the meaning of being, but about the "being" of meaning, its place in logical space. Phenomenological grasp of meaning as the object of logic implies recognition of a third sort of reality in addition to sensible (psycho-physical) and supersensible (metaphysical) being, for which "Lotze has found the decisive expression in the treasury of our German language," viz., that "in addition to an 'it *is*' there is an 'it *holds* [*gilt*]'" (GA1 170). Meaning, the object of logic, does not exist but "holds," is "valid." It is neither sensible nor supersensible, but "non-sensible." An ontological difference obtains between meaning and everything that is or occurs. Meaning "holds without having to be."

This phrase is taken from Emil Lask,[13] for though the concept of *Gel-*

tung was initially introduced by Lotze (and was accepted in some form by virtually all anti-psychologistic logicians), it is primarily Lask's elaboration of the term that stamps Heidegger's views. Lask replaces the traditional Platonic theory of two worlds—the physical and the metaphysical—by a new two-world theory: the "universe of the thinkable" is divided into what exists and what is valid. The consequences for the theory of categories are two. First, it resolves the question of whether logical categories are metaphysical entities (Aristotle) or psychic *Denkformen* (Kant). Categories are neither; they belong to the region of "validity."[14] Second, and decisive for Heidegger, it establishes what may be called a "transcendental" priority of meaning over any and every object domain. Since categories are not forms of thought but forms of meaning, the realm of logic is unlimited; there can be no domain of "what is" (including that of metaphysics) that would be "metalogical," beyond the reach of categorial validity. As Lask says, "metaphysics may prove to be all deception and folly, but no kind of epistemological, logical considerations has the power to convince us of it"; the theory of categories "is not at all in a position to decide this question" (LP 128). Lask's logic thus undoes Kant's "critical" resignation and restores the "unlimited reach of truth" (LP 125), a notion echoed in Heidegger's talk of logic's "absolute hegemony over all object worlds." The relation between meaning and the object thus becomes the central issue of Lask's (and Heidegger's) logical investigations.

The term *Sinn* was initially introduced to designate the logical judgment, but the antinomy of truth already points toward a widening of the concept, one Lask undertakes in his *Logik der Philosophie*. On Lask's view logical categoriality pertains to the objecthood of the object itself (LP 29), and thus it is to this latter, the object of transcendental logic, that the term "meaning" ought apply. Judgment meaning is a "derivative," secondary, artificial construct. Meaning "in an absolute sense" is "the unity or clasp of form and material" (LP 34). Such unity is not a relation between existing parts or pieces, but an *Urverhältnis* "incomparable to any sort of relation obtaining within the sphere of the sensible" (LP 175).

If the object as understood by transcendental logic is thus paradigmatic (*urbildlich*) meaning, not representational (*nachbildlich*) meaning, the *Urverhältnis* between category and material, this concept of meaning is nevertheless inscrutable to non-philosophical ways of thinking. It, and not some metaphysical concept like substance or subject, is the primary "philosophical epithet" for what is (LP 123), but it is a specifically transcendental notion, intelligible neither in the terms of straightforward experience nor those of empirical science. For there the concern is exclusively with what Lask calls the object *material* (LP 122); one simply "lives" in the realm of meaning without "knowing" it as such (LP 191f). But "if we as logicians characterize the existing object as meaning," we have turned our attention to categorial form as such in reflection upon what implicitly makes our first-order cognitive grasp possible (LP 123). In transcendental logic we "know" the object as meaning because we grasp the category as form, understood in terms of the existence/validity distinction.[15]

Heidegger explicitly adopts Lask's concept of categorial form. He notes that "the concept of form plays an equally decisive role in Aristotelian and transcendental philosophy," though it is not always "clearly and above all unambiguously conceived" (GA1 223). In Aristotelian philosophy, form has "metaphysical significance as a forming principle of psychical, physical, and metaphysical reality," i.e., it is a metaphysical entity. But if form is an entity, and if it is supposed to be that which constitutes an entity *as* an entity, there is an infinite regress (GA1 221). Kant "raised the concept of form to its decisive position of power within the region of the logical" (GA1 223) but did not decisively break free of psychologism.[16] For Lask, however, categorial form simply has the character of "holding," and since to hold is always to hold *of* something (*Hin-gelten*), form is intrinsically bound up with particular material. It is thus unthinkable that form could either exist apart (Aristotle) or be imposed on the material by thinking (Kant). Moreover, if there is a plurality of forms (a "table" of categories), the principle of differentiation must lie in the material itself. From this, Lask's principle of the "material determination of form," it follows that the "discovery" of categories will be, as Heidegger demanded, an empirical phenomenological affair (LP 63).

The principle of material determination means that the object cannot, in Hegelian fashion, be sublated into the (logical) concept, even at the infinite remove of Hegelianizing Neo-Kantianism. But if form is not an existing element of the object either, e.g., as the branches or DNA of a tree are its elements, how is its "holding" to be conceived? Lask answers that form is "nothing other than a particular objective *Bewandtnis* pertaining to . . . the material" (LP 69), a certain ordering inherent in the material itself.[17] It is a "moment of clarity," that by which the way things stand with the material is "lit up" (LP 75). Object material cannot be reduced to logical form ("Panlogism"), but is instead *logos*-immanent, "held" within form as within its own involvements ("Panarchy of the *logos*") (LP 133). For Heidegger, too, form is neither an entity nor an existing element of entities, but a "moment of clarity"; the category "brings nothing new" to the object material, it only brings "more clarity." It is nothing but a "certain *Bewandtnis* with the object," the arrangement or involvement of the material itself (GA1 224, 235). As "a moment of order in the given," the category makes it "graspable, cognizable, intelligible," i.e., it holds (GA1 224). For Heidegger as for Lask, then, form is not a metaphysical principle but a principle of intelligibility; yet it belongs to the material itself and does not arise first through the constitutive activity of thinking.

This view of logical form, and thus of the object as paradigmatic meaning, undergirds Lask's concept of truth. Cognitions, judgments, can strictly speaking be called "in accord with truth" or "contrary to truth" only, since they arise from an "artificial" destructuring of the object in the subjective process of empirical knowledge. That against which their contrariness or accordance is measured is truth in the genuine sense, viz., the object itself as *"übergegensätzlich"* meaning, beyond the opposition of truth and falsity.[18] As a unity of valid form and material, the object can rightfully be called "true": "Particular objects are particular theoretical meaning unities, particular truths." For example, "spatio-temporal objects *are* truths," though they are not "cognitions, judgments, propositions" but "unities of meaning in the paradigmatic sphere" (LP 41). Lask's transcendental object concept thus satisfies the condition laid out above for a logical account of correspondence, viz., that it show how the object can in principle serve as the measure of truth in the judgment. For if "the object itself is nothing other than meaning," it follows that the "distance between meaning and the object" (the sceptical distance between judgment meaning and the thing itself) "amounts to a distance between meaning and meaning" (LP 43; LU 394).

We cannot further examine Lask's attempt to show how the moments of the paradigmatic object (categorial form and material) are taken up into the structure of the judgment.[19] Lask's views have been introduced here only to suggest the source of Heidegger's thinking about the logical object and to prepare for locating what is new in his account. Lask enables Heidegger to frame the Neo-Scholastic appeal to ontological truth in a critical, logical way, but he does not fully resolve the antinomy.

Heidegger formulates Scotus's doctrine of ontological truth—the convertibility of *ens* and *verum*—in a logical idiom: "every object is a true object" (GA1 265). Though sharing a motive with Neo-Scholasticism's appeal to ontological truth (viz., to incorporate the thing itself into logic as the measure of judgment), Heidegger's reconstruction replaces the latter's metaphysical "encumbrances" with logical considerations grounded in the theory of validity. To say that every object is a true object is not to make a metaphysical claim (a metaphysical judgment always pertains to supersensible object material, and not to the object as such). Instead, it is to register the categorial nature of the category itself, to identify the *Bewandtnis* pertaining to validity as such, viz., "the possibility of a relation to knowledge" (GA1 267). But such a *Bewandtnis* is unintelligible without reference to the knowing subject. If the object, as the unity of category and material, is true, as a unity of meaning "beyond the opposition" of truth and falsity (GA1 268), and if thus "in mere givenness consciousness may be oriented toward 'the true'" (GA1 285), Heidegger nevertheless emphasizes that this object "contains only virtually" (GA1 271) those moments which are brought out explicitly and conjoined into a unity of meaning in the judgment: "the true constitutes itself in cognition" (GA1 271). Through the "position taking acts of the subject" the categorially formed "true" object, i.e., "the significative content of the object material which has come to givenness together with its particular form of reality," is "taken up into the judgment" (GA1 270).

It would seem that the elements for a logical account of correspondence are now in place. The theory of categories has been grounded in the object by way of the third "form of reality," valid meaning. The idea of material determination of form clarifies the object of knowledge in the various regional sciences without reductionism, and it establishes the "hegemony of logical meaning" without metaphysical dogmatism or Kantian sceptical resignation. But does this transcendental recasting of ontological truth suffice? How is the "taking up" of the object into knowledge—the very *Bewandtnis* of validity upon which the transcendental sense of the object as "true" depends—to be understood? Here Heidegger finds it necessary to go beyond Lask, for reasons he hints at in the second bit of unfinished business in the *Schluss*.

4. Logic and Subjectivity

The first horizon of the category problem is to delimit the region of reality of the object domain of meaning. This cannot be approached without the second, viz., its "insertion into the subject and judgment problem" (GA1 401). A logic of truth demands that a certain lacuna in Scotus (and thus in contemporary Neo-Scholasticism) as well as in Lask (and thus in contemporary Neo-Kantianism) be filled. So long as a theory of categories remains, like Lask's, focussed wholly on "genuine transcendence" (the object "untouched by all subjectivity"), it has not yet shown how knowledge, as knowing, is possible.[20] The antinomy still arises, since "it is simply not possible to compare judgment meaning with the real object" (GA1 273). Lask's isomorphism between the elements of object meaning and judgment meaning (LU 394) is only a necessary condition for knowledge. A sufficient condition would involve showing how that isomorphism could be *given*.

In contrast to Lask, Heidegger addresses this problem phenomenologically. Knowing is not comparison but *Erfüllung*. That is, the object as given, "the significative content of the given, the intuited state of affairs *simpliciter*," is "the measure of judgment meaning; from it the latter derives its objective validity" (GA1 273). But this implies that the givenness of Lask's sphere of *logos*-immanence (the site or "clearing" of the object as paradigmatic meaning) must be situated logically. The logical clarity of the object is unintelligible without reference to the subject; hence ontological truth must be grounded in a "correctly understood concept of immanence" (GA1 273), one toward which Scotus already points. The convertibility of *ens* and *verum* implies Lask's thesis, "the convertibility of the '*ens logicum*' with the objects" (GA1 279). But for Heidegger/Scotus the *ens logicum* (the object from the transcendental logical viewpoint) is an *ens in anima*. This cannot be an existing, psychically real entity, an act or representation, but only "what today one expresses as 'noematic meaning'" (GA1 277).

The allusion to Husserl is crucial to Heidegger's understanding of the *Bewandtnis* between knowledge and object. The noema, the significative content of the given, is nothing but the thing itself grasped in the *secunda intentio* of reflection, where consciousness is not oriented (as in the *prima intentio*) toward the "real object in its immediate reality" but "toward its own content" (GA1 279), i.e., the intelligibility "of" the real object, thus also its categorial structure. For Heidegger, the logical distinction between object of knowledge and knowledge of the object falls *within* an immanence governed by the (phenomenological) distinction between reflective and unreflective consciousness. The "cardinal distinction among modes of reality is that between consciousness and reality; more precisely, between non-valid modes of reality which can in turn always only be given in and through a context of meaning having the character of validity" (GA1 279). If it is true that "only because I live in the realm of validity do I know anything concerning what exists" (GA1 280), it is also true that only because I can reflect on such "living" can I know anything concerning the realm of validity.

With his phenomenological concept of immanence Heidegger can place Lask's theory of categorial validity "within the subject and judgment problem." If categories, which Heidegger here calls "elements and resources for interpreting the meaning of the experienceable" (GA1 400),[21] are not something "copied" from the real but ordering principles "with respect to" the material, then what needs explaining is, roughly, their *Erfullüngsbedürftigkeit* (Lask) or semantic quality, their *Hin-gelten* or holding "of" the material. Where Lask takes validity to be an irreducible transcendental category, Heidegger argues that it must be grounded in intentionality: "Intentionality is the 'defining category' of the logical realm" (GA1 283), i.e., the "moment which determines the order and characterizes the realm of logic" (GA1 281). Without taking this "subjective side" of logic into account, then, an "objective logical" theory of categories "necessarily remains incomplete" (GA1 404).

The category is the "most general determination of objects," but to speak of an object already implicates the subject (GA1 403). First, in the "mere givenness" of life consciousness is "oriented toward the 'true'" (GA1 285); and second, one becomes "conscious of it as true, valid meaning only through the judgment" (GA1 285). The theory of categories thus confronts the traditional problems of givenness and "predication" (GA1 403). How is the object as valid meaning ("the 'true'") given, such that the subject can "become conscious of meaning" through its "accomplishments" as "position taking" judging subject (GA1 285)? To ask how this predicative activity and its immanent logical construct—judgment meaning—can hold of transcendent objects ("non-valid modes of reality") takes one from the theory of categories to the theory of signification, and so must remain untreated here. But in the *Schluss* Heidegger sums up: only "by beginning with the judgment" can the "problem of the 'immanent' and 'transeunt' (lying 'outside of thinking') validity of the categories can be solved," since "without taking 'subjective logic' into account it makes no sense even to speak of immanent and transcendent validity" (GA1 404).

Heidegger had already touched on issues of subjective logic, though without developing them, when he introduced the term "projection" (*Projektion*) in discussing how an object domain is constituted by the category. For example, only by "projecting them into a homogeneous medium" or "*Lebenselement*" governed by the category can I count otherwise radically particular object-materials as "two *trees*" (GA1 255). And Husserl helps him unravel the hints of subjective logic in Scotus when the latter appeals to a subjective or "act" analysis in distinguishing between modes of givenness (*essendi, intelligendi, significandi*) (GA1 321).[22] But in Scotus, too, there is a lacuna: he lacks a "precise concept of the subject" (GA1 401). Together with the predominantly "objective-noematic orientation" of Scholastic psychology (GA1 205), this means that Scotus never fully coordinates a logic of the object (theory of categories) with the subjective logical problems of givenness and the constitution of objectivity in judgment.[23]

If medieval logic fails finally to co-ordinate subjective and objective logic, Heidegger is quick to note this same failing in contemporary logical theories as well. He contrasts two rival modern positions—Külpe's critical realism and Neo-Kantian transcendental idealism—to suggest that neither successfully clarifies the connection between knowledge and the object.

The critical realist position distinguishes between empirical (psychical) and rational (categorial) aspects of knowledge and holds that the latter, the categories, allow us to move from merely "positing" a transcendent object (on the basis of subjective givenness) to predicating something of it truly.[24] This avoids psychological idealism since categories are not principles of association working upon the givens of perception. But Heidegger notes that on Külpe's view the "real-world objects to be determined by knowledge" are not as such "present in perception, not simply given in consciousness, but only first of all to be grasped through the process of knowing, in particular, through scientific research," and that this is just the principal claim of Marburg (formal) idealism: the object of knowledge is not the given, but the valid judgment achieved by an infinitely pursued science, an Idea in the Kantian sense. Failing to recognize the significance of the problem of judgment (built into its own scientistic object-concept) for the "grounding of objectivity" (GA1 403), critical realism is not critical enough.[25]

But Marburg idealism also falls short, though in the opposite direction. First, it sidesteps the problem of givenness by treating space and time as categories. With this logicizing of Kant's Transcendental Aesthetic, formal idealism fails, on Heidegger's view, to "incorporate the principle of the material determination of form organically into its position" (GA1 404). If categories receive their sense from the material, they cannot be understood apart from phenomenological recourse to the givenness of different types of material. And second, out of fear of psychologism, it relegates the noetic or act sphere to the status of a categorial construction in "rational psychology." But if the material is given first of all not to a "theoretical" subject but to consciousness engaged in the pretheoretical, pragmatic life of the world, then such a formal reconstruction of "objectively valid" thinking will bypass the very dimension in which the origin of categories can be sought, viz., the intelligibility or clarity present in "life."

It was Lask who came closest to overcoming the inadequacies of current realism and idealism. He "unquestionably achieved something significant" with his theory of materially determined categorial form (GA1 405). But the problem of *how* the material determines form—the site of the *Urverhältnis*—ultimately opens onto a "new sphere" in which Lask was unable to "take sufficient account of the difference between sensible and non-sensible material" (GA1 405). That is, if the category is itself the "material" for transcendental logical knowing, Lask's elision of the question of how the category can be given (as sensibly-existent material is given in perception) will not do. Lask's "aletheiological realism" of meaning thus also remains finally uncritical, since he deems all such questions psychologistic. Heidegger points toward a solution to this problem by grounding validity in intentionality; and his preoccupation with Husserl's "categorial intuition" shows how seriously he took it in his later work.[26] Here, however, he simply remarks that without first getting clear about the "judging subject" one will "never succeed in bringing out the full sense of what one designates as 'validity'" (GA1 405).

Regarding the second horizon of the category problem, then, Heidegger suggests the need to bring the motives of critical realism and transcendental idealism "into a higher unity" (GA1 404). Külpe's realism properly preserves the transcendence of the object of knowledge, but its naturalism does not do justice to the problematic of meaning. Marburg idealism properly insists on the logical primacy of valid meaning but does not recognize, as Lask did, that "the most elemental problems of logic only show themselves to those logical investigators who take 'pre-scientific' knowledge into account" (LP 185) where the origin of materially determined form is to be sought. But if Lask grasped the material determination of form, his treatment of the relation between judgment and category remains stuck in a quasi-dogmatic sphere of "genuine transcendence," concerned with "structural problems" in abstraction from how structure is achieved or uncovered in immanence. The issue of material determination does not lead him to the "unavoidable principled investigation into the value and limits" of the form/matter dichotomy itself (GA1 405), and thus his "extremely fruitful" concept of meaning as the object "beyond the opposition" of truth and falsity drives him to "metaphysical problems of which he perhaps never became fully conscious" (GA1 406).[27] But then, what sort of "higher unity" does Heidegger propose? This is the third horizon of the category problem.

5. The Question of Metaphysics

The previous two problem areas belonged to logic as such, implying a co-ordination between its objective and subjective aspects. The third issue, however, requires a move beyond logic and thus raises the question of the relation between logical inquiry as a whole and what Heidegger here calls "metaphysics." On the basis of the foregoing we are now in a position to say something about the problematic character of this move.

If the first problem (categorially delimiting the logical realm of meaning) cannot be solved without appeal to the second (the subject and judgment problem), Heidegger goes part way toward this goal by appeal to Husserl's notion of immanence. Husserl's *Ideen I* has provided "decisive insight into the riches of 'consciousness' and has destroyed the oft-expressed opinion concerning the emptiness of consciousness in general" (GA1 405), but finally this is not enough: "One is not at all able to see logic and its problems in their true light unless the context from which they are interpreted becomes a translogical one" (GA1 405). In particular, the concept of immanence which contextualizes the subjective (phenomeno-) logical problems cannot be understood on the model of any traditional or current idealism or realism. Evidently the categories which would clarify this immanence itself are not to be gained by reflecting on the *Bewandtnis* of knowing, i.e., on the logical "epistemological subject." It is necessary to go beyond logic, beyond the "theoretical attitude," which "is only *one* among a wealth of formative directions of living spirit." The third horizon of the category problem thus appears as "the task of an ultimate metaphysical-teleological interpretation of consciousness" in terms of the notion of "living spirit" (GA1 406). Since this is "essentially historical spirit" (GA1 407), it is necessary that "history and its culture-philosophical, teleological interpretation" become an "element which determines significance within the category problem" (GA1 408); i.e., history belongs to the meaning-determining *material* in a theory of categorial form.

These notions raise a number of issues crucial to a full account of Heidegger's early logical work. For instance, though the call for metaphysics reflects his proximity to the Neo-Scholastics, Heidegger's own terms are far from the Aristotelian realism of a Geyser or a Sentroul; they derive from Hegel, or rather, from Dilthey's post-Hegelian *Lebensphilosophie*. But here we shall simply indicate the way Heidegger's call for metaphysics pertains to the logic of truth. It is the "truth problem," says Heidegger, that demands a "metaphysical-teleological interpretation of consciousness" in which philosophy leaves the logical "study of structures" and "breaks through to true reality and real truth" (GA1 406). If logical meaning (truth) is neither psychical nor metaphysical, Heidegger nevertheless demands that what might be called its "ontological" status be specified in some way. The structural form/material unity may suffice within logic, but "logical meaning must be made into a problem with respect to its ontic significance as well" if one is to ground logic's ability to "guarantee us true reality and objectivity" (GA1 406).

These elliptical remarks amount to the claim that transcendental logic fails to answer the question, What is meaning? "Metaphysics" is supposed to provide access to "ontic significance," but it is clear that Heidegger's usage in the *Schluss* does not correspond to the sense of metaphysics (a science of supersensible entities) found in the main text. What is ontic significance? When Heidegger suggests that this would be a "transcendental-ontic interpretation of the object concept," it is possible to hear in the term "ontic significance" what he will later develop as ontology, viz., a (transcendental) investigation of the meaning of the being of entities, the successor-discipline to the transcendental logical investigation of paradigmatic meaning as the ground of truth.

That a "metaphysics of meaning" arising from transcendental logic calls finally for something other than metaphysics is evident in the problem of trying to co-ordinate metaphysics and logic in the systematic terms of the main text. Given the absolute hegemony of logic as the theory of theory, its principles hold for metaphysics as a theory of supersensible entities as well. And given that object, form, and material are all logical principles, an ontic interpretation of the object could only be a grasp of the "ontic" significance of the *Urverhältnis* of form and material. For example, what does it mean to say that material "determines" form, or that form "clarifies" material? But if metaphysics is the science of supersensible entities, what can it tell us about that relation that logic cannot, since it already presupposes it? Whence come its "translogical" principles? Heidegger does not say, but two remarks point up the difficulty.[28] First, Heidegger insists that metaphysics and mysticism "belong together" in medieval philosophy, that "philosophy as a rationalistic construction cut off from life is powerless, mysticism as irrationalistic experience is purposeless;" thus rationalism and irrationalism must be seen in some sort of higher unity (GA1 410). And second, in connection with the problem of material determination he promises to show the philosophical relevance of Eckhart's mysticism for "the problem of truth" (GA1 402).[29] It thus appears that the form-determining material does not call for metaphysics as a "science" of supersensible entities. Instead, a breakthrough to the "true reality and real truth" of logical meaning, its "ontic significance," seems to imply an incorporation of mysticism. Yet it is also to have the character of a "*transcendental* ontic interpretation," meaning, I take it, that it remains focussed on the critical, phenomenologically understood "unique relation of being conscious" (GA1 277).

Hence the metaphysical horizon of the category problem calls for a transcendental ontic interpretation of the subject as well. The "true reality" of the subject, in whose immanence the problem of truth is structured and answered logically, is historical. The category cannot be deduced from a timeless consciousness in general, since it is a *Bewandtnis* of the material itself. Thus the discovery of categories—the emergence of the "resources for interpreting the meaning of the experienceable"—is an historical issue that must be brought to bear on an "ontic" interpretation of the nature of categories. If it is not first of all in science but in the pretheoretical intelligibility, the "living in validity," of everyday life that the *Bewandtnisse* of the material originally show themselves, it is artificial to limit the theory of categories to the principles of intelligibility of science. Intelligibility, categoriality, is not found only in theoretical life; consequently logic must recognize that the origins of meaning (and categories) lie in all the meaning-full formative directions of living spirit. Only by grasping the "fundamental metaphysical structure" of this historical living spirit "and its relation to the metaphysical 'origin'" can one understand how the "uniqueness and individuality of *acts* is amalgamated into a living unity with the universality and subsistence in itself of *meaning*" (GA1 410).[30]

Here then is the ultimate horizon of a metaphysics of meaning, a "metaphysics of the truth problem." The difference between meaning (the logical object) and acts in the psychological sense is presupposed, while Husserl's theory of intentionality shows that this is not incompatible with a non-psychological, logical investigation of acts. But at the metaphysical or "ontic" level there is still need to understand the being of the relation between individuality and universality, act and meaning, by investigating the fundamental metaphysical structure of historical living spirit. Making logic philosophical again demands a "transcendental ontic" interpretation of the phenomenological sphere of immanence, of consciousness. Epistemological immanence must be referred to the translogical context of historical living spirit as the original site (though not, apparently, the origin) of meaning. Heidegger does not say how one is to do this, nor what the logical status of such interpretation would be.

It would be possible to show that this demand very soon led Heidegger to one of his central innovations, viz., abandoning the transcendental *logical* identification of meaning with the "object" for the transcendental *ontological* concept of meaning as "world." But this would require consideration of his early Freiburg lecture courses, as would a complete account of how and why he came to drop the 1916 idea of the "deeper, essentially worldview character of philosophy" (GA1 410) underlying his mystically tinged metaphysics. Here we will only recall that the demand for a theory of categories, for philosophical science, continues to exert a hold on that text which investigates the "existentials" of Dasein. In its own way, and in spite of radical advances, *Sein und Zeit* continues to heed the challenge laid out in the logical truth problem, viz., that it clarify how true knowledge is possible in all the different modes of scientific inquiry, including its own. This does not represent a metaphysical resolution to the problem of knowledge, but a transcendental ontological reinterpretation of it.

4

Phenomenology, Hermeneutics, *Lebensphilosophie*: Heidegger's Confrontation with Husserl, Dilthey, and Jaspers

István M. Fehér

With the recent publication of some of Heidegger's early Freiburg lecture courses (GA56/57, GA58, GA61, GA63), as well as of related manuscripts such as the "Natorp essay" (PIA) and the lecture on the concept of time (BZ), we have been placed in a better position to understand Heidegger's philosophical path leading up to *Being and Time* (a path long closed to us by a decade of silence preceding *Being and Time*) and thereby to understand also this magnum opus itself. Another important early document from Heidegger's postwar period, his unpublished extensive review of Jaspers, has been available for some time now (GA9 1–44). So has the text of Heidegger's apparently most comprehensive and detailed confrontation with Husserl's phenomenology on his way to *Being and Time*; namely, his lecture course of SS 1925 (GA20).

In the following chapter I wish to focus upon Heidegger's hermeneutic turn, viz., his transformation of Husserl's phenomenology into his own project of fundamental ontology, which is conceived in terms of an existential analytic as a hermeneutic of human existence. In addition to the texts referred to above, I wish also to draw occasionally upon student transcripts of some of Heidegger's hitherto unpublished lecture courses.[1]

The thesis I wish to illustrate is that Heidegger's confrontation and critique of Husserlian phenomenology ran parallel to his growing sense for hermeneutics, and was partly influenced by his encounter with the thought of some other important thinkers of the time, such as Dilthey and Jaspers. The hermeneutic transformation of phenomenology is clearly anticipated in the review of Jaspers. The historicist rejection of Husserl's transcendental ego is likewise hardly conceivable without the influence of historicist thinkers such as Dilthey. As a matter of fact, there is a whole complex of criss-crossing influences at work in the young Heidegger's development, each of which deserves autonomous treatment one after the other—an undertaking that necessarily falls outside the scope of this paper. I propose to focus on Heidegger's confrontation with Husserl, and I will refer to other influences and encounters, mostly with an eye to his absorption of the *lebensphilosophisch*-hermeneutic problematic, only insofar as this perspective makes it indispensable.

In order to delimit the hermeneutic horizon of this paper, three additional preliminary observations should be made. First: hermeneutic phenomenology as elaborated in *Being and Time* is also ontology (i.e., not anthropology); thus, to speak of a hermeneutic transformation of phenomenology amounts to speaking of an ontological transformation of it. Husserl's phenomenology—which confined itself to an investigation of the constituting acts of transcendental consciousness, thereby suspending assertions concerning being—is in Heidegger reoriented toward the being-question and turned into a phenomenological ontology. For Heidegger, the *Sache*, the "thing," which phenomenology must let us see, is being. However, he transformed not only phenomenology in an ontological way, but also hermeneutics itself. Like phenomenology, hermeneutics was also given an ontological dimension that it formerly did not have. The hermeneutic turn of philosophy that Heidegger carried out implies not only the elaboration of the operation called *Verstehen*. More importantly, it implies that interpretation is no longer seen as an auxiliary discipline of the human sciences, as dealing with the rules of the interpretation of texts. Rather, it emerges as an autonomous philosophical perspective, insofar as the human being is viewed as an interpreting animal in all the modes of everyday activities and not just in the handling of classical texts in the human sciences. This obviously also holds for the activity we call philosophical research, i.e., questioning. As an interpreting animal, the human being interprets being as well, and Heidegger formulates his being-question specifically as a question of the *meaning* of being. Phenomenology, hermeneutics, and ontology accordingly become fused in Heidegger's elaboration of the being-question. He gave phenomenology a hermeneutic dimension, such that this hermeneutically transformed phenomenology was assigned the role of serving as fundamental ontology. This perspective emerges in virtue of a prior fusion of a number of significant influences. And some of these have not yet been mentioned, such as the Aristotelian-Scholastic, Neo-Kantian-logical, and Christian-theological influences. In the following discussion I shall exhibit a cross-section of this philosophical landscape, highlighting some influences, and eclipsing and forcing others into the background.

Second observation: a distinction must be made between carrying out the transformation and offering an explicit critical evaluation of that which is transformed. The hermeneutic-ontological transformation of Husserlian phenomenology is one thing; giving a detailed critique of Husserlian phenomenology following from (by basing itself upon) a previous transformation of it is quite a different matter. The former is obviously a presupposition of the latter. Now the first seems to have been well under way from KNS 1919 onward (or even earlier), whereas a detailed confrontation and critique of Husserl is not offered (as far as we can see today) until the lecture course of SS 1925. Obviously, Heidegger must have already worked out an autonomous stance toward Husserl—must have transformed his phenomenology—in order to gain a view on it. The transformation thus clearly has two phases. First comes the phase of the transformation proper, which may (but need not) be accompanied by important critical remarks and hints, but hardly by any extensive confrontation. After the transformation is realized, and the new perspective sufficiently consolidated, it becomes possible to give a detailed critical reconstruction of the thing transformed. In any case, one may legitimately claim that the discussion of Heidegger's relation to and critique of Husserl cannot be restricted to the lecture course of SS 1925, while it is presumably also correct to maintain that this course contains the most mature and developed discussion of Husserl's phenomenology on the way to *Being and Time*.

Third observation: to speak of Heidegger's *transformation* of Husserl's phenomenology, insofar as this term is applied, not so much to characterize part of the history of "the phenomenological movement" but rather to describe Heidegger's own development, must in several important respects be regarded as erroneous, or at least as ambiguous and misleading. Indeed, one's transformation of something clearly presupposes one's first getting hold of the thing as it is in itself in order then to modify or transform it. This way of putting things tacitly assumes that Heidegger had first appropriated phenomenology in its original, i.e., Husserlian form. But as we shall see, this is precisely not the case. His appropriation of Husserl's phenomenology was far from being a neutral assimilation; rather, it showed from the very beginning a highly critical attitude prompted by the simultaneous assimilation of some leading motifs of life-philosophy. Appropriation and transformation (if we stick with the latter word) were apparently going on hand in hand, giving us a good example of Heidegger's own theory of the fore-structure of understanding in *Being and Time*.

I. Proto-hermeneutic motifs in the young Heidegger's student and academic writings

Heidegger's first philosophical writings are embedded in, and thoroughly permeated by, the philosophical perspective of anti-psychologism common to the two prominent German philosophical schools of the day, namely, phenomenology and Neo-Kantianism. Some of the essential motives inspiring both of these tendencies centered around their common battle with positivism and naturalism, i.e., against the attempt either to dissolve philosophy into the kind of positive knowledge exemplified by the triumphant natural sciences or to absorb it into the new form of psychology, namely, experimental psychology—psychology "without soul." Here the argument ran roughly as follows: epistemology and logic are the central philosophical disciplines; knowing, however, is just one phenomenon, in addition to "feeling" and "willing," occurring in the psyche of the living being called human. Scientific, i.e., no longer "speculative," philosophy should therefore find its fundament in psychology. Central to the philosophical outlook of anti-psychologism was the distinction between "psychic act" and "logical content," i.e., between the *fact* of cognitive acts going on in the psyche of existing human beings, on the one hand, and the *validity* or *truth* claims pertaining to those acts, on the other. What is "true" or "valid" for the anti-psychologists is the "ideal content"; psychic acts, by contrast, can only be said to take place or not to take place, to occur or not to occur—similar to any kind of natural event or process such as an eclipse—but can in no way be called "true." The subject matter of logic or epistemology is constituted by those ideal contents, while the psychic act does not belong in the realm of logic at all. What was at stake for the anti-psychologists was thus the autonomy of philosophy, the existence of "truth" and "validity," which psychologism threatened to relativize and make subject-dependent.

From the start, when the young Heidegger took an interest in philosophy, he became an enthusiastic defender of anti-psychologism (see GA1 7). He had, however, his own reasons for doing so. His mentor, the theologian Carl Braig, who decisively influenced the young Heidegger's career through his book *Vom Sein: Abriß der Ontologie*, orienting him towards the ontological problematic, was a fervent apologist of Catholic doctrine over against all forms of "modernism" (a word coined by him). Braig held Kant to be a subjectivist.[2] In one of his first philosophical writings on the problem of reality in modern philosophy, the young Heidegger also claimed that Kant was "a classical representative of phenomenalism" (GA1 9). From the realistic standpoint proper to Scholasticism, Braig attacked the tendency, going back to Schleiermacher, to subjectivize concepts of God, theological assertions, and faith in general—a subjectivization connected to the claim that all they amounted to was the subject's *Erlebnisse*, but not objective truth. What Braig basically attacked was the psychologistic conception of the day, which permeated all areas of culture, including religion. Heidegger himself, in the introduction to his dissertation, also called his time an "age of psychology" (GA1 63). So it is plausible to assume that Heidegger's approach, or "access," to the psychologism debate was motivated by this theological background. It thereby makes understandable the rationale he had for taking sides with anti-psychologism.

In both phenomenology and Neo-Kantianism, the distinction between "psychic act" and "logical content" gave anti-psychologism the character of a Platonic two-world theory, which Heidegger would sharply criticize throughout the twenties. This criticism is in fact an integral part of his deconstruction, and thereby also transformation, of the philosophical presuppositions of both phenomenology and modern epistemological philosophy in general, a point to which we shall return in the course of this chapter.[3] If we consider the deconstruction of the two-world theories of transcendental phenomenology and Neo-Kantian epistemology as crucial for Heidegger's hermeneutic breakthrough (and we have reasons to do so), then the zero point of this development may be seen to lie in Heidegger's early adherence to the anti-psychologistic perspective, an adherence that is not exempt from some characteristic reservations from the very beginning.

In his 1912 article on "Recent Developments in Logic," Heidegger suggests (despite his appreciation for the distinction delineated above) that "the sharp delimitation of logic against psychology is perhaps not feasible" (*durchführbar*). For, he argues,

> it is one thing whether psychology founds logic in a fundamental way . . . and another whether psychology is assigned the role of becoming a first ground of activity, an operational basis [for logic]. And the latter is the case, for we have to do here with a specific state of affairs implicating a series of problems that we may perhaps never be able to wholly illuminate—namely, that *the logical is embedded* [eingebettet] *in the psychic*. (GA1 29f.; my emphasis)

It is at this point that Heidegger announces his first tentative doubt about the sharply dualistic perspective proper to anti-psychologism. This critical stance will be developed in the twenties and will underlie both his criticism of the transcendental outlook and his own autonomous perspective growing out of such criticism. It is of course not a matter of indifference, he adds immediately after the above-cited passage, in what way psychology—or what kind of psychology—may lay claim to a relation to logic. Experimental psychology is naturally of no use here. And even introspective psychology can be relied upon only if we assume a specific comportment, namely, if attention is directed toward *meanings*, the *sense* of acts. But that is exactly what Husserl's phenomenology of consciousness aims at; it is in this sense, Heidegger concludes, that "psychology will always have a connection to philosophy" (GA1 30).

Psychology conceived in terms of a phenomenology of meaning, providing an "operational basis" for logic, and remaining, in this sense, forever relevant to philosophy: we may find here the seeds for what Heidegger will come to elaborate as the hermeneutics of facticity, viz., existential analytic. Indeed "logic," the doctrine of *logos*, assumed for him the meaning of theoretical comportment as such in the broadest sense. At the same time he saw traditional ontology obtaining its access to being from within the horizon provided by the theoretical attitude. Thus an ontological thematization of the being of *logos*, i.e., of theoretical comportment, aiming to probe into its deeper dimensions by showing it to be a derivative attitude of those beings called humans, will provide an "operational basis" for the posing of the being-question. This thematization of *logos*, here of the human being as that being which possesses *logos*, will be provided in *Being and Time* under the name of "existential analytic." And, in fact, Heidegger writes in *Being and Time* that "the 'logic' of the *logos* is rooted in the existential analytic of Dasein," a claim made hermeneutically plausible "by demonstrating that assertion is derived from interpretation and understanding" (SZ 160/203).

We already saw that for the young Heidegger "*the logical is embedded in the psychic*." We now see that, insofar as (logical) assertion is derived from interpretation and understanding, logic later gets embedded in the existential analytic which is carried out in *Being and Time*. The latter is a hermeneutic radicalization (its primary structures are "understanding" and "interpretation") of what is outlined in Heidegger's early paper as psychology in the sense of a phenomenology as a doctrine of meaning.[4] Psychology, so defined, "will always have a connection to philosophy."

Both Heidegger's dissertation and his *Habilitationsschrift* are permeated by the perspective of anti-psychologism. I wish to single out only a few methodological considerations here. These bear a proto-hermeneutic character in regard to the hermeneutic circle.

In his dissertation, in the midst of his criticism of psychologism, Heidegger stops at one point to formulate general methodological questions. What is at issue is whether the most efficient criticism conceivable (the Husserlian sort) can ever succeed in refuting the psychologist conclusively, i.e., convincing him about the absurdity of his position. Any science can be considered, so argues Heidegger, as a questioning of a given domain of objects. The meaning of a question must first be oriented towards the object under inquiry. There are questions that cannot be answered because they are *a priori* incompatible with the characteristics of the object under question, so that any kind of answer one can give would be meaningless with regard to it. These are questions, e.g., about the weight of a geometrical object, that fail to be oriented towards the object, i.e., misunderstand it from the very beginning. Psychologism is a questioning of just this sort, for the characteristics of psychological objects are incompatible with those of logical objects. The psychologist does not merely misunderstand logic; he or she simply does not understand logic at all! In other words, it is not merely a matter of insufficient or false knowledge of logic; the psychologist has no knowledge of it at all! (GA1 161) The psychologist can hardly be persuaded, for he or she is simply blind to logic. How can you prove to the psychologist that there is a domain called logic? No proof of any sort can be provided, because reality, that which is, can only be shown (GA1 165; cf. 213).

The hermeneutic concept of preunderstanding, as well as that of the circle, are obviously at work here. Unless one has some preliminary knowledge of the object of inquiry, no science can be put into motion, no reasonable or meaningful question can be asked. Preunderstanding is a necessary prerequisite of knowledge. Preliminary acquaintance with the object and the resulting development of explicit knowledge of it constitute at the same time a circle within which alone anything like "proof" is possible. That there are limits to demonstration will then become a well-established claim of Heidegger's throughout his career (e.g., GA61 166; SZ 229/271; GA65 13; SD 80/72). The hermeneutic logic, the mutual conditionality, of question and answer (GA61 153), as well as the formal structure of questioning in general, to be elaborated in detail in §2 of *Being and Time*, are not only clearly anticipated but also fairly well delineated at this point in Heidegger's doctoral dissertation.[5]

II. The postwar turn

To speak about the presence of proto-hermeneutic elements in the young Heidegger's student and academic writings is not to speak about the hermeneutic transformation of phenomenology. Although the young Heidegger seems to have been fairly familiar with Husserl's phenomenology and to have adhered to its basic anti-psychologism without reservations, it is unclear how far he had appropriated phenomenology in its complexity by the end of the First World War. We know from an October 8, 1917, letter by Husserl to Natorp that Heidegger's first in-depth confrontation with phenomenology ("seeking to come to grips with [it] from within") took place near the end of the war.[6] Last but not least, the young Heidegger can in no way be said to have had a philosophical outlook of his own. Had he not published a work with the title *Being and Time* in 1927, the student and academic writings would presumably be of no importance today. In other words, the significance of these early writings lies clearly in their anticipatory character.

Heidegger was to find his own voice and start the move toward *Being and Time* only after the war. Seeking to confront the leading philosophical movements, Heidegger's strategy strives to uncover what he perceives to be the common deficiencies inherent in the philosophical positions of the day—positions that often stand in sharpest opposition to each other. Epistemologically oriented scientific philosophy is criticized for not being scientific enough, life philosophy is accused of failing to grasp life itself, existential philosophy is charged with not seizing upon existence, historicism is called to account for losing sight of history, and, last but not least, phenomenology is accused of not being phenomenological enough—indeed, of being "unphenomenological." Underlying Heidegger's critiques is a new hermeneutic concept of philosophy, allowing him to develop all of these criticisms from a single intuition. The various aspects of *critique* later coalesce within the project of fundamental ontology into the concept of *destruction* (an integral part of the redefined phenomenological method). Unravelling the different lines of criticism would require more space than is available here, so I shall confine discussion to considerations centering around phenomenology.[7]

II. 1. The Emergence of the Hermeneutic Viewpoint

It is somehow the prerogative, or perhaps the fate, of every great philosopher to rethink and redefine the concept of philosophy itself. Small wonder then that Heidegger, when he set out on his own, repeatedly reflected upon philosophy itself, reexamining its very concept and meaning.[8] That is exactly what he is doing with regard to phenomenology as well. Or, more precisely, since phenomenology provided him with the "method" for reexamining the concept of philosophy, the rethinking of philosophy became for him inseparable from coming to grips with phenomenology. While his remarks on phenomenology in the academic writings scarcely amount to more than a faithful recapitulation or exposition, the postwar observations display a tendency toward a comprehensive confrontation with its basic concepts and theoretical fundaments. The lecture course of WS 1919–20, bearing the title *Grundprobleme der Phänomenologie*, begins with the following characteristic sentence: "For phenomenology, the most original and decisive problem of phenomenology is phenomenology itself" (GP 10-10-19; GA58 1; see also GA9 36).

The Platonizing-*wissenschaftstheoretisch* perspective of the prewar student and academic writings quickly gives way to a radical reorientation. The new password sounds: back to life in its originality![9] This in turn implies a twofold claim: to go back to original experience (i.e., to gain a new access to life), and—together with it—to find appropriate means for its description, to develop a conceptuality adequate to it. One of Heidegger's basic insights is that contemporary philosophy's descriptions of everyday life, the environing world, etc., stem from and are rooted in theoretical comportment and conceptuality. They therefore fail to do justice to factical life, its comportment and the language it speaks, precisely insofar as the theoretical attitude is a derivative mode of factical life.

This endeavor bears in itself some basic characters of phenomenology. The proclamation of returning to "the things themselves" was Husserl's battle cry in his programmatic *Logos*-essay.[10] It implies the suspension of traditional philosophical strategies, dismissal of authorities, and, with regard to method, the preference for description over construction.[11]

Heidegger heartily welcomed this innermost tendency of phenomenology, and it may well have been that under its spell he soon proceeded to radicalize it in such a way as to turn it against itself. In fact, for Heidegger phenomenology became identical with philosophy. From this postwar period to his last years he repeatedly maintained that phenomenology was not just a philosophical "trend," one "standpoint" among many possible others, but was, in the radicalized sense he came to give it, equivalent to the innermost possibility of philosophy itself (GA56/57 110; GA58 139, 233; GA61 187; GA63 72; PIA 247; GA19 9; GA20 184/136; GA21 32, 279f.; SZ 38/62; GA24 3/3; GA29/30 534; US 95; SD 90/82). Phenomenology was a possibility for Heidegger, not just something to be taken over in its actuality from someone, not even from Husserl. On the contrary, "Higher than actuality stands *possibility*. We can understand phenomenology only by seizing upon it as a possibility" (SZ 38/63).

Against phenomenology in the name of phenomenology itself: that is one way in which we might characterize Heidegger's postwar efforts to come to grips with phenomenology and with contemporary philosophy in general. Philosophy was to be renewed phenomenologically—a renewal that was to affect deeply the innermost character of phenomenology itself.[12] KNS 1919 already shows some important reservations about Husserl's actual phenomenology, as well as the outlines of another possible phenomenology. These remarks are woven into a criticism of the epistemological Neo-Kantian philosophy as such, and appear in the form of an attack against the primacy of the theoretical. Heidegger observes that the distortive representations of life and the environing world are due not simply to the prevalence of naturalism, as Husserl thought, but to the domination of the theoretical in general (GA56/57 87; see also GP 10-10-19). Heidegger here interprets Husserl's "principle of all principles" by noting that it is not at all theoretical in character, but expresses the most original attitude (*Urhaltung*) of life, that of remaining close to its own experiencing (GA56/57 109f.).[13] It expresses indeed a fundamental attitude (*Grundhal-*

tung) rather than a scientific method. To claim that phenomenology is a standpoint would be a "mortal sin," simply because it would restrict its possibilities. But, Heidegger immediately asks, is it not already a deviation, having the character of a hidden theory, to turn the sphere of living experience into something given? (GA56/57 111; cf. GA58 221) This doubt is one of the first signs of Heidegger's basic dissatisfaction with Husserlian phenomenology, which will lead up to the grandiose critique of SS 1925. Here Husserl will be charged with the unphenomenological attitude of dogmatism with respect to nothing less than the delimiting of the field of research of phenomenology itself to transcendental consciousness (GA20 159/115, 178/128). The world of lived experience knows of no such duality between object and knowledge.

In 1921–22 Heidegger suggests, proceeding along much the same lines, that phenomenological constitution is not necessarily tied to the concept of the transcendental (GA61 173; cf. GA58 229). He urges that the meaning of Descartes' "I am" should be investigated more deeply, and warns, in accordance with his "formally indicative" method, against allowing traditional views of the "I" to infiltrate surreptitiously. If life is to be brought to self-showing, then it is the "am" rather than the "I" which must be stressed (GA61 173ff.; later SZ 46/71, 211/254). In the third part of the course, in developing significant hints given in 1919–20, Heidegger provides the first detailed analysis of what in 1923 will be called "hermeneutics of facticity" and in *Being and Time* "existential analytic"—a description put under the heading of "factical life."

In conjunction with Heidegger's postwar dissatisfaction with the basically theoretical character of contemporary philosophy, including Husserlian phenomenology, we find repeated attempts to redefine the original character of the description of factical life. As early as KNS 1919, in outlining the idea of philosophy as "*Urwissenschaft*," primal science—whose circular character is accentuated several times[14]—and, more specifically, in the interpretation of phenomenology as pretheoretical "*Urwissenschaft*," Heidegger presents his alternative in terms of "hermeneutical intuition," to which he assigns the role of remaining close to *Erleben*, living experiencing. What is meaningful, or is of the character of linguistic expression, need not necessarily be theoretical—in fact, this springs from life, "lives in life itself" (GA56/57 117; see also GA61 88, 99). In Heidegger's redefinition of the specific descriptive character of phenomenology, the coupling term "phenomenological hermeneutics" appears several times between 1919 and 1922, until hermeneutics attains a detailed reinterpretation and consolidated initial meaning in the coining of the phrase "hermeneutics of facticity" in 1922–23.[15]

As part of the rethinking of the methodological devices of phenomenology, we find sketches and outlines of a theory of understanding with its characteristic pre-structure (GA56/57 116f.; GA61 41ff., 59; GA9 9, 32, 38f.; GA63 79f.; for later, see GA20 416/300). A result of this reconsideration is the exposition of what Heidegger calls "formal indication," which is taken to be *the* method proper to philosophy or phenomenology (GA9 9f., 29; GA58 248; GA61 20, 32ff., 60, 66f., 113, 116, 134, 141, 175; GA21 410; GA29/30 425ff.). Generally speaking, it is due to Heidegger's search for proper methodological devices for an adequate conceptual expression of "factical life" that the hermeneutic problematic emerges in the postwar lecture courses. Theoretically (and ahistorically) neutral knowledge is opposed to, and gives way to, existentially (and historically) involved understanding (or preunderstanding) and interpreting, whereby knowledge becomes at best a subdivision of understanding. All these efforts are in the service of seizing "life." The main character of the latter is care (*Sorge*) rather than knowledge (GA61 89ff.; PIA 240).

It is in his effort to gain a new access to life, as well as to reject the theoretical conceptuality and comportment proper to transcendental philosophy, that Heidegger formulates his hermeneutic concepts and formal indication, and so comes to the elaboration of a hermeneutics of facticity. "Facticity" is a term adopted to substitute for the vague and ambiguous concept of life employed by life-philosophy, as well as for that of "existence" employed by Jaspers and Kierkegaard.[16] "Hermeneutics," "hermeneutical," have the sense of rival concepts to "theory," "theoretical," understood in terms of "theoretically neutral." The description of life, or "facticity," obtains an overall hermeneutic character precisely in virtue of the insight that interpretation cannot be regarded as something added, as a kind of extension or annex, as it were, to some theoretically neutral (and allegedly "objective") description of a state of affairs. Rather, preliminary "interpretedness" is inherent in all kinds of description, in all kinds of seeing, saying, and experiencing. (See GA61 86f.; PIA 241, 264; for later, see GA20 75/56, 190/140, 416/300; SZ 169/213, 383/435.) If there is no "pure" theory (for "theory" is a derivative mode of being or comportment of a particular being called human), there is also no pure description. What this insight implies for an adequate description of life or facticity is that theoretical concepts, as well as the language that theory speaks, should be abandoned in favor of a language growing out of everyday life and able to let things be seen in their interpretedness, that is, in exactly the way we encounter them and deal with them; a hammer, e.g., is primarily encountered as a tool for pounding nails into the wall, etc., rather than as a neutral thing out there having the property of weight (SZ 154ff./195ff.). We shall return to this point in the discussion of Heidegger's criticism of Husserl.

This reevaluation of interpretation implies that hermeneutics cannot remain a subordinate discipline of the human sciences, but becomes, as Heidegger explicitly states, "the self-interpretation of facticity" (GA63 14). It is important to see that this "self-interpretation of facticity" is not a kind of anthropology, simply a matter of our having to do with ourselves, implying that other beings of the world are left untouched.[17] Insofar as humans are precisely the beings who describe the world in its entirety, hermeneutics gets linked to ontology—a major reason why, in the title of the SS 1923 lecture course, "hermeneutics of facticity" and "ontology" occur together, clearly anticipating the correlation of fundamental ontology and existential analytic in *Being and Time*. The relation of hermeneutics to facticity, moreover is, not such, Heidegger adds, that facticity is the "object" of hermeneutics, it is just a question of grasping this object adequately. Hermeneutics is rather a way of being pertaining to facticity itself, so that if we define the latter as the "object" of hermeneutics, hermeneutics itself is affected intrinsically with regard to its "object."[18]

II. 2. The Husserl-Critique of 1925

This rough sketch puts us in a position to leap forward to Heidegger's critique of Husserl's phenomenology in the lecture course of SS 1925. At the risk of oversimplifying Heidegger's complex treatment, I will condense the discussion into one basic issue. This is the delimitation of the specific field of research of phenomenology itself, in other words, the self-concretization of phenomenological philosophy out of its initial principle or maxim. The basic issue is whether and how phenomenology gets access to and comes to delimit its own field of research, whether the procedure thereby employed is phenomenologically coherent or not.

Heidegger begins by defending Husserl's phenomenology, its central concept of intentionality, over against the charges of dogmatism, viz., metaphysical speculation. Indeed, owing to its Scholastic origin and the fact that Husserl took it over from Brentano, Rickert claimed this concept was permeated with "traditional metaphysical dogmas" (GA20 35f./28f.). After a detailed examination of this charge, Heidegger comes to the conclusion that it is not intentionality as such that might legitimately be claimed to be dogmatic, but rather that to which intentionality gets tacitly linked or bound, that of which it is claimed to be the specific structure. In fact, intentionality is held to be the specific structure of the psyche, reason, consciousness, etc. (rather than, say, of nature), all of which are ontological regions naively, traditionally, and so dogmatically assumed rather than phenomenologically discussed, delimited, and elaborated. Rather than an ultimate explanation of psychic reality, Heidegger observes significantly, intentionality is a way of overcoming such traditional ontological realities as psyche, consciousness, reason.[19] The question is whether access to that of which intentionality is declared to be the structure is attained in a phenomenological way.

Insofar as the principle of phenomenology ("To the things themselves!") requires suspension of unwarranted constructions and subjection of the unquestioned domination of philosophical theories to critical examination, Heidegger's objection strikes home; it turns out to be eminently phenomenological. From it Heidegger infers the inevitability of the being-question. The issue concerns the delimitation of the "thing itself" in a phenomenological way—the question of whether the linking of intentionality to pure consciousness, or to the transcendental ego, is carried out phenomenologically, and not simply by taking over the leading idea of modern philosophy.[20] That phenomenology may be shown to be intrinsically incoherent or inconsistent, i.e., "unphenomenological,"[21] affected with metaphysical bias, is significant enough. However, it is not yet clear whether the posing of the being-question is really inevitable, i.e., whether and why phenomenology is to be radicalized ontologically. Can the being-question be dispensed with? The inevitability of this question follows for Heidegger from the fact that—although Husserl fails to pose it, claiming to suspend "assertions concerning being," although he leaves the being of intentionality in obscurity—he nevertheless answers it tacitly by linking it to an ontological region called transcendental consciousness. Moreover, he makes distinctions of being like the one between being as consciousness and being as transcendent being, which he himself, symptomatically, calls "the most radical of all the distinctions of being."[22] Remarkably enough, while prohibiting the making of assertions about being, he tacitly commits himself to certain ontological positions without thematizing the access to those positions phenomenologically.[23]

The immanent reexamination and renewal of phenomenology thus shows the necessity of an ontological transformation. To achieve this renewal, can we receive some help from phenomenology itself? How, in what kind of experience, do we gain access to intentional being? Can we experience this being more originally, more unprejudiced, as it were? (GA20 152/110f.) The experience of the distinction between empirical reality and pure consciousness is characterized by Husserl in terms of a change in attitude. Performing phenomenological reductions, the being of the outside world (including my empirical consciousness) is bracketed so as to gain access, through reflections, to pure "*Erlebnisse*," experiences, and their "essences." Let us look more closely at what is going on here. What exactly is it that gets bracketed; what precisely characterizes the region that now, at the moment it gets left behind, is put out of action? In the natural attitude, the world is present as a spatio-temporal sequence of events including the psychic processes going on in the minds of empirically existing people, as opposed to the new realm, i.e., the pure region of consciousness, which we are about to enter, where man appears merely as a living being, a zoological object among others.

Let us stop at this point. We may legitimately ask whether one really experiences oneself in the manner described here in this alleged "natural attitude"? In other words, is this attitude indeed so natural? Is it not rather artificial or, in any case, theoretical? Do I really experience myself "naturally" as a living being, a zoological object, out there, present-at-hand as any other? Do I not rather experience myself as someone engaged in a particular activity, job, and the like?[24]

It suffices to have followed Heidegger's criticism up to this point to see how the previously accomplished transformation of phenomenology (a more original phenomenology as a "science of the origins of life" [GP 10-7-19, 11-7-19], as a hermeneutics of facticity) enables Heidegger to uncover the hidden dogmatic, i.e., "theoretical," presuppositions of phenomenology, as well as to make Husserl's transcendental elaboration of it superfluous and indeed empty.[25] And because the primacy of the theoretical is not a modern development, but rather goes back to the Greeks,[26] this calls for a destruction of the conceptuality of the history of ontology—not simply a turn away from (as Husserl urged) but a radical new turn toward the history of philosophy.[27]

The implications of the above criticisms for a transformation of phenomenology in terms of its ontological-hermeneutic renewal are simple enough: an attempt should be made to experience intentional being more originally, i.e., in a more unprejudiced way, in its "natural" setting, thereby no longer taking the traditional definition of man as *animal rationale* for granted.[28] This is exactly what *Being and Time* will do under the heading of an "existential analytic."

A good example of Heidegger's modified outlook: by adopting a hermeneutic way of seeing, traditional empiricism can be shown to be insufficiently "empirical," indeed, laden with a multitude of dogmatic "theoretical" presuppositions. In turning to "factical life," Heidegger might have been expected to embrace empiricism, but the "experience" Heidegger has in mind is something entirely different from the concept of experience employed in empirical philosophy. "Experience" is a key word for the young Heidegger, but as he elucidates it "experience is not understood here in a theoretical sense, as empiricist perceiving in contradistinction to something like rational thinking" (GA61 91). What we perceive in the first place is, hermeneutically seen, emphatically not "sense data." "What we 'first' hear," writes Heidegger in *Being and Time*, "is never noises or complexes of sounds, but the creaking wagon, the motorcycle. We hear the column on the march, the north wind, the woodpecker tapping, the fire crackling." And then he adds, significantly: "It requires a very artificial and complicated comportment [*Einstellung*] to 'hear' a 'pure noise'" (SZ 164/ 207; cf. GA20 367/266). In other words, to claim that we first perceive a "pure noise" requires a change of comportment, the assumption of a theoretical attitude. In like manner, what we do see in the first place is not anything like colored surfaces, or, still less, "sense data," but, e.g., the professor's chair, a ready-to-hand object in our surrounding world.[29] What is immediately given is not acts of consciousness. An immediate, unprejudiced experiencing knows of no acts of consciousness, sense data, pure sounds or noises, complexes of colors and surfaces, and the like.

The emergence of the hermeneutical dimension in Heidegger's thought, as well as the hermeneutical reshaping of phenomenology, are, as we have seen, inspired to a considerable extent by Heidegger's effort to develop an original, "unprejudiced" approach to life. It is therefore in order, finally, to focus a bit more on his confrontation with life-philosophy.[30]

II. 3. The Lebensphilosophisch-Existentialist Motif

One crucial point of criticism that runs through the early courses is that the alternative of scientific, rational, or theoretical philosophy *versus* irrationalism, life-philosophy, or historicism is not a genuine one. These major trends (in short: metaphysical *versus* anti-metaphysical traditions) are indeed complementary to one other. Epistemologically oriented philosophy fails to seize upon life because its outlook and conceptuality are rooted in theoretical comportment, and in a derivative mode of it. But the opponents, life-philosophy, historicism, and any kind of irrationalism, remain dependent on it precisely to the extent to which they claim life, history, or existence to be inaccessible to concepts, a claim that does not make sense unless one tacitly assumes that the concepts developed by theoretical, epistemological philosophy (as well as the comportment from which they spring) are unchallengeable, to which we cannot even conceive alternatives. In the course of various devastating criticisms, Heidegger more often than not takes great pains to note that there is a positive and original impulse inherent in life-philosophy, that he indeed appreciates this impulse very much, while what he rejects is rather its insufficient (because parasitic) realization (GA61 82, 117; GA9 13f.; GA63 69, 108; GP 10–7–19; PhA 6–20–20; PhR 38). We should note that when Heidegger, for all his criticism, emphasizes the positive tendencies of life-philosophy, the philosopher he most frequently has in mind is Dilthey (see GA63 42; further GA9 13f.; PhA 6–20–20; GA61 7). And we can hardly conceive of

Heidegger's historicist opposition to Husserl's transcendental ego and the stress upon "*das Historische,*" the historical, without Dilthey's influence.[31] Heidegger seems to suggest that the basic effort of life-philosophy is correct. He seems even to share the view of contemporary philosophy that the object primarily to be approached and investigated is "life."[32] But rather than developing conceptual means adequate to its ownmost object, to "life," life-philosophy relies upon the tools of the adversary for its own concepts, tends to borrow them from there.[33] That is also the reason why, having realized that their tools are not equal to the task, life-philosophers tend to come inevitably to the conclusion that life, history, and existence are irrational. The point Heidegger makes could be put as follows: irrationalist philosophy is really too rational. In claiming its objects to be irrational, it uncritically borrows the measure or concept of rationality from the adversary rather than developing or elaborating a rationality or conceptuality of its own, one conforming to its "object."[34]

Heidegger's objections to Jaspers move in the same vein. He maintains that the way "existence" is characterized by Jaspers is reifying, containing as it does Bergsonian overtones.[35] It is in the course of these observations that he first presents his decisive alternative, namely, "hermeneutical concepts" (GA9 32).

In summary we can say that, in several important respects, it was the appropriation and radicalization of the *lebensphilosophisch*-existentialist problematic that led Heidegger to transform Husserl's phenomenology hermeneutically. But we may perhaps express this even more radically by saying that the hermeneutic transformation of phenomenology is in several important respects *the* consistent radicalization of the *lebensphilosophisch*-existentialist problematic, and not just one implication of it— something that may arbitrarily follow or may not. Heidegger's primary effort seems to have been directed toward gaining a new and genuine access to "life"—one without unwarranted constructions, uncontrolled prejudices, and presuppositions—an attempt in which the means were to be provided by phenomenology. That is how and why phenomenology was to undergo a transformation or, since it was shown to be laden with "unphenomenological" prejudices, even "purification."

Finally, I may refer to a further interesting connection of phenomenology, hermeneutics, Dilthey, and historicism in Heidegger's thought. Heidegger emphasized several times that what Dilthey was striving to get access to was, although he himself was not fully aware of it, historical *reality*, historical *life*, rather than historical *knowledge*.[36] We may assess what this implies by coupling two passages from the young Heidegger. In W. Bröcker's transcript of Heidegger's Kassel lectures there is the sentence, "Hermeneutics is a discipline which will attain fundamental importance in the present and the future." For the understanding of this sentence, which at first may sound arduous as well as enigmatic, a passage from the recently published lecture on the concept of time (1924), which sounds no less provocative, may give us a clue—a passage that formulates what Heidegger calls "the first principle of all hermeneutics":

> *The possibility of access to history is grounded in the possibility according to which, from time to time, a present age is capable of being futural. This is the first principle of all hermeneutics* . . . . Philosophy will never come to find out what history is so long as it analyzes history as an object for methodical observation. The enigma of history lies in the question, what does it mean to be historical.[37]

5

Philosophy as Primordial Science in Heidegger's Courses of 1919

George Kovacs

Heidegger regards philosophy as "one of the human being's few great achievements."[1] But in his "Wege zur Aussprache" (written in 1937) Heidegger also warns that philosophy is overestimated by expecting immediately useful results from philosophical thinking. Philosophy is underestimated if one finds in philosophical concepts merely an abstract, removed, rarified form of what already has been secured through experiential acquaintance and dealings with things.[2] Genuine philosophical knowledge does not limp after beings already known by way of an addendum of their most general representations; it, much rather, leaps ahead and opens up a new range of questions and views on the always afresh "self-concealing essence of things" (GA13 18). Philosophy is neither the abstract representation of beings nor the unquestioned acceptance of what is already obvious in our practical and concrete dealings with them. Philosophy calls into question and regards as most question-worthy beings, one's self-understanding, and, ultimately, Being. As essential thinking (GA13 17), it remains a stranger to merely utilitarian, calculative knowing. Philosophy is neither abstract nor merely empirical; it is, according to the early Heidegger's struggle with Neo-Kantian thinking, a primordial way of knowing, a "primordial science" (*Urwissenschaft*), quite different from the taken-for-granted notions of science and knowledge.

The meditation on the question "What is Philosophy?" leads Heidegger to a dialogue with the sciences, with the philosophical trends of the times, with the philosophical tradition, with worldview and forms of ideology, and, quite significantly, with poetry and art. His journey of thought, i.e., his search for the "matter" (*Sache*) and way (*Weg*) of thinking, as his early lecture courses at the University of Freiburg indicate, reaches a decisive turn, a breakthrough, through his encounter with Husserl's phenomenology. Though the young Luther was his companion in the search, Kierkegaard gave him the "push," and Aristotle was his exemplar of thinking, it was Husserl who "gave" him his "eyes" and taught him how to see (GA63 5).

How does the early Heidegger define the essence of philosophy? The following reflections respond to this question in the light of his early courses at the University of Freiburg given in 1919. They include (1) an examination of the way the question of the essence of philosophy originates in the early Heidegger, (2) the analysis of his idea of philosophy as primordial science, as his search for the "matter" and method (way) of thinking and knowing, and (3) an assessment of the significance, limitations, nature, and final sense of the horizon and direction of his insights.

1. The recent publication in the *Gesamtausgabe* (GA56/57) of the texts of Heidegger's two 1919 courses ("The Idea of Philosophy and the Problem of Worldview" and "Phenomenology and Transcendental Philosophy of Values") at the University of Freiburg under the title *Zur Bestimmung der Philosophie*[3] makes an essential, much needed contribution to the understanding of the early origins, development, and primal intention of his thought. There can be no substitute for reading his texts in appropriating and interpreting his way of thinking, and in discerning his insights and his oversights. The attentive reading of his texts is an experience of immersion into his thought. Reading, according to Heidegger, is "the gathering together" of what is said in the writing as well as of "the unspoken in that which is spoken" (GA13 11, 108). Genuine reading is attentive to, gathers, that which without our knowing "claims our essence" even though we may not correspond to or refuse it (GA13 111). Reading a text is an experience of discerning and retracing the emergence of meaning; the good reader knows that the word is not an end but a beginning, i.e., an eruption of meaning.

What is the significance of these two early courses for retracing the early beginnings of Heidegger's teaching, of his philosophical perspective? These texts show that his teaching is a gradual dawning of his own mind; they include a critical confrontation with the philosophical trends (Neo-Kantianism, phenomenology, psychologism) of his own time as well as the finding of his pathway of thought. His reflections are focused on, and thus try to determine, what genuine research, worldview, and philosophy are; they are guided by the question, "What is Philosophy?" These courses are engaged in a rethinking of the essence (*Wesen*) of philosophy; they are indeed underway in finding a "philosophizing response" to this question, according to the words of Heidegger's essay on what philosophy is, written in 1955.[4] In the final analysis, according to Heidegger's *Beiträge*, written in 1936–1938, the yet hidden essence of philosophy "springs forth from the essence of Being itself" as essential thinking that "prepares the truth of Being" beyond beings.[5] The question, "What is Philosophy?" is at the core of Heidegger's thinking in 1919, as the two lecture courses given in this year clearly indicate, as well as in 1936–1938 and in 1955. The texts of

1919, then, let their readers see that which shines forth in them, i.e., the emergence of Heidegger's own philosophy. In the beginning of his teaching, his own unique thought is already there, even if it remains undeveloped; the return to these texts, then, is an experience of thinking, a retracing and a beginning of the event of questioning.

How can the idea of philosophy as "primordial science" (GA56/57 12, 4, 15) constitute a rethinking of the concept of philosophy? To what extent does this new idea of philosophy represent the early formulation and origin of Heidegger's thought as a meditation on the question of Being (*Sein*)? How radical, i.e., how deeply rooted, is his examination of the very nature and task of philosophy? Why is his attention focused so intensely on defining philosophy as a very unique way of thinking, as, in the final analysis, something irreducible to any other type of knowing? The following reflections respond to these questions. The course "The Idea of Philosophy and the Problem of Worldview," included in *Zur Bestimmung der Philosophie*, develops the idea of philosophy as primordial science; its introductory §1 is a clear formulation of Heidegger's approach to defining philosophy.

Heidegger's introductory reflections on the traditional, historically accepted view of the relationship between philosophy and worldview (*Weltanschauung*) lead to the questioning of the existence of any serious connection between the two, and from there to the unearthing of the essence of philosophy. Although based on seemingly divergent justifications, everyone claims to be in the possession of a worldview. Thus, for example, the farmer's worldview coincides with the teachings of his religious convictions; the factory worker, in contrast to the farmer, may find the seed of his worldview in thinking of religion as something dead, outdated, and useless. Political parties and the educated have their own worldviews. Philosophy is regarded as worldview based on autonomous thinking free from religious and other dogmas. Philosophers are called "great thinkers" because of the depth and breadth of their thought, not merely because of the sharpness and logical consistency of their thinking; they experience and contemplate the world in its "ultimate meaning" (*Sinn*) and "origin" (*Ursprung*) (GA56/57 7). Philosophy strives for an ultimate understanding of the natural world (i.e., of nature as the system of laws of motion, of energy) as well as of the spiritual world (i.e., of artistic, social, and political life). The final problems of the natural and spiritual worlds, the questions about the meaning and goal of human existence and culture, find their solution (some form of ultimate response and understanding) in the great philosophical systems, e.g., in the dualism of Nature and Spirit, in the reduction of the two (natural and spiritual) worlds to a common origin (God) thought of as being outside the world or as being identical with all that is (*Sein*), in the interpretation (reduction) of Nature as (to) Spirit or in the interpretation (reduction) of Spirit as (to) Nature. Thus philosophy in all its forms leads to an ultimate view of life and of the world. These considerations allow for the conclusion, according to Heidegger, that "all great philosophy culminates in a worldview," that, according to the unfolding of its inner tendency, every philosophy is metaphysics (GA56/57 8). In the final analysis, then, philosophy and worldview are basically the same (*im Grunde dasselbe*). The elaboration of a worldview is an intrinsic task of philosophy (GA56/57 8, 18, 19; see also GA1 410, 406 [399–410 were written in 1916]). This first view of the relationship between philosophy and worldview leads to the identification of the meanings of these two forms of thought, and thus, according to Heidegger, to the discovery of the metaphysical nature of philosophy, to the assignment of an ideological task (i.e., the final explanation of the world and the establishment of an ideal of living) to philosophical reflection. It seems, then, that the tradition of metaphysics is the historical realization of this task.

According to these introductory considerations, there is a second view of the connection between philosophy and worldview, in the light of the critical theory of knowledge. The possibility of the old precritical metaphysics is undermined by the impossibility of obtaining valid knowledge of realities, forces, and causes beyond the realm of experience. The scientific foundation of philosophy is the critical theory of knowledge. Thanks to the critical attitude, the philosophical disciplines of ethics, aesthetics, and philosophy of religion lead to ultimate values and absolute validity, i.e., to a system of values. According to Heidegger's assessment, the system of values represents the "scientific means," the methodological tool, for developing a "critical, scientific worldview," i.e., for interpreting the meaning of human existence and culture from the perspective of the system of absolutely valid norms of the "True, of the Beautiful, and of the Holy" (GA56/57 9). Philosophy, then, remains within the domain of consciousness; it is the conscious activity of thinking (logical values), willing (ethical values), and feelings (aesthetic values). The harmony of these values constitutes the Holy, i.e., their coming together is religious value. Thus, in the critical approach, philosophy culminates in a scientific worldview (GA56/57 10). The individual, personal attitude of the philosopher toward life, world, and history is governed by the results of scientific philosophy as the science of the system of values. Philosophy is the foundation of a critical, scientific worldview. Worldview is situated at the boundary (*Grenze*) of philosophy (GA56/57 10). Modern critical consciousness adopts this interpretation of the relationship between philosophy and worldview; it does not regard critical science (i.e., philosophy as the critical science of the system of values) as being identical with worldview.

Heidegger's reflections lead to a third alternative, to a radically new way of understanding the nature of worldview and the notion of philosophy. For Heidegger, the main issue is not the identity or nonidentity of philosophy and worldview (always based on some connection between them according to the history of philosophy), but, on the contrary, their incompatibility (*Unvereinbarkeit*), i.e., their radical separation (*radikale Trennung*) (GA56/57 11). This third alternative (Heidegger's new understanding of the relationship between philosophy and worldview) includes the demand for discovering an entirely new concept of philosophy that is beyond any relation to the ultimate questions of humanity. In this way, according to Heidegger's claim, philosophy would lose its ancestral privileges, its royal, superior vocation. This new understanding of philosophy cannot be viewed as a critical science of values built on the acts and norms of consciousness, and characterized by the necessary inclination to become a worldview. This third alternative represents a new view of the essence of worldview and a rethinking of the essence of philosophy. It leads to the "catastrophe" (*Katastrophe*) of all philosophy up to the present (GA56/57 12). Thus Heidegger speaks of the end, of the termination of philosophy, in 1919, though the full significance of this insight comes to its now classical expression, in his "The End of Philosophy and the Task of Thinking," in 1964.[6] The task of philosophy does not consist in building and developing a worldview, not even at the limits of philosophy. Worldview is a "stranger" to philosophy; it is "unphilosophical" in character even when its opposition to philosophy is shown by a philosophical methodology (GA56/57 12). The nature of worldview thus becomes a problem for philosophy. What is a worldview if it is something totally other than philosophy? But the main issue at stake in this question is still the essence, the concept (*Begriff*) of philosophy (GA56/57 12). And the answer given in these preliminary considerations to this central question of "What is Philosophy? is that the latter is to be defined essentially not as worldview, but rather as "primordial science."

2. The main intention of the course "The Idea of Philosophy and the Problem of Worldview" consists in showing that the true essence of philosophy is something quite unique, beyond any connection with ideology, worldview, and teachings about the ultimate destiny and meaning of human living. Philosophical thinking is more rigorous, more primordial than scientific knowing; it is more radical, more essential than the exploration of nature and life by the theorizing attitude of the sciences. It is more radical and essential than the critical-teleological method of the Neo-Kantian philosophy of values. For Heidegger, philosophy is not a theoretical, speculative science at all; it is a way of disclosing (living) experience. It is a primordial, pretheoretical science that is able to reach and describe (phe-

nomenologically in hermeneutic intuition) lived experience prior to its disruption and deformation by the theoretical attitude. The idea of philosophy as primordial science does not stand for a set of teachings, but for a way of knowing; it is not the content of some new discipline, but a method of disclosure, a search for the "matter" of philosophy. According to Heidegger's remark made toward the end of the course in §20, the main theme of the entire course is centered around the problem of method (GA56/57 110). Thus the idea of primordial science (ultimately, the notion of phenomenology as pretheoretical science) represents Heidegger's search for a method that originates from the essence of philosophy, thus for the "matter" and the way of thinking and knowing. This task of the lectures leads Heidegger to reexamine and develop the logical (methodological, epistemological) but not the ethical (volitional) and the aesthetic (emotive) aspects of Neo-Kantian transcendental philosophy.

The following reflections do not represent a summary review of all the ideas contained in the entire lecture course; they focus their attention on, and thus try to think with Heidegger, the notion of philosophy as primordial science, as the method of disclosure of living experience, of the "primordial sphere" (*Ursphäre*) (GA56/57 60, 61) given prior to the predominance (*Vorherrschaft*) of the theorizing and hypothesizing attitude. Heidegger develops his definition of the essence of philosophy as primordial science by exposing the primacy of the theoretical attitude in Neo-Kantian methodology and philosophy of values (Natorp, Rickert, Windelband) at the expense of its background in the primordial sphere of the pretheoretical (the task of the first part of the course, i.e., §§2–12), and by overcoming the primacy of the theoretical attitude with basic insights of hermeneutic phenomenology (thus appropriating Husserl's phenomenological method) as pretheoretical science (the task of the second and last part of the course, i.e., §§13–20).

How does the "regression" from the theoretical to the pretheoretical attitude represent a rethinking of the essence of philosophy, an end to the conception of philosophy as the highest theoretical science? What is the true essence of philosophy? Why is philosophy totally other than, and without comparison to, the other (natural, physical, and spiritual) sciences? In what sense is it then still a science? The response to these questions may be found in the following analysis of and reflections on the basic elements of Heidegger's search for the method and the "matter" of philosophical thinking, for the disclosure (*Erschließung*) of the "origin," of the "something" (*Etwas*) that "is given" (*es gibt*), of the primordial realm of living experience (*Erlebnis*) as event (*Ereignis*) (GA56/57 67–76).

a) The idea of philosophy as primordial science cannot be derived from surveying the history of philosophy; it is rather presupposed by the history of philosophy. Primordial science cannot be found by the method of induction; it cannot be obtained from or discovered by means of the individual sciences, not even the highest of them, because it is not at all one of the particular (e.g., empirical) sciences that are limited to a determinate field of objects. However, it is possible and even necessary "to go back methodically" to primordial science as the source or origin of all individual sciences (GA56/57 24–25). Primordial science is not the result of the conclusions of the individual sciences; it is not identical with the natural sciences as a whole, not even with theology as the teaching about God as the Absolute (though in some sense theology may be labelled as primordial science), because both the natural sciences as well as theology are particular sciences with their particular field of objects. Primordial science is not identical with the dialectical construction of the science of the ultimate causes of Being nor with the elaboration of the general idea of Being. The idea of primordial science, i.e., of absolutely primordial science, is not a formal theoretical construct. It is not identical with inductive metaphysics (GA56/57 26–27). Primordial science is not a field of knowledge, but a phenomenon of knowing; it is not the objective content of knowledge, but the knowledge of objects, a way of knowing them (GA56/57 28). Primordiality can be grasped only in and out of itself; genuine scientific method springs forth from the essence of the object of the science in question (GA56/57 16; also 39). Philosophy as primordial science is understood by Heidegger as a method, as primordial disclosure, as a way of knowing prior to and thus more radical than any theoretical construction and presupposition. This is the way out of the logical-epistemological circularity of the idea of primordial science, that is, the methodological recognition of the mutual presupposition of each other by the concept of primordial science and by that of a particular science.

Thus the idea of primordial science is misunderstood by the critical-teleological method of knowing because it is filled with presuppositions; its emphasis on the theorizing attitude merely presupposes what it cannot deliver, i.e., the ideal of and for thinking the norms of absolute validity and truth (GA56/57 44, 52). The critical-teleological method (e.g., in Windelband), the main feature of the Neo-Kantian philosophy of values, claims to justify the validity of those axioms that render science possible by relating them as means to the ideal or "end" (*das Telos*) of truth as norms that are necessary for obtaining the "end" called "truth" (GA56/57 35, 39). The teleologically necessary norms and forms of thinking can be discovered and brought forth (*herausgestellt*) in their "rough" structure by means of the psychological characterization of the processes of thinking, with the help of the activity of consciousness. According to Heidegger's critique, however, the forms and norms of thinking, ideality and absolute validity, cannot be found empirically; they are not empirical in nature, i.e., are not the object of a particular science (GA56/57 33, 34). They cannot be derived from a particular, empirical science (e.g., from psychology). Ideality and validity are beyond the realm of experience, beyond the reach of an individual, empirical science. The teleological justification and dialectical construction of the forms and norms of valid thinking, another characteristic of the Neo-Kantian philosophy, is based, according to Heidegger's emphasis, on the adoption of the primacy of the theoretical attitude (hypothesis, pre-supposition, dialectic) and the objectification of living experience (GA56/57 59, 76, 61).'

Heidegger's extensive analysis and systematic critique of the critical-teleological method of value-metaphysics bring about a methodology-consciousness of knowing and thinking; it shows the need to break the primacy of the theoretical attitude and thus the way back to the pre-theoretical attitude and lived experience, in which the theoretical attitude is itself rooted. The teleological method is full of presuppositions; as primordial science, philosophy cannot be derived from psychology, which is a particular, empirical, and thus hypothetical science. Thus the teleological method in the value-philosophy of Windelband and Rickert does not measure up to the idea of primordial science, which is non-hypothetical and reaches the primordial phenomena. In the final analysis and according to Heidegger's most radical criticism, the methodological confusions and assumptions of the critical-teleological method and of its philosophy of values are rooted in the fact that this method fails to grasp the ontological sphere, i.e., the primordial nature of the Being-dimension (*Seinsmässige*) of all philosophical questions, and makes a radical separation (*Scheidung*) between Being (*Sein*) and value (*Wert*) (GA56/57 54, 55, 52). The teleological method is fascinated by the partition between Being and value; it destroys the connecting bridge between them, remains on one side, i.e., on the side of value, and transforms philosophy into a philosophy of values. Value is not the same as "ought" (*Sollen*), it is even less a Being (*ein Sein*). Not every "ought" is founded on a value; even a Being can be the foundation of "ought" (GA56/57 46). Being-true (*Wahrsein, aletheia*) is not the same as being-a-value; though value plays a role in the historical constitution of truth (GA56/57 49). "I experience [*erlebe*] value[s], I live [*lebe*] in the truth as truth" (GA56/57 49). Truth is not grasped through an experience of value. The primacy of value over Being is, according to Heidegger's critique, the ultimate presupposition of the Neo-Kantian philosophy of values. The phenomenon of "ought," the relationship between truth and value, and their connection with Being, that is, their ontological dimension, remain unexamined in the teleological method. This mode of thinking, then, is not really primordial; it does not reach the sphere of primordial phenomena, except by making unexamined presuppositions about them. Heidegger's critical reflections unmask these presuppositions; they intend to overcome them by "breaking" the predominance of the theoretical over the pretheoretical attitude and by recovering the ontological roots of thinking and knowing. In this way, his search for a method, the unfolding of the new definition of philosophy as primordial science, becomes a rethinking of the essence of philosophy, a new understanding of the task of thinking.

b) Heidegger's way of defining the essence of philosophy as primordial science does not consist in choosing between Aristotle and Kant, between realism and idealism, but rather in overcoming the dilemma of realism and idealism. The emphasis on the pretheoretical and on the theoretical attitude does not represent a choice between the horns of the dilemma between critical realism and critical idealism; it is, much rather, Heidegger's way of finding and exposing their common misunderstandings about the primordiality of philosophy, as well as their epistemological and ontological shortcomings. These aspects of Heidegger's thinking, focused on the analysis of living experience and on the presuppositions of the primacy of the theoretical attitude, clearly indicate his way into phenomenology and his idea of primordial science as phenomenology.

As a method of disclosure and not a theory of theories, phenomenology tries to reach the primordial sphere; it intends to return to living experience as phenomenon (i.e., as it is given prior to its disconnection from life) and to the phenomena of living experience. The knowledge of living experience is, however, obstructed by the general sway and unjustified absolutization of the theoretical sphere in critical realism as well as in critical idealism, both being influenced by the natural sciences (GA56/57 87). Living experience (*Erlebnis*) is not merely a process (*Vorgang*), but an event (*Ereignis*) (GA56/57 73–75). The unity of living experience includes the subject or "I," the attitude and role of the questioner, which includes a sense of wonder, and the immediate givenness in it of a primary significance; it is a basic form of living in the world prior to the theorizing view of it by the detached observer. Science, e.g., natural science, objectifies and dissects, analyzes and "theorizes" about and away from living experience, even doing away with it occasionally; it is a cognition of objects, of things. The theoretical attitude is not the rule but the exception in living; the living experience of the world around us is the essence of life (GA56/57 88, 98). In the final analysis, the basic problem with the theorizing attitude, with its primacy in philosophy as well as in the sciences, consists in the fact that it misunderstands and forgets the root, the origin (*Ursprung*), of theorizing itself in "living" (GA56/57 91, 96). The sciences of experience (*Erfahrung*) and philosophical reflection presuppose the lived experience of the world. Primordial science, phenomenology, is the method of disclosure of living experience, of the lived world (GA56/57 98, 127).

c) How is primordial, pretheoretical disclosure possible? According to Heidegger, the response to this question does not consist in a "theory of theory," in the "theory of the theoretical," but in learning to see "how" we see, i.e., in disconnecting all essentially theoretical opinions or prejudice (*Vormeinung*). This recognition and putting aside of any theoretical prejudgement and pre-view can be identified already as the door to, as the preliminary phase of, the phenomenological method elaborated by Husserl. The decisive function of this method is precisely to allow us to see the living-experiencing comportment (*das erlebende Verhalten*) as differing from the objectifying cognition of the sphere of objects (GA56/57 98).

The living experiences, however, become looked-upon (perceived) experiences by means of reflection. According to Husserl, we know of the stream of lived-through living experiences only by means of reflectively-experiencing acts (GA56/57 99). Reflection on lived experience transforms lived experience into a looked-at experience. Even reflection itself is a living experience and as such it too can be considered reflectively, and so *ad infinitum*. "The phenomenological method advances through acts of reflection" (GA56/57 99). Thus reflection itself, according to Heidegger, belongs to the realm of living experience; it is a basic trait of living experience. In reflection, the stream of living experience becomes describable. The science of living experience, therefore, is a descriptive science; it is characterized by the method of descriptive reflection. According to Husserl, every descriptive science has its justification in itself (GA56/57 100). It is clear, then, that in this way the living experience "perception," the living experience "reminiscence," the living experience "representation" (*Vorstellung*), the living experience "judging," as well as the person-experiences of "I," "you," and "we," become describable. These living experiences are explained by bringing out and setting forth (*herausstellen*) "what lies in them" (GA56/57 100). This descriptive method is not the same as a psychological explanation, since it makes no reference to physiological processes and physical dispositions. It includes no construction of hypotheses, but rather a respect for living experience; the explanation measures itself on and remains faithful to the living experience.

Is the method of descriptive reflection, or reflective description, capable of investigating the sphere of living experience? Can this method make living experience scientifically accessible? These questions are raised by Heidegger in the light of Natorp's objection to Husserl's phenomenology, to which Husserl had not responded at the time of Heidegger's 1919 course. According to Natorp, the "stream" of living experience is brought to a halt by reflection: "There is no immediate grasp of living experience" (GA56/57 101). He maintains that description already includes the use of concepts; it is "subsumption"; it is transcription (*Umschreibung*) of something into generalities; it presupposes the formation of concepts, abstraction, theory, and mediation (GA56/57 101). Reflection does not live-through the lived experience; it views the experience and its meaning. The reflective attitude is directed to the object, it makes the experience into an ob-ject (*Gegen-stand*). The theoretical comportment does not re-live the lived (living) experience; rather, it divests ("de-lives") the lived (living) experience. In the final analysis, the reflectionless living experience becomes a "looked at" experience through the reflective turning of the look (GA56/57 100).

Natorp's critique comes from the basic position of the Marburg school which, according to Heidegger, is characterized by the "absolutization" of the theoretical attitude (GA56/57 103). Thus there can be only a mediate grasp of living experience, i.e., only objectification (*Objektivierung*) of the subjective (GA56/57 102). According to Natorp, the absolute givenness of living experience does not mean that it is immediately and absolutely reachable, as the phenomenological view claims. Knowing represents and elucidates experience. The mediate grasp and objectification of living experience is possible, for Natorp, by means of the method of reconstruction.

d) What is Natorp's method of reconstruction? Reflective analysis (e.g., in self-observation) infringes upon, transforms, and deforms the living experiences. Natorp claims that this devastation can be undone, that analysis and interpretation can "regain" (reconstruct) "theoretically" the "wholeness of the subjective" (i.e., of that which is immediately given prior to the analysis) from the primordial life of consciousness (GA56/57 103). The synthetic unity, the wholeness, that which was devastated (*zerstört*) by the analysis, can be "reconstructed" (GA56/57 104, 105). According to Heidegger's critique, however, the method of reconstruction cannot deliver what it promises; it cannot bring about the scientific disclosure of the sphere of living experience. Even reconstruction is objectification; it consists in construction, in theorizing. Natorp's method represents the "absolutization of the logical" and thus the "most radical absolutization of the theoretical" (GA56/57 107, 108). This method objectifies the realm of living experience (e.g., the living experience of the *Umwelt*, the immediate world around us); it remains a theoretical object-consciousness, according to the legitimacy of constitution. This systematic, panlogistic, absolute theorizing orientation, which absolutizes the logical, hinders free access to the sphere of living experience, to consciousness. The theoretical attitude accounts for the misunderstanding of phenomenology by Natorp and for the futility of the critique of phenomenology from the standpoints of transcendental philosophy, empirical psychology, and post-Hegelianism (GA56/ 57 109).

e) The final methodological conclusion of Heidegger's reflections, of his identification of primordial science, consists in breaking the primacy of the theoretical attitude through the phenomenological disclosure of living experience. The way, the "method," of the scientific disclosure of the realm of living experience, the methodologically basic problem of phenomenology, belongs to the "principle of principles" (the first principle) of phenomenology. According to Husserl's statement in §24 of his 1913 *Ideen I*, no theory can mislead us about "the *principle of all principles*: *that very primordial dator Intuition is a source of authority* [*Rechtsquelle*] *for knowledge, that whatever presents itself in 'intuition' in primordial form* (as it were in its bodily reality), *is simply to be accepted as it gives itself out to be*, though *only within the limits in which it then presents itself*."[8]

This principle is the foundation of all principles; it precedes (*vorausliegt*) them as an absolute beginning. Heidegger remarks that, although Husserl does not speak of it, this principle is "not theoretical in nature," that it is the "primordial intention [*Urintention*] of true living," i.e., the "primordial attitude [*Urhaltung*] of living experience and of life as such" (GA56/57 110; see also 125–27, 211). The basic disposition of life, the living experience, is not reached by a conceptual system; it can be discovered and disclosed only by living in it, by adopting the primordial habit (*Urhabitus*) of the phenomenologist (GA56/57 110). The problem of method retains a central position in phenomenology. In the final analysis, the entire course "The Idea of Philosophy and the Problem of Worldview," i.e., the idea of philosophy as primordial, pretheoretical science, is concerned with the problem of method (GA56/57 110). The phenomenological method, according to the appropriation of Husserl by the early Heidegger, is not a dialectical, theoretical construct; it consists in making oneself free from the theoretical attitude and in orienting oneself toward the primordial pretheoretical intention of true life and of living experience, i.e., immersion in phenomenological living. Thus phenomenology's "rigor" is not comparable with that of the derived, nonprimordial sciences; it comes from its basic disposition. It is something intrinsic and not extrinsic to the scientific attitude awakened by it. The "rigor" of phenomenology proves itself from within itself, from phenomenology, and not by some extrinsic justification. Phenomenology, then, is not a point of view (*Standpunkt*) (GA56/57 110), not a theorizing, objectifying attitude toward something (GA56/57 112), but a way of disclosure of living experience in "hermeneutic intuition" (*hermeneutische Intuition*) (GA56/57 117; see also 131).

For Heidegger, phenomenology as primordial science is a pretheoretical science or way of knowing; it is a method of disclosure, of reaching—

at least to some extent—the primordial intention(ality) of life and of non-objectified, non-theorized, living experience. In the final analysis, philosophy as primordial science is not a "content," not a system of ideas about life and the world, but a "way" of opening up, disclosure, and encountering of the "stream of living," of that which is given in lived understanding (GA56/57 115, 125). Intuitive eidetic phenomenology, i.e., "philosophical primordial science," is, then, an "understanding science" (eine verstehende Wissenschaft) (GA56/57 208). According to Heidegger's other early Freiburg courses documenting his way into phenomenology, as well as his deconstruction of the tradition and his encounter with Aristotle and Husserl, philosophy is rooted in the "facticity" of "concrete life" (GA61 169); the idea of hermeneutics of facticity enables Heidegger to drive philosophical inquiry back to its wellspring (Sachquellen), to the source of its matter, to Being as its "object," as its main concern (GA63 75, 76).[9] For Heidegger, the way of thinking is determined by Being, i.e., by the "matter" (Sache) of thinking and not by the thinker. According to GA65, the more genuinely the way of deep thinking (Erdenken) is the way to Being (Seyn), the more unconditionally it is determined (bestimmt) by Being itself (GA65 86); "thinking out of Being" (Erdenken des Seyns) is impelled by Being itself as its work and gift (GA65 428).

3. What is the significance and what are the limitations of the idea of philosophy as primordial science in the early Heidegger? Is it possible to think the essence of philosophical thinking as primordial, pretheoretical science in the light of the final, radical claims made by Heidegger according to the preceding considerations? What is primordial disclosure? Does the search for a method of disclosure include the identification of the at least tentative and guiding topology of primordial disclosure? Can the search for a method, i.e., for the "matter" and the way of philosophical thinking, lead to "only," or perhaps to "more" than, a nameless pathway of thought? The concluding phase of these reflections constitutes a concise response to these questions, as well as some indications for their more comprehensive development with and even beyond Heidegger.

a) The notion of phenomenology, the idea of hermeneutic intuition with which Heidegger's insights finally conclude, and many other aspects of the new way of thinking and knowing are not explored fully in the course "The Idea of Philosophy and the Problem of Worldview." However, in the light of the task of finding a hermeneutic phenomenology (and thus going beyond merely criticizing the philosophical trends of his time), Heidegger examines, though briefly, some objections to phenomenology. Thus, for instance, he rejects the identification of phenomenological viewing with description, as well as the objection that description is always theorizing. He also rejects the prejudice that all language is inevitably objectification, as well as the claim that descriptive verbal expression as "putting-into-words" is always generalization (GA56/57 111). From a thematic perspective, the trend of thought in "The Idea of Philosophy and the Problem of Worldview" ends almost abruptly, i.e., without harvesting all of its possible conclusions, without giving a full account of hermeneutic phenomenology. Its main significance consists in documenting Heidegger's way into hermeneutic phenomenology and his break with Rickert and the entirety of Neo-Kantian philosophy (GA56/57 180, 181).[10]

The elaboration of the well-focused theme of his reflections is not inconclusive, since it defines philosophy as a way of disclosure, as primordial science; it is, however, somewhat incomplete. It does not respond to many of the issues raised in the introductory reflections. Thus, for instance, the essence of worldview and the significance of the idea of primordial science for the final assessment of the "place" of worldview in human living and in the human search for knowledge do not receive their promised and deserved attention. Is the worldview of a great thinker just a metaphysical illusion? Perhaps there is "more" to worldview than what the early Heidegger seems to admit. In 1936–1938, he analyzes the dangers of worldview as a substitute (*Ersatz*) for "lost ground" and as the result (*Folge*) of modern metaphysics; he claims that worldview destroys the will to philosophy and that it uses philosophy as an instrument of propaganda (GA65 37, 38, 41, 435). This diagnosis, however, remains abstract and incomplete; it fails to discern and distinguish between the diverse concrete, historical forms of worldview (e.g., Nazism, communism, imperialism, racism).

b) In the final analysis and even in the courses examined in this study, the search for a method in the early Heidegger does not lead to the discovery of one specific procedure and thus to a methodic one-sidedness, but much rather to the recovery of the sense of wonder in questioning and in the practice of thinking. The idea of primordial, pretheoretical science is basically a way of questioning the historically transmitted essence of philosophy; it is a dialogue with the tradition. The understanding of the nature and function of this strong method(ology)-consciousness (*Methodenbewusstsein*) is essential for the elaboration and resolution of the questions raised earlier about the significance and the limitations of Heidegger's insights. According to his "Die Kategorien- und Bedeutungslehre des Duns Scotus" (first published in 1916), method does not consist in the definitely fixed forms of the presentation (*Darstellung*) and communication of thoughts (*Gedanken*), but, much rather, in the "spirit" of the research and in the "posing of the problem" (*Problemstellung*), in the liberation of the inquiry from the "one-sided direction of the glance of the life of the spirit" (GA1 199), from the one-sidedness of the thinker. Methodology-consciousness, a basic aspect of the very early works of Heidegger, shows the development of the impulse as well as of the courage of questioning (*Fragetrieb, Fragemut*), the awareness of the nature of the problems and of the way to get hold of them, and the "steady control of each step of thinking" (GA1 198). Thus, for instance, the "absolute surrender" (*absolute Hingabe*) to authority and to tradition (a main feature of the medieval outlook and sense of transcendence), as well as the overestimation of the theoretical attitude (a key characteristic of especially modern teleological metaphysics and epistemology), represent a "fatal error," a mistake in principle of philosophy as "worldview" (GA1 197–99, 406–410).[11] Heidegger's reflection on transcendental philosophy is motivated by his judgement that it is since Kant that one can speak of the theory of science (*Wissenschaftslehre*) in the strict sense (GA1 274).[12] Thus philosophy as "science" reaches a higher degree of maturity; it acquires a greater sense of "rigor," i.e., a more and more genuine method-consciousness. This development is also true in, and conditioned by, the methodology-consciousness of the particular sciences.

The idea of primordial science in the early Heidegger of 1919 constitutes a deepening of methodology-consciousness in philosophy, of the search for the "matter" and the way of thought. The terms "method" and "science" will acquire a more restricted meaning in the course of Heidegger's development. According to GA65, he abandons the project of philosophy as primordial science; his critique of modern science, as marked by the abandonment of beings by Being, by truthlessness, tries to build knowledge on a more originary founding of the truth of Being (GA65 144, 140–57, 435). However, the ideas about primordiality, the direction and task of thinking, the essence and types of thinking, the nature of science, always remain at the core of his philosophy, and become more and more substantial in it. The search for a method, then, is a pathway of thought that never comes to a halt; it is always open toward new possibilities.

c) According to Heidegger, phenomenological critique is in essence never negative in nature (GA56/57 125, 131); it always leads "somewhere" with a sense of direction, i.e., it is positive in nature. What is the sense of the direction of his trend of thought, of his search for a method, according to the phenomenological criticism of basic systems of philosophy? The essence of philosophy, the nature of worldview, the concept of science, the nature of culture and ideology are reexamined by Heidegger in his many writings. This dialogue with the tradition leads to the radicalization of the search for a method, to the relearning of the art of thinking, i.e., to essential questioning as "listening to" that which "addresses itself to" the questioner (GA13 131). According to Heidegger's claim in 1969, the net of dialectic—be it Hegelian or Marxist, teleological-metaphysical or techno-

logical-scientific—"suffocates" every question; the superpower of calculative thinking and the fascination with modern rationalization, with the
help of modern science, "consolidate the flight" from noncalculative, essential thinking (GA13 211–22). The analysis of the structure and of the
presuppositions of questioning and the clarification of the phenomenological method of research (a new possibility of thinking, not a technique)—
main issues in seminal works by Heidegger—indicate the depth of the
struggle for a new, more essential way of thinking.[13] The idea of philosophy
as primordial science, developed in GA56/57, is Heidegger's search for the
"matter" and thus the way of thinking; it is the unfolding of his thought as
a breaking away from Neo-Kantian philosophy (Rickert) and as a breakthrough to hermeneutic phenomenology (GA58, GA61, and GA63 develop
and clarify this breakthrough).

   In the final analysis, the search for a method leads to its self-overcom-
ing, to the insight that, as Heidegger hints at it in his "Der Fehl heiliger
Namen" (written in 1974), the immense number of methods chokes off
thinking, that method (*Methode*) and way (*Weg*) of thinking are not the
same, that their identification is a characteristic of the age of technology
and the culmination of modernity. "The way (*he hodos*) is never a method
(*mepote methodos*), never a technique [*Verfahren*, procedure]." The insight into the way-quality (*Wegcharakter*) of thinking is the first experience of awakening to the forgottenness of Being; it is the journey toward
the lighting-process of Being (*Lichtung des Seins*). The way, then, "knows
no method, no proof, no mediating." It is described by Heidegger poetically: "The way is way in being-underway; it leads and clears because it
poetizes." (GA13 233–35)

   The idea of philosophy as primordial science is Heidegger's early way
to reawaken the essential element of the sense of wonder in philosophy; it
is the beginning of the journey to that way of thinking which is under way
"to listen to the voice of Being" (*auf die Stimme des Seins zu hören*).[14]
According to his "Das Wesen der Philosophie" (a short, undated manuscript written probably in the early 1940s), to think the essence of philosophy means "simply to think" (*einfach denken*).[15] This "simple thinking,"
however, is described not as scientific, not as primordial science, but as
"poetic thinking."[16] Thus the search for the essence of philosophy entails a
dialogue with the essence of poetry. The topology of primordial disclosure,
then, can be found in "simply thinking." The indifference of thinking in
science as well as in philosophy reduces everything to being(s); it leaves
unclarified and unquestioned not only what is Being and what is meaning,
but also what is a being (GA56/57 198–99). This remark of Heidegger in
1919 suggests that his questioning of the true essence of philosophy, i.e.,

his idea of primordial science, is underway to the "matter" and to another way of thought.

d) According to a poem written by Heidegger in 1947, "the sail of thinking keeps trimmed hard to the wind of its matter [*Sache*]" (GA13 78).[17] Thus the course and movement of thinking is governed by its "matter," i.e., by Being. For Heidegger, thinking is the thinking of Being; philosophy proper consists in listening to, in corresponding with Being. Philosophical thinking is more, and other, than the work of the faculty of human subjectivity; it is an event of Being. A way of understanding Being is at work even in thinking about particular beings. The essence of philosophy is to think and to prepare for the intimations of Being itself. The revealment of Being is, however, also a withdrawal, a sheltering; the primordial knowing of beings, i.e., "science," reaches the primordial depth of beings in Being. The idea of philosophy as primordial science shows the movement of the responding of Heidegger's thought to this primal depth.

Part III

Destruction

6

Heidegger's Ontological "Destruction" of Western Intellectual Traditions

Jeffrey Andrew Barash

The year 1989 marked the centenary of the birth of the Freiburg thinker Martin Heidegger, and the thirteenth year since his death in 1976. However one might judge Heidegger's contribution to twentieth century thought, there can be little doubt concerning the profundity of its influence in the decades following the publication of his work *Being and Time* in 1927.[1]

During the years before and just after World War II, *Being and Time* constituted the primary source of Heidegger's influence. In this work Heidegger introduced the central query which, from that point onward, he addressed ever and again: the *Seinsfrage*, or the question concerning the meaning of Being. Whatever changes his later thought underwent, the *Seinsfrage* constituted the central leitmotif that unified the different topics of his work, whether they dealt with the foundations of Western logic, the origin of the work of art, the essence of language and poetic expression, or any other of the manifold themes of his investigation.

In view of the seemingly recondite character of this leitmotif, it may seem paradoxical to refer to a profound "influence" of his thinking. Few questions, indeed, would seem farther removed from the standard discourse of philosophy in the current century than the question of Being. In what terms, therefore, might one speak of the meaning of Heidegger's endeavors in the perspective of the twentieth century?

In the following pages, I will examine Heidegger's thought in relation to a central aim that the *Seinsfrage* engaged during the early period of his work which culminated with the publication of *Being and Time*: the "deconstruction" of Western intellectual and cultural traditions. When examined against the backdrop of the period of its formulation, this deconstructive intention of the *Seinsfrage*, as I will argue, underscores the significance of Heidegger's thought as it articulated the key presuppositions that have come to expression in an ongoing crisis in the human sciences. In identifying the precise target of the *Seinsfrage*'s deconstructive intention during the period of its elaboration, I will attempt to set in relief a key source of this crisis.

In the years following World War I, and before envisaging the full implications of this theme in light of the question of Being, Heidegger began to call for a "deconstruction" (*Abbau*) or a "destruction" (*Destruktion*) of Western intellectual and cultural traditions.[2] In his review of Karl Jaspers' book, *Psychology of Worldviews*, which Heidegger wrote between 1919 and 1921 and sent to Jaspers in June 1921, but which was not published until 1973, the Freiburg thinker proposed that Western intellectual traditions might have unwittingly strayed from the fundamental themes which stood at their origin and, through an "unwarranted concern to save culture" (GA9 5), had mistaken merely secondary matters for fundamental problems. Such a concern to "save culture" proved wholly inadequate for the purpose of retrieving the original meaning of the past, just as did all approaches to the past in terms of objectified categories—like the "ideal of humanity" or the cultivation of "personality"—that a declining tradition had bequeathed (GA9 34). At the outset of a biting attack against the contemporary interpretations of the cultural task of philosophy, Heidegger stipulated in the 1923 Freiburg lecture course "Hermeneutics of Facticity" that "philosophy as such has no warrant to concern itself with universal humanity [*allgemeine Menschheit*] and culture [*Kultur*]." He then called for a reinterpretation of this task from the vantage point that later became *Being and Time*'s central focus: he proposed that the "destruction" or "deconstruction" of intellectual traditions should proceed from a reexamination of the original Greek interpretation of Being, which had been completely misunderstood due to the influence of more recent academic styles of analysis (GA63 51–77, 91, 108).

Well before the publication of *Being and Time* in 1927, Heidegger rose to prominence in Germany on the basis of his reputation as a teacher. A number of his former students, including Karl Löwith, Hannah Arendt, and Hans-Georg Gadamer, have attributed his renown to the originality of his attempt to disengage interpretation of the seminal thinkers of the past from the conventional assumptions of contemporary academia. As these former students have emphasized, Heidegger's critical appraisal of traditional, culturally-oriented contemporary philosophy was warmly received among students and younger professors who, following the devastation wrought by World War I, questioned the soundness of the Western cultural heritage and the purport of any attempt to evaluate philosophy in relation to its contemporary cultural significance.[3]

In the years following World War I, Heidegger's deconstruction of intellectual and cultural traditions directed particular attention not only toward the attempt to adapt philosophy to a cultural role, but also toward the more specifically philosophical connotation that the term "culture" had acquired during the course of the nineteenth century. What was the purpose of this critique? What was the precise relation between the "destruction" of cultural traditions and the more original interpretation of the question of Being he sought to elaborate?

The recent publication of some of Heidegger's early Freiburg and Marburg lecture courses (1919–28) for the first time in the framework of his collected works (*Gesamtausgabe*) enables us to place these questions in a new perspective. It becomes possible to identify the central target of Heidegger's deconstruction of contemporary ideas of "spirit," "tradition," and "culture": namely, the historical and historicist orientations responsible for the elaboration of these ideas since the late nineteenth century. From Heidegger's standpoint, it was these orientations that obstructed the approach to the past requisite for the reformulation of the originary question of Being. This is why the debate concerning historical consciousness evoked by terms like "spirit," "tradition," and especially "culture" is so closely bound to the interpretation of Heidegger's *Seinsfrage*. Let us turn to Heidegger's early lecture courses in which he examined the idea of "historical consciousness," which the term "culture" had come to represent over the course of the nineteenth century. From there we will proceed toward an elucidation of Heidegger's *Seinsfrage* through an analysis of its relation to the "deconstruction" of cultural and intellectual traditions in his writings of the 1920s.

Heidegger provided a detailed analysis of the idea of "culture" or "historical culture" in the 1919 course, "Phenomenology and Transcendental Philosophy of Values." Here he explained that the idea of "culture" or "historical culture" served as the basis for interpretations of German thought, most specifically in relation to the theme of historical consciousness, from the period of J.G. Herder and F. Schlegel onward (GA56/57 133f.). In the course of the nineteenth century, "culture" in this sense, according to Heidegger, had come to signify an "accomplishment" (*Leistung*) and an "achievement" (*Errungenschaft*) in a long process of historical development (130). This idea of historical development, as Heidegger noted, was most immediately spurred by the emergence of scientific consciousness and by the ensuing progress of natural science and technology (130f.).

What stood most directly in question in this and other of Heidegger's courses of the 1920s was not so much the emergence of modern historical consciousness or of science and technology per se. He sought above all to reveal the way in which the one-sided focus on the development of culture had tended to obscure other interpretive possibilities which could not be readily measured in terms of cultural values. Heidegger directed his polemics of this period at philosophers who had most strongly influenced the idea of culture that marked contemporary German thought: the Marburg Neo-Kantians, above all Hermann Cohen, and the Baden Neo-Kantians Wilhelm Windelband and Heinrich Rickert. Heidegger labeled the "philosophy of culture" (*Kulturphilosophie*) of Windelband and Rickert (the latter of whom had directed Heidegger's doctoral dissertation at Freiburg) as "the typical philosophy of the nineteenth century" (GA56/57 131). Heidegger did not hesitate to take to task other thinkers, most notably Max Weber and Ernst Troeltsch, in so far as they shared similar ideals.[4] Even the contemporary "philosophy of life" (*Lebensphilosophie*) came under fire for its affirmation of the ideal of universal validity (*Allgemeingültigkeit*) in the study of objectifications of cultural life, in spite of the fact that Dilthey's "philosophy of life" seemed to Heidegger to anticipate a more radical interpretation of human existence toward which he himself was groping at this time (GA61 79–89; GA9 1–44).

In the context of these early years of the Weimar Republic, the broad appeal of Heidegger's critique of intellectual traditions and of "culture" might seem to bear a certain resemblance to other contemporary expressions of radical doubt about the Western heritage. In this regard, one need only think of the enormously popular work of Oswald Spengler, *The Decline of the West* (1918). On the basis of an all-encompassing typology of cultural forms, Spengler interpreted the waning of Western spiritual values and religious faith in favor of the pragmatic and technological orientation of a materialistic civilization as the unmistakable sign of the West's impending decline. If Heidegger reproached what he took to be the dilettantism of Spengler's historical method, he nonetheless heartily applauded the boldness of Spengler's prediction. It demonstrated nothing more clearly, for Heidegger, than the groundlessness of historical methods in the human sciences in their attempt to elaborate objective, universally valid criteria of judgment as a basis for comparison of typical patterns of cultural expression (GA63 35–57).

Much closer than Spengler to Heidegger's own concerns in this period stood a group of young neo-orthodox Protestant theologians who berated nineteenth and twentieth century liberal theology for what they took to be its too-exclusive focus on the role of religion in the development of culture. In this regard, the polemics that theologians like Friedrich Gogarten and Rudolf Bultmann directed against Adolf von Harnack and Ernst Troeltsch, whose orientation had been deeply influenced by the Neo-Kantian *Kulturphilosophie*, ran directly parallel to the early philosophical critique enunciated by Heidegger. Indeed, Heidegger himself evoked the theological implications of his endeavors in his early Freiburg courses, above all in "Einleitung in die Phänomenologie der Religion" (WS 1920–21) and in "Augustinus und der Neuplatonismus" (SS 1921). In these courses Heidegger, like Bultmann and Gogarten, directed his concern toward the eschatological, otherworldly striving at the heart of the pristine religiosity of the original Christian community; like these theologians, he censured a long tradition of interpretation of the essence of Christianity in terms of the objective manifestations of the Christian contribution to the development of culture.[5] It is this affinity between philosophical and theological concerns which enables us to comprehend the close collaboration between Heidegger and Bultmann during the Marburg years (1923–28), when Heidegger was engaged in the composition of *Being and Time*.

For our interpretation of Heidegger's deconstruction of Western intellectual traditions, we might extend our analysis of affinities that Heidegger shared with other authors in an attempt to derive his radical critique of tradition and of culture from a broader "spirit" of the times. In order to account for the significance of Heidegger's thought and for the magnitude of its influence, we might also search for a sociological basis to his orientation by attempting to trace it to a given ideological milieu. As suggestive as such methods might be for the comprehension of Heidegger's intellectual biography, they would hardly seem to indicate how the deconstruction of the historical "consciousness" or "spirit" bequeathed by cultural traditions might be related to the philosophical meaning of the question of Being at the heart of *Being and Time*.

Nonetheless, even a superficial reading of *Being and Time* illustrates the difficulty involved in the identification of this relation. While the question of Being is central to this work, Heidegger hardly ever refers in it to the idea of "culture," which had been a focus of his earlier critique and, more generally, of radical doubt in Germany during the decade following World War I. Indeed, two years after the appearance of *Being and Time*, during a public debate at Davos in 1929 with Ernst Cassirer, Heidegger insisted that one should not attempt on the basis of that work to understand "culture" and the "realms of culture": "When one asks this question in such a way, it is absolutely impossible to say something from what is given here."[6]

This deliberate neglect of a philosophical concept whose significance Heidegger himself had underscored in his early Freiburg courses by no means indicates a suspension of Heidegger's critical thrust in this direction but rather a broadening of its focus. Indeed, one of the principal tasks of *Being and Time* was to encompass the deconstruction of "culture" and of the related topics of historically oriented philosophies of the post-Hegelian world, such as history of the "spirit" or "intellect" (*Geistesgeschichte*) and "world history" (*Weltgeschichte*), in a broader deconstruction of traditional metaphysics.[7] The originality of Heidegger's interpretation stems from his elucidation of modern philosophies of history and of historical consciousness in view of what he took to be their tacit affirmation of presuppositions inherited from a long tradition of thought concerning the meaning of Being. Since to Heidegger's mind the predominant contemporary philosophies of history and of culture had unwittingly imbibed the presuppositions of traditional metaphysics, deconstruction of the metaphysical residue at the basis of these philosophies aimed at a fundamental reinterpretation of the past—and, above all, of the question of Being it had bequeathed—from a vantage point that, by virtue of their very dependence on the presuppositions of traditional metaphysics, these philosophies had thoroughly obstructed.

This attempt to designate the post-Hegelian philosophies of history and of culture as the unwitting exponents of traditional metaphysical presuppositions may indeed seem strange to readers familiar with the works of the theoreticians against whom Heidegger's polemics were directed in *Being and Time* and in lecture courses of the late 1920s. Here, as in the early 1920s, Heidegger's critique was levelled at theories of objectivity and universal validity in the works of the Baden Neo-Kantians Wilhelm Windelband and Heinrich Rickert, as of Max Weber, Georg Simmel, and Wilhelm Dilthey. But what could be farther from traditional ontology or metaphysics than these theories, which have in large measure provided the methodological foundations for present-day social or human science? Had these authors, after all, not redefined such terms as "culture" (Windelband, Rickert) and "spirit" (Dilthey) as a means of critically refining them by separating them from the metaphysical presuppositions of the Hegelian philosophy of history? In spite of all the differences between these thinkers, were they not united, as Heidegger himself stressed in his early Freiburg courses, in the pursuit of a "critique of historical reason" (GA63 68f.), for which the historical contingency of consciousness—the rootedness of its grasp of truth in a singular historical and cultural perspective— precluded knowledge of an ultimate truth beyond the limits of any given perspective and capable of encompassing the ultimate metaphysical meaning of history as a totality? Was not the much-touted relativism of the human sciences in general, and of modern historical methods in particular, a direct result of the abandonment of metaphysical claims to an ahistorical, absolute foundation for truth?

The answer to these questions depends upon what one identifies as traditional in the history of metaphysics. For Heidegger, the claim to have uncovered ultimate ontological knowledge of the world in itself constituted only one aspect of this tradition. Indeed, according to Heidegger's argument in *Being and Time*, this claim to ultimate knowledge of the world in itself is rooted in another, more significant character of metaphysics: the presupposition of the temporal permanence and perdurability of Being that ultimate knowledge designates, which was originally introduced into the Western metaphysical tradition by the Platonic claim to the eternity of ideas and the Aristotelian doctrine of substantial permanence.

From the standpoint of *Being and Time*, this identification of Being with permanence and unperishing presence constitutes the fundamental presupposition of the Western metaphysical tradition, whatever its historical variations. This presupposition re-emerged in the predominant interpretations of Being that oriented the concept of truth in the ancient, medieval, and modern periods of Western intellectual history. And in each period this identification was founded on a tacit, unexamined omission: the question of Being, of what truly "is," overlooked or set aside as insignificant the temporal finitude of the questioner. It was this supposedly insignificant omission that Heidegger sought to take into consideration as fundamentally constitutive of the interpretation of Being and of truth throughout the Western intellectual tradition.

According to the renowned argument of *Being and Time*, the identification of permanence and continual presence with the very criteria of Being in Western intellectual traditions, far from constituting a merely theoretical hypothesis, derives from an all-pervasive, if usually hidden quest rooted in Dasein's (finite man's) everyday being-in-the-world: Dasein's quest to interpret its existence in terms of a semblance of perdurability and permanence as a tacit means of dissembling the finitude of its own Being as being toward death. In a complex series of finely-constructed arguments which cannot be reproduced here, Heidegger supported the argument that the ultimate criteria of Being acknowledged by the predominant strands of the Western metaphysical tradition were theoretical expressions of Dasein's everyday attempt to seek refuge from the finitude of its own mortal being.

A mountain of existentialist literature since the 1950s has widely popularized Heidegger's analyses of human finitude in relation to the Western intellectual heritage. But what of the line of argumentation which will enable us to interpret these analyses in light of Heidegger's deconstruction of the "spirit" and the "historical consciousness" present in contemporary cultural traditions?

This line of argumentation is advanced in Heidegger's interpretation of world history in *Being and Time*, which places his earlier critique of culture in a more comprehensive framework. In spite of modern insight into the historical character of human understanding, rooted in variations of historical viewpoint relative to evolving cultural perspectives, the idea of world history as a broad framework of cultural and spiritual continuity shared one essential presupposition with earlier metaphysical assumptions it had supposedly superseded. Setting aside any consideration of human finitude in the elaboration of the criteria of truth, the modern idea of world history located the source of historical meaning in the continuity of processes of development. Like earlier metaphysical traditions, with their emphasis on the timeless and immutable character of truth, modern historical reflection had adopted continuity and perdurability as the criteria of truth per se. And nowhere was the predominance of these criteria more evident than in the ideal of fixed scientific "objectivity" and "universal validity" posited by all the post-Hegelian philosophies of history. This ideal involved the identification of criteria capable of subsisting beyond the temporal finitude of singular, mortal beings, providing a permanent standard to encompass the resolute historicity of human existence. It signified to Heidegger nothing less than an unspoken attempt to overcome the finite perspective of temporal and historical existence through the comforting illusion of the timeless presence of the past in the continuous development of an overarching cultural and world historical context. This context supposedly constituted the basis for the permanent, "objective" accessibility of the past's meaning (SZ 387–404/439–55). And precisely here the modern methodologies of the social and human sciences revealed their unacknowledged debt to an ancient way of positing the meaning of Being. For Heidegger, the deconstruction of the ontological tradition was tantamount to unveiling the illusory character of this attempt in order to delve beyond the objective interrelation of cultural and world-historical processes, and to reveal the finite temporality of Dasein as the primary source of historical truth.

We recognize today with what force Heidegger's deconstruction of intellectual and cultural traditions, in proposing to ground the criteria of objectivity and universal validity in the temporal finitude of Dasein, rekindled the debate concerning the problem of truth in the human sciences. The analysis in *Being and Time* of Dasein's temporal modes played a central role in the shift in our way of envisaging this problem. It is above all in this work that Heidegger rooted "authentic being-toward-death" in "finite temporality" as the hidden foundation of Dasein's historicity (SZ 386/438). Only being-toward-death, conceived in terms of the temporal future of the singular Dasein which interprets history, proves to be capable of conferring an authentic meaning on the past. It is in relation to this futural possibility open to a singular Dasein that Heidegger places in question the privilege traditionally accorded to the stability of ever-present criteria presumed to be capable of identifying the "reality" of the past. Heidegger thus shifted the criterion of truth from that of stability and permanence in the mode of interpretation of past reality to that of "repetition" (*Wiederholung*) of authentic meaning implicit in the past in light of the *possible future* of the interpreter. A decisive sentence in *Being and*

Time places the depth of this shift in relief in relation to its temporal horizon: "Higher than actuality [*Wirklichkeit*] stands possibility [*Möglichkeit*]" (SZ 38/63). Heidegger's historical reflection devalues the contextual reality of cultural and world history in favor of another approach to history for which the futural possibilities of the interpreter of the past provide the essential criteria for uncovering its authentic significance.

For the purposes of our present investigation we are concerned less with the specific mode of elaboration of Heidegger's ontology than, to return to our initial question, with the significance of his deconstruction of tradition in the perspective of the twentieth century. By questioning the fundamental meaning of traditions or other objective processes of development, Heidegger placed in doubt the role of contextual interpretation that aims to retrieve an autonomous significance presumed to emerge within such processes. Certainly it is true that Dasein's being, marked by the facticity of its being-in-the-world, is always situated within the shifting framework of its given place in the world. But this Heideggerian notion of being-in-the-world must be distinguished from an historical, sociological, or cultural *context*. Indeed, where the notion of context presupposes the autonomy of historical, sociological, or cultural processes as a primary source of the meaning of human existence, for Heidegger, on the contrary, Dasein's own finite possibilities, oriented by its authentic or inauthentic choices, determine how its existence as being-in-the-world is to be made significant. Here any unequivocal, self-subsistent meaning of the context in its traditional sense dissolves as the finitude of Dasein's being, governing the plurality of its possible choices, becomes the fundamental guide toward interpreting itself and its world.

For two key reasons this Heideggerian doubt concerning the role of contextual interpretation proved consequential. First, this devaluation of contextual significance simultaneously involved a depreciation of the attempt to identify, on a contextual basis, the past intentions of an author and the circumstances which marked the reception of his or her thought. Second, the placing in question of contextual significance implies a refusal of the assumption characteristic of post-Hegelian philosophy of culture, as well as of cultural and intellectual history, of a multiplicity of historical contexts as the source of transhistorical meaning, and thus of "progress" or spontaneous development in the historical process. Once historicity is rooted in the temporal modes of singular Dasein, the problem of transhistorical continuity no longer finds an authentic counterpart in a purpose or task of the "subject," of culture, or of humanity, but is *primarily* posited in *Being and Time* in terms of a tacit, inauthentic forgetfulness of the fundamental issue of Dasein's finitude, manifested in traditional ideas of Being and of truth. If there exists an ontological principle of world-historical cohesion, it must be above all comprehended in terms of the manifold ways in which great texts of the tradition obscure this issue, independently of the express awareness of their authors.

Rather than continuity in the traditional lines of thought, *Being and Time* thus aims to uncover the transhistorical horizon delineated by the fundamental problem of human finitude as it has traditionally been left *unthought*. Fundamental historical reflection proposed in this work is by no means limited to an examination of authors in relation to criteria specific to the periods in which they wrote. Moreover, hermeneutic discussion is no longer confined to the problem concerning whether one may address an issue which is situated "entirely outside the horizon" of an author (SZ 98/131).[8] Beyond any merely doxographic examination of a given set of ideas, the analysis of Dasein provides the ontological leitmotif for historical discussion (ibid.). In *Being and Time* this theme furnishes a touchstone for the determination of the fundamental link between authors of the tradition, from Plato and Aristotle to Descartes and Leibniz, Kant and Hegel, right up to Dilthey.

In the decades following Heidegger's critique, and partly because of his influence, it has become a commonplace of intellectual life to posit the dissolution of the subject, spirit, or consciousness understood as a uniform structure underlying historical continuity; in light of the historical variability of the ground of experience, the idea of an essential historicity of interpretation has become a standard presupposition in the hermeneutically oriented human sciences. At the same time, intellectual history has been in a state of continual crisis since thinkers like Heidegger, and those he has influenced have undercut the assumption that cultural processes or continuity in the development of the human spirit constitute, in the idiom of Dilthey, Burckhardt, or Meinecke, the generative matrix of historical meaning.

Here is not the place to evaluate Heidegger's role as one of the earliest and most radical spokesmen for the dissolution of the subject, nor the scope of his influence on the anti-contextualist presuppositions put forward by different waves of contemporary post-structuralism and post-modernism.[9] Whatever one might think of the specific hermeneutic method proposed in *Being and Time*, Heidegger unquestionably gave expression to a radical break with earlier methods of interpretation and, consequently, to the problematic character of any contemporary attempt to resuscitate traditional historicist conceptions of human identity. If traditional ideas of the subject constituting a coherent, transhistorical basis of human historical experience hardly seem capable of enlightening us in regard to our current condition, it remains an open question whether "authentic" meaning in history indeed becomes accessible on the basis of

Heidegger's specific mode of deconstruction of the subject, of culture, of world-history as the traditional bearers of historical meaning. On one score, however, it is legitimate to conclude our analysis of the deconstructive intent of Heidegger's *Seinsfrage* on a critical note: Heidegger himself simply presupposed that what he designated as an ontological problem ultimately corresponds to the fundamental *historical* problem. He thus never envisioned the possibility that, in the name of an ontological issue, his mode of analysis might render inaccessible essential dimensions of the past which a close analysis of authorial intentions within the linguistic horizon of a specific socio-political context might best be capable of, independent of recourse to traditional assumptions of the "subject" or spirit underlying the development of world history.

7

Repetition and Tradition:
Heidegger's Destructuring of the Distinction
Between Essence and Existence
in *Basic Problems of Phenomenology*[1]

Robert Bernasconi

Heidegger is clear in *Being and Time* that a destructuring of the on-tological tradition is a necessary precondition for posing the question of Being concretely, and that it is toward this that the book is directed (SZ 26/49). To that extent, not only the first division of the first part of *Being and Time*, the "Preparatory Fundamental Analysis of Dasein," but the whole of the first part of *Being and Time*, had it been completed, would have to have been understood as only provisional, awaiting the destructur-ing that was set to take place in the book's second part (SZ 39–40/63–64). Nevertheless, *Being and Time* has usually been read without reference to this rubric.[2] The way in which the work was supposed to contribute to a destructuring of the history of ontology has been left virtually unclarified or, worse still, the notion of destructuring has been given a wholly nega-tive sense, contrary to Heidegger's own explicit warnings to the contrary.[3] The most prominent exception to this tendency is, of course, the decon-structive reading, though I believe that the deconstructive reading of *Be-ing and Time* has also introduced its own distortions. In spite of the fact that Derrida traces his conception of *déconstruction* back to Heidegger's *Destruktion*, it can readily be shown that Derrida draws more heavily on the later Heidegger, the Heidegger of the history of Being.[4]

So long as the complex relation between Heideggerian *Destruktion* and Derridian *déconstruction* remains unclarified, deconstruction inevita-bly tends to approach *Being and Time* more as the later Heidegger subse-quently wanted the book to be reread than in accordance with the reading *Being and Time* itself invites, following its own directions to its readers.[5] In the first section of this chapter I rehearse Heidegger's programmatic statements about destructuring, both as they are found in *Being and Time* and in contemporaneous lecture courses. The contemporary discussion of Heidegger's destructuring of the history of ontology is largely confined to a compilation of such statements. The remaining sections of the chapter are more innovative. In the second section, I direct attention to Heidegger's critical appropriation of that history in *Basic Problems of Phenomenology*. In the third section, I bring Heidegger's own discussion of historicality in *Being and Time* to bear on the possibility of any such history, and thereby attempt to open the way to another, richer, notion of destructuring.

I

What is often treated by commentators and critics straightforwardly as Heidegger's own philosophy is rather to be read under the rubric of repetition (*Wiederholung*).[6] Repetition is never a simple reiteration of the past; it includes reconstructing the tradition to which each of us is said to belong. To the extent that reconstruction has been carried out successfully, it does not call for acceptance or rejection. Faced with the tradition to which one already belongs, the decision one is called to make is not that of whether the tradition is correct or incorrect. Rather, if one decides not to remain largely indifferent, the further decision to be made is between either owning or disowning one's tradition. However, so stated, the choice is not a genuine one. As Heidegger learned from studying the relation of Descartes' philosophy to its predecessors, one can never simply turn one's back on tradition and start anew: "Even the most radical attempt to begin all over again is pervaded by traditional concepts" (GA24 31/22). What Heidegger calls "destructuring," and is often talked about by commentators as if it was a disowning, is in fact an owning or an appropriation (*Aneignung*) that is not separated from the constitution of the tradition. Tradition is never simply given and then decided upon. Heidegger does not reject the traditional conception of truth. He derives it from the primordial phenomenon of truth that is preserved in the Greek word *aletheia*. Heidegger understands this, not as a shaking off of tradition, but as an originary appropriation of tradition (SZ 220/262).

The basic features of the destructuring of the history of ontology are set out by Heidegger in §6 of *Being and Time*.[7] The decisive statement is this one:

> If the question of Being is to have its own history made transparent, then this hardened tradition [*Tradition*] must be loosened up, and the concealments which it has brought about must be dissolved. We understand this task as the *destructuring* of the traditional [*überlieferten*] content of ancient ontology to the primordial experiences in which the first and subse-

quently governing ways of determining the nature of Being were
achieved, a destructuring that is *guided by the question of Being.* (SZ
22/44)

It is clear from this statement that the problem to which destructuring the
history of ontology is the remedy is a problem posed by the hold of a
rigidified tradition. That is why the negative side of destructuring, its critique, is aimed not at the past, but at "today;" that is to say, destructuring
aims at "the prevalent way of treating the history of ontology," be it Neo-
Hegelian, Neo-Kantian, or naively historiological (SZ 22–23/44; see already PIA 239). The tradition is to undergo "a positive appropriation"
(GA24 31/23), one that frees philosophy not so much from the past as from
certain fashions of the present (GA24 142/101). In keeping with this,
Heidegger presents falling prey to the tradition as a form of *Verfallenheit*
(SZ 21/42). Indeed, he emphasizes the relation between this form of *Verfallenheit*, and the better known form that arises when Dasein interprets
itself in terms of the world (SZ 21–22/43). Nor was this an afterthought.
Already in the 1924 lecture *The Concept of Time*, Heidegger associated
tradition with *das Man*: "On average, the interpretation of Dasein is governed by everydayness, by what one traditionally [*über-lieferter*] says about
Dasein and human life. It is governed by the 'One,' by tradition [*Tradition*]" (BZ 14/2). That is to say, it is governed by a tradition that has not
been appropriated in the sense of destructured.

"The discovery of tradition" (SZ 20/41) imposes a task on Dasein that
cannot be met at the level of a mere historiological study of tradition. The
assignment is to "positively make the past our own" by appropriating the
tradition (SZ 21/42). However, it is important for understanding what
Heidegger means by "tradition" that one notice how he specifically draws
attention to the way in which concentration on alien cultures represents a
form of uprootedness: "Dasein has had its historicality so thoroughly uprooted by tradition that it confines its interest to the multiformity of possible types, directions, and standpoints of philosophical activity in the most
exotic and alien cultures; and by this very interest it seeks to veil the fact
that it has no ground of its own to stand on" (SZ 21/43). Tradition, for
Heidegger, is not just any tradition, but one's own tradition awaiting being
owned. Under the phrase "the hardened tradition" Heidegger emphasizes
that what the tradition transmits can appear obvious and to that extent
may have its evidence obscured. Although the context of this observation
is Heidegger's attempt to raise again the question of Being, he explicitly
focuses, not so much on the tradition's inhibiting of questioning, as on its
concealing of the "primordial experiences" that serve as its "sources":[8]
"Tradition takes what has come down to us and delivers it over to self-

evidence: it blocks our access to those primordial 'sources' from which the categories and concepts handed down to us have been in part quite genuinely drawn. Indeed it makes us forget that they have had such an origin, and makes us suppose that the necessity of going back to these sources is something which we need not even understand" (SZ 21/43). Heidegger explicitly advises that this process has nothing to do with a misguided relativizing of the ontological standpoint of the tradition. The point is not to transcend the limits imposed by the tradition, but by marking those limits to stake out its positive possibilities (SZ 22/44). If commentators have not given that rubric sufficient attention hitherto, it is in large measure because the negative connotations of the word "destructuring" overwhelmed the positive description Heidegger gave of it.[9]

Heidegger thought of destructuring less as an overcoming and more as a genealogy, although ultimately neither term suffices. The term "overcoming" (*überwindung*), which later came to be so prominent in Heidegger's presentation of his thought, played only a limited role in the Marburg period and was not applied to metaphysics or the tradition. Destructuring is not an overcoming. It is true that in *Basic Problems* Heidegger writes that Hegel must be overcome, but the context of this remark should not be forgotten (GA24 254/178). Heidegger is here saying that Hegel, who dissolved ontology into logic, can be overcome only by a radicalizing of the latter's thought which at the same time appropriates it. Heidegger writes, "This overcoming of Hegel is the intrinsically necessary step in the development of Western philosophy which must be made for it to remain at all alive" (GA24 254/178). In other words, what is here described as the overcoming of Hegel is not the same as the overcoming of metaphysics that takes place at the end of philosophy. Of course, it was Hegel himself who proposed the idea of the end of philosophy, as Heidegger acknowledged: "In Hegel, philosophy—that is, ancient philosophy—is in a certain sense thought through to its end" (GA24 400/282). However, it was an end only in a limited sense, as one could not say that Hegel had exhausted all the possibilities of the beginning (GA24 400/282).

In order to focus attention on the beginning, Heidegger twice employed the word "genealogy." The reference to "genealogy" in *Being and Time* is merely in passing. In the course of outlining the character of ontological inquiry, Heidegger observes that, recalling Plato's phrase, "even the ontological task of constructing a non-deductive genealogy of the different possible ways of Being requires that we first come to an understanding of 'what we really mean by the expression "Being"'" (SZ 11/31). The more important use of the word is in *Basic Problems*, where Heidegger associates the notion of genealogy with Kant's notion of "establishing the birth certificate" of a concept (GA24 140/100; cf. SZ 22/44).

Heidegger asks whether the birth certificate of the concepts of "essence" and "existence" is genuine or whether the basic ontological concepts take a quite different course. Heidegger's genealogy reveals in the Middle Ages and antiquity "a different horizon for the interpretation of existence as actuality than in Kant or, more accurately, . . . *a different direction of vision within the same horizon*" (GA24 142/101). The task of the genealogy is to expose this horizon and so secure the unity of the tradition that stretches "from antiquity to Hegel" (GA24 4/3). Heidegger therefore adopts the twofold task of showing the difference between the Kantian and ancient interpretations of Being, while at the same time insisting that at some deeper level they coincide.

What unites the tradition is not only the idea of a scientific philosophy (GA24 3/3), but also a recognition of Being as philosophy's proper and sole theme. The claim that previous thinkers did not recognize that they were in some sense saying Being, a claim later developed by Heidegger in the course of articulating the history of Being, is absent here. Being as a theme "comes to life at the beginning of philosophy in antiquity, and it assumes its most grandiose form in Hegel's logic" (GA24 15/11). Since antiquity, philosophy has been ontology "in the widest possible sense" (GA24 15/11). All ontological investigations are determined by their historical situation, including not only the limitations on the specific possibilities governing one's approach to being, but also "the preceding philosophical tradition" (GA24 31/22). The unity of tradition, and indeed a sense of its linearity, pervades Heidegger's remarks about the history of philosophy at this time. Within this perspective, Heidegger privileges the origins of philosophy and "the primordiality of antiquity." Ancient philosophy is presented as "a gigantic beginning," containing within itself "a wealth of truly undeveloped and in part completely hidden possibilities" (GA26 11/9). The task is to gain access to what is "old enough" to allow us to learn to comprehend what was prepared by the "ancients" (SZ 19/40).

By making the question of Being the central issue of philosophy, Heidegger had a more secure basis for identifying philosophy with the Western tradition of metaphysics and locating the origin in Greece than is the case with academic philosophy more generally, whose decision in favor of Greece is more arbitrary. It has to be recognized that Heidegger's focus on Western metaphysics, his virtual exclusion of everything else, the subsequent references to Buddhism notwithstanding, are not a casual mistake nor an oversight that can easily be corrected: "My essential intention is to first pose the problem and work it out in such a way that the essentials of the entire Western tradition will be concentrated in the simplicity of a basic problem" (GA26 165/132). Fundamental ontology alone provides access to "the inner and hidden life of the basic movement of Western philosophy" (GA26 196/154). There is, Heidegger acknowledges, "a definite viewpoint" (GA26 196/154), "a specific, concrete shape" to the way the problems are posed at the beginning of Western philosophy (GA26 197/ 155). However, it has to be asked whether Heidegger ultimately attempts at this time to locate the sources of the tradition in a historical beginning.

That the destructuring of the history of ontology is not limited to tracing concepts back to their sources, disturbing the self-evidence into which those concepts have fallen, and then opening up the way to their appropriation, is already clear from *History of the Concept of Time*. When Heidegger, in these lectures from 1925, describes "genuine repetition" as a taking up (*Aufnahme*) of the tradition that is quite different from traditionalism, he asks about the prejudices that accompany tradition. In traditionalism, what is taken up is not subjected to critique; in repetition, one goes back prior to the questions which were posed in history to appropriate them "once again originally" (*erst wieder ursprunglich*) (GA20 187–188/138). But Heidegger insists that a genuine repetition shows further that Greek philosophy is *inevitably* conditioned. To recognize the prejudices underlying the tradition is not only to discover within the Greek formulations an origin that the Greeks failed to see. To understand that Greek thought is necessarily conditioned is to acknowledge the finitude of thought.[10]

II

The thesis that "to the constitution of a being there belongs essence and existence" is the second of four theses discussed in Part One of *Basic Problems* under the heading "Phenomenological Critique of Some Traditional Theses about Being." The first thesis discussed is Kant's "Being is not a real predicate." The third thesis concerns the distinction between *res extensa* and *res cogitans*, and, although it is mainly concerned with Kant, it also rehearses the analyses of environmentality and worldhood found in §§15–18 of *Being and Time*. The fourth thesis, "the thesis of logic," rehearses the discussion of assertion and truth from *Being and Time*, following an examination of the Being of the copula in Aristotle, Hobbes, Mill, and Lotze. The historical portion of the discussion of the fourth thesis appears to be the least successful portion of the first part of *Basic Problems*, although the discussion of Hobbes is not without interest.[11] Perhaps for that reason Heidegger returned to the issue the following year and, using Leibniz as his text, performed what he described as a "destructuring of logic" by showing how logic is not independently grounded, but must be referred back to metaphysics (GA26 70–71/56–57, 126–127/102–103).

Although Heidegger does not explicitly describe his discussion of the medieval distinction between essence and existence in *Basic Problems* as a destructuring, it would seem appropriate to understand it as such for a number of reasons. Firstly, Heidegger repeatedly refers to the self-evidence of the traditional distinction, thereby invoking that characteristic of the history of ontology which, according to *Being and Time*, is unlocked by destructuring (GA24 110/78, 120–124/87–88, 140/100). Secondly, just as the unpublished Second Part of *Being and Time* was to have passed in reverse historical order from Kant through Descartes to Aristotle,[12] so the "Phenomenological Critique" in *Basic Problems* of the medieval distinction between essence and existence exemplifies Heidegger's claim that it is with reference to the subsequent history of philosophy that the fundamental orientation of Greek ontology first becomes comprehensible (GA24 121/86). Although the focus appears to be on medieval philosophy, Heidegger is ultimately more concerned to find the original sources of the distinction in Greek philosophy. Heidegger's view is that the medieval period shows no new approaches. His discussion of Aquinas and Scotus closely follows Suarez's discussion of them (GA24 124–139/88–99),[13] and he judges that Suarez's attempt at a detailed circumscription of the concept of existence remains "wholly within the framework of traditional ontology" (GA24 144/102).[14] The medieval terms are mere "translations of ancient concepts" (GA24 148/105) whose sources have been forgotten, but by reading the history of philosophy backwards, the alienation produced by the tradition can be reversed. Thirdly, although Heidegger's discussion in *Basic Problems* of the medieval distinction between essence and existence is initially directed toward its origin in Greek philosophy, he also takes the opportunity to show how together they both determine Kant's discussion of Being (GA24 107–108/76–77). The stock of ontological categories that Kant inherited from antiquity was in his thought "deracinated and deprived of its native soil, its origin no longer understood" (GA24 166/117). More specifically, Kant's thesis that "Being is not a real predicate" was anticipated by Suarez who himself drew explicitly on Aristotle.[15] This does not mean that Kant's thesis had no purchase. The claim that "Being is not a real predicate" is found to "unhinge" (GA24 42/32) a longstanding tradition that reaches back beyond Anselm to Boethius, Dionysius the Areopagite, and finally to Neoplatonism (GA24 40/30–31). These are names one rarely hears about from Heidegger, again, thereby indicating in some measure the process of selection by which Heidegger sought to establish the lineage that identified which thinkers and which ideas constituted *the* tradition.

The underlying theme of Heidegger's discussion of the origins of the distinction between essence and existence is the contrast between, on the one hand, the primacy of the productive view within Greek ontology, where the form (*morphe*) is grounded in the look (*eidos*), and, on the other hand, the priority of sensory intuition within modern philosophy, where the look is founded in the form (GA24 149/106). The dominance of the horizon of production is said to be reflected in the fact that Plato's key term, *eidos*, originally meant the anticipated look of the thing to be produced (GA24 150/106). And yet the Greeks themselves defined the mode of access to the extant primarily as an intuitive perception (*noein*) (GA24 154/109). The same is true of Kant. Kant's thesis that Being is not a real predicate is interpreted by Heidegger to mean that Being is perception and presence (*praesens*). At the same time Heidegger is clear that the intelligibility of the *Critique of Pure Reason* depends on recognizing that for Kant, even though he was unaware of it, to be is to be a product (GA24 216/152). Whether the focus is perception or production, the thrust of Heidegger's discussion is to show the "undeviating continuity of tradition" (GA24 165/117; see also 213–214/150). Heidegger's statement in *Being and Time* that "we have deprived pure intuition of its priority, which corresponds noetically to the priority of the present-at-hand in traditional ontology" (SZ 147/187), has been interpreted as his attempt to overcome the primacy of intuition as the ideal of knowledge from antiquity to Kant and Hegel (GA24 167/118) in favor of the primacy of production. But this not only presupposes that Heidegger was aiming at the "overcoming metaphysics"; it also assumes that depriving intuition of its priority entails the priority of practice, as if *Being and Time* did not problematize the distinction between theory and practice.

Heidegger contests the priority of intuition not by referring it to production, but by referring both intuition and production to Dasein. The longstanding privilege accorded to intuition arises from the fact that it has to a higher degree a quality that it also shares with production, the character of release and setting free from Dasein (GA24 160/114, 166–167/118). This apparent independence of Dasein in intuition, the fact that Dasein is pushed into the background, is what allows Dasein to be overlooked, even though it is "that to which all understanding of being-at-hand, actuality, must be traced back" (GA24 169/119). According to Heidegger, the Kantian interpretation of Being as *actualitas* privileges apprehension or perception, whereas the ancient and Scholastic interpretation is governed by the process of actualization and thus implies a reference to the creative or productive Dasein. In both cases the extant (*das Vorhandene*) is being referred back to Dasein (GA24 143–147/101–105). It is true that Heidegger claims that these are not just two rival interpretations, and that there is an ordering between them, such that the modern interpretation presupposes the ancient one, which is to be understood as ontologically prior (GA24 147/104), but the thrust of Heidegger's interpretation is against choosing between them. Instead it is directed to the hitherto unrecognized concept of world (GA24 234/165; also GA15 110) and the hitherto unacknowledged problem of Dasein's transcendence (GA24 231/162).

So long as intuition is considered the primary way of access to beings, the phenomenon of transcendence disappears. That is why it was necessary in *Being and Time* to challenge its primacy. That does not mean that transcendence is attained simply by the addition of the practical comportment, whether "in an instrumental-utilitarian sense or in any other," to the theoretical (GA26 235/183). Rather, transcendence precedes every possible mode of activity. "The genuine phenomenon of transcendence cannot be localized in a particular activity, be it theoretical, practical, or aesthetic" (GA26 236/184). Hence Heidegger is much less concerned to determine the relative priority of the theoretical and the practical, than he is to find their common root. Nevertheless, Heidegger insists that transcendence "must have already come to light in some form, even if quite veiled and not formulated as such" (GA26 234–235/182). The destructuring of the history of philosophy seeks "the connection between the transcendent intended by the *idea* and the root of transcendence, *praxis*" (GA26 237/184). Plato's *idea tou agathou* points to the *hou heneka*, found also in Aristotle, which organizes the ideas in their totality while at the same time transcending them. Hence the need for a repetition of the *hou heneka* as the for-the-sake-of-which (*das Worumwillen*) in *Being and Time*.

The Greeks did not know the original context of their interpretation of Being. They did not know that their interpretation of beings as present-at-hand or extant was governed by a conception of time in which the present dominates. Heidegger understood his task to be that of radicalizing Greek philosophy by submitting it to repetition (*Wiederholung*) (GA24 449/315–316), even if this is only "the first necessary step that any philosophy in essence has to take" (GA24 157/111). Ancient ontology was naive. Its reflection remained within the rut of pre-philosophical knowledge. It did not get beyond a conception of Dasein and its comportments that belongs to Dasein's general everydayness (GA24 156/110–111). Heidegger does not simply dismiss "the everyday, pre-philosophical productive behavior of the Dasein" (GA24 162/114). He appears to be impressed by its wide application: it provides "the basis for the universal significance assignable to the fundamental concepts of ancient philosophy" (GA24 164/116). Nevertheless, "the inadequacy of traditional thought" cannot be attributed simply to the loss suffered during the process of transmission. There is a sense in which it rests on an "inadequate foundation" (GA24 158/112).

The inadequacy of the foundation becomes apparent as Heidegger undertakes what he calls "the necessary positive task" of providing "a *more original* interpretation of *essentia* and *existentia*" (GA24 158/112). Heidegger proceeds by examining the double philosophical meaning of *ousia*, as it was already explicated by Aristotle.[16] Whereas in everyday pre-philosophical language *ousia* means disposable possessions, goods, property, and wealth (GA24 153/108 and 448–49/315; see already GA61 92),[17] philosophically *ousia* means, firstly, the produced extant being or its extantness, its at-handness (*Vorhandensein*), and, secondly, *eidos*, the pattern which is first merely thought or imagined and which corresponds to the appearance or look of the product (GA24 215/151). *Ousia* is a richer term than *essentia* (GA24 153/109). Heidegger underlines this point in *The Metaphysical Foundations of Logic*, where he is more direct in saying that *ousia* also includes *existentia*.[18] The double sense of *ousia* embraces therefore both terms of the distinction between the *modus existendi*, corresponding to Being in the sense of presence at hand, and the *modus essendi*, as whatness or the *idea* (GA26 183/145).[19] Hence Heidegger can be said not only to have offered a more original interpretation of the concepts of essence and existence in terms of the twofold meaning of *ousia*; at the same time he finds their common origin in Dasein's productive comportment (GA24 155/110).[20] This example not only shows how destructuring reveals the way in which beings come to be conceived in their relation to Dasein, it also confirms that, although Heidegger proceeds historiologically, he is not in search of an historiological origin.

Much more could be said, but the essential point that emerges is that the themes evoked in the preparatory analyses of the first division of *Being and Time* take on a new appearance when seen in the light of the historical studies set out in *Basic Problems of Phenomenology* and *Metaphysical Foundations of Logic*. These exercises in the destructuring of the tradition extend our understanding of what is meant by destructuring beyond anything found in the Introduction to *Being and Time*. By juxtaposing the historical studies of the late 1920s with the discussion of the distinction between essence and existence in the 1941 text "Metaphysics as History of Being," one of the few places where the later Heidegger returns to medieval philosophy, the contrast between Heidegger's early program of destructuring the history of ontology and his subsequent approach to metaphysics in terms of the history of Being can be clarified. In 1941 Heidegger dismisses as "easy" the attempt to establish historiologically the connection of the distinction between *essentia* and *existentia* with the thinking of Aristotle.[21] He says explicitly that tracing the terms of that distinction to their origin in Greek thought is insufficient for his purposes, even though this was a major concern of the first part of *Basic Problems*.[22] The next section will confirm that there was always more to destructuring than uncovering the origins of the concepts that subsequently dominated philosophical thought. Nevertheless, when Heidegger in 1941 opts to retain the word "destructuring," as he does only rarely after the 1920s, it is to say that destructuring "has not yet been thought in terms of the history of Being."[23] Until that rethinking of destructuring, which in fact amounts to its transformation, Heidegger's account of the history of philosophy is governed by the notions of repetition and tradition, the elucidation of which takes place in the Second Division of the First Part of *Being and Time*, to which I now turn.

III

Part of the confusion surrounding the notion of destructuring is, as I suggested in the first section, a consequence of the fact that Heidegger's readers have drawn solely on the programmatic statements located at the outset of *Being and Time*.[24] As a result, not only have previous discussions tended to proceed without concrete illustrations of destructuring such as I developed in the previous section, but, more importantly, they have also proceeded on the basis of formulae and concepts that have not yet been subjected to the radicalization that transforms them once Heidegger's analyses of temporality and history are considered. In the remainder of this chapter, I turn to the discussion of historicality in Chapter Five of the Second Division of *Being and Time* in an effort to reconstruct the appropriate conceptual framework in which to discuss destructuring. Commentators have largely overlooked the fact that in that chapter Heidegger announces that his projection of the ontological genesis of historiology in terms of Dasein's historicality is meant to prepare the way for the clarification of the historiological destructuring of the history of philosophy (SZ 392/444).[25]

Chapter Five of the Second Division, "Temporality and Historicality," shows that to understand the tradition as simply a past that imposes a burden from which the present can be freed only with great difficulty, if at all, is to remain within an inauthentic conception of temporality. This conception of freedom remains bound to an idea of time whose self-evidence itself needs to be destructured. And yet this is the conception of time that dominates the way in which commentators tend to construe Heidegger's notion of destructuring. Heidegger's discussion of historicality, however, shows that tradition need not always appear as an irredeemable weight dragging Dasein back to the past. Tradition can also serve as a heritage in terms of which the possibilities of authentic existing are disclosed and taken over (SZ 383/435).

Heidegger argues that historiology (*Historie*) has its existential origin in Dasein's historicality (*Geschichtlichkeit*) (SZ 392/444).[26] The significance of this claim extends beyond the philosophy of history to the understanding of the historiological destructuring of the history of philosophy itself. What is at stake is apparent from observing the fate of another task. Heidegger repeatedly expresses his concern over the possibility that the question governing Division Two of the First Part, the question of the connectedness of life, might have derived from inauthentic historicality (SZ 387–390/439–442). Just as that question proved inappropriate, so the suspicion arises that the explication of destructuring remains inadequate until Dasein's temporality has been clarified. So long as destructuring relies on a historiology that is not rooted in Dasein's authentic historicality, destructuring would not reverse, but would only magnify, Dasein's alienation (cf. SZ 396/448). Heidegger thereby rejects any approach to Dasein's historicality that would take its start from the present (SZ 395/447). In §76 of *Being and Time* it becomes apparent that the central theme of destructuring must be "the *possibility* of existence which has-been-there": "Even historiological disclosure temporalizes itself *in terms of the future*" (SZ 395/447). By contrast with this clear emphasis on the future, §6 "The Task of Destructuring the History of Ontology" gives no indication of this except for the single phrase, somewhat enigmatic in that context, where Heidegger says that one must "stakeout the positive possibilities of that tradition" (SZ 22/44).[27] It is no wonder that exclusive reliance on that section has led to a somewhat flat or diminished conception of destructuring.

In §74 Heidegger argued somewhat paradoxically that Dasein's possibilities are inherited, yet they are also chosen (SZ 383/435). He produced a formula which was presented in the context of a discussion of the authentic resoluteness in which Dasein hands itself down to itself free for death, but which is equally illuminating when transferred to the issue of destructuring:

> Die Wiederholung ist die ausdrückliche Überlieferung, *das heisst, der Rückgang in Möglichkeiten des dagewesenen Daseins. Repeating is handing down explicitly*—that is to say, going back into the possibilities of the Dasein that has-been-there. (SZ 385/437)

A detailed analysis of this sentence is not possible here. It would not be possible without rehearsing the web of concepts that underlie it.[28] I shall concentrate on the word *Überlieferung*.

In Heidegger there are at least two senses of the word "tradition," corresponding most often, although certainly not always, to the two terms *Tradition* and *Überlieferung*. *Tradition* is the term most often used in §6 of *Being and Time*, where the emphasis is on history as an obstacle blocking access to the sources, but it is virtually absent from the discussion of historicality in the fifth chapter of the Second Division where *Überliefe-*

rung and its cognates are more prominent. The verbs *überliefern* and *Sichüberliefern* contribute to the way in which tradition comes to be thought with reference to Dasein's possibilities. It is in the same spirit that Heidegger thirty years later in *The Principle of Reason* contrasts the way a tradition (*Überlieferung*) can degenerate into a burden and a handicap, or be, "as its name says, a delivering [*Liefern*] in the sense of *liberare*, of liberating."[29] Liberation is not from tradition but by way of tradition. Heidegger would presumably also say that it is liberation from the present. It is in this way that it can be understood as critical.

This explication of *Überlieferung* recalls Nietzsche's conception of critical history in "On the Uses and Disadvantages of History for Life," as Heidegger himself appeals to it in *Being and Time*. Nietzsche describes three species of history: the monumental, the antiquarian, and the critical. Each belongs to a different soil or climate and only to it. Critical history, for example, is for one who is "oppressed by a present need and who wants to throw off this burden at any cost."[30] Heidegger, in taking up Nietzsche's analysis of the three kinds of historiology, insists, in contrast to Nietzsche, on the factical unity of the three possibilities in any authentic historiology (SZ 396/448). So, then, it is as monumental and antiquarian that authentic historiology is a critique of the present. It is thus in terms of the analysis of temporality that Heidegger explains how the negative side of destructuring is, as he said in §6, aimed at detaching oneself from the falling publicness of the 'today' (SZ 397/449), even though this negative function is "unexpressed and indirect" (SZ 23/44). The claim that repetition and tradition (*Überlieferung*) are both rooted in the future (SZ 386–387/438–439) makes clear that there can be no return to the past that brings it back; the possibility of that existence which has-been-there cannot be actualized again. It is the rejoinder to that possibility that is at the same time "a *disavowal* of what in the 'today,' is working itself out as the 'past.'" (SZ 386/438).[31] But it is not just the "moment" of disavowal or rebuttal (*Widerruf*) that is "destructive," as one commentator seems to suggest in an otherwise illuminating discussion.[32] Destructuring embraces all the "moments" of repetition.

The impact of Heidegger's analysis on how the concrete tradition in its conventional sense comes to be conceived is too large a topic to be entered into here, beyond offering a few pointers. In the Introduction to *Being and Time*, Heidegger introduced the task of destructuring by remarking that worldhistory (*Weltgeschichte*) is possible only on the basis of Dasein's historizing (SZ 19/41), but that statement only becomes intelligible as the book unfolds. In particular, the term "worldhistory" cannot be understood in its familiar sense. Heidegger explains in §73 that "it can be shown that the ordinary conception of 'worldhistory' arises precisely from our orientation to what is thus secondarily historical" (SZ 381/433). But there is a further sense of worldhistory at stake. Heidegger hyphenates it as "world-history" (*Welt-Geschichte*) to emphasize the specifically Heideggerian sense of the world as an existential concept and so to bring out what is elsewhere called the return to Dasein.[33] This separates Heideggerian world-history from Hegelian worldhistory, let alone a more vulgar conception. Heidegger notes the double signification of the expression, world-history, which means both the historizing (*Geschehen*) of the world in its essential existent unity with Dasein and "the 'historizing' within-the-world of what is ready-to-hand and present-at-hand, insofar as entities within-the-world are, in every case, discovered with the factually existent world" (SZ 389/440–441). Heidegger explicitly decides to abstain from exploring the ontological structure of world-historical historizing, but it would seem that this notion of world-history opens up the possibility of acknowledging a multiplicity of traditions, although Heidegger himself does not pursue the idea.[34]

In sum, Heidegger does much more in the first part of *Basic Problems* than attempt to establish that certain traditional theses about Being form a linear tradition. Destructuring is more than genealogy. The tradition initially presents itself as an obstacle to questioning, because of its tendency to impart to certain concepts an aura of self-evidence. It becomes, in the course of Heidegger's analyses, the means by which that self-evidence gives access to what, concealed, underlies it. In other words, the tradition is found to give access to what at first it seemed to obscure. What it obscures is not a beginning, a historiological origin, but the unthought as the space from which previous philosophers have thought.[35] In the first part of *Basic Problems*, this takes the form of the common root of theory and practice. To paraphrase the end of Heidegger's lecture on "The Principle of Identity," only what has already been thought gives access to what is still to be thought.[36] Tradition in the Heideggerian sense of *Überlieferung* prevails precisely in this conception of the unthought as what is yet to be thought. So conceived, it is not *necessarily* narrow or unitary, even if questions have to be raised about Heidegger's own initial construction of the tradition as exclusively that of Western philosophy.[37]

8

Destruction and Moment

Otto Pöggeler
Translated by Daniel Magurshak

The word "destruction" [*Destruktion*] is one of those terms that permeates Heidegger's philosophy from the outset, and as if its meaning were self-evident. After all, wasn't the gesture with which the Privatdocent Heidegger came onto the scene generally destructive? His lecture courses, and even more pointedly his letters to Karl Löwith, manifest rejection, the desire to clear away, and dissatisfaction with everything. Such destruction nevertheless fell in with Edmund Husserl's philosophy, which wanted to allow nothing but the things themselves [*die Sachen selbst*] to speak. But the question remained to what extent these things (the phenomena of phenomenological philosophy) manifest themselves only in a process whose motivating core must constantly be reopened through destruction. Is it not the case that the proper relation to "the last things" is granted us only in the moment [*Augenblick*] that is not at our disposal? Existing itself repeatedly falls away from this moment; it tends to understand itself "ruinously" in terms of things [*Dingen*] self-evidently given like the tables and chairs of everyday life. Still, can the fleeting moment really yield something constructive?

For phenomenological philosophy, constructions were precisely what had to be deconstructed [*abgebaut*] as speculations that do not do justice to the things themselves. It is in this negative sense that Heidegger introduces the term "construction" in *Sein und Zeit*. In the course of the treatise, however, the word does gain a positive sense, such that the summer course of 1927, *Grundprobleme der Phänomenologie*, places construction as the systematic part of philosophy alongside destruction as its historical part. Construction is a showing and letting be seen of the lawfulness of a thing. One can, for example, construct a right-angled triangle with regard to the lawfulness expressed by the Pythagorean Theorem. Philosophy itself is assumed to be concerned not only with the lawfulness of mathematics, for in it systematics and history, that is, construction and destruction, cannot be separated. In fact, this interplay of construction and destruction constitutes the appropriation of the tradition in which we always already stand. But this appropriation is the appropriation of what has been forgotten, of what is necessitated from out of the things and thus remains to be freed up. However, what has to be freed up in Western philosophy through destruction could well be the orientation to the moment. As Heidegger says in *Die Grundbegriffe der Metaphysik*: "The spell of the times can be broken only by time itself, by that which belongs to the most proper essence of time and what we in conjunction with Kierkegaard call the moment." Heidegger emphasizes at the same time that "what we characterize here as the 'moment' is what Kierkegaard actually conceptualized for the first time in philosophy—a conception that for the first time since antiquity initiates the possibility of a completely new epoch of philosophy." (GA29/30 225f.)

The lecture course just cited was held in the winter of crisis in 1929–30, which points to another crisis in Heidegger's philosophizing that prevented him from writing the sequel to his fragment, *Sein und Zeit*. An initial self-critical question concerned the tradition: Can thinking follow Kierkegaard who took up Socrates' questioning but, with the Apostle Paul, oriented it toward the eschatological moment? In this lecture course, Heidegger indicated that our own time is determined by a Nietzscheanism that plays life or "soul" off against spirit in various ways. Max Scheler, on the other hand, had spoken of an age of balance that now has to connect anew the traditions of East and West, as well as the masculine and feminine forms of life, and above all the Dionysian immersion in the drive for life and the Apollinian participation of the spirit in all essences. Heidegger took up the struggle between the Dionysian and the Apollinian as a basic law of history. Seeking to restore this struggle to its full intensity, he also recalled Nietzsche's formulation "Dionysos versus the Crucified." Thinking was directed back to that tragic age in which it stood next to poetizing as its partner, and *logos* had not yet opposed itself to *mythos*. If the first course on Hölderlin [WS 1934–35] and the first course on Nietzsche [WS 1936–37] begin with the struggle of the Dionysian and the Apollinian as a basic law of our historical Dasein, they then regard this struggle to be more purely and simply expressed in Hölderlin as the struggle between the inspirational fire from heaven and the sobering form. From Hölderlin's letters to Böhlendorff, Heidegger drew the insight that this struggle presents itself to us differently than it did to the Greeks. We therefore cannot merely write a commentary on the Greeks.[1] It is out of the experiences of Hölderlin that Heidegger speaks in *Beiträge zur Philosophie*, his main work from the years 1936–38, first published at the centenary of his birth. Here he referred to Kierkegaard, Nietzsche, and Hölderlin as those who direct thinking to the task of uncovering the forgotten dimension of truth as the site of the moment. Indeed, Heidegger noted that of these three who had broken down so prematurely, it was the one who came first, Hölderlin, who points farthest into the future.

At the beginning of the forties Heidegger's thinking had to cope with a crisis that once again demanded a fundamental transformation. The illusion that the creativity of great creators, about which Nietzsche had spoken, could ground history anew out of a tragic experience of the world had to be put aside. By means of Heraclitus' fragments and Hölderlin's later ventures, one should at least hold onto traces in the darkening of the world that could someday lead to a transformation of life. In the summers of 1946 and 1947, Heidegger attempted with the help of a Chinese acquaintance to actualize Lao-tzu's pictorial signs and their diversely interwoven interplay. The term 'Tao' or 'Way' emerged from another origin in contrast to the Heraclitean key word 'Logos.' It was no longer simply a matter of translating from Greek into one's own element (as Hölderlin had attempted to do when he allowed himself to be drawn to his own poetizing by translating Pindar and Sophocles). What mattered now was a conversation in which the difference between the speakers was based not only on the different historical origins of East and West, but also on different ways of groping forward into the future.[2]

In 1933, Wolfgang Schadewaldt had nominated the young professor Heidegger to be the rector of the University of Freiburg (so that, one thought at the time, a moment fraught with many dangers would not be completely missed). In October 1947 he wrote to Heidegger, "The world is now filled with your name. Should one congratulate you or lament for you on this occasion?" According to Schadewaldt, words remain ambiguous—should not thinking play in them as poetry does? Even Plato does not abandon his most serious thought to the mercy of words, but rather puts it under wraps. Heidegger replied, "Lofty play blossoms only for the serious, never for the playful and casual. For the *sudden* 'play,' Plato had to make an effort to think as he did in the *Sophist* and other dialogues, running the risk that his thought would remain concealed in the future except for those rare moments of illumination on the part of the few."[3]

The "sudden" is the *exaiphnes*, that suddenness about which Plato speaks in the *Parmenides,* which prepares for the *Sophist*, as well as in the Seventh Letter. Does the late Platonic dialectic, and thereby the logic of philosophy, allow for its own destruction in such a way that what is at stake (the aforementioned rare moments of illumination of the few) clearly appears? For the sake of this question, I would now like to develop as briefly as possible how Kierkegaard, following Plato's indications, tried to free up the moment—to be sure, according to Heidegger, without the necessary destruction of the logic or dialectic presupposed here. The second section will indicate at least suggestively how Heidegger himself since 1929 tried to understand the moment as the site of the moment [*Augenblicks-Stätte*] with the help of Nietzsche and Hölderlin. Given this two-fold program, the rest of Heidegger's path, his conversation with Lao-tzu, for example, can and will not be addressed here.

I. From Plato to Kierkegaard: Freeing Up the Moment

It is well-known that the young Heidegger wanted to revitalize medieval Aristotelianism with its theory of the analogy of being. In his postwar courses, Heidegger tended to take his point of departure 1) from Bergson, for whom the new motives of thinking culminated in the experience of time, and above all 2) from Dilthey, who had made this experience the theme of a multilevel hermeneutics.[4] Heidegger, the former theologian, also brought other elements into play, especially the new discovery of eschatology in primal Christian faith. The course entitled *Einleitung in die Phänomenologie der Religion* from the winter of 1920–21 set the oldest document of the New Testament, the first letter of Paul the Apostle to the Thessalonians, over against the new philosophy of religion and Ernst Troeltsch's metaphysics of religion. This letter refers to the unavailable moment beyond our control in which the crucified proclaimer of God's power is raised to the measure of history, and the last things come to pass. Heidegger was not concerned, however, with apocalyptic mythology and not at all with theology, but rather with the philosophical indication that life-experience in general is factical, historical, and thereby oriented to the unavailable moment beyond our control.

Is such a moment capable of conceptualization, or is philosophy, ever concerned with a universally binding conceptuality, at its end when the moment in all its uniqueness becomes the theme? Heidegger believed that through phenomenology one could offer a methodology to the new philosophy demanded by the moment. Husserl's phenomenology thus became a hermeneutical phenomenology, a hermeneutic, however, that formally indicates, as Heidegger developed this in the aforementioned lecture course by starting with Husserl's distinction between generalization and formalization. What is formally indicated is, in the first place, the region to which something belongs: one cannot treat a human being like a thing [*Ding*], taking its existence to be present-at-hand being. This means, secondly, that the matter indicated need not present itself in theoretical evidence; rather, the formal indication points to a decision (for example, a decision of faith) which itself remains outside thinking. As a formally indicating hermeneutics, this phenomenology is therefore fundamentally "atheistic";

that is, as philosophy it knows nothing about God, though it does point to the dimension of the last things. But in this way, the freedom of God could be preserved for revelation in the moment precisely through the eyes of faith.[5]

Crucial for Heidegger was his friendship with a philosopher schooled in psychiatry who, as an outsider, could set himself against the academic guild. This was Karl Jaspers, Heidegger's senior by a few years. In 1919 Jaspers published his *Psychologie der Weltanschauungen*. Heidegger then wrote a long review of it which remained unpublished for half a century. However, he was concerned not with critique of a book but rather with motives for a new philosophizing. He vacillated between admiration for the breakthrough to new ways of questioning and disappointment over the cataloguing presentation that was coupled with existentiell appeals. He did not hesitate to offer the strange advice that the book should be completely rewritten and the point of departure taken from its most important chapter, the theory of limit-situations. The limit-situation presupposes the situation, and immediately in 1919 a discussion of the situation then became fundamental in Heidegger's courses. Indeed, in his own analyses Heidegger distinguished historical situations from those that comprise our everyday life: even without a developed theory of things, we deal familiarly with what is ready-to-hand and significant for us in our environing world. We can then pursue our goals in various situations, though a limit can appear in these situations or even as a situation itself.

According to Jaspers' formulations carried over into Heidegger's review, the limit-situations arising in this way are "the ultimate" for those living; in them the consciousness of existence is raised "to the consciousness of something absolute."[6] With the limit-situation of struggle, Heidegger stressed above all the limit-situation of death. All is reduced to nothing for us not in the mere knowledge of death and transitoriness but in the limit-situation of death, in one's own experience of mortality; the experience of perishing has a "total character." Heidegger admired the "highly unusual capacity and energy to open up and evoke 'psychic conditions'" that Jaspers acquired from Nietzsche and Kierkegaard. When Jaspers plays Kierkegaard off against the totalizing thinking of Hegel, he counts him among the "prophets of indirect communication" who radicalize Socrates' attitude of appealing to the other only in order to thrust him back upon his freedom and direct him toward himself. Heidegger nevertheless wanted to derive the method, that is, a binding logic, of philosophy directly from Kierkegaard.

Coming out of Kierkegaard, Heidegger took a critical stance toward Dilthey and Weber. Dilthey regarded life externally and in terms of states, that is, imagistically and aesthetically. Max Weber's sociology (for example, the theory of types) is indeed valid for economic processes and commerce, but hardly applicable to the authentic phenomena of existence.[7] Heidegger himself sought to develop the drawing-attention-to performed by indirect communication as a formally indicative hermeneutics. Formal indication must first of all make sure that the regionally anticipatory "preconception" avoids the alien "viewpoints of construction," improper "construction-perspectives," for example, one that treats human being categorically as a thing. If human being is defined as existence, then this existence is not to be had in "theoretical reflection" but only in the enactment [*Vollzug*] of "I am." A human being is not merely a particular case of the realization of a universal. In theoretical work as well as in everyday dealings, we take a thing as an indifferent case of a universal's instantiation. For example, I must be familiar with what a desk is so that I can comprehend this desk here as a useful instance of a desk. Human being cannot understand itself in this way, because, due to its facticity, it opens itself up for the universal only historically at a particular time. If indirect communication is unfolded as a formal indication, then one is denied the possibility of following Kierkegaard's or even Nietzsche's specific conception of existence "uncritically." Kierkegaard was not taken up by Heidegger as the edifying writer he had ultimately wanted to be; rather, precisely through the indirect communication of his pseudonymous works, he points to that which remained undeveloped in his own work, that is, to the logic of philosophy whose method immediately presupposes a destruction of tradition. Heidegger could not find this necessary destruction in Jaspers any more than he could in Kierkegaard. Jaspers all too quickly uses, for example, the Kantian concept of antinomies for the limit-situation. In spite of every ethical motivation, his work is supported by an observational and indeed even an aesthetic attitude (thus he can parade worldviews like patients before the classifying gaze of the director of a clinic). What Heidegger found missing was that this understanding [*verstehende*] psychology should be determined as an "understandingly constructive psychology," where "constructive" is taken in the good sense as a "formation of types" drawn from understanding intuition and realized by constantly taking its measure from this intuition.

Remarkably, Heidegger's review does not touch upon what became the decisive impulse for him, namely, Jaspers' discussion of how Kierkegaard transformed the "sudden" of Plato into the moment. Among many possible attitudes, Jaspers also recognizes the attitude oriented to the moment, taking his point of departure from the detailed comment on the moment that Kierkegaard gave in *The Concept of Anxiety*. Heidegger's reference to the eschatological moment of the Apostle Paul raised the question as to how Kierkegaard could arrive at this interpretation or reinterpretation of Plato. Still, *Sein und Zeit* was able to culminate in the theory of the moment only after a slow groping around with this problematic. In the process, the concept of the situation is introduced only very late in *Sein und Zeit* and then oriented beyond the limit-situation (especially of death and guilt) to the moment. One reads that Kierkegaard saw the existentiell phenomenon of the moment, but he remained captive to the ordinary concept of time and thereby lacked the necessary existential (formally indicative) interpretation. Like Jaspers, Heidegger refers to Kierkegaard's work on anxiety which he distinguishes favorably within the Christian theory of affects.[8]

Kierkegaard's work on anxiety has a formally indicative character in that it wants to approach the dogmatic problem of original sin "psychologically" in terms of the anxiety familiar to any person. This anxiety tears human being out of the state of innocence and relegates it to the dizziness of freedom. Psychology can show only how sin can arise, but not that it actually belongs to human being. Indeed, Kierkegaard's "psychology" commits its analyses to a mood (especially earnestness) in which individuals, alone with themselves, must decide for themselves about themselves. Since Kierkegaard investigates the history of the interrelationship of anxiety and consciousness of sin, he has to make note of the lack of the consciousness of sin among the Greeks, but also has to draw attention to the fact that the Church Fathers nevertheless considered the Greeks as heathens who lived in sin. Can this ambivalence also be understood from the philosophy of the Greeks? Kierkegaard attempts this by way of comments in his reflections on the sudden and the moment. From the outset, he opposes Hegel's attempt to absorb the dialectic of the sudden into his speculation while evading the genuinely Christian sense of the moment. Hegel consequently transformed the Christian faith into a new paganism. The possibilities of philosophy were overtaxed.

Can Kierkegaard show that Plato understands the task of a logic of philosophy, but in the end must fall short due to Greek innocence? The dialogue about the sophists is supposed to show how the sophist, appearing to be omniscient, himself represents nullity when he passes untruth and deceit off as something null and trivial, thus sacrificing both their difference from truth and morality and so truth and morality themselves. The dialogue *Parmenides* can indeed point to the moment, but cannot grasp it adequately. This dialogue takes up the originary philosophical question of the one in the all. The young Socrates meets the old Parmenides who regarded being as the one. Zeno attempted to safeguard this relation to being, rescuing it from the shortcomings of sensory intuition by way of a dialectic of the one and the many. Is the one the one being [*Sein*] or is it the one entity [*Seiendes*], that something which belongs to the many? Here one must not only intuit and perceive, but also think. This thinking seeks that *eidos* in which the many participates in the one. This participation, which could lead to the separateness of the world of ideas, succeeds only for dialectic, i.e., for the self-movement of the one that manifests itself in the sudden transformation of fundamental concepts (*metaballein*).

For Plato, the sudden remains an *atopon*; the transformation of basic concepts has no place in time because it leads temporal being to a limit, that is, it refers it to the eternal. In contrast, Kierkegaard grasps this limit as the now in order to clarify it as the moment. That blink of an eye which is swifter than any gesture can provide a metaphorical expression that, according to Kierkegaard, is found in "poetic" guise in the Apostle Paul. According to the First Letter to the Corinthians (15:52), the world is to pass away in an atom and in an *Augenblick*, a moment, a blink of the eye (*en atomo kai en rhipe ophthalmou*). The moment of downfall permits simultaneously the emergence of eternity, thus placing time under the measure of eternity. Time as a continuous series of levelled now-points knows no distinctive point of demarcation separating the future from the past. As an unqualified endless succession, time has no present. Only the eternal is the present, a presence in the sense of the presencing gods (*praesentes dii*) in the Latin language. Only when this eternal intersects with time in the moment can time draw an atom of eternity into itself, maintain the present, and thus distinguish future and past.

Kierkegaard does not follow the philosophical tradition on the courage of reason that overcomes fear (and hope) as a vice. Rather, with the tradition that appears in the Apostle Paul, he wants to direct one in fear and trembling to the moment of judgment and salvation and thus to taking responsibility for one's own constantly threatened existence. Consequently he distinguishes fear, which fears something specific, from the anxiety in which existence, related to the moment, announces itself in its reality. Anxiety is the anxiety of existence over itself, and therefore anxiety over death together with anxiety over birth. According to Kierkegaard, animals do not feel anxiety, nor do they die. Even the Greeks, and especially the Greek philosophers, could not let the anxiety of existence over itself arise. They are familiar with delusion and deception; indeed, their philosophy grows out of the struggle against them. However, when Plato deals with the illusion of sophistical omniscience, he is dealing with a non-being that exists in the sophist as that which is not supposed to be. Christians, on the other hand, start by maintaining that the world is created out of nothing and that non-being in the sense of illusion, vanity, and sin, remains present everywhere in creation. Anxiety brings experience face to face with this groundlessness; the dizziness of the freedom to be seized thus points to the fact that existence must be seized in its unsecured possibilities. The transition here belongs in the sphere of historical freedom in which something new can begin in a qualitative leap, that is, the overcoming of sinfulness in repentance as the beginning of another life.

In their "naivety," the Greeks cannot tie the sensory and temporal together with the psychical and eternal from out of the distance of spirit. They understand the moment, and with it the opening-up of the distinction between past and future, in such a way that they seek an eternal present from out of the past and include the future in this connection. The life of the cosmos becomes a cycle. Philosophy requires that dying which in *anamnesis* recollects the eternal. This concept of the eternal as the past to be recollected can be understood historically; for example, the *Book of Daniel* names the Godhead the "ancient one" (as Kierkegaard notes in the outline of his text). If the Jewish concept of time is transposed into the historical sphere, it takes the moment as the moment of discrimination or turning point; thus the futural is accented as the whole that also contains the past (as the earlier future). According to Kierkegaard, the eternal thereby arises in the future only *incognito* and thus remains incommensurable with time. For Christian experience, on the other hand, the moment is the eternal as the fullness of time. The moment is the moment of decision on whether the eternal is won or lost, such that concepts like conversion and redemption, judgment and resurrection, receive their world-historical and individual-historical sense. To recollection is added repetition, which as repentance leads to a leap. Plato's experimental dialectic turns into an existentiell dialectic which places the human being at different stages and ultimately brings philosophy before the faith that cannot be anticipated. Since Christianity brings the sensory and temporal sphere into the dialectic of eternity and time, it can itself, like the demons in the New Testament, demonically refuse the eternal life of the spirit. In a perversion of the moment, there then arises an enjoyment of isolated moments, as in the case of Don Juan.

One can consider *Sein und Zeit* as Heidegger's first attempt to work out a philosophy of the moment. He appropriates a Kierkegaardian concept when he characterizes Dasein's manner of being as existence. But from the very start he approaches Dasein's basic structure in another way. No longer are sensibility and understanding contrasted with one another and related to reason; rather, thrown finding-oneself-in is combined with projective understanding toward articulation or speech. This approach undercuts the traditional starting point of relating temporality to sensibility and of opposing this to the timeless forms of the intellect. When Heidegger begins with an analysis of our dealings with things having significance in our environing world, he breaks the one-sided orientation to theory that, according to him, has persisted from Parmenides to Husserl. Here Heidegger already introduces the moment not only when he talks about the "appropriate moment," but also when he speaks of the sudden on-slaught of the threatening that is "possible at any moment."[9] Heidegger follows colloquial speech here as well as the linguistic usage of the Greeks, whose poets and sages (Hesiod, Pindar, and the school of Pythagoras, for example) denote the favor of nature and the divine at a particular hour and special place with words like *kairos* [the fitting moment], *hora* [the fitting hour and season), and *acme* [high time].

In his lecture course on the *Grundprobleme der Phänomenologie* in the summer of 1927, Heidegger even claims that, in the sixth book of the *Nicomachean Ethics*, Aristotle saw and delimited the phenomenon of the moment, but was unable to connect the specific temporal character of *kairos* with what he formerly recognized as time (as the *nun* or now) (GA24 409/288). Working in this tradition, Kierkegaard was thus wrongly inclined to understand the moment in terms of the now. In fact, the second book of the *Nicomachean Ethics* holds that there is no exact and definitive prescription for the *kairos* or the given occasion. Here agents must discover for themselves what is fitting, even what is necessary, say, in the arts of healing and navigation. The beginning of the third book also emphasizes that mixed involuntary-voluntary action appears as freely cho-sen when it is being carried out; the goal of the activity is directed in each case toward the *kairos*. One can understand the sixth book of the *Nico-machean Ethics* as a development of that truth-relation and that *logos* which can provide orientation in the situation. What since Kierkegaard has been associated with the moment first emerges by intensifying the situa-tion into the limit-situation, especially historically in the experience of the moment in the Christian faith. Among the Greeks this experience is hardly concealed by the representation of time that Heidegger, using modern rep-resentations of time, attributes to Aristotle; it is rather concealed by the relation to eternity that Aristotelian theology brings into play (for example, in the twelfth book of the *Metaphysics*, which Heidegger disregards).

In *Sein und Zeit* as well, it is anxiety which allows the moment to come into prominence. The analysis of the anxiety in which Dasein as being-in-the-world trembles before itself leads from the first division of *Sein und Zeit*, the analysis of the basic structure of Dasein, to the second division, the interpretation of this basic structure in terms of temporality. Only in this second division, that is, after the analysis of the environing world, does Heidegger introduce the concept of the situation. The intro-ductory discussions immediately ask about the "hermeneutical situation" in which the analysis itself stands. When anticipating death and wanting-to-have-a-conscience are exhibited, the there of being-there is determined more precisely in terms of the "constitutive moments of the existential phenomenon that we call a *situation*, which up to this point has been passed over."[10] The situation is a "being-on-the-spot [*Lage*]" which is disclosed when the call of conscience calls Dasein forth into the situation. The resoluteness that belongs to disclosedness is in itself an action that lies beyond the distinction between practical and theoretical capability. Such a situation cannot be reckoned in advance nor given in advance as something present-at-hand. Resoluteness should not "stiffen up" in the situation, but rather keep itself free (along with the "truth of existence") for its possible withdrawal and retraction. A situation is a situation at a particular time (*jeweilig*). The situation and thus the there of Dasein arrives in all its intensity only when it becomes a limit-situation. Ultimate limits loom in the situation when Dasein anticipates the death upon which every potentiality-for-being shatters. Guilt is also a limit-situation. In acting, one cannot command a complete overview and mastery of the situation in which one stands; one falls into guilt, since one must let oneself be guided by one-sided perspectives. Since this limitation is unavoidable, Heidegger repeats the saying from Goethe that Jaspers quoted: "The one who acts is always without conscience." He nevertheless formalizes guilt into an ultimate having-to-accept-responsibility-for-oneself on the part of the Dasein that did not bring itself into the world. Heidegger takes the concept of the limit-situation from Jaspers; indeed, one can understand the two initial chapters of the second division of *Sein und Zeit* as an elaboration of the limit-situations of death and guilt. (Even chance as a limit-situation is briefly intimated when it is stated that only disclosedness of the situation unleashes the facticity of Dasein in all its harshness.)

When the situation becomes a limit-situation, it is capable of setting the moment free; conversely the situation can become a limit-situation only from the moment. Heidegger leaves no doubt that every situation as a being-on-the-spot carries with it a temptation for Dasein to lapse self-forgetfully into what is situationally given. Dasein must time and again tear itself away from the "inauthenticity" which thus arises. This happens when the apparently fleeting glance of the eyes lights upon the situation; then a resolved Dasein fetches itself back out of fallenness "in order to be 'there'" all the more authentically in the *glance* of the 'moment' ['Augen*blick*'] toward the disclosed situation."[11] When Dasein ecstatically endures every dimension of time authentically, it is enabled to fetch itself back out of lostness in the given "in order to disclose the situation at the particular time and the primordial 'limit-situation' of being toward death as a moment that is held in reserve." When Dasein is not merely afraid of this or that, but rather trembles in anxiety as being-in-the-world itself, then the present of anxiety holds "the moment (as which only the present itself is possible) *at the ready* [*auf dem Sprung*]." Every moment that deserves the name is unique; the coming moment never allows itself to be anticipated and mastered from any preceding moment. The being-at-the-ready of the moment is rather the constant openness for something new. Heidegger takes up the talk that death is "possible at any moment." He does not evade the question of what the anticipation of this death that is possible at any moment, thus accepting one's mortality and finitude, has to do with the "concrete situation" of action. The answer must be that in this antici-pation of death every purpose and goal becomes null and void. But this anticipation affords a distance from which remove Dasein can return to itself and its goals as free. The moment is effected by and interwoven with the future, which is not merely a set goal but an open possibility. This moment is interwoven just as much with the past which, as having-been, is likewise taken in accord with its being-possible. Repetition is a "re-joinder" to the "possibility of precedented existence, its having been there," by putting this possibility up for renewed decision; thus as an ele-ment of the moment, repetition is "the *revocation* of what is working itself out in the today as 'the past and gone.' Repetition neither abandons itself to the past nor does it aim at progress. In the moment, both alternatives are a matter of indifference to authentic existence." Memory, which only recalls the past theoretically, presupposes the forgetting of this repeatedly required revocation. It thus retains the past only on the basis of this for-getting.

The moment in which future and past join in the authentic tempo-ralizing of time stands in contrast to the inauthentic, self-forgetful tempo-ralizing of temporality in mere making-present. To be sure, this making present—the representing of the present-at-hand and the dealings with the ready-to-hand—belong to the disclosure of the situation. The moment must be torn away from self-forgetful "everydayness"; in turn, however, existence can even "master the everyday in the moment and indeed often only 'for the moment.' But it can never eradicate the everyday."[12] The mode of the present that results when Dasein falls, dispersed, rootless, and alienated, into the midst of the given is "the most extreme counter-phe-nomenon to the moment." If the situation becomes a limit-situation, then it leads beyond mere environmental worldhood toward the historical world, which in *Sein und Zeit* is characterized more as a breakthrough of world as such. Dasein can indeed be thoroughly "in the moment for 'its time.'" It is not by possessing a substance but by entrusting itself to exist-ing openly that existence receives its constancy, which must be maintained moment to moment. This momentariness is "a de-presenting [*Entgegen-wärtigen*] of the today and a weaning from the conventions of the They." Resolutely handing oneself over to the there of the moment is the action that Heidegger calls "fate." He differentiates the fate of the individual from the destiny of a generation and a people, but he also relates fate and destiny to the world-historical and the relationship with nature. Here many distinctions are necessary, and they must be expressed philosophically and scientifically, for instance, by distinguishing the different kinds of concept formation and respective preconceptions belonging to physics, history, and theology.

The motto of *Sein und Zeit* asks, with Plato's *Sophist*, what the expression 'being' really means. This indicates that for Heidegger the question of the formation of philosophical concepts is really the fundamental problematic of Platonic philosophy, as it was, for example, albeit in a one-sided and inadequate way, for the Neo-Kantian Natorp, who was hardly concerned with the splendid myths and the doctrine of eros. Of course, questions about Plato remain: Should one refer to opposites like "being and non-being" as the supreme genera, as if they could be attained by generalization? Can one seek to derive the single characterization of the idea from the mathematical model (for instance, the so-called Platonic solids) as well as by way of the virtues? Heidegger began his course on the *Sophist* with an interpretation of the sixth book of the *Nicomachean Ethics*: Aristotle claimed that the situations "here under the waxing and waning moon" had their own relationship to truth, their own *logos*, so that the structure of the situation had its own way of being. This mode of being can be brought to language only if one considers the temporal character of the situation and questions it expressly, as is done in *Sein und Zeit*. A particular ontological option, that of taking being as constant presence, hinders this question in Aristotle and perverts his experience of time.

Nonetheless, Aristotle's hermeneutics and dialectic, together with rhetoric, point out a way forward. Aristotle delimits the assertion, which is ruled by the "true-false" dichotomy, from other modes of the truth-relationship. Heidegger endeavors to place the assertion, and with it the prevalent way of doing theoretical work, back into the comprehensive context of linguistic usage (to which, for example, the question and oath also belong) and thus back into the more encompassing setting of being-in-the-world. He consequently distinguishes the apophantic "as" that lets something be seen as something and be addressed in the assertion from the hermeneutical "as" in which, for example, a hammer is ready-to-hand for a worker as a hammer. When, in the winter semester of 1925–26, Heidegger abruptly breaks off his interpretation of Aristotle and, contrary to plan, turns to an interpretation of Kant's doctrine of schemata, he elaborates the doctrine of schemata as that of the twofold "as," and thus sticks to his theme. Formally indicative hermeneutics is transformed into schematizing; this makes it possible to distinguish different modes of being, such as existential being, being-ready-to-hand, and being-present-at-hand, in terms of the varied interplay of the schemata of the dimensions of time: if the "for-the-sake-of" is actively in play as the schema of authentic futurity, then the dimension of wanting-to-have-a-conscience and religion opens up. If this schema is dimmed down to the "what-for" [*"Wozu"*] as the schema of inauthentic futurity, then the worker can self-forgetfully get down to work. If this latter schema is itself dimmed down and the "hermeneutical as" transformed into the "apophantic as," then pure theory is emancipated from the many technical functions that are, for example, absolutely necessary in the work of physics.[13] To develop a philosophy of the moment in no way means to abandon philosophy to existentiell decisions. Rather, it means to show in structural analyses that human being has to lead its life in different spheres of the world in accordance with different modes of being. But why did Heidegger not portray the hermeneutics of formal indication as the logic of his philosophy—why was the third division of *Sein und Zeit* never published?

II. Hölderlin: The Site of the Moment

I can only briefly indicate the question of whether *Sein und Zeit* was broken off due to its immanent aporias, and how Heidegger, after this breakdown, then found a new beginning that led to his genuine magnum opus, the *Beiträge zur Philosophie*. In *Sein und Zeit*, Heidegger clearly affirms what he will always reiterate later: Kierkegaard grasped the existentiell problem of existing, but the existential problematic remained so foreign to him "that his ontological orientation is completely dominated by Hegel and by ancient philosophy as seen through Hegel's eyes."[14] The destruction that the ontological problematic was supposed to awaken did not have to be enkindled by Kierkegaard's polemic against Hegel's use or misuse of ancient dialectic; it could just as well have begun with Augustine's relationship to Neoplatonism, with Luther's relation to Aristotelianism, or with an interpretation of Aristotle, Kant, and the pitfalls in their philosophizing. Heidegger's own time (Jaspers, for instance) did not seem to see the necessity of destruction. Heidegger could only scoff when Tillich's religious socialism apparently wanted to establish a journal called *Kairos* next to the journal *Logos*. And without any relation to philosophy since the second edition of the *Letter to the Romans*, Karl Barth, following Kierkegaard, wanted to assert the dialectic of time and eternity within the moment. At this time, Heidegger traversed these other paths of philosophy, and this meant first and foremost: the ways of destruction.

The question remained as to whether this destruction was approached in such a way that it allowed an orientation towards the moment, which alone makes destruction possible. Construction and destruction, systematics and history, ought to be interconnected; but was the circle that binds the two also traversed to its conclusion? Doesn't the [*temporale*] interpretation bring in the schemata of time as a timeless framework of principles? To be sure, *Sein und Zeit* declares at the outset that all formations of ontology, and so also the doctrine of schemata, are historical and are to be expressly inserted into history by way of the destruction in the second half of the treatise. A schema like "for-the-sake-of" has both the features and the dismissal of the tradition written all over its face. Aristotle also has a say, but in refraction through Kierkegaard; Meister Eckhart's "without why" stands just as much in the background as Kant's insistence on the sanctity of the moral will and the impossibility of relativizing it. Heidegger put in question whether one could with Kant assign space to the outer sense and time to the inner sense, and yet in Heidegger space and time are once again coupled in similar fashion. He cannot accept the idea that the "present" or "the standing now" has to be the character of the eternal. But does he really get beyond a mere counter-move against the tradition when he asks whether eternity can be construed *via eminentiae* or *via negationis* as original time, that is, "infinite" time?[15] Kierkegaard's reinterpretation, or his misunderstanding, of Plato's *Parmenides* has its roots in his equating the sudden with the *nun*, the caesura between past and future. Yet even Heidegger, here perhaps oriented to Husserl's relating of time to the impression, believes that he can understand Plato's and Aristotle's concept of time as a series of now-points.

It was above all else Heidegger's Freiburg inaugural lecture "Was ist Metaphysik?" in 1929 which embarked upon entirely new paths with the question: "Why is there Being at all rather than *Nothing*?" Heidegger later insisted that the word "Nothing" is capitalized here since he is not repeating Leibniz's question, which only sought to show the superiority of being over nothing.[16] The capitalization does not imply the hypostatization of the nothing, but rather the following question: Why does being, its fullness with the multiplicity of modes of being, move us, but not the nothing, namely, that which withdraws and withholds itself in all of this fullness and multiplicity? In making metaphysics problematic with this question, Heidegger had found, along with Brentano and Husserl, the leading determination of being in *ousia*, which of course was to be set back into the forgotten horizon of time. Now he problematized the very region that required this repositioning. Consequently, he had to insist that the leading determination of being is that *energeia* which contains open *dynamis* within itself. If *dynamis* is grasped as appropriation [*Eignung*], then *energeia* becomes an appropriating event [*Ereignis*] that is no longer to be supported by *entelecheia*. Around the same time, Oskar Becker took a similar step within a specific discipline when he advanced from mathematical intuitionism to the development of a modal logic. Husserl at least published this sketch of modal logic in the last volume of his yearbook (1930), but the conversation with his students then broke off. Discussions about *Sein und Zeit* or schematization could still take place, but now those among whom Husserl hoped to find co-workers appeared to turn into mere antagonists. Did they not thereby betray philosophy altogether? In fact, does the intent of Plato and Aristotle not get lost when being and non-being are no longer distinguished from one another, but become so interwoven that an untold wealth of constellations can be produced? This question forgets that within any particular constellation the aforementioned distinction is also once again possible!

Don't even the sudden conceptual changes in the *Sophist* allude to Heraclitus and ultimately play into the hands of the lightning flash that steers all things?[17] In any case, Heidegger henceforth sought with Heraclitus that which still echoed in a word like *energeia* and resonated together with words like *physis, aion, aletheia*, and *logos*. Here he also assumed that even in the conjugation of the verb *'sein'* ['to be'] in forms like *"ich bin"* ["I am"] those roots that point to a becoming still resounded. Aware of this, Nietzsche too reached back to the beginning of philosophy when he grasped the struggle of the Dionysian and the Apollinian as a law of history: the limiting form is to be won from the suffering of becoming. But actuality as a being-at-work cannot be made visible simply from exemplary modes of being like being-present-at-hand, being-ready-to-hand, and existential being. In 1929–30, then, Heidegger sketched out a philosophy of the organic; he saw poetizing and thinking as partners and related them back to the *mythos* that cannot simply be contrasted to *logos*.[18] Must one not show how philosophy unfolds in history? *Sein und Zeit* indicated questions of this sort when the fate of the individual was related there to the encompassing destiny of a generation and of a people or folk [*Volk*]. When the text stated that this destiny works itself out in communication and struggle [*Kampf*], it resorted again to one of the limit-situations (struggle). This question and especially its treatment of concepts that have long become obsolete, like *"Volk,"* "people" or "folk," contained a disastrous power of seduction. Still, these questions belong to philosophy, even to the beginning of *Sein und Zeit*, since laying the ground for a philosophy must clarify how this philosophy belongs to the happening of history.

Jaspers had discussed in detail the "antinomic" structure of Dasein as it emerges in limit-situations, and this in terms of the contrast between Kierkegaard and Nietzsche: Kierkegaard understands human being in terms of suffering, while Nietzsche overcomes the woe of suffering in the desire that wills "deep eternity" and affirms becoming with its woe for the sake of the inexhaustible desire of becoming. Jaspers thus had quoted the "drunken song" with which *Zarathustra* ends: woe and lust, high noon as the time of greatest brightness and midnight as the time of deepest darkness, are bound together.[19] Heidegger puts this very same song at the end of his lecture course in WS 1929–30. When he spoke of the struggle of the Dionysian and the Apollinian, he made clear that he understood this strife in terms of the later Nietzsche who locates it within the one god Dionysos. But the tragic philosophy that Nietzsche unfolds as a disciple of this god does not, according to Heidegger, escape the Socratic-Platonic or metaphysical tradition that it rejected. This "tragic" philosophy can only be understood from its self-entanglement in this tradition. This means, however, that this philosophy is still oriented to the moment, if only finally to dissimulate it.

For Nietzsche's *Zarathustra*, the moment is the gate of eternity in which the infinite paths of future and past meet. Yet the eternal return which is to be understood only from the moment teaches that these ways are interwoven into a circle. The experience of high noon, in which the world is complete and rushes into the fountain of eternity, teaches that this circle is complete in itself and that nothing new or different can or should enter into it. Anyone can have the experience of such a high noon in rare moments; the only question is whether Nietzsche's interpretation of this experience is valid. Shouldn't one relate not only the rise and fall of day, but also the life of the individual human being and indeed history as a whole, to the culmination point of a "great noontide?" Doesn't this high noon provide an experience not only of the rare, the unique, the transitory, and the endangered, but also of a "thus again and again?" According to Heidegger, Nietzsche must insist upon the "again and again" because he thinks metaphysically. The will-to-power in Heidegger's view does not show that each interpretation of the world rests perspectivally on a standpoint of power, such that one interpretation overtakes the other and there is thus no one definitive metaphysical interpretation. The doctrine of the will-to-power for Heidegger is rather a metaphysical doctrine about what beings are. In this doctrine, the hold on things that was slumbering from the beginning in the doctrine of the being of beings comes forth. And in the doctrine of the eternal return, this hold on things then yields the constancy of the "again and again." Metaphysics seen in this way governs the uprising in which the struggle for world-domination occurs today. Heidegger can accordingly interpret the age of the struggle for world-domination and the mobilization of all resources with the slogans of metaphysics and of Nietzsche. Since the moment of meaningful living gets lost in the tumult of revolt, Nietzsche must yield in order to allow Hölderlin to show a way to another future.

The *Beiträge zur Philosophie* are constructed from the experiences and formulations of Hölderlin, into which the hints and suggestions of Kierkegaard and Nietzsche are intertwined into a new beginning. This new and different beginning weaves destruction and construction directly into one another. Thus, thinking hears the "echo" [*Anklang*: II] of the truth of being in nihilism's abandonment of being. It takes the earliest Greek thinking along with German Idealism's experience of history as the "play" [*Zuspiel*: III] of another future; it thereby ventures the "leap" [*Sprung*: IV] into the "grounding" [*Gründung*: V] of the truth of being itself as the temporal space of play [*Zeitspielraum*] that can become the site of the moment (according to the wording of the titles of Divisions II-V in the *Beiträge*). If this site of the moment is experienced, this experience transforms human beings into "the coming future ones" [*Zu-künftigen*: VI] who are prepared for the passing of "the last god" [*Der letzte Gott*: VII] (as the two concluding chapters of the *Beiträge* put it). Heidegger starts with the formulation of the preliminary drafts of Hölderlin's "Celebration of Peace," which refers to everything heavenly as rapidly passing; "for only a moment" does the god touch the dwelling of humans. Thus in his first Hölderlin course, Heidegger can already find the eternity of the heavenly or divine in a passing [*Vorbeigang*], in the "fleetingness of a scarcely perceptible nod" [*Winken*], whereby "in the flash of passing all blessings and all terrors" can still manifest themselves.[20] When the *Beiträge* speak of the last god, they do not mean the last in a series or even an idealistic synthesis. Rather, the experience of nihilism at once enables us to think the divine in an ultimate experience according to its highest essence, that is, in terms of eternity as the passing which again and again has its hour but is never at our beck and call. In this experience time swings into eternity and can with its finitude withdraw in favor of another time; in this experience the human being becomes a "momentary one." In his first letter to the Corinthians, Paul, to whom Kierkegaard appeals, calls the time in which human beings are judged and transformed the *Augenblick*, the moment, the blink of an eye. According to a later fragment ("You solidly built Alps . . ."), Hölderlin wanted to lie buried as a "momentary one" on the wine terraces of Stuttgart—there, where the path from Swabia opens up a vista of the city, seeing it as the dwelling that can be touched in the moment by the divine.

Heidegger undoubtedly believed that the experiences upon which he built had to be maintained against ever increasing distortions and in ever more modest beginnings. When in 1962 he discussed his lecture *Zeit und Sein*, the protocol of the discussion closed with a statement from Hans Erich Nossack's *Impossible Trial*: "One has to be there when one is called; but to summon oneself—that is the most wrongheaded thing that one can do."[21] At that time Nossack had just had his novel *After the Last Uprising* published, in which an outsider also appeals to a "last god" in the emotional verses of the motto. To the question whether he believed in such a god, Nossack answered that he could sooner believe in angels. Perhaps this statement is not entirely consistent, since angels are actually the messengers of a god or its adversary. In any case, the novel has a young man in a critical situation of life encounter such an angel just as he is about to cross Leopold Street in Munich. One can scarcely doubt the reality of this angel since the young man is about to be run over by a car when this angel suddenly steps up to him. The only question is how to understand this reality. Is it perhaps a projection from the concealed depths of the soul (for instance, the image of a friend from youth who had gone into the foreign legion because of an unconditional refusal of all compromises)? The novel makes it clear that such an interpretation would sidestep the issue. Human beings naturally tend to clutch avariciously after the divine in cults, rites, and dogmas. According to Nossack's novel, the experiences of the rare moments of human limit-situations fare better, for example, as they are presented occasionally in the theater, or in the quiet hours outdoors on an estate where nuns care for the handicapped. Do such experiences carry weight? Perhaps the "last uprising" succeeds less by making the religious dimension of life unnecessary than by employing it functionally to give human beings even now the right god to fit their needs.

Can "being called" in the singularity of the moment still be claimed for our life today? When Heidegger first came to Marburg in 1923, he took part in Rudolf Bultmann's seminar on the ethics of the Apostle Paul. There he referred to Luther's interpretation of the third chapter of *Genesis* and to chapters 33 and 34 of the Book of *Exodus*: human beings, who fall into sin follow the promptings of the serpent, liken themselves to God and talk "about" God; they thereby lose their relationship to God. It can be regained only in God's call out of that passing in which God only shows His back to the human being.[22] At that time Heidegger took Max Scheler to be the philosopher who corrupted phenomenology by mixing it with theology by way of uncontrolled speculations, and so spoke "about" God. But when *Sein und Zeit* appeared, Heidegger, along with his new friend Scheler, placed the fundamental ontological question of "why at all?" back into metaphysical perspectives, as these are pregiven by human life's place in the cosmos and by the question of God. In that "transcendental" sphere of the sense or truth of being which was now understood in its character as destiny and appropriating event [*Ereignis*], an indication of the pregivens of nature and life and of the relation to God was supposed to be given prior to all problems belonging to the regional ontologies and special metaphysics. The "situation," which Heidegger now left to the analysts of the situation of the times, thus became the "constellation" that sets the gathering of earth and world or sky, as well as the divine and the mortal, in the fourfold [*Geviert*] over against the technological grip of the enframing [*Gestell*]. The appeal became the *Wink*, the hinting wave, wink, or nod, in which that which is passing and departing once more signals in the site of the moment. When Heidegger with Hölderlin spoke of the *Wink* as the language of the gods, he still wanted to keep it free from the sudden "*numen*" familiar to religious studies.

When the Second World War had finally exposed Europe's catastrophe, Heidegger understood the *Wink* also as trace [*Spur*] (in the essays on Rilke and Anaximander in *Holzwege*). If the *Wink* is an immediately comprehensible gesture, the trace points more forcefully to the absence of what is indicated. Emmanuel Levinas believed nonetheless that this conception of the trace had to be turned against Heidegger: Heidegger's purported critique of metaphysics still remains within the metaphysical orientation to identity, which in Heidegger becomes historical identity. Yet we are set on the trail and trace [*auf der Spur*] not only of the ownmost, the proper [*Eigenen*], but also of the other, and therewith of God's having passed (as Levinas tried to show through an interpretation of *Exodus* 33). This difference and alterity, this passing, must be preserved in thinking. But the question remains whether this focus on the other merely reverses that concentration upon the ownmost, the proper, which (according to the criticism of Keiji Nishitani, for example) characterizes the Western tradition since its Iranian beginnings. According to Nishitani, the decisive breach among the authoritative traditions of the contemporary world occurs not between the European-American West and the Soviet East, but rather between both of these parts of the Western tradition and the East-Asian tradition (as Toynbee also claimed).[23]

There can be no doubt that through its options philosophy, too, has led to the horrors committed during our century in the camps of Siberia, in Auschwitz, and in Hiroshima. Can philosophy with its different traditions also help to find paths beyond these horrors? A poet like Paul Celan, with whom Heidegger had communicated since the fifties, sought the "unerring trace" in the "countryside," in the death camp out there on which a star still shines (in the poem "*Engführung*"). In the course of Heidegger's philosophical efforts, the connection between moment and destruction becomes the connection between site of the moment and path, and finally that between nearness and trace. His thinking has in this way contributed to the question of how philosophy with its history might be able to provide an orientation for our lives.

Part IV

The Retrieval of Primal Christianity

9

Martin Heidegger, Martin Luther

John van Buren

Karl Jaspers recalled that "in the spring of 1920" he "visited [Heidegger], sat alone with him in his den, watched him at his Luther studies, saw the intensity of his work."[1] Julius Ebbinghaus recounted that, apparently due to the financial grant of the Canadian philosopher Winthrop Bell in 1921,[2] Heidegger "had received the Erlangen edition of Luther's works as a prize or gift—and so on the evenings we spent together we read Luther's reformation writings for a time."[3] We do indeed find Luther being mentioned and discussed repeatedly along with Paul, Augustine, the medieval mystics, Pascal, Schleiermacher, and Kierkegaard in Heidegger's courses from 1919 to 1923,[4] as well as in those following. In 1922 he actually planned to publish a journal essay on "The Ontological Foundations of Late Medieval Anthropology and the Theology of the Young Luther."[5] This theme was sketched out roughly also in the 1922 introduction to his planned book on Aristotle (PIA 250–52/372–73). By SS 1923 Heidegger and Ebbinghaus were giving a seminar together on "The Theological Foundations of Kant's *Religion within the Limits of Mere Reason*," which explored Luther's influence on Kant and German Idealism.[6] In his lecture course during this semester, he wrote that "companions in my searching were the young Luther and the paragon Aristotle. . . . Kierkegaard gave impulses, and Husserl gave me my eyes" (GA63 5). The Luther-scholar Edmund Schlink even went so far as to maintain that "Heidegger's existential analytic of human Dasein is a radical secularization of Luther's anthropology."[7] After moving to Marburg in the autumn of 1923, Heidegger continued his Luther studies in the context of seminars with the theologian Rudolf Bultmann in Marburg.[8] Here Heidegger is reported to have held a seminar with Bultmann on the young Luther,[9] delivered a lecture on Luther's commentary on Paul's Letter to the Galatians,[10] and taken over the theological seminar of a colleague who had fallen ill.[11] Later, we still find him having assisted the Luther-scholar Gerhard Ebeling in his 1961 work on Luther's *Disputatio de Homine*.[12] Heidegger even had a line from Luther's translation of the Old Testament engraved in wood above the door of his house in Zähringen: *Behüte dein Herz mit allem Fleiss; denn daraus geht das Leben.* Shelter your heart; for from it life goes forth (*Proverbs* 4:23).[13]

Heidegger's turn to Luther after the First World War has to be situated within the history of his theological interests, which can be broken down into at least three phases: 1) The Catholic Neo-Scholastic and Antimodernist Phase from 1909 to around 1913, when Heidegger studied theology for two years (1909–1911) with the aim of entering the priesthood, and published a series of articles in the antimodernist Catholic journal *Der Akademiker*.[14] 2) The Neo-Neo-Scholastic Phase from 1913 to 1916, when he pursued the project of developing a new type of Neo-Scholasticism that would revive medieval Scholasticism and mysticism with the help of the modern language of Husserlian phenomenology, Neo-Kantianism, Hegel, the German Romantics, and Dilthey. It was to be nothing less than a "philosophy of the living spirit, of active love, of worshipful intimacy with God" (GA1 410). 3) The Protest-ant and Mystical Phase which began around 1917 with his growing interest in Schleiermacher.[15] In a letter of January 9, 1919 to Father Engelbert Krebs, Heidegger officially announced his confessional turn to a free Protestantism: "Epistemological insights, extending to the theory of historical knowledge, have made the *system* of Catholicism problematic and unacceptable to me—but not Christianity and metaphysics, these though in a new sense."[16]

Heidegger now began from the assumption that, as he wrote in WS 1919–20, "the ancient Christian achievement was distorted and buried through the infiltration of classical science into Christiantity. From time to time it reasserted itself in violent eruptions (as in Augustine, in Luther, in Kierkegaard)," which also included "medieval mysticism: Bernard of Clairvaux, Bonaventura, Eckhart, Tauler."[17] Heidegger's "phenomenology of religious consciousness," as he called it in 1919,[18] attempted to follow in the footsteps of these Christian thinkers by carrying out a destruction (*Destruktion*) or deconstruction (*Abbau*) of the Aristotelian and Neoplatonic conceptuality of western theology and philosophy. He wanted to uncover the original experiences of the personal "selfworld" and "kairological" time in primal Christianity (*Urchristentum*) (GA56/57 134), and then explore the universal significance of these phenomena in a phenomenological ontology. Again we read from the WS 1919–20 course, which was originally supposed to be a course on "The Philosophical Foundations of Medieval Mysticism"[19]:

> The great revolution [of Christianity] against ancient science, against Aristotle above all, who, however, actually prevailed once again in the coming millennium, indeed should have become the Philosopher of official

Christianity—in such a manner that the inner experiences and the new attitude of life [of Christianity] were pressed into the forms of expression in ancient science. To free oneself and radically free oneself from this process, which still has a deep and confusing after-effect today, is *one* of the innermost tendencies of phenomenology. (GA58 61)

Here Heidegger modeled his thinking especially on the young Luther's theology of the cross (*theologia crucis*) and its scathing attack against the theology of glory (*theologia gloriae*) in Aristotelian Scholasticism and against the *philosophia gloriae* of the so-called "blind heathen master Aristotle" himself, about whose writings Luther had also scoffed that here it is "as if someone were exercising his talents and skills by studying and playing with dung."[20]

If Heidegger planned to illuminate ontology through his phenomenology of religion, he also simultaneously took the conceptuality for this phenomenology from his ontology.[21] Between WS 1919–20 and 1922 he was pursuing the question about the sense of being in terms of a complex configuration of intentional moments creatively drawn from Husserl's concept of intentionality (GA58 260–61; GA61 52–53). These moments included the sense of the content or, in short, the content-sense (*Gehaltssinn*) of intentional experience, that is, the sense of the world that is experienced. Relational sense (*Bezugssinn*) encompasses the modal senses of intending the world, which include understanding, mood, and language. Enactment- or fulfilment-sense (*Vollzugssinn*) has to do with how the prefigured intentional person/world relation is enacted or fulfilled interpretively in concrete situations. Finally, temporalizing-sense (*Zeitigungssinn*) is the deeper sense of this enactment as historical time with its interwoven moments of having-been, futural coming-towards, and making-present. In 1919 Heidegger had called this temporalizing an "it worlds," (*es weltet*) "there is/it gives" (*es gibt*), and *Ereignis*, event/enownment (GA56/57 73–75), terms that carried strong overtones of the "*mysterium tremendum*" (GA58 107) in the mystical tradition.

After the first ontological and methodological part of his WS 1920–21 course "Introduction in the Phenomenology of Religion," Heidegger focused in the second part on Paul's letter to the Galatians, the second letter to the Corinthians, and the two letters to the Thessalonians in order to get at the specific content-, relational, and temporalizing-senses of primal Christianity (DMH 36–37; IPR 319). Here the content of Christian experience was centered pivotally on the unique historical facticity of the hidden God (the *Deus absconditus* rediscovered in the *mysterium tremendum* of the mystics), who had been encountered in the Incarnation and Crucifixion, and was to be encountered again in the Parousia, the Second Coming.

In order to get at the factical relational sense of New Testament experience, Heidegger took up Paul's theme of the "thorn in the flesh" in 2 Corinthians 12:1–10, and his renunciations of mystical charisma, eschatological speculation, and apocalyptic visions (DMH 37–38). Earlier in WS 1919–20 he had shown that, against objective Greek metaphysics, "the most profound historical paradigm for [the concentration of factical life on the selfworld] is given to us in the emergence of Christianity. What lies forth in the life of the primal Christian communities signifies a radical reversal of the directional tendency of life, and is here mostly thought of as denial of the world and asceticism." This "great revolution against ancient science" then reasserted itself in Augustine's *Confessions*, the mystics, Luther, Kierkegaard, and the general tradition of confessional autobiography. For example, Augustine's "*crede, ut intelligas*," believe in order to understand, means: "live your self in a living manner—and only on the basis of this experience, your ultimate and fullest self-experience, does knowing get built up. In the phrase '*inquietum cor nostrum*' [our heart (is) restless], Augustine saw the great unceasing restlessness of life" (GA58 56–62, 205, 212). During the early twenties Heidegger showed that the basic sense of life in primal Christianity is that of care (*merimna* or *phrontis* in the New Testament). "In its widest sense," he wrote, "the relational meaning of life is: anxiously caring for one's 'daily bread'" (GA61 90; cf. GA20 418–19/302–303 and GA2 264 n. 3/243 n. vii). Care in the New Testament takes two forms: either care for the self/God relation, or worldly care that falls away from this relation into the present world, a contrast that Paul expresses between "care for the things of the lord" and "care for the affairs of the world" (1 Cor. 7:32–33).

Heidegger's WS 1920–21 course also pointed out how this care is defined by a particular type of understanding, mood, and discourse.[22] He did this through analyses of the first twelve verses of the First Letter to the Thessalonians, noting that there is a distinctive repetition here of the term "to know" (*eidenai*) (IPR 320–21). For example, Paul writes: "But concerning the time and the moment [*kairos*] [of the Coming] I do not need to write to you, for you already know well. . . ." (5:1). This kind of knowing means not a theoretical knowledge, but rather a practical understanding that Heidegger called "experiential knowledge" and "comprehension of the situation" in which God is encountered historically. Elsewhere in the New Testament this situational understanding is often being referred to as *phronesis*, practical wisdom. For example: "He has made known to us in all wisdom and practical insight [*phronesei*] the mystery of his purpose according to . . . the fullness of the fitting moment [*ton kairon*]" (Eph. 1:9–10). In the first twelve verses of 1 Thessalonians there is also an emphasis on mood. For example: "your labor prompted by love, and your endurance inspired by hope"; "in spite of much anxiety, you welcomed the message with joy"; and "we had previously suffered." Heidegger also noted that "the situation of the epistle is designated as 'preaching,'" the bringing of a message (*euangelion*), which is a thoroughly practical mode of discourse. For example: "From you the word has sounded forth," "we dared to tell the message to you," etc. (1:6–2:2).

In order to show how the intentional believer/God relation in the New Testament generates authentic kairological time, Heidegger's WS 1920–21 course turned to an analysis of the notion of the Second Coming within the Kairos, the eye-opening moment (*Augenblick*), as this is developed especially in the fourth and fifth chapters of 1 Thess. and the second chapter of 2 Thess. (IPR 317–22). Heidegger showed here how the "situation of historical enactment," the "context of enactment with God," includes a dimension of "already having become," an "already having been" (*genesthai, Gewordensein*), or "now being" (*jetziges Sein*), which is disclosed in "remembering," "knowing," affectivity ("tribulation," "joy"), and "preaching." But this present perfect of "having been" is always already taken up into and shapes precisely the hopeful waiting toward the *Zukunft*, the future (literally, the coming-towards), which means here the *Second Coming*. This interwovenness of having-been and futural coming is expressed in Paul's statement that "you *have* turned to God and away from idols in order . . . to *wait* for his son from heaven" (1 Thess. 1:9–10; emphasis added). This Coming will arrive in the Kairos as "the fullness of time." However, the time and content of this arrival are not objectively available in advance to be awaited, expected (*erwartet*), represented, and calculated, but rather are to be determined only out of the Kairos itself, which will happen with a "suddenness" and in "the twinkling of an eye" (1 Cor. 15:52). "Concerning the times and moments," says Paul, "we need not write to you, for you yourselves know that the Day of the Lord will come like a thief in the night" (1 Thess. 5:1–2). The situation of the parousiological and kairological temporalizing of the intentional believer/God relation is thus a futural Coming that is textured by a having-been and will be determined only out of the incalculable eye-opening moment of arrival. The original Christians live in "a constant, essential, and necessary insecurity . . . a context of enacting one's life in uncertainty before the unseen God," in "daily doing and suffering" (IPR 322, 317). They live in a resolute and open *wachsam sein*, being-wakeful for the incalculable Coming within the eye-opening moment. Thus Paul writes: "But you are not in the darkness for that day to surprise you like a thief. For you are all children of the light and children of the day; we belong not to the night and the darkness. So then let us not sleep like the others, but rather remain wakeful, watchful, and sober. Sleepers sleep at night, and drunkards get drunk at night, but we who belong to the day wish to be sober" (1 Thess. 5:4–8). Heidegger pointed out that the words "day" and "light" in these passages mean both the "Day of the Lord" itself and also the light of self-comprehension, that is, the disclosedness or illumination of both God and the believer's own authentic self in the historical situation.

Here Heidegger also contrasted this authentic kairological time with *chronological* time, that is, time-reckoning, calculating time. This is the time of those who await or expect the Coming by objectifying, representing, and calculating it in advance as an already available, determined, and datable event. This is what happens especially in eschatological and apocalyptic speculations, visions, and prophesies about the coming of the last days (DMH 36). Heidegger showed how the Pauline notion of the Parousia differs radically from earlier Jewish prophecy and eschatology concerning the "Day of the Lord" and the coming of the "Messianic Man," as well as from Iranian-Babylonian notions of eschatology and even from the Synoptic teaching of the coming of the Kingdom of God. What one seeks in such chronological time is an escape from anxiety, insecurity, and difficulty into the security and tranquillity of an objective present-at-hand reality that can be observed and counted on. Heidegger pointed to Paul's statement that "when people say 'peace! security!,'" then suddenly destruction will come upon them as travail comes upon a woman with child, and there will be no escape" (1 Thess. 5:3). These people, says Paul, live in darkness, sleep, drunkenness. According to Heidegger, this means that they have fallen away from the historical situation and from their authentic selves into the present world. Their "'waiting' is all for this world" (IPR 322). Their authentic selves within the historical situation have been closed off to them. Asleep and drunk, they will be away when the Parousia arrives in the Kairos, they will miss it, and they will be ruined.

In his SS 1921 course "Augustine and Neoplatonism" and in his following courses on Aristotle, Heidegger argued, as he had already begun to do in WS 1919–20, that the eclipse of authentic kairological time by inauthentic chronological time is just what happened when Christian thinkers, including St. John and St. Paul, began to use the conceptuality of Greek and Roman philosophy to speak about New Testament experience. Apostolic literature itself and the theology developed in the patristic and medieval periods often cried out: "peace! security!" A conceptual "Hellenization" of primal Christianity took place (GA61 6). In SS 1921 Heidegger showed how Augustine in particular falsified his own understanding of primal Christianity by adopting *inter alia* the Neoplatonic concept of *fruitio Dei*,[23] the enjoyment of God in contemplation, which brings about a "theorizing" or ocularizing of the whole intentional configuration of primitive Christian experience. In this concept, the historical content-sense of

Incarnation, Crucifixion, and Second Coming is levelled off into the Greek notion of the divine as a present-at-hand, objectively available highest being (*summum ens*), highest good (*summum bonum*), and most beautiful being in a hierarchical-teleological order of beings. The hidden God of the Old and New Testaments is reduced to a *prae oculis esse*, a constant being before the eyes (DMH 42). Simultaneously, the original relational sense of care, anxiety, situational understanding, and preaching is dimmed down to the ocular-aesthetic relation of beholding, contemplating, theorizing, enjoying. Finally, the movement, absence, and incalculability of the kairological temporalizing-sense of primal Christianity is brought to a standstill in the *esse praesto* of God, a being constantly present in the dead eternity of a *nunc stans* for the believer's *praesto habere* or having-present, that is, for the believer's awaiting, objectifying, representation, calculation, enjoyment. Kairological time is levelled off into chronological time. Anxious, insecure, and resolute being-awake for the Kairos is quietistically lulled to sleep in the speculative vision of the heart that "rests in thee," in the *tranquillitas* of the *visio beatifica*, the happy and blessed vision—the *vita beata*, the happy and blessed life of contemplative enjoyment of God. Intoxicated, asleep, and darkened by these contemplative and speculative visions, the self falls away from itself into the world and closes off the historical situation of its relation with God. All in all, the Neoplatonic concept of the enjoyment of God means that the original intentional configuration of *Deus absconditus*/being-awake/kairological time is displaced by the foreign Greek configuration of *summum ens*/contemplation/presence.

Through the intitial adoption of such Greek conceptuality, Augustine and other patristic figures helped pave the way for consolidating the reception of Neoplatonism and Aristotle in late Aristotelian-Scholasticism. In his 1922 essay on Aristotle Heidegger wrote:

> The late-Scholastic doctrines of God, the trinity, innocence, sin, and grace operate with the conceptual means that Thomas Aquinas and Bonaventura provided for theology. But this means that the idea of human being and the Dasein of life that is initiated in advance in all of these spheres of theological problems is based on Aristotelian "physics," "psychology," "ethics," and "ontology." . . . Simultaneously, Augustine is also decisively at work here and, through Augustine, Neoplatonism. . . . (PIA 250/372)

But thereby the believer/God relation of original Christianity is forced into the foreign Aristotelian concept of the presence-at-hand of pure and constant being-in-act (*energeia*) that belongs to the activity of contemplation and eminently to the divine unmoved mover, which is thought thinking thought.

> The *theion* [the divine] is *noesis noeseos* [thought of thought] . . . . This being *must* be pure beholding, i.e., free from every emotional relation to its [intentional] towards-which. . . . the specific ontological explication of this being [makes up] the motivational sources for the basic ontological structures that later decisively determine divine being in the specifically Christian sense (*actus purus*), the divine inner life (trinity), and therewith simultaneously the being of the relation of God to human being and therewith the sense of the human being's own being. (PIA 263/386)

However, Aristotle's divine *nous* "does not have the slightest thing to do with the God of Thomas" (GA21 123). Thus, "Christian theology, the philosophical 'speculation' standing under its influence, and the anthropology that always also develops in such contexts all *speak in borrowed categories that are foreign to their own field of being*" (PIA 263/386).

Heidegger held that the understanding of time in primal Christianity was reawakened by Augustine himself, the medieval mystics, Pascal, and Kierkegaard, but in SS 1921 and elsewhere he focused on the young Luther's violent critique of Aristotelian Scholasticism. "Luther's counterattack," he wrote in WS 1921–22, "was now enacted religiously and theologically against the Scholasticism that had been consolidated through the reception of Aristotle . . . . What is at stake here is something decisive" (GA61 7). In his WS 1920–21 course on Paul's letters, he said "that Luther *did* understand [the] basic experience of temporality [in the New Testament] and for that reason opposed Aristotelian philosophy so polemically" (IPR 322). In SS 1921, he introduced Luther's critique in his early 1518 *Heidelberg Disputation* and focused on the contrast in the nineteenth and twentieth theses between the *theologia gloriae* of Aristotelian Scholasticism and Paul's *theologia crucis* (DMH 40). Thesis 19 attacks the Scriptural basis in the Letter to the Romans that had been used to justify the adoption of Greek philosophical methods and concepts: "That person is not rightly called a theologian who looks upon the *invisible* things of God as though they were *perceptible* through things that have been made [Rom. 1:20]." Thesis 20 states: "He deserves to be called a theologian, however, who understands the visible and manifest things of God seen through suffering and the cross. The manifest things of God, namely, his human nature, weakness, and foolishness, are placed in opposition to the invisible. . . . he is hidden [*absconditus*] in [the] suffering [of the cross]. . . . Isaiah says, 'Truly, you are a hidden God'" (WA I 361–62/XXXI 52–53; emphasis added). The theology of glory is not content with belief in the unseen, the absent, the incalculable, but rather desires precisely to see "God in his glory and majesty," that is, to have God present as the first cause and highest good that is manifested through created works.

> A theologian of glory (that is, someone who does not know along with the Apostle the hidden and crucified God, but sees and speaks of God's glorious manifestation among the pagans, how his invisible nature can be known from things visible and how he is present [*presentem*] and powerful in all things everywhere) learns from Aristotle that the object of the will is good . . . . He learns that God is the highest good [*summum bonum*]. (WA I 614/XXXI 227)

Here Luther uses the term "theology of glory" to describe in effect the intentional configuration of *summum ens*/contemplative enjoyment/presence that defines Scholasticism and the Greek metaphysics from which it derives. "Glory" (*doxa, gloria*) is Luther's term for the Greek and Scholastic experience of being as an exalted radiant divine presence that is enjoyed in quietistic, aesthetic-ocular contemplation.[24]

It is here in his *Heidelberg Disputation* that Luther fatefully uses the Latin term *destruere*, destroying, dismantling, or—if you will—deconstructing, to translate Paul's talk in 1 Cor. 1 of "destroying" the "wisdom" of "the Greeks" with the the concrete historical "*logos* of the cross." Paul writes: "For it is written: I will destroy [*apolo*] the wisdom of the wise . . . . Greeks seek wisdom, but we preach Christ crucified . . . [which is] foolishness to Gentiles . . . . God chose . . . non-being [*ta me onta*] in order to bring to nothing being [*ta onta*], so that no one may glory before the face of God." Luther comments:

> God "*destroys* [*perdit*] the wisdom of the wise." . . . So also, in John 14:8, where Philip spoke according to the theology of glory: "Show us the Father," Christ immediately dragged back [*retraxit*] his flighty thought and lead him back [*reduxit*] to himself. . . . through the cross works are *destroyed/dismantled* [*destruuntur*] and the old Adam . . . is crucified. . . . [one must be] *destroyed/dismantled* and reduced [*redactus*] to nothing through the cross and suffering . . . .

Like all other types of *hyperbia*, pride, which glory in "works," speculative theological visions of God as glorious exalted presence (being, *eidos/ species*) that have been built up (*aedificatur*), "puffed up, blinded, and hardened," must be dismantled and led back in a kind of theological reduction to the concrete historical realities of "the cross," the absent *Deus absconditus*, "suffering," "sin, foolishness, death, and hell," the "poor and needy" (non-being, nothing in the sense of *me on, privatio*, and *defor-*

matio). The "love of the cross . . . turns to where it does not find good it may *enjoy* [*fruatur*]." (WA I 362–65, 357/XXXI 53–57, 44; emphasis added)

The *theologia gloriae* must be subjected to a destruction back to a living *theologia crucis*, whose *logos* arises out of and returns to the intentional configuration of an anxious wakeful faith (relational sense) that is related to an absent God hidden in the cross (content-sense), and that enacts and suffers (enactment-sense) the mysterious parousio-kairological time of this relation (temporalizing-sense). In his 1515–16 *Lectures on Romans*, which Heidegger knew well,[25] Luther comments on Paul's statement at 8:18–27 that "our sufferings of the present moment [*tou nun kairou*] are not worth comparing to the coming futural [*mellousan*] glory . . . . creation anxiously waits . . . . Hope that is seen is not hope. . . . And he who searches our hearts knows the wisdom [*phronema*] of the spirit" (WA LVI 371–72/XXV 360–62; emphasis added). Here Luther provides a destruction not just of Scholastic theology, but also of Greek and Scholastic metaphysics of presence itself. Whereas "we [metaphysicians] *enjoy* ourselves and *glory* in knowledge" of the present suffering world:

> The Apostle philosophizes . . . in a different way than the philosophers and the metaphysicians do. For the philosophers so direct their eyes to the *present* state of things [*in presentiam rerum*] that they speculate only about essences and qualities of things. . . . the Apostle recalls our eyes away from the intuition and contemplation of the present, away from the essences and accidents of things, and directs us to the *future*.

With destruction comes also repetition of that which is uncovered. For Luther suggests that, as the first philosopher to think the connection between being and time, Paul makes a new non-metaphysical beginning that needs to be radicalized:

> . . . . in a new and amazing theological vocabulary he speaks of the "expectation of the creation" . . . . Therefore, you will be the best philosophers and the best speculators of things if you will learn from the Apostle to consider the creation as it waits, groans, and travails, that is, as it turns away in disgust from *that which is* and desires *that which is not yet* and in the *future*.

Similarly, the twelve "philosophical theses" of Luther's 1518 *Heidelberg Disputation* carry out a destruction also of the *philosophia gloriae* of Aristotle himself.[26] In the "proofs" to these theses, one finds Luther moving freely about in quoted passages from one end of Aristotle's corpus to the other. Luther had studied Aristotle's writings in detail and lectured on them. "I understand him," Luther maintained, "better than Thomas or Duns Scotus" (WA VI 458/XLIV 201). In 1517, he was working on a commentary on the first book of the *Physics* in which he planned to unmask the inability of Aristotle's philosophy to express Christian realities, but it was never completed in this form (WA *Briefwechsel* I 88/XLVIII 38). It became instead his 1517 *Disputation Against Scholastic Theology* and 1518 *Heidelberg Disputation* (WA IX 170/I 70), whose philosophical theses open with the declaration that "he who wishes to philosophize in Aristotle without danger must first become completely a fool in Christ. . . . But Christ is hidden in God. . . . 'The wise person does not glory in wisdom.'"[27]

According to Luther, "it is not that philosophy is evil" in itself for the Christian, but rather its "misuse." One should "philosophize well."[28] The Luther-scholar Ebeling, with whom Heidegger later collaborated, argues that Luther defends the "true Aristotle" against Scholastic misinterpretations.[29] Indeed, despite Luther's sweeping rhetorical condemnations of Aristotle, his *destructio* of Aristotelian Scholasticism and of Aristotle's own theological metaphysics entails simultaneously not only a retrieval of primal Christiantity, but also (as in Kierkegaard)[30] a highly creative and non-Scholastic appropriation of Aristotle's concepts of *physis, kinesis, dynamis, steresis*, etc., in his physics and practical writings. For example, Luther's *Lectures on Romans* applies these concepts to interpret Paul's exhortation to "those who have already become Christians" that they constantly "be transformed by the renewal of your mind and heart" (Rom. 12:2). Luther explains that "the condition of this life is not that of having God but of seeking God" again and again in repetition. The "way to God," as well as human life in general, is a constant circular *kinesis* and becoming (*genesthai*), since what one has become and is in actuality (*energeia*) is never cut off from the lack, privation (*steresis*), not-yet, and non-being of possibility (*dynamis*), in terms of which life is to be repeated and renewed. Thus "human being is always in non-being":

> Their life is not something in quiet rest and repose [*in quiescere*], but in movement . . . . just as there are five stages in the case of the things of nature: non-being, becoming, being, action, passion, that is, privation, matter, form, operation, passion, according to Aristotle, so also with the spirit . . . human being is always in privation, always in becoming and potentiality . . . . Aristotle philosophizes about such matters, and he does it well, but he is not understood in this sense.[31]

Luther had a great respect for Aristotle's practical writings, stating that "Aristotle is the best teacher one can have in moral philosophy."[32] We find

Luther in his *Lectures on Romans*, *Commentary on Genesis*, and elsewhere creatively appropriating also Aristotle's notions of *phronesis*, *kairos*, the mean, excess and deficiency, the fitting (*to deon*), and justice or equity (*epieikeia*). "Aristotle," Luther praises, "deals with these matters in a very fine way." Luther uses these notions precisely to get at the Christian sense of the situational *kinesis* towards God, the Spirit of love, and the Second Coming in contrast to the excessive *superbia* and deficient falling-away of the Law and metaphysical *theologia gloriae*.[33]

Remarkably, in these passages from Luther's *Lectures on Romans*, in his *Heidelberg Disputation*, and in his *Commentary on Genesis*, Chapter 3 (Heidegger studied closely here the treatment of the "fall," "care," "anxiety," "death," "flight," and "conscience"[34]), we find not only the basic idea of Heidegger's own deconstructive repetition of Aristotle, but also many of the major terms that he used in his own descriptions of falling in his first course on Aristotle in WS 1921–22, namely, "falling away," *securitas*, "self-satisfaction," "presuming" or "mismeasuring" (*Vermessen*), "the hyperbolic" (excess; cf. *superbia* in Luther and *hyperbole* in 2 Cor. 12), "the elliptic" (deficiency), "blinding," "going wrong," and "ruinance" (GA61 100ff.). Most telling is the similarity between Luther's term *obex* (bolt, bar, barricade; as in the phrase "they are their own *obex* against the divine light") and Heidegger's very prosaic term *Abriegelung* (bolting, barring, barricading) for how the self "barricades" itself off from itself (WA LVI 238–39/XXV 224–25; GA61 105–108). We also find that much of the terminology of this lecture course on Aristotle actually consists of Germanizations of terms gleaned from the Latin texts of Augustine, Luther, etc.: for example, *das Quietive* (the quietive), *das Alienative* (the alienative), *das Tentative* (the tentative), *Ruinanz* (ruinance), *Larvance* (larvance), *Horrescenz* (horrescence). The Latin term *horror*, dread, is found often in Luther's commentary on Genesis 3 (GA61 138; WA XLII 127–34/I 171–80).

According to Heidegger, Luther's *destructio* of Aristotelian Scholasticism and his return to the concrete historical consciousness of primal Christianity simultaneously provided the basis for and underwent a "derailing" in the development of Melanchthon's Aristotelian "Protestant Scholasticism," which became "the soil of German Idealism." Heidegger noted that "Fichte, Schelling, and Hegel were [Lutheran] theologians, and Kant is to be understood theologically" also. They "come out of *theology* and take from it the basic impulses of their speculation. This theology is rooted in Reformation theology, which succeeded only to a very small extent in achieving a genuine explication of Luther's new basic religious position and of its immanent possibilities" (GA61 7; PIA 250/372; cf. GA63 26). Heidegger also thought that the later Luther himself, Kierkegaard, and Dilthey all fell short of unfolding the immanent possibilities of Luther's new position because they fell back under the spell of Greek conceptuality

(DMH 41; GA63 41–42). Neither Luther nor the following theological and philosophical movements pushed to its radical conclusions the deconstructive commentary on Aristotle and Aristotelian Scholasticism that Luther had started in his youthful period.

It was Heidegger who, as it were, finished it when he began lecturing and writing a book on Aristotle (PIA) in WS 1921–22. Writing to Paul Natorp in 1922, Husserl reported that, in its oral form, Heidegger "opened his Aristotle course on November 2, 1921 by citing Luther's condemnation of the *Metaphysics*, *De Anima*, and *Ethics* of the 'pagan master Aristotle'"[35] in *To the Christian Nobility of the German Nation*: "What else are the universities . . . than what the Book of Maccabees calls *gymnasia epheborum et graecae gloriae*? . . . Aristotle's *Physics*, *Metaphysics*, *De anima*, and *Ethics* . . . should be completely discarded along with the rest of his books that glory in natural things" (WA VI 457–58/XLIV 200–201). Indeed, we find in the published text of this very first lecture course on Aristotle a loose page titled "Motto and Grateful Indication of Sources." It contains two quotations from the Erlangen edition of Luther's works (GA61 182). The one consists of the last two lines of the following passage in Luther's *Preface to St. Paul's Letter to the Romans*, which criticizes the *theologia gloriae*: "And here we must set a limit for those arrogant and high-climbing spirits . . . . without suffering, the cross, and the distress of death, one cannot deal with predestination without harm . . . . The old Adam must die before he can suffer and endure this thing and drink the strong wine of it. Therefore, see to it that you do not drink wine while you are still an infant. Every doctrine has its measure, time, and age."[36] The other motto is from Luther's *Commentary on Genesis*, in which he describes life as a perpetual *cursus ad mortem*, which Heidegger will translate in his courses and in "Being and Time" as *Vorlaufen zum Tode*, anticipatory running ahead toward death: ". . . [Life] is nothing else than a constant running ahead toward death. . . . [Heidegger's quotation starts here:] Right from our mother's womb we begin to die" (WA XLII 146/I 196). The other two mottos are from Kierkegaard, who, as the great destroyer of modern speculative thought, is the modern counterpart to Luther's deconstruction of medieval Scholasticism. The first is from Kierkegaard's *Training in Christianity*: ". . . philosophy floats in the indefiniteness of the metaphysical. Instead of admitting this and so directing human beings (individual human beings) to the ethical, the religious, the existential, philosophy has created the illusion that human beings could, as one prosaically says, speculate themselves out of their own good skin and into pure light."[37] And then we read from Kierkegaard's *Either-Or*: "'But what philosophy and the philosopher find difficult is stopping.' Kierkegaard, *Either/Or*, Vol. I. (Stopping at the genuine beginning!)"[38]

The young Heidegger saw himself at this time as a kind of philosophical Luther of western metaphysics. In WS 1921–22 and in his other courses on Aristotle, Heidegger modelled his project on Kierkegaard and especially on Luther's *destructio*, from which he derived his odd philosophical term "destruction" (*Destruktion*). In SS 1919, Heidegger, following Kant, had rather used the term "phenomenological critique," and had been modelling his regress to primal Christianity more on Schleiermacher and the mystics (GA56/57 9–12, 127, 134). Jaspers recalled seeing Heidegger at work on his Luther studies in the spring of 1920, and it was indeed at the close of his WS 1919–20 lecture course (which mentions Luther's attack on Aristotle) that Heidegger first used the term *Destruktion* (GA58 139ff., 61–62, 205). After the quasi-Lutheran destructions back to primal Christianity in his two religion courses of WS 1920–21 and SS 1921, it was in his first lecture course on Aristotle in WS 1921–22 that Heidegger now ventured the more ambitious project of a quasi-Lutheran destruction of 1) the entire philosophical tradition based on Aristotle, including Aristotelian Scholasticism, and 2) Aristotle's metaphysics itself, so as to effect what he already in WS 1921–22 called "the end of philosophy" (GA61 35). Again following Luther's and Kierkegaard's appreciative readings of key Aristotelian concepts such as *physis, kinesis, phronesis, kairos*, etc., Heidegger's destruction prepared the way for uncovering and repeating on an ontological level the historicity of factical life in 1) primal Christianity and 2) Aristotle's own practical writings, so as to effect what he called a new "genuine beginning" for the question about being (GA61 35, 186; cf. GA63 19–20, 5, 57). The intentional configuration of Aristotelian metaphysics, namely, substance (*ousia*)/theory/always-being (*aei on*), was to be dismantled back to the more primal configuraton of *polis-oikia-ethos/ phronesis*/kairological *kinesis* in Aristotle's practical writings, which was in turn to be repeated in the intentional configuration of Heidegger's new beginning, namely, world/wakeful care/kairological time.[39]

Heidegger continued this project in his early Freiburg and Marburg periods. For example, in laying out his plan for a "destruction" of the "Greek conceptuality" of the philosophical tradition, the 1922 introduction to his unfinished book on Aristotle stated clearly that, "for the sake of carrying out the task of the phenomenological destruction [of the history of ontology], these researches set their sights on late-Scholasticism and Luther's early theological period" (PIA 249–252/370–73). In SS 1923, when the outlines of his reading of Aristotle had already been worked out in preceding courses, Heidegger again proposed a "deconstruction [*Abbau*] . . . to Aristotle," replacing the page of mottos in his WS 1921–22 lecture course with the simple introductory statement that "companions in my searching were the young Luther and the paragon Aristotle, whom Luther hated" (GA63 76, 5). By the time Heidegger wrote *Being and Time* in

1926, this "Grateful Indication of Sources" had almost been entirely eclipsed by his turn to Kant's transcendental philosophy.

The young Heidegger's concern, however, was to find a new "genuine beginning" not only in a new ontological language, but also in the end of Aristotelian-Scholastic theology and the initiation of a new Lutheran theological language in his phenomenology of religion. As Gadamer has maintained, Heidegger's thinking in the early twenties was also his attempt, after giving up the Aristotelian-Scholastic system of Catholicism, to "become a Christian."[40] Influenced by Schleiermacher's Romantic Protestant mysticism, as well as by Natorp's synthesis of Meister Eckhart and Luther, and exploiting the symmetry of intentional configurations between medieval mysticism and Pauline parousio-kairology (namely, *Deus absconditus*/ faith/kairological time and *mysterium tremendum*/surrender/analogical emanation), the Heidegger of the early Freiburg period seems actually to have been moving for a time toward a kind of free mystical Lutheranism or Lutheran mysticism.[41] In a theological discussion in which he participated in 1923, he made the challenging statement that "it is the true task of theology, which must be discovered again, to find the word that is able to call one to faith and preserve one in faith."[42] This statement was reiterated in SS 1925 and in section 3 of *Being and Time*: "Theology is seeking a more original interpretation of the being of the human being toward God, prescribed from the meaning of faith and remaining within it." After centuries it is only now "slowly beginning to understand once more Luther's insight that its dogmatic system rests on a 'foundation' that has not arisen from a questioning in which faith is primary, and whose conceptuality is not only not adequate for the problematic of theology, but rather conceals and distorts it" (GA20 6/4; GA2 13–14/30).

If Heidegger's phenomenology of primal Christianity, along with his readings of Dilthey, Emil Lask, Husserl, and Aristotle, was to help make possible a new ontology, then the latter was in turn supposed to provide the former with the ethico-religiously non-committal and "atheistic" formal indications of ontology, which are indeed not restricted in their application to the sphere of Christian life, but can nonetheless be concretized interpretively therein (GA61 197; PIA 246/367). This back-and-forth movement between theology and ontology is the sense of Heidegger's statement in 1921 to his student Karl Löwith that "I am no philosopher . . . . I am a 'Christian theo*logian*,'" that is, one whose *logos*, language, arises out of his own factical Christian heritage and returns to it.[43] Similarly, he had written to Blochmann in 1919 that his philosophy was "preliminary work for a phenomenology of religious consciousness."[44] Since the conceptual basis of theology had after all been provided originally by Platonic and Aristotelian philosophy, theo*logical* reform presupposed ontological reform of the question about being. This is exactly the point Heidegger made in section 3 of *Being and Time* and in his 1927 lecture "Phenomenology and Theology" before the Protestant theological faculty in Tübingen. Here he showed the theologians how the new formally indicative, ontological language of *Being and Time* indirectly made possible a new theological language that could do justice to Luther's statement that "faith is surrendering oneself to matters that cannot be seen."[45] However, by this time Heidegger's Christian theological interests had already been on the wane for a long time. Treatment of a fourth phase of his theological interest, and how he used it as a model for the question about being, needs to show that sometime around 1930 he began to identify with the experience of "the death of God" in Nietzsche and Hölderlin, as well as with their aspirations toward the Parousia of a new and more Greek God.

10

Heidegger (1920–21) on Becoming a Christian:
A Conceptual Picture Show

Theodore Kisiel

Heidegger had planned once before to give a course of the phenomenology of religion. But several weeks before WS 1919–20 began, he wrote to the dean requesting that the two-hour course already announced under the title "Philosophical Foundations of Medieval Mysticism" be cancelled, and that the more methodological one-hour course entitled "Basic Problems of Phenomenology" be expanded to two hours. Looking beneath the surface, we find that there may have been more to the cancellation than the stated reason, namely, lack of time to prepare an extra course in an already crowded postwar academic year. For Heidegger's extant notes for that cancelled course on mysticism betray an overriding concern for the phenomenological methodology required to develop an atheoretical dimension like religious life, especially in articulating the notoriously inchoate and amorphous experience described by mystics like Meister Eckhart, Bernard of Clairvaux, and Theresa of Avila.

The concern for a phenomenology not only applicable to put perhaps even drawn from the religious life is deeply rooted in Heidegger's Catholic past. Already in the Introduction to his habilitation of 1915 on Scotus, Heidegger notes that a non-psychologistic sense of phenomenology's "intentionality" was after all first discovered by Scholastic psychology. In order to bring this out, he proposes the task of a "phenomenological elaboration of the mystical, moral-theological, and ascetic literature of medieval Scholasticism" (FS 147), and concludes by singling out "Eckhartian mysticism" (FS 344n.) as a particularly fruitful vein to explore in order to bring out the full scope and depth of the phenomenological notion of intentionality. Thus, it is not surprising that Heidegger's notes for his cancelled course underscore the importance of an intentional dynamics within the religious world, one which "is centered on the movement of a conative experience which is detaching itself in the process of finding God." He accordingly plans to map the entire gamut of negative and positive movements of the religious life, beginning with the repulsiveness of a corrupt

175

world, around Eckhart's master concept of "detachment" (*Abgeschieden-heit*), which is oriented toward not a theoretical but rather an "emotional nothing," "the God-ignited emptiness of form" reached by a progressive suspension of all multiplicity, particularity, and specificity. This accounts for Heidegger's interest in the forms and figures of practical guidance provided by devotional manuals, which tell us *how* the religious life is to be actualized, what he would soon call its "actualization sense" [*Vollzugs-sinn*]. With that aim in mind, Heidegger at this time is reading not only Eckhart's hortatory tracts and popular sermons, but also Bernard's *Sermons on the Song of Songs*, Theresa's *Interior Castle*, Francis of Assisi's *Fioretti*, and Thomas à Kempis's *Imitation of Christ*. There are even early signs that this map of the itinerary of the soul to God would in part include a grammatical mapping of its formal directives. Following Deiss-mann's reading of Pauline mysticism, the young Heidegger is pondering the senses of "in" in the Pauline formula, "Christ in me, I in Christ."[1]

But Heidegger does not go public on this religious side of his phe-nomenologizing until WS 1920–21, and even then with great reluctance, despite his obvious deep involvement in the topic. For one thing, he com-plains, in a letter to Karl Löwith shortly before the course began, that "the Old Man" (*der Alte*), namely his mentor Husserl, does not even regard him as a philosopher, but as "still really a theologian" (October 20, 1920). He also complains of the poor theological grounding of his students, and so refuses to hold a concurrent seminar on the same topic. "For, to be frank, all that would come of it is the kind of babble on the philosophy of religion that I want to eliminate from philosophy, this talk about the religious that is familiar to us from the secondary literature" (September 13). "I would like to do away with 'talking' about the religious, but it is perhaps inevita-ble. It is also a false expectation regarding my lecture course, if anyone thinks that is what I plan to do. It is probably best to say so from the start" (September 19).[2]

And this is precisely what Heidegger does on the opening day of his course entitled "Introduction to the Phenomenology of Religion," in an obvious effort to disenchant those who might have signed up for the course for something that would "stir the heart" or, at the very least, provide some "interesting" content. He then notes that the philosophically operative word in the course title is not really "religion" or even "phenom-enology," but rather the seemingly incidental word "intro-duction." Never arriving at answers but always "leading-into" questions: that is the essence of philosophy. "I wish to aggravate this need of philosophy to be ever turning upon the preliminary questions so much, and to keep it before your eyes so relentlessly, that it will in fact become a virtue."[3] And this is precisely what Heidegger proceeds to do in the next month of the course.

Hardly an introduction in a pedestrian sense, aimed at attracting non-majors into philosophy. Accordingly, the main term of this intense phenomenological exercise in the self-understanding of philosophy as perpetual intro-duction becomes the "formal indication," which had been the very core of Heidegger's hermeneutic method ever since he had made his breakthrough to his lifelong topic in KNS 1919. Thus, for the next ten hours of this two-hour lecture course, Heidegger's students are overwhelmed with an ever more abstruse treatment of phenomenological method and its object, of the subtle distinctions between *Objekt, Gegenstand,* and *Phänomen,* of the central phenomenon of factic life experience which is always at once active experiencing and the passively experienced, of the need to approach this middle-voiced identity of experience through its inescapably situated and historical character, how this elusive historical quality can only be explicated by way of formally indicative concepts, or better, provisional "preconcepts." The method of formal indication calls for a closer look at how philosophical concepts are formed, of the difference between generalization and formalization, between generic universals and formal universals, since, as we already know from Aristotle, "being is not a genus." Accordingly, the ontology of human experience is to be a formal ontology. But the ontology that would articulate the full immediacy of human experience cannot be the then-current formal mathesis of objects, but a more non-objective formalization of "intentionality" that would seek to preclude the classical distinction between subject and object.

Precisely at this ponderous point in the course, in the midst of specifying the special kind of formalization involved in the formal indication of intentionality, something untoward and unexpected occurs. For, despite Heidegger's forewarnings on opening day, the non-majors are still in attendance, by now thoroughly at sea in this increasingly abstruse discussion of the classical philosophical "problem of the universals." Upon getting word that the less methodologically minded students had gone to the dean to complain about the lack of religious content in a course purported to be about the philosophy of religion, Heidegger, in the tenth hour of the course, abruptly—and angrily—cuts short his abstruse methodological discussion with the announcement that, beginning with the next class, the course will henceforth be concerned solely with concrete religious phenomena. WS 1920–21 thus turns out to be a *cursus interruptus,* prematurely thwarted in its original thrust and carried to a climax other than the one originally intended. The interruption is most unfortunate for us who follow, since Heidegger was then still in the middle of the one and only truly sustained treatment of the "formal indication" that we are likely to get from his *Nachlass.* He will never again return to this vital but esoteric subject in the deliberate and systematic way that he had begun here, usually preferring instead to mention it in passing, with little or no explanation, as he applies this method of philosophical conceptualization in one context or another in the years to and through *Being and Time*. The formal indication thus becomes the "secret weapon" in Heidegger's methodological armory, dictated by the need to find words to articulate the peculiarly inchoate and purportedly "ineffable" immediacy of the human situation, Heidegger's lifelong topic. The course of WS 1920–21 has over the years become justly famous for its discovery of the kairological character of lived time, in its second part glossing the concrete religious phenomena described in the Pauline letters. But no less important is its development of the formal indication in the first part of the course. There is thus a doubly significant hidden trajectory from WS 1920–21 to *Being and Time*, as it was finally drafted in March 1926, inasmuch as kairology and formal indication together constitute the *most* essential, but largely unspoken, core of the book published in 1927.

The two, formal indication and kairology, are of course intrinsically connected. One can literally see this double connection with *Being and Time* by taking a closer look at a hitherto unknown aspect of WS 1920–21, left unreported by the two principal previous commentators on this course, Otto Pöggeler and Tom Sheehan. For after the interruption of his exposition of the formal indication, Heidegger, master pedagogue that he was, recovers his losses by visually illustrating the pedagogical power of his formalizing approach, by baring the underlying structures operative in the koine Greek of Paul's First Letter to the Thessalonians and, in the following semester, in the rhetorician's Latin of Augustine's *Confessions*, Book 10. These two blackboard diagrams of the dynamics of becoming (= being) a Christian graphically illustrate the kind of "prefiguring power" (*vorzeichnende Kraft*) for sketching out and schematizing experiential structures that formally indicative master concepts like intentionality possess. The formalizing of life experience leads to the schematizing and outlining of structures, not so much in the Venn diagrams familiar to us from formal logic, but more akin to the formal grammar that we learned in grade school when we diagrammed the flow and interrelations of phrased sentences. Heidegger's venture into the classical languages by way of formal concretization rather than generic abstraction also demonstrates where he hopes to find his formal ontology of the human situation: not in a formal mathesis of objects à la Leibniz, but in the reformulation of the non-objective grammar of tenses by way of a reexamination of the grammatical structure of the exclamatory impersonals of happenings, middle-voiced infinitives, "reflexive" constructions, the double genitive relationship, transitive-intransitive relations, and the like. The best known fruit of this grammaontology is the strange new language game of prepositional and adverbial schematisms that made *Being and Time* so difficult to read even for native Germans.

But let us now get graphic and take the student's tour through the courses after the First World War, when Heidegger first developed his formally indicative approach to the facticity (occasionality) of life, being, existence. It is time, in short, to examine the diagrams and conceptual schemas that Heidegger actually did draw—or could have drawn—on the blackboard in class, as he began to develop his lifetime topic and how it is to be approached. All three diagrams, which can be found at the end of this chapter, are drawn from as yet unpublished student transcripts of these courses.

Figure 1: The KNS-Schema

It all began in the KNS of early 1919. In the dramatic closing minutes of the course, Heidegger put on the board *by hand* this four-part overview scheme which immensely clarifies the theme and upshot of the entire course for his students. The schema with its double homology (A-A, B-B) at the threshold between the theoretical and the pretheoretical, between the universal and particular, language and being, is however nowhere to be found in the published GA-edition of this course, the so-called *Ausgabe letzter Hand*, "edition of the dead hand," but only in the unpublished student transcripts, and now here, as a visual aid to this discussion.

The diagram is a culmination of the young student Heidegger's seven years of deliberation in the seminal period 1912–19 on the classical problem of the universals and the resulting "logic of philosophy," which condenses thousands of years of the history of philosophy, from Aristotle's analogy of being, which is never a genus but a far more concrete universal, through Duns Scotus' speculative grammar of *haecceitas* (thisness) to the Neo-Kantian Emil Lask's distinction between the constitutive and the reflexive category. The latter is the already mentioned phenomenological distinction between generalization (B-B) and formalization (A-A). The schema seeks to point out that generalization (B-B) yields an abstract "object-like" universal occurring stepwise and typewise according to species and genera drawn from particular lifeworlds or regional spheres of experience. By contrast, formalization (A-A) yields its master formal universal, *das Etwas überhaupt*, the "anything whatsoever," in one fell swoop directly from *das Ur-etwas*, the "primal something" of life as such, life in and for itself. It is thus formalization and not generalization which puts us directly in touch with the very concreteness of being itself. But now we must be careful to distinguish between traditional logical formality, whose *Gegenstand* is always an *Objekt*, and phenomenological formality, whose *Gegen-stand* is first a relation, the intentional relation which defines and articulates life as such, gets at life in and for itself. It is at this point that Heidegger applies his secret weapon, "intentionality" dynamically and formally understood, to name the sheer movement of life, the original self-motion of experience, first in terms of the non-substantifying indexicals expressed in impersonal sentences.

At this stage of Heidegger's development, the formal indication is intentionality itself in its relational sense, in contrast to its content or containment sense, the "worldly something" of a particular lifeworld. If we project forward a bit, in the three drafts of *Being and Time* various permutations of intentionality, understood dynamically as "directing itself toward," become the formal indication designed to guide our concept formation of life, Dasein, being: first the seemingly static being-in-the-world in the first draft of 1924, then the muscularly active conative "to-be" (*Zusein*) in 1925, third the etymologically stressed ex-sistence in the final draft of 1926, and, after *Being and Time* appeared, transcendence in SS 1927. But in KNS 1919, the first fruits of intentionality as a formal indication are expressions that point to the sheer dynamics of the primal something, of the event of life: *Es weltet*, It's worlding, It contextualizes; *Es ereignet sich*, It's properizing, It happens by singling out and appropriating, much like "It's raining" points to the unique global action that is happening right now, here. As we know, the later Heidegger will return to the prolific German impersonals like *es gibt* to specify the sheer activity of being. But in the interim it should be noted that Heidegger transfers the same grammatically indicative function, which like the impersonal sentence points to a sheer impersonal action, to the simple infinitive form, beginning of course with *Sein* (SZ 54), but also with the clusters of Greek and Latin infinitives that we shall soon be examining.

It is important to note that Heidegger, in the period of his juvenilia of 1919–1922, resolves intentionality not only into the two formal senses already noted in the KNS-Schema, the relational sense of life as "directing itself toward" and the containing sense of a world and the objects it holds. These two together receive their completion and fulfillment in a third vectorial sense which, as it were, follows and repeats them in their vectorial course and sense of direction, and so pulls them to a completion, to a *Vollzug*, a "full-pull." A Husserlian would call this moment of intentionality its fulfilling sense, while an Aristotelian reading of its potentialized dynamics would translate *Vollzugssinn* as the actualizing sense. As we know from Husserl, the "vital impetus" of intentionality is the inseparable coincidence of expression and intuition, empty intending and its intuitive fulfillment. The transitional synthesis of fulfilling presence with privative absence is accordingly a temporal synthesis. The moment of fulfillment and coincidence, traditionally called truth, finds its ultimate account in an underlying temporalizing sense that comprehends the other three senses of direction. But this comprehensiveness is already achieved in the covering moment operative in the sense of actualization.

What precisely is this covering moment in less formal language, this overlay that comes from fulfilling an initially empty intention? In response to Natorp's objections against phenomenology, i.e., against the very possibility of accessing and expressing the full immediacy of experience, Heidegger from the start rejects describing this intentional overlay in the divisive subject-object terms of reflexivity, which would serve to dissect and "still the stream" of experience (GA56/57 101). Instead of Husserl's "intuition," modeled after perceptual experience, the early Heidegger variously describes this covering moment as a spontaneous experience of experience which already gives life a certain familiarity with itself, the streaming return of experiencing life upon already experienced life, in this active-passive relation accordingly an immanent historicity already inherent in life itself. This self-referring familiarity of life with itself, this covering moment inherent in life which is formally called its sense of actualization, is the very structure of what Heidegger now calls prereflective understanding, whose inherent familiarity with life phenomenology in its expositions needs but to repeat. But how to repeat this self-retrieving moment without reflective distortion and intrusion? Precisely in the way it repeats itself, by an empathetic going-along-with, a devoted yielding to it to let it be, a *Hingeben* and not a *Hinsehen*, a looking-at, replies the early Heidegger, echoing Lask and Schleiermacher. But this problem of repeating the intrinsic repetition already in life, as well as a description of its intrinsically non-reflective self-reference, will nag the early Heidegger into *Being and Time*, and beyond. A non-reflective "full pull" effectively precludes a satisfactory diagram of the triple-sensed schematism of intentionality, although the image of the "circle" of hermeneutic return continues to be evoked throughout the twenties. It has become the custom to supplement the apparently self-reflective circle of sameness with the image of a spiral of a temporally driven understanding of being, where both the "circular" repetition intrinsic to the lived question of being and the more methodological repetitions of content from Division to Division in *Being and Time* accordingly always repeat something different.

The self-referential character of a prereflective understanding of being is in fact the very first and so most central formal indication in *Being and Time* itself, in the attempt to found an ontology on "the being which in its being *goes about* this very being" (SZ 12). Note that the whole structural problem of the dynamics of a non-reflective repetition of being is totally masked when *es geht um dieses Sein* in this recurrent formula in *Being and Time* is so obfuscatingly translated as "for whom this being is an issue."

The grammar of the earlier triple-sensed schematism of intentionality poses yet another diagrammatical complication, inasmuch as all three senses grammatically articulate middle-voiced phenomena. *Sich richten auf* translates into both active and passive voices, as "directing itself toward" as well as "being directed toward." In the terms of 1919–22, it is either a tending motivation or a motivated tendency, which in *Being and Time* becomes the thrown/throwing project of time. The containing power of intentionality is likewise doubled where, for example, the holding done by an active tendency can in turn become the motive passively entering into other tendencies. The holding sense is thus formally left open, flexible enough to formally indicate both activity and passivity, as diverse as the containment of objects within the meaningfulness circumscribed by a world or region, as well as the captivation of the self by the objects thus "beheld," in attachments that border on addiction (GA61 53, 55). Finally, the sense of actualization can be a matter of both self-actualization and being actualized by another, as we see in the following two diagrams of the self-actualization involved in becoming a Christian.

Figure 2: First Thessalonians

We are greeted by a cluster of Greek infinitives that play the same role as the impersonal sentence in formally indicating a sheer action, both subjectless and objectless, at the destructured non-substantive frontiers of immediate experience. Especially in this Biblical context, γενέσθαι = γενέται = "It's happening, coming to be, taking place!" The middle-voiced infinitives, in their indeterminacy between the active and the passive, in particular point to the amorphous boundary of undifferentiated immediacy. What they verbally indicate is clearly not the sheer "Being" doomed to be an "empty word, full of vapor and smoke" (Nietzsche), but rather an empowering action and δύναμις as the milieu for the emergence of the I from the primal It of "becoming" and "knowing."

This diagram of the most central concepts of Paul's letter reflects Paul's experience of the Thessalonians' already hav*ing*-become followers of Christ, and the concomitant "knowledge" that "goes with" this having-become. Paul's recollection of this "event" in terms of the present perfect tense is itself middle-voiced, inasmuch as their facticity of having-become is not wholly past and bygone, but at once constitutes their present being. This present perfect apriori (SZ 85) of their 'genetic' becoming accompanied by its tacit knowledge, i.e., a pretheoretical understanding of the being of this becoming, thus places the entire diagram squarely on the level of the sense of actualization. Here, "knowing" (or understanding) and becoming (or actualization) are one to the point that becoming makes up the being of knowing, and knowing the very being of becoming.

By proceeding more deeply (i.e., toward the right) into the diagram, we find that this becoming is a *reception* of the Word *accepted* in great tribulation and *appropriated* as our own condition. As if to underscore the ordeal of suffering the Word as a gratuitous destiny, Paul marshals a second Greek word to describe this receiving. This even more "receptive reception" of the "word *of* God" (double genitive) prompts us to acknowledge its operation in us as basically *of* God, *from* God (παρα-λαμβάνειν = "taking-from"), thus as "genitive subjective." With this more receptive reception, we enter into the operative context of God, in a working relation to and from and in His presence. To receive is to change before God and through God. The decisive determination in becoming is accordingly (at the very pivot of the diagram) our "turning *to*" God; the turn from idols here is secondary. This turn then manifests itself in two more temporally concrete receptive stances toward God: becoming through serving God in an authentic everydayness and through awaiting Him in the anticipation of hope.

Even the most superficial explication of the conceptual connections manifested here suggests that the counterstance (*Gegenstand*) *of* "the living and true God" in Christian actualization is hardly an object (*Objekt*) of speculation, but a much more temporally subtle and gratuitous relation of "standing-toward" (*Gegen-stand*), whose richness is to be explicated by theology. For our part, what it means to be "before God" or "in the presence of God," in His Parousia, will depend on whether we understand the "waiting for God" in terms of an objective time or in the vitally persistent element of hope. The sheer persistence of hope leads us to a kairological sense of time. The ultimate message of First Thessalonians is that the καιρός (moment of opportunity, insight, decision) is maintained by, and so contains, a steadfast persistence, "to stand fast in the Lord" (1 Thess. 3:8), to hold out and endure not only in absolute "fear and trembling" but also in and through the everyday works of faith and labors of love. This expectant openness in the travail or waiting is the relational sense connected with the expectation of the Parousia, which stands toward me only in the full temporal actualization of a steadfast life, and not in a momentary passing When. In short, look not to the actual timing of the Parousia in objective history, look instead to yourselves. For the real decision implied in the question of the Second Coming depends on your own life, on your "having become," the status of which "you yourselves know only full well" (5:2), says Paul, as he ex-hortatively emphasizes the full "token-re-flexive" and "indexical" character of the kairological situation of "I, here, now."

Through this dia-grammatic reading of First Thessalonians, Heidegger not only demonstrates how "Christian religiosity lives temporality as such" (his most pressing formal indication here), but also relates this temporality to a kind of authentic everydayness, which gives a stable infra-structure to the Christian travail. This indexical portrayal of the plight of Christian facticity and receptivity at the same time gives us an intimate introduction into Paul's own self-world, in terms of the specific parameters which dynamize his own situation at every moment and motivate his own becoming.

Figure 3: Augustine's Confessions

The Pauline schema for becoming a Christian, centered on the "turn-ing to," emphasizes the actualizing sense. The Augustinian schema, the diagram of SS 1921, stresses the relational sense of "caring," where the infinitive *curare* immediately catches our eye as central to the diagram. But by way of a crucial sentence that Heidegger makes central in his read-ing, sharing center stage with caring is the goal of all our cares, delight, in which the happy life (*vita beata*) finds it locus. *Finis curae delectatio est* (*Enarrationes in Psalmos* 7:9). But trial also resides in the same arena as delight, and in this delight holds two basic possibilities within itself, that of being dissipated into multiplicity or contained in the One. But repeated emphasis on the end of delight gives this diagram of the relational sense a decidedly aesthetic and quietistic tone. Even Augustine's less Neoplatonic and more Christian goal of life in *fruitio Dei*, the enjoyment of God, ulti-mately culminates in repose and quietude. The present life consists of trouble and toil, but in hope it consists of rest. Contrary to Paul's kai-rological reading, the full historical (i.e., unsettling) character of the con-cept of trial is defused in this goal-oriented schematism. Likewise defused is the note in *cura* of *quaero*, seeking, and its concomitant tribulation and anxiety. And yet the onslaught of trial and the insecurity of caring is be-hind Augustine's famous line, *quaestio mihi factus sum*, "I am become a question to myself." If trouble and hardship (*molestia*) belong to the es-sence of facticity, the burden and locus of factic life is in the questing question, and not in the satisfying delight. *Curare* is first divided by the middle voice. Heidegger's basic translation of *curare* here is not yet *Sor-gen*, "caring," but the passive *Bekümmertsein*, "being troubled," and the first response to this facticity of life's troubling situation is the action of taking the trouble to trouble oneself. Even Augustine's usufruct theory of reality, which constitutes caring by dividing it into an active using and receptive enjoying, misses the full passion and action of the life of the self in its trouble and toil, restricted as it is by a Neoplatonic hierarchization culminating in a *summum bonum*. Only the highest good, God, is to be enjoyed, all else can only be of use as a means to that end. Any other end is much like money, and so would be the grossest perversion of life. If the life of man on earth is a trial, then such a life is to be endured and not loved and enjoyed, which is restricted to the *fruitio Dei*. And yet the Psalmist writes: "The fear of the Lord is pure, and endureth forever" (Ps. 18:10 [19:9]). Heidegger thus concludes the course by exploring Augustine's development of this pure fear (*timor castus*) that goes with the enjoyment of God for eternity. The experience of God is an everlasting "mysterium *tremendum* et fascinans," a *terrifying* as well as fascinating mystery, just as Paul's Christian experience of "before God" is from the start a joy wrapped in dread (1 Thess. 1:6).

The Crucifixion Schematism

With this last of two conceptual schematisms of Christian actualization, Heidegger is not yet done with the blackboard in these religion courses of 1920–21. He now prepares for an especially figurative traditional schematism of the experience of God drawn from the devotional manuals, by way of the young Luther's distinction between a theologian of the cross and the theologian of glory. The theologian of glory receives his justification from the oft-quoted Romans 1:20 to see the invisible things of God from the created world. But this long-standing Patristic-Scholastic misreading already finds its refutation in the very next lines of Paul's letter, which identifies this "wisdom" aesthetically oriented to the things of the world as a speculative form of idolatry, and calls such would-be theologians "fools" (Romans 1:21–23). Such an aesthetic gloating, which craves for signs and wonders in the spectacle of the world, not only concludes by calling sensory things God, but is also entangled in the vain since insatiable quest related to the second temptation of Christ (Matt. 4:3) that Augustine calls "the lust of the eyes," curiosity. Instead of observing God aesthetically in terms of objective content, the theologian of the cross, by contrast, like the philosopher of factic life, seeks to actualize the experience of God that is found in a life of care and travail.

Heidegger's gloss of Luther in Catholic Freiburg is quite sparse, but in the coming hours he quietly makes his point on the ways of the theologian of the cross who, like Augustine, seeks to actualize God in human experience as He is found in the historical movement of *confiteri*. For

Augustine likewise urges us to put aside all human constructions and cosmological reifications of God, and instead to divine His Presence in the
sense of actualization of the inner life. It is not in the measures of the
cosmos but in the intimate facticity of life that we discover God in His
infinite nature. "The breadth, and length, and depth, and height" of the
"fullness of God" in the "love of Christ" (Eph. 3:18f.) are not cosmological
dimensions. Breadth is in the reach and full stretch of His good works
whose latitude extends even to one's enemies. Length is in the long-suffer-
ing perseverance to the very end. Height is in the elevation of hope seeking to attain what lies well beyond us. Depth, the part buried and hidden,
is in the unsearchable judgments of God, the secret of freely given grace in
which we are founded and rooted as Christians. These accordingly are dimensions of the sense of actualization of God within factic Christian life,
and can be located, Augustine proceeds, upon the figure of the cross, the
breadth of its transverse beam, its upright beam in its height and length
and hidden rooting. Thereupon drawing the sign of the cross on the blackboard, Heidegger insists that it is not meant to be merely an objectively
palpable symbolism, "a vainly fictitious but usefully true" interpretation,
but is rather an "outline" (formal indication!) serving to restore factic
Christian life back to its full actualization. Augustine is thus here assuming the role of what Luther later calls a theologian of the cross, rather
than a theologian of glory. This theological side to factic life experience is
undoubtedly also what Heidegger had in mind at this time when, a month
later, still caught up in the euphoria of his course, he identified himself as
a "Christian theo-logian," in a letter to his student, Karl Löwith.[4]

Figure 4: The Schematism of Existence in *Being and Time*

Long before I came upon these various conceptual schematisms in
the student transcripts of Heidegger's early Freiburg courses, I had quite
independently developed my own schematism of the hoard of existentials
of Dasein in *Being and Time*, as a pedagogical aid in the difficult problem
of communicating these same esoteric structures to beginning students in
simple terms.[5] This schematism of the existentials articulated into vectorial directions and contexts bounded by horizons is perhaps most reminiscent of the triple sensed schematism of intentionality of 1919–22. It
therefore graphically indicates how intentionality is transformed into its
formally indicative replacement in *Being and Time*, ex-sistence. The three
axes intersecting at the "Here I am!?" point, which situates Dasein in three
equiprimordial existential contexts, correlate with those very same three
senses of intentionality. The horizontal "time" axis, life's irretrievable

movement from birth to death, is now the relational sense, where the internal relation of motive to tendency (or passion to action) is in *Being and Time* replaced by the unified movement of thrown project. The vertical world axis, with its inner horizons or worlds of among-things and with-others, and its outer horizon of in-the-world, is the containment sense. The diagonal axis of the self ever "ahead-of-itself," as the vectorial summation of the other two axes, is poised to sketch the integrating movement of self-actualization that foreruns its own death and retrieves its birthright, bringing both "ends" from the horizons of life to bear upon the fullness of the present moment of opportunity and decision. This move comprehending life from its outermost horizons of death, birth, and the world is the temporalizing sense, "authentic temporality" in *Being and Time*. It is thus not surprising that the majority of the existential categories cluster around the two opposing poles of the diagonal "self" axis. *Being and Time* itself, which for the first time stresses ontology's inescapable reference to the ontical, is, like the Pauline schematism, basically about the actualization sense. On this diagonal axis of self-actualization, we find the inertial drag of falling or decadence holding back transcendence to the self from opening onto its full being, by an involuting closure which clings to the narrow horizon of the everyday, in contrast to the horizon of a lifetime. This opposition between the tendencies of decadence and transcendence recalls Augustine's Neoplatonic juxtaposition between dissipation and containment. The major difference in *Being and Time*, however, is that the schematism is clearly self-centered and not God-centered, it goal resides in the formal fruition of the individual human *being* and not in *fruitio Dei*, its usufructuary relations are guided more by Aristotle's distinction between human making and human deeds, where living well is its own end, in self-referential actions which are performed for their own sake. *Being and Time* is indexically (but not formally) an Aristotelian humanism.

Conclusion

Of course, this diagram of Dasein, just like those of the precursors of Dasein in the religion courses, also has its limitations, stemming from its depictive character: it does not include all of the existentials of *Being and Time*, the less visual ones perhaps; the represented holism, as if viewing life from above or outside, might prompt one to forget the essentially unfinished "underway" character of ex-sistence always developing from the inside out. There are dimensions of Dasein, like intentionality, that resist depiction. *Formal* indications, after all, are not meant to be definitive. They are only meant to suggest a promising "on-set" (*An-satz*) of determination or "first cut" in the inchoate topic of life, in search of promising beginnings and directions that would trace, prefigure, and outline its ever fluent self-motion, like maps drawn lightly in filigree to show the way, only to be recast to point to an entirely new way. Like Superman's X-ray vision of Lois Lane, formality has a way of baring underlying structures, but discreetly, with tact and modesty. The immediacy of experience, if not sayable, is at least showable, and it is worth a lifetime of effort and an endless variety of inductive probes and inducive leads if only to maintain our orientation to the pretheoretical start that is the one matter of thought. At the undifferentiated threshold between language and being, often at a loss for words, one is sometimes left only with "body English," beginning with the primitive gestures of pointing, joining, and disjoining that are already built into words. But not grasping and seizure. Heidegger's arsenal of linguistic gambits is telling not only for its light touch but also for its recurrent fluent topic of never-ending transitions: transitive-intransitive relations, exclamatory impersonals of happenings, infinitives, reflexive reversals, the middle voice and double genitive, the vectorial permutations of prepositions like "in" and "out." Here, we have only wanted to illustrate the peculiar *dia*grammar and largely non-metaphorical 'poietics,' which literally builds with words and thereby naturally prefigures this formal grammar and grammaontology of time and its tensors. By no means has it resolved the question that naturally springs to our lips from this consideration of formality in the early Heidegger, namely: How graphic can you get, how far can one go with this form of scrutiny of the existential spatiotemporality of Indo-European grammars? But before you jump to judgment to head off such a blatant return to the representational thinking that the later Heidegger would roundly condemn, it might be noted that the courses that immediately follow the publication of *Being and Time* begin to abound in such conceptual diagrams.[6]

KNS - SCHEMA

Kriegsnotsemester 1919: "Die Idee der Philosophie und das Weltanschauungsproblem"
Heidegger GA - Band 56/57, *Zur Bestimmung der Philosophie*, vom Anfang bis S. 117.

1. Ergänzung zu S. 116 aus den Nachschriften von F. J. Brecht, Gerda Walther und Oskar Becker:

I. Das <u>vortheoretische Etwas</u>   II. Das <u>theoretische Etwas</u>

A. Das vorweltliche Etwas   B. Welthaftes Etwas   A. Formallogisches   B. Objektartiges
(Grundmoment des Lebens   (Grundmoment bestimmer   gegenstandliches Etwas   Etwas
überhaupt)   Erlebnissphären)
                                                              (motiviert in   (motiviert in
<u>Ur-etwas</u>   <u>Genuine Erlebniswelt</u>   Ur-etwas)   genuiner Erlebniswelt)

2. Mein Überblick über die Vorlesung durch die Folge der Impersonalien:

es gilt (29, 50), es soll (34), "es wertet" (46) — es gibt (62) — "es weltet" (73), es er-eignet sich (75) ..
Erster [Neukant.] Teil   Zweiter [Phän'log.] Teil

FIGURE 1

Lecture Course by Privatdocent Heidegger:
WS 1920-21 – Introduction to the Philosophy of Religion
Text being diagrammed: Paul's First Letter to the Thessalonians
Lecture date: January 28, 1921

Oskar Becker's version of the "FORMALE'S SCHEMA" in Greek:

$$\gamma \epsilon \nu \acute{\epsilon} \sigma \theta \alpha \iota \left\langle \begin{array}{l} \delta \acute{\epsilon} \chi \epsilon \sigma \theta \alpha \iota \\ \epsilon \pi \iota \sigma \tau \rho \acute{\epsilon} \phi \epsilon \iota \nu \\ \pi \alpha \rho \alpha \lambda \alpha \mu \beta \acute{\alpha} \nu \epsilon \iota \nu \end{array} \right.$$

εἰδέναι

δουλεύειν   τὸ ἔργον τῆς πίστεως
    ὁ κόπος τῆς ἀγάπης
ἀναμένειν   ἡ ὑπομονὴ τῆς ἐλπίδος

Ἰῆ   ※   Χϛ

ἔμπροσθεν
τοῦ θεοῦ

English rendition:

becoming   receptive appropriating
    turning to
    receptive receiving

knowing

serving   working of faith
    labor of love
waiting   patience of hope

Jes. ※ Chr.

before
God

Textual Source	in 1. Thessalonians
'knowing' (13), becoming (12 times)	passim
receptive receiving, receptive appropriating	2:13
turning to	1:9f
waiting, serving	1:9f
patience of hope, labor of love, working of faith	1:3
before God	1:3

FIGURE 2

Lecture Course by Privatdocent Hiedegger:
SS1921 – Augustine and Neoplatonism
Text being diagrammed: Augustine's <u>Confessions</u>, Book 10
Lecture date: end of June 1921

The "Übersichtsschema der Phänomene" in the Latin (O. Becker's notes):

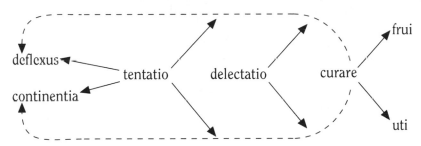

English:

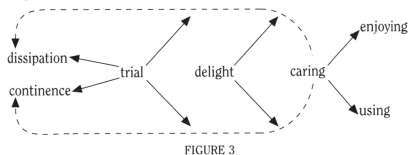

FIGURE 3

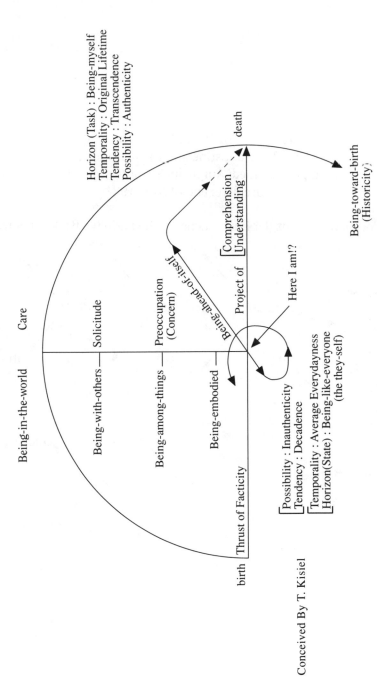

THE SCHEMATISM OF EXISTENCE

Being-in-the-world   Care

Horizon (Task) : Being-myself
Temporality : Original Lifetime
Tendency : Transcendence
Possibility : Authenticity

Solicitude

Being-with-others

Preoccupation
(Concern)

Being-among-things

Being-embodied

Being-ahead-of-itself

Project of

Comprehension
Understanding

Here I am!?

death

Being-toward-birth
(Historicity?)

Possibility : Inauthenticity
Tendency : Decadence
Temporality : Average Everydayness
Horizon(State) : Being-like-everyone
(the they-self)

birth   Thrust of Facticity

Conceived By T. Kisiel

FIGURE 4

Part V

Aristotle

11

Being and Time: A "Translation" of the *Nicomachean Ethics*?

Franco Volpi
Translated by John Protevi

1. If Aristotle Were Alive Today

A respected scholar of ancient philosophy, Jonathan Barnes, once said—indeed wrote—that if Aristotle were alive today he would undoubtedly live in Oxford, taking a few side trips to Louvain perhaps. A no less respected Italian specialist in Greek philosophy retorted that, if Aristotle were to have lived in our century, he would have at least spent his vacations in Padua. Overworking the anachronism, I would add: had Aristotle lived in our century, he would not have lived in Oxford for the sake of discussion with Jonathan Barnes, nor would he have stayed over in Louvain or Padua; rather, he would have preferred philosophizing in the Black Forest with Heidegger.

What this bon mot is trying to convey is clear: Heidegger's work is the most significant philosophical confrontation of Aristotle in our century. To understand this claim, one must of course momentarily put aside an interest in the historical truth of the Greek world and instead pay attention to the unbiased and uninhibited way that Heidegger seeks to draw from Greek philosophy as the first and originary repertoire of philosophizing. He does not wish to determine the historical facts of the matter; rather, he seeks to appropriate—and this means for all of us and the entire century—the founding questions first thought by the Greeks and especially by Aristotle, in order thereby to obtain a fundamental doctrine. Thus Heidegger has not only restored to us a sense for the problems that Aristotle first set forth (and indeed Heidegger has done so with a radicality unmatched since Hegel), but he has also simultaneously shown us again, after the crisis of grand philosophy, what it means to philosophize in the grand style.

With this as my background, my reflections on Heidegger's confrontation of Aristotle will try to make my opening bon mot convincing in all its truth. In particular, I will examine this confrontation of Aristotle in the crucial ten-year silence preceding the publication of *Being and Time*.[1] I intend thereby to show how the genesis of the terminology in *Being and Time* can be explained by paying attention to its zealous appropriation of Aristotle's practical philosophy. To put it in a nutshell, I will ask the following provocative question: is *Being and Time* a "translation" of the *Nicomachean Ethics*?

2. Methodological Access To and Thematic Focus of the Early Heidegger's Confrontation of Aristotle

A brief word is necessary at the outset to sketch the general context in which I see Heidegger's confrontation of Aristotle at this time playing itself out. This confrontation is methodologically and thematically determined in the following manner. 1) Methodologically, it is stamped by the critical comportment that generally characterizes Heidegger's mode of access to traditional philosophy up until his turn; termed "phenomenological destruction" in *Being and Time*, it is understood together with "reduction" and "construction" as one of the three essential components of phenomenological method. This term is thus to be used not in the trivial sense of everyday speech, but in the sense of de-construction, that is, as a dismantling [*Abbau*] and dissection of the essential elements of traditional philosophic constructions, in order to effect a truly radical reconstruction [*Wiederaufbau*]. 2) Thematically, Heidegger's confrontation of Aristotle up until *Being and Time* is oriented to the basic problems that also stand at the center of his *magnum opus*. These are at least three in number: the question of truth, the question of the mode of being of human being (*Dasein*), and the question of time. The unitary horizon within which these questions are treated is undoubtedly the horizon of the question of being, which is here still developed in the sense of the question of the being of beings and thus as the question of the determination of the fundamental modes of being.

Of these three major problems (truth, Dasein, time), I will primarily treat the one that is for me decisive, namely, the problem of Dasein, that is, the problem of the ontological constitution of human life (its fundamental and unitary manner of being). How does Heidegger come to pose this question, and indeed pose it in the horizon of the question of being that occupied him ever since he read Brentano's *Von der mannigfachen Bedeutung des Seienden nach Aristoteles*? My supposition, in which I consider Heidegger's autobiographical portrait "Mein Weg in die Phänomenologie" (SD 81–90/74–82) not as a self-stylized account of his school years but as a sincere testimony, is that he arrived at the three major problems of truth, Dasein, and time (and indeed in their systematic nexus) by investigating the ontological problematic of *on hos pollachos legomenon*, "being as said in many ways." Overall, the leading threads of Heidegger's philosophical questioning in the twenties developed, as he himself explains, in the search for the unified basic sense of being sustaining the manifold meanings of beings; it may be supposed further that in pursuing this goal Heidegger tested each of the four basic meanings of beings as to their ability to function as the sustaining basic sense of being. Quickly dissatisfied with the ousiological solutions of the question offered by the Scholastic tradition (and by Brentano), Heidegger immersed himself during his ten-year silence before *Being and Time* in investigating the meaning of beings in the sense of the true (to which, by the way, Brentano had also directed his gaze). Here one can clearly see a pervasive intention to test whether this meaning can serve as the basic sense of being. Heidegger's 1922 introduction to a projected book on Aristotle, "Phänomenologische Interpretationen zu Aristoteles (Anzeige der hermeneutischen Situation)" (PIA), and his course of WS 1925–26, *Logik. Die Frage nach der Wahrheit* (GA21), as well as the conclusion to his course of WS 1929–30, *Die Grundbegriffe der Metaphysik. Welt-Endlichkeit-Einsamkeit* (GA29/30), and the first part of the course of the following semester, *Vom Wesen der menschlichen Freiheit* (GA31), make manifest just how decisive the equation of truth and being, worked out in interpreting Aristotle, was for Heidegger. With the same intention of discovering the unitary basic sense of being, Heidegger later also sounded out—so goes my supposition—the basic meaning of beings in the sense of *dynamis* and *energeia*, potency and act, as one can see in the course of SS 1931, an interpretation of *Metaphysics* Theta, 1–3.[2]

I will now pursue the way that Heidegger, starting from his interest in the problematic of the manifold meaning of beings, arrives at a reconstruction of Aristotle's practical philosophy, in particular, of the questioning in Book Zeta of the *Nicomachean Ethics*. One should consider at the outset the circumstance that Heidegger's access to Aristotle's practical philosophy takes place in the context of an investigation of beings in the sense of the true, and that this investigation was determined by Heidegger's in-depth confrontation of Husserl's *Logical Investigations*. This confrontation can now be followed in all its details in the course of SS 1925, *Prolegomena zur Geschichte des Zeitbegriffs* (GA20).

3. The Phenomenological Treatment of the Phenomenon of Truth and the Locus of Truth in Aristotle

In critically examining the theory of truth developed by Husserl in the *Logical Investigations*, Heidegger comes to the conviction that, as is also already clear in Husserl's own work, the judgment, the assertion, a *synthesis* or *diairesis* of representations, is not, as is traditionally maintained, the original locus of the appearance of truth, but merely a localization that, compared with the ontological depth of the happening of truth, constricts the phenomenon. For this reason he wants to place in question the three traditional theses on the essence of truth, which maintain that: 1) truth is an *adaequatio intellectus et rei*, an adequation of intellect and things; 2) the original locus of its appearance is the judgment as a combining or separating of representations; and 3) the authorship of these two propositions is to be attributed to Aristotle.

With his thesis that not only relational and synthetic acts, but also monothetic acts of simple apprehension can be true, Husserl had already put in question the traditional concept of truth as an *adequatio* occurring in a judgment; consequently, he distinguished propositional from intuitional truth, assigning the latter a founding and more original role. Moreover, Husserl had introduced a decisive innovation, namely, the idea of a categorial intuition; in analogy with sensory intuition, it was to explain the cognitive apprehension of the elements of a judgment, which traditionally belong in the sphere of the categorial. Their identification therefore exceeds sensory intuition. These reflections in the sixth of Husserl's *Logische Untersuchungen* provide Heidegger with clues to push ahead in the direction indicated here. Thus he comes to distinguish terminologically the pure logical meaning of "being-true" from the more original, ontological meaning of "truth." He is here convinced that this distinction can be found prefigured in Aristotle. In Heidegger's eyes, the originary ontological depth of the phenomenon of truth is in fact the determining one for Aristotle, even though the latter surely also knew the more limited meaning of being-true belonging to assertion. Heidegger's questioning of the traditional concept of truth, set in motion by Husserl's phenomenology, thus proceeds by way of a strongly ontologizing interpretation of certain key texts of Aristotle, such as *De interpretatione* 1, *Metaphysics* Theta 10, and *Nicomachean Ethics* Zeta, which he seeks to restore to their full ontological force.

Heidegger thus arrives at something like a topology of the loci of truth. In drawing it up, he assimilates certain basic determinations of the Aristotelian concept of truth and restores their validity through an ontologizing refiguration. In broad outlines this topology can be summarized in the following manner: 1) Beings themselves [*das Seiende selbst*] are primarily true in the sense of their being-manifest, being-uncovered, being-unconcealed. Here Heidegger re-establishes the Aristotelian determination of *on hos alethes*, being as true. 2) In addition, then, Dasein, human life, is true in the sense of its being-uncovering, that is, on the basis of its comportment that uncovers beings. Here Heidegger assimilates the Aristotelian determination of the *psyche hos aletheuein*, the soul as being-in-truth. Furthermore, Heidegger believes he can with some justification draw from Aristotle, especially from the 6th Book of the *Nicomachean Ethics*, a complete phenomenology of the uncovering comportments, of being-in-the-truth, belonging to human life. These comportments can be detailed as follows. The human *psyche*, Dasein, can in the first place be uncovering through its specific capacity of combining that belongs to *logos*; this occurs in the five ways of being-in-truth, of the *aletheuein* of *psyche* that are named in *Nicomachean Ethics* Zeta: *techne*, technique; *episteme*, science; *phronesis*, prudence; *sophia*, wisdom; *nous*, reason. But the human *psyche*, Dasein, can also be "intuitively" uncovering in immediate apprehension; it can be this in *aisthesis*, sensation (which is related to its *idion*, its proper object, and is thus *aei alethes*, always true) or in *noesis*, reason (which apprehends its object through as it were a *thinganein*, *thigein*, a touching, and thus cannot be false, but rather only actualized [*vollzogen*] or, on the other hand, absent in *agnoein*, ignorance). The above-named combining comportments are grounded in the immediately uncovering ones. 3) Finally, what is true is the explicit form of *logos*, namely, the *logos apophantikos*, the predicative assertion in its two forms of *kataphasis* and *apophasis*, affirmation and denial. The being-true of the assertion is, however, a derivative mode of the originary happening of truth in which it is grounded.

By means of this ontologizing reconstruction of Aristotle's theory of truth, Heidegger disengages the understanding of the phenomenon of truth from the structure of the assertion and opens up the ontological horizon in which he unfolds the problem of beings in the sense of the true. It is in the context of the analysis of this basic meaning of beings in the sense of the true that Heidegger devotes himself in the twenties to determining the basic ontological structure of human life, Dasein, the *psyche*, and indeed in its specific character of being-uncovering. It is thus in the context of the typical phenomenological question of the basic constitution of "subjectivity" that Heidegger interprets the Aristotelian determination of *psyche* as *aletheuein*, being-in-truth, and it is with this combination of a phenomenological mode of access and Aristotelian components that he gets the existential analysis of *Being and Time* going.

But why and whence the central significance of the *Nicomachean Ethics* and the concept of *praxis*, action, as I have announced this in the title of this chapter? There are to my mind more than enough indications that lend weight to the thesis that Heidegger had recourse to the *Nicomachean Ethics* and the Aristotelian determination of *praxis* in order to extricate himself from the problems into which he must have been necessarily led by Husserl's concept of transcendental subjectivity.

4. The Nicomachean Ethics as an Ontology of Human Life: Focusing and Ontologizing of Praxis

In Heidegger's eyes, Husserl's determination of subjectivity actually leads into a real dead end, namely, into the aporia of the I belonging to the world and the simultaneous constitution of the world by the I. Heidegger could not subscribe to Husserl's proposed solution that sharply distinguished between the I that psychologically belongs to the world and the I that transcendentally constitutes it, between the reality of the one and the ideality of the other. Certainly, Heidegger agreed with Husserl that the constitution of the world could not be explained by recourse to beings that have the same manner of being, the same ontological status, as the world. Nevertheless, he distanced himself from Husserl's determination of transcendental subjectivity, since he thought this was acquired primarily and one-sidedly within the horizon of a privileging of rationalistic and theorizing determinations.

As is clear from his analysis of the phenomenon of truth and from his topology of the loci of truth, Heidegger was convinced that theory is only one of the manifold uncovering comportments in which human beings have access to and grasp beings. Next to and before *theoria*, theory, stand, for example, *praxis* and *poiesis*, action and production, which are likewise modes of the comportment of human being to beings. Consequently, Heidegger went back anew to Aristotle who, according to Heidegger, remained open to the multiplicity of Dasein's uncovering comportments and was in fact able to describe them on human life's own terms. In an interpretation of Aristotle on which he had worked since 1919 and whose traces can be seen in the Marburg courses and in *Being and Time*, Heidegger interprets Book Zeta of the *Nicomachean Ethics* in this direction. He thereby discovers in Aristotle's treatment of the intellectual virtues just so many determinations of human life, which Husserl had never recognized or thematized in its full richness. It is precisely in the horizon marked out by the resistance to Husserl's theorizing concept of the subject and by the productive assimilation of the wealth of Aristotle's thought that the existential analysis of *Being and Time* is to be understood. So I think one has a good chance of understanding Heidegger's philosophical work in the twenties if one rereads the Dasein-analysis anew in the light of the phenomenological interpretation of Aristotle, especially of the *Nicomachean Ethics*, and if one here pays attention to the fact that the fruits of Heidegger's eager assimilation of Aristotle often turn up in places where there is no mention of Aristotle. I would like to highlight just this Aristotelian horizon of some basic determinations that can be unearthed and singled out in the existential analysis. I do this by showing correspondences that reveal how Heidegger, in several basic terms of his analysis, reappropriates, reformulates, and reactivates the substantial sense of just as many basic concepts of Aristotle's practical philosophy.

The first and in itself fairly conspicuous correspondence is that between the three ways of the being of beings differentiated in *Being and Time* (namely, readiness-to-hand, presence-at-hand, and Dasein) and the Aristotelian determinations of *poiesis, theoria,* and *praxis*. 1) *Theoria*, theory, is the comportment of an observing and describing knowing, which sets itself the goal of apprehending the truth of beings, and whose specific knowing is *sophia*, wisdom. When Dasein holds itself in this disposition, it encounters beings in the manner of being that is presence-at-hand (a term with which Heidegger recovers in an ontologized translation the Aristotelian determination of *ta procheira*, what is close at hand; see *Metaphysics* Alpha 2, 982b 12–13: *dia gar to thaumazein hoi anthropoi kai nun kai to proton erxanto philosophein, ex arches men ta procheira ton atopon thaumasantes*, "for it was astonishment that now and at first led human beings to philosophize; at the start they were astonished at strange things close at hand.") 2) *Poiesis*, production, is the comportment of productive, manipulative activity, whose goal is the production of things made, artifacts. The corresponding disposition is *techne*, technique, whereby we encounter beings in the manner of being that is readiness-to-hand. 3) Finally, *praxis* is action that occurs for its own sake and whose goal is a unique type of success, namely, *euprattein*, acting well. *Phronesis, prudentia*, prudence, is the knowing that belongs to and orients it. With Heidegger, the uncovering comportment of *praxis* is enlisted, according to my thesis, to serve as the distinguishing mark of the manner of being belonging to Dasein.

Before we consider this last correspondence, which seems to me to be the most significant but at the same time also the most thought-provoking one, a general remark on the nature and style of Heidegger's reappropriation of Aristotelian concepts is necessary. It is obvious that Heidegger not only re-establishes the above-named determinations, but also at the same time reinterprets and transforms them to a great extent. The most noticeable alteration seems to me to be the emphasizing and indeed absolutizing of the ontological feature of the determinations, that is, their interpretation as ways of being in the strict sense, such that all ontic meaning is excluded in principle. What interests Heidegger is manifestly not the individual *praxeis* (actions), *poieseis* (producings), and *theoriai* (theorizings), but rather only the ontological potential of these determinations. Certainly, one can find points of contact in the Aristotelian text on which to fix this ontologizing interpretation. For instance, if one were to read the differentiation between *poieseis* and *praxeis* in Book Zeta of the *Nico-*

machean Ethics in conjunction with *Metaphysics*, Theta 6, one would clearly recognize that an ontic differentiation is not at issue, that is, a differentiation with reference to individual actualizations of action, where there are *poieseis* on the one hand and *praxeis* on the other. Rather, this differentiation has an ontological character; it distinguishes two different ways of being that do not ontically stand out from one another. For example, giving a speech can have the way of being of a *poiesis* (in the sense of the production of *logoi*, statements, by an orator), but it can also have the way of being of *praxis* (in the sense of a political speech); on the ontic level this difference does not appear. It is thus exclusively this ontological content of the Aristotelian concepts that Heidegger extrapolates and absolutizes in distinguishing the modes of being of Dasein, readiness-to-hand, and presence-at-hand.

Another decisive transformation is the displacement of the hierarchy in which the three determinations stand to one another. Among the possible ways of being-uncovering belonging to *psyche, theoria* is no longer viewed as the highest vocation that is to be preferred for human being. Rather, in the context of Heidegger's ontologizing, *praxis* in each of its components is elevated to serve as the basic determination of the way of being belonging to the human being, that is, as its ontological structure. On the basis of this structural shift, the relation of *praxis* to the other two determinations is altered as well: readiness-to-hand (in which the determination of *poiesis* is taken up) and presence-at-hand (which corresponds to *theoria*) characterize the ways of the being of beings not of the order of Dasein; these are conditioned by the ways in which Dasein comports itself to beings, either in an observational and veridical or in a manipulative and productive manner. Still another hierarchic structuring ensues. *Poiesis* and *theoria* are now both understood as two ways of a comportment that Heidegger names "concern." With this move Heidegger arrives at two things: on the one hand, he exhibits a unitary connection between readiness-to-hand and presence-at-hand, *poiesis* and *theoria* (and between these two and Dasein); on the other, he makes it possible for himself to maintain that *theoria* is not an originary comportment, but merely a derivative mode of *poiesis*.

Ontologizing, hierarchical displacement, and unitary ordering are thus the decisive refigurations that underlie Heidegger's assimilation of Aristotle's concepts of *praxis, poiesis*, and *theoria*. There still remains the question, however, why I interpret *praxis* as the determination that forms the basis for characterizing the manner of being belonging to Dasein. I do so because it seems to me that the characterization of Dasein and its basic structure is conducted in an eminently practical horizon obtained from an ontologically reinterpreted concept of *praxis*.

5. Dasein as Praxis: Aristotle's Practical Philosophy as the Watermark of the Existential Analysis

It seems to me that the characterization of the manner of being of Dasein as a to-be [*Zu-sein*], which Heidegger introduces at the beginning of the existential analysis (*Being and Time*, §§4 and 9), can in the first place be interpreted in a practical sense. With this characterization Heidegger wants to say that Dasein, human life, originally comports itself to its being not in a contemplative, observational, and veridical attitude, that is, in a theorizing, reflexive introspection of itself, in an *inspectio sui*; rather, it comports itself to its being in a practical-moral attitude, in which its being is itself in each case at issue in the sense that it has to decide about this its being and, before its willing or non-willing, take on the burden of this decision. This means that Dasein primarily relates itself to its being not in order to fix and describe it in its essential traits (e.g., as *animal rationale*), but rather in order to decide what is to be made out of it, to choose and actualize [*vollziehen*] its own possibility from among a variety of possibilities. Here Dasein cannot bypass the burden of this decision, this choice, and this actualization. In this sense Dasein has to take upon itself the unbearable lightness of its being.

Only the insight into the basic practical-moral structure of Dasein makes it possible to apprehend the unifying context of the other determinations of Dasein that Heidegger discovers. For example, only in this way can one understand why Heidegger designates the mode of "disclosedness" by a determination drawn from practical philosophy, namely, care. Care, with which Heidegger is able to comprehend more primordially the phenomenon that Husserl had characterized as intentionality, is in my view the ontologizing of the basic trait of human life that Aristotle designated with the concept *orexis dianoetike*, noetic desire. The proof for this claim? It would suffice to collate the places in those Aristotelian texts commented upon by Heidegger in which the term *orexis* or the verb *oregomai* appears so as to be able to establish the important point that Heidegger translates them each time with his term "care." The most conspicuous passage in this regard is the beginning of the *Metaphysics*, whose first sentence, *pantes anthropoi tou eidenai oregontai phusei*, reads in Heidegger's translation: "the care for seeing is essentially inherent in the being of human being" (GA20 380/275; SZ 171/215). What should be noted here is, of course, the correspondence between *orexis* and "care," but also the ontologizing of *pantes anthropoi*, all human beings, with the phrase, "in the being of human being."

Heidegger draws several fundamental conclusions from the ontologizing of *praxis* and the practical determination of the manner of being belonging to Dasein: 1) Against the metaphysical privilege of the present and presence, Heidegger advocates the priority of the future. Precisely because Dasein comports itself to itself in a practical sense by deciding about its being, this being that is at stake is in each case futural. For, as Aristotle teaches in the *Nicomachean Ethics,* deliberation (*bouleusis*) and decision (*prohairesis*) always have to do with something futural. 2) The being to which Dasein comports itself is Dasein's own being that is in each case proper to it; Heidegger therefore ascribes to it the character of "mineness." I suspect that through this determination he takes up and ontologizes the sense of a basic trait belonging to the types of knowing appropriate to *phronesis,* which is characterized by Aristotle as an *hauto eidenai,* a knowing of oneself, and thus as a knowing about *ta hauto agatha kai sumpheronta,* one's own goods and expediencies (*Nicomachean Ethics* Zeta, 1140a 26–27, 1141b 34). 3) In view of all these findings Heidegger advocates a radical differentiation between the ontological constitution of Dasein and that of beings not of the order of Dasein, for only Dasein is constituted as a to-be, only Dasein comports itself to itself in an eminently practical-moral sense. On the basis of this differentiation Heidegger can then criticize the insufficient radicality of the metaphysical distinctions between human being and nature, subject and object, consciousness and world, above all because they are not based on insight into the originary ontological constitution of Dasein. 4) Finally, the practical determination of the manner of being of Dasein implies a critique of the traditional theory of self-consciousness as an observational and reflexive self-knowledge accomplished by the inward turning of human being into itself. According to Heidegger, the identity of Dasein is rather constituted by recovering itself in its to-be, in its action as well as in its knowing, and this occurs not merely in the transparency of the rational, but just as much in the opacity of moods.

My thesis has now acquired precise contours: the understanding of the practical structure of human life, which Heidegger claims to be the ontological constitution of Dasein, originates from a type of speculative sedimentation—in the starting point and indeed in the terminology of *Being and Time*—of the substantial determination of the moral life and being of human being carried out in the *Nicomachean Ethics.* We now can see more clearly what else, in addition to the treatment above, comes to the fore regarding Aristotle. To begin with, the general horizon of the Aristotelian problematic is reconstituted. In the context of *episteme praktike,* practical science—a term that Heidegger, I would like to emphasize, translates with "ontology of human Dasein"—Aristotle deals with human life as *praxis,* and this in turn as the type of movement (*kinesis*) that is specific to human being. *Praxis* is not simple *zen,* that is, mere life and

self-preservation of life, but rather *bios*, that is, a life-project that is unfolded beyond the self-preservation of life with a view to the problematic
choice of a form of life and indeed the good and best possible life (*eu zen*,
living well) and of the appropriate means to such a life. This means: as
zoon politikon logon echon, the social-political living being having *logos*,
human being is supposed to deliberate (through *bouleusis*), choose, and
decide (through *prohairesis*) which ways and means of its life are to be
taken hold of with a view to the best possible form of life for it. As is
known, it is the prudent, wise human being, the *phronimos*, to whom
deliberating well (*euboulia*), deciding well, and acting well (*euprattein*)
belong, and who thus attains happiness (*eudaimonia*).

This fundamental intuition is taken up and reactivated by Heidegger
through a reinterpretation in which its basic sense undergoes an ontologization. In fact, Dasein is also for Heidegger the exceptional being to
whom its being (in Aristotle's ontic expression: *ta hauto agatha kai sumpheronta*, one's own goods and expediencies) is in each case an issue, and
indeed in the sense that it must decide about the possibilities and ways of
its actualization, even in the extreme case where this decision is a willing-
not-to-decide and an evasion of its having to decide. The actualization of
existence can take place authentically only when, hearing the call of conscience, Dasein recognizes this having to decide, and thereby its to-be, and
takes this upon itself in the projection of its possibilities, thus accepting
the difficult weight of its being as its ownmost without relinquishing this
with the help of the "they."

To be sure, the Heideggerian ontologizing of *praxis* in each of its
determinations necessarily leads to fundamental alterations and displace-
ments. I do not, of course, want to suppress or indeed to dispute this
ontologizing, but neither do I want, so to speak, to turn it against myself
as an objection. Thus, in laying out the correspondences that, despite all
the differences, stand out between Aristotle and Heidegger, I would like to
push on and show how, in the determination of the disclosedness of Dasein, Heidegger again goes back to the Aristotelian understanding of the
moral being of human being.

As the basic trait of Dasein's way of being, disclosedness obviously
arises from the originary unity of Dasein and world. The unitary sense of
disclosedness inclusive of the existentials is care, whose three major determinations are moodfully finding oneself [*Befindlichkeit*], understanding,
and discourse. To comprehend these concepts one should consider that
Heidegger here reappropriates several fundamental determinations of the
human being as an acting being and, ontologically deepening them, radicalizes them in the context of fundamental ontology. With *Befindlichkeit*,
he magnifies in an ontological-transcendental sense that determination of

the actor which has been thought in the traditional theory of affects as the moment of the passivity, receptivity, finitude, and corporeality of the actor. A significant piece of evidence for this association I am suggesting is the fact that in his interpretation of Augustine the young Heidegger translates the term *affectio* precisely with *Befindlichkeit* (BZ 11). Analogously, then, Heidegger—so goes my further assumption—ontologizes in "understanding" the active, projective moment of productivity and spontaneity.

Without examining at this time the third equiprimordial moment of discourse, I would like to suggest that the two moments of *Befindlichkeit* and understanding correspond to two central determinations of Aristotle's theory of action. *Befindlichkeit* represents for Heidegger the ontological ground for the possibility of ontic moods [*Stimmungen*]; in it Dasein opens itself up with regard to its to-be, is placed before its "that it is and has to be" (as one reads in §29), and indeed in such a way that its whence and whither remain hidden from it; this is its thrownness. What Heidegger wants to indicate here is that to the structure of Dasein belongs not merely the pure, transparent, and rational moments of spontaneity and self-determination, but equally a murky and opaque side that has been understood traditionally as the affective, and whose ontological condition of possibility Heidegger seeks to determine with the concept of *Befindlichkeit*. In other words, the identity of human life is actualized, according to Heidegger, not simply in the transparence of purely rational self-presentation and self-determination, but equally in the inaccessible opacity of its moods. Telling for my thesis concerning Heidegger's relation to Aristotle is the fact that his discussion of *Befindlichkeit* (§29) explicitly refers to the doctrine of *pathe*, affects, expounded in the second book of the *Rhetoric*. Heidegger extricates this doctrine from the context of oratory in which it stands for Aristotle, and voices the conviction that it is "the first systematic hermeneutic of the everydayness of being-with-one-another," after which no progress was made in the ontological interpretation of the affects until phenomenology (SZ 138/178).

The determination of understanding (§31) is in my view the complementary moment to *Befindlichkeit*, that is, it is the ontological ground for the possibility of the active and spontaneous ontic determinations of Dasein. It is the determination that expresses the productivity of the can-be of Dasein. In contrast to the commonplace meaning of the word in which understanding is a specific type of knowledge, Heidegger has this term characterize the basic ontological constitution of Dasein, insofar as Dasein is activity and self-determination, that is, has the character of projection and thus anticipates and shapes its own being in an eminently practical stance. That Heidegger determines understanding as an ontological mode of the can-be in its existentiality, that he ascribes to it the structure of projection, that he defines its meaning as "being able to do something" or "being able to manage something"—all this shows that the Heideggerian determination of understanding is to be interpreted in relation to a practical horizon. Certainly, as a rigorously ontological determination it precedes the distinction between theory and practice. But this by no means prevents Heidegger's characterization of it from being oriented to a specific frame of reference, and this is surely not that of *theoria*, but rather precisely that of *praxis*. So it is no wonder that practical elements nevertheless slip through Heidegger's ontological filter. If one consults, for instance, the discussion of understanding in the SS 1927 course *Die Grundprobleme der Phänomenologie*, in which the filter of Heidegger's repression of the ontic is even more encompassing than in *Being and Time*, one finds there the statement—very telling for my thesis—that understanding "is the authentic sense of action" (GA24 393/277). And in light of my thesis one then also understands why Heidegger is so anxious to shield the determination of understanding from any epistemological misinterpretation in the sense of a type of knowledge opposed to explanation. It is obviously intended to safeguard the practical character of understanding.

The practical horizon of Heidegger's concept of understanding is also clearly visible in the determination of the knowing that accompanies and guides understanding. Understanding has the structure not only of a projection, but also of a knowing, a "sight" that orients the projection. This is the knowledge and sight of one's self in which Dasein achieves self-transparency or, as Heidegger puts it, "perspicuity" [*Durchsichtigkeit*]. Heidegger has recourse to this term, as he himself explains, in order to avoid the misinterpretation of the selfhood of Dasein within the horizon of perception, apprehension, inspection, intuition, that is, within the context of the theorizing type of understanding that defines traditional theories of self-consciousness.

Without wishing to overlook or indeed deny the obvious and deep differences involved, I want to point out here another correspondence, which should be taken *cum grano salis*. In the background of Heidegger's determination of understanding stands the substantial sense of that which is conceived in Aristotle's theory of action as *nous praktikos*, practical reason. Just as this functions as the complement to *orexis*, desire, and is essentially bound up with it, so understanding is the determination that complements *Befindlichkeit*. Certainly, understanding is not confined to a theory of action, but concerns Dasein in its entirety; thus it is developed as "concern" (encompassing theoretical as well as poietic comportments) in relation to the things of the environing world, as "solicitude" in relation to the with-world of others, and in relation to itself as the "for-the-sake-of-which" (an ontologizing of the Aristotelian *hou heneka*, for the sake of). Understanding has its unitary roots in care, and is thus seated in a completely different way than *nous praktikos*. And yet, in thematizing the complementarity and equiprimordiality of *Befindlichkeit* and understanding, of passivity and activity, receptivity and spontaneity, of thrownness and projection, relucence and prestructuring, Heidegger has again raised in an ontologically radicalized context the same problem that Aristotle took up in the sixth book of the *Nicomachean Ethics* when he stated that human being is the *arche*, the origin, which is simultaneously *orexis dianoetike* and *nous orektikos*, noetic desire and desiderative mind (1139b 4–5). And just as Aristotle sees the bond of *orexis* and *nous* as always occurring in the medium of specifically human *logos*, so Heidegger maintains the equiprimordiality of discourse with *Befindlichkeit* and understanding.

Heidegger of course insists on the deep ontological radicality of his problematic and thus on the differences between Aristotle and himself; for instance, he declares that care precedes any differentiation of theory and praxis (§41) and therefore cannot be explained on the basis of a return to traditional concepts such as will, craving, and inclination. But the fact that he finds this declaration necessary betrays that in the end a thematic relationship between care and the Aristotelian concept of *orexis* persists; exactly this is what makes necessary the distinction he sets forth.

In the context of these correspondences one then understands also why Heidegger, as Gadamer has reported, could exclaim regarding the difficulty in translating the term *phronesis*: "it's the conscience!"[3] He was obviously thinking of the proper determination of conscience as the locus in Dasein at which its to-be, its practical-moral determination, announces itself to Dasein. (Heidegger also believes he can see the same problem in the Kantian determination of the "feeling of respect.") In *Being and Time* (§§54–60) conscience is characterized as the locus of an "attestation on the part of Dasein to its authentic can-be"; this attestation takes place when, in the attitude of wanting-to-have-a-conscience, Dasein hears the call of conscience and thus authentically exists. Analogously, *phronesis* for Aristotle forms the horizon within which good action, *euprattein*, becomes possible. And thus just as in Aristotle *phronesis* requires an acquaintance with the *kairos*, so in Heidegger conscience is constantly related to the *Augenblick*, the moment.

There are thus good grounds for saying that conscience in Heidegger corresponds to *phronesis*, that it is indeed the ontologizing of *phronesis*. In fact, one can even cite the passage in the *Nicomachean Ethics* that offers a decisive motive for ontologizing *phronesis*. It is found in the conclusion of the fifth chapter of Book Zeta: after having defined *phronesis* as *hexis meta logou alethe*, a true habit involving *logos*, Aristotle explains that even this definition is insufficient for fully comprehending the essence of *phronesis*, for it is more than a *hexis*, a habit. Remarkably, Aristotle does not say what it is supposed to be then, but merely offers evidence for his assertion: one can forget every *hexis*, but *phronesis* can never be forgotten. In interpreting this passage—so goes my surmise—Heidegger must have attended to precisely the question as to what "more" *phronesis* might genuinely be. If it is more than a *hexis* and cannot be forgotten, then it must be a characteristic of *psyche* itself; it has to be ontologically understood.

One can persist in laying out such correspondences and show how Heidegger also performs a similar ontologizing of other determinations of Aristotle's practical philosophy. But I have to be content here with simply enumerating them. With the term "mineness" Heidegger ontologizes, as I have previously indicated, the determination of *phronesis* as an *hauto eidenai*, a knowing of oneself. Furthermore, the characterization of Dasein as the "for-the-sake-of-which" represents in my view the ontologizing of the *hou heneka* (for the sake of which) of *praxis*; it is proper to *praxis* not to be for the sake of something else (*heneka tinos*), but rather to have its principle and goal (*hou heneka*) in its own self, and since Dasein is ontologized *praxis*, it must have the character of the *hou heneka* in a special manner. For this reason Heidegger characterizes Dasein as the for-the-sake-of-which. Finally, the determination of "resoluteness," which is often interpreted in connection with contemporary decision-theory, is in my view the ontologizing of the substantial sense of Aristotle's *prohairesis*, decision, with the difference that the latter designates a specific act in Aristotle's theory of action, while resoluteness amounts to a basic trait of the very constitution of Dasein. This correspondence is also confirmed by the fact that Heidegger translates *prohairesis* with "resoluteness." Here I can merely refer to a significant passage in the SS 1926 course *Grundbegriffe der antiken Philosophie* (GA22) where Heidegger interprets the passage from the second chapter of Book Gamma of the *Metaphysics* in which Aristotle distinguishes the philosopher from both the dialectician and the sophist. Heidegger translates: "Dialectic and sophistry have in a certain manner put on the same clothes as philosophy, but they are fundamentally not the same; sophistry only appears to be such. Dialectic is differentiated by its type of possibility: it has only limited possibilities, it can only experiment; philosophy, on the other hand, gives understanding. Sophists are differentiated by the nature of resoluteness to scientific research: they are not serious." One should notice that with "resoluteness to scientific research" Heidegger translates the Greek *prohairesis tou biou*, a choice of life.

6. From Heidegger to Aristotle and From Aristotle to Us

I hope that if the correspondences indicated above have not in fact proven my general thesis about Heidegger's re-establishment of basic questions and determinations of Aristotle's practical philosophy, then they have at least indeed rendered it plausible. But seeing that I have concentrated almost exclusively on, as it were, the pieces of the puzzle, that is, on the individual correspondences between specific concepts and terms, I would like in conclusion to come back to the general correspondence between the understanding of human being in Aristotle's practical philosophy and Heidegger's analysis of Dasein. I want to do this in the form of a citation that very clearly shows Heidegger's attempt to return to a proximity with Aristotle and also to bring Aristotle closer to himself. Near the end of the SS 1926 course *Grundbegriffe der antiken Philosophie* Heidegger concludes his discussion of the five ways of being-true belonging to *psyche* with this definition of human being: "*anthropos* [human being] is the *zoon* [living being] to which *praxis* and moreover *logos* is fitting. These three determinations go together: *zoe praktike tou logon echontos* [the practical living being that has *logos*] is the essence of human being. The human being is the living being that has, in accord with its type of being, the possibility to act." The continuation of the text is likewise very significant: "This very same determination of human being turns up again in Kant: the human being that can speak, that is, act with grounds." The equation of "speak" and "act with grounds" should be noted here—a hint for interpreting the existential called "discourse"?

In re-establishing the Aristotelian determinations, Heidegger certainly radicalizes them from an ontological point of view, but having completed this ontologizing, he takes a critical distance from Aristotle, maintaining that Aristotle did not get as far as comprehending the unitary ontological nexus of the basic uncovering comportments belonging to human *psyche* (i.e., *theoria*, *praxis*, and *poiesis*), that he was unable to see the basic ontological constitution of human life, and that this was because he remained captive to the horizon of a naturalistic, chronological, and thus non-kairological understanding of time that denied him insight into originary temporality as the ontological ground of human *psyche*. Even the celebrated aporia of the relation of time and the soul that Aristotle after all explicitly posed as a problem, and of which Heidegger offers us a magisterial interpretation, does not suffice in Heidegger's eyes for reinterpreting Aristotle beyond the naturalistic metaphysical understanding of time. And yet even here there is again something that counts, namely, that it is precisely Aristotle who, at least on an ontic level, anticipates—so it may once again be surmised—the intuition that Heidegger later magnifies ontologically with the equation of Dasein and temporality. One sees this in a truly controversial passage from *De anima* Gamma 10 where Aristotle seems to ascribe to human being, in distinction from other living beings, the characteristic of *aisthesis chronou*, the sensation of time. The reason and occasion for my surmise is the fact that Heidegger knew this passage well and commented upon it in the following manner in the context of his interpretation of *praxis* as the basic trait of human life: "The opposition of drives and authentically resolute, reasonable action is a possibility only for living beings who have the possibility of understanding time. Insofar as that which is alive is abandoned to drives, it is related to *to ede hedu*, that which immediately is there and stimulates; drives strive uninhibitedly towards this, toward the present, the available. However, since *aisthesis chronou*, the sensation of time, is found in human being, the latter has the possibility of presenting *to mellon*, the future, as something possible for the sake of which it acts."

Heideggerians will say: in this manner Heidegger is simplified and levelled down to Aristotle such that in Aristotle a correspondence, indeed even an anticipation, is found for Heidegger's decisive philosophic discovery in *Being and Time*, namely, the identification of the unitary ontological structure of Dasein with originary temporality. Conversely, non-Heideggerians will perhaps protest that what is passed off as Aristotelian has really little to do with him and appears more like speculation scraped together with an Aristotelian implement.

To these objections I would answer: I was clear about this risk, but still had to take it. If I have given the impression of levelling Heidegger down to Aristotle or vice versa, this entails merely a perspectival distortion. Contrary both to the old existentialist interpretation and to the new interpretation that somewhat carelessly would like to see in Heidegger's thought only the overcoming of metaphysics, I simply wanted to show, in the example of his early confrontation of Aristotle, how intensely Heidegger thought through the metaphysical tradition, confronted its decisive and founding moments, and thereby restored to our century a sense for the fundamentality of a confrontation of the Greeks.

12

The Place of Aristotle
in the Development of Heidegger's Phenomenology

Walter Brogan

Heidegger tells us in "My Way to Phenomenology" that his reading of Aristotle was decisive in his more radical formulation of the project of phenomenology (SD 81–90/74–82). The appropriation of Aristotle, he says, led him to develop his own unique "way" to phenomenology. In this chapter, I will attempt to show the Aristotelian character of Heidegger's early phenomenological pathway, a pathway that led to the publication of *Being and Time*. Specifically, I will examine two seminal texts that substantiate, I believe, the claim that a careful investigation of Aristotle was a necessary and crucial part of Heidegger's phenomenological project.

The first of Heidegger's early texts that I want to examine is the recently recovered lost manuscript, often referred to as the 1922 "Aristotle Introduction," which has now been published in English translation under the title "Phenomenological Interpretations with Respect to Aristotle: Indication of the Hermeneutical Situation."[1] This essay, more than any other, capsulizes the Husserl-Aristotle-Heidegger interconnection and offers a remarkable opportunity to gain insight into the development of Heidegger's thought. It was on the basis of this Aristotle manuscript that Heidegger obtained his first academic position in Marburg. In this text, in the context of his retrieval of Aristotle, Heidegger already lays out in programmatic form many of the key components of *Being and Time*.

One of the most significant "discoveries" that Heidegger recovers from Aristotle is a phenomenological, non-propositional, originary sense of truth. In the second text that I will treat, his 1925–26 *Logik* course, published with the subtitle "the Question of Truth," Heidegger first discusses Husserl and then Aristotle before developing his own philosophy. On a superficial level, we see here that Heidegger's lengthy treatment of the problem of truth in Aristotle comes directly after his discussion of Husserl's critique of psychologism and before his own analysis, in the second part of the course, of the question of truth as the question of time. But I will try to show, through an analysis of §§10–14 of this text (GA21),

213

that this placement is more than just a happenstance. Heidegger works through Aristotle to dismantle the priority of truth as assertion in the post-Aristotelian tradition and show its derivative character in relation to phenomenological truth in Aristotle. The decisive turn toward Aristotle that is evident in the sketch of his project that he gives in his 1922 "Aristotle Introduction" unfolds in the 1925–26 *Logik* course and lays out the basis for the rethinking of truth and time in his 1927 publication of *Being and Time*.

I. Heidegger's Discovery of Aristotle: The Lost Manuscript

Heidegger claimed on many occasions that his discovery of Aristotle was decisive for the genesis of *Being and Time* and the development of his own philosophy. In "My Way to Phenomenology," he wrote: "The clearer it became to me that the increasing familiarity with phenomenological seeing was fruitful for the interpretation of Aristotle's writings, the less I could separate myself from Aristotle and the other Greek thinkers. Of course, I could not immediately recognize the decisive consequences my renewed preoccupation with Aristotle would have" (SD 86/78).

Much of Heidegger's teaching prior to the publication of *Being and Time* was related to his work on Aristotle.[2] Indeed, many of his early students went on to become Aristotle scholars in their own right.[3] The recent recovery of the seminal essay manuscript on Aristotle, which Heidegger had sent to Marburg and Göttingen in support of his nomination for a position at these institutions, should help to further our understanding of the important link between his early work on Aristotle and the development of his own method of phenomenology.

The essay "Phenomenological Interpretations with Respect to Aristotle" falls into three distinguishable parts. In the first part, Heidegger gives his explanation of philosophy as hermeneutic phenomenology and addresses the implications of this for a genuinely philosophical interpretation of the history of philosophy and of philosophy itself as historical. Heidegger here argues that "every interpretation must over-illuminate its thematic object" (PIA 252). Only then, by retracting this excessive illumination, can it possibly hope to restore the appropriate boundaries to the object of investigation. Heidegger practices such a hermeneutics in this essay. Only after illuminating, through a phenomenological destruction that is carried out in the second part of the essay, the context of his own inquiry—the problem of facticity—does Heidegger turn, in the third part of his essay, to his interpretation of Aristotle. There he shows that Aristotle posed the question of factical human life in an originary way.

Phenomenology, Heidegger demonstrates, is not just a hermeneutically naive appeal to the things themselves, as if it were a matter of recapturing or approximating some lost original position. It is the self-address of factical life. Heidegger's pervasive claim in this essay is that philosophy is life, that is, the self-articulation from out of itself of life (PIA 246). This is why he says that genuine philosophy is fundamentally atheistic (PIA 246). To the extent that theology takes its cue from outside of factical life, it can never do philosophy. All philosophical research remains attuned to the life situation out of which and for the sake of which it is inquiring. The first sections of this essay are entirely about this situatedness, this overwhelming facticity, that defines the being of life.

What Heidegger emphasizes in his "destruction" of the history of philosophy in the second part of the essay is not the ability to point out the various trends and interdependencies that can be traced through the history of philosophy. The more important task of destruction is to bring into focus and set apart the central ontological and logical structures at the decisive turning points of history. This is accomplished through an originary return to their sources. Though the source is never an "in itself" that is captured, so that Aristotle's philosophy could no more capture this origin than could that of his followers, Heidegger considers the turning of Aristotle's thinking to be especially crucial (PIA 251). This is certainly, at least in part, because of Aristotle's peculiarly phenomenological bent.

One of the clearest indications of the legitimacy of efforts that have been undertaken to show the link between the genesis of *Being and Time* and Heidegger's work on Aristotle[4] is found in this lost "Aristotle Introduction" when Heidegger announces that the question he is asking as he approaches Aristotle's texts is the question of the being of human being (PIA 238). He makes clear that his projected reading of Aristotle is to be a *Daseinsanalytik*, a questioning about the being who experiences and interprets being. His aim in reading Aristotle is to uncover *der Sinn von Dasein*, the various "categories" that constitute the way of being which in some manner always already is in relationship to being. The fact that Heidegger looked to Aristotle for help in clarifying the many ways of being and knowing that found the possibility of hermeneutic phenomenology complicates the traditional explanation of Heidegger's destruction as a critical movement back through the history of philosophy in order to overcome it. In the case of Aristotle at least, Heidegger discovers that the very future of philosophical thinking has already been prepared for but covered over by the scholasticism of the tradition.

It is indeed fascinating and informative that so many of the sections of *Being and Time* were already so cogently and compactly presented here in outline form. Already in place in 1922 was much of the philosophical vocabulary of *Being and Time*, words like *Sorge, Besorgen, Umwelt, Umgang, Umsicht, Bedeutsamkeit*, etc. This is the text where Heidegger begins to speak of the notion of *Verfallen* (PIA 242, 248), not as an objective event that happens to one but as an "intentional how," a way of being directed toward life that constitutes an element of facticity and is the basic character of the movement of caring. What is not so clearly fixed in these pages are the strategy and divisions of *Being and Time*. Themes like death, the averageness of *das Man*, individual existence as possibility, truth as unconcealing wrestling from concealment (a notion of truth, as we will see, that Heidegger attributes to Aristotle), the tendency of life to drift away from itself in fallenness—these themes are not so clearly divided in these pages as they are in *Being and Time*. In some regards, in reading this essay, one gets a better sense of the interdependence of each of the parts of *Being and Time*.

Heidegger does use the words *Dasein* and *Existenz* in this text, but for the most part he speaks of factical life. Facticity is the fundamental way of being that constitutes human life. The movement of facticity is what Heidegger calls care. Existence as a possibility of factical life can be retrieved only indirectly by making facticity questionable. To do this—to make factical life questionable—is the task of philosophy. Heidegger calls this questioning movement of retrieve the decisive seizing of existence as a possibility of factical life. But this existential return is also a recovery from the movement of fallenness that Heidegger calls an *Abfall*, a descent from itself, and a *Zerfallen*, a movement of dispersion and disintegration. Yet, it is the movement of fallenness that Heidegger says opens up world and that he explains through the care structure.

Existence, as a countermovement to the movement of fallenness, has a temporality other than that of being in time. It occurs in the kairological moment and is not called care but the *Bekümmerung*, the worry or affliction of being. Yet, in a footnote, Heidegger suggests that we should think care (*Sorge*) as middle voice, as a movement and countermovement, as a recoil of being, in which case, he says, *Bekümmerung* would be *die Sorge der Existenz*, the care that belongs to existence (PIA 243). This probably marks the place of a major shift in Heidegger's thinking that prepared the way for *Being and Time*. The back and forth play between fallenness and existence that is signalled by Heidegger's invocation of the middle voice also indicates a suggestion by him on how to read the relationship between facticity and existence, even in his later work. As care reveals being in the world, so the existential moment opens Dasein to the whole of being. But the existential *Gegen* (against) and the *Nicht* (not) belong essentially to factical life. Heidegger suggests that Aristotle recognized this in his notion of *steresis* (privation, lack), and even remarks that Hegel's notion of negation needs to be returned to its dependency on Aristotle's more primordial conception (PIA 266).

It is not just accidental that Heidegger inserts a discussion of death and the finality of life into the text at this juncture. Factical life is such that its death is always somehow there for it, always in sight as an obstinate and uncircumventable prospect of life. What Heidegger discovers here, then, is a kind of double movement, a movement and a countermovement, a dual movement of descent and recall that unfolds the span within which human life is. This middle-voiced *kinesis* is the very being of life, as Heidegger later shows in his brief exposition of Aristotle's *Physics*.

One of the most powerful aspects of this essay is Heidegger's cogent characterization of the nature of philosophy. One could argue that the entire essay is about this. Philosophical research is the taking up and carrying out of the movement of interpretation that belongs to factical life itself. Philosophy is radical, concernful questioning because it positions itself decisively at the movement wherein the threatening and troubled character of life—*die Bekümmerung der Existenz*—unfolds and holds itself steadfastly out towards the questionability of life. Thus Heidegger describes philosophy as letting the difficulty of life gain articulation by engaging in an original, unreduplicable and unrepresentable moment of repetition. Philosophical movement discloses the movement of being of factical life as possibility. The investigation of this movement, this peculiar kinetic activity, this original *kinesis*, is the primary task of philosophy.

Having thus prepared the way through an illumination of his phenomenological position and a destruction of the history of philosophy, Heidegger announces in outline form his plans for an interpretation of Aristotle that spans the corpus of his works. It was this section that led Natorp to anticipate that Heidegger would be working out a revolutionary new reading of Aristotle during his time in Marburg.

A significant portion of Heidegger's treatment of *Nichomachean Ethics* VI in this essay has to do with the meaning of *aletheia* and its relationship to *logos* and *legein*. Already we find an indication of the analysis of truth that Heidegger later offered as part of his 1925–26 *Logik* course, which, as I will demonstrate in the next section of the chapter, is one of the places where Heidegger worked out in detail part of the interpretation of Aristotle that he outlines in this "Aristotle Introduction." As in the *Logik* course three years later, Heidegger here distinguishes two modes of truth. Noetic truth necessarily comes before and makes possible the kind of truth displayed in the propositions of language. This more original revealing discloses the *arche*, that out of which beings emerge and that which is responsible for their being. This is the original *legein*, the gathering into the oneness of being. Aristotle calls this *aletheia*, this mode of

revealing, philosophical thinking—*he theorei to on he on*, a beholding of
being as being, a letting beings be seen as being. Philosophical knowledge
is in part a simple standing in the presencing of being. Aristotle says that
no falsity or deception is possible in this noetic way of seeing, this pure
Hinsehen.

But then Heidegger makes a rather remarkable claim. He says that for
Aristotle this noetic activity that secures the truth of being is fulfilled
principally in two ways of revealing: *sophia* and *phronesis* (PIA 255). It
seems to me to be important that Heidegger does not see Aristotle as tying
phronesis to *sophia* in a hierarchical way, such that *sophia* would be the
disclosure of the *arche* while *phronesis* would be the equivalent of an apophantic disclosure of the synthesis of the true and the false. Both *sophia*
and *phronesis* are noetic activities, ways of carrying out and fulfilling our
primordial relationship to what is. What then is the difference between
sophia and *phronesis*?

Heidegger translates *phronesis* as *Umsicht* (circumspection). He also,
at least implicitly, offers *Sorge* (care) as another translation. In this text,
Sorge has mostly to do with one's dealings in everyday factical life, what
Heidegger calls *Sorgensumsicht*. *Phronesis*, Heidegger says, is only possible because it is primarily an *aisthesis*, an ultimately simple view of the
moment (the *kairos*). It is in *praxis* that this phronetic moment of factical
life is revealed in its fullness and brought to fruition. But this practical
situating of oneself out of an overview of one's being is for Aristotle a
noetic activity, a *nous praktikos*.

What specifically concerns Heidegger here is the movement of this
practical disclosure wherein the fullness of the moment of being can draw
back into itself its past and future. *Phronesis* is here understood as a way
of having one's being, a *hexis*. Just as the earlier analysis of death belonged to the broader context of the question of factical life, so here also
Heidegger has not so clearly worked out the primacy of the future and of
possibility as he later formulated it in *Being and Time*. In this regard, his
analysis here of Aristotle's project is still close to Husserl and Husserl's
concept of phenomenology. But, as Heidegger shows, this way of having
its being that belongs to human factical life is peculiar. There can be no
pure, atemporal beholding of such being since the moment of *praxis* is
always already caught up in the coming to be of factical life. Therefore,
phronesis, though a kind of revealing and a noetic activity, is always a
doubling regard ("*eine Doppelung der Hinsicht*") (PIA 255). Human life is
situated in this double regard of *phronesis* as a way of revealing and seeing
being.

In contrast, Heidegger's treatment of that other noetic activity,
sophia, is ambiguous. He clearly attempts to show that *sophia* has to do

with divine movement, not with the movement of living being. The mistake that has pervaded the tradition, namely, interpreting all being on the basis of what is revealed in *sophia*, has its roots in a certain theological bias, as Heidegger explained in an earlier part of this text. But it also can be traced to a certain ambiguity on the part of Aristotle. To a certain extent, Aristotle's concern about divine being causes him to define living being in terms of what it is not, that is, in terms of its not being necessary and eternal. This blocks, to some extent, a more original and positive access to the peculiar kind of movement and being that is involved. But, more importantly, Heidegger also finds that the dominant concern with the movement of production—with *techne* and *poiesis*—and the use of produced beings as exemplary beings in Greek ontology has its roots in this same failure to properly distinguish *sophia* and *phronesis*. For *sophia* is also the appropriate basis for the way of revealing that is involved in production. In other words, *techne* is governed by a kind of understanding of *sophia*. When beings from *techne*, produced beings, become the exemplary beings for the analysis of living being, then this double movement we discussed earlier, the movement of being whose *arche* belongs to its being and does not come from outside, gets separated out into two separate regions of being and beings.

Heidegger goes from his brief study of Book VI of the *Nichomachean Ethics* to a study of *Metaphysics* I, 1, 2 and *Physics* II, 1. In his analysis of the *Metaphysics*, he points to the primacy Aristotle gives to experience as the fund out of which philosophical thinking arises and returns. What Heidegger finds here is an understanding of *sophia* understood in relation to *techne*. What he shows is that for Aristotle philosophy is the desire to know more, *mallon eidenai*, to see more, to go beyond, to explore, to propel oneself more deeply into the thick of things. *Sophia* is not some sort of abstract theoretical activity. Heidegger says: "The why has a primordially practical sense" (PIA 262). That is, the why that the one who is wise asks is practical and not theoretical.

It is easy to see the importance of Heidegger's brief analysis of these crucial passages from Aristotle. Natorp was certainly correct to recognize that they imply the need for a radical rethinking of the entire traditional understanding of Aristotelian philosophy. But he could not have predicted that these discoveries about Aristotle would provide the foundation for Heidegger's own treatment of concernful dealings, understanding, and being in the world in a very contemporary philosophical work called *Being and Time*. The driving questions of this book are the question of the possibility of a genuine revealing and disclosure, that is, the possibility of truth, and the question of time. But even these overriding questions are generated out of his reading of Aristotle, as we will see by turning to the course

on Aristotle that he delivered in Marburg three years after he wrote the
"Aristotle Introduction" that won him the position there.

II. The 1925–26 Logik Course: The Place of Aristotle in Heidegger's Development of the Question of Truth

Heidegger treats the question of truth in Aristotle in §§11–14 of the
Logik course. Prior to these sections, Heidegger shows the contribution
that Husserl made to a genuine, philosophical understanding of truth
through his critique of psychologism. However, in §10 Heidegger raises
countercritical questions concerning Husserl's critique of psychologism
that serve to delimit Husserl's analysis and demonstrate the inadequacy of
Husserl's own approach to the question of truth. He summarizes the results of his investigation in three points: 1) The question of truth is not a
question that belongs to psychology, as Husserl has shown in his critique
of Brentano. Rather, truth must be understood *"aus den Sachen selbst."* 2)
Die Sache selbst is not given by representation (*Vorstellung*) but by intuition (*Anschauung*), i.e., truth is not determined primarily in propositions
or in relation to assertion, but in respect to knowing as intuition. 3) The
question of the connection between truth of assertion and truth of intuition requires a return to Aristotle (GA21 109).

According to Heidegger, Husserl establishes that the proposition, as
the structure of relation, is founded on the truth of the intuition of identity. Of Husserl's sense of the truth of identity uncovered in intuition,
Heidegger says: "With Husserl's typically encompassing and fundamental
formulation of intuition, namely, the giving and having of a being in the
fullness of its bodily presence [*Leibhaftigkeit*], a formulation that is not
restricted to any particular field or possibility but instead defines the intentional meaning of the concept of intuition, Husserl has thought
through to its end the great tradition of Western philosophy" (GA21 113).
But the critical point that Heidegger raises is the question of why intuition
is held to rank prior to the logic of assertion in the matter of truth and
what the nature of this *Vorrang* is. In other words, what is the relation
between the truth of intuition, the immediate givenness of the being fully
in itself, and the truth of assertion, the givenness of the being in this or
that way, as this or that. Despite Husserl's claim of priority for intuition,
the character of the relationship between intuition and assertion is determined from the model of propositional relationships. Thus the kind of
truth that is held to be a founded mode comes to dominate the way of
thinking about truth in general. Husserl has uncritically taken over the

structures of assertion, such as synthesis and correspondence, into his way of thinking about what is uncovered in all modes of truth.

Before turning to Aristotle in an effort to untangle this confusion, Heidegger goes through a destruction of the history of philosophy to show that philosophy has, throughout its history, stood in one way or another under the dominance of two fundamental starting points of ancient thought: *logos* and *nous*. Yet, Heidegger calls the equation of the truth of *nous* with the truth of intuition and that of *logos* with *Satz* (logical proposition) "a somewhat comical linkage of Greek and German" (GA21 110).

Heidegger's project in investigating Aristotle is an attempt to win back in an originary way an access to the phenomenon that lies before the truth of *logos* and the truth of *nous*, and that constitutes the sphere in which both are brought into relation and, in fact, the horizon out of which both emerge. This turns out to be time. Thus, in the second division of this text, Heidegger exposes how time governs the meaning of *nous* and *logos*, of the truth of being and the being-true or being-false of beings in relation to their being (GA21 207). This recognition, developed out of a rethinking of Aristotelian notions, provides the basis for Heidegger's treatment of time as the central focus of *Being and Time*. His investigation of truth in Aristotle leads him to raise the question of time as the central issue of phenomenology. In order to retrace Heidegger's path, I will first consider his treatment of the *logos* of assertion which is the kind of saying (*kataphasis*) related to beings and a thinking (*dianoia*) about beings (GA21 138). Then I will examine the saying which is always presupposed and which has already occurred in the disclosure of assertion, namely, the simple saying (*phasis*) and thinking (*nous, noein*) which reveals the being as such, as it is in itself, that is, the being of what is. Finally, I will try to pose the question of the relation of these two ways of thinking and saying, a question which provides the impetus for Aristotle's and, I believe, Heidegger's thought.

In this regard, both Aristotle and Heidegger attempt to situate their thinking about truth in a confrontation with Parmenides, who forbade those who would truly think from bringing together the two paths of speaking in regard to being. This is why Heidegger says that it is only through Aristotle that Parmenides's fundamental thinking can be understood (PIA 252). For Aristotle, it is precisely this contra-diction, this prohibition, that is the matter of thinking for the philosopher. He calls it "the *arche*, the source of all understanding that everyone must have before he can relate knowingly to beings" (*Metaphysics* 1005b15). He calls this *arche*, this principle, "the most certain of all" in the sense that it allows beings to be seen in their being. Aristotle has several formulations of this law of non-contradiction, all of which are important, but I will call attention to that formulation at 1005b29: "It is impossible for the one who understands to tolerate or permit it to be said together in relation to one and the same being, and at the same time [*hama*], that it be and not be."

Heidegger's discussion of this *aporia*, this impasse, at the heart of thinking hinges on the question of the relationship of *nous* to the *logos* of assertion. He shows that the issue at stake in Aristotle's discussion of *nous* and *logos* is truth, the disclosure of the being of beings. In turn, falsity, non-being and non-disclosure, is central to Aristotle's concern about truth. What Heidegger finds in Aristotle is, first of all, a radical separation of the saying of *nous* and the way of addressing beings involved in assertion. He then traces in Aristotle the decision to rank *nous* higher and prior to the other kind of discourse. Finally, he identifies the source of the untransversable difference between these two, a source which Aristotle himself failed to articulate but which he nevertheless stood near to, and which can be deciphered in the above formulation of the law of non-contradiction. The source is there named *hama*, a word for time and togetherness in time. In other words, with the importation of time into the Parmenidian radical separation of these two discourses, Aristotle uncovers the horizon of the twofoldness of Parmenides's thought, a horizon that, in turn, went unnoticed and unthought in the metaphysical tradition that followed Parmenides.[5]

The *hama* opens up the relationship of being and non-being. Non-being can be disclosed precisely because being, the *eidos*, is always already uncovered before we come to the disclosure or non-disclosure of beings in time. The "not being said together" and the "not being at the same time" indicate the derivative character of the *logos* of assertion, which always follows after an original disclosing and is true to the extent that it brings together what can and does belong together in this disclosure and keeps apart what is not together (GA21 146). But, although derivative, this kind of *logos* does uncover beings, those whose way of being is such that they can be with other beings in the way of being-together or synthesis. Aristotle differentiates beings on the basis of their way of being revealed. Thus there are beings which can be only in that they are together with another, namely, those whose way of being is *symbebekos*, accidental. Black can only be, for example, in that it belongs to another being. Other beings such as natural beings do have their being in themselves and are therefore always already what they are, before they are together with others. These beings are *aei on*, enduring being in itself, one and unchanging (GA21 180). They do not have their being as a coming and going with another. Nevertheless, natural beings, while dwelling simply in their being, do have their being in a way that can be shaped and determined in different ways. But it is only by being directed out from their *eidos* that they become determined in this or that way. It is in the *logos* of assertion that the disclosure of a natural being as having this or that characteristic takes place. This disclosure first of all takes the form of addressing the being as something, a making specific and thematic what the being is and keeping it in this disclosure. Such a disclosure takes the being as already disclosed in its present-at-handness and identifies it as something.

Naming can be an example of this kind of uncovering—a horse, a dog, a deer, etc. What is presupposed and taken for granted in naming is the prior disclosing that makes it possible for me to recognize this particular being as having such and such a being. This requires that I already know and be in touch with (*noein* and *thigein*) the being of beings (GA21 182). The being-true of my identification depends on the being's truly having the kind of being I have ascribed to it. For I could be mistaken. Heidegger uses the example of a man walking in the woods who sees something approaching. It is a deer, he says. But he is mistaken. Upon getting closer and focusing his attention on the object, he discovers that it is after all only a bush (GA21 187).

Thus, according to Heidegger's analysis, both the naming that identifies what the being is and the activity of ascribing properties to the being are part of apophantic discourse or assertion. Neither are the kind of noetic revealing of being that it always presupposed in this other way of revealing. Husserl's treatment of truth remained, therefore, confined to a mistaken assumption that all truth is found within the framework of assertion.

It may not be immediately clear how it is that naming involves *synthesis* and *diairesis*, the primary characteristics of the *logos* of assertion. But, for example, in exhibiting the being as a deer, there is a denying to it all those ways of being that are not what a deer is. Likewise, letting the being be seen in this way ascribes to the deer those characteristics which it can have and which are appropriate to its way of being. Such affirmation and denial belong to naming precisely because synthesis and division are the ways in which beings such as natural beings give themselves to us to be disclosed. Assertion involves first of all the making present of a being. Only on the basis of such a way of disclosing a being can it further delineate the being in terms of categorial properties. The statement, "the board is black," says that being-black is something that belongs to the board. Something, namely a board, is seen as something else, as black. In being seen as black, the board is seen as not gray or yellow.

But the structure of this kind of revealing is even more complex in that two beings—board and black—must be already disclosed before putting them present at hand together. Why must this be so? For one thing, being black does not belong necessarily to the being of the board. The latter could still be what it is if it were a green board (GA21 137). It must already be seen as separate from and other than its blackness before it can be put together with it. Also, the mode of being of these two kinds of beings is different. Black never is except as together with a being that has its being in itself, whereas the board has its being in itself, albeit not in the same way that natural beings do.

The upshot of Heidegger's analysis of the *Metaphysics* up to this point is that the revealing of both substantial being and accidental being belongs to the *logos* of assertion. Naming, as well as ascribing properties to what is named, belongs to apophantic discourse. But both presuppose another disclosure, one that is prior to the representation of something as something. The simple saying of *nous* is not what occurs in the disclosure of substances in relationship to accidental properties. The revealing of beings as present at hand, substantial beings is a derivative meaning of truth.

The possibility for the being true and false of beings arises with the *logos* that is operative here, as well as with the way of being that is uncovered in this way of revealing beings. In Heidegger's rendition, Aristotle says: "For it is not for the reason that we in our uncovering take you in your being present at hand as white that you are white, but it is on the basis of your being at hand as white, that is, because we let this being at hand as white be seen in our speaking, that our comportment uncovers" (*Metaphysics* 1051b6–9/GA21 175). What makes our comportment towards a being such that it is false is that our discourse does not reveal the being as it truly is in its togetherness with others. It covers over the being. It lets the being be shown as other than it is. But even in being led astray in this manner there is only a partial closing off of the being. All being false is always also a letting the being be seen in a privative way. The not being seen is due both to the *logos* and to the being that is disclosed. It can be true, when I say it, that the board is black, and yet false tomorrow after the painters come.

On the other hand, it can never be true, as Aristotle points out, that a triangle has two right angles. The way of being of a triangle resists such determinations (GA21 177). The being in itself, the *eidos*, directs what can and cannot and what does or does not belong together with it. But for this to be so, non-being must, in fact, belong to the very character of the *eidos* that is disclosed in advance. The privative character of being cannot be only a factor of apophantic discourse or synthetic judgment. A more deep-rooted, prior falsity belongs to the very heart of being. This non-being is the source of the failure to disclose that lies at the heart of the kind of uncovering that Aristotle describes in his treatment of *apophansis*, the propositional statements of assertion.

Aristotle differentiates between two different ways of being and thus two different ways of revealing beings. Beings which can be other than they are have their being as a being together with. Synthesis is the way these beings are revealed in their togetherness. However, beings that have their being in themselves cannot have their being as such revealed in this way. Their being is *aei on*, an always being, always (as long as they are) not being other than they are. Such beings are made manifest in their being, not through *kataphasis*, not by a saying something in respect to something else ("*kata*"), not in a bringing together of something in terms of something else, but in a simple saying (*phanai*) and being in touch with (*thigein*), which is given by *nous* and to *nous* in the selfsame showing of the being that is uncovered. Heidegger says that Aristotle here posits the identity of thinking and being in a way that is yet to be understood, but which Aristotle insists cannot be understood as in any way parallel to the uncovering of being in the synthesis of assertion (GA21 190). In synthesis, the uncovering and discovering that takes place is also a covering over. Being false as well as being true belongs to this way of disclosing. Whereas, in the truth of *noein*, in the disclosing that takes place in the thinking and seeing of being in itself, no being led astray (no *Täuschen*) is possible. One either sees it or one does not. Here the alternative is not between a knowing that discloses truly and a knowing that fails to disclose what is intended, but between knowledge and ignorance. For Aristotle, the possibility of revealing something falsely lies in the *synthesis* character of assertion, which does not belong to the seeing of the being as what it is in itself.

I must always already have the being as a whole in a predeterminate way and retain the being as it is in itself in advance of any determination of the being as having this or that specific character. The calling attention to the being as manifest in a determinate way presupposes the prior disclosing of the *eidos*, the aspect in which it shows itself as such. The being together of something as something requires a turning back to the being as it is in itself, which must always already be disclosed in order for the truth of synthesis to occur. But what is turned back to cannot itself be disclosed in a synthesis, for it is because of this prior disclosure that synthesis is even possible at all.

For Heidegger, it is here that the essential question lies. Dasein's *Besorgen*, its concern for beings, involves this coming back to that with which Dasein is always already dwelling, that which governs and first of all makes possible the unity of thinking and being, the logos of synthesis, and the relationship of the two. Aristotle did not make this thematic, although it is the horizon upon which his philosophy is based. In Aristotle's presentation, the relationship between *nous* and *logos* and between being and beings is one of priority. The presentation of being is prior to and governs the manifestation of beings. Aristotle's question and problem—really the entire question under which Greek philosophy emerges—is the question: how can beings be? This question attempts to expose the being's way of being. The Greeks, Heidegger says, already dwelled in an understanding of being itself, and therefore left unspoken the meaning of being. From the point of view of beings, the prior disclosure—the prior presence—of being is necessary. Thus, for Aristotle, the truth or disclosure of *eidos* must always come before and be independent of the truth of beings. Yet as the *arche* and *aitia*—that out of which beings emerge and that which is responsible for their being what they are—it lets beings be. It gathers beings into the oneness of being. This oneness with being is what Aristotle calls truth. How then are we to understand this *thigein* that is in touch with being and this *nous* that occurs as always the same as being, in a togetherness that is not a synthesis?

Aristotle says that no falsity or deception is possible in this way of seeing. Only ignorance, *agnoia*, is possible (GA21 185). He points out that ignorance is not the same as not-seeing at all or being incapable of knowing. It is only the one who can see—whose way of being is to see—who can fail to see. But this indicates that there is, for us, an incompleteness in the identity of *noein* and *eidos*, thinking and being. It is a sameness that does not have to occur, but without which no truth, no disclosure, is possible. The possibility of not seeing has two sides. That which is to be seen can be there, and I can fail to see it. Likewise, I can be looking for it, and it can turn out not to be there. In the latter case, we need to ask: what is the character of this complete not being and not having, which Aristotle says is not the same as the partial being true and being false, which we have already discussed as the combining and dividing that occurs in assertion and the *logos* of propositions. This complete not-seeing, like the oneness of seeing and being, must be prior to the other kind of truth and falsity. This prior concealment and not being (*ouk on* rather than *me on*) must be a simple not-being there that is different than the coming together and departing of a being that is already there. In Book IX of the *Metaphysics*, Aristotle says that, "with regard to being itself, there is no coming to be and passing away; otherwise being would have to come to be out of something else." He says further that, "with respect to being, there is no motion" (225b10). The always being there as it is of the *eidos* is what makes possible the movement and passage of beings. But there are beings whose being is such that they not only can move and be altered, but can also not be. The movement from not being to being that characterizes these beings is not of the same order as that kind of motion which comes and goes within the oneness and sameness of a being. Aristotle names this other kind of movement which is prior to motion *genesis*. The difference between these two kinds of movement is not a differentiation between two ontic kinds of motion, say, alteration and locomotion, but the difference between the *kinesis* of beings and the being of *kinesis*, the difference between being and beings. In the *Physics*, Aristotle says: "Therefore it is impossible for that which is not to move. This being the case, *genesis* cannot be *kinesis*, for it is that which is not which comes to be. It is a sudden change [*metabole*] which implies a relation of contradiction [*antiphasin*], not motion . . . , change from not being there to being there, the relation being that of contradiction, is *genesis*" (225a25ff.). Aristotle has said that the *eidos* is what being is. The *eidos* cannot be lacking in the fullness of being. But he also says in the *Physics* that *steresis*, privation and not being, is a kind of *eidos*. In the *Metaphysics*, at 1004b27, he says: "Thus the other of opposition corresponds to *steresis*; that is to say, everything leads back to being and not being, and oneness and manyness. And nearly all thinkers agree that beings that are present are and endure out of opposition. At any rate, all address the *arche* as this kind of opposing." In *genesis*, the movement of *eidos* from not being to being, a being comes forth into presence and sustains itself in its being as long as it is.

Thus Aristotle says that "such beings do not stay in their being as a single unit would, . . . but rather they endure inasmuch as their *genesis* is also an absence of change with regard to not being" (230a10, b11). The twofoldness of *genesis* and *steresis* is the enduring presencing of beings. The being of beings is the sudden emerging forth out of hiddenness into the unhidden. This emerging forth maintains itself in its emerging and thus is. Unconcealment always stands in relation and opposition to concealment. These opposites do not exclude each other, but grant the disclosure of beings. Thus Aristotle's thought remains faithful to that of Heraclitus, who said, *physis kruptesthai philei*, being loves to hide itself. Hiddenness and *steresis* are not to be banished from being. Because being loves to hide itself, the philosopher's task is to place oneself within the drawing power of being and understand beings by holding them out toward their being. In Aristotle's thought, *a-letheia*, truth, belongs to being and is a way of being because human being stands essentially in relation to being.

This task of the philosopher is carried out as phenomenology in *Being and Time*. There Heidegger unfolds the derivative character of the truth of assertion and the primordial meaning of truth as unconcealment. The indebtedness of his analysis to his reading of Aristotle is only alluded to in that text. His earlier courses make this debt manifest.

Part VI

Husserl

13

Heidegger's Critique of Husserl

Daniel O. Dahlstrom

> There is scarcely a need to acknowledge that even today, opposite Husserl, I still consider myself a novice.

Heidegger, SS 1925

In lectures delivered by Heidegger just prior to the publication of *Sein und Zeit*—in other words, at a time when he still considered it necessary to philosophize under the banner of "phenomenology"—Heidegger refers to Husserl's *Logische Untersuchungen* as a "breakthrough"; Husserl's masterful achievement is to have "thought the grand tradition of western philosophy to end."[1] There is an obvious edge to these remarks, revealing a basic tension informing Heidegger's regard for Husserl's thought. If, as Heidegger contends, the history of western philosophy displays an endemic proclivity to sidetrack the fundamental question of being, then this *Seinsvergessenheit* should display itself in the sharpest possible fashion where that tradition is brought to its conclusion. However, at the same time, it would seem that Husserl, precisely by thinking the tradition to its end, first puts himself and Heidegger in a position to see the tradition's limits, to regard it as a whole and see what lies beneath and beyond it.

In his Marburg lectures Heidegger presents his students with a picture of Husserl as traditional philosophy's Moses, at once its liberator and its victim, pointing the way out of the desert through a clarification of intentionality, but unable to enter the promised land of existential analysis. A central objective of this chapter is to ponder the accuracy of this image. To this end, the first part of the chapter elaborates Heidegger's explicit criticism that Husserl's phenomenology fails to bracket fatal prejudices of "the grand tradition of western philosophy." The second part demonstrates the extent to which Heidegger's own project, precisely where it purports to move beyond those fatal prejudices, nonetheless iterates Husserl's reflections on the absolute flow of time-consciousness. Besides considerably mollifying the force of Heidegger's objections to Husserl's analysis of intentionality, the iteration raises the question why it is not

231

acknowledged. In a final segment, reasons are suggested for Heidegger's silence on the ways his account of temporality is anticipated by Husserl.[2]

1. Heidegger's Critical Presentation of Husserl's Phenomenology: Lotze and the Neo-Kantian Connection

In the Marburg lectures that focus on Husserl prior to the publication of *Sein und Zeit*, Heidegger begins by taking exception to the Neo-Kantian dismissal of Husserl's achievement in the *Logical Investigations* (LU). Given Kant's and Cohen's insistence on the difference between transcendental and psychological standpoints, Natorp observes that "there does not remain much for us to learn . . . from Husserl's fine discussion (in the first volume of the LU)."[3] As for the investigations themselves, they were regarded as a relapse into psychologism (a misinterpretation admittedly abetted by Husserl's own initial characterizations of his phenomenology [GA21 88; GA20 31]). Heidegger's problem with this Neo-Kantian viewpoint is not simply its fundamental misunderstanding of Husserl's account of intentionality, but also its pretense of having mastered the problem of the relation between psychology and logic.[4] Yet, in the end, Heidegger faults Husserl for a similar—not the same—pretension.[5] In order to specify both Husserl's breakthrough and his share in that pretension, Heidegger turns to the thinker who, in his view, set the terms for the entire controversy over psychologism: Hermann Lotze.

a. The Logical Prejudice: Truth and Fact

Opponents of psychologism, Heidegger avers, were united in maintaining that the way in which truth is regarded as functioning in a particular kind of logic, namely, as a property of a proposition (assertion, belief, or judgment), represents a kind of first principle or closure of epistemological or ontological analysis. This conception may be aptly labelled 'the logical prejudice,' by which is meant a prejudice, not of logicians, but of those engaged in elaborating or analyzing what in various contexts 'to know,' 'to be true,' and even 'to be' might mean. 'The logical prejudice' stands for the unquestioned but questionable presumption that the understanding of truth in terms of a judgment constitutes the end of this sort of analysis.

Heidegger traces the roots of the logical prejudice to Hermann Lotze's delineation of four irreducible modes of actuality (being, happening, obtaining, validity).[6] Truth, on Lotze's conception, is not a thing, event, or relation but a proposition that is valid.[7] That by virtue of which a proposition is considered true, that is to say, in Lotze's words, its validity (*Gelt-ung*), is nothing other than its constancy and independence of any instances or entertaining of it. A valid proposition is something ideal, something that, in contrast to things and events, always obtains and, in that sense, is said to have "the actuality of validity."[8] With this conception of truth's "actuality," developed in tandem with his influential interpretation of Plato's ideas, Lotze assigns to truth the kind of being, Heidegger observes, "that the Greeks characterized as authentic being . . . designating presence and present-at-handness of *physis* in the broadest sense" (GA21 77). While its constancy is only accessible to an "inner intuition," truth in this sense of a valid proposition refers to the constant features and lawlike connections of things present-at-hand, in short, the objectivity of things, binding on every knower (GA21 80–81).

While this sort of ontological differentiation of truth contributed to the ready acceptance of the critique of psychologism (valid propositions not being things, events, or relations, including psychological ones), it raises several unanswered (in some cases, unanswerable) questions. What is the basis of the differentiated, yet common grouping of those four modes of actuality? What is the status of the relations between these modes? More to the point, how am I able *actually* to think what only *ideally* obtains (GA21 89–92; SZ 216–217)? The act of thinking, considered something psychologically real, is so severed from what is thought, indeed, what is true, construed as something ideal ("the actuality of validity"), that the question of the precise meaning of their relation—the question of knowing at all (GA21 99–100)—is rendered unanswerable, if not meaningless. Why, finally, is truth construed in terms of propositions or judgments (as a proposition or the property of a proposition)?

In Heidegger's view, a major accomplishment of Husserl's *Logische Untersuchungen* is to have provided some answers to these questions. The center of gravity for Husserl's determination of truth is *not* the proposition, but rather knowing's intentional character, specifically, knowing as a fulfilled intention, an intuition.[9] Knowing is not some bare intuition, to be sure, but an act of identification where what is intuited (something 'in the flesh,' precisely as it presents itself) is the *same* as what was meant or intended (conjectured, entertained, judged) in its absence.[10] Truth in the primary sense of the word is precisely this identity: "*the complete agreement between the intended and the given as such*," the intentional correlate to the act of knowing or identification.[11] What, furthermore, 'to be' means, in contrast to the copula, is precisely this "objective first sense of truth."[12]

Propositional truth, in Lotze's sense of validity, proves to be "a derivative phenomenon," founded on the truth in the sense of the identity

yielded through (sensible or categorial) intuition.[13] A proposition (assertion, belief, or judgment) is said to be 'true' insofar as it is understood or
employed as part of one side of the relation constituting the truth. In
other words, what the proposition means is the same as what is intuited,
and, because of this identity (truth in the primary sense of the term), the
proposition is true. "Because truth in the sense of identity *obtains*, the
proposition is then *valid*," and what obtains—in this deliberate reversion
to Lotze's terminology—is truth as "a relation of the identity of the intuited and the meant."[14]

It should now be clear why Heidegger considers Husserl's determination of truth such an advance over that of Lotze and those like Natorp or
Rickert who, under the influence of Lotze, readily concurred with Husserl's critique of psychologism without appreciating his account of intentionality. For Husserl truth is not in the first place a property of a proposition (or assertion or judgment), but an identity realized in intuition, a
sameness obtaining between something merely meant or "emptily entertained" (*ein Leervorgestelltes*) and what is intuited, viz., what presents
itself in the flesh (*leibhaftig*).[15] While Lotze merely postulated the ideal
being of truth and its distinctness from real beings, Husserl is able,
through his critical appropriation of the notion of intentionality, to explain
the difference as a difference between what is the correlate of an act of
knowing and what is a subject for empirical psychology (GA20 59–61,
160). Because they presumed a psychology that did not appreciate the intentional structure basic to the psyche or consciousness, proponents and
critics of psychologism alike were incapable of elaborating the intuitive
character of the act of knowing and what that entails concerning the nature of truth, viz., the structure of empty and filled intentions such that
truth in the primary sense of the term is the identity of what is meant or
asserted[16] and what is intuited.

Yet what precisely does it mean to say that the truth, that identity of
what is only emptily entertained and what is confronted face-to-face, "obtains"? Husserl's elucidation of the character of the intentionality involved
in emptily entertaining as well as in directly intuiting something removes
the bogus difficulty of trying to explain the union of some kind of self-
contained psychological reality with the ontologically distinct, ideal being
of truth (that is to say, something non-psychological). That the analysis of
knowing cannot, need not, and should explain not the fact of transcendence, but rather its possibility and structure, was a lesson of Husserl's
phenomenology long before it graced the pages of *Sein und Zeit*.[17] Nevertheless, Heidegger insists, it is still incumbent on Husserl to explain the
relation of intended and intuited, constituting truth in the primary sense.

In an attempt to single out the distinctiveness of this relation, Heidegger refers to it as *Wahrverhalt*, the relation constituting truth, or *Wahrsein*, inasmuch as it is equivalently the primary sense of 'to be.' In these terms, Heidegger's criticism is that Husserl, despite broaching their primary significance as *Wahrverhalt*, characterizes both truth and being literally, substantially, and fatally as a *Sachverhalt*, a fact or state of affairs that, in Husserl's terminology, is the objective correlate of a "categorial intuition," specifically, a judgment.[18] Heidegger thus couches his criticism in a word-play on the difference between two sorts of relation (*Verhalt*), that of truth (or, equivalently, being) and that of facts. Husserl is charged with failing to respect this difference; his characterization of truth as a fact, Heidegger avers, moves the relation between meant and intended, as far as its structure is concerned, "into the same line as the fact [*Sachverhalt*] S is P, the table is black, the relation of black and table. . . ."[19]

As an illustration of the difference between these two ways of construing 'truth' and 'to be,' Heidegger calls attention to two ways the sentence 'the chair is yellow' can be taken. The sentence could be meant with the emphasis on 'is' ('the chair *is* yellow') to indicate that the chair 'actually' ('truly') is yellow. In this sense the word 'is' signifies the identity of intended and intuited or, in other words, that the *Wahrverhalt* obtains.[20] The emphasis could also, however, be placed on the predicate ('the chair is *yellow*'), in which case 'is' functions as a copula to indicate an attribute of what is designated by the subject, namely, the fact that the chair is yellow.[21]

To construe truth in the primary sense (*Wahrverhalt*), namely, the relation (identity) of the intended and the intuited, as a fact (*Sachverhalt*) is in effect to assimilate or reduce that relation to the kind of relation obtaining between a thing and its determination. Heidegger's contention is that Husserl's analysis is guilty of doing just that. The result, Heidegger concludes, is that truth is assigned "the same type of being as the proposition, namely, the ideal being [of a proposition]. We have returned on a curious path back to the point of departure [Lotze]. The proposition as member of the relation is found in the intuitive truth of the identity, identity itself in turn as fact [*Sachverhalt*] has the kind of being of a proposition or relation within a proposition: ideal being."[22] Husserl, in Heidegger's eyes, thus remains caught up in a version of the logical prejudice. Husserl clearly recognizes the inadequacy of the Neo-Kantian characterization of truth as a kind of judgment; what is more, he uncovers the distinctive relation obtaining in the most basic, prejudgmental sense of truth. Yet, for all that, Heidegger charges, he continues to regard "truth primarily as a phenomenon that is to be construed originally in terms of assertions or, better, in terms of objectifying acts in the broad sense."[23]

b. Methodological Infidelity: Being and Intentionality

In lectures of SS 1925 Heidegger sketches the self-critical evolution of Husserl's thinking. In LU, Heidegger claims, "the discussion and description of intentionality still move completely within the structure of the indicated disciplines of psychology and logic and their questions," but in *Ideen I*, through the process of bracketing, intentionality "first becomes accessible."[24] Nevertheless, Heidegger sets out to demonstrate how Husserl's phenomenology, despite this development, essentially leaves the questions of what intentionality is, and what 'to be' means, unposed, and does so by being unfaithful to its central methodological precept.[25]

Thematizing the acts of consciousness themselves and their respective objects *precisely and only as they are given* in those acts, and without regard for any way they belong to me or are part of my individual stream of experiences, is not the same as having those perceptions or objects the way we do in a "natural attitude" (*Ideen I* 52–57). By "turning off" (*ausschalten*) that natural attitude through these transcendental and eidetic reductions, a sphere is won in which nothing can be denied.[26] The transcendental and eidetic reductions are thus intended to unpack or arrive at what is "absolutely given," and Husserl explicitly dubs the absolutely given the "immanent or absolute being" (*Sein*) in contrast to every other, particular being (*Seiendes*) or reality (*Realität*) (*Ideen I* 92–93). Husserl accordingly declares the distinction between the "ways of being" of consciousness and reality "the most cardinal of distinctions."[27] "Between consciousness and reality a veritable abyss of meaning yawns" (*Ideen I* 93; also 76–87, 91–94).

Yet it is precisely this contrast between absolute being, given in "pure consciousness," and the reality of consciousness that raises in Heidegger's mind the questionable question of their connection, much as Lotze's modes of actuality had done.

> How is it at all possible that this sphere of absolute position, the pure consciousness that is supposed to be separated from every transcendence through an absolute breach, at the same time unites with reality in the unity of a real human being that itself as a real object turns up in the world? How is it possible that the experiences constitute an absolute, pure region of being and at the same time turn up in the transcendence of the world? (GA20 139)

The comparison with Lotze goes even deeper. Lotze employed 'actuality' equivocally, buttressing it on some vague sense of 'affirmedness' (*Bejahtheit*), when in fact, according to Heidegger, he was unknowingly relying on the traditional conception of being as presence. So, too, for Husserl when terms like 'being' and 'objective' are used in regard to both the "immanent or absolute" and "transcendent" spheres, it is "only in terms of the empty logical categories" (*Ideen I* 93). This appeal to the purportedly empty logical category of 'to be' and the radical disengagement of immanent and transcendent senses of 'to be' go hand-in-hand, in Heidegger's view, signalling that, as in the case of Lotze, an unexamined conception of 'to be' is at work in Husserl's analysis.

Heidegger presents these misgivings in the form of an immanent critique, based on the principle that supposedly distinguishes phenomenology, namely, the principle of making its determinations, not on the basis of traditional presuppositions, but on the basis of the things themselves. Rather than examine what it means for intentionality (the "thing that is the theme most proper" to phenomenology) to be, Heidegger charges, Husserl's account of intentionality relies on traditional preconceptions; rather than clarify what 'to be' means, Husserl takes as given a categorical, elementary distinction of consciousness and reality as two particular beings (GA20 178, 147). Husserl's specific characterization of being in a primary sense, as what is absolutely given in pure consciousness, is based on an attempt to elaborate, not what 'to be' means, but rather what is necessary for consciousness to constitute an "absolute science."[28] For the phenomenologist above all, the failure to raise the question of what 'to be' means is of a piece with a failure to unpack what 'to be' means in the case of a particular sort of being (*Seiendes*), namely, consciousness, understood as 'intentionality.' This twin failure is, moreover, the direct result of an infidelity to phenomenology's most basic principle. Heidegger locates one source of that infidelity in the method of reduction (GA20 151–152). In the interest of attending to the essential structure of the intentional act, the transcendental reduction brackets the reality and the eidetic reduction the individual character of the intentional experience, effectively sabotaging any attempt to determine what it means to say that intentionality exists. To clarify this criticism, Heidegger reverts to the Scholastic distinction of *essentia* and *existentia*. For example, the essence of color can be determined, set off from that of sound, without inquiring into its manner of being, its existence. Similarly, through the method of reduction, the existence of consciousness is ignored in the interests of determining its essence.[29]

It might well be objected that, in the first place, while not what Heidegger means by 'existence,' the reality of consciousness is nevertheless clearly recognized in the phenomenological reduction as its starting point, namely, the natural attitude, and that, in the second place, while at first bracketed, consciousness is itself in turn, like any other reality, to be determined as it presents itself in pure consciousness or, as Husserl himself puts it, as "a correlate of pure consciousness" (*Ideen I* 105–107; GA21 153–154). Heidegger is quite ready to concede these points, since in his opinion they merely underscore his basic contention. The sort of being attributed to consciousness, he observes, both in the point of departure and in the analysis following the reduction, is that of something "objectively present-at-hand" or, in Husserl's own words, "a real object like others in the natural world."[30] The problem in the end is not so much the phenomenological reductions as their contrived starting point: the natural attitude that, Heidegger argues, is nothing "natural" at all, but something "naturalistic" and fatal to the question of what it means for consciousness 'to be.' "By virtue of the fact that this attitude affords itself as natural, the prejudice is reinforced that in this type of attitude the being of the acts is given in an original and authentic way, and that each inquiry into the being of the acts is forced to have recourse to this sort of attitude" (GA20 156). Again, as in the case of Lotze, 'being' is tacitly assumed to mean as much as it does for the study of nature, namely, a kind of presence in nature, and human being is construed as an instance of the same, a natural thing (GA20 156–157).

In the first half of "Philosophy as Rigorous Science," Husserl himself criticizes "the reigning naturalism" and, in particular, "the naturalization of consciousness" as he explicitly argues for "a *phenomenology of consciousness* in contrast to a *natural science of consciousness*."[31] In fact, he asks point-blank what sort of "being" is investigated when the object is "what is immanent to the psyche," since the latter is "in itself not nature." What is investigated, Husserl maintains, is "an essence," something capable of being directly perceived, absolutely given, and immanent within a pure intuition (for example, "perception in itself" as something identical in any passing instances of perception).[32]

This answer, Heidegger contends, simply reinforces his criticism that Husserl inquires into the essence, but not the existence, of consciousness. "'To be' means for him [Husserl] nothing other than true being, *objectivity, true for a theoretical, scientific knowing.* Here there is no inquiry into the specific being [*Sein*] of consciousness, of the experiences, but rather into a *distinctive manner of being an object for an objective science of consciousness*" (GA20 165). In this connection Heidegger briefly reviews Husserl's repeated and largely unpublished attempts, at least since 1914, to develop a personalistic psychology. Heidegger, in fact, qualifies his criticisms, noting that they are already somewhat "antiquated" by Husserl's more recent efforts to respond to them; completely in character, Husserl's queries are "still fully in flux."[33] Yet, despite Husserl's best efforts, in Heidegger's mind the basic criticism remains. At odds with its guiding principle "To the things themselves!," Heidegger charges, phenomenology determines the "thing" that is the theme most proper to it, not on the basis of the thing itself, but on the basis of traditional preconceptions. *"Not only the being of the intentional,* thus the being of a specific, particular being, *remains undetermined, but categorial distinctions of the most original sort in regard to particular beings are given* (consciousness and reality) *without the principal aspect,* in terms of which the distinction is made, *being clarified or even simply inquired into, namely, what 'to be' means* (GA20 178; also 149). Heidegger thus faults Husserl for infidelity to the phenomenological method due to a failure to bracket a certain kind of scientific and naturalistic preconception of what 'to be' means. 'To be' is equated with 'givenness' or 'presence' (to consciousness) and any talk of what it means for consciousness or intentionality 'to be' becomes equivocal or, worse, tacitly reductionistic. In his opposition to naturalism, Husserl remains in Heidegger's eyes a victim, like Lotze, of a more subtle and fundamental naturalism, the inheritance of an ancient identification of being and presence, where 'to be' signifies the presence fulfilling an act of intending or, paradigmatically, of making a judgment about something present.

2. Internal Time-Consciousness and Ecstatic-Horizonal Temporality

How fair is Heidegger's criticism? On the one hand, despite his enthusiasm for Husserl's intentional analysis of knowing, Heidegger's criticism effectively discounts the essential role Husserl accords the mere, or even empty, intending of things in the constitution of the primary significance of 'truth' or 'being.' Yet this fundamental feature of Husserl's analysis belies the reproach that he crudely equates being with sheer presence.[34] Heidegger's critical exposition of Husserl's phenomenology is, moreover, highly selective, ignoring several other nuances and details of its analyses and development.[35] On the other hand, as amply documented in the preceding section, there are certainly grounds for Heidegger's contention that the basic structure of objectifying acts or, more specifically, an ontology of presence dominates the horizon against which accounts are given of truth, being, and intentionality in LU, *Ideen I,* and several subsequent studies.[36] In this respect, however, in his lectures prior to the publication of SZ it is curious that Heidegger, though freely expounding on Husserl's ongoing, at the time unpublished work, only gives bare mention to the latter's *Untersuchungen über das immanente Zeitbewußtsein* (GA20 126). In these investigations Husserl plainly addresses the ultimate horizon for objectifying acts that is accordingly itself neither an object nor an act. There is still a kind of consciousness involved, but it is not the objectifying consciousness or intentionality that Heidegger criticized as prejudicially scientific; if anything, internal time-consciousness is prescientific, even "preobjective," starkly contrasting with the sketch Heidegger gives in his lectures of Husserl's account of intentionality. Nor is Heidegger unaware of this significance. In the preface to the published part of these manuscripts he writes that what is particularly telling about them is "the growing, fundamental clarification of *intentionality* in general," a remark that must have surprised the students who listened to him during the summer semester of 1925.[37]

In what follows, in the interest of keeping the discussion within certain limits, no attempt is made to provide anything like an adequate review of each philosopher's complex account of time. Yet even a cursory sketch of similarities is instructive. Both analyses (in loose accord with Kant's account of time as the form of sensibility) distinguish time from things or parts of things in time, while denying that time somehow exists apart from constituting or forming (in the sense of making present-able) those things (Zb 22–23, 296, 377; SZ 330–33). Through phenomenological reductions, both thinkers aim at unravelling a phenomenon more fundamental than the so-called "objective time" of watches and clocks, determined by the relation between earth and sun, in other words, a phenomenon more fundamental than "the real time of nature in the sense of natural science and even psychology as a natural science"; for this reason, both analyses distinguish themselves from empirical and\or psychological analyses of the genesis or origins of the consciousness of time (Zb 4–10, 124; SZ 45–50, 326). Yet both analyses also purport to show how the derivative senses of 'time' are constituted in the more fundamental phenomenon (Zb 64–79, 107–109; SZ 333, 406–27).

In their analyses, both philosophers labor to avoid what Brough calls "the prejudice of the now,"[38] the view that past or future are knowable only by way of some representation or image of them in the present. Instead Husserl emphasizes that the past is "given" (and, indeed, neither as being now nor by way of the presence of some "real" replication, but rather "intentionally") in retention; retention is the originary consciousness of an inexorable elapsing, the ongoing and direct cognizance of the flow's fading phases with-and-in their fading (Zb 31, 41, 316, 327, 368, 417–18). In Brough's apt formulation, "Retention does not transmute what is absent into something present; it presents the absent in its absence."[39] This point is echoed by Heidegger's insistence that, as far as temporality in its original sense is concerned, "the future is *not later* than the having-been and the latter is *not earlier* than the present" (SZ 350). (As discussed below, Heidegger is more emphatic about the sense in which the original present [the presenting of something] depends on a primordial sense of the future, a "coming" to oneself from which, with equal primordiality, the past, a "having been" first springs.)

In keeping with this last point, both analyses distinguish the way the past is originally (retentionally) given to us from its replication in memory (Zb 33–37, 45–50, 312, 316, 360; SZ 339) and the original future from expectation (Zb 52–53, 154–156; SZ 337). "The idea of the realized expectation necessarily includes the idea that the expectation itself is over" (Zb 156). In Heidegger's formulation, the original future "must have already disclosed the horizon and range out of which something can be expected" (SZ 337).

Both analyses emphasize the thick character of the original phenomenon of time. For Husserl the now is "always and essentially the border of a stretch of time" (Zb 70), the now has a "temporal fringe" (Zb 35, 40, 201, 210), it always refers to a past and vice versa (Zb 68, 179, 397). "Each perceptual phase has intentional reference to an extended section of the temporal object and not perchance merely to a now-point" (Zb 232). Correspondingly, in Heidegger, time is a "unified phenomenon"; the sense of "having-been" springs from an original future, a way of "coming" to itself that, in the process, renders present what is at hand (SZ 326).

The primordial time-consciousness uncovered by Husserl is more basic than "objective time" and "subjective time," that is to say, than the time of temporal things and the time of perceiving such things (Zb 22, 73, 76).[40] This time-consciousness is the "flow" within which each individual object, including each individual act of consciousness, is constituted as an identity, "the time-constituting phenomena" as opposed to "the phenomena constituted in time" (Zb 74–75). This distinction resurfaces in Heidegger's distinction between the original temporality (Zeitlichkeit) constituting world-time, in terms of which particular beings within the world are encountered, and the time-determination of a particular being within the world (Innerzeitigkeit) (SZ 333, 414, 419).[41]

To speak of an object at all there must be "something" that alters and thus also persists, something that transpires and thereby must be said to endure as a unity for a certain stretch of time. Meaningful talk of objectness presupposes notions of alteration and endurance, contemporaneity and succession, which in turn presuppose the flow of time. ('Object' here refers to both "transcendent" and "immanent" objects, as Husserl dubs them, for example, the perceived tree as well as the act of perceiving the tree.) However, while and because the absolute flow of time consciousness is a prerequisite for speaking meaningfully of the alteration and persistence of objects or acts, the flow is not itself the altering or transpiring of an object or an act. The flow of time is "preobjective" or, more literally, "prior to being objectified" (Zb 72). As Husserl puts it: "There is nothing there that alters itself and for that reason there can also be no meaningful talk of something that endures" (Zb 74; also 370). Similarly, since this absolute flow of inner time-consciousness is no object, the meaning of 'time' in regard to it is unlike the meaning of 'time' when applied to objects and to consciousness itself if it be construed solely as the act of being conscious of an object.[42] *"The flow of the modes of consciousness is no occurrence, the now-consciousness is not itself now"* (Zb 333).

Both these characterizations of inner time-consciousness are applied by Heidegger to temporality. Just as inner time-consciousness is no object, so "temporality 'is' no particular being at all," and since temporality is not "a particular being," temporal predicates, at least as they are used in regard to particular beings, are simply inapplicable to it (SZ 326–29).[43] In practically a paraphrase of Husserl, Heidegger notes: "'Time' is not something present-at-hand either in a 'subject' or in an 'object,' it is neither 'inner' nor 'outer,' and 'is' *'earlier'* than any subjectivity and objectivity, because it presents [*darstellt*] the condition of the possibility itself for this 'earlier'" (SZ 419). As an original presencing tied to a way of coming to itself that profiles its having-been, temporality makes possible the very presence of something present.

Inner time-consciousness is the consciousness of the unity of the continuous running-together of primal impressions, retentions, and protentions, that is to say, the unitary structure of ever-new phases of the present that, for all their newness, are continually bound with ever-fading phases of the originary past, precisely as fading and ever-coming phases of the originary future as coming (Zb 76–83, 379–80). This consciousness can be considered a consciousness of itself, though not as an object or even as an act. Rather it is the consciousness of itself as originally successive (involving a distinct structure) that makes identification of a succession of objects and acts of consciousness possible. This flow or succession (internal time-consciousness) is, unlike those objects and acts, not constituted by anything else, and hence it is in an important sense the end of the analysis of intentionality (Zb 381–82).

In much the same way, temporality is for Heidegger the end of the analysis of what 'to be' means in the case of *Dasein*. Like the absolute flow of inner time-consciousness, moreover, temporality is the end of this analysis precisely inasmuch as it makes the presence of things present possible and, in so doing, constitutes their horizon. As Heidegger compendiously puts it, temporality is "ecstatic-horizonal."[44] Just as Husserl uncovers the time-consciousness at the root of intentionality (Zb 76), explicable neither as an object nor as an act of intending one, but rather as what at the most fundamental level makes them possible, so Heidegger uncovers the temporality that grounds being-in-the-world. "The *transcendence* of *being-in-the-world* in its distinctive entirety *is grounded in the original ecstatic-horizonal unity of temporality.*"[45]

3. Silence and Differences

Why is Heidegger silent about these similarities between his and Husserl's analyses of time? One possible explanation, offered by Bernet, is that Heidegger simply had not worked over Husserl's manuscripts on time-consciousness during the period of writing SZ.[46] Yet even if Heidegger did not have the manuscripts (especially the B manuscripts) in his actual possesssion, both the considerable similarities recounted and the close contact of the two thinkers up to 1926 strongly suggest that Heidegger's analysis was influenced by Husserl's investigations of time.[47]

Thomas Prufer gives a more plausible explanation, namely, Heidegger's need to distance himself from Husserl because of the dangerous closeness in their thinking, dangerous because Husserl remained beholden to the "matrix of the language of acts and their objects, especially the objects which acts themselves become when they are reflected on by other acts."[48] According to Prufer, "the means of persuasion and demonstration are different," as Heidegger "transposes" Husserl's analysis into a quite different nomenclature. This thesis has the considerable merit of accurately reflecting both Heidegger's explicit criticisms of Husserl's investigations (reviewed in the first part of this chapter) and his appropriation of Husserl's analysis of time (sketched in the second part of this chapter). Nor does Prufer intend to leave the impression that Heidegger merely provided another rhetorical matrix for the same basic account, transplanting it into analyses of themes such as tools and death; Heidegger also explicitly situates the analysis of time in the gravitational field of the *Seinsfrage*.

Heidegger clearly does utilize features central to the sort of time-analysis previously made by Husserl. However, Heidegger does not so much transplant as graft that analysis onto his account of temporality. To be sure, for Husserl as well as for Heidegger, a distinction between an authentic and an inauthentic temporality or experience of time is fundamental: an inauthentic sense of 'time' must be bracketed as part of the reduction and its derivativeness from an authentic one demonstrated (Zb 9; SZ 329). However, what the two philosophers respectively mean by 'authentic' time is radically different, and the core of that difference lies in the conception of the original or primary future.[49]

Husserl notes that there is a freedom, an openness to the original future that is radically closed off in the case of the original, inexorable past; he also calls attention to the fact that perception does not simply pass from now to now while intimately retaining the "just been," but also is always "previewing" (*vorblickend*) what is coming (Zb 106–107, 52). In Husserl's account, however, the future is basically indeterminate, and his analysis focusses primarily on "the comet tail of retentions," the distinctive fusion of retentions and primal impressions (Zb 29–33). For Heidegger, on the other hand, *"the primary phenomenon of the original and authentic temporality is the future,"* and even in the case of the derivative sense of time this primacy evidences itself (SZ 329).[50]

Moreover, the future is the primary phenomenon of temporality because it is finite. This sense of the finitude of the future, of time, is not integral to the absolute flow of internal time-consciousness in Husserl's account. Indeed, it would seem that for Husserl talk of a finite future is meaningful only in regard to temporal objects, acts, events, in short, only in regard to derivative senses of 'time,' not in regard to the absolute flow of internal time-consciousness.[51] By contrast, for Heidegger the finite, original future is protentional, but with a definitiveness that pervades all the indeterminacies of coming phases. 'Dying' is not the same as 'perishing' or 'expiring'; Dasein "does not have an end at which it simply ceases, but rather it *exists finitely*" (SZ 247, 329). As inexorable as the original past, the original future is either being anticipated or being occluded, and as such, together with the past it profiles or releases, it is defining the manner of making present: the original, ecstatic sense of the present (now).

Conclusion

Heidegger's silence about the stark similarities between his account of temporality and Husserl's investigation of internal time-consciousness contributes to a *misrepresentation* of Husserl's account of intentionality. Contrary to the criticisms Heidegger advances in his lectures, intentionality (and, by implication, the meaning of 'to be') in the final analysis is not construed by Husserl as sheer presence (be it the presence of a fact or object, act or event). Yet for all its "dangerous closeness" to what Heidegger understands by temporality, Husserl's account of internal time-consciousness does differ fundamentally. In Husserl's account the structure of protentions is accorded neither the finitude nor the primacy that Heidegger claims are central to the original future of ecstatic-horizonal temporality.

14

Phenomenological Reduction and the Double Life of the Subject

Rudolf Bernet
Translated by François Renaud*

After undergoing too long a purgatory, the problematic of phenomenological reduction is again, and deservedly, occupying the forefront of phenomenological thought, especially in France.[1] Everyone seems willing to consider this reduction as a return or leading back (*Rückführung*) of philosophical thought to phenomena. Which phenomena? Those whose manifestation requires a particular procedure or event, which is precisely that of phenomenological reduction! This reduction thus has the task of making manifest phenomena that are usually hidden; it leads to the phenomenalization of that which otherwise would never have become a phenomenon. By awakening dormant phenomena, the phenomenological reduction appeals to the vigilance of the subject. Here is a second point that all agree upon: the phenomenological reduction is unthinkable without a subject capable of receiving the givenness of the phenomena that this reduction makes manifest for the first time.[2] These phenomena in the phenomenological sense are not only covered over by the phenomena of ordinary life, but at the same time constitute the foundation from which ordinary phenomena receive their significance. The given which phenomenological reduction offers is therefore a fundamental given, that which founds all other givens. Beyond this third point of agreement, however, opinions begin to differ on what it is that phenomenological phenomena make manifest, on the form of manifestation peculiar to them, and on the way in which they differ from and are linked to ordinary phenomena.

What is made manifest by the phenomenological reduction? *Husserl* says that it is transcendental subjectivity insofar as it constitutes the world. What becomes a phenomenon is therefore just as much the world,

*Translator's Note: I heartily thank Carol Fiedler, Theodore Kisiel, and John van Buren for their countless valuable comments on preliminary versions of the translation.

insofar as it is constituted by transcendental subjectivity, as it is this subjectivity itself insofar as it constitutes the world. In this manner, the phenomenological reduction brings to light the "transcendental correlation"
between the being of the constituting subject and the being of the constituted world by also showing how this constitution was already at work in
natural life without itself becoming manifest. For *Heidegger* also, it is
being, and especially the being of beings, that becomes manifest through
the phenomenological reduction: the being of tools, the being of the environment, the being of Dasein in its various modes of existence, and finally
the sense of being in general. However, this phenomenological manifestation no longer appeals to a detached spectator, as in Husserl, but is carried
out within Dasein's actual existence. Beyond this manifestation of the being of different beings, Heidegger examines the phenomenality of these
phenomena, already in his first phenomenological writings. *J.-L. Marion*,
finally, attempts to go beyond a Husserlian "transcendental" or Heideggerian "existential" understanding of reduction in order to make manifest
"the giving of turning to *or* fleeing from the demands of the appeal." This
giving appeals to "the addressee" and is carried out each time there is a
call, whatever the content of this call may be. By making manifest *"the* call
as such," this reduction opens up a field of giving that is much larger than
the phenomenon of transcendental correlation or the ontological phenomenon.[3]

The question of what is made manifest through the phenomenological
reduction has thus been given a clear answer in the course of the history
of phenomenology, even if the answers differ and the nature of this difference is far from clear. *M. Henry* rightly points out that many phenome-
nologists have, on the other hand, failed to deal with the question of what
"appearing phenomenologically" means. According to Henry, their neglect
of this question results from their presupposition that things necessarily
appear in the form of intentionality or of ecstatic transcendence.[4] Rather
than presupposing that givenness is an affection of the subject's immanence by something that transcends it, one should, according to him,
make room for "the duplicity of appearance" and face the fact that the
manifestation of transcendence is only a derivative form of manifestation:
"Neither affection by the world nor, as a result, that by an entity would
occur, if this ecstatic affection did not affect itself in Life, which is nothing
other than primitive auto-affection" (23, 16).

We do not intend to discuss here these new reflections on the reduction developed (in various ways) by Marion and Henry. But we want to
bear them in mind while proposing in turn a new reading of the significance of phenomenological reduction in the works of Husserl and Heidegger. Our aim is not to go beyond the ontological phenomenon in the man-

ner of E. Levinas and Marion toward a mode of givenness that would be "other than being," nor, as Henry does so subtly,[5] even to inquire into the ambiguities of this identity between being and appearance to which both Husserl and Heidegger appeal. In rereading Husserl and Heidegger to ask ourselves once again what is made manifest in the phenomenological reduction, to whom and how it appears, we are working toward an end that meets some of Henry's concerns, in particular what he calls "the duplicity of appearance." We want to bring to the fore the double life of the transcendental subject and of Dasein as it becomes manifest in the phenomenological reduction and in turn seems to pursue a double objective. We will try to show how the phenomenological reduction makes manifest a subject that, on the one hand, clings to the world and, on the other, turns away from it. More precisely, we will try to show how the transcendental subject or Dasein appears through the phenomenological reduction to lead a double life, and how thereby it becomes manifest to itself in a double manner. If phenomenological reduction does indeed introduce a split or separation, then it has to do less with an alleged opposition between the rationality of phenomenological phenomena and the irrationality of ordinary phenomena than with the phenomenological phenomenon itself, namely, with the manifestation of the transcendental subject or Dasein.

Husserl accounts for the double character of the transcendental subject by making a sharp distinction between, on the one hand, the subject insofar as it constitutes the world and, on the other, the subject insofar as it watches this constitution as an "impartial spectator." The first case concerns the transcendental subject as seen through phenomenological reduction, the second concerns the transcendental subject as the agent carrying out this phenomenological reduction. The first subject becomes manifest to itself through the work it accomplishes in and for the world; the second becomes manifest to itself in an immediate manner, that is, independently of all reference to the world. But we are in both cases dealing with one and the same transcendental subject. In *Heidegger*, this split within the transcendental subject assumes the form of Dasein's double mode of existence. In "inauthentic" or "improper" [*"impropre"*] existence Dasein attends to the practical matters of its familiar world, while in "authentic" or "proper" [*"propre"*] existence it is led to care for its own proper being. Phenomenological reduction thus reveals, in the first instance, the readiness-to-hand of tools and the significance of the familiar world and, in the second instance, Dasein's authentic being as it becomes manifest when the significance of the world collapses. In these instances of phenomenological reduction, Dasein becomes manifest to itself differently and does so in different ways: on the one hand, as involved in the world and, on the other, as exiled from the world; on the one hand, in the loss of itself and, on the other, in a return to itself that looks very much like an auto-affection. However, here we are again dealing with the same Dasein, whose ontological predicament consists precisely in being unable to escape this ambiguity of its existence, this duplicity encountered as double disclosure of the truth of its own being.

While both assign to phenomenological reduction the task of making manifest the double life of the subject, Husserl and Heidegger are far from saying the same thing. The mode of appearance of the transcendental subject and of Dasein is fundamentally different. Equally different is the analysis of the relationship that unites and divides the two modes of appearance of the transcendental subject and of Dasein.

1. Husserl

It may seem surprising that we are going to use a text from E. Fink to show how the reduction, as conceived by Husserl, makes manifest a double life in the transcendental subject. However, this text of the *Sixth Cartesian Meditation*[6] was written in 1932 upon the request of Husserl, as a follow-up to a reworked version of the *Cartesian Meditations*. Fink was then Husserl's private assistant, and his text was written at a time when the collaboration between teacher and pupil was very close. Husserl closely followed the genesis of this text, carefully reread it several times, and copiously annotated it, especially where he wanted to indicate his disagreement with Fink's way of presenting his thought. It goes without saying that we will not fail to take these critical notes into consideration. This allows us at the same time to consider the rest of the text as an authorized version of Husserl's thought.

The *Sixth Cartesian Meditation* is entitled "The Idea of a Transcendental Doctrine of Method." There Fink takes on the task of bringing to light the ontological significance of Husserlian phenomenological reduction. The reduction is meant to make manifest the difference between the "being" of the world and the "pre-being" of transcendental consciousness. Since this consciousness is at once the object made manifest in phenomenological reduction and the subject carrying out this reduction, the ontological difference thus extends to the core of the transcendental subject itself. Fink even thinks that it is at the transcendental level that the ontological difference is most profound; while between constituting subject and constituted world an "analogy" of being prevails, the constituting subject and the phenomenological spectator of this constitution are, on the contrary, separated by a profound "chasm," by an "opposition" of being.

1.1 The Being of the World and the Being of the Constituting Consciousness

For Husserl and Fink, both the phenomenological reduction and the non-worldly phenomenon that is made manifest by the reduction still rest upon the world. It is true that the phenomenological reduction makes manifest the constituting consciousness outside the world, but it also makes the world manifest as being constituted. One can say then that it makes the being of the world manifest from its origin in the transcendental subject. The being of constituting consciousness and the being of the constituted world are therefore different, but not indifferent to one another. By dislodging the constituting consciousness from the world, the phenomenological reduction thus does not change the fact that this consciousness is-in-the-world. Since the being of the constituting consciousness consists in being concerned with the world, consciousness is quite naturally led to integrate itself in the world by becoming a worldly or "empirical" subject. It is precisely this fascination with the world that leads the transcendental subject in daily or "natural" life to become aware of itself as a part of the world and thus forget the ontological difference that holds sway between itself and the world. This difference between the being of constituting consciousness and the being of the constituted world appears only by way of the artificial procedure of the phenomenological reduction, which produces a new mode of life for the transcendental subject. In this new mode the subject is no longer involved in the task of constituting the world. This agent of the phenomenological reduction, this "phenomenologizing spectator," although separated from the world and refraining from taking part in its constitution, nevertheless still honors the world by allowing it to become manifest as being-constituted. The spectator cannot take action and develop the form of transcendental life that is peculiar to it except on the basis of an already fulfilled constitution of the world, of a world that is "pre-given" to it.

The *Sixth Cartesian Meditation* examines at length the motives implied in the phenomenological reduction that lead a subject to introduce this radical change in its life. At the end of this investigation none of the possible motives have proved to be compelling: no difficulty encountered in natural life, no desire for clarification, no will to accomplish scientific work has the power to draw human beings out of their immersion in the natural life that takes place within the world. As Husserl says in a marginal note, the human being that tears itself from its fixation on the world, that transcends (*übersteigt*) "its natural self, its [empirical] being human," makes a "leap" (*Sprung*) (36). Though phenomenology is a science, the entry into phenomenology must therefore be considered as an act of faith devoid of all anticipation or foresight (*Vor-Sicht*) (40). The "leap" Husserl speaks of is a leap into phenomenological reduction and a leap out of the world. Although what one finds on both sides of the leap is the same subject, nevertheless, in the course of this leap the subject splits into constituting subject and constituted subject. By leaping out of the constitution of the world, the subject settles into the position of spectator who observes the constitution of the world without taking part in it (*unbeteiligter Zuschauer*). By creating such a spectator, the phenomenological reduction makes the constituting subject and the constituted world appear differently than in natural life, and thus makes their difference manifest. The reduction strips the constituting subject of its empirical apperception and makes manifest the constituted world as the universal ground of natural life. Indeed it is only by annexing such a spectator to itself as its "exhibitor" (*Exponent*) that constituting consciousness can appear to itself as different from the world it constitutes (44, 65). In order for the unity of correlation peculiar to the constitution and the difference of being between transcendental consciousness and the world to become manifest, the transcendental subject must split itself in two so as to become both a constituting consciousness and a phenomenologizing spectator.

When Husserl says that the phenomenological reduction makes manifest how, in the course of natural life, transcendental consciousness constitutes the world without realizing it, this seems to be very much an act of reflection. By making manifest the constitution of the world, the phenomenon as understood by phenomenology would then be a simple reflective vision of a phenomenon as understood by natural life. Upon closer examination, however, this passage from natural phenomenon to phenomenological phenomenon is the work of a reflection or thematization of a very particular kind. Rather than bringing the constituting subject before one's gaze by separating it from the constituted object, and rather than making constituting consciousness the object of a second constituting consciousness, phenomenological reflection interposes the gaze of a spectator who super-vises the work of constitution without taking part in it.

Phenomenological reduction is much more than a mere reflective redoubling of consciousness, since it effects a genuine split. This split concerns not only the relation between constituting consciousness and constituted world, but also transcendental consciousness itself insofar as it is agent, on the one hand, and spectator of the world's constitution, on the other. The phenomenon made manifest for the first time by the spectator is the ontological difference between constituting consciousness and constituted world. It is this difference that the natural life is unaware of and that reestablishes the correlation between subject and world within the work of constitution. The aim of phenomenological reduction is therefore quite ontological. "To reflect" phenomenologically on the work of the world's constitution is therefore not only to awaken transcendental consciousness from its sleep in the world, but also and above all to make manifest the ontological difference between the transcendental subject and the world.

How then is one to understand the sense of this ontological difference between the being of constituting consciousness and the being of the constituted world? What is the horizon within which this ontological difference is to be understood? Within what perspective must the phenomenological spectator place itself in order to perceive it? The *Sixth Cartesian Meditation* remains strangely mute in this respect. It confines itself to a purely conceptual response by distinguishing the "being" (*Sein*) of the world from the "pre-being" (*Vor-Sein*) of transcendental consciousness. Although there is a certain "affinity" or even an "analogy" between the two forms of being [*être*], transcendental being [*l'étant*] and worldly being are nevertheless not to be subsumed under the same general concept of being (105, 82).

While Fink's text may not be entirely satisfactory with regard to the analysis of the ontological difference between the being of the world and the being of constituting consciousness, it is much more explicit on "the ontological opposition" (*Seinsgegensatz*) that prevails within the pre-being of the transcendental subject and that separates the phenomenological spectator from constituting consciousness (89, 117, 119). However, several of Husserl's marginal notes attest to a profound uneasiness over Fink's way of hardening the "division" (*Entzweiung*) and the "dualism of transcendental life," and of emphasizing "the chasm" (*Kluft*) separating the phenomenologizing spectator from constituting consciousness (157, 22, 29). Without calling into question a certain duality within the life of the transcendental subject, Husserl thus doubts, and rightly so it seems, that the spectator of the constitution of the world has lost all interest in the world and totally ceases to refer to it. This same attention accorded to the task of a phenomenological elucidation of the world's being furthermore leads Husserl to underscore another ontological difference oddly neglected in Fink's text, namely, the one concerning the difference between the being of things belonging to the world and the being of the world itself (38, 40, 103).

1.2 The Being of Constituting Consciousness and the Being of the Phenomenological Spectator

It is in the analysis of the double life of transcendental consciousness that the *Sixth Cartesian Meditation* demonstrates its greatest speculative strength. Let us recall that the splitting (*Spaltung*) of the transcendental subject follows directly from the phenomenological reduction: "In universal *epoché* . . . the phenomenological spectator generates itself" (25, 43). It separates itself from constituting consciousness in order to make the latter manifest by positing it as its counterpart. The spectator that generates itself in the phenomenological reduction does not, however, generate this constituting consciousness which it brings to light. For transcendental consciousness constitutes the world well before, and independently of, all phenomenological reductions. But before phenomenological reduction is carried out, transcendental consciousness remains so buried within the world and so fixed on the things of the world that its own activity of constitution is unable to be disclosed to itself. In natural life, constituting consciousness lives in ignorance of itself, and the spectator's intervention is needed for this blindness to be overcome. There exists, however, no phenomenological spectator that would be unaware of itself while working in the anonymity of natural life. The spectator does not exist before the reduction. While presiding over the radical change of constituting consciousness that leads it to self-recognition, the spectator remains selfsame and unchanged, that is, it remains a passive (*unbeteiligen*) spectator of the world's constitution. Its work consists in drawing transcendental consciousness out of the world in order to "cross out" its self-apperception as worldly subject and to reveal the ontological difference between the pre-being of constituting consciousness and the world that it constitutes.

If the phenomenological spectator is responsible for making constituting consciousness manifest, then this also implies that the self-relation (*Selbstbezug*) of constituting consciousness is characterized by heterogeneity or alterity. For the self-relation in this constituting consciousness occurs through the medium of a different self, namely, the spectator that is another self of the same transcendental subject. The fact that constituting consciousness is completely turned toward and entangled in the world prevents it from becoming manifest to itself in an immediate manner. On the other hand, the phenomenological spectator is indeed endowed with an immediate self-consciousness, even though it remains implicit so long as it continues to observe the world's constitution instead of looking at itself. There is therefore an important difference between the phenomenological spectator and the constituting consciousness in that, for the spectator, self-recognition occurs in the context of homogeneity, while for consciousness the recognition of itself implies a form of alterity or heterogeneity within transcendental life. Constituting consciousness needs the spectator in order to appear to itself, but the phenomenological spectator depends only on itself for reflection on its activity as spectator. At the level of spectator, that is, at the level of the activity exerted by the phenomenologist, there is an iterability of reflection in homogeneity. There is, however, heterogeneity between the consciousness that constitutes the world and the phenomenological spectator who brings this constituting consciousness to self-recognition.

How then is one to understand this "heterogeneity," this "difference," this "chasm," this "split" at the heart of transcendental life? What is the sense of this opposition (*Seinsgegensatz*) between two different modes of being that belong to the same transcendental being? In what way "is" the phenomenologist different from the transcendental subject that constitutes the world? Fink constantly repeats that it is, above all, the absence of any *interest in the world* which distinguishes the life of the phenomenological spectator from every other form of life. This spectator lacks the "tendency to being" (*Seinstendenz*), as well as the "finality of a realization of and in the world" (*Finalität der Weltverwirklichung*) that inhabits all constituting consciousness, whether it is "operative" (*fungierend*) in natural life or recognized as such through the phenomenological reduction and through the spectator (24). This spectator is driven by a completely different tendency, which, instead of being directed toward the world's being, prompts the spectator to become interested in the pre-being of transcendental consciousness and especially in the pre-being of the transcendental consciousness that constitutes the world. It would then surely be more accurate to say, as does Husserl in his criticism of Fink, that the phenomenological spectator is indeed interested in the origin of the world within transcendental consciousness, rather than to contend that it has no interest in the world at all.

It is therefore the complete absence of a spontaneous desire to join in the affairs of the world that allows the phenomenologist to make manifest the being of the world in its dependence on the pre-being of constituting consciousness. But the illuminative intervention of the phenomenological spectator will not change the fact that this constituting consciousness will continue to follow its "tendency to being." Even under the scrutiny of the phenomenological spectator it will not give up its work of constituting the world. The phenomenological self-elucidation (*Selbsterhellung*) of its own constituting activity will not prevent constituting consciousness from plunging into the world once again and into the blindness that this act entails.

Led by a different interest, constituting consciousness and the phenomenological spectator also realize themselves in a different task. The constituting consciousness constitutes, organizes, and enriches the world, and the spectator develops a phenomenological analysis of this uninterrupted work of constitution. The phenomenological spectator acts *in soli-tude*, whereas different constituting subjects associate with one another quite naturally and collaborate in fashioning a world that is *common* to them.

> Phenomenological reduction leads the phenomenologizing subject . . . out of the situation of common-intersubjective reference [*Bezogenheit*] to intra-worldly being that is accessible to everyone and exposes it to the solitude of its transcendental-egological existence . . . The "Others" exist in a transcendental mode as constituting monads with which the ego finds itself in a community of constitution, but not in a community of transcendental self-knowledge [*Selbsterkenntnis*]. (134, 135)

If it is true that there is a solipsism of the transcendental subject in Husserl, then it does not concern the subject that constitutes the world, as a too hasty reading of the *Cartesian Meditations* might lead one to believe. The world's constitution is a communal work, and the being of the constituted world is a common-intersubjective-being. But this common-being of the constituted world reveals itself only in the solitary evidence of a solitary subject that, by means of the phenomenological spectator, has become aware of its individual contribution to the communal work of the world's constitution.

The discrepancy between the different interests and tasks of transcendental consciousness and those of the phenomenologizing spectator should not, however, lead us to forget that this opposition arises within one and the same transcendental subject. We must conclude that "the unity of transcendental life [is] identity in difference, opposition within what remains equal to itself [*Sichselbstgleichbleiben*]" (119, 25–26). The transcendental subject brought into play by the phenomenological reduction is therefore never a constituting consciousness nor a phenomenological spectator exclusively. In order to recognize itself as a constituting agent, consciousness involved in the world's constitution needs a spectator; but, on the other hand, "the 'non-participation' [*Unbeteiligtheit*] of the spectator [is only] possible if that in which it does not participate, namely, the world's constitution, takes place" (65). Being neither mere constituting consciousness nor mere phenomenological spectator, the transcendental subject is necessarily both. It emerges from the world to become manifest to the phenomenologist's gaze, while remaining in other respects immersed in the world. The identity of this subject is a composite unity. It can be itself only by being itself in various ways. When it knows itself, it at the same time does not know itself. When it becomes manifest, it is always manifest only in one of its two faces.

2. Heidegger

As is well known, Husserl blamed existential phenomenology and especially Heidegger for abandoning the phenomenological reduction due to the lack of a thorough understanding of it. This judgment has been accepted and repeated by most commentators on the works of Husserl and Heidegger. One can then understand their great astonishment when there became available in 1975 a lecture course taught by Heidegger in the same year as the 1927 publication of *Being and Time*, in which he presented "the phenomenological reduction" as a "basic component of the phenomenological method" (GA24 29ff./21ff.). It is likewise noteworthy that Heidegger's clear statement of allegiance to the method of phenomenological reduction is immediately followed by an objection directed at Husserl:

> *For Husserl*, the phenomenological reduction . . . is the method of leading phenomenological vision from the natural attitude of the human being whose life is involved in the world of things and persons back to the transcendental life of consciousness and its noetic-noematic experiences, in which objects are constituted as correlates of consciousness. *For us* phenomenological reduction means leading phenomenological vision back from the apprehension of a being, whatever may be the character of that apprehension, to the understanding of the being of this being (projecting upon the way it is unconcealed). (GA24 29/21)

In what follows, we would like to show not only how such a phenomenological reduction is indeed at work within *Being and Time*, but also that it does not differ as much from the Husserlian presentation of it, at least in the *Sixth Cartesian Meditation*, as Heidegger seemed to believe. For Husserl and Fink, the task of phenomenological reduction is to bring to light the "transcendental" correlation between constituting consciousness and the constituted world. And it is true that making this correlation manifest also means showing that it was already at work in the anonymity of "natural" life without natural life realizing it. But this in no way gives Heidegger the right to say, as he does repeatedly, that Husserl is not interested in the issue of the being of constituting consciousness.[7] On the contrary, by revealing the correlation between constituting consciousness and the constituted world, the phenomenological reduction makes manifest precisely the (pre)-being of this consciousness and the being of this world as well as the difference between them.

For Heidegger, natural or daily life assumes above all the form of the circumspective concern of a Dasein turned toward the practical use of equipment (*Zeug*) belonging to a familiar environment (*vertraute Um-*

welt). In daily life, Dasein pays attention neither to the way in which equipment refers to the world or to its own proper concernful existence, nor to the way in which this existence inserts itself into the world by organizing it. It is only the *first* phenomenological reduction that, through a certain *malfunctioning of natural life*, reveals this correlation between Dasein's (inauthentic or improper) existence and the familiar world to which it refers. Exactly as in Husserl and Fink, this first reduction, by making manifest the equipment's intraworldly being in its relation to the being-in-the-world of concernful Dasein, reveals the hidden being of the world and of Dasein, their difference and their bond. While insisting on the fundamentally practical or rather poetic character of Dasein's existence as well as on the involvement of Dasein and world, Heidegger, however, avoids speaking again of an activity of "constitution" on the part of the "transcendental" subject.

Husserl and Fink took a second step toward elucidating the being of the transcendental subject by stating that the transcendental subject's life is not limited to its constituting activity. By making manifest the hidden work of the world's constitution by the transcendental subject, phenomenological reduction at the same time effects a split within this subject. The transcendental subject is at once a constituting subject and an observer of the activity of constitution. As opposed to the constituting subject, this phenomenological spectator of the world's constitution does not in any way pre-exist in natural life. It is a new transcendental subject existing only in and through phenomenological reduction. Contrary to constituting consciousness, it shows no particular interest in the world. While one may speak of constituting consciousness operating unknowingly within natural life, there is no phenomenological spectator that does not know itself, that is, does not know what it is doing.

In what might be called a *second* phenomenological reduction, Heidegger reaches similar conclusions. In the experience of *anxiety*, Dasein realizes how ridiculous and futile its unceasing concern for things within-the-world can be. In anxiety and especially in the call of conscience, Dasein discovers itself divided between, on the one hand, the flight into the everyday affairs of worldly life (what Pascal called "*le divertissement*") and, on the other, the care it preserves for its own proper potentiality-for-being. Even if anxiety cannot abolish Dasein's being-in-the-world and eradicate the world as such, the fact remains that the concerns by means of which Dasein usually fits into a familiar, anonymous, and common world are put aside. Like the phenomenological reduction in Husserl and Fink, anxiety therefore sees to it that Dasein, when confronting itself and alone with itself, meets for the first time not only a new self, but also the phenomenon of its own authentic or proper being.

While the differences between the Husserlian and the Heideggerian conceptions of phenomenological reduction are therefore not as radical as Husserl and Heidegger seemed to think, we will see that these differences nevertheless do exist. It is true that in the *Sixth Cartesian Meditation* phenomenological questioning about the phenomenon of being is much more developed than in the first book of the *Ideas*, against which Heidegger's critique was directed.[8] But while this late text of Husserl and Fink does indeed examine the being of transcendental consciousness, it still continues to assume that this being appears in the form of an intentional object, albeit of a higher order. Appearance is always and everywhere appearance before an intentional consciousness. This is the case whether it concerns the constituting consciousness that appears and disappears, which by disappearing also makes manifest its difference from the world as well as from the phenomenological spectator, or whether it concerns the phenomenological spectator that makes the constituting consciousness manifest, but which in turn needs only itself in order to appear. When Heidegger speaks of that "transcendence" that characterizes Dasein's "being-in-the-world," he does much more than simply give a new name to Husserlian intentionality; on the contrary, he inaugurates a new inquiry into the phenomenality of the phenomenon.

2.1 The Being of Beings-Ready-to-Hand and the Being of Concernful Dasein (Inauthentic Existence)

What Heidegger says about daily life corresponds fairly well to Husserl's notion of "the natural attitude." For Husserl, natural life is turned entirely toward things. Things are endowed with a sense that is primarily of a practical nature and unceasingly refers the subject from one thing to another. Other persons are made manifest with regard to their influence on things, but they are nevertheless not mistaken for those things. If it is true that things are endowed with a sense that meets the practical aspirations of the "natural" subject, then it follows that the natural relations between human beings have the form of an interaction or a collaboration. In natural life, subjects meet and quarrel about particular things on the basis of a general and common lifeworld (*Lebenswelt*).

In *Being and Time* Heidegger develops and illustrates this Husserlian conception of natural life without adding much that is very new. Besides, the distinction between things that manifest themselves as being ready-to-hand (*zuhanden*) or as being present-at-hand (*vorhanden*) was already sketched within the second book of the *Ideas*,[9] whose manuscript Heidegger had consulted as early as 1925. Heidegger only further emphasizes the fundamentally practical character of natural life by presenting presence-at-hand (*Vorhandenheit*) as a "deficient" mode of readiness-to-hand (*Zuhan-denheit*). What Husserl, using a visual metaphor, had called "horizon," Heidegger immediately terms "world" or, more precisely, "environment" (*Umwelt*). For Heidegger also, this "environment" is not devoid of all visual connotation, as is evidenced in his use of the term "circumspection" (*Umsicht*) that usually accompanies it. As with "horizon" in Husserl, this environment is never taken into account for itself in the course of daily life, even though it underlies and makes possible circumspective concern for things. This environment is the framework of multiple references (*Verweisungen*) that is woven among things within-the-world. Insofar as it is the condition for the appearance and the understanding of the practical sense of things, environment radically differs from things within-the-world and even from totalities or groups of inter-worldly things. Husserl had also taken account of these differences between things and the world already before the publication of *Being and Time*, although it is true that the significance of this distinction only gradually forced itself upon him.[10]

All these similarities between Heidegger and Husserl deserve to be examined in more detail. However, they suffice to underline that it is not in the description of natural, daily or ordinary life that Heidegger has made the most innovations. Does this mean that one should seek Heidegger's original contribution in the fact that he is the first to have questioned the being of things within-the-world as it stems from concernful Dasein by underscoring the difference between these two modes of being? Heidegger certainly tried to convince us of this. We have, however, seen that the phenomenological examination in Husserl and Fink of the constituting correlation between the transcendental subject and things within-the-world also leads to this same conclusion.

If there is a radical difference between Heidegger and Husserl, then it involves less the ontological concern for a proper understanding of the difference and link between the sense of the being of things within-the-world and the sense of Dasein's being, than the phenomenological *access* to the disclosure of these different modes of being and their specific sense. In other words, the difference concerns the concept of phenomenological reduction and the manner in which it is carried out. For Husserl and Fink, the phenomenological reduction, which provides access to the difference between the being of worldly things and the being of constituting consciousness, as well as to the difference between the being of the constituting consciousness and the being of the phenomenological spectator, requires a "leap" (*Sprung*). But this leap out of natural life is ventured, dared by the subject who *wants* to know more, who *wants* to have a clear mind, who *wants* to give a verdict in the name of scientific evidence. There is nothing of this sort in Heidegger. The disclosure of being is a giving that offers itself in a givenness (*Gegebenheit*) that is out of the ordinary. Concernful Dasein receives the disclosure from the readiness-to-hand (*Zuhandenheit*) of equipment, and Dasein is subjugated to the sudden illumination of its own being. While there is in Heidegger a double reduction (one that is carried out within inauthentic life and another that provides access to the authentic understanding of Dasein's being), these two reductions nevertheless have in common the fact that they are both the result of an event that imposes itself upon Dasein unexpectedly and in a "no-place." Moreover, in both cases being manifests itself against a backdrop of absence.

What we have called the first reduction involves the manifestation of the being ready-to-hand of equipment within the circumspective concern characterizing Dasein's daily existence. In *Being and Time* the movement of such a reduction is initiated at least three times concerning: 1) the referential reference (*Verweisung*) that is constitutive of the being of equipment (§§16–17); 2) the spatiality of a tool occupying a specific place within a region (*Gegend*) (§22); 3) the being-with (*Mitsein*) that for concernful Dasein takes the form of an interaction between subjects who conform to the implicit norms of an anonymous community, which Heidegger calls the "they" (*das Man*) (§§26–27). These three instances of the first reduction have in common the function of presenting the being of equipment and of concernful Dasein against a backdrop of *absence*. The being of a thing reveals itself when this thing is defective, and being-with others manifests itself most clearly when the others turn out to be missing. It is only through their absence that beings come to manifest their being.

1) The sense of the being of what is ready-to-hand is not restricted to serving an occasional user in the realization of some particular work. The tool's utility (*Dienlichkeit*) acquires its sense first of all through a whole complex network of a priori references (*Verweisungen*) or essential references whose different dimensions Heidegger patiently dismantles. These references all fit into a totality of references that Heidegger calls "world" or, more precisely, "environment." However, this world is not merely the sum total of these references. Rather it is the framework of these assignments, that is, what allows concernful Dasein to let itself be referred from one thing to another, without losing itself. This Dasein cannot understand the practical sense of a thing with which it is referentially involved, in short, "what is going on" and "how matters stand" (*Bewandtnis*) with it [*ce dont il retourne avec elle*], and cannot let itself to be guided by this (*Bewendenlassen*), except on the condition that it had first familiarized itself with the significance (*Bedeutsamkeit*) of the world to which this thing belongs. Familiarity (*Vertrautheit*) with the world, however implicit, is the chief presupposition for the proper use of the frame of references that

constitutes the being of things ready-to-hand. For concernful Dasein, the proper use of things consists in letting itself be carried along by these references without stopping to think about them. Forgetfulness of these references, forgetfulness of the world, and finally forgetfulness of the being of the beings ready-to-hand is therefore the best guarantee of their proper functioning. Familiarity with an environment and efficacious understanding of a thing's sense consist precisely in its being a matter of course and passing unnoticed. One stops to think about things only to the extent that they, and more precisely their references and their sense, are no longer a matter of course in that they halt and suspend the natural course of Dasein's concerns.

In §16 of *Being and Time*, Heidegger distinguishes between three different modalities of such a "disturbance of reference": Something can prove to be unusable (*unverwendbar*) and what then catches the attention (*Auffälligkeit*) of concernful Dasein is its *not* being ready-to-hand (*Unzuhandenheit*) (SZ 73/102). One can also find something wanting at the very moment one needs it to carry out an assignment. It then asserts itself as obtrusive (*Aufdringlichkeit*). Finally, a thing can also become an obstacle to the fulfillment of a concern and thus oppose Dasein in an obstinate manner (*Aufsässigkeit*). In these three cases, "circumspection comes up against a void and now sees for the first time *what* the deficient article was ready-to-hand *with*, and *what* it was ready-to-hand *for*. The environment announces itself afresh" (SZ 75/105). Furthermore, in these three cases the tool's being reveals itself precisely in that the tool escapes the control of concernful Dasein. To be able to appear in the truth of its being, the tool needs to give itself room in relation to a subject that wants to make use of it. And this room for the disclosure of the tool's being is that of *atopia*, that is, a place on the fringe of the places of the familiar world. The first phenomenological reduction makes manifest the being of equipment and of the environment by detaching it from the influence of the subject of natural life. Making the being of things manifest also means giving freedom back to things.

No tool is exempt from such a malfunctioning, and concernful Dasein remains constantly at the mercy of such a disarray, which has however the virtue of making Dasein attentive to the being of the beings that are in default to it, that is, to their being ready-to-hand. Heidegger also mentions the peculiar case of a tool whose normal function is precisely to attract the attention of concernful Dasein to the references constituting the being of the things of practical life. It concerns the *sign* (§17) that Heidegger judiciously calls a "tool for indicating" (*Zeigzeug*) (SZ 78/108). Rather than referring to other tools, this exceptional tool excludes itself from the world of ordinary equipment and refers to intersecting references that such equipment bears. In other words, the sign, rather than following the lead of references in order to point to other tools as normal tools do, is instead an abnormal tool that shows how ordinary tools refer, that is, how their being ready-to-hand is inseparable from their act of referring. The sign is thus a tool that points to what a tool is; it is a being that points to the appearance of beings and thereby *offers* itself to the phenomenologist as "an ontological clue" for grasping the being ready-to-hand of tools as the particular beings that they are (SZ 77/108).

Heidegger gives the illuminating if obsolete example of an "adjustable red arrow" that indicates the direction the motor vehicle will take to all drivers at a common intersection. This directional indicator guides people's conduct by revealing a "total tool-complex to expedite and regulate traffic" (SZ 78/109). The arrow of the vehicle cannot fulfill this function of indicating a traffic situation involving a group of vehicles except insofar as it presents itself as a sign and not as a tool or as a mere part of the tool, the vehicle, on which it is affixed. While both can be sold as "spare parts," the sense of being of an arrow differs fundamentally from the sense of the being of a wheel. The sign indicates to the extent that it commands attention or is conspicuous, and it commands attention to the extent that it emerges from the whole context of utilitarian references that link the wheel to the vehicle, the vehicle to the driver, the driver to other drivers, to cyclists, to pedestrians, etc.

Thus, the case of the sign is like that of a missing tool: it indicates the references that are interwoven between things within the environment because it excludes itself from this normal function, because it does not integrate itself into this world. The sign is conspicuous by being out of the ordinary, and it indicates by making itself inconspicuous. The sign presents the being ready-to-hand of things by absenting itself from their utilitarian context. Thus I can indicate something by pointing only to someone who, unlike my dog, does not abandon himself to the entranced contemplation of my forefinger. In order for a tool to become a sign capable of indicating the "kind of being that belongs to whatever equipmental totality may be ready-to-hand in the environment and to its worldly character," it must be understood and grasped by a Dasein that knows how to give sense to absence (SZ 79/109).

2) Heidegger adopts this same line of reasoning concerning the spatiality of tools and being-with others (§22). The spatial being of a tool, that is, the "place" it occupies within a "region" (*Gegend*) of the world is most clearly manifested to Dasein when it does not find the tool in its usual place. One would be tempted to say that this location, where a tool is manifested, is a no-place, an *a-topos*. At any rate, it is clear that this revelation of the tool's spatiality is accompanied by a temporary disorienta-

tion of Dasein within its familiar world. A tool has its place in the environment in accordance with its reference to other places which are all situated within the same region. Without its familiarity with this region,
concernful Dasein would be totally lost in the exercise of its daily business.
It would never find anything for want of knowing where to look for it. In
ordinary life, Dasein finds things without having to look for them, and if it
must look for its equipment it is forced to interrupt its work. This existential difficulty that impedes the efficient management of Dasein's daily concerns is nevertheless rich in ontological lessons for Dasein. In having to
look for something, Dasein discovers for the first time what it had already
found without having to look for it and without thinking about it, namely:

> The readiness-to-hand that belongs to any such region beforehand has
> the *character of inconspicuous familiarity* [*unauffällige Vertrautheit*],
> and it has it in an even more primordial sense than does the being of the
> ready-to-hand. The region itself becomes visible in a conspicuous manner
> [*Auffallen*] only when one discovers the ready-to-hand circumspectively
> and does so in the deficient modes of concern. Often the region of the
> place does not become accessible explicitly as such a region until one fails
> to find something in *its* place. (SZ 104/137f.)

3) In this region, tools occupy a place that concernful Dasein assigns
to them by virtue of what Heidegger calls its "re-moval" (*Ent-fernung*) and
its "orientation" (*Ausrichtung*) (§23). Even though the spatiality of the
environment seems thus endowed with a concentric structure polarized by
a single Dasein, this environment is for Heidegger unquestionably an *in-
tersubjective world*. This world that concernful Dasein's work fits into is a
common rather than a shared world, a world prior to sharing and prior to
a mine and yours in their communion. It is the world of "everyone" and no
one, it is the world of anonymous Dasein that Heidegger calls the "they"
(*das Man*). This they is not a trans-individual subject; it is one of Dasein's
modes of existence that is ruled by conformism, commonplaces, and conventional outlooks. Even in isolation, concernful Dasein still acts in the
mode of the they. However, while being-alone does not necessarily call
into question what Heidegger calls the "dictatorship" of the they, the absence of others nevertheless has the peculiar effect of making Dasein attentive to the fact that its existence always has the form of a being-with
(*Mitsein*) others (SZ 126/164): "Being-with is an existential characteristic
of Dasein even when factically no Other is present-at-hand or perceived.
Even Dasein's being-alone is being-with in the world. The Other can *be
missing* only *in* and *for* a being-with. Being-alone is a deficient mode of
being-with; its very possibility is the proof of this" (SZ 120/156).

Here again, it is the task of absence to make Dasein conscious of what underlies its daily existence without its being aware of it. The being-alone of concernful Dasein is part of those existential difficulties that Dasein would gladly do without, but which at the same time instruct it much more on the being of things and on its own being than does a life without difficulty. In looking for a piece of equipment that is not in its place, Dasein finds out what it neither looked for nor wanted, namely, the manifestation of the readiness-to-hand of equipment and its insertion into the world's space. In finding itself alone, Dasein discovers that in the entirety of its preoccupied existence it has acted, without knowing it, in accord with its being-with others. Thus these experiences do indeed have the effect of a *phenomenological reduction*, but of a phenomenological reduction undergone in the disturbance brought on by disarray. Far from wanting this reduction and its countless revelations, Dasein would much rather avoid having to undergo its unexpected occurrence again. It is anxious to repair the disturbance (*Störung*) to which it owes the discovery of the being of the familiar world and its dependence on Dasein's concernful existence. This flight from circumstances capable of making manifest the phenomenality of worldly phenomena to (inauthentic) Dasein can be explained by the fact that this ontological disclosure happens at the cost of losing the usability of tools and the smooth functioning of Dasein's concerns.

2.2 The Being of World as World and the Being-in-the-World of Dasein (Authentic Existence)

The *first* phenomenological reduction exposes the mode of the tool's worldly being and the mode of being of concernful Dasein's communal existence to the scrutiny of a Dasein that continues to exist under the form of concern even if this concern is disturbed. The *second* phenomenological reduction, the one carried out in anxiety (§40),[11] no longer owes anything either to concern or to its disturbance. The opening toward being made possible by anxiety departs resolutely from the natural bounds of daily life. But this does not mean that in anxiety Dasein is deprived of all connections with daily life or with the ontological lessons that follow from its disturbance. While it is true that in anxiety Dasein is struck by the disclosure of its own being, it is no less true that, in this stunning disclosure of the truth about its being, its concernful and inauthentic existence also appears in a new light, namely, as a flight from truth. This disclosure concerning the futility of its daily existence is accompanied by the collapse of the familiarity of the environment in which Dasein's inauthentic existence takes place. Anxiety thus reveals to Dasein that which the world that is no longer the familiar world of things ready-to-hand really is, and from which this familiar world of the things of practical life nonetheless receives its sense. One can therefore say that the second phenomenological reduction incorporates the ontological lessons of the first by deepening them. By confronting Dasein not only with a piece of equipment that is no longer in its proper place, but also with a world in which Dasein no longer feels "at home" (*Un-zuhause*) (SZ 189/233), the second reduction goes deeply into the sense of this atopia, of this no-place where being can manifest itself in its truth. It effects a new type of sight and a new "care" (*Sorge*) that brings Dasein "before itself" (*vor sich selbst*) (SZ 182/226), and measures the being of things and of the familiar world, as well as Dasein's concernful existence, by the standard of the authentic disclosure of Dasein's proper being.

This manifestation of the authentic being of Dasein and of the world that takes place in anxiety is again the result of a confrontation between Dasein and absence. This time it concerns not the absence of a tool, but the absence of this being ready-to-hand that the absence of the tool had already made manifest. Thus anxiety is the experience of a redoubled absence, the disclosure of this radical nothingness that Heidegger calls "the nothing ready-to-hand" (*Nichts von Zuhandenheit*) (SZ 187/232). In anxiety one watches a shipwreck of "the beings within-the-world to which Dasein clings [*klammert*] proximally and for the most part" (191/235). Whereas in the disturbance of usage, equipment alone loses its purposiveness [*finalité*] (*Bewandtnis*) and thus becomes "un-employable" (*unverwendbar*), anxiety, on the contrary, brings about the collapse of all significance (*Bedeutsamkeit*) in the familiar world. In anxiety "the world has the character of complete in-significance [*Unbedeutsamkeit*]" (SZ 186/231).

How could things and the world come to this? How can it be that suddenly they "don't matter anymore" to Dasein? For Heidegger, this loss of interest in the world and the disorientation that follows from it are the result of Dasein's painful and obstinate encounter with its own being. Faced with the unfathomable facticity of its existence and with its being-toward-death, Dasein loses its taste for the things of the world. Struck by anxiety, circumspective concern for what is ready-to-hand appears futile. By tearing Dasein away from its habitual concerns within the world, anxiety also expels it from the undifferentiated community of the "they." Anxiety abolishes the security of what Lacan would call an "imaginary" identification with others. In experiencing anxiety and in bearing this anxiety without falling into phobic fear, Dasein finds itself alone in the face of its ipseity, its "*solus ipse*" (SZ 188/233). In the solitude of anxiety, the sense of Dasein's being is manifested to itself, which sense, according to *Being and Time*, is meant to serve as the basis of inquiry into the sense of being in general. In the solitude of anxiety, in listening to the silent voice of conscience (*Gewissen*), Dasein hears the call of its "vocation."

But what more exactly is the sense of this solitude that accompanies authentic existence? What is the sense of this solipsism to which anxiety, acting as phenomenological reduction, constrains Dasein? Anxious Dasein's disinterest in the world irresistibly reminds us of that impartiality that Husserl and Fink ascribed to the phenomenologizing spectator (*unbeteiligter Zuschauer*). This spectator was also alone, owing to the simple fact that one sees clearly only by oneself. Despite appearances, it is not the same with anxiety-ridden Dasein. For even if Dasein is indeed anxious of itself, that is, of its own self, it does not, for all that, offer itself as an object to its own gaze. Dasein experiences itself rather in that particular mode of feeling that Heidegger called "affection" (*Befindlichkeit*). Anxiety is a self-affection in which Dasein experiences its individuality as an incomparable and irreplaceable character. It is true that in anxious care for its own being, Dasein hardly pays any attention to other Daseins, but despite this its solitude is still always a mode of being-with. Unlike the phenomenologizing spectator, the Dasein that undergoes the disclosure of its own being as a result of anxiety is also very far from having broken all contacts with the world. Even if the truth of its own being becomes manifest to Dasein in the solitude and disorientation of anxiety, this does not change the fact that to-be-with other Daseins and to-be-in-the-world (*In-der-Welt-sein*) belongs to Dasein's being. On the contrary, through the world's in-significance experienced in anxiety "the world as world" announces itself for the first time (SZ 187/232). In anxiety, "Dasein is isolated and individualized [*vereinzelt*], but *as* being-in-the-world" (SZ 189/233).

When Heidegger opposes authentic existence to inauthentic existence, he does it somewhat in the way that Fink and Husserl oppose the phenomenologizing spectator to constituting consciousness. This opposition in principle, that is, in structure, between these two forms of existence does not, however, prevent their cohabitation within the same subject. The "double life" of one and the same Dasein manifests itself most explicitly in what Heidegger calls "*the call of conscience*" (*Ruf des Gewissens*) (§§54–60). This "call comes *from me* and yet is imposed *upon* me" (*aus mir und doch über mich*) (SZ 275/320). It comes from me since, according to Heidegger, no one can care so much about my own being as myself. Even so, it imposes itself upon me because I have always already lost myself in my worldly concerns. This call that expresses itself in silence and this return to myself that answers it, this whole drama of vocation and conversion, occurs nonetheless between me and myself. While it does violence to me, in the end this calling requires of me only that I take hold of (*Ergreifen*) my existence, that I choose myself rather than allow myself to be carried along by the conformist attitudes and conventional outlooks of the "they" (SZ 179/223–24). This call sees to it that "Dasein specifically brings itself back to itself from its lostness in the they" (SZ 268/312). It recollects the self that has been "dispersed [*zertreut*] into the they" (SZ 129/167). Does not Dasein's recognition of its own being remind us of the way in which the phenomenologizing spectator extracts constituting consciousness from its immersion in the world in order to disclose it to itself?

The authentic existence to which I am called nevertheless retains the status of a "modification" of inauthentic existence (SZ 267/312, 130/168). Consequently, it cannot aspire to the status of an autonomous way of life: "The irresoluteness of the 'they' remains dominant notwithstanding, but it cannot impugn resolute existence" (SZ 299/345). In the second phenomenological reduction, the one accompanied by anxiety and the call of conscience, and the one that discloses the being of Dasein's authentic self, the trace of Dasein's double life is thus made manifest: "Disclosed in its 'there,' it maintains itself both in truth and in untruth with equal primordiality" (SZ 298/345).

By making Dasein's being manifest, phenomenological reduction makes a double phenomenon manifest, each aspect of which has its own mode of manifestation. By making manifest Dasein's inauthentic and authentic existence in different ways, phenomenological reduction at the same time discloses the difference and the split that traverse that peculiar being which is Dasein. Indeed, if Dasein's "being" is its "existence," and if Dasein exists "with equal primordiality" in an authentic and an inauthentic manner, then Dasein's being cannot be protected from contamination by this double life that Dasein leads. Phenomenological reduction, which makes Dasein's being manifest, presents it as torn between truth and untruth. There is then no Dasein whose being could epitomize authentic existence, no more than there was a pure phenomenologizing spectator for Husserl and Fink. Dasein's life, much like that of the transcendental subject, is a life both in authenticity and in unauthenticity, in the care of the self and in the concern for the world. For Dasein, as for the transcendental subject, "being" means "being otherwise" or "being always different from itself," in short, never coinciding with itself. If difference is thus inherent in the being of the transcendental subject and of Dasein, it follows that the phenomenological reduction, called upon to make this being manifest, will forever be incapable of exhibiting a "pure" phenomenon.

However, even if Husserl and Heidegger agree that phenomenological reduction consists in making manifest the being-divided of the transcendental subject and of Dasein, they have a completely different conception of the manifestation of this being. For Husserl, this "manifestation" of being means to appear [*comparaître*] *before* the inquisitive gaze of an "impartial spectator." Becoming manifest as the intentional object of a gaze filled with evidence, the being [*l'être*] of transcendental consciousness still becomes manifest in the manner of a being [*étant*]. Regardless of whether the being of constituting consciousness, the being of the phenomenological spectator, or else the difference between the transcendental subject's two modes of being is at stake, their manifestation always consists in presenting themselves before the intentional gaze of a "supervisor." Nothing escapes the phenomenologist's gaze, not even the internal division of a two-faced transcendental subject who sees to it that the subject cannot appear on one side without disappearing on the other. Finally, phenomenological manifestation is only distinguishable from ordinary forms of manifestation by the quality of the phenomenologist's gaze, who will not rest until the manifesting *object* is given to it "in person" and in its entirety (*Selbstgegebenheit*) without holding anything back. For Heidegger, on the contrary, Dasein's being never gives itself as an object to be displayed in its entirety before a spectator. Marion is therefore not wrong in juxtaposing the Heideggerian conception of phenomenon to Husserl's "flat phenomenon," where for Heidegger it is a question instead of probing the phenomenon's "enigmatic" depth.[12]

An initial aspect of the depth of the phenomenon's being consists in the fact that Dasein is far from being able to govern this phenomenon. Regardless of whether it concerns the being of a tool, of the world, or of Dasein, the manifestation of being is inseparable from the way in which Dasein's existence is carried out. It is therefore no accident that Dasein's authentic being does not present itself under the form of an object of intuition, but instead receives its disclosure in the state of anxiety, that is, by being moved in its existence and more particularly in its "affection" (*Befindlichkeit*). Being can thus become manifest without betraying its invisible character. A second aspect of the depth of the phenomenon's being is linked to Dasein's double life. The manifestation of Dasein's authentic or proper being is inseparable from its recovery through its inauthentic or improper being. Untruth is an integral part of the way in which the truth of Dasein's being becomes manifest. Thus, to probe phenomenologically the depth of the phenomenon of Dasein's being does amount, as Marion also says, to "making manifest not only the unmanifested, but also the play of the manifest with the unmanifest in the manifestation."[13]

15

The Husserlian Heritage in Heidegger's Notion of the Self

Jacques Taminiaux
*Translated by François Renaud**

This is an attempt to locate traces of a Husserlian heritage in a specific theme found in Heidegger's text. The theme is the *Selbst*, the self understood as *ipse*.

I chose this theme for two reasons. The first is self-evident, the second is a wager. It is evident that the self is a central theme of Heidegger's existential analytic and, more generally, of fundamental ontology. On the other hand, it is, at first sight, quite unclear how Dasein's *ipse*, its very own answer to the question *"who?"*, could testify to any kinship with Husserl's *Bewußtsein*. This "first sight," however, is precisely what I want to overcome.

What first prompted me to undertake this endeavor are observations made by Heidegger himself in the last seminar in Zähringen, in which I participated. Asked by Beaufret whether the *Seinsfrage* could appeal to a Husserlian heritage, Heidegger in that seminar replied that the doctrine of categorial intuition proclaimed by Husserl in the *Logical Investigations* had in effect provided him with the basis for the problematic of *Being and Time*. This confession, however guarded, never ceased since then to alert me to Beaufret's question and gradually led me to the conviction that a certain Husserlian heritage governs the problematic of fundamental ontology at its very core. Indeed, it governs it at its core to the point of including the question of the self. This conviction is what I shall try to justify here.

As recalled above, it is, by Heidegger's own admission, an intuitionist theme from the *Logical Investigations* that allows him to articulate the *Seinsfrage* into a problematic. The theme around which my reflections will revolve is accordingly intuitionism.

Heidegger in *Being and Time* does not refrain from expressing some

*Translator's Note: I am grateful to John van Buren, Carol Fiedler, and Theodore Kisiel for their numerous and insightful comments on my translation.

reservations with respect to Husserl's descriptions. However, on closer examination, one realizes that when he refers his readers to Husserl's writings without adding critical comments—and this he does most often discreetly in footnotes—the texts to which he refers are precisely among those that insist on the privileged status of intuition. This is the case with the first, fourth, and sixth *Logical Investigations*. At this point in my exposition, it is sufficient for my purpose to outline briefly Husserl's view in the first *Logical Investigation*. More specifically, I will outline the beginning of that investigation, the one so brilliantly examined by Jacques Derrida in *Speech and Phenomena*. Heidegger himself alludes to this investigation and, in his lecture course on the *Basic Problems of Phenomenology* in SS 1927 (the year of the publication of *Being and Time*), affirms that he subscribes to it. For example, he writes: "Only in recent times has this problem of the sign been pursued in an actual investigation. In the first of his *Logical Investigations*, "Expression and Signification" [*Ausdruck und Bedeutung*], Husserl gives the essential definitions of sign [*Zeichen*], indication [*Anzeichen*], and designation [*Bezeichnung*], taking them all together in distinction from *Bedeuten*, signifying" (GA24 263/185). To agree with Husserl about that distinction, to consider it as essential, amounts to drawing a clear demarcation between, on the one hand, the order of *Bedeutung* and, on the other, that of the symbolic. The first is capable of offering itself to an adequate seeing in an immediate manner. The second is not capable of it because it is intrinsically affected by an inescapable mediation. In Husserl, the distinction is justified by the phenomenological privilege of *Bedeutung* and the marginalization of the symbolic. Indeed, *Bedeutung* in the Husserlian sense is properly a phenomenon insofar as it is an ideality capable of exhibiting itself with evidence in full presence before an intention of signification which is in turn present to itself, an ideality that, further, finds in this its own fulfillment. It is, however, this possibility of evidence that in general is lacking in the order of indication whose characteristic is the simple motivation defined as follows: "[Here] certain objects or states of affairs of the world, of whose existence someone has actual knowledge, indicate to him the existence of other objects or states of affairs in the sense that the belief in the being of the one is experienced as the motivation (and as a non-evidential motivation) for the belief or surmise in the being of the other."[1] The order of indication is one where absence intrinsically affects presence, where what offers itself is not a full phenomenon, but a mere *Erscheinung*, appearance, of that which does not offer itself to a seeing. This order must be put aside if one is to gain access to the phenomenological phenomenon proper.

　　1. These observations define the first aspect of my inquiry, namely, the *method*. Husserl's phenomenological procedure, as recalled above, is

based from the outset on the clear demarcation between an intuitive and a purely symbolic order. My first question is whether this demarcation can also be found in Heidegger's concept of method as employed in *Being and Time* in order to arrive at the self, understood as Dasein's *ipse*.

The concept of self is defined, at least provisionally, in the famous first pages of the introduction. There Heidegger carries out the elucidation of the respective components of the word "phenomenology," phenomenon and *logos*. As to the first component, he claims that the expression "phenomenon" signifies "that which shows itself in itself" (*das sich-an-ihm-selbst-Zeigende*), the manifest (*das Offenbare*). From this phenomenon in its original and positive sense, Heidegger derives by way of privative modification what is commonly called "semblance" (*Schein*). To say that "semblance" is a privative modification of the phenomenon in the original sense amounts to saying that semblance in its very derivation remains grounded in that which it modifies. Indeed, semblance is what "shows itself as that which it in itself is *not*." "Now, only to the extent that something claims, in its sense, to show itself, that is, to be a phenomenon, *can* it show itself *as* something that it is *not*" (SZ 29/51). Semblance is only an alleged phenomenon, but in this pretension it is nonetheless a phenomenon.

It is therefore appropriate, Heidegger insists, to find something that is opposed both to the phenomenon in the original positive sense and to its negative modification which is semblance, that is, find something which is neither the one nor the other. Heidegger calls it the *Erscheinung*, the appearance. The meaning of the term *Erscheinung* is very closely linked to the term *Anzeichen*, indication, as employed by Husserl in his first *Logical Investigation*. The scope of the Heideggerian notion of *Erscheinung* includes: "all indications [*Indikationen*], *Darstellungen*, symptoms and symbols" (SZ 29/52). Husserl, for his part, evokes stigmata, the flag, distinctive markings, traces, mnemonic signs, designations, etc., but, as he says, "these distinctions and other similar ones do not abolish the essential unity pertaining to the concept of indication."[2] Its function is to indicate and to set up a non-evidential (*uneinsichtig*) relation between an indicator that is given and something indicated that is not given. This is precisely how Heidegger defines the *Erscheinungen*, the "occurrences which show themselves and which in this very self-showing 'indicate' [*indizieren*] something that does *not* show itself." And one reads further: "The *Erscheinung* as *Erscheinung* 'of something' precisely does *not* mean showing-itself, but the announcing-itself by something that does not show itself through something that does show itself" (SZ 29/52). It is not unjustified to decipher Heidegger's distinction of *Erscheinung* as a mere terminological transposition of the Husserlian description of *Anzeige*, indication. Where Husserl speaks of *Anzeichen*, Heidegger speaks of *Erscheinung*.

Where Husserl speaks of *Anzeige*, Heidegger, despite his sparse use of words of Latin origin, speaks of *"Indikation"* or *"indizieren."* Where Husserl says *"kundgeben,"* Heidegger says *"melden,"* "to announce." These expressions are nevertheless interchangable, for they respectively signify the same thing.

Consequently, just as Husserlian phenomenology rests from the outset upon the clear demarcation between the intuitive and the symbolic order, the phenomenon in Heideggerian phenomenology, understood as "something that shows itself in itself," is distinguished at the outset from the order of mediation and that of the symbolic in general. In this connection, the SS 1925 lecture course on the *History of the Concept of Time*, which may in many respects be regarded as the first version of *Being and Time*, includes the following passage: "To indicate something by means of something else means not to show the former in itself, but to present it indirectly, mediately, symbolically" (GA20 112/82). The order of phenomenon, although monitored and threatened by its privative modification which is semblance, distinguishes itself, therefore, clearly from the symbolic order.

Now, the demarcation can be found again in Heidegger's elucidation of the second component of the word "phenomenology": the Greek word *logos*, which he translates as *Rede*, discourse. On this theme, it is revealing to consider the relevant section in *Being and Time* in connection with the more explicit one in the SS 1925 lecture course. Every discourse, Heidegger maintains, has the function of revealing, of making the subject of its discourse manifest (*offenbar machen*), of showing it (*zeigen*). However, within the function of discourse in general, it is, according to him, appropriate to distinguish carefully between two modes of showing. On that question, Heidegger appeals to Aristotle, who affirms in *De Interpretatione* that while every *logos* is semantic, not every *logos* is apophantic. Every *logos* is semantic, according to the Heideggerian commentary, in that every *logos* shows something understandable. Only a portion of *logos* is apophantic in that what this portion shows consists "in making something visible in itself and this—*apo*—from itself," thereby bringing it to a seeing, to a *theorein* (GA20 115/84). There is, therefore, a clear distinction between a merely semantic and a properly apophantic discourse. The latter alone, as stressed in *Being and Time*, has the property of a showing "in the sense of a making visible that exhibits identification" (*im Sinne des aufweisenden Sehenlassens*) (SZ 32–33/56). It seems to me noteworthy that the verb *Aufweisen* figures also in the first of Husserl's *Logical Investigations*. There it characterizes, in opposition to the mere *hinweisen* (to refer) carried out by the indication and the symbolic in general, fulfillment through making visible what it aims at, which aim is inherent in the act of *Bedeutung*, signification. The echo of this oppositon can be found also in Heidegger's distinction between the apophantic and semantic *logos*.

It is, Heidegger insists, only to the extent that *logos* is apophantic, i.e., makes visible, that it can be true, i.e., unveiling that about which it speaks. And just as phenomenon, in the original and positive sense (that which shows itself in itself), is monitored by its privative modification under the mode of semblance (that which shows itself as that which it in itself is not), so the revealing power of making visible characteristic of apophantic *logos* is monitored by its privative modification of falsehood in the mode of a misleading concealing. Concealing consists in allowing something to pass for what it is not by placing it before the thing of which one speaks.

In contrast, the merely semantic discourse is neither true nor false in the sense of unconcealing and concealing. Heidegger lists the following as lying within the scope of this discourse: exclamation, request, wish, prayer. One might be tempted to add, given the close isomorphism between the elucidation of *logos* and of phenomenon, that this list of a few examples of merely semantic discourse concerns precisely that part of symbolic discourse in which what is shown refers to what cannot be made visible. In any case, both elucidations betray a clear demarcation between the intuitive order, which is open to phenomenon as "that which shows itself in itself," and the symbolic order where self-manifestation does not occur.

As to *logos*, Heidegger emphatically confirms the primacy of the intuitive order by insisting that *logos*, even the apophantic one, is not the primary locus of truth understood as unconcealing. The primary locus is instead *aneu logou*, without *logos*. *Aisthesis*, for instance, is what never fails to refer to the sensible objects proper to it, such as colors for seeing, sounds for hearing. However, "in the purest and most original sense," he writes, "what is 'true', that is, what limits itself to unconcealing in such a manner that it can never conceal, is pure *noein*, the pure and simple observational [*hinsehende*] apprehension of the simplest determinations of the being of beings as such."

In relation to noetic seeing, *logos*, even the apophantic one, occupies a subordinate place. Heidegger proves to be the heir of Husserl also in regard to the secondary character of the apophantic *logos* in relation to noetic seeing. He himself indirectly recognizes it when he points out in a footnote in *Being and Time* that pages 255 and following in *Ideas* I radicalize the problematic of the first *Logical Investigation* (SZ 166/209). What is the subject matter in these pages? Husserl begins by inviting his readers to reflect upon their experience of reading, to pay attention to the apprehension of what is called the "content of thought" of the readings and, to consider "that which, in the understanding of what is read, accedes to a truly originary actualization with regard to what can be called the infrastructure of thought in expressions."[3] This actualization is the subject matter of § 124 in *Ideas* I. It is entitled "The Noetico-Noematic Stratum of 'Logos': Signifying and Signification [*Bedeuten und Bedeutung*]." According to that section, the infrastructure of thought in expressions resides in expressive acts, that is, following Husserl, in the stratum of specifically logical acts. The stratum of a specifically logical act in an expressive act consists in the act of signifying, *Bedeuten*. This act is intentional and has therefore a noetico-noematic structure. Its intentionality, however, is only that of a medium "whose peculiarity is in its essence to reflect as it were every other intentionality" (257/320). In other words, "the stratum of expression—and here lies its originality—is not productive apart from the fact that it confers an expression upon all other intentionalities" (258/321). To express is merely to explicate by means of *Bedeutungen* "pre-expressive" or even "non-expressive" intentionalities, which are endowed with a productivity proper to them. Thus, perception as intentional act corresponds noematically to a "pure object of seeing [*visé*] as such" in a perceptual order, of which it is the primary apprehension pure and simple (*die erste, schlichte Erfassung*). When one states that "this is white," the expression, as an act that occurs by means of significations, is only a secondary stratum that, in its noetico-noematic structure, copies and reflects strictly the noetico-noematic structure of the primary apprehension pure and simple. This apprehension is the intentional substructure upon which the expression is dependent. Such a substructure is accessible to "a glance of the I [*Ichblick*] constituted by a single ray (which is) directed toward it, and grasps the noematic object envisaged in a single indivisible apprehension" (255/318).

The fact that Heidegger in his analysis of *logos* appeals to Aristotle and not to Husserl is beside the point. For it is hardly questionable, it seems to me, that he reads the former in the light of the latter.

On the basis of this double elucidation, it is evident that the very notion of phenomenon merely concentrates the close relationship between what is thought by the term phenomenon and what is thought by that of *logos*. Phenomenology, therefore, signifies "making visible from itself that which shows itself in the very way that it shows itself from itself." This is, Heidegger says, what the motto *"Zu den Sachen selbst,"* "To the things themselves," expresses (SZ 34/58). One could not suggest more effectively that the *Selbst*, the self, the "themselves," is capable of an access that is not symbolic, but intuitive.

2. a) The question is—and this is the second step of my inquiry—

how this methodological demarcation, of Husserlian origin, between the intuitive and the symbolic governs the analysis of determinations of Dasein's being, that is, the existential analytic conceived of as an ontology of Dasein. One of the first versions of this ontology is delivered in the 1925 lecture course on *The History of the Concept of Time* cited above. This version is prefaced by Heidegger's recall of the three Husserlian discoveries upon which his own investigation admittedly depends. It seems to me significant that the intuitionist theme plays a decisive role in Heidegger's reflections on each of these discoveries.

The first discovery is that of intentionality. It is a structure, Heidegger insists, that concerns "the being itself of comportment" and designates in it a "directing-itself-toward" (GA20 40/31). However, we have a "traditional tendency not to question that of which it is presumably the structure and what this sense of structure itself means" (63/47). This is why it is important, Heidegger says, to resist this tendency and to adopt as a "methodological rule for the initial apprehension of intentionality . . . not to be concerned with interpretations, but only to keep strictly to that which shows itself, regardless of how meager that may be." He continues:

> Only in this way will it be possible *to see, in intentionality itself and through it*, equally that of which it is the structure and how it is that structure. Intentionality is not an ultimate explanation of the psychic, but an initial approach toward overcoming the uncritical application of traditionally defined realities such as the psychic, consciousness, the continuity of lived experience, reason. But if this task is implicit in this basic concept of phenomenology, then "intentionality" may least of all be used as a phenomenological slogan. (63/47; emphasis added)

The realities in question (consciousness, continuity of lived experience, etc.) are no doubt an integral part of Husserl's terminology, and for this he is here being criticized. But this criticism is directed at his disregard of the rule of intuitive vigilance that he himself imposed. It is in the name of this vigilance that Heidegger blames Husserl for leaving undiscussed the question of the being of the being endowed with intentionality. It is in the name of that same vigilance, which is ultimately the reduction, that he directs the "phenomenological seeing." The latter is no longer directed toward the transcendental life of consciousness and the noetico-noematic correlations inherent in intentionality, but toward Dasein's openness to beings and to itself, as well as toward the understanding of the being inherent in this openness, in short, toward transcendence.

The second Husserlian discovery praised by Heidegger is that of categorial intuition. The elucidation of this discovery is an occasion, he says, to "pursue intentionality to its concretion" (63/47). It is therefore a discovery, of an intuitive nature, as its name indicates, that plays a privileged role with respect to that of which intentionality is the structure. It also plays a privileged role with respect to the manner in which it is that structure, which is to say, with regard to the being of intentional beings, that is, with regard to transcendence as an understanding of the being of beings.

Indeed, from the very outset, Heidegger underscores the ontological scope of this intuitive discovery. "The discovery is the demonstration first," he says, "that there is a direct apprehension [*ein schlichtes Erfassen*] of the categorial, that is, of the constituents of beings, which are traditionally designated as categories and which were seen in crude form quite early on," that is, in Plato and Aristotle (64/48). More fundamentally, among the categorial intuitions dealt with in the *Logical Investigations* appears that of being. Insofar as it is a *surplus* with regard to the real properties of the states of given things, or, according to the Kantian formula cited by Husserl, insofar as it is not a real predicate, being is accessible to an intuition. This is Husserl's discovery which, according to Heidegger's own late acknowledgment, was to provide him with the basis of the existential analytic. This discovery made him realize that the understanding of being, insofar as it differs from beings, is a matter of *seeing*. If it is true that this understanding is not just one intentionality among others, but is rather the primordial and most basic constitution of the being that we are, then it prompted him to *see* that the concretion of intentionality consists in the movement that exceeds beings toward being, that is, in transcendence. It seems to me significant in this respect that Heidegger, in one of his most condensed expositions of transcendence as he understands it, can say that it is *überschüssig*, excessive. *Überschuß*, excess, is the word that describes the status of categorial intuition in comparison with sensible intuition (GA26 248/192). It is no less significant that the exposition to which I am alluding appears in the lecture course on *The Metaphysical Foundations of Logic*.

Husserl's third discovery praised by Heidegger is that of the a priori. Here Heidegger also credits Husserl with undertaking the task, despite certain limitations, of giving a universal ontological scope to this discovery. This discovery as such is independent of the traditional division between the subjective and the objective sphere. Husserl is also credited with recognizing that the a priori is accessible "to itself from within itself" in a "simple apprehension," an "originary intuition" (GA20 102/75). Finally, Heidegger credits Husserl with "preparing the determination of the structure of the a priori as a feature of the being of beings" (103/75).

Since Heidegger's remarks on this third discovery underscore at the outset that the elucidation of the sense of the a priori presupposes the understanding of time (as already suggested by the terms *prius, proteron*), it is perhaps no exaggeration to see here in Heidegger an acknowledgment of his dependence on Husserl when he in the end makes temporality the principle of transcendence as the understanding of being. It seems to me significant in this respect that Heidegger in his lecture course on *The Metaphysical Foundations of Logic*, while referring to the subtitle "Transcendence and Temporality," briefly evokes the *Lectures on the Phenomenology of Inner Time-Consciousness*, and credits Husserl with "seeing, for the first time, by means of the intentional structure, the phenomena" of expecting, retention, and presentifying. Although this praise is accompanied by the reservation that Husserl remained a prisoner of the problematic of consciousness, Heidegger nevertheless makes the following acknowledgment: "That which Husserl still calls *Zeitbewußtsein*, that is, consciousness of time, is precisely time itself in its original sense [*im ursprünglichen Sinne*]" (GA26 264/204).

In any case, what Heidegger brings to the fore with respect to these three Husserlian discoveries, ontologized by him, is really an intuitionist theme.

This ontologization implies an analysis of Dasein, the being that in its being questions being itself. It is, therefore, fitting to ask ourselves whether and how the privileged status of the intuitionist theme governs the analytic of Dasein and concerns Dasein in itself, in its self.

2. b) The analytic of Dasein rests upon a distinction in principle between the manner in which Dasein acts in everyday life, proximally and for the most part, and the manner in which it is proper [*en propre*] or authentic. This distinction, on the one hand, deals with everydayness where Dasein, concerned with tasks and with the means or instruments to carry them out, tends to reflect on its proper condition in the mode of the being of things, i.e., *Vorhandenheit*, presence-at-hand, and, on the other hand, deals with Dasein's resolute sight carried out by itself in the mode of being that is proper to it, i.e., existing. This distinction, as a more careful study shows, closely corresponds to the distinction between the symbolic in general and *Bedeutung*. Heidegger regards this latter distinction, set up at the very beginning of the *Logical Investigations*, as essential. More specifically, this distinction, given the ontologization evoked above, is the object of both a reappropriation and a metamorphosis. One may even say that it is precisely because the tension between the proper and the improper governs Dasein's comportment ontologically that Heidegger, in his detailed description of everydayness, can analyse the order of the symbolic. Now, it is precisely this order which Husserl in the *Logical Investigations* characterized only briefly, hastening to highlight the sphere of the purely logical.

We said that it is in Husserl's wake that Heidegger set up a demarcation between, on the one hand, the phenomenon in the phenomenological sense (that which shows itself in itself) as well as the semblance, the privative modification of the phenomenon, and, on the other hand, the mediate order of the symbolic in general. Now, if a phenomenon proves to be for the most part not itself, if it proves not to manifest itself from within itself precisely because it is interwoven in the mediate order of the symbolic in general, then it goes without saying that this notional and formal demarcation must be described with more nuance. One could not simply say that there is, on the one hand, the phenomenon and its privative modification (semblance) and, on the other, the mediation of signs. One would have to say rather that semblance is a privative modification of the phenomenon proper insofar as it is interwoven in the mediate order of signs. Now, such is indeed Dasein's everyday status, a status that Heidegger through his ontologizing of Husserl's discoveries sets out to analyze. To the degree to which it is preoccupied with signs, Dasein in everydayness succumbs to the sway of semblance in relation to its proper phenomenality. This explains why Heidegger, in his 1927 lecture course on the *Basic Problems of Phenomenology*, can present §17 of *Being and Time*, which consists in a thematization of the sign in general, both as a "complement" to Husserl and as a radicalization of his view, understood as a "principial orientation," that is, as an ontological orientation. This ontological orientation is what permits Heidegger to thematize the signs and references that Husserl describes briefly in order to quickly reduce them. But this thematization, as we shall soon see, is in no way a rehabilitation of the symbolic. It instead aims at an ontological justification of the reduction that in Husserl's *Logical Investigations* opens up the realm of *Bedeutung* beyond all symbolism.

Let us recall the outline of this thematization and the reduction. The thematization, as suggested above, occurs in §17 of *Being and Time*. This section, inseparable from those surrounding it, is entitled "Reference and Signs" (*Verweisung und Zeichen*). It demonstrates that a sign, far from being something present before us (*vorhanden*), which as such would find itself in a relation of reference indicating another *vorhanden*, appears as a sign only in regard to Dasein's everyday comportment that is given over to the production and manipulation of tools within an environment (*Umwelt*). As a result, a sign is but one particular case of the handy (*zuhanden*), and the reference displayed is based upon a deeper reference of "useful for." This ontological characteristic of everything *zuhanden* in general is there for a Dasein that relates to it out of its concern. This *um zu*, in-order-to, insofar as it ontologically founds the sign, is not itself a sign. By virtue of this ontological foundation, what the sign shows in the first instance or a priori is not the relation of this particular thing given to another thing that is not it. Rather, it shows "the 'wherein' one lives, the in-conjunction-with-which one is concerned, the conjuncture of relations [conjoncture: Bewandtnis as a relation that permits Dasein to be next to this by means of that] that is a matter of concern" (80/111). And since any given conjuncture of relations stands out against a totality of conjuncture of relations, what the sign a priori shows is that totality in which everyday Dasein is inscribed.

Such is, schematically exposed, the general thematization of the symbolic in *Being and Time*. The fact that this thematization does not consist in privileging the symbolic becomes manifest as soon as one realizes that it is in no way complete in itself, but rather is only a first step toward the ontological equivalent of a reduction, that is, of a suspension of the symbolic. Indeed, immediately after this thematization, §18 stipulates that the totality of conjuncture (*Bewandtnisganzheit*) itself effects

> a return in the end to a for-which [*Wozu, pour-quoi*] that is no longer inscribed within any conjuncture of relations, that is not itself an intra-worldly readiness to-hand, but a being whose being is defined as being-in-the-world with the constitution of being characteristic of worldhood itself. . . . This primary 'for-which' or 'why' [*pourquoi*] is a 'for-the-sake-of-which' (*Worumwillen*). However, the 'for-the-sake of' [à-dessein] always pertains to the being of Dasein, for which, in its being, this being itself is essentially an issue. (SZ 84/116–17)

It is this return, this reversal of *Wozu* and *Um-zu* into *Worumwillen*, that makes the thematization of the symbolic slip into a reduction of it. Indeed, while the symbolic is everywhere present in the order of *Um-zu*, it has no place in the order of *Worumwillen*. The relation of Dasein to its being, the design [*dessein*] of being that properly constitutes it, has no need of symbols, signs, indications, etc. To distinguish between *Um-zu* and *Worumwillen* in fact amounts to setting up a demarcation between the symbolic order and the intuitive non-symbolic order of pure vision.

Some might perhaps object that the characterization of Dasein by a fundamentally hermeneutic mode of being makes such a demarcation problematic. Does not the very choice of the word "hermeneutic" denote a concern for the symbolic, for the interpretation of signs? Upon closer examination, however, the symbolic proves to be essential only at the first level of the famous hermeneutical circle, or circle of interpretative understanding.

This initial level is that of concern referred to an everyday environment already familiar and clarified by a specific seeing, namely, that of foreseeing circumspection. In general, this concern is filled with interpretative understanding in that Dasein immediately grasps those beings with which it is involved "as such and such." It therefore interprets those beings immediately in accordance with its projection of its own being on intraworldly possibilities on the basis of what it has already acquired, that is, on the basis of its familiarity with an environment. Its environment therefore appears to it as endowed with sense or significance (*Bedeut-samkeit*), or, put differently, as inhabited by signs. And since each sign is connected with others on the backdrop of a region of conjuncture of relations that in turn distinguishes itself from other regions upon a backdrop of a totality of conjuncture of relations (*Bewandtnisganzheit*) that functions as a horizon, concern is inscribed within an endless circuit of interpretations. At this level, the order of the symbolic may be said to be inexhaustible.

The situation at the second level of the hermeneutic circle is quite different. This level is no longer that of concern, but instead that of care. In caring, Dasein does not project its being upon intraworldly possibilities, but rather upon the ownmost proper [*la plus propre*] possibility, that is, upon its own proper [*propre*] end. At this level, instead of being absorbed in the indefinite circuit of references that is the correlate of everyday concern, Dasein refers, in pulling itself together, to its ownmost proper can-be. It is at this level, and in an ontological framework, that Heidegger's reappropriation of *Bedeutung* comes in, a concept that Husserl had separated from the symbolic in general. The reappropriated *Bedeutung* is not a logical ideality. Rather, for Dasein it consists in "giving itself an originary understanding of its being and its can-be with regard to its being-in-the-world" or, to state it differently, realizing that it exists for the sake of itself (SZ 87/120). This *Bedeutung* as auto-reference in no way belongs to the symbolic order. Rather, it belongs to the intuitive order in that, after the fashion of Husserlian *Bedeutung*, it offers itself to a seeing. Heidegger writes: "Understanding, in its projective character, constitutes existentially what we call Dasein's 'seeing' [*Sicht*]. . . . the seeing that is directed upon being as such for the sake of which [*umwillen dessen*] Dasein is each time as it is. The seeing that is related primarily and on the whole to existence we call 'transparency' [*Durchsichtigkeit*]" (SZ 146/186). This is not the order of the symbolic, nor the encroachment of the visible and invisible, nor again the indefinite movement of interpretation. Rather, this is the order of integral transparency at which Dasein arrives when in anxiety it acquires an instantaneous and resolute vision of its ownmost proper possibility.

In this ontology of Dasein, the thematization of the symbolic is therefore accompanied by its reduction. Given primordial *Durchsichtigkeit*, symbolism in general, far from having a privileged function, proves to be in a state of falling. Indeed, according to Heidegger's analytic, it is inevitable for everyday concern, in taking seriously the signs that inhabit its environment due to the a priori, that is, to the *Um-zu* structure, to forget that this structure itself has a more profound ontological foundation, namely Dasein's reference to its own proper can-be. To take signs seriously is to forget the fundamental.

Someone might here reply that my analysis is confined to too narrow a notion of the symbolic and tends to identify the world of symbols with the system of signs with which everyday concern is confronted when absorbed in technical tasks. The elements of great myths preserved in humanity's memory are also symbols. It would be surprising, one might say, if Heidegger reduced these symbols to types of readiness-to-hand as such.

I therefore open a parenthesis on myth. In point of fact, the theme of myth is not absent in *Being and Time*. Shortly after its publication and initial impact, Heidegger wrote a fairly detailed book review of the second volume of Cassirer's *Philosophy of Symbolic Forms*, which was devoted to *Mythical Thought*.[4] Despite their relatively narrow scope, these texts are nevertheless detailed enough to enable us to determine the status that Heidegger attributes to mythical symbols.

The most lengthy treatment on myth in *Being and Time* can be found at the end of the very section on "Reference and Signs" discussed above. What does Heidegger say? On the basis of the analysis invoked above, he begins by recognizing that it would be tempting to consider the "abundant use of 'signs' in primitive Dasein, especially in fetishism and magic" as an illustration of the "remarkable role they play in everyday concern for the very understanding of the world." But he rejects the temptation: "On closer examination, it becomes clear that the interpretation of fetishism and of magic by way of the idea of sign is insufficient to grasp the kind of 'being ready-to-hand' [*Zuhandensein*] that belongs to the beings encountered in the primitive world." In other words, even assuming that this world relates to something *zuhanden*, it does not, strictly speaking, relate to signs. Indeed, "for primitive man a sign coincides with what it 'indicates,'" "the sign itself always *is* the indicated." This remarkable coincidence shows that in this world "the sign has not yet liberated itself from what it indicates," and that therefore here "the intraworldly *zuhanden* does not have the mode of being of the tool" (SZ 81–82/112–13).

The primitive world is therefore characterized in terms of a "not yet." Here signs are not yet signs, tools are not yet tools, and perhaps the *zuhanden* is not yet *zuhanden*, if it is true that *Zuhandenheit* and toolness are nearly inseparable. To characterize the primitive world with the indication of the "not yet" clearly means to postulate that its myths and the symbols inhabiting them could not address the philosopher, much less lead him to think. More fundamentally, to characterize it with the indication of the "not yet" clearly entails a prior decision to consider the so-called primitive Dasein solely with respect to a teleology of Dasein's *Eigentlichkeit*, of its ownmost proper being, in short, to a teleology of the understanding of being whose key the philosopher supposedly already possesses.

This is indeed how Heidegger himself characterizes his method at the end of §17 in *Being and Time*:

> If an understanding of being is constitutive for primitive Dasein and for the primitive world, then it is all the more urgent to elaborate the 'formal' Idea of worldhood, that is, the idea of the phenomenon modifiable in such a way that all ontological assertions, which postulate that in a given phenomenal context something is *not yet* such and such or is *no longer* such and such, may acquire a *positive* phenomenological meaning on the basis on what it is *not*. (SZ 82/113)

The view that the ultimate methodological criterion is a phenomenological seeing enjoyed by the philosopher can hardly be stated more clearly. It is this seeing that operates as a *telos*. This seeing is also what makes it possible to say that the only "positive sense," for instance, of mythical symbols, consists, strictly speaking, in being the "not yet" of the order of *Zuhandenheit*, as treated in the analysis of everydayness in the Dasein-analytic.

And yet, someone might say, Heidegger nonetheless attributes to primitive Dasein an understanding of being. What about this understanding? Its thematization is to be found not in *Being and Time*, but rather in the review of Cassirer's book. This thematization confirms the teleological presupposition just spoken of. In order to respond to the question of what sort of understanding of being determines mythical existence, "it is of course necessary," Heidegger insists, "to presuppose a preliminary elaboration of the ontological constitution of existence [*Dasein*] in general. If this constitution lies in 'care,' understood ontologically [Heidegger on this point refers to *Being and Time*], then being-thrown [*Geworfenheit*] reveals itself as the primary determination of mythical existence" (1009/43). To be thrown means to be delivered over to that to which one is exposed, and to be exposed to its overwhelmingness [*Übermächtigkeit*]. Since the primary determination of mythical existence consists in *Geworfenheit*, this existence "thus refers to the overwhelming . . . is 'captivated' by it and therefore cannot be experienced except by belonging and being akin to this reality itself. Consequently, in *Geworfenheit*, every unconcealed being will, one way or another, have the existential character of overwhelmingness (mana)" (1009–1010/43). It follows from the priority in it of *Geworfenheit* that mythical existence is driven (*umgetrieben*) by the beings to which it is exposed, possessed by a mana which is itself represented in such a way that "the ontic interpretations of mana are not altogether false" (1010/44).

However schematic, this portrayal of the understanding of being inherent in mythical exigence betrays its teleological presupposition. It is as though the understanding of being, as portrayed above, precisely because it is governed by *Geworfenheit* alone in the absence of the *project* that is the counterpart of authentic existence, is doomed to disregard the onticoontological difference, to flatten being to the level of beings and to understand itself in terms of the latter. From then on, it is as though existence in myths and symbols can only exercise a narrow understanding of being, which turns out to be only a truncated and blind "modification" of the authentic understanding of being. This modification as such presupposes, it is true, that mythical Dasein "has already understood itself" (cf. SZ 313/361). It also presupposes that it has already understood the distinction between existence and "reality." But, in fact, it understands it without understanding it, since it interprets the former in terms of the latter.

A reduction of the symbolic therefore does take place here. It is as though fundamental ontology did not allow itself any kind of inspiration for its proper task.

Someone might perhaps further object that this reduction, seen in the light of the texts on which the foregoing reflections are based, only pertains to so-called "primitive" Dasein's symbols and myths, and that this is no clear indication that the same reduction affects the myths that Greek and Roman antiquity has transmitted to the west. It seems to us that this objection does not withstand scrutiny. In point of fact, *Being and Time* does make an allusion, the only one to our knowledge, to classical mythology. The latter is obviously the basis for the fable of Caius Julius Hyginus on "*cura*" cited and analysed by Heidegger in §42. Heidegger recalls that Goethe, who in turn received it from Herder, was inspired by it in the second part of his *Faust*. This very allusion, however, seems to us of significance for the reduction under discussion. First, the allusion to the ancient myth is made through the medium of a fable, that is, through a literary document that tends to turn myths into mere allegories, into a cloth of imagery holding a philosophical sense that can supposedly be apprehended beyond this envelope. Moreover, the cited fable was written in Rome during Augustus' century, which is to say at a time and place no longer dominated by myths, but rather by late philosophical movements such as Stoicism that precisely reduced myths to mere allegories. Finally, it is as though Heidegger further stressed these reductive tendencies by attributing no other sense to the mythological and symbolic elements of the fable than the one which illuminates his own analysis of Dasein. Thus, when the fable relates that Saturn is, in the end, the one who is to arbitrate the quarrel between Cura (Care), Tellus (Earth), and Jupiter about the name to be given to the human being moulded by Cura, Heidegger immediately translates: "this being whose being originates from Care" and "the decision as to the 'originary' being of this creature is left to Saturn, 'time'" (SZ 199/243).

The symbol is not here the trace of a lost treasure or of an enigma that could make one wonder. Symbol does not lead to thinking anything unusual. It can at the most illustrate, by confirming it, that which fundamental ontology claims to be able to see by itself.

Let us close the parenthesis. It confirms the extent to which the Husserlian distinction of the symbolic and the intuitive was regarded by Heidegger as essential in relation to his own project. This distinction is really what governs the existential analytic and the polarity set up between the improper and the proper.

3. On this point it will no doubt be objected that these considerations are confined to a merely formal analogy insofar as the question "Who is Dasein?" has no equivalent—not even a remote one—in the Husserlian problematic. The objection prompts us to ask ourselves—and this is the third point of my paper—whether there might not still be traces of a Husserlian heritage in Heidegger's determination of *Selbst*, self, the *ipse* of Dasein. Put differently and more specifically, it prompts us to ask ourselves whether the movement of the ontologization of intentionality, categorial intuition, and the a priori, a movement carried out in the direction of transcendence, still betrays a kinship with the movement which, in Husserl, leads to constitution by the transcendental ego. What do the transcendental ego and Dasein's *Selbst* have in common?

As is known, the access to the original region of transcendental experience in Husserl rests upon successive levels of epoche. First, the suspension of empirical inscription in the totality of occurrences that constitute the "natural world," so as to discover the immanent order of the purely psychic; then, the suspension of the purely psychic in order to arrive at transcendental consciousness. Nevertheless, Husserl insists, "phenomenological psychology and transcendental philosophy are allied with one another in a particular and inseparable manner, in virtue of the alliance of difference and identity between psychological ego (that is, the worldly human ego in the spatio-temporal world) and transcendental ego."[5] One must say that the transcendental ego, at the same time, is and is not the psychological ego. This strange alliance of difference and identity is characterized by Husserl as parallelism. A parallelism that nevertheless is in no way a mere doubling. For the transcendental ego remains what it is in spite of the destruction of the world, that is, in spite of the totality of spatio-temporal occurrences that constitute nature. It is, further, a monad without a body and without a soul, which is nevertheless the ultimate constituting element (not in their existence but in their phenomenality) of the body, of the soul, of other human beings, and of the world. The transcendental problematic of constitution is the fruit of successive neutralizations and purifications in relation to all that constitutes the initial experience, namely, that of the natural and human I, whose ultimate condition of possibility, however, is the transcendental ego.

One might think that Heidegger in his search for an answer to the question "Who is Dasein?" is worlds apart from this monadological purification, which can be regarded as the final avatar of the philosophies of the *cogito*. Not only is his question no longer Husserlian, but Dasein, unlike the Husserlian *cogito*, is at once characterized as being-in-the-world. Hence we are tempted to think that Dasein is essentially incarnated, that it dwells close to things, and that its ipseity is not separable from intercourse with others. What the movement of the Dasein-analytic institutes is, nonetheless, a monadological purification.

The sequence of the Husserlian reductions is, on the whole, a matter between me and myself, and it is a matter of seeing. The Heideggerian way toward the ownmost core of the self is the same matter. The same Dasein which is in each case mine is at times absorbed in the field of its everyday concerns, and at times relates itself to its ownmost proper possibility of being. This is so much the case that Heidegger can say both that everyday Dasein is a modification of authentic Dasein, and, inversely, that the latter is a modification of the former. Everyday Dasein is my self in a state of falling with respect to my ipseity. Authentic Dasein is my self freeing itself from everything to which this falling binds it. Jacques Derrida observes, regarding the psycho-transcendental parallelism and Husserl's struggle against transcendental psychologism, that "there is a difference which in fact does not distinguish anything, which does not separate any beings," and "which nevertheless, without altering anything, changes every sign . . . . Transcendental consciousness is nothing other than psychological consciousness. Transcendental psychologism misunderstands that if the world needs a *supplement of soul*, the soul, which is in the world, needs this supplementary nothingness, which is the transcendental and without which no world would become visible."[6]

Husserl, it goes without saying, does not name this nothingness; nothingness is simply not one of his themes. For Heidegger, however, it became imperative to name this "supplementary nothingness" and to make it a central theme precisely in accordance with his ontologization of Husserl's discoveries, especially of the categorial intuition of being. This discovery teaches us that being is not a real predicate, that therefore it has *nothing* in common with *beings*, and that it nevertheless gives itself to a seeing in this very difference. If the understanding of being is the task of phenomenology, then the epoche ought at the same time to assume the appearance of a reduction to nothingness [*néantisation*]. And if this understanding (which is the understanding of the ontico-ontological difference) concerns each Dasein in its mineness at the level of what it is proximally and for the most part, in the same way that Husserl's transcendental ego is what the empirical ego presupposes, then it is imperative to demonstrate at various depths the ontic and pre-ontological attestation of this ontological reduction to nothing that constitutes a metamorphosed epoche. This is achieved by successive analyses of the everyday experience of the malfunctioning of tools, of anxiety, of the relation to one's own death, of *Gewissen*. These analyses are well known, and I refrain from returning to them. I do, however, note that the description is, at every step, accompanied by a warning against confusion between the ontic and the ontological, or between the *existentiell* and the *existential*, that is, against a confusion akin in form to the one denounced by Husserl as "transcendental psychologism." I note, moreover, that at every step it is a matter (for a Dasein that is each time mine) of a suspension combined with a corresponding seeing. This is what the analysis of *Gewissen* shows remarkably well.

As already noted, it follows from the ontologization of Husserl's logical discoveries and from the privilege attributed, consequently, to the intuition of being that the originary *Bedeuten* of *Bedeutung* consists for Dasein in a self-giving of the understanding of its being and of its can-be. This understanding no longer proceeds by means of signs, but rather resides in an intuitive elucidation, namely, in the seeing of *Durchsichtigkeit*. This is that to which the phenomenon of *Gewissen*, in the Dasein that is each time mine, attests ontically—and preontologically.

The word *Gewissen* cannot be translated by "moral conscience," since Heidegger's analysis of this phenomenon explicitly excludes every moral connotation and attributes the ontological origin of the notions of good and evil and, more generally, of the notion of value to *Vorhandenheit*, the mode of being of beings that precisely does not belong to Dasein's mode. On the other hand, since the prefix *Ge-* in Heidegger's usage denotes a gathering, a collecting, a centering, I see no inconvenience in translating it by one's "internal tribunal" *(for interne)*. However, since in *Gewissen* there is *Wissen*, that is, knowing, I prefer to translate it by "internal knowledge" or "intimate knowledge" [*"science interne" ou "savoir intime"*].

"Intimate knowledge" is presented by Heidegger as an existentiell attestation of an "authentic can-be-itself [*Selbstseinkönnen*]." It is no exaggeration to say that Heidegger, in listing the characteristics of "intimate knowledge" attributed to the self, institutes a monadological purification of phenomenon and *logos*, while also joining them to one another on the register of intuition alone, where every sign is absent. In so doing, Heidegger remains faithful to the spirit of Husserl.

A monadic purification is really involved here, since Dasein, with all the characteristic traits of that intimate knowledge, makes a circle with itself. These characteristic traits are the existentials themselves, albeit here detached from every referent other than the can-be-itself. Here the only disposition mobilized is the fundamental disposition of anxiety insofar as it unveils nothing other than the nudity of facticity, the pure strangeness and radical "isolation and individualization [*esseulement*] [*vereinzelt*] that characterizes the fact of being thrown into the world" (SZ 276/321). Here again, the only understanding in question has nothing to do with an interpretation: it gathers itself in the resolute clarity of the glance of the eyes (*Augen-blick*) upon one's own proper can-be. Here also, discourse (*Rede*), *logos*, purifies itself of every communication, of every expression, and even of every monologue in order to gather itself in silent listening to a call that has no other reference than the one calling, no other aim than the self insofar as it is indebted (*schuldig*) to its own proper can-be.

This is the ultimate joining of phenomenon and *logos*, since what this call gives to understand/hear [*entendre*], and which is ultimately nothing, mere nullity (*Nichtigkeit*), is also what the call gives to see and be seen.

Heidegger himself insists that intimate knowledge moves in its own proper circle. Listening to the call of *Gewissen*, he says, has no other sense than wanting-to-have-intimate-knowledge (*Gewissen-haben-wollen*).

The fact that we are really dealing here with a legacy of Husserl's monadology, however great the metamorphosis to which it is subjected, is in my mind confirmed by two indications with which I conclude. As noted, Heidegger's project of fundamental ontology rests upon an ontologization of logic. Heidegger admits to this ontologization as early as the first lines of the text which in 1922 he sends along with his application for a position in Marburg and Göttingen. The text outlines an interpretation of Aristotle in the light of what Heidegger then called "hermeneutics of facticity." This hermeneutics, which is his topic at the beginning of the Freiburg years, is still the subject matter of the final Marburg course of SS 1928 to which I alluded earlier, namely, *The Metaphysical Foundations of Logic*. This course, which characterizes itself as phenomenological, consists of two parts, one historical, the other thematic.

The first indication that appears to support my reflections can be found in the historical part. This part consists essentially of a debate with a certain monadology. The fact that it concerns Leibniz's monadology and not Husserl's is not a valid objection, since Heidegger was fond of practicing textual overlappings. I gave an example of this practice in connection with his analysis of the notions of phenomenon and *logos* that is carried out in Aristotle's language, but closely coincides with and confirms a certain Husserlian view. The second indication is to be found in the thematic part. It consists in a metaphysics of the principle of sufficient reason that announces the text *On the Essence of Reasons* and provides a number of clarifications on the self. After recalling that his question is the fundamental problem of metaphysics—"what does 'being' mean?"—and that it alone governs the analytic conducted in *Being and Time*, he enunciates a number of principles that guided this analytic.

First and foremost, the notion of Dasein is neutral. Its *neutrality* is characteristic of the essence prior to every actual concretization in an ontic individuality, prior therefore to every incarnation and consequently also to all gender distinction. This neutrality goes hand in hand with the most intimate (*innerlichst*) isolation. Heidegger grants an originary and transcendental status to this isolated neutrality. Neutrality is the ultimate condition of possibility. The transcendental origin of scattering (*Zersplitterung*) in a body and of sexual division (*Zerspaltung*) is therefore to be sought in it. More fundamental than this bodily scattering and sexual division, still ontic, is the ontological and transcendental dispersion (*Zerstreuung*) at the very [*même*] heart itself of Dasein's metaphysical neutrality and isolation. Transcendental dispersion, which goes hand in hand with a no less transcendental *Mitsein*, being-with, is grounded in *Geworfenheit*. Finally, the world to which neutral and isolated Dasein refers turns out really to be nothingness. *"Die Welt: ein Nichts, kein Seiendes—und doch etwas; nichts Seiendes—aber Sein."* "The world: a nothing, not a being—and yet something; nothing that is—but being" (GA26 252/195). One may rightly suspect in this hypertranscendental characterization of Dasein an echo, as well as, certainly, a profound ontological metamorphosis, of Husserl's transcendental reduction considered in its monadological core as the pivotal point of the problematic of incarnation and subjectivity. This suspicion is confirmed when one learns that such Dasein, transcendentally neutral and isolated as well as dispersed, constitutes what a *Selbst* properly is. It is to such Dasein that the following statement refers: "Dasein exists for the sake of itself." With an approach whose style is equally of Husserlian origin, Heidegger insists that this statement not only does not express a *Weltanschauung*, a worldview, but that it concerns an ontological and metaphysical ego-ity [*égoité*], identical with ipseity itself, with *Selbstheit*, selfhood (cf . SS10 and 11). This suspicion is strengthened when one realizes that the transcendental problematic, called by Heidegger "fundamental ontology," constitutes "the internal and hidden life of the fundamental movement of western philosophy," a status that Husserl always, right up to the *Krisis*, accorded for his part to pure phenomenology. The suspicion grows stronger when one learns that this transcendental problematic, which is radical, is also universal in that it ends meta-ontologically in a thematization of beings as a whole. Does not Husserl, for his part, make pure phenomenology into the science of the foundation of every science and of the regions to which they are related?

A final observation. There is a paradoxical character in this search for an answer to the question "Who?" because, in agreement with Husserl, it disregarded at the outset the symbolic as such. And because it is a deliberate revival of the Platonic denial of every narrative (one is supposed to cease telling stories [*mythoi*]), it has in the end little to do with the vicissitudes of the embodied life of a mortal at the heart of plurality and the interlocution that accompanies it. The *ipse*, dealt with through the series of successive reductions, is ultimately an *idem* of final appeal.

Heidegger takes great pains to specify that Dasein, intimately isolated and transcendentally dispersed insofar as it is thrown, is free. Its freedom is also both transcendental and metaphysical. He adds that the conquest of metaphysical neutrality and isolation is itself possible only in a free projection, which in turn is found only in its exercise. As such, this projection springs from the existentiell implication (*Einsatz*) of a projecting Dasein. This implication is called "extreme," since it consists for a projecting Dasein in the "constructive articulation [*Konstruktion*] of one of the most extreme possibilities of authentic and total can-be" (§10). This construction is identical with the philosophical activity. Heidegger specifies: "The more radical [the philosopher's] existentiell implication, the more concrete the ontologico-metaphysical project. But the more concrete this interpretation of Dasein is, the more it leads to the fundamental misunderstanding that the existentiell implication as such is what is essential and the only thing of importance, while the very implication reveals itself precisely only in the project considered in all of its indifference toward the particularity of the person" (*in seiner jeweiligen personalen Belanglosigkeit*) (GA26 177/140). This amounts to saying that in the end—this is the paradox I am getting at—the true and proper response to the question of *Selbst*, the self is given by the philosophical act. Or to put it differently, an individuation can only be speculative.

One must take care not to claim that at least on this point Heidegger is not in any way Husserl's heir, for the passage just cited can be read as showing the vanishing point—in the pictorial sense—of Heidegger's reappropriation of Husserl's struggle against transcendental psychologism. In the margin of his copy of *Being and Time*, Husserl scribbled a large number of annotations that generally accuse Heidegger of anthropologism. One of them reads as follows: Against all this "I opposed the natural apprehension of the world in natural worldly life to the philosophical transcendental apprehension of the world—and therefore to a life which is not naturally devoted to a naive valorization of the world, which for the human being does not consist in remaining in a naive valorization, but rather is the Idea of a philosophical life, determined by philosophy" (SZ 16, ll. 38–41). I have suggested that it is this kind of opposition which, whatever Husserl may have thought of it, and in spite of considerable metamorphoses, governs Heidegger's notion of *Selbst*. In so doing, I have on the whole done nothing other than to take literally a well-known footnote in *Being and Time*: "If the present investigation has taken some steps forward in disclosing the 'things themselves,' the author thanks first of all Edmund Husserl who, by providing his own incisive personal guidance and by very freely turning over his unpublished investigations, familiarized the author with the most diverse areas of phenomenological research" (SZ 38/489). This may be regarded as more than a courtesy. Inversely, one may think that there is more than blindness to Husserl's note in his copy of the book: "Everything here is a translation and transposition of my thought. Where I say *Bewußtsein*, Heidegger says Dasein, etc." I wanted to discuss the *etc.*

Part VII

Back to Kant

16

Heidegger's Kant-Courses at Marburg

Daniel O. Dahlstrom

During his last few years at Marburg, a breeding ground of "Neo-Kantianism," Heidegger generated his own controversial interpretation of Kant's critical philosophy. The interpretation was first elaborated in two lecture courses, given in the winter semesters of 1925–26 (GA21: *Logik, Die Frage nach der Wahrheit*) and 1927–28 (GA25: *Phänomenologische Interpretation von Kants Kritik der reinen Vernunft*), which in turn served as the basis for Heidegger's Davos lectures in 1929 and for the book composed shortly thereafter, *Kant und das Problem der Metaphysik* (KPM).[1] These Marburg Kant-courses contain a far more extensive interpretation of what Heidegger calls "the positive part" of the *Kritik der reinen Vernunft* (KrV) than does his Kant-book. While the chapter on schematism is treated only in the first of these courses (not surprisingly, the one coinciding with the completion of SZ), both elaborate in considerable detail Kant's account of time and his references to time at key junctures in the Transcendental Aesthetic and the Transcendental Analytic. The content of these courses corresponds to the announced but unpublished first division of the second part of SZ, entitled "*Kants Lehre vom Schematismus und der Zeit als Vorstufe einer Problematik der Temporalität*" (SZ 40). They present the conception of time in KrV as a first step or introduction (*Vorstufe*) to the problem of temporality.

Heidegger's reflections on Kant's philosophy during his final Marburg years are not limited to these two courses, nor does his interest in critical philosophy wane after his move to Freiburg. In addition to KPM (1929) and the courses already mentioned, two additional courses between 1926 and 1930 and yet another course in 1935–36 are largely devoted to critical philosophy. In SS 1927 (GA24: *Grundprobleme der Phänomenologie*) Heidegger takes up themes from the Transcendental Dialectic, the "negative" part of KrV, notably Kant's thesis about being and rejection of an ontological account of the "I think." At Freiburg in SS 1930 (GA31: *Vom Wesen der menschlichen Freiheit*) and in SS 1935–36 (GA41: *Die Frage nach dem Ding*), Heidegger returns to the "positive" part of the first critique, but with a different emphasis. In the Marburg courses, as in KPM, Heidegger refers to the schematism chapter as the "core" of KrV; in the Freiburg courses, on the other hand, Kant is said to have taken "the decisive step" with his Analytic of Principles, "the middle," according to Heidegger, "carrying the entire work from within" (GA41 130, 146).[2]

In the Marburg lectures during SS 1927 and in the final portion of the Freiburg course of SS 1930, Heidegger makes a rare excursion into Kant's practical philosophy, sketching the extent of Kant's capacity to articulate the ontological distinctiveness of human being.[3] Despite the relatively few occasions upon which Heidegger explicitly addresses Kant's moral thought, Kant's practical philosophy is fundamental for analyses in SZ, not only for the analysis of 'conscience,' as Heidegger himself attests (SZ 272, note), but also for the analysis of 'care.' Here, once again, a glance at Heidegger's courses proves illuminating. In the middle of WS 1925–26 he claims that care is the very phenomenon on which Kant focussed when articulating the basis for the categorical imperative with the words: "the human being exists as an end in itself" (GA21 220).

Of all Kant's doctrines, however, the most important to Heidegger, so important that they were to be treated in a separate section of the unfinished argument of SZ, are the doctrines of time and of the schematisms. As noted earlier, Heidegger's reading of these doctrines is contained in the two Kant-courses at Marburg thematically and temporally most proximate to the composition of SZ. The following essay is an attempt to sketch some of the main lines of Heidegger's interpretation of the critical philosophy in those winter semesters of 1925–26 and 1927–28. The aim of this exercise is to explain the significance of the critical philosophy for the project of SZ and, in the process, to unpack what Heidegger means when he characterizes Kant's conception of time as a "first step towards the problematic of temporality."

The first part of the following discussion briefly details the composition and central theses of both courses, including the themes and sections from KrV treated in them. Parts two and three are attempts to illustrate the distinctiveness of Heidegger's interpretation by contrasting it with its counterpoint, the Neo-Kantian interpretation by Heidegger's Marburg predecessors, Hermann Cohen and Paul Natorp. The contrast is defined by the different challenges each interpretation makes to the ordering of the first half of KrV and by their incompatible interpretations of the meaning of "manifold" at the outset of KrV. After outlining what Heidegger plainly rejects in critical philosophy and his reasons for doing so, part four summarizes how Kant's account of time anticipates, in Heidegger's eyes, his own account of temporality.

1. Heidegger's Marburg Commentary

Though Heidegger addresses the doctrine of the schematism in only the first of the Marburg Kant-courses, the course in WS 1925–26, unlike that in WS 1927–28, is not devoted solely to Kant's theoretical philosophy, nor was it originally intended to treat Kant's philosophy at all. In the first half of the course Heidegger sets out to do three things: first, to establish the dominance of the logical prejudice that the meanings of 'true' and 'to be' are properties of judgments (or at least circumscribed by the structure of judgments); second, to show that Husserl's intentional analysis of the intuitive character of truth (his articulation of truth as the coincidence of the givenness or presence of something intuited with something meant or judged) at once exposes and reinforces this prejudice; and third, to demonstrate that for Aristotle, in spite of his reputation for being the originator of the logical prejudice, neither judgments nor intuitions constitute the last word as to the meaning of 'true' and 'to be.'

As often happens in such courses, Heidegger departs from his original plan for the course and, in the place of a systematic treatment of "the radicalized question: what is truth?," he sets out in the second half of the course to outline a "phenomenological chronology," demonstrating how temporality underlies what 'true' and 'to be' are taken to mean (GA21 26, 197–207). In words repeated practically verbatim in SZ, he notes that Kant is the only philosopher to have broached "this obscure domain," though, to be sure, "without having gained an insight into the fundamental significance of his effort" (GA21 200, 194; SZ 23). In the last third of the course Heidegger attempts to show why and how Kant again and again comes back to the basic phenomenon of time "in all the decisive parts of KrV" (GA21 270, 305). The course pursues this objective in regard to the following four "foundational parts" of KrV: (1) the Transcendental Aesthetic (GA21 272–305), (2) the revised Transcendental Deduction (GA21 305–347), (3) the First Analogy of Experience (GA21 347–357), and (4) the Doctrine of Schematism (GA21 357–415). On the basis of KPM, Heidegger is often linked with Schopenhauer (for whom, incidentally, he appears to have had little regard) as an advocate of the first edition of KrV. There the imagination is not, as in the second edition, explicitly subordinated to a sentience standing in contrast to the understanding (B151), but rather figures as one of the "three subjective sources of knowledge" (A115; A94). It is worth noting, however, given the controversy over the merits of the two editions, that Heidegger's first Kant-course concentrates exclusively on the second, revised edition of KrV. Moreover, the explicit focus of this course is time and not the productive imagination.

Heidegger remarks that, in the context of this first Marburg Kant-course, he must forego a more extensive elaboration of his interpretation (GA21 272). A year and a half later the stated goal of his course, "Phenomenological Interpretation of Kant's Critique of Pure Reason," is to work out a philosophical understanding of KrV as a unified whole (GA25 6). As is often the case in such undertakings—think of Vaihinger!—this course, which most approaches the style of a commentary, falls far short of its goal, addressing barely a quarter of Kant's text.

Heidegger begins his phenomenological interpretation of KrV, not with textual scrutiny of the prefaces and introductions, but with "a freer presentation of the basic problem of the 'critique,'" the ontological significance of the Copernican turn, "Kant's fundamental discovery" (GA25 9–76). The body of the course is then devoted to a detailed, occasionally line-by-line consideration of five sections of KrV: (1) the Transcendental Aesthetic together with some of Kant's subsequent remarks on space and time (GA25 77–163); (2) the Introduction to the Transcendental Logic, in connection with the thesis of Kant's Logic lectures that reflection is the logical origin of concepts (GA25 165–255); (3) the so-called "metaphysical deduction" of the categories, specifically paragraph 10, which, in Heidegger's view, contains all that is most essential to the basic problem of KrV (GA25 257–302); (4) the original version of the Transcendental Deduction with its reference to three syntheses and cognitive faculties (GA25 303–391, 403–424); and (5) the relation between self-affection and apperception in the revised Transcendental Deduction (GA25 391–402).[4]

The theme common to the interpretations of these last three sections in particular is the centrality of the productive imagination, integrated now with the central themes of the first Kant-course. At the same time, though the transcendental schemata are generated by the productive imagination, in the second Kant-course there is only a brief concluding remark about the significance of the schematism chapter, extensively interpreted in the first Kant-course.[5] In this and other respects the two courses are complementary, amounting to a kind of commentary on the first two hundred and more pages of KrV.

The theses of Heidegger's interpretation of critical philosophy in KPM, those that most enraged some scholars of Kant and enthused others, are generally developed at far greater length in his Marburg courses. Five central theses of his interpretation may be summarized as follows:

Thesis #1 (the 'hermeneutical' thesis): "KrV is nothing other than the laying of the foundation for metaphysics as science" precisely because it raises the pre-ontological and prescientific question of "what it means for a particular being 'to be,' on the basis of which every objectification of being in science rests" (GA25 10, 51f.; GA21 306f., 312f.; KPM 1, 5f., 225).

Thesis #2 (the 'epistemological' thesis): "all *knowing in general* is primarily intuition" (GA25 83; GA21 114f., 56f.; KPM 21).

Thesis #3 (the 'phenomenological' thesis): "the productive synthesis of the imagination" is (a) the common root of sentience and understanding (GA25 417f.), (b) the origin of the categories, that is to say, the key to the "metaphysical" deduction (GA25 270–292), (c) the presupposition for the transcendental unity of apperception (GA25 410f., 421), and thus (d) the ultimate source of the categories's objective validity, in other words, the foundation of the "transcendental" deduction (in both versions!) (GA25 368, 403–423).

Thesis #4 (the 'ontological' thesis): the productive synthesis of imagination is rooted in time, "understood no longer in the sense of the vulgar concept of time, but rather as temporality in the sense of the original unity of the ecstatic constitution of Dasein" (GA25 426).[6]

Thesis #5 (the 'historical' thesis): Kant "pulled back or recoiled" from the implications of his account of transcendental imagination and the original significance of time (SZ 23; GA25 412, 426; KPM 155). (Heidegger's account of the reasons for Kant's retreat is outlined in the last section of this chapter.)

There is a basic unity to these five theses: together they present critical philosophy as an anticipation of SZ (GA25 426, 431; GA21 403f.). Kant is paid the tribute of having raised the question of ontology and even indicated the path fundamental ontology must take if the question is to be answered, though he does not himself continue down that path and even sets up considerable roadblocks to it. Heidegger argues that, by raising the question of the conditions of the possibility of experience, Kant institutes an earthshaking shift from (ontic) studies of particular beings (*Seiende*) and what they are to an (ontological) investigation of what it means 'to be' (*Sein*) (GA25 55f.; KPM 12f.). This often misunderstood "Copernican turn" in no way signifies that actual things are somehow dissolved into subjective representings, but rather that access to beings is only possible on the basis of a foregoing understanding of what it means 'to be' (GA25 55f.). "Kant's fundamental discovery," Heidegger tells us, is to have recognized that these principles (synthetic judgments a priori) represent our knowledge of what is (*Seienden*), but are themselves based upon neither experience nor mere conceptual analysis (GA25 47, 51). The basic question asked in KrV is the question of the possibility of these judgments, in which that understanding of what it means 'to be' is formulated. The question of the possibility of synthetic judgments a priori is thus, in Heidegger's view, equivalent to the question of the possibility of ontological knowledge. "How is the pre-ontological or, better, explicitly ontological understanding possible, that is, the understanding of what it means for (a particular) being 'to be,' on the basis of which every objectification of being in science rests?" (GA25 51f.)

By locating the union of those conditions in the transcendental imagination, Kant even broaches the task of "fundamental ontology," namely, the investigation of what it means for Dasein 'to be' that is the basis for any inquiry into the meaning of 'being' (SZ 7, 132). Just as ontology must begin with fundamental ontology, so Kant's ontological investigation, on Heidegger's interpretation, takes its bearings from the study of the human faculty in which are joined, in Kant's own terms, the two necessary but radically disparate sources of human knowledge, sentience and understanding (GA25 281). In Heidegger's interpretation, the productive imagination is best described, however, not as the a priori mediation of receptivity and spontaneity as such, but rather as the basic phenomenon underlying Kant's account of what makes experience possible. Indeed, in relation to the imagination, sensations and concepts alike are mere abstractions.

In effect, the productive imagination is construed by Heidegger in such a way that it coincides in crucial respects with his account of temporality. Or, to put it more accurately, since this notion of temporality *expressis verbis* is missing from Kant's account, Heidegger urges that the various roles assigned the productive imagination in KrV and thereby the success of the work's argument as a whole (see the phenomenologial thesis above) are understandable only when the productive imagination is interpreted in terms of temporality. Just as temporality makes Dasein possible, so, on Heidegger's interpretation, the temporality of transcendental imagination, as elaborated in KrV, makes specific synthetic a priori judgments and therewith experience itself possible. "Through the interpretation," Heidegger declares, "we will show that this *third basic faculty* [imagination] does not, however, grow up next to the other two stems [sentience and understanding] as a third stem, as it were, and that it also does not only mediate as something placed between them, but rather is, as it were, a piece of the root itself. Still more, it will be shown that this root is nothing other than *time*, radically conceived in its essence" (GA25 93, 341f.).

From even this cursory review of the basic theses of Heidegger's Kant-courses, it is obvious that they correspond to the general project, announced in SZ, of the *Destruktion* of the history of ontology. This destruction, as Gadamer is wont to emphasize, is not the annihilation (*Zerstörung*) but rather the dismantling of a philosophy in the attempt to see how it is put together and what intuitions underlie its construction or hold it together. A *phenomenological* interpretation of KrV deserves that name only if it is able to strip away the layers of preconceived notions (on the part of both Kant and his critics) about the genuine phenomena (in the Husserlian sense) addressed in KrV, and is able to give a more adequate account of those phenomena (SZ 23f.; GA24 31). The purpose of the interpretation is thus to articulate, not what Kant explicitly said or even wanted to say, but what he "should have said" (GA25 338; KPM XVII). Critics often fault what they perceive as a lack of argumentation or, more significantly, as a lack of criteria for what counts as a sound argument in Heidegger's thinking. However, in his courses on Kant's critical philosophy Heidegger identifies the criterion of a successful interpretation. After paying close heed to Kant's treatment of certain phenomena, a successful interpretation demonstrates that it is demanded by those very same phenomena; that is to say, it takes its bearings from Kant's own account of those phenomena, but also demonstrates that this account has unacknowledged roots and connections (GA21 346, 309).

Heidegger's 'argument,' then, is that Kant himself at crucial junctures in KrV has recourse to the underlying phenomenon of temporality. Those key passages include Kant's accounts of time in the Transcendental Aesthetic, productive imagination in the Transcendental Logic (the metaphysical as well as the transcendental deductions), and the productive imagination's a priori temporal determinations of the categories in the Doctrine of Schematism. For example, Heidegger makes much of the fact that Kant, in the midst of the metaphysical deduction (the derivation of the pure concepts of the understanding from the logical forms of judgment), refers to the indispensability of an imaginative synthesis *in advance of* the unifying logical function of the understanding. Seeing in these remarks an anticipation of the schematisms, Heidegger leaps to the conclusion that the table of judgments "is not the primary and sole source for the origin of the concepts of the understanding" (GA25 284, 287, 290–293). This conclusion (Thesis #3b above) is, at least ostensibly, utterly at odds with Kant's stated intentions. If, however, Heidegger's argument is in fact sound, and the productive imagination is only understandable as the ecstatic temporality underlying human subjectivity (including human understanding), then it becomes necessary to reinterpret Kant's claims for the understanding alone (and sentience alone) as philosophical abstractions, drawing what legitimacy they enjoy from "the original, pure, time-related synthesis of the imagination" (GA25 422).

2. Marburg Neo-Kantianism and How to Read KrV

Heidegger's Marburg courses on KrV are defined by two coordinates: the Neo-Kantian reading of the work and the account of ecstatic-horizonal

temporality in *Sein und Zeit*. In common with the Neo-Kantian interpretation of critical philosophy (chiefly the Marburg school of Cohen and
Natorp, with occasional references to Windelband and Rickert), Heidegger
attempts to resolve the issue of Kant's epistemological dualism. As is elaborated in what follows, Heidegger's understanding of this issue is decidedly
different from that of his predecessors at Marburg. "Kant," Heidegger was
fond of saying, "was no Kantian" (GA21 117). Nevertheless, Heidegger
praises Cohen and Natorp for recognizing and not hesitating to confront a
fundamental philosophical difficulty informing Kant's thought. The Marburg school interprets KrV as a unified whole with a clear understanding
that such an interpretation demands a resolution of the problem of the
unity of intuition and understanding.

Superficially, at least, this problem is mirrored in the uneven structure of the first critique's Doctrine of Elements. If sentience and understanding are both irreducibly necessary for knowledge in the strict sense of
the term (B103, B146, B157), why is the first part (the Transcendental
Aesthetic) so disproportionately shorter than the second part, namely,
forty pages to six hundred and fifty-nine pages? More to the point, why
does the explanation of their synthesis nevertheless occur in the second
part (specifically, the Transcendental Analytic of the Transcendental
Logic), devoted allegedly to the understanding's pure concepts and judgments, rather than in a third part? Without denying Kant's "unmistakable
gift" for architectonic, Heidegger observes: "The entirety of the Critique's
problematic is, in its structure and its formation, not adequate to the originality of the insight to which Kant comes in the most central part of the
Critique" (GA25 213; 198f.).

Though the problem of finding the right presentation of critical philosophy clearly plagued Kant himself (as his correspondence with Beck
indicates), there are also unmistakable virtues to the ordering of KrV. In
the first place, the realm of sensibility is given a kind of emphasis by the
fact that the Transcendental Aesthetic is presented first. This emphasis is
patent from the opening sentence of the Transcendental Aesthetic (a
line—see the epistemological thesis above—tirelessly quoted by Heidegger
from course to course and repeated in KPM as a challenge to the Neo-
Kantian interpretation), in which Kant awards a primacy to intuition as
the sort of knowledge that relates immediately to objects and is the aim of
all thought (B33). In addition, by not presenting the doctrine of the synthesis of sensibility and understanding as a separate part of KrV, Kant
underlines the distinctiveness of his transcendental account of knowing, a
distinctiveness apparently lost on his idealist critics.[7] For a finite mind,
there is no knowable third realm or underlying ground for the synthesis
that makes the experience of objects possible. This transcendental syn-

thesis is precisely the spontaneous structuring of the a priori intuition of time by the understanding, employing the same forms of judgment that it employs in formal logic.

Still, this notion of an a priori intuition of time is, historically and systematically, a philosophical hybrid, threatening to blur Kant's own bifurcation of passive sentience and spontaneous understanding. On the one hand, as an intuition and thus belonging to sentience, time is something given to the knower and not the product of its thinking processes (conceptualizing, judging, inferring). On the other hand, inasmuch as time is a pure intuition, it presents no object (contrary to that opening line of the Transcendental Aesthetic), but only relations of succession and contemporaneity; as a form of sensibility it determines these sorts of relations for things insofar as they are present to the knower (B67, B349).

A central part of the Marburg Neo-Kantian "correction" of critical philosophy was the effort to rid it of this troubling notion of intuition, replacing it with the notion of the "complete thought of an object."[8] For the Marburg Neo-Kantians, Kant's lasting contribution is what they take to be his insight into a transcendental method. This method, on their view, is a critical and immanent pursuit of the laws of objective formation, at odds as much with empiricist or psychologistic pretensions to forego or deconstruct such laws as with metaphysical pretensions to rise above them. Underlying this understanding of transcendental method is the notion that all being reduces to "a movement of thought" and that no givenness is irreducible to the basic unity of knowledge.[9] Given this understanding of the transcendental method, Natorp argues, the dualism in Kant's epistemology, the opposition of the givenness of intuition to the spontaneity of thinking cannot be sustained. "There can no longer be any talk of a given 'manifold' that the understanding . . . would merely have to classify, to bind together, and—afterwards—to recognize."[10] It is simply an "error," Cohen observes, albeit an error to which Kant himself was liable, to believe that something might be *given* to thinking or, in other words, that the content of thinking is not itself the product of thinking.[11] Not surprisingly, Natorp regards the positioning of time and space prior to the categories, in other words, the placing of a transcendental aesthetic before a transcendental logic as "a serious blunder" (GA25 77f.).[12] Because the Neo-Kantians construe apperception as "the proper center" of Kant's critical inquiry, they set the Transcendental Aesthetic as a self-sufficient inquiry aside and read the entire KrV from the standpoint of the Transcendental Analytic. Time itself (at least as a pure intuition) is reinterpreted as a category.[13]

In the light of this Neo-Kantian interpretation, the point of Heidegger's emphasis on the irreducible and primary role of intuition in critical philosophy—Thesis #2 in the list above—becomes patent. As far as the reading of KrV itself is concerned, Heidegger's interpretation reasserts the integrity of the Transcendental Aesthetic. Nevertheless, as noted earlier, he concurs with the Neo-Kantian view that the uneven structure of KrV, most notably the account of the synthesis of intuitions and concepts within the Transcendental Logic (GA25 209f.), betrays substantive difficulties and prejudices.[14] In this connection Heidegger calls attention to an unmistakable parallel between the Transcendental Aesthetic and the Analytic of Concepts. Just as the task of the Transcendental Aesthetic as the first part of KrV's doctrine of elements is the isolation of "what sentience can deliver a priori" (B36), encompassing metaphysical and transcendental accounts of space and time, so the Analytic of Concepts is intended to "pursue the pure concepts to their origins and foundations in human understanding" (B91) with corresponding metaphysical and transcendental deductions of those concepts (B159). Heidegger argues that Kant's reason for ending the enumeration of paragraphs at the end of the transcendental deduction (in the second edition) indicates that Kant himself has this parallel in mind. Kant writes: "Only up to here do I consider the division by paragraphs necessary, because we had to deal with elementary concepts" (B169). The phrase "elementary concepts" in this sentence refers, Heidegger maintains, not simply to the categories, but to all the elements of knowing, the elements of sentience and understanding. By ending the enumeration of paragraphs for the reason given, Kant is signalling the end of the *analytic phase* of KrV, according to Heidegger. "But this breakdown into *elements* by way of *isolating* them—and that is indeed the function of the Aesthetic and the Logic—is a first step toward the investigation of the *entirety* of knowledge, that is, the *unification* of sentience and understanding, with respect to its possibility" (GA25 166).

Heidegger suggests, then, that we read KrV as though the Transcendental Aesthetic and Analytic of Concepts provide the analytic phase of the positive part of the work, the analysis of sentience and understanding into pure intuitions and pure concepts respectively. The *synthetic phase* begins (at least explicitly) with the Analytic of Principles (GA25 196). Both the Transcendental Aesthetic and the Analytic of Concepts are to be re-read from the standpoint of the account of schematisms, the first chapter of the Analytic of Principles (SZ 23f.).[15]

Heidegger thus takes his cues from the Marburg Neo-Kantians' attempt to uncover the unity of the Doctrine of Elements by unraveling the philosophical issue at its core. However, this unity is to be achieved, not at the cost of the Transcendental Aesthetic, as the Marburg Neo-Kantians propose, but only by showing "how both [Aesthetic and Logic] rest upon a common and original foundation, still hidden from Kant" (GA25 78). That foundation is temporality, surfacing in Kant's accounts of time and the schematisms of the productive imagination. *"To make this foundation visible and to determine it positively is an essential task of our phenomenological investigation"* (GA25 79, 93).

3. The Horizon of Pure Intuition, the Ecstasis of the Form of Sentience, and the Problem of the Original Manifold

Kant characterizes time as a form of sentience and as a pure intuition. "Form" in this context signifies what makes it possible for there to be an ordering of "the manifold of appearance in certain relations" or, in other words, "that within which the sensations alone can be ordered" (B34). Time is the form of sentience in that it "lies at the basis of all intuitions" (B46); it is "the subjective condition under which all intuitions take place within us" (B49). That time is a "pure intuition" indicates that it is known neither by reference to something else (i.e., conceptually) nor by being itself sensed (i.e., empirically). The original ordering of time itself—its successiveness and contemporaneity—is distinct from any empirical sequence or contemporaries (B46).

But what exactly is a *pure* intuition? Can the manifold of the senses in general be accounted for, or is it merely a highly plausible, but unsubstantiated, point of departure for Kant? Is there any connection between time as a pure intuition and its function as a form of sensibility? Heidegger answers all three of these traditionally troubling questions by taking the pure intuition of time to be a foregoing, unthematic view of sheer succession (an horizon for constituting the encounter of anything at all). This succession is the original manifold, indeed, an original order belonging to time itself. Precisely as the implicit regard for this original before-and-after, the pure intuition of time is formative of every other sensible manifold.

Heidegger introduces his interpretation as an attempt to remove some of the obscurity attaching to Kant's talk of the 'form' and 'matter' of sensibility by exposing its phenomenological content. Each of the senses presents me with a manifold of colors, sounds, and so on. Together, the senses yield manifolds of manifolds. Those manifolds may be in apparent disorder (like a film clip run at quadruple its normal speed or the random sights and sounds of a city corner) or highly ordered (like a musical score or mosaic). In each case, however, the manifold is encountered as such "on the basis of a foregoing view of what allows the manifold to be encountered as a manifold" (GA21 274). "What Kant saw," Heidegger insists ("as we now, phenomenologically, more sharply interpret it"), is precisely this "view toward or of something" and its constitutive necessity for the encounter of a manifold as such (GA21 274).

Whatever is given to us, whether objects or sensations, has the character of being a manifold. A manifold is in fact "the first order, the order first yielding itself," lying at the base of every subsequent order and disorder (GA21 287, 281). That in view of which every manifold is determined as such is the character of being successive or contemporary. However else it be ordered (or disordered), a manifold is characterized as a manifold by being ordered from the outset in view of time, a view so basic that it is largely taken for granted ("*unthematisch*").

In this way Heidegger explicates the phenomenological content of Kant's account of time as a pure intuition. "Pure intuition" signifies that time as the original manifold is unthematically intuited. Time is entertained but in a quite distinctive, original manner; in Kant's own words, it is "the original representation" (*die ursprüngliche Vorstellung*) (B48). Time presents itself to us independent of any conceptual understanding of it, that is to say, prior to any attempt to determine it conceptually, as though it could be derived from comparison with something else or generalized from specific experiences (empirical intuitions) (GA21 276).

The significance of Heidegger's insistence on interpreting "the pure intuition of time" to mean that time itself is intuited precisely as an original, "pure" manifold is once again best seen against the backdrop of the Neo-Kantian reinterpretation of Kant's reference to a manifold.[16] For Natorp Kant's talk of a manifold wrongly suggests something merely given and indeterminate, when in fact it necessarily already contains the determinations by the categories of quantity and quality (which, of course, stem from "pure" understanding, not "pure" sentience). The Neo-Kantian project of Cohen and Natorp is to demonstrate that a manifold as well as a unity spring from one and the same primordial act of thinking. "In no way is it any longer permitted to speak of a manifold of the senses, which is to be united synthetically through thinking as a second, subsequent act of knowledge."[17]

In contrast to this Neo-Kantian proposal, Heidegger upholds Kant's apparent presumption of a preconceptual manifold. The manifold of time is "the primary order" such that all other manifolds are from the outset ordered *in view of* time. The intuition of time itself remains, nonetheless, an *intuitus derivativus* in contrast to the divine *intuitus originarius*. For human beings time is something immediately given, not created, in the act of intuiting (GA21 276).[18]

On the basis of these same considerations, time must also be considered to be a nonconceptual ordering ("the primary order"), a notion that the Marburg school considers implausible and alien to at least the spirit of

Kant's critical project.[19] According to Heidegger, "not nothing, but rather a manifold is given," not produced by a synthesis of the understanding, and this original order is one with which we get along quite well in the "natural environment," though it be sheer disorder for the purposes and standards of scientific thought (GA21 281). This construal of time, then, introduces an ordering that is both prescientific (lived) and preconceptual (present not by reason of a synthetic act of understanding). "What is essential and, again, what Kant saw," Heidegger insists, "is that it lies in pure intuition that the pure manifold is immediately given and that it requires no synthesis of the understanding. The interpretation of KrV, as the Marburg school seeks to carry it out, miscarries on this fact" (GA21 276, 282).

In direct opposition to the Marburg interpretation, then, Heidegger is insisting (and here, at least, *with* Kant) on the self-sufficiency of the forms of intuition. Time and space contain nonconceptual determinations, the pure manifolds of being-after-and-next-to one another, in the absence of which no specific (one might add, no "empirical" or "ontic") manifold can be given. To be sure, Kant does not speak as such of the lived time and space that Heidegger interprets as prescientifically given.[20] Nor does Kant's meager description (in the Transcendental Aesthetic) of the relation between sentient forms and matter suggest that the former are unthematic viewpoints (horizons) on the basis of which the latter are ordered. Yet Heidegger is faithful to Kant when he emphasizes that those spatial and temporal determinations of the manifold are themselves given, that "in all eternity I can never, by merely thinking, conjure up these specific characters (next to, behind, before, below) from the empty distinctions of something in contrast to something else; they must be *given*" (GA21 299f.).

On Heidegger's interpretation, there is a pure intuition of time precisely because time is a form of sensibility (and vice versa).[21] The claim that time as this pure intuition is also the form of sensibility is a way of affirming that time is the horizon in view of which a manifold may be encountered as such (and, as Kant himself notes, an empty intuition without an object is one of the senses of "nothing" [B348]). Thus, in the complementary characterizations of time as pure intuition and form of sensibility, Heidegger sees a clear intimation of his own view of the complementary horizonal and ecstatic aspects of temporality. As a pure intuition, time is the unthematic but original and ineluctable, sheer manifoldness of succession, simply being-after-one-another.[22] Kant's claim that the pure intuition of time is also an a priori form of sensibility is, on Heidegger's interpretation, a way of expressing that both the fact that manifolds are "always already" encountered and the way that they are so encountered coincide with having that original manifold in view precisely in the sense of projecting unthematically upon it as an horizon.

Even this brief sketch illustrates how far Heidegger's interpretation departs from Kant's account of time. Though Heidegger chastizes the Neo-Kantians for reinterpreting intuition as a function of thought, he in turn invests pure intuition with an active character that Kant seems clearly to reserve for understanding. For Heidegger that pure intuition of time alone, albeit unthematically, yields the order of time.[23]

Yet, while Heidegger's interpretation does "violence," as he puts it, to Kant's own elaborations of time, it does provide a way to resolve several traditional quandaries. The characterization of time as a pure intuition (and, thus, neither empirical nor conceptual) is explained by Heidegger as a way of articulating the unthematic horizon of temporality, indeed, as the original sense of the "a priori." The characterization of time as a form of sensibility is a way of indicating that the encounter of any particular being (and thereby the unthematic disclosure of its own way of being) is already shaped by an original projecting (future) that is at once also a way of having been and being present. This phenomenological interpretation of Kant's characterizations of time even meets Fichte's demand for an explanation of the "manifold" of sensibility, ostensibly prior to any synthetic activity by the understanding.

Because this last point is particularly difficult, not to say, obscure, the following example may help to elucidate it. A musician playing to sheet music takes the sheet music unthematically as a series of notes, that is to say, as a manifold, though, to be sure, a manifold with a direction or *telos*. Taking the sheet music as such a manifold coincides with taking it (just as unthematically) as something ready-to-hand.[24] The presencing and absencing of the notes in their use, that is to say, their directional sequence or ordinality, comprise the source of their manifoldness (*that* presencing and absencing is nothing other than their readiness-to-hand, namely, their way of being). The "disclosure" of the notes' readiness-to-hand, in turn, rests upon a projection or anticipation of the end of their use, sustaining the manner in which they are both unobtrusively "at hand" (or present) and "retained" in their absence. This unthematic projecting, out of which the presencing of the notes (as ready-to-hand) springs and is retained, is, in Heidegger's terms, the ecstatic character of temporality. Empirical temporal "manifolds" (for example, the sequence of the notes, the movement of the second hand) and the character of being "within" such manifolds (what Heidegger calls *Innerzeitigkeit*) presuppose the original, hardly discontinuous manifold constituted by the ecstatic horizon of temporality.

The example is, of course, more readily compatible with Heidegger's interpretation of a pretheoretical, hermeneutical understanding than with Kant's basically theoretical conception of *Verstand*. With this weighty caveat, however, the implications of the foregoing example for the problem of the "manifold" in the argument of KrV may be summed up in the following way: (sensible) experience presents itself from the outset as a manifold precisely because time is both a pure intuition and the form of sensibility or, in other (Heidegger's) words, is the horizon upon which, in the understanding (use) of any particular thing (*Seiendes*), human beings unthematically project themselves (and thereby the world). It is precisely due to time, so interpreted, that experience from the outset always presents itself as a manifold. Kant's conceptions of time as a pure intuition and a form of sensibility, as well as his assumption of an original manifold, can thus be reconciled with one another and sustained, Heidegger is arguing, by taking the phenomenological turn and interpreting time as ecstatic-horizonal temporality.

4. Kant's "Wavering"

In Heidegger's first Kant-course, as in KPM, Kant is said to have retreated or pulled back from a more fundamental interpretation of time, already implicit in his characterizations of time as a pure intuition and form of sensibility. In his second Kant-course Heidegger advances a similar, but far more broadly based criticism, charging Kant with "vacillating" or "wavering" (*schwanken*) in his accounts, not only of the productive imagination (GA25 216, 280, 412), but also of the thing in itself (GA25 100), the table of judgments (GA25 259, 289), the transcendental deduction (GA25 305), and appearances (GA25 339).[25] Specifically, Kant's accounts are said to vacillate between psychological and logical points of view (GA25 323f.), between "notions" and "categories" (GA25 301f.), and between psychological and transcendental concerns (GA25 343). KrV, to its credit, contains an ontology and even a fundamental ontology, yet it vacillates between (phenomenological) investigations required by ontology and the (methodological) determinations of the presuppositions of an ontic science.

Heidegger advances three principal reasons for Kant's failure to exploit the genuine breakthrough that critical philosophy otherwise constitutes. First, Kant's analysis remains dogmatically fixed on "the peculiarly rigid separation" of sentience and understanding (GA21 203). This dogmatic commitment prevents him from successfully elaborating the status of the imagination in regard to both sentience and understanding (GA21 283), as evidenced by his altered, but no less ambiguous characterization of it in the second edition of KrV. Even more significantly from Heidegger's point of view, Kant feels compelled, on the basis of this dogma, to sever time and apperception from one another (GA21 203, 406).

Kant's conception of time, on the one hand, and of apperception, on the other, are respectively sabotaged by two other prejudices. Though Kant does, indeed, differentiate between empirical intuitions of time and the pure intuition of time, his elaboration of the latter remains oriented, as are the analyses in KrV as a whole, toward nature as it is conceived by mathematical science. Under this conception, nature is the set of things present-at-hand, and time is not the ecstatic projection that originally retains-and-makes-present, but merely a hollow series of nows, co-extensive with nature's present-at-handness (GA21 203f., 247f., 269f., 294, 313–320).

Fatal to critical philosophy is, lastly, its embrace of "the Cartesian position" or "Descartes's dogma" that "what is given immediately and above all, that is to say, a priori, is the *ego cogito*" (GA21 278, 289–291). With this presupposition in hand, Kant construes whatever is a priori as a *cogitatio*, as though it were necessarily and exclusively bound up with human subjectivity, understood as a realm of consciousness to which each individual has a private and privileged access. The intuitions of time and space are reduced to mere conditions or activities of the mind (GA21 289), time is itself confined to the inner sense (GA21 340), and self-consciousness itself becomes saddled with the illusory problem of its connection with the world—a sure sign of Kant's misconstrual of the problem of transcendence (GA21 353; GA25 314–324).

Heidegger's phenomenological interpretation of KrV is perhaps best summed up as an attempt to demonstrate that critical philosophy's fundamental insight into the constitution of time and human subjectivity not only does not presuppose, but in fact contradicts these three dogmas. There is an original, concrete sense of the a priori, the ecstatic horizon of temporality or, in Kant's terminology, the productive synthesis of the imagination, and it is neither reducible to sentience or to understanding nor explicable as somehow their joint product. Moreover, it would be as egregious a "category mistake" (in Ryle's sense of the term) to subordinate the being of temporality, its thick horizon of being-before-and-after, to the presence-at-hand of natural entities or to a mere series of nows as it would be to confuse the pure intuition of time with empirical intuitions of comparative motions (for example, lunar motions, the hands of a clock).[26] Finally, the temporality of human subjectivity is not some sort of "mediating station" (*Vermittlungsstation*) for the subject to enter into a world (GA21 406f.). What it means for Dasein "to be" is, among other things, precisely a form of presencing, a presencing of things ready-to-hand and present-at-hand, whereby it is always already "outside itself." Kant's account of time as the form of sentience is nothing less than a "first step" (*Vorstufe*) toward an understanding of this ecstatic character of temporality.[27]

17

The Kantian Schema of Heidegger's Late Marburg Period

Frank Schalow

Heidegger's preoccupation with Kant's transcendental philosophy emerges suddenly into the forefront of his lecture course *Logik: Der Frage nach der Wahrheit* after the Christmas break in WS 1925–26 (GA21). Heidegger had become familiar with Neo-Kantianism during his student years (1909–1915) while working under the guidance of his mentor Rickert; this introductory period proved crucial for shaping the approach Heidegger would later take in re-asking the question of being (GA56/57 121–203). In his early lecture courses Heidegger had stressed the process of forming categories in its importance for outlining the task of ontology.[1] But it was not until the rather abrupt association with Kant in 1925–26 that Heidegger began to recognize the significance of retrieving Kant's doctrine of schematism. As Heidegger later summarized this dramatic development in his WS 1927–28 course *Die Phänomenologische Interpretation von Kants Kritik der reinen Vernunft*: "When I began again to study Kant's *Critique of Pure Reason* a few years ago and read it, as it were, against the background of Husserl's phenomenology, it was as if the blinders fell from my eyes, and Kant became for me the confirmation of the correctness of the way for which I was searching" (GA25 431). For Heidegger, the retrieval of Kant's thought holds the key to how temporal schemata can provide the configuration of meaning that shapes Dasein's precomprehension of being.

What remains somewhat of a mystery, however, is whether Heidegger had taken a step forward by adopting the Kantian view of time as the universal form of understanding being, or whether instead this allegiance involves turning away from the earlier insights of the particularized enactment of factical life.[2] Indeed, how does the earlier concern for being, world, and truth get refracted through the lens of Kantian thought and thereby recast in light of the adjacent problem of temporality?

My aim here is to show how the formulation of the question of being determines the path of Heidegger's retrieval of transcendental philosophy, beginning with the *Logik*, leading up through the 1927–28 lecture course,

and culminating in the book *Kant and the Problem of Metaphysics* (1929).[3]
Needless to say, we must also include in this development such texts as
Heidegger's SS 1927 lecture course, *The Basic Problems of Phenomenol-
ogy*, and *Being and Time* (1927); while more explicitly aimed at developing
Heidegger's phenomenological task, these texts nevertheless betray an un-
mistakably Kantian legacy.

Two considerations emerge immediately into the foreground. First,
Heidegger's way of juxtaposing Kant's concern for a priori synthesis with
his own regard for the character of human existence presupposes an attempt to relocate the origin of truth in disclosedness. This development
allows for greater input of the "practical" in terms of Dasein's factical,
worldly engagement, and for the recovery of the more affective dimensions
of human experience in which even the Kantian disposition of moral respect is rooted.[4] Second, the transposition of the focus of inquiry, from
human reason to the situated occurrence of human existence as care, entails something more than a recovery of subjectivity; it involves instead
Dasein's appeal to itself as immersed within an ensemble of signifying relations, the referential context through which the individual in his/her facticity is disposed vis-à-vis an "it worlds" (*es weltet*) or "it happens" (*es
ereignet sich*) (GA56/57 73–75). In this manner the retrieval of transcendental philosophy clears the way for thinking *how meaning comes to be
determined through a horizon*. Accordingly, the Kantian way of denoting
temporality through an imaginative synthesis (schematism) can provide
the key for delimiting truth in terms of finite transcendence.

Logic and the Self-Critical Move of Phenomenology

Heidegger seeks an alliance with transcendental philosophy due to a
common concern for transplanting metaphysics onto the soil of human
finitude. He thereby characterizes Kant's task as one of "laying the ground
of metaphysics" (GA3 1/1). Insofar as Kant implements a "critique of pure
reason" in order to place metaphysics on the right footing, Heidegger suggests that the germ of his own inquiry into being must in some way be
prefigured through this critical enterprise. But, these similarities not with-
standing, it requires closer scrutiny to discover the important points of
correlation between Heidegger's task and Kant's that allow for a creative
appropriation of the latter in terms of the former.

The correlations that are to be gleaned, for example, between the
Heideggerian theme of human finitude and Kant's delimitation of reason,
must arise from the movement of questioning being; their discovery must
contribute to the radicalization of that questioning in such a way that

Kant's more narrowly epistemic concerns can be juxtaposed with adjacent onto-logical issues and unfolded on Heidegger's broader front. *Only through such a transposition in the fulcrum of inquiry* could Heidegger's retrieval of transcendental philosophy mark a decisive historical exchange that both maps out the terrain of the philosophical tradition and distinguishes the originality of his own project.

For Heidegger, it is through the dispositional unfolding of being-in-the-world that the germ for any configuration of meaning and the disclosiveness constitutive of it can first be experienced within the flux of factical life. Another way of eliciting intelligibility more concrete than that of a calculative, logistic model is required.[5] Inevitably, Heidegger must consider not only what defines the occurrence of truth, but must also outline the very groundplan for such an examination that traditionally has fallen under the banner of "logic." From our perspective, the question then arises as to the various influences shaping Heidegger's approach in his study of logic in the 1920s. Only by taking this detour can we begin to appreciate what is distinctive in his "turn" to Kant, as well as what may be problematic about it when contrasted with Heidegger's initial emphasis on the role of "formal indication."

From his analysis of Emil Lask's work as early as 1916 and 1919, Heidegger had looked to factical life as the inroad for developing concepts to bring what is hidden on a pre-philosophical level to an explicit philosophical understanding. In the way of "formal indication," which Kisiel describes as the "real hermeneutic method," Heidegger recognized the possibility of identifying such basic occurrences as the "it worlds."[6] For Heidegger, the recognition that an embryonic idea of being stems from the formative roots of experience provides him with the clue for developing his hermeneutic phenomenology. Subsequently in *Being and Time* Heidegger conceives phenomenology as the letting be seen (*logos*) of what shows itself from itself. What becomes problematic in this transition, however, is whether he views the *logos* according to the same immediacy of formal indication, or whether there is instead a slippage back into metaphysical constructs due to invoking a "transcendental" scheme of meaning found in Kant.

There is an important difference that should not go unnoticed between the hermeneutics practiced in *Being and Time* and that arising from the problem of formal indication in the attempt to orient philosophy from the immediacy of factical life.[7] Specifically, in *Being and Time* Heidegger considers how meaning arises from and takes shape within a horizon. In a way that keeps an eye on the contributions of both the medievals and Kant, Heidegger defines this horizon "transcendentally" as arising from a point "even beyond being" in such a way as to determine the unity of being's many senses (GA24 406/286). But what now distinguishes this transcendental characterization of meaning? The answer lies in the shift that Heidegger makes in locating the origin for such a horizon in the projective structure of "understanding" (*Verstehen*), which in turn displays the most radical enactment of care, namely, its *finitude*. Insofar as human finitude emerges as the fulcrum for this shift, temporality comes into view as the chief concern for hermeneutics; the opportunity then emerges to draw upon parallel sources within the tradition to embody further this development, most notably drawing upon Kant's account of time and imagination.

As Heidegger recognizes in the second division of *Being and Time*, the fore-concept (*Vorgriff*) marking the unification of the structures of care, of existence, facticity, and falling proves to be temporality. Within the broader scope of Heidegger's ontological project, temporality supplies the clue for raising anew the question of the *meaning* of being; this occurs both in recognition of and in contrast to the way that he, in his earlier thought, construed factical life as the most direct access to the enactment of care and also to how being reveals itself according to formal indication. The influx of a primordial historizing movement realized in each of us as care, the influx of enactment-sense (*Vollzugssinn*), concretizes the relational context from which the understanding of being arises. When recast with an emphasis placed more on Kant than on Dilthey, the issue of temporality becomes especially important, for its very advent provides a transcript whereby the fragmented assortment of signifying relations that comprise factical life can coalesce to form the background upon which (*woraufhin*) to project the meaning of Dasein's being. Under the provision of such a transcript, fundamental ontology becomes nothing else than the exercise whereby Dasein *"can put itself into words for the very first time"* GA2 1/4, 417/362).

Recounting the provisional steps in which Heidegger can address the *logos* of phenomena, we can begin to seek a link between the issues of truth and temporality. But why does Heidegger's subsequent attempt to explore this link prompt him to retrieve transcendental philosophy? The answer lies in the fact that the variable which contributes most to the determining quality of the fore-concept is human finitude. In the early 1920s Heidegger had already been familiar with Jaspers' idea of the "limit situation" as a concrete sense of finitude.[8] In 1926 Heidegger then recognized a parallel to this that would become decisive for redefining temporality. The locating of boundaries and the delimiting movement thereby accomplished not only has its analogue in Kant's critical or "transcendental" survey of reason. More importantly, Kant's effort to seek the denotive character of the categories—their power to refer to objects according to those very same conditions that constitute human finitude—provides a new point of departure for ontological inquiry in concert with Heidegger's. As becomes more explicit later, Heidegger extends the narrow Kantian sense of the "transcendental" from a concern for the precursory conditions of cognition intrinsic to any knowing act to include more broadly the parallel interest in human existence and the precomprehension of being issuing from it. Heidegger ultimately equates transcendental philosophy with the problem of transcendence (GA24 423–24/298).

In Heidegger's view, the need for such an expansion suggests that Kant's problematic is severely restricted by its confinement to an ontology of the present-at-hand; this ontology employs categories for the objective determination of nature as a nexus of cause-effect relations. Yet at the same time Kant's thinking reveals a greater depth that harbors a sense of human nature as finite. Thus Heidegger effects a transposition in which the a priori synthesis of experience—the combination of receptivity and spontaneity—becomes juxtaposed with a regard for the unification of the components of care within individual Dasein. For Heidegger, the chief challenge is not simply to compare his own task and Kant's, given the common concern for human finitude.[9] Indeed, Heidegger can accomplish the desirable transposition only by showing how his own hermeneutical mandate comes to fruition through a retrieval of transcendental philosophy. Just as the integration of the components of care occurs within the movement of factical life, so the denotive character of the categories exhibits a pre-predicative origin in an even more rudimentary organizational stem, i.e., the occurrence of the "I think" as "pure self-affection." With the appeal to this origin, Heidegger shows that the enactment of understanding (*Verstehen*) indicative of factical life provides a deeper origin for the formal unities of thought or categories belonging to *Verstand*. When viewed phenomenologically, the idea of the "a priori" delineates what comes before or precedes, and thereby displays the sense of "alreadiness" that stems from facticity (GA21 344ff., 405). Within the confines of Heidegger's *Logik*, the idea of Kantian "critique" gives way to a hermeneutical exposition of the finite, circular enactment of *Verstehen*.

We need not undertake a detailed account of the *Logik*, of what for Heidegger becomes an analysis of the phenomenon of self-affection.[10] Of particular importance for us is the way in which the self betrays a latent affinity with time insofar as the "I think" precedes the organization of the manifold of sense; it thereby exemplifies that purest unity that traverses all at once each of the stages of the cognitive synthesis of an object. Time must be understood as a dynamic formation of the present, of making-present (*Gegenwärtigen*), that bears an affinity with the being of the subject; the subject is not an isolated "I" in the Cartesian sense but consists of the standing out beyond itself of Dasein as being-in-the-world (GA21 406). Given that the characteristics which define time and the self are one and the same, Heidegger can then establish the parallel between Kant's theme of the threefold synthesis of apprehension, reproduction, and recognition and the unity of care as falling, facticity, and existence in his own existential analysis.

In order to distinguish in 1925–26 the link between his own concern for finitude and Kant's, Heidegger suggests that temporality provides the common root for the organization of the components of both care and synthetic a priori knowledge. In this regard, any comportment toward beings, even that involved in cognition, must exhibit the threefold unity of care and the corresponding interplay of the temporal ecstases of future, past, and present. Moreover, insofar as care is defined primarily in terms of its own "can be" (*Seinkönnen*), which arises from the future, we must look to the futurity of Dasein to show how we can develop an understanding of ourselves. Any guidelines or principles that delineate the finite, factical occurrence of our understanding—even Kant's analysis of synthetic a priori knowledge—must exhibit this circular movement of temporality and thereby "have the character of hermeneutical indication." The transposition that Heidegger undertakes becomes complete insofar as his attempt to recover the temporal root of the categories implies the parallel, more inclusive insight of "time as an existential" (GA21 409–415).

For Heidegger, the more radical move of seeking an isomorphism between temporality and imagination occurs three years later in his Kantbook. In 1925–26 he does not yet look to imagination as the more encompassing origin in which to root the threefold synthesis and ultimately the unifying capacity of the "I think." But is it equally evident that he had already planted the seeds for the later analysis that will constitute the origin of the Kant-book, and for the further transposition in which the role of imaginative synthesis will be correlated with the openness of care. As he states in discussing the role that schematism plays in ascribing the characteristic of permanence to the pure concept of substance: "The condition of the possibility for the basic principle for the empirical determination of time is the schematism of the understanding itself."[11] The determination of time as a sequence of instants must give way to a more basic unification of time through the overlap of each of its dimensions, i.e., its ecstatic origin.

Ultimately, we must ask whether Heidegger's appeal to the schematism of imagination is a departure from or a continuation of his earlier emphasis on "enactment-sense," in which the historical and cultural factors defining one's situation contribute to a thematic understanding of human existence. No longer is the activity of schematism restricted, as it was in Kant, to defining the conformity of natural events to law, e.g., according to synthetic a priori principles as cause and effect. The *schematized* categories, or those recovered in their temporal origin, point to a more encompassing understanding of being that previously had been restricted by Kant to what can manifest itself within the scope of the assertion. As the cornerstone of Heidegger's exchange with Kant, the *Logik* identifies the link between a hermeneutics of human existence and an inquiry into the transcendental conditions of knowledge. Let us now turn to the next step in the development of the Heidegger-Kant dialogue as documented in the development of the Heidegger-Kant dialogue as documented in the WS 1927–28 course comprising the *Phenomenological Interpretation of Kant's "Critique of Pure Reason."*

The Reformulation of Kantian Schematism

The development of an overt concern for being is one that seems to have escaped Kant for the most part, even by Heidegger's own admission. Yet Heidegger maintains that Kant alluded to being, and the discourse by which Kant did so, no matter how cryptic it may be, nevertheless proves instructive. In *Basic Problems*, Heidegger considers Kant's thesis that being is "not a real predicate." To be sure, Kant conceives being rather starkly as mere "existence" within the ontology of the present-at-hand.[12] As such, he recognizes that existence is not merely one property among others of an object, a determination within our concept of it. Instead, the concern for being pertains to the perceptual givenness of the object that marks its separateness from us, our recognition of its opposition, of "position" or "positedness" that presents the ob-ject (*Gegen-stand*) precisely in its otherness (GA24 32ff./45ff.).

Heidegger's discussion of Kant's thesis about being early in *Basic Problems*, which follows in the footsteps of the *Logik*, provides the point of departure for all his subsequent analyses of transcendental philosophy. Indeed, his way of raising this issue constitutes the leading edge of the attempt to transpose the epistemic concerns of transcendental philosophy into analogous ontological ones. For the consideration of the appearance of the object in its otherness requires a questioning that can move from the fact of that otherness to the pre-thematic interval or space, the prior advent of openness, that facilitates our finite encounter with the object.

In line with his attempt to formulate the question of being with temporality as the clue, Heidegger describes this prethematic arena as a "horizon." For him, what becomes important is how the occurrence of such a horizon calls forth the priority of the precomprehension of being that governs all comportment toward beings. In this light, the primary challenge in reinterpreting transcendental philosophy lies in determining how the definitive metaphysical problem that Kant formulates under the aegis of a priori synthesis marks the trajectory in which the precomprehension of being can unfold. In the WS 1927–28 course, Heidegger describes this trajectory as one of "anticipation" (*Antizipation*). He states that "*the possibility of such anticipation of the objective determinateness for all experience, the meaning and correctness of such anticipation is the basic problem of transcendental logic*"(GA25 195).

The interjection of these finite conditions of transcendence harbors the riddle of defining a priori synthesis, and the innovation that unravels the puzzle of synthetic a priori knowledge. Heidegger writes: "This task is the problem that we have already focused upon provisionally: How are synthetic a priori judgments possible? . . . In every knowledge of beings, ontically, lies already a certain knowledge of the constitution of being, a pre-ontological understanding of being. The possibility of this knowledge is the problem for Kant" (GA25 81). Kant describes this innovation as the Copernican revolution in philosophy. For Heidegger, the transposition of the problem of a priori synthesis in terms of finite transcendence marks the mature grasp of this Copernican move, namely, an appreciation for the distinction between the ontic and the ontological, as well as the corresponding vision of truth resulting thereby. "The Copernican revolution says simply: ontical knowledge of being must already be oriented according to the ontological."[13]

Though Heidegger succeeds in bringing the issue of ontology to the fore, he does not simply dismiss the epistemic concerns of the first *Critique* in a wholesale fashion, as he may be said to do later in the Kant-book. The categories are to be viewed no longer simply as predicates determining the nature of objects, but instead as contributing to the understanding of being itself. As such, they betray an affinity with that pre-predicative area of openness through which a rudimentary access to the object is first granted and which is experienced factically as the affectivity of intuition. As Heidegger states, "The finitude of this intuition is factically determined through affection" (GA25 87). Affectivity is not merely a passive occurrence, but as *pure* intuition it entails an advance orientation to the manifestness of the object. Spontaneity as well as receptivity are essential to intuition. Likewise, the categories are not merely constructions of thought for superimposing meaning on experience; rather, they too must enter into partnership with intuition so as to achieve that "gathering" (in the more primordial sense of *logos*) for the object's appearance according to a consistent and universal standard. In this way Heidegger's analysis reaches into the inner heart of a priori synthesis to define thought as a receptive spontaneity and intuition as a spontaneous receptivity. By conceiving of the stems of knowledge in this bilateral fashion, Heidegger succeeds in recasting the Kantian concern for cognition on the other side of the subject-object dichotomy. In that pre-predicative region where we can witness the horizon of objectivity a still deeper root of a priori synthesis first becomes evident, namely, the temporal activity of imagination. Such a horizon is to be taken not as a limit marking an enclosed area, but rather as the outward unfolding of the temporal ecstases that define the process of disclosure.[14]

In the WS 1927–28 course Heidegger redirects his analysis of imagination by conceiving imagination in its richest synthetic unifying power, namely, as the mediator in the cognitive process and hence as activating the determinative power of the categories. "The *imagination* is only possible in its temporal unfolding, or formulated more strictly; it is itself time in the sense of the primordial time that we name *temporality*." Despite this important insight, Heidegger does not yet go so far as to suggest, as he will in the Kant-book, that all cognitive structures can be dissolved into the autonomous and creative organizational patterns, the schemata, processed through the power of imagination. But we do find precisely a precedent for imagination assuming this encompassing ontological role. That is, the temporalizing process suggested in it must sustain the movement of anticipation. For Heidegger, anticipation is the primary feature of human existence as care (being-ahead), which in its cognitive form allows the advance comprehension of the object to occur. By radicalizing the Kantian notion of time, Heidegger brings to the fore the definitive elements of care, namely, "being-ahead" and "alreadiness." He captures their dynamic character without reference to a preset view of substance or presence-at-hand. It is symptomatic of Kant's confinement to an ontology of the present-at-hand that he remained oblivious to the enactment-character of care, despite raising the question of human finitude. "Kant still could not see the essence and the task of a pure *phenomenological* interpretation of Dasein in the sense of a *fundamental ontological explication of its basic structure*" (GA25 318, 342).

When recast phenomenologically, cognition itself emerges as a kind of comportment that exhibits the constitutive elements of human concern and can be seen as depending on the same interplay of the ecstases that governs the unification of care. Herein lies the fruition of Heidegger's initial belief beginning in the *Logik* that the retrieval of transcendental philosophy provides the key for working out in detailed form the possibility of understanding being through time. The further development of this insight resides, of course, in Heidegger's radicalization of Kant's treatment of imagination so as to establish its role in the genesis of ecstatic-horizonal temporality. In respect to Kant, Heidegger can then elevate the Husserlian concern for a primal categorial intuition of the constitutive structures of being to the pinnacle of the more actively engaged process of transcendence.[15] Thus for Heidegger the opportunity arises to undertake a more radical reading of transcendental philosophy.

Let us briefly turn to his celebrated analysis of transcendental philosophy that marks the crowning fulfillment of his philosophical investigations in Marburg. What becomes prominent now is the strategic pattern of Heidegger's retrieval of Kant along a historical front, that is, its place within the wider task of undertaking a destruction of the history of philosophy.

The Science of Imagination

The attempt to evolve a *logos* appropriate to address the preontological understanding of being governs Heidegger's ontological inquiry. The achievement of this end yields what he first describes in *Basic Problems* as the "science of being." But we need to qualify what he means by "science." We must distinguish between a science that addresses a predetermined subject matter and one that accepts the challenge of the fluidity of content given in factical life. Science in the latter sense then responds appropriately to the innovativeness of questioning. In this more originary sense of science, questioning draws forth the intelligibility that is carried, as it were, embryonically within factical life, so that the hermeneutic move of interpretation creates a forum in which to reveal experience in a more universal, conceptual manner. The uniqueness of this scientific knowledge lies in the way that ontology resists arbitrary concept-formation, deferring instead to the nuances of self-showing in relation to which the boundaries of determinateness, of concepts, can be identified. As Heidegger states in *Being and Time*, the aim of such an investigation is not to construct an arbitrary, technical vocabulary, but instead to draw from the prearticulated sources of intelligibility in order to "preserve the *force of the most elemental words in which Dasein* expresses itself" (GA24 14–15/11; GA2 291/262).

A science open to the plenitude of human experience, then, is one that also welcomes that which most epitomizes the ingenuity and innovativeness of questioning, namely, imagination. Precisely in this way Heidegger can appeal to the power of imagination and to its affinity with time in order to fulfill the role of enactment-sense that he depicted in his writings in 1919 and the early twenties. But this association cannot so easily be made unless we recognize that Kant's treatment of imagination can be retrieved in terms of those subtleties that reflect Heidegger's appreciation for the uniqueness of the science of being. According to Heidegger, the distinctive character of this science lies in accentuating the distinction between being and beings.[16] The development of this concern for the ontological difference and the quest to direct the *logos* of phenomenology from it constitute the central stage of the science of being. This awakening does not occur in a vacuum, but instead arises on a historical level as an attempt to counter the inertia in the tradition's tendency to forget the question of being. Heidegger aims to recover the ontological difference as the hidden root of metaphysics. Yet this recovery must traverse various historical periods in such a way as to retrieve, from the recesses of other philosophers' thought, concerns parallel to those of fundamental ontology. Through a more radical questioning, these concerns are to be transposed and thereby retrieved in a way that traces the broad outlines of the concealed relation of being to time.

The retrieval does not simply occur on one front—as it were, backward—so as to reap the fruits of the philosophical tradition. It moves on another front as well, namely, forward, so as to yield the historical backdrop for the appropriation of Heidegger's own task and the clarification of the uniqueness of his way of couching the question of "being and time." In this way, his dismantling of the philosophical tradition takes its clue from the tendency of human existence to hide from itself; his task of "destruction" thereby remains anchored within the hermeneutic plan for retrieving the experience of factical life. For Heidegger, Kant becomes the prominent figure not only for initiating the destructive retrieval, but also for formulating its strategy as a plan to accentuate the hidden dynamics of temporality.

As an outgrowth of the concern for factical life, the task of destructive retrieval attempts to pull back from the absorption in beings in order to redirect attention to the understanding of being. To a certain degree, a faint glimmer of the inevitability of "forgetting" being underlies the appeal to a dimension of time, namely, the "present," in order to explain the manifestation of an object in a perceptual act. This is the case in Kant's thesis about being. On the one hand, the attempt to resolve the enigma of the distinctive character of being as an offshoot of the perceptual act of "positing" an object testifies to how an absorption in beings prevails over a vague sensitivity to the ontological difference. On the other hand, the negative formulation that being is "not a real predicate" preserves the insight that its meaning can never be captured by the ostensive act involved in singling out beings; for it instead depends on a prior uncovering presupposed in the act of perception. The need to appreciate this ambiguity in the Kantian thesis, and thereby to bring forth the ontological difference as the central problem of transcendental philosophy, defines the heart of

Heidegger's destructive retrieval of Kant. As Heidegger states at the beginning of *Basic Problems*:

> It is easily seen that the ontological difference can be cleared up and carried out unambiguously for ontological inquiry only if and when the meaning of being in general has been explicitly brought to light, that is to say, only when it has been shown how temporality makes possible the distinguishability of being and beings. Only on the basis of this consideration can the Kantian thesis that being is not a real predicate be given its original sense and adequately explained (GA24 23–24/17–18).

Though the Kantian thesis appears in the second half of the *Critique of Pure Reason*, in the Dialectic, the steps that are required to extract its ontological import are made in the first half, in the Analytic. For Heidegger, an adequate reinterpretation of Kant's thought must knit together these two sides of the first *Critique* and thereby establish a deeper unity for the task of Transcendental Logic. The concern for offsetting the downward absorption in beings requires an ascent to an antecedent horizon in which the understanding of being can first arise. For Kant, this ascent involves identifying the synthetic a priori conditions that regulate in advance any encounter with an object. Insofar as these conditions translate into sensibilized concepts or temporal schemata, the schemata demarcate the horizon and hold forth the area in which the manifestness of an object can occur. Thus, a re-examination of the doctrine of schematism provides Heidegger with the key by which to dismantle the tradition's emphasis on reason and uncover a deeper root for both its theorectical and practical employments in the power of imagination. In retrospect, what excited Heidegger so much about Kantian schematism was not simply its temporal character; rather, he was moved by how that account offered the clue to extract the entire organizational structure of fundamental ontology and thus a "metaphysics of metaphysics" (GA3 156–60/107–110, 230/157).

When conceived radically, imagination becomes a way of holding forth that ever elusive area, that play-space or leeway (*Spielraum*), within which the manifestness of beings arises. In its temporal occurrence, imagination determines how the overlap and play of all the temporal ecstases recedes into the "nothing," into the absence that, by contrast, renders explicit the advent of the opposite, namely presence, through an objectifying act. The way in which imagination initiates the primeval upsurgence of possibility suggests that it bears the extreme tension of distinguishing being and beings. But that tension is nothing other than what yields to being its ownmost determinateness, rendering it intelligible and thereby inverting its own tendency toward self-concealment (*forgetfulness*) in the direction of disclosure. But what else can accomplish this process besides time? Couched in his retrieval of imagination, then, Heidegger uncovers the problem of "being *and* time."

At first it might seem strange that an archaic concept like imagination should prove so crucial to Heidegger. But the answer lies in the fact that the activity of imagination serves as a medium for tracing all the twists and turns whereby being becomes narrowly conceived in terms of a specific dimension of time, the present; time is then addressed only secondarily, as a sequence of moments, and hence is considered only as an *afterthought* rather than in its reciprocity with being. What we might describe as the *economy* of imagination thereby makes explicit all the transmutations and variations permeating both the forgetfulness of being and the countermovement of recalling its historical disclosure through time. Within this economy, imagination suggests a discourse in which the *finitude* of human experience, of factical life, can be shown to shape more directly our understanding of being. As Heidegger considers this problem at the close of the Kant-book:

> The essence of time as first put forward by Aristotle in the way that has proven decisive for the subsequent history of metaphysics gives *no* answer to this [problem]. On the contrary: it can be shown that precisely this analysis of time was guided by an understanding of being that—concealing itself in its action—understands being as permanent presence and that accordingly determines the "being" of time from the "now," i.e., on the basis of the character of time that is always and constantly presencing [*anwesend*], i.e., which strictly speaking *is* in the ancient sense.[17]

With his destructive retrieval of transcendental philosophy Heidegger extends the frontiers of his project. Yet we cannot help but wonder whether his introduction of Kantian motifs like schematism and the portrayal of time as the backdrop for the discursive "objectification of being" mark a departure from the seemingly more concrete itinerary of describing factical experience that he developed in his earlier courses and writings. An ontology that seeks its direction through imagination constitutes a *"temporal* science" in contrast to the positive sciences. As such, "all the propositions of ontology are *temporal propositions"* and its insights comprise *"temporal truth."* We must appeal to temporality as the medium for transcribing the most basic grammatical allusions to being, e.g., the "earlier," the "a priori." In this way, temporality emerges as the linguistic prism through which the various senses of being shine forth or achieve illumination (GA 457/322, 460/323).

For Heidegger, temporality is not just a foil for logic abstractly construed, but instead captures the animating spark of factical life. Is recognition of this insight sufficient to counter the objection posed by some scholars that Heidegger's turn to Kant is so abrupt that it constitutes a break with the earlier plan of hermeneutic phenomenology?[18] In part, an appropriate answer depends on whether we maintain that Heidegger's plan for a destructive retrieval of transcendental philosophy supplements rather than departs from the "unbuilding" (*abbauen*) of the tradition carried out in re-examining factical life. According to Heidegger, destructive retrieval does not simply end with supplying a prepackaged answer to an ontological riddle posed long ago. Rather, the very attempt to lay the ground of metaphysics must undergo a shift of boundaries away from any conclusion and back to a beginning that initiates questioning even more radically through Dasein itself. The staging of this return defines the movement of *metontology* that sustains the doubling of the original inquiry and thereby interweaves into the concern for truth an ever more intricate set of practical issues arising from our thrownness into the midst of beings (GA26 199/157).

The insertion of this *repetitive* movement within philosophy yields the factical impetus for Heidegger's undertaking the destructive retrieval *practiced* in the Kant-book. Conceived in its finite possibility, ontology defines a basic form of praxis whose questioning is enriched by a re-examination of those kinds of issues that traditionally have been reserved for ethics. The importance of re-interpreting Heidegger, both from the perspective of his earlier courses on factical life and then later refracted through the lens of Kant's account of moral respect, cannot be underestimated; for it indicates the *Denkweg* that crisscrosses the path of ethics and may offer a critical perspective on Heidegger's later allegiance to National Socialism. As Heidegger remarks in his SS 1930 Freiburg lecture course: "And so the question concerning the essence of freedom is the basic question of philosophy, in which even the question concerning being is rooted."[19]

Just as in *Being and Time* Heidegger criticized Kant for dogmatically taking over Descartes' position, so there remains a sense in which Heidegger in the late 1920s overzealously attempts to reconcile his hermeneutic phenomenology with the transcendental character of Kant's approach. Indeed, Heidegger saw in transcendental philosophy the prospect of uniting Husserl's formalist agenda for conceptual rigor, for science, with the concerns precipitated by Dilthey's life-philosophy in emphasizing the interpretation of cultural and historical experience. The possibility that a retrieval of Kant's thought could provide this "fusion of horizons," despite Heidegger's dramatic allusion to the "blinders" falling from his eyes upon reading the *Critique*, may have been too much to ask. As suggested above, when compared with the early period of his thought, this subsequent development may look like an "aberration."[20] The question then arises whether a more genuine form of phenomenological, hermeneutic practice may not have been attained earlier by recognizing the role of formal indication vis-à-vis the "it worlds" than by later implementing a transcendental plan to project being upon time. Yet even for those who most pointedly advance this claim, it appears just as evident that the importance of the "Kantian phase" cannot simply be discounted. At the very least, the development of this controversy suggests that much of the continued allure of Heidegger's thinking lies in the rich crossfertilization of ideas pervading it.

Part VIII

The Question of Ethics

18

Sorge and Kardia:
The Hermeneutics of Factical Life
and the Categories of the Heart

John D. Caputo

Heidegger had it right early on, at the very beginning of his work, when he said that philosophy needed a new start. Philosophy, the young thinker proposed, should return to its prephilosophical beginnings, to the long neglected conditions of what he called in those early days "factical life" (*faktisches Leben*) or, giving it a slightly more transcendental abstractness, "facticity" (*Faktizität*) (GA63 §6). Philosophy can do no better than to return to this most unphilosophical, theoretically impenetrable fact, the fact of facticity. Having hitherto taken the side of clear and distinct ideas, philosophy can get new life, he argued, only if it reattaches itself to the density of the beginning from which it must always set out. In the beginning is the fact that cannot be turned into an essence, the facticity that cannot be transcended, muted, neutralized, or put in brackets.

Facticity was to be the means for radicalizing phenomenology (GA61 57–60, 195–97). Heidegger demonstrated the impossibility of getting beyond factical being-in-the-world, of gaining some transcendental high ground in which the facticity of human being could be neutralized. He showed the illusoriness of thinking that one could philosophize from this fantastic point, that one could adopt the view from nowhere. On the contrary, Heidegger said, it is always already too late. We can never get back past (*re-ducere*) our factical beginning. The density of the beginning is always already at work on us, behind our back. We are always already there.

The young philosopher hoped thereby to start a revolution, one that would transform and reinvigorate academic philosophy (and the academy itself) by turning philosophy into life itself taking categorial form (GA61 62–73). Kisiel has shown with meticulous care the birth of Heidegger's project in a transformation of the table of categories from the logico-grammatical categories of presence at hand (*ousia*), the task of the habilitation dissertation on the Pseudo-Scotus, to the categories of factical life.[1] The whole idea behind the revolution the young Heidegger wanted to start was to think Aristotle's *Metaphysics* back down into his *Ethics*, to think the *ousia* of the *Metaphysics* back down into factical life, into *ousia* taken as *oikos*, everyday household life, house, and hearth (a sense that is still alive in English usages like "a man of substance" in the sense of "a man of means").

Van Buren has shown that it is not too much to say that Heidegger first really learned that the question of Being needed to be raised anew from Luther's critique of Aristotelian metaphysics.[2] The prototype for the destruction of the history of ontology, van Buren has persuasively argued, is Luther's attempt to deconstruct medieval Scholastic metaphysics in order to recover the authentic categories of biblical life. That whole Lutheran project also lay behind Kierkegaard's revolutionary rethinking of the categories of Christian "existence." It is this uniquely biblical and pre-philosophical experience of life, the young Heidegger claimed, that makes the Greek philosophical notion of Being as presence tremble. Paul and Pascal, Luther and Kierkegaard, first instructed Heidegger that Being does not reduce to the static presence (*stetige Anwesenheit*) of the Greeks, but is rather, in keeping with its temporal key, historical movement. It was here that he first learned that human being is adequately conceived not as *animal rationale* but as the temporality of a being faced with decision and expectation, uncertain of its future but resolved to act. Heidegger found in the New Testament narratives a wholly different set of (pre)philosophical paradigms: not of neutrality and the *epoche*, not of the disinterested, objectifying thinking of Greek metaphysics, but rather paradigms of concernful struggle, of fear and trembling, of passion and resolve.

But Heidegger put this discovery to work not as a way of dismissing Aristotelian metaphysics (like Luther, who thought that Aristotle had been sent into the world as a punishment for our sins), but rather as a way of rereading and rewriting it. Heidegger submitted Aristotle to a hermeneutic violence that drew students to Freiburg from all over Germany and that, very much as he hoped, resulted in a fundamental reorientation of phenomenology. Indeed, he succeeded, perhaps beyond his expectations, in shaking philosophy in this century to its very foundations.

Home fresh from the war, the young philosopher was very much taken with Kierkegaard's sense that Christianity has not been brought into the world in order to comfort us in our old age and allow us to sleep at night. Christianity had to do with the terror of Abraham and the battle of the knight of faith. We ought not to believe ourselves prematurely enrolled in the church triumphant, Johannes Climacus said, while we are still paying our dues to the church militant. That would be to behave like an army that, "drawn up to move in battle, were instead to march back to the city barracks in triumph."[3] Christian life is "repetition," Constant Constantius said, by which he meant movement forward, putting your hands to the plow and not looking back, as opposed to the headlong retreat of Greek philosophy into an eternity left behind (*anamnesis*) and the pseudo-movement of Hegelian *Aufhebung.* Heidegger loved the rhetoric of vigor and robustness, of the "difficulty of life." We recall Johannes Climacus sitting in Fredericksberg Garden, puffing on a cigar, and conceiving it to be his life's work to make life difficult (whence Heidegger's reading of *Nicomachean Ethics* 1106b28; see GA61 108–110), inasmuch as the authors of the encyclopedias had already done enough to make life easy. Heidegger loved all this Christian militancy and Christian soldierism. Everywhere he looked he saw a battle. Even his Socrates was a soldier (GA61 49–50).[4]

Heidegger well understood the sense in which Christianity had not come to bring peace but the sword and to warn us against those who shout "peace and security" just when we need to be on the alert (I *Thess*. 5:1–3).[5] But it is hard to come away from these early Freiburg lecture courses without the feeling that something important was missing from this *hermeneia,* that some sort of new "reduction" or exclusion was being enforced. Heidegger let the prephilosophical biblical paradigm shake the metaphysical understanding of human "existence" (factical life) as *substantia, animal rationale,* and even of Being itself as *ousia, Anwesenheit.* But he showed no interest in certain striking differences between the biblical narratives and Aristotle's metaphysical categories, a failure that I want to say was fateful and in one respect fatal. If anything, he seemed to think that once Aristotelian metaphysical categories were deconstructed down into the factical categories embedded in the *Ethics,* and once the categories of Scholastic metaphysics were deconstructed down into the factical experience of life in the New Testament, the results would be pretty much the same. Either way, the same table of factical categories would emerge and would serve as the basis of a universal ontological framework that was neither Greek nor Christian.

He seemed not to notice, or not to consider relevant, that in comparison to the Aristotelian ethics in particular, the biblical narratives are not at all oriented to the *phronimos,* the prudent man (sic), the well-educated, moderate man of judgment, the aristocratic gentleman whom the younger aristocratic set should learn to emulate. Indeed it was of just these well-to-do, respectable gentlemen that the biblical experience of life was most suspicious. Instead of this mainstream prudent man, the biblical attention is directed to everyone who has been marginalized by the mainstream, to everyone who is out of power, out of money, out of luck, uneducated, and despised. Instead of the uprightness of the man of good judgment, the biblical narratives turn to those who are bent and laid low. Instead of the cultivation of health, these narratives concern themselves with the infirm and afflicted, with lepers and cripples. MacIntyre is quite right to find a world of Aristotelian virtues and vices in the novels of Jane Austen.[6] But the biblical world is not to be found in the country estates and comfortable parsonages of the well-to-do, but in the slums and alleyways where the "victims" of these wealthy Austenians dwell. Aristotle was surely right to say that a man ought not to seek honor but that in virtue of which he deserves honor, viz. virtue. But the biblical narratives were preoccupied not with honor but with dishonor, with all those who were humiliated and dishonored, everyone whom the "world" had made despicable, with all those who had never gotten as far as the debate between true honor versus false, with all those whom, as Paul said "are not" as far as the world is concerned.[7] Aristotle was on this point—and this is not surprising, not a criticism—very Greek. He wanted his *phronimos* to shine with glory, to glitter with all the *phainesthai* at his command, but he insisted that this be earned glory, not a false shine. His was a hermeneutics of *aristos* and *arete*, of excellence, of those who make themselves beautiful because they make themselves men of good judgment and taste, of sense and sensibility. It was a hermeneutics of the best and the brightest, the most beautiful and honorable, the upper percentiles who would all get into the best schools and have seminars with Allan Bloom. The biblical narratives on the other hand consorted with outcasts and the rejects who drop out of school.

So the fabric and texture of factical life was decidedly different in the two cases. On the one hand, a hermeneutics of excellence and *arete*, of putting everything in order with the order of rank. On the other hand, a hermeneutics not of glory but of humiliation, not of the strong and erect but of those who have been laid low, not of the great but of the small, not of the straight but of the crippled and bent, not of the beautiful but the ugly, not of athletes but of lepers, not of *eudaimonia* but of misery, not of prudence but of mercy, not of the order of rank but of all those who drop to the bottom wherever a *logos* and a *polemos* shake things down and distribute them into an hierarchy.[8]

The whole point of the biblical narratives seems to have been to put the best and the brightest on the spot, to single out those who are not hungry, not naked, not in prison, and to ask them "Why not?," to disturb and question their autonomy and freedom with troubling analogies about camels squeezing through a needle's eye. The biblical favor is bestowed not on the *aristos* or *archon*—on the prudent man, on the rulers, or the wealthy, or the ones who have the power—but on those who drop through the cracks, those who are cast out and ground under, on the remnants and left-overs, the disenfranchised and different, on everyone an-archical, outside the *arche*. That deeply offended Nietzsche's exceedingly Greek palate.[9] On this point, even the young Heidegger is very Greek.

One point in the Aristotelian text that Heidegger seizes upon in particular is the notion that *phronesis* is precisely the ability to operate without hard and fast rules. Unlike the knowledge of unchangeables, *phronesis* is the know-how that knows how to cope with a changing market, a shifting scene, that has the wherewithal to operate in a world that is mutable through and through. That captured Heidegger's interest, and the work he did with *phronesis* in those early days set the work of Arendt and Gadamer into motion and pretty much put hermeneutics in the twentieth century sense on the map. Heidegger quite rightly saw *phronesis* as the sort of knowing that is uniquely tailored to fit changeable being, the sort of knowing keyed to being as movement, not presence, and this was an insight of enormous moment for contemporary philosophy. But it is also the stuff of a significant contrast with the biblical narratives.

The biblical narratives were concerned with softening the bite of the Law, and so something like *phronesis* seems to come into play every time these stories put healing above the sabbath laws and more generally put human well-being ahead of keeping rules. But Heidegger made nothing of that point of comparison; it did not draw his interest. Furthermore, he never noticed the revealing difference between the Aristotelian and the biblical paradigms. The flexibility of *phronesis* is of a dominantly cognitive or noetic sort. *Phronesis* is a kind of *nous* that consists in having a sense for the mobility of loosely fitting principles, of what Aristotle called *schemata*, and hence a matter of a certain practical-cognitive adroitness in their application. The biblical sense of flexibility about the Law, on the other hand, was driven not by *nous* but by mercy, and was far less a cognitive matter than a deeply praxical one. *Phronesis* is a sense of what the individual situation demands, an *insight* (*nous*) on the part of practical understanding into the idiosyncrasies of the particular, whereas mercy is a giving way on the part of what the biblical narratives call the *heart* (*kardia*), which is not so much "insight" as a certain giving in to the needs of the other.[10] Mercy is a tenderness of heart that takes the demands of the one who is afflicted to override and trump the Law, to lift the Law from the backs of the ones who need help, especially when they are afflicted by the Law itself. It is not so much insight and practical *nous* as a kind of melting or succumbing to the needs of the other. This biblical flavor also shows up in Thomas Aquinas's version of Aristotelianism, when Thomas argues that it is *caritas*, not *prudentia*, which constitutes the form of the virtues, that without which the virtues are hollow rule-keeping.[11] It is possible to compare and contrast and even temporarily to confuse *phronesis* and *techne*, but it would never be possible to confuse mercy with *techne*. The biblical "cardia-logy" (or even "hetero-logy") could never look like a "technology."

The biblical stories proceed from a different conception of factical life, one that was enamored neither with rules, as in modernity, because they favored a kind of radical mercifulness over rule-keeping, nor with "excellence" (*arete*), because their heart was with the outcast, with the worst not the best. Heidegger fixes on the first point and misses or ignores or just is not interested in the second point. His implicit ontology of the biblical lifeworld was guided chiefly by his interest in *phronesis* and *techne* as kinds of practical knowing, and in knowing as a kind of unconcealing. However many clues he took from the biblical discourses, his interest remained on this point at bottom very Greek. His concerns turn entirely on the phenomenological question of the "constitution" of the "world," with how "it worlds," with *techne* and *phronesis* as kinds of practical knowing, knowing how, which as it were light up the public space. He was not at all interested in the notion of those whom the world cast out, the shadows who inhabit the margins and crevices of the world. In Heidegger's "everyday world" there are no beggars, lepers, hospitals, homeless people, sickness, children, meals, animals. In general, there is very little room in the early Freiburg courses for the category of what Merleau-Ponty would call "flesh." Yet the "kingdom of God" (*basileia theou*) is a kingdom of flesh, of banquets and of hunger, of cripples made whole, dead men made to live again, a realm of bodies in pleasure and pain, of flesh and blood. In Heidegger's factical lifeworld there are, however, plenty of tables, chairs, houses, tools, and instruments of all sorts, including even automobile turning signals—"table, jug, plough, saw, house, garden, field, village, path" (GA63 90)—all beings of concernful "care" (*Sorge*). Heidegger heard the *Sorge* in "*sorgen um das 'tägliche Brot'*" (GA61 90), but he underplayed the *Brot*, the sphere of bread and flesh.

Heidegger thematized the materials of factical life, not of uppercrust Austenian or Aristotelian factical life, which was much too comfortable and bourgeois a scene for Heidegger (cf. GA61 187–88) and so not factical enough. Most of the wrinkles of facticity have been smoothed out for the Austenian set. When Heidegger thought of facticity he thought of struggle and work, and so he incorporated Kierkegaard's attack upon the comfortable bourgeoisie of "Christendom" into his story. Now let there by no mistake about this: it was a startling and revolutionary proposal on Heidegger's part to say that such workaday "things" were the fitting subject matter of philosophy's venerable and ageless pursuit of the *Ding an sich*. My complaint here is only that his conception of "factical life" is not factical or perhaps praxical enough. *Faktizität*—which is after all a Latinism coming off *facere, factus sum*: making, made—is too strongly oriented to this artisan world, too much taken with the paradigm of practical goods and the unique sort of cognitivity it requires. It ignores the scenes of *praxis* and afflicted flesh, the *praxis* of afflicted flesh, which is essential to the biblical lifeworld.

Heidegger had at least a partial glimpse of this category. In an interesting passage in the early lectures, when Heidegger is describing the world of everydayness, he writes:

> In *the* room stands *the* table (not "a" table alongside many others in other rooms and houses) at which one sits *in order to* write, eat, sew, play . . . . Its standing there in the room means: it plays a role for such and such a use; this or that is impractical, unsuited for it . . . . Here and there it shows lines—the boys made themselves busy at the table; these lines are not just occasional interruptions of its coloring, but rather: the boys have been here, and still are. This side is not the easterly side, the small side is not so many cm. shorter than the other, but rather this is the side at which my wife sits if she wishes to read; earlier we had this or that discussion at the table; here a decision was made with a *friend*; there a certain *work* written; that *holiday* celebrated. (GA63 90)

There is an interesting quality in this account of the world of everyday things. For while his eye is on the table, he sets out the concatenation of the table with other elements: the boys, my wife, the friend, i.e., with the elements of the other. That is an opening to be pursued. The kitchen table still bears the marks of "*die Buben*," the scallawags who marked it up. The table points to the presence of the boys, who are still there. Had Heidegger followed this up, had he pushed it harder, he might have brought the world of utensility closer to the sense of factical life that I am here pursuing and that I think is systematically excluded or even suppressed.

What he needed was a still more radical account of the factical world, a still more concrete facticity rooted in the *praxis* and flesh of life, in the griefs and joys of everyday life and concrete being-in-the-world. For the factical world is a world of family meals around the kitchen tables, or of friends one has welcomed into one's home, and Heidegger captures that in this passage, although he tends to mute it in *Being and Time*. That is an opening, but only privatively. For factical life is no less the world of those who have no food, a world quite literally of *Darbung* (GA61 90), of *steresis*, *privatio*, of the hungry and homeless, and of children abandoned by their parents. The world of everydayness is the familiar piece of clothing of someone close, the sort of thing that grieves the heart when it is come upon after their death; and Heidegger catches sight of that. But it is also the grief of those who go unclothed, who dress in rags, who leave nothing behind when they die, who vanish without a trace, without provoking a memory, perhaps even without a name. The world of everydayness is the broken pair of skis in the cellar—"that is my youth," he says quite acutely (GA63 91). But it is also the world of the lame and the crippled. "This book was a gift from so and so"—but it is also the world of those who cannot read. The factical world is the world of living bodies surrounded by the sphere of utensility, but it is also the world in which those bodies have been shattered, shamed, disabled. Now it is always the latter, the *steresis*, the privation and the deprivation, which is the special focus of the biblical narratives, the preferential option it exercises. Biblical factical life is a world not of able-bodied being-in-the-world actualizing its potentiality for Being, but of disabled beings whose potencies have been cut short.

Heidegger's revolutionary impulse lay in seeing that these matters, hitherto considered altogether beneath the dignity of philosophy, were in fact the very prephilosophical materials from which philosophy itself is forged, to which philosophy seeks to give "ontological-categorial" form. But his impulse was aborted or narrowed by a certain philosophical prejudice in favor of the cognitive-aletheiological features of the world that had the effect of neutralizing the flesh. His impulse was cut short by a new and more subtle *epoche* that enforced a new and different neutralization of factical life. In Husserl, the philosopher carried out a reflective disengagement from and neutralization of factical life that turned being into permanent presence and philosophy into an impossibly pure *theoria*. For Heidegger, the philosopher is situated from the start in the pre-reflective, pregiven world of factical being-in-the-world. But Heidegger in turn enforces a whole new layer of reductions. Fundamental ontology shuts down, excludes, or neutralizes the whole dimension of being-dis-abled (instead of having a *Seinkönnen*), of being cast-out of the world (instead of being projected into it), of suffering and enervating grief (instead of moodful tuning), of illiteracy or aphasia (instead of *Rede* and *Gerede*). The full measure of facticity is suppressed by the ontology of everydayness and the world of work and care. Heidegger had quietly closed down the operations of the flesh, the whole "economy" or "world" of bodily diminishment, distress, and vulnerability, in short, the "world" of those whom the world casts out, those who are despised by the world and "world-poor" in a more literal sense than Heidegger gives to this word. "It worlds" (GA56/57 73), but it also "de-worlds" one down into poverty and destitution. That is the "world" that in biblical terms was called the "kingdom."

These are matters that go to the heart of what Aristotle called *steresis* (*privatio*) and that Heidegger translated, almost ironically, as "*Darbung*," neediness and literally "starvation." Yet no one in the hermeneutics of facticity is starving—or ill, disabled, diseased, suffering, in need of help and succor[12]; and no one ministers to the needy. It is a world of able-bodied artisans and equipment, of a busily engaged but thoughtless bourgeoisie, and above all of able-bodied knights of anticipatory resoluteness. Everyone seems to go skiing on the weekends. Nowhere is anyone laid low. Sometimes the equipment breaks, but bodies do not break. There is an implicit ontology of the body, to be sure, in Heidegger's hermeneutics of facticity, but it is very much an agent-body, not a patient; it does not suffer. There is no flesh, no real feeling. On the contrary, *Gefühle*, feelings in their most concrete and factical sense—pleasures and pains, feeling ill and feeling well—are explicitly barred from the scene of "ontology (the hermeneutics of facticity)."

Heidegger's conception of "factical life" fails to address the range of life, the totality of the "interest" we take in life, of "*inter-esse*," which means being radically inserted in the midst of the rush of existence. "Facticity" needs to include the movements of pleasure and pain, the exclusion and neutralization of which simply reenacts, this time on an existential-phenomenological level, the transcendental reduction, i.e., the attempt to purify, decontaminate, and disengage thinking. The "world" is not only the disclosive features of being-in-the-world but the shattering of the world, not only utensility but palpability, not only resoluteness but the dissoluteness of shattered lives. The world includes the gaunt faces of real *Darbung*, of those whose bodies are being "eaten away." The thought of being eaten, of having one's body consumed by a parasite or a disease, is an *Angst* not provided for in the hermeneutics of anticipatory resoluteness. Such consumptiveness is always implicit in the grim metaphorics used to describe the archi-diseases, the diseases that over the centuries have done emblematic service for the ultimate vulnerability of our bodies—leprosy, the plague, cancer, and nowadays AIDS.[13] The relentless consumption of the body by a virus for which there is no cure: that surely is *Darbung* and surely part of "the difficulty of life." Eating—the haleness of people gathered around a plentiful table in friendship, the "hearty appetites," the hunger of those in good health—and being eaten away belong to the same economy. That economy is an essential part of the revolutionary "other" in the prephilosophical materials supplied by the biblical "world." Heidegger just did not hear or see or show any interest in any of it. The biblical materials projected a "world" of banquets and beggars, lepers and cures, bodies wrapped in death cloths and bodies emerging from tombs. But Heidegger assimilated all of that into Greek terms, into *energeia*, *phronesis*, and *techne*, silencing the terms of mercy and *kardia*, which were the most distinctively non- or pre-philosophical categories of the biblical narratives, the categories most likely to scandalize philosophy, to shock it, to radicalize it—since that was Heidegger's whole idea.

Heidegger made no room for *kardia*, flesh, disablement, affliction. He had an implicit phenomenology of the body as a tool-user, as a being of a certain spatiality, and as subject to death, which was organized around the concept of *Sorge*. But he missed or neutralized the unique quality of the body as "flesh," as "vulnerability," the body in need, the body of the suffering, the bodies of those who lay claim to those who are well-off. Being well-off and being laid low go to the core of factical life, of a thrownness in the sense of being thrown out, which would be a different kind of ek-sisting, which antedates and is older than my freedom. But *kardia* and the flesh fell before a new *epoche* that was driven by a very Greek, phenomeno-logical-aletheiological reduction.

Heidegger's view of "feeling" in the early Freiburg courses is very telling and entirely consistent with his later views. In the discussion of "kairological" time Heidegger speaks of something that "torments" factical life, gnaws at it, bothers it; something matters to factical life inasmuch as much factical life is full of care and concern. "Torment" (*Qual*, GA61 137–138) of course belongs to the sphere of flesh and affliction that was the-matized by the biblical narratives. But then Heidegger adds: "It is not sufficient, i.e., in terms of interpretive categories it is on the wrong track, if one wants to characterize these (formal) characters as "feelings." "Feel-ing" is a psychological category, whose categorial structure is confused, at least is not definite enough to amount to anything in the present inter-pretation" (GA61 138). The reason for this is familiar, and it represents a constant view of Heidegger's from these early Freiburg courses to his last writings. Feelings are purely private, subjective states without the power to "disclose" the world. Against the reductionism of the empiricists, which reduced feeling to private mental states, Heidegger actually gave unprece-dented importance to the affective sphere. He did this by interpreting feel-ings in terms of "*Stimmung*," a very rich German word that means mood and has a strongly intentionalist quality. Literally *Stimmung* means "tun-ing," the way factical life is tuned to the world, its at-tuning, and hence its being-toward the world. To have a feeling in this sense is to be responding to the world in a certain way, a way that was ultimately determined in *Being and Time* as "finding oneself" (*sich befinden*) in the world into which one has been thrown (GA2 §29). That in turn means that mood "discloses" the world as that which is always already there. The most im-portant of these moods is anxiety, whose central ontological role in dis-closing the Being of Dasein in *Being and Time* and in disclosing Being itself in *What is Metaphysics?* is quite rightly famous. Far from being private states, moods disclose the Being of Dasein, the Being of the world, and meaning of Being itself and hence enjoy the highest phenomenologi-cal prestige, far outstripping anything merely psychological.

That I take to be an impressive demolishing of the empiricist notion of private mental states on the basis of a brilliant phenomenological inter-pretation. I have no desire to detract from the importance and originality of this analysis that represents in my view a major superseding of the mind-body dualism that has confounded philosophy since the seventeenth and eighteenth centuries, indeed since Plato himself. But I am interested in the new set of eliminative and reductionist tendencies that this highly phenomenological-disclosive view itself sets in motion. The success of Heidegger's analysis turns on his ability to redescribe feelings as disclosive-intentionalist structures and to take moods as their paradigm. But not all feelings are moods. There is a considerable importance to be attached to feelings just insofar as they are not disclosive, indeed insofar as they remain, to use the most classical vocabulary, quite "inside" the "psychological" sphere. There is a considerable difference between a "feeling" like "anxiety" on the one hand, which has a stongly intentionalist value—its whole import is to be a certain kind of apprehensiveness, an apprehension of I know not what—and a "feeling" like "pain," where the disclosive value is not the only value. We are more likely to describe pain as "blinding" than as disclosive. Pain tends to cut the world off from us, to turn us in upon ourselves. A being in pain folds in upon itself, "curls up" in pain, contracts upon itself in an "inner agony," in worldlessness, in the loss of one's world. Pain closes us in on ourselves, closes down our worldly life, and hence is not primarily a dis-closive event.[11]

This is not to say that pain is without its disclosive value, for pain discloses in the mode of a symptom (GA2 §7a), and this is so true that the most insidious diseases cause no pain until it is too late. But the symptomatic view of pain, in terms of the function it performs, tends to disengage from the pain and to look on at it (*anschauen*). It requires another party, like a physician, to "diagnose" it. The disclosiveness of pain is not its only feature. As a lived state, pain does not primarily indicate something else; it "is" what is. For pain is an event of the "flesh," of a being *in* pain who suffers, who is humiliated and laid low, and who calls for help or relief. Pain on its *nondisclosive* side, inhabited from within, the suffering of an individual *in* pain, is precisely an event of the "flesh" and hence the precisely factical datum in which Heidegger is not interested. That is the side of pain which is overridden by the phenomenology of disclosiveness, which consigns pain to something "psychological."

Pain belongs to another register of events—to that of suffering and of ministering to suffering—than the "disclosiveness" by which everything is monitored in the "hermeneutics of facticity." Even as he radicalized phenomenology, Heidegger perpetuated its prejudices. He turned the phenomenology of intentionality, which still took the thetic propositional mode as paradigmatic, back to its prethematic base in concernful factical life. Later on, he continued the same radicalization of phenomenology by pushing back even further to the event of *aletheia*. But this radicalization remained within the horizons of phenomenogy's valorization of manifestness and truth, of *phainesthai* and *aletheia*, and left the issue of the flesh, of pleasure and pain, and of *kardia*, which is sensitivity to afflicted flesh, on the shelf, bracketed as ontico-psychological cases of the structure of the disclosiveness of *Befindlichkeit*, outside the pale of "fundamental ontology" or the "thought of Being."

To that extent, the early courses fail to stay with the facticity of life, with its situatedness and concreteness, with all of its prethematic immediacy. The significance of pain lies not in its ability to disclose the world but in its power to close the subject down, to shut it in on itself, to deprive it of worldly life, to reduce it to "ruins" in a far more radical and literal sense of *Ruinanz* than the early courses allow (GA61 131ff.) Again—and this as the far side of the same point—the pain of the "other" has the capacity to draw the subject out of itself, to draw into an "ek-sistence" of a different sort, in a uniquely powerful way. Pleasures and pains go right to the core of the existing individual, to the concrete case of life that is ever mine, which is this body, here and now, at this time and place. Pleasures and pains concretize us, draw us back down into the most immediate situatednesss of our lives, and constitute in a unique way all the intensity and "feel," all the flavor and quality, of our embodied, living being-in-the-world.

Pleasures and pains establish a new register of events, with a table of categories of their own, which is simply missing from Heidegger's aggressive, able-bodied ontology. The significance of pleasures and pains lies not in their world-disclosiveness as in the way they close factical life in upon itself and deprive it of a world. The "subjectivity" of "feelings" is an objection to them only if one is enforcing a transcendental-ontological reduction. In fact, feelings explain how the "subject" in one important sense is constituted. Postmodernist critics have done considerable damage to the modernist notion of subjective agency, individual autonomy, reflective transparency, and prelinguistic interiority. They have in effect finished the job of demolishing the Cartesian subject first launched in *Being and Time*. But the result of this critique is to bring to the fore another subject, the subject as patient, as subject to grief and misfortune, power and oppression. What I mean by "my" life, by "I" myself, in the most elemental sense is the incommunicability of "my" pain, "my" pleasures, the pleasures and pains, the feelings, which define my factical life. What I mean by the subjectivity of the "other" is the one in pleasure or pain, the one whose face is twisted with torment or streaked with a smile. That is the sphere and the subject matter of the categories of *kardia*.

Heidegger tended to take two closely related views on the question of feelings and in particular of pain. On the one hand, he devalued them as purely psychological because they do not have ontological significance, i.e., do not disclose the world. That, as I have argued, is a transcendentalist prejudice that fails to see that their ontological significance goes in a different direction, not in disclosing the world but in constituting a whole new register of events keyed to *praxis* and suffering.

In the second place, because Heidegger regarded feelings as purely subjective states, as defining a purely interior sphere or mental state, he tended to treat them as something to be mastered. This is connected with all the military bravado in these early courses, a militarism that rears a very ugly head in the following decade. Heidegger valorizes struggle and strife, hard work and strenuousness, a taste for the difficult. He is contemptuous of the love of comfort, of bourgeois ease, of making things easy. He wants factical life to gather itself together, to press ahead in a primal decision, to stand its post in the battle of life, and not to blink in the face of difficulty. He wants to be hard, not soft; hard on the self, pushing the self to the limit, and hard on the other, no coddling of others, no robbing them of their anxiety, taking away their shot to stand on their own. Pain is always my pain, a psychologico-empirical state, something to be overcome, a test of my strength. There is no room in this ontology of factical life for the pain of the other as exercising a claim over me, as mattering to me, as calling and soliciting me. In short, there is no room for the categories of *kardia*. The pain of others will make others hard and strong (so long as it does not kill them).[15] Van Buren has shown that in the early Freiburg days Heidegger was very much taken with Luther's *theologia crucis*, with Christian life as a matter of taking up one's cross, putting one's shoulder to the heavy weight of life.[16] But Heidegger omitted the entire framework of mercy and *kardia*, of lifting the burden of the other.

Heidegger was drawn to the idea of the Christian soldier, but he was deaf to the solicitousness about the flesh in the biblical narratives: healing the crippled, making the blind to see, feeding the hungry crowds, even raising the dead. The fortunes of the flesh, its well-being as well as its debilities, are at the center of these stories, but they do not so much as register on Heidegger's attempt to bring the factical life of the biblical narratives to ontological-categorial determination. He has no category of the flesh and no category of the claims of the flesh of the other on my flesh. He takes the biblical narratives off in the direction of Aristotelian *phronesis* and *techne*, of Kierkegaardian resoluteness and temporality, but he leaves the healings behind. He was very responsive to the *Sorge*, the care for one's being-in-the-world, but he entirely missed the *cura*, the healings, the caring for the flesh of the other, the *kardia*. For *cura* also means healing the flesh of the other, tending to the other's pain and afflicted flesh. To put this as ironically as possible, the author of *Being and Time* never really thought *cura* all the way through.

Conclusion

This omission, I said above, was fateful and in an important respect fatal. Eventually it caught up with him. Sometime around 1928 or 1929, shortly after he returned to Freiburg from Marburg as Husserl's successor, the whole thing took an ugly turn. What started out as a vigorous effort to return philosophy and the university to concrete life ended up in the 1930s as a kind of *Kampfphilosophie*, a philosophical celebration of danger that easily accomodated his notorious politics.[17] The call to engage life in all its hardness became a celebration of danger, battle, and strife. The "militancy" of life, first framed within the horizon of Aristotle and Kierkegaard, was fatefully recast in the terms of Nietzsche and the zealous militarism of Ernst Jünger (whose influence on Heidegger Zimmerman has documented).[18] The "difficulty" of hitting the Aristotelian "mean" gave way to a love of heroic excess, to the Heraclitean theme that *polemos* (which Heidegger translated in the 1930s as *Kampf*) is the father of all things. The Pauline warning not to fall asleep now was recast to say that the one real danger is to lack danger. Safety is the most dangerous thing of all. In the "safe" is the real danger (virtually the exact inverse of the later formula from Hölderlin that he would come back to again and again after 1936: "in the danger, the saving grows.") Danger makes one "great"; danger is the stuff of "destiny" and great nations. The rectorial address ends with a citation from the *Republic* (497d9) that Heidegger translates as "Everything great stands in the storm." The Greek *oikos* and the New Testament *ekklesia* have become the German *Volk*, and the church militant has become German militarism. The call for a university that really philosophizes is transformed into a politically radicalized National Socialist university.

Heidegger was ripe for the picking when he read Jünger's *Über den Schmerz* (1934), which included among other things the statement, "Tell me what you think of pain [how inured to it you are, how tough you can be about pain] and I will tell you who you are."[19] Jünger's philosophy of danger and pain utterly transmuted the sense of "difficulty" that Heidegger had first learned from the *Nicomachean Ethics* and the New Testament.

Even the question of Being was made to wear a steel helmet. We must not expect philosophy to make things easy but to make things hard.[20] Hence it is only by raising the question of Being, which makes everything questionable, which makes the whole totality of beings waver over and against the possibility of non-being, that "our people," the great metaphysical people—as opposed to thoughtless American pragmatists and Russian positivists—will become great and assume its historic destiny. Only the question of Being will give the revolution its truly spiritual bearings. He warned the Germans that their models ought to be Aeschylus and

Heraclitus, not (the prizefighter) Max Schmelling whose fortunes with Joe Louis had nothing to do with the real *polemos*. The Party regulars were largely baffled by all this. They did not see why their revolution needed to be backed up with the question of Being instead of a modern "philosophy of values," nor did they quite see how making everything tremble would consolidate the new order. In fact, as Ott and Farias show, they suspected that Heidegger was an anarchist. While they were glad to have such a prestigious professor on their side, they had no intention of allowing him real power.

After 1936, when he gave up his political ambitions and took still another "turn"—this one keyed not to Aristotle and Kierkegaard (1919–23) or to Nietzsche and Jünger (1928–29) but to the poetry of Hölderlin—and after the war, when the pain and torment of millions were plain to see, Heidegger still had learned little about pain, flesh, and *kardia*. I do not share the view of many Heidegger commentators who think that by 1936 or at the latest by 1945 Heidegger had learned his lesson. His baffling silence about the holocaust, the scandalous comparison of the gas chambers to modern agriculture, the mythologizing of pain into the "rift" between Being and beings in the commentaries on Trakl, the notion that real homelessness is not the lack of housing (in post-war Europe!) but failure to think the essence of dwelling, that real killing (said in 1943!) is not the loss of human life but murderousness towards Being—these are all scandalously insensitive to real "factical" pain and concrete human suffering. Beyond insensitivity, they represent what I have argued is a kind of "essentializing" tendency in Heidegger that transcends the concrete and suffering subjects of actual history. It is still essentialism whether one chooses to think in terms of a verbally understood *Wesen* (Greco-German) or a nominatively understood *essentia* (Latin and Romance), because the result is the same, viz., the loss of facticity, of the concretely existing and situated subject of real historical events. Such essentialism does not merely depart from or move beyond the original project of the first Freiburg period, namely, to return philosophy to the concreteness of "factical life." It flatly contradicts it. Such essentialism represents a new, higher, and still more abstract and austere reduction.[21]

Heidegger had dropped all reference to the idea of "factical life" and "facticity" after the 1920s. He turned more and more toward the search for the Origin (*Ursprung*) and Essential Being (*Wesen*)—of truth, of poetry and art, of technology, of thinking, of human being, of Being itself. He made it plain that "onto-theo-logic"—the fateful joining of Christian theology and Greek metaphysics—only served to block off the Origin. His was to be a task of thinking back beyond metaphysics and beyond the fateful Latin-Christian distortion of early Greek experience to the "First Beginning," a mythical Great Greek Origin (now mono-manically conceived so as to *exclude* the biblical origin and a lot of other origins, too). Such thinking would be at the same time a thinking forward, back to the Future, back to what is coming, a kind of second coming, or "Other Beginning," to Being's possible turn back towards us. What has all along slumbered in the essence of Being (*Gewesen*) may, if thinking prepares a space for it, come again toward us: *Wesen* is *Gewesen* and *Anwesen*. Such a task was hardly to be described as a "hermeneutics of facticity"—it was nothing of the kind, nothing so meagre—but as the "thought of Being" (*Seinsdenken*), the thinking of essential Being (*wesentliches Denken*). Factical life had given way to essential thinking, to thinking Being's own history (*seinsgeschichtliches Denken*).

Such a project is aboriginally Greek, for the Origin is Greek. The idea behind *wesentliches Denken* was to be as Greek as possible, maybe even more Greek than the Greeks themselves. The idea was to keep thinking purely in the element of what is Greek and not to let it be contaminated by what is not Greek, e.g., by what was Jewish or Christian, Latin or French. Of course it goes without saying that Greek is not contaminated by German, because German is Greek, spiritually, essentially. German and Greek: in essence the same.

At that point the project of the deconstructive retrieval of early Christian experience, which was a centerpiece of the early Freiburg courses on the hermeneutics of facticity, and of the correlative retrieval of Aristotle's ethics, had been entirely renounced. Heidegger even made the attempt to expunge it from the record, from the official intellectual biography, the one given out in brief strokes for public consumption. At one point he and his literary executors even planned to exclude these courses from the *Gesamtausgabe*.

The repudiation of the hermeneutics of facticity, along with the hyper-essentialism that characterizes the later writings, reveal the most ominous side of Heidegger's thinking. Heidegger never heard, or never attended to, the "call of the other," which is the call of the most concretely situated and factical being of all. If one asks, from a Levinasian perspective, what has become of the call of the "widow, the orphan, and the stranger" in Heidegger's later writings, the answer is that it was never there, that it was omitted from the earliest Freiburg period on, that it was excised from his hermeneutics of the factical life of the New Testament right from the start in favor of the machismo of Christian soldiering. That omission was from my point of view both fateful and fatal. Its fatal effects were delayed for ten years. They were first felt in the political disasters of the 1930s and then after that in the scandalous omission of human grief from the "History of Being" in all of the writings after 1936, an omission that led him into a scandalous silence and then into obscenely tasteless pronouncements about essential homelessness or essential destruction, as opposed to real factical homelessness, destruction, and suffering.

One can only imagine how a new Johannes de Silentio would react to this new speculative leap into *Seinsgeschichte*, to this gigantic meta-narrative about the march of Being through History that leaves factical life in the dust. "The present author is by no means a *Seinsdenker*," Johannes would say. "He has no such prodigious head for the History of Being, and he has no information for the reader about the scheduled arrival of the Other Beginning. As for himself, he is stuck in between the two beginnings, hardly able to move an inch. He is still trying to cope with the difficulties of factical life and it will be some time, he fears, before he can turn his life's task over to recovering the Great Greek Origin."[22]

Johannes de Silentio, where are you when we need you?

19

The Ethical and Young Hegelian Motives in Heidegger's Hermeneutics of Facticity[1]

Jean Grondin

The absence of an ethics has been singled out almost routinely as one of the most glaring lacunae in Heidegger's philosophical endeavor. In France, Emmanuel Levinas was the first and foremost philosopher to regret this vacancy of the ethical dimension. His protest was directed mainly against the alleged primacy of ontology and the question of being. The preeminent motivation of our existence and thus of philosophy is not being, but the ethical imperative presented by the other. The irreducible alterity of the other challenges my own being, thus laying bare its essential "secondarity," its peripheral status in the face of the other. By holding fast to the question of being so tenaciously, Heidegger—in spite of his self-proclaimed critical ambitions—would have fallen back into classical ontology and renewed its claim to totality that swallows every form of alterity. The reduction of individual beings to the sameness of being that is constitutive of ontology had to make the ontological question blind to the defiance of being and sameness that proceeds from the plea of the other.

This accusation that Levinas set forth as early as 1951 received little attention in the beginning.[2] It rapidly gained a new urgency in the wake of the widespread discussions and suspicions raised by Heidegger's entanglement in National Socialism. The events of 1933 led some to believe that the political error had something to do with a certain typical ontological blindness toward the ethical dimension. Seen from an outside perspective, that is, regardless of the precise circumstances and the specific context of Heidegger's own Janus-like involvement, there is something to the suggestion, reinstated by Adorno among others, that the claim to totality on the part of philosophy can translate into a tendency to some form of political totalitarianism. In this blindness that one could date back to Plato, if not earlier, Heidegger would be just one of the latest links in a long chain of philosophers that also includes many of his contemporaries, such as Lukács or Sartre who were prone at one time to celebrate Stalinism as progress toward the conscience of freedom. Intuitively, one could actually think that philosophy, with its inner drive toward clear, ultimate, and certain principles, has always had a hard time reconciling itself with such a gray element as democracy, which rests on the wavering ground of public opinion and its seductiveness. Philosophers, whose science Plato once described as being of a kingly nature, have never been outstanding democrats.[3]

It would certainly be hazardous to dispute any relationship between Heidegger's philosophy and his political error. Heidegger, for one, was the first to recognize it: his political proclamations drew all their authority and substance from his philosophy, as if he had wanted to stamp on the political events of his time the seal of a "philosophical spirit," as Jacques Derrida has recently pointed out.[4] In view of the intensity of the philosophical as well as of the political involvement, it appears doubtful, however, whether this engagement has to be attributed—as is customary in large parts of the literature—to any absence of an ethics in Heidegger, as if ethical philosophers of the time did not find their peace with National Socialism (which to most did not yet in 1933 appear to be clearly totalitarian; the Röhm Putsch of June 30, 1934, opened the eyes of everyone, including Jaspers and Heidegger). Heidegger certainly possessed an ethical awareness. When Jean Beaufret asked him right after the war, "when are you going to write an ethics?," he responded instantly, thus demonstrating his sensitivity on this matter, with a long letter on humanism, which became the first public testimony to his newly accentuated thinking in the wake of his *Kehre*.[5] To this day, the letter has remained one of the most representative, evocative, and readable texts of the later Heidegger. Insofar as an ethics has to reflect on the *ethos* or dwelling of humankind on this earth, replied Heidegger to Beaufret, this type of thinking was already underway in the ontology of *Sein und Zeit*. The ontology of Dasein, he provocatively stated, was in itself an originary ethics (*ursprüngliche Ethik*).[6] Here Heidegger anticipated the accusation of Levinas: ontology is not outside ethics; rather, it provides its most radical realization.

But in what sense can ontology claim to be the original form of ethics? Was this ethics really to be found in the fundamental ontology of 1927? This claim is far from obvious since, if it were, no one would have dreamed of faulting Heidegger's main work with the absence of an ethics. In order to sort out this important question, we can now fortunately go beyond, or behind, *Sein und Zeit* and take into account the earlier lecture courses. *Sein und Zeit* is in a way so cryptic and formal that it is hard to take it at face value. For instance: did Heidegger really intend to set forth the pure idea of Being and to decline its generic variations? Furthermore, to what extent did he still understand himself as a phenomenologist after exposing his anti-phenomenological notion of *phainomenon*? Why did he outline such an ambitious table of contents that he had no certainty of bringing to completion? Why did he question the whole project of the book on its last page? Was existential, even theological self-understanding more important to him than ontological, phenomenological inquiry? What or who were his true inspirations, Luther or Husserl, Augustine or Kant, Kierkegaard or Dilthey? Then came the numerous reinterpretations after *Sein und Zeit* that meanwhile have been discovered to be just that—reinterpretations.

For a long time, readers who did not have the privilege of following Heidegger's notorious lecture courses were left in the dark as to the ultimate intentions of *Sein und Zeit*. The publication of these texts could offer a new key to the understanding of his whole philosophy. In a sense, Heidegger appeared more "honest" in these earlier courses, philosophizing ingenuously on the issues that preoccupied him without a philosophical system in his back pocket or, despite his obvious self-awareness, wanting to make a name for himself (otherwise he would have published some of his work). When pressed by his students to be more specific on theoretical issues, such as his relation to Husserl's phenomenology, he bluntly told them that he was "not a philosopher" and went so far as to say that he might even be something like a "Christian theo*logian*."[7]

Wherever Heidegger speaks of ontology in his earlier courses, he always associates it with the general task of an ontology of Dasein that would spring from the "self-preoccupation" that inhabits every human. The strongest indication of this can be seen in the title of the SS 1923 course (a relatively late stage of the "early" Heidegger): "Ontology" with the subtitle "Hermeneutics of Facticity" in parentheses, as if the terms were equivalent.[8] Facticity means our own specific being insofar as it is something that we have "to be," that is, to assume and take into our care. This idea of a *Zu-sein*, namely, that we have "to be" this specific being that we are, will enter into the concept of "existence" in *Sein und Zeit*. It suggests, simply put, that our being, our Dasein, is a task for ourselves. Whether it realizes it or not (the latter means for Heidegger fleeing from oneself), our Dasein is characterized by the fact (thus the facticity) that it is open to its own being. In classical terms that Heidegger is trying to avoid, one could say that our Dasein is distinguished by a capacity of self-reflection concerning its own possibilities of existing—a self-reflection that has an utterly ethical import, since it deals with a decision we have to assume concerning our being in this world. To be a Dasein, to be "there," means that this "there" that we are can be elevated into consciousness and, yes, into our conscience as something that each one of us has to take up according to the possibilities that are at the time specifically (*jeweils*) available to and only to us.

I would like to expound on this point by saying that for Heidegger, our Dasein is constituted by something like an "inner dialogue" with itself, since it knows or can always know how things stand with its own self, that is, what possibilities of existence are being offered to oneself. Our "self" is nothing but this ongoing tacit discussion on what we should, could, or must be. That we are confronted by such a "choice" or "resolve" can be confirmed by the negative experience we can have of ourselves when we realize that we could have done things differently, that we missed this or that possibility. Without a doubt, the early Heidegger could find this idea of inner dialogue in the work of Saint Augustine, one of the most notable mentors of this period, even though Heidegger did not write or speak much about him. Beyond this historical link to Augustine that forthcoming publications of the earlier Heidegger will document more extensively, it is more important to see the issue itself, the fact that Dasein is a self-dialogue in a state of permanent confrontation with its own self and thus with others (who can very well dwell within us).

Sein und Zeit retained this idea of an inner dialogue of facticity by defining Dasein as the being whose own being is constantly at issue. In the same breath, Heidegger could write that Dasein is singled out as a being of care (*Sorge*) and more specifically (lest we be indulged by the later Heidegger in thinking that care only concerns being in itself!) the care of oneself (*Selbstbekümmerung*). In this way, the "ontology" of Dasein was not only unmistakably directed toward ethics; even more, it was in itself an ethical enterprise. Humanity is not originally characterized by the purely theoretical, intellectual, or rational grasp of the world expressed in the definition of the human being as *animal rationale* that dominated the rationalist tradition of philosophy from Plato to Husserl; it is more specifically circumscribed by the task that it is for its own self, by its dialogical existence as something that it has to take in its care. This task can be described in Kantian terms as a *Sollen*, an imperative "to be" that is inscribed in everyone of us, regardless of whether we want to heed it or not. It is therefore not surprising that Heidegger could rely on Kant's practical philosophy in a lecture course of SS 1930 on the essence of human liberty, what was conceived as nothing less than an introduction to philosophy.[9] To be "free" means that we are not fixed in reality, that we rather have to assume ourselves as a project, a future that we can open up for ourselves. Even where human beings appear to be preoccupied by theoretical pursuits, they remain governed by the fundamental imperative of the "care" of Dasein. There is no knowledge which is not an answer to a specific quest that is worth caring for. The primary mode of our relationship to the world is thus for Heidegger *befindliches Verstehen*, moodfully situated understanding. And here understanding does not primarily signal a form of "knowledge," as it did, say, for Schleiermacher or Dilthey, who saw in this knowledge the specific method of the human sciences. Originally, Heidegger claims, understanding is not to be regarded as a mode of cognition. Rather, it alludes to a "possible being" (*Seinkönnen*), that is, more to something that we can do than to something that we can know. Heidegger relies on the German locution *sich auf etwas verstehen* (to be able, to be up to the task, to know-how) to suggest that understanding is more like a "competence," an ability to run things, to "know one's way around," than any specific form of theoretical insight. To "understand" something is to be able, to be up to it, to cope with it, even to master it. It is thus in such a mode of "understanding" that Dasein muddles through existence, that it sorts out how it can manage its affairs. One could say that this understanding is thought of as a mode of self-orientation for Dasein that is a means not so much to know as rather to know-how. Some interpreters have pertinently suggested that this analysis brought Heidegger into the vicinity of pragmatism.[10]

According to Heidegger, Dasein already finds itself immersed in possibilities of understanding, that is, in more or less conscious projects whose function it is to forestall a potentially threatening course of events. In order to stay afloat in this world into which we are and feel "thrown," our understanding clings to different possibilities of being and behaving that represent just as many interpretive, fore-caring preconceptions (*vorsorgende Vorgriffe*) of the world. Before we become aware of the world, we find ourselves entangled in historical perspectives and ways of understanding the world (and thus ourselves, since we are, as Heidegger emphasizes, essentially "being-in-the-world"). "Those viewpoints, which stand at our disposal more often than not in an implicit manner and into which factical life enters much more through habit than through any explicit appropriation, open up avenues of enactment [*Vollzugsbahnen*] for the movement of care" (PIA 241/363). However, as Dasein, better still, as potential Dasein, we do not remain inexorably captive to these interpretive possibilities. We have the opportunity to elaborate and to raise them to consciousness. This unfolding of our specific situation of understanding is what Heidegger terms *Auslegung*, which ordinarily means "interpretation," but here amounts to a rendering explicit of what guides our understanding. The possibility of this "explicitation" necessarily belongs to a being that is already characterized by self-care and self-awareness, even if it is always limited. This (self-) interpretation is not a process that is added to understanding. It is nothing but understanding carried through to its own end. We understand in order to keep abreast and to sort out our way in our world. Consequently, we are also capable of sorting out our way in *Verstehen* itself and shedding light on the anticipations of understanding.

Thus, as a "self-understanding of understanding," so to speak, interpretation merely brings understanding to itself. Heidegger writes: "The development of understanding is what we call interpretation [*Auslegung*]. In it, understanding becomes aware of what it has comprehensively understood. In interpretation, understanding does not become something else, but itself" (SZ 148/188).

The philosophy that is willing to reflect on this self-interpretation accomplished in the name of a practically oriented understanding has to go by the name *hermeneutics*. Hermeneutics, specifies Heidegger, is here understood "in the original meaning of the word, where it signifies the task of interpretation" (SZ 37/62). In turn, interpretation has to be taken in its Heideggerian sense of the development of the preconceptions of understanding. As a philosophical project, hermeneutics will thus bring to completion the reflective task of interpretation that Dasein naturally performs out of itself. The hermeneutics of facticity will thus offer an interpretation of the interpretation of Dasein, a self-interpretation of facticity.[11]

Its intent is eminently critical and in accord with the tradition of enlightenment. This self-interpretation wants to pave the way to a level of self-transparency (*Selbstdurchsichtigkeit*) that has to be won by every Dasein.[12] Heidegger's hermeneutics promises to announce to Dasein the fundamentally open ground-structures of its own being so that the particular Dasein can take hold of them. This specific announcement (*Kundtun*), says Heidegger, is called for since these structures and this openness are more often than not missed by factical Dasein. It misses its own self because it recoils from the task of defining and developing its own avenues of understanding through a process of reflective interpretation or appropriation. Instead, Dasein lazily takes over the prevailing and public view of things that alleviates the burden of self-determination. Of course, no one can avoid stumbling into the "proven" interpretations that are already there before us. No single Dasein can take upon itself the creation of its own modes of understanding out of the blue. We all depend on the performance of tradition. But if we do so without self-awareness, without acknowledging what we are doing by repeating what has been transmitted to us, we succumb to a certain fall or forfeiture (*Verfallen*). One could easily single out the "theological" origins of this notion of fall, but again it is more urgent to see why it is so appropriate for the being called "Dasein." For in this fall from the possibility of self-determination, we in a certain way stop being a Dasein in the sense of being-"there" where and when the determining decisions concerning ourselves take place. The earlier Heidegger spoke of an essential ruin (*Ruinanz*) to evoke this self-abolition of Dasein. In lecture courses after *Sein und Zeit* and in his recently published *Beiträge zur Philosophie* of 1937–39, Heidegger coined the term *Wegsein*, being-away, to describe this avenue of a Dasein that "is not there" (GA29/30 94ff.; GA65 301, 323ff.). It is not there (*da*), but away (*weg*) from itself by letting someone else, namely, *das Man*, the they, conduct the self-dialogue of Dasein. It has to be stressed that this fall or ruin is in a sense unavoidable. Heidegger will therefore single it out as an existential, as a foremost category or predicament of our existence. Nevertheless, the notion of Dasein is constituted as a possible and even perhaps Sisyphean counterinstance against this fall from oneself. And the reflective unfolding or explicitating interpretation of our hermeneutical situation is the means by which we can become aware of ourselves as Dasein and control our tendency to fall into anything and everything but this debate with ourselves, to which we are invited or compelled as Dasein.

As a self-interpretation of our self-interpretation, the philosophical hermeneutics of factical existence will take up this declaration of war against the falling tendency of Dasein in the name of a more authentic and Dasein-like way of comprehending ourselves. Thus one has to acknowledge that its point of departure is thoroughly ethical. It aims to combat the cover-up of facticity that holds sway wherever Dasein takes its self-determination "from the world" instead of from its inner dialogue, as this is inscribed in the fundamental structure of Dasein as a possibility that we all have before our eyes. Heidegger qualifies this self-definition of Dasein out of the world (the they) in the strong terminology of the young Hegelians as nothing less than self-alienation (*Selbstentfremdung*). The expression is rigorously justified, since Dasein is no longer itself, that is, the virtual agent of its own self-determination, but the mere exponent of an unquestioned self-interpretation that stems from elsewhere. It is "away" from itself and thus literally self-alienated. The avowed program of the hermeneutics of facticity will be to fight against this self-alienation in the hope of reminding Dasein of its virtual possibility of liberty or self-determination, however limited it may be according to the always different situations we are in or that we are. "It is the task of hermeneutics," writes Heidegger in his SS 1923 lecture course, "to make the Dasein that is in each case my own accessible to itself in its own character of being, to communicate it, to pursue the self-alienation that is plaguing Dasein" (GA63 15). To remain in the terminology of the young Hegelians, what is envisioned is something like an autonomous self-consciousness of human being that Heidegger identifies as a "wakefulness" that needs to be fought for. "The theme of hermeneutical inquiry is the Dasein that is in each instance my own, and indeed hermeneutically interrogated regarding its character of being with a view to developing a radical vigilance toward itself" (GA63 16).

These potent formulations carry a tone that is reminiscent of the critique of ideology. In reality, the enterprise of the early Heidegger is not so distant from the concerns of the young Hegelians. The prime objective of this generation of students that was disillusioned by Hegel's system was to do away with the merely theoretical and idealistic perspective of classical philosophy and make way for a more practically oriented form of critical reflection. This motive found its expression in the famous eleventh thesis of Marx on Feuerbach: "Philosophers have only interpreted the world in different ways; what is important is to change it." In spite of Heidegger's well-documented aversion to communism, it is not surprising that we find a text as late as his "Letter on Humanism" expressing sympathy for Marx's notion of alienation as an essential dimension of our historical destiny.[13] It corresponded all too well to his earlier motivations at a time when he was certainly unable to read anything from Marx or even Freud.

Marx is certainly not the most fashionable of authors nowadays. Nevertheless, a form of critique of ideology is at work wherever one attempts to unmask a doctrine that aims to hamper the exercise of human freedom, be it propagated by the metaphysical understanding of humanity, by capitalist ideology, by the "politically correct" movement, or by self-proclaimed liberators—in short, by every form of prevailing wisdom that does not question its own foundations. What Heidegger espouses is not any of the particular forms of critique of ideology as they are to be found in the young Hegelians, for example, a socio-political version or a critique of religion (though one could encounter some traces of these in his work). Heidegger teaches only that the ethical motive for a critique of ideology or false consciousness is already inscribed in the fundamental structure of a being potentially understood as Dasein. Heidegger reminds us that this "authentic" structure of Dasein always has to be won anew by each and everyone, and that it has to be preserved from any dogmatic claims to exhausting the promise of liberty. Dasein is marked by a fall, by a being-away-from-itself—in Kantian terms, by a "self-inflicted minority." Out of this universal philosophical horizon it becomes possible to differentiate and appreciate different forms or applications of critique of ideology. The Marxist version is but one possible realization and has to accept other forms next to itself.

One of the opportunities the hermeneutics of facticity offers philosophy today could be to help us relativize the prevailing and unquestioned oppositions of schools and traditions, most prominently the opposition of hermeneutics and critique of ideology that has dominated the scene ever since the attacks by Lukacs and Adorno against Heidegger and up to the more recent debates between Habermas, Gadamer, and Derrida. It is not surprising that students of Heidegger like Marcuse, Löwith, or even Apel could start off with Heidegger and then feel completely at home in the critique of ideology of the Marxist tradition. Through Heidegger they had learned that the fundamental impetus of philosophy lies in a fundamental critique of the levelling effect of prevailing dogmatisms that restrict the possibilities of human freedom and self-awareness.

Heidegger certainly shares the unsatisfied feeling of the young Hegelians concerning philosophical concepts that remain strictly theoretical. The theoretical ambition of traditional philosophy has been to grasp the totality of the world, but more often than not its results appeared irrelevant to the practical concerns of our Dasein. What the concept can never encompass, because it is in principle open, is the particular and specific realization of the possibility of existence that each individual represents. Besides Augustine, it was Kierkegaard who imparted to Heidegger this "young Hegelian" suspicion regarding self-sufficient speculation, thus awakening in him a sensitivity for the higher urgency of the ethical.

Nevertheless, Heidegger knew that his philosophical endeavor could not entirely forfeit the theoretical medium. This is why he took extra care to propose his own conceptual framework (significantly never ceasing to modify it before and after *Sein und Zeit* in order to protect it with more or less success from any scholastic rigidity) under the provision that he was just offering a formally indicative orientation. The notion of formal indication (*formale Anzeige*) means that the terms used to describe existence require a specific and non-prescribable process of appropriation on the part of the reader or listener. This process is not contained in the concept itself, it can only be awakened, encouraged, urged by the concept. Formal indication would be totally misunderstood as the description of an objective state of affairs. As an exhortation to self-awareness on the terrain of every specific Dasein, it needs to be "filled" with concrete content according to our different situations. The formal indicative can thus only suggest or "indicate" the possibility of Dasein, the openness of self-determination. Heidegger stresses this point clearly: "As uttered sentences, all expressions about the being of Dasein . . . have the character of indication: they only indicate Dasein, though, as uttered sentences, they at first mean something present-at-hand . . . but they indicate the possible understanding of the structures of Dasein and the possible conceptualizing of them that is accessible in such an understanding. (As sentences indicating such a *hermeneuein*, they have the character of hermeneutical indication)."[14]

Such formal indications are what the Jaspers review of 1921 alluded to under the heading of "hermeneutical concepts" that are "accessible only in the renewal of interpretation that is always beginning anew."[15] Formal indication introduces us to a situation of decision, but its concrete realization must remain open[16] since it has to be performed (*vollgezogen*) by each specific Dasein in its own unique way. As a free accomplishment, the vigilance to which Dasein is exhorted has to go against the flow of self-alienation. This self-illumination of existence is what Heidegger's hermeneutics of facticity is all about.

This appellative, exhortatory dimension of wakefulness will go on to command the entire problematic of conscience (*Gewissen*) in *Sein und Zeit*. As an existential, conscience only takes the form of a call (*Ruf*) to "wanting-to-have-a-conscience" (*Gewissen-haben-wollen*). This call thus remains formal in nature, and critics were quick to point out here yet another lacuna of Heidegger's analysis. But, according to Heidegger, it doesn't fall in the immediate competence of philosophy to recommend any concrete models for our edification. His existential hermeneutics is content with the task of "recalling" this call of conscience that has to be fulfilled by each one of us in our own way, and whose structure is strictly identical with that of Dasein. As a potential *da* or "wakefulness" regarding its existential decisions, the human being is characterized as a being of conscience that is aware of a debt (*Schuldigsein*) to its own self. Dasein is "in debt" insofar as it has the tendency, in falling away from its possibilities, to let someone else make its decisions for it instead of confronting them resolutely and with full responsibility. Here again one can perceive in Heidegger's analysis of *Gewissen* an echo of Kant's ethics of *Sollen*. Kant also wanted only to recall the appellative character of moral duty that stems from every human reason—and to do this against the primacy of theoretical, syllogistic metaphysics. We cannot avoid being touched and perhaps even shattered by a compelling moral law, the application of which, however, can only occur at the level of our own specific maxims and judgments. For the application of the moral law, there are in turn neither rules nor edificatory examples. Every Dasein must take full responsibility for its own self. Similarily, moral wakefulness also retains for Heidegger the status of a "task" that lies before everyone and from which we can never recoil, so long as we exist and feel summoned by the call "to be" our own Dasein. Human being as Dasein is thus characterized from the outset as a being of possibility (*Seinkönnen*) and of "having-to-be," of *Sollen*.

Through this understanding of humanness from the vantage point of an existence approached in purely ethical and practical terms, through the terminology of care, Heidegger certainly contributed immensely to the rehabilitation of practical philosophy in our century. It has to be noted that his earliest courses were followed by students like H.-G. Gadamer, L. Strauss, H. Arendt, and H. Jonas, all of whom were later credited with a revival of practical philosophy.[17] One could also evoke later students like J. Patocka or E. Tugendhat who clearly perceived the ethical import of Heidegger's ontology of facticity. Even if this rehabilitation of practical philosophy took on many different forms, some of which are clearly at odds with Heidegger's own intentions, it is more than likely that its possibility has to be traced back to Heidegger, more specifically to the rediscovery of the human being as an essentially caring and ethical being that was made by his hermeneutics of facticity. This rediscovery of our situated and ethical humanity was outlined as a counter-model against the strong epistemological bent of Neo-Kantianism and the methodological perspective that was dominating the development of philosophy in the twenties and also prevailing in some circles of phenomenology. It was grounded in a mainly theoretical, contemplative understanding of human subjectivity. For it, humanity is defined primarily through its intellectual competence, through an attitude of theoretical perception of the world. The issue of the cognitive relationship between the subject and its object thus became the central concern of philosophers. In his early courses, Heidegger discovered that this academic question was not up to the urgencies of his time, which he found in a state of moral disarray that was manifest in all-pervading nihilism, in a crisis of the values of modernity and its scientificity. A new beginning was called for. Under the "young-Hegelian" influence of Kierkegaard, Heidegger called into question the entire epistemological background of his contemporaries and attempted to win a more radical—that meant a more ethical—understanding of our human being-in-this-world. That this momentous step was followed by a multifarious rehabilitation of practical philosophy was nothing but the logical outcome of his ambitious hermeneutics of facticity.

If Heidegger did not develop any specific "ethics," it is only because his entire project, founded as it is on the self-preoccupation of Dasein, which is also "there" collectively, was ethical from the ground up. For a hermeneutics of facticity, the clear-cut division of philosophy into disciplines like logic, aesthetics, epistemology, and then, beside the others, ethics corresponded to a false reification and fragmentation (cf. GA29/30 §10, 52ff.) of philosophical inquiry that is always directed to the whole of our experience (*das aufs Ganze geht*)—a reification from which all young Hegelians are immune. This ethical motive remained predominant in Heidegger's later work, even though the high-flown discourse of conscience, indebtedness, and authenticity seemed to fade in order to make room for the more prudent and serene approach of our dwelling on this earth. The thinking of the destiny of being that we encounter in the later Heidegger clearly results from a radicalization of the experience of human thrownness (*Geworfenheit*). In view of its being-thrown-into-the-world, human Dasein ceases in a way to emerge as the sole architect of its projects of existence, as appeared to be the case in the early courses as well as in *Sein und Zeit*. It now receives its possibilities from the history of being that has already decided before us how being is to be grasped. The somewhat peripheral character of humanness in respect to this seemingly over-bearing history of being does not have to lead to resignation to a *fatum* before which we always come too late and thus have to renounce any attempt at enlightenment. On the contrary: Historical enlightenment has now become the main task of philosophy. Out of its thrownness, Dasein comes to reflect upon the projections and paths of intelligibility that have constituted its history. With respect to his interpretive praxis, Heidegger's thinking remained thoroughly hermeneutical. The ethical motivation that distinguishes his hermeneutics did not cease to command his attempt to clarify the history of being. The "destruction" of this history of being still aimed "to prepare a transformed dwelling of human being in this world," as Heidegger reiterated in a text of April 1976 that could have been his last philosophical pronouncement.[18] This quest that directs his lifelong work is obviously ethical from the outset and in its consequences.

What one could find questionable is thus not the absence of any ethics in Heidegger, but perhaps the somewhat utopian character of this idea of a wholly new type of dwelling on this earth. This revolutionary zeal also goes back to the young Hegelians. It could very well be that such a utopianism might also have been a determining factor in Heidegger's po-litical engagement. He wrote explicitly that Hitler's "revolution" implied the "complete transformation" (*Umwälzung*) of our own Dasein,[19] as if Na-tional Socialism would be the opportunity finally to carry out the revolu-tion sought by the young Hegelians!

It would be erroneous to ascribe the political error of 1933 (that we will have to learn to differentiate from what later became manifest as the reality of National Socialism) to some "absence" of ethical consciousness. Hopefully one will not be misunderstood on a issue as sensitive as this, but one could also see in Heidegger's political errancy the consequence of an exacerbated moral consciousness. There is no doubt that the hermeneutics of facticity was animated by an ethical motive. One will also not call into question the fact that Heidegger jumped into the fray in 1933 *because* he felt he could not remain indifferent to the requirements of his time, thus putting into practice his own idea of resolute existence.[20] Events proved Heidegger wrong in a humiliating way, but he did not lack a principle of responsibility. Far from it: since Dasein must carry responsibility for its situatedness and thus its community, Heidegger entered, with great risk to his personal reputation, into the political arena in the hope that he could direct what he took to be a promising revolution in the direction that was appropriate. Whether Heidegger had any right to see some positive possi-bilities in the "revolutionary" outburst, born out of many motives in 1933, is a moot point. To be sure, there were at the time more lucid and much braver evaluations of what the "awakening," the *Aufbruch*, was all about.

But the mistake that is relevant for philosophers could lie in the expectation that a *fundamental* and *ethical* revolution of Dasein could be brought about through political means. It is the illusion that concrete politics could some day satisfy the requirements of the ideal state. The point is that the sense of the ethical dimension is possibly overburdened here. It could very well be that the radicality of human finitude and the limits it sets on any dream of total revolution are not heeded in such an expectation.

In conclusion, one will have to recognize that the revolutionary point of departure of Heidegger's early hermeneutics of facticity had the often overlooked merit of calling attention to the primacy and the urgency of the issue of the ethical for a being such as Dasein. Against the backdrop of an epistemological and methodological self-restriction of philosophy that he saw in Neo-Kantianism, in the epistemological orientation of Dilthey's hermeneutics, and even in phenomenology itself, Heidegger contributed greatly, by reappropriating some tenets of young Hegelianism, to the re-awakening of an original ethical consciousness that led to a rehabilitation of practical philosophy. But we could also learn from this new sensitivity for the ethical sphere that there are also limits to the possibilities of a philosophical ethics, such that these can underscore the problematic nature of any messianism that would promise to revolutionize Dasein by finally bringing it back to its forgotten essence. Isn't the young Hegelian hope for a total political revolution the expression of an overexcited moral conscience and a seduction that surpasses the realm of what is possible for our finitude? A practical philosophy that would take into account this finitude of moral conscience would have many lessons to learn from Heidegger's example.

Part IX

Toward the Later Heidegger and Back

Part IX

20

The "Factical Life" of Dasein:
From the Early Freiburg Courses to *Being and Time*

David Farrell Krell

"Life" is not an existential structure of Dasein. And yet Dasein dies. Indeed, it is even born to that end: birth is one of the two ends of an end-like or finite existence—Dasein natal, Dasein fatal. In this regard Heidegger entertains the testimony of a medieval Bohemian peasant, one who has recently become a widower, and who has a complaint against Death. However, Heidegger follows the lead of his anonymous medieval predecessor by allowing Death to have the last word. *Der Ackermann aus Böhmen* begins:

> *Grimmiger tilger aller leute, schedelicher echter aller werite, freissamer morder aller menschen, ir Tot, euch sei verfluchet!*

> Malevolent subverter of all the people, thoroughly malignant to all the world, murderous devourer of all mankind, thou Death, my curse upon you!

Death, offended by the farmer's accusation, replies:

> *Weistu des nicht, so wisse es nu: als balde ein mensche geboren wird, als balde hat es den leikauf getrunken, das es sterben sol. Anefanges geswisterde ist das ende. . . . [A]ls schiere ein mensche lebendig wird, als schiere ist es alt genug zu sterben.*

> If you knew it not before, know it now: as soon as a human being is born it has drunk from the proffered chalice, and so it is to die. The end is akin to the beginning. . . . The instant a human being comes to be alive it is old enough to die.[1]

In an early lecture course at Freiburg, Heidegger cites Luther's commentary on Genesis to similar effect: *Statim enim ab utero matris mori incipimus*. "For as soon as we abandon our mother's womb we begin to die" (GA61 182).

We, who? How many of "us" are there? How many mother's sons and mother's daughters? How many peasant men and women? How many living creatures? If the classical and perdurant definition of human being is ζῷον λόγον ἔχον, "the living being that is essentially determined by its capacity to speak," Heidegger resists "life" as an earmark of Dasein. The birth and death of Dasein will have to be interpreted in a way that does not depend on the unclarified, unexamined categories of traditional ontologies, especially the category of the "living." Almost always, "life" will appear in "scare-quotes" in *Being and Time*. Almost always, "life" will have to be shooed away, for example, in the following moments of the analysis, which one ought to examine quite closely.

1. Section 10, where the fundamental ontology of Dasein is demarcated or delimited over against anthropology, psychology, and, *a fortiori*, biology;

2. Section 12, where human being as *embodied* being is affirmed, albeit in a way that leaves the human body, the body of Dasein, largely undetermined;

3. Sections 35–38, on the "falling" of Dasein, which is the very animatedness (*Bewegtheit*) of existence;

4. Sections 40–42, where "anxiety" and manifold "care" define what it is to be human by spilling over into other receptacles of life; and in subsections 43b–c, where the principal ontological problem of "reality" is the being of *nature* and of the sort of thing we call *life*;

5. Sections 47–49, where the *death* of Dasein is set in relief against the *perishing* of animals and the mere *demise* of a forlorn, inappropriate Dasein;

6. Subsection 68b, where the ecstatic temporalizing of having-been, mood, and anxiety is made to *bedazzle* an already bedazzled and benumbed life;

7. Sections 78–81, in which the path of the live-giving sun rises once again (as it did in section 22) in order to pose the timely question of the *life* of Dasein, a question eventually posed to beings as a whole;

8. Sections 72–74, where Dasein finally turns to the "end" of its birth, destiny, heritage, and history in the world-historical fate of a "generation" and a "nation."

In each of these locations in Heidegger's *Being and Time*, locations we will not be able to visit in this brief space, "life" proves to be both essential to existential analysis and utterly elusive for it, quite beyond its grasp. Life falls into the gap that yawns between beings that are of the measure of Dasein and beings that are altogether unlike Dasein. Life neither precedes nor succeeds existential analysis but remains outside it, being both necessary to it and inaccessible for it. In short, life supplements Dasein, and like all supplements it is the death of Dasein. Fundamental ontology discovers a kind of being-there that is born and that dies, an existence it "fixes" terminologically as *Dasein*; what it is unable to determine is whether such a being is ever properly alive, or what such "life" might mean.

Oblivion seems to seal the fate of Dasein, as unneeding, unheeding. Like Nietzsche's herd of cows at pasture and child at play, like Kafka's ape roaming the rainforest before the circus troupe captures him, oblivious Dasein is indifferent to the question of being. A remarkable complacency (*Bedürfnislosigkeit*) surrounds the question with an impenetrable fog; a remarkable lack of need (*Unbedürftigkeit*) characterizes the "they" in their quotidian concerns (SZ 177, 189). The tradition of philosophy exhibits such complacency in its neglect of the question of being (21, 46); it is as though philosophers too were Cartesian extended substances (92), more like mindless, indifferent stones and animals than vital thinkers.[2]

However much Dasein declines to heed and neglects to need the question of being, it nonetheless moves within and is animated by something like an "understanding of being." Not a theoretical observation of entities or a scientific comprehension of their being, to be sure, but an understanding (in) which Dasein *lives*. Being is not only the most universal and undefinable concept, but also the most evident one: "That we in each case already live in an understanding of being and that the meaning of being is at the same time veiled in obscurity demonstrates the fundamental necessity of fetching back again [*wiederholen*] the question concerning 'being'" (44).

What does it mean to "live" (in) an understanding of being? Can we ever understand such "living," if the living itself encompasses understanding? Can living leap over its own shadow?

Whether or not we can ever understand it, such living within an understanding of being, Heidegger assures us, is a fact (5: *ein Faktum*). Thus the formal structure of the question concerning being yields a particular facticity and a certain movement or motion. We move (*wir bewegen uns*) in a vague and average understanding of being, not insofar as we theorize and construct ontologies, but simply by being alive. Such animation or, better, animatedness (the passive form of *Bewegtheit*, "movedness," is not to be overlooked) is Heidegger's principal preoccupation both before and after *Being and Time*, from the period of his hermeneutics of facticity (roughly 1919 to 1923) to that of his theoretical biology (1929–1930) and well beyond. Moreover, our factical animatedness within an understanding of being, which is an understanding in which we *live*, directs us to something very much like *being*. Nietzsche, in a note that will become important for both Heidegger and Derrida, writes as follows: "'Being'—we have no other notion of it than as '*living*.'—For how can something dead 'be'?"[3]

If the earliest form of *Being and Time* is a hermeneutics of facticity, the fact of facticity (to repeat, the facticity by which we understand something like being, which is something like being alive) is a fact of life. Heidegger's project sprouts (in part, but in good part) from the soil of Dilthey's philosophy of factical-historical life.[4] We know that already from sections 10, 43, and 72–77 of *Being and Time*. However, the early Freiburg and Marburg lecture courses demonstrate the point even more forcefully.

For example, during his lecture course on the hermeneutics of facticity in SS 1923, Heidegger says, "*Facticity* designates the character of the being of 'our' 'own' Dasein" (GA63 7). Why the quotation marks or "scare-quotes" around "our"? Because Dasein lingers or tarries there in each case as this particular Dasein: *Jeweiligkeit* is under way to what *Being and Time* will call *Jemeinigkeit*, Dasein whiling away its hour of existence as in each case "my own." Why the scare-quotes around "my" or "our" "own"? Because what may seem to be the property of Dasein is swept away in the larger questions of life, being, and (not quite yet, but lingering on the horizon, *as* the horizon) time. For the moment it is the being alive that captivates Heidegger: *Sein—transitiv: das faktische Leben sein!*" Being is to be understood transitively; it means that we *are* factical life—not as a soporific solipsism but as active vigilance (*Wachsein*). "If we take 'life' as a way of 'being,' then 'factical life' means our own Dasein [now without scare-quotes] as 'there' in every sort of ontologically explicit manifestation of the character of its being" (GA63 7).

Yet the larger questions posed to "our" "own" factical Dasein will not disperse, not even in *Being and Time*. If fundamental ontology appears to be constructed on the axis of the proper and the improper, the appropriate and the inappropriate (*Eigentlichkeit/Uneigentlichkeit*), the quotation marks around "own" have in fact already replaced more drastic question marks, or, rather, as we shall see, a single, drastic, ironic exclamation point (!). The scare-quotes and exclamation point cause that axis to tremble and perhaps even to shatter. Any reading of *Being and Time* in terms of "authenticity" would be put to riot by this catastrophe, inasmuch as the only authentic Dasein would be a dead Dasein. And yet such trembling, such shattering of the axis of propriety, would be a sign of *life*.

Hence hermeneutics is not the chilly science of facticity, not a methodology that allows us coolly to approach life matter-of-factly; rather, hermeneutics is factical life caught in the act, vigilantly caught in the act of interpreting itself. Hermeneutics of facticity is not like the botanics of plants (GA63 15; cf. SZ 46), whereby vegetable life is the object of a botanical science; rather, to say *facticity* is to say *interpretation*—as though

Dasein were goldenrod catching itself going to seed. In a sense, the genitive in "hermeneutics of facticity" is subjective as well as objective: factical life does the interpreting as well as the living. Yet what does factical life include? What does it exclude? These questions Heidegger does not raise, perhaps because of a certain solidarity of life, solidarity *with* life, or perhaps because of insufficient vigilance. Nevertheless, we gain some insight into the sort of life Heidegger means when we hear him say, toward the end of his lecture course, "Life addresses itself in a worldly way whenever it takes care" (GA63 102, *Das Leben spricht sich im Sorgen weltlich an*). Life, the sort of life that fascinates Heidegger, is what has a world, relates to a world. In his remarks on theoretical biology in 1930, nothing essential will have changed with regard to the world–relation of life. And if among the scattered pages of notes for the 1923 lecture course on the hermeneutics of facticity we find a potpourri of names—Aristotle, the New Testament, Augustine, Luther, Descartes, and Kierkegaard—two names stand out, to wit, Dilthey and Husserl. What Heidegger wishes to pursue is a phenomenological hermeneutics of factical historical life, a task that he reduces to two words: *Dilthey destruiert*, "*Dilthey deconstructed.*" (106–7).

Factical life receives even fuller treatment in the WS 1921–1922 lecture course, a course whose title ("Phenomenological Interpretations to Aristotle: Introduction to Phenomenological Research") does not do justice to its extraordinary contents. The entire third part of the course is devoted to "factical life" (GA61 79–155). These pages would amply repay the most meticulous reading. For the moment let me recall only a few of its most striking theses on factical life, theses that are well under way to *Being and Time*.

The overarching theme of the course is the imbrication of phenomenological research and factical life. Research cannot extricate itself from its situation; nor should it ever desire to do so. For if it did so it would only succeed in being uprooted, after the manner of the Neo-Kantian schools of the day, with their doctrines of epistemology, values, and worldviews. Nor can philosophical research simply force its way into life; it must wait upon a maturation or temporal unfolding of its own access to life (GA61 37, *Zeitigung des Zugangs*). Indeed, phenomenological research is cast adrift on the seas of factical life. Its life is the life of Ishmael:

> Our situation is not that of the rescuing coast; it is a leap into a drifting boat. Everything depends now on our taking the sails' tack into our hands and looking to the wind. It is precisely the difficulties that we must see: illuminating them will first disclose the proper horizon of factical life. Only by appropriating to myself the structure of my having to decide;

only by realizing that it is within and upon such having that I shall come
to see; only in this way can illumination sustain the fundamental motivation for the temporal unfolding of philosophizing. (GA61 37)

In this regard, life-philosophy seems to offer phenomenological research
some hope, even if its own situation is duplicitous.

On the one hand, Heidegger seems to criticize "modern *Lebensphilosophie*" precisely in the way his mentor, Heinrich Rickert, did in *Die
Philosophie des Lebens*.[5] The tendency of Rickert's book is betrayed by its
subtitle and its dedication: *A Presentation and Critique of the Fashionable
Philosophies of Our Time*, "dedicated to the life of philosophy," rather than
to the philosophy of life. Rickert (28) spares none of the enthusiasts of life-
philosophy: Schelling, Scheler, Simmel, Dilthey, Bergson, Nietzsche,
Spengler, William James, and even Husserl are tainted with it and are
accordingly excoriated; all have surrendered rigorously defined concepts
and principles for the sake of "the intuitive," "the ingenious." It may well
be that some of Heidegger's own polemics against *Lebensphilosophie* (for
example, those in the Nietzsche lecture courses of 1936–1940 and the
1936–1938 *Contributions to Philosophy (Of Propriation)* borrow from the
tract of his former mentor. Yet for the moment Heidegger champions
Scheler, Nietzsche, Bergson, and Dilthey against their detractor. He cites
the penultimate page of Rickert's monograph, where the relationship of
research to life touches on the crucial word "repetition," *Wiederholung*. I
cite Rickert's text (194) somewhat more fully than Heidegger does (at
GA61 80): "One should finally give up trying to see this philosophizing
about life as a mere repetition [*ein bloßes Wiederholen*] of life; one should
give up trying to measure the value of philosophizing on the basis of its
vitality. To philosophize is to create." Heidegger interjects at this point, in
good Nietzchean fashion: "Is not creation life?" Rickert's text continues:

> Insight into the distance that separates what is created from the life that
> is merely lived must leave both life and philosophy content. For even the
> life-philosophy of our own day has in its own way contributed a great deal
> to this separation, in spite of its unscientific life-prophecies and the an-
> titheoretical bias of its value accents. Only one who has understood that
> living life diverges from knowing it can be a philosopher of life—one who
> both loves life and thinks about it.

Heidegger repudiates such a complacent, not to say smug, separation of
living from knowing. In so doing he points to the "repetition" that will
characterize his own conception of fundamental ontology. "Repetition" is
vigilance, fetching itself back from oblivion and complacency. It rescues

life from degeneration and decrepitude, "properly" restoring life to itself: "'Repetition': everything depends on its sense. Philosophy is a fundamental 'how' of life itself [*ein Grundwie des Lebens selbst*], so that in each case it properly retrieves life, snatching it back from decline [*es eigentlich je wieder–holt, aus dem Abfall zurücknimmt*]. Such snatching back, as radical research, is life" (80). In Rickert, cognition and the concept are "sheer ghosts," says Heidegger; and Rickert's philosophy of values and of *Weltanschauungen* is as vapid as his anemic life.

On the other hand, Heidegger concedes that the expression "life" is remarkably fuzzy, perhaps because life itself, as he will later say, is "hazy" (*diesig*). He sets aside all "biological" conceptions of life, a gesture he will make repeatedly throughout his career, insisting always on the priority of philosophy over the sciences. He attempts to trace the very multiplicity of those familiar uses of the word *life*—he lists a few of them: "political life," "a squandered life," "he's got a hard life," "he lost his life on a sailing voyage," which is, one must hope, not the voyage of the phenomenologist adrift—back to what he takes to be the sense of the ultimate meaning of the word. The task of phenomenological research, of philosophy, and even of thinking, will be to show that "life" means something "ultimate"; that "*das Leben" ein Letztes bedeutet*, "life" signifies an ultimate (81).

Before he spells out "the fundamental categories of life," Heidegger emphasizes such ultimacy, even if linguistic usage should be ambiguous (82). The verb *leben* may be intransitive: Heidegger's examples are, "he lives intensely," "he lives headlong [*wüst drauflos*]," "he lives a sheltered life [*zurückgezogen*]," "he's only half alive [*er lebt nur halb*]," "I'm surviving [*man lebt so*]." Yet it may also be used transitively ("to live life," "to live one's mission," "to survive [*überleben*] this or that," "to spend one's years," or "live out one's years," or even "fritter away one's years." [*die Jahre verleben*], and, "above all," Heidegger says, "to undergo a lived experience of something ['*etwas erleben*']"). Yet no matter how we use the word, "a concrete experience [*Erfahrung*] is to be presentified," even if we can only account for that experience as a mere "feeling." Thus Heidegger takes care to defend himself against the charge of grammarification (*Grammatisierung*): even if early on, with the Greeks, grammar was taken over by "a particular theoretical outgrowth and articulation of life," the grammatical categories "have their origin in the categories of living speech [*des lebenden Sprechens*], the immanent speech of life itself" (82). If that is so, one may expect that the grammatical categories will be rooted in the fundamental categories of (speaking) life. One might also expect two grammatological problems to arise, problems with which the early work of Jacques Derrida has familiarized us: (1) What about those forms of life that do not speak, forms that are not marked by *des immanenten Sprechens des Lebens selbst*, forms that are deprived of the vaunted interiority in which humanity hears and understands itself (while) speaking? (2) Why and how did the categories of grammar, as soon as they were formulated by the Greeks, become complicit with Stoic logic? We should retain these questions concerning the privilege and the ruination of speaking life as we discuss the fundamental categories of life.

Heidegger begins with three propositions concerning life: (1) life is a "sequential unity and process of maturation" (*Einheit der Folge und Zeitigung*), the temporalizing of a bounded stretch of time, a process-manifold (*Zeitigung, Erstreckung, Vollzugsmannigfaltigkeit*) that coheres and "hangs together"—even if cohesion occurs by way of an original distancing that can become "an original aversion" (*Ursprungsabständlichkeit*) and even "direct hostility",[6] (2) the temporal stretch of life brings with it a sequence of *possibilities*, which are to be taken in a strictly phenomenological sense, not as logical possibilities or as transcendental *a priori* possibility; (3) life combines the senses of (1) and (2) by being the collapse—or, perhaps, the imposition—of possibilities (*möglichkeitsverfallen*), the saddling of life with and by possibilities (*möglichkeitsgeladen und sich selbst ladend*), or the very shaping and cultivating of possibilities (*Möglichkeiten bildend*; cf. *weltbildend* in the 1929–1930 biology lectures). The whole (*das Ganze*) of life, as the temporal process of a bounded stretch of possibilities that we shape and that shape and befall us, is called actuality, *Wirklichkeit*, "indeed, reality in its specific imprevisibility as power, destiny [*Schicksal*]." If we try to reduce this complex tripartite description of life into a single assertion, we may say that life proceeds as a bounded stretch of possibilities, some which we choose and cultivate, some with which we are saddled, all such possibilities—but especially those over which we exercise no control—constituting the destined or fateful character of life.

One is struck by the dour and even dire mood of the fundamental categories of life. Life is a bounded stretch, a finite process. It involves an original distantiation that can readily become aversion and hostility. Itself a sequence of possibilities, life succumbs to possibilities: *verfallen* is the very first word attached to *Möglichkeit*. If life lives out its days caught on the horns of the modalities of necessity and possibility, its reality will always be a bleak one: reality will of necessity hinge upon possibilities that are essentially susceptible to degeneration. Life is loaded (*geladen*) and is self-burdening. Such is its reality. Such is the power of its impenetrable destiny. Such are life, existence, and even "being" itself: "Life = Dasein: in and through life '*being*'" (85).

Heidegger does not speculate on the origins of the apparently irremediable degeneration of life. Yet the very parataxis of his analysis says some-

thing about the source of declivity and decline. That in which, on the basis
of which, for, with, and toward which life lives; that from which life lives,
on the horizon of which it lives, Heidegger calls *world*. "Life in itself is
related to the world [*weltbezogen*]" (86). It is the world-relation of life that
will continue to haunt Heidegger, not only in the first division of *Being
and Time*, where a modally neutral description of the everyday life of Dasein continually breaks down and becomes a pejoration of the everyday as
somehow "improper," *uneigentlich*, and not only in the 1929–1930 biology lectures, where the "world-relation" is that which invariably binds the
life of Dasein to the squalid life of animals, but also throughout Heidegger's later career of thought. Here, of course, we are near the outset of
that career. Here the process-meaning of life is its being drawn to the
world, as our everyday speech shows when it identifies *life* and *world*. To
stand in the midst of life is to confront the world; to live in a world of
one's own is to lead one's own special life. Life inevitably interprets itself
in the refracted light of the world. Life, in a word, is relucent, *reluzent*
(117ff.; cf. SZ 16, 21). If much later, in the Nietzsche lectures, Heidegger
is suspicious of the ambiguous identity of life, world, and (human) existence, he early on accepts the concatenation of *Welt, Leben, Dasein*, and
Sein as evidence of the meaning-content of life-in-process. Phenomenological research dare not try to forge or force such concatenations. Nor
forget them. It can only respond to the compelling character of factical
life, even if the world-relation of life seems to contaminate all of life, existence, and being. In the fundamental categories of life, says Heidegger,
suddenly ventriloquizing the spirit of Hegel, *"life comes to itself"* (88). Yet
life tends to misunderstand itself, fall away from itself, precisely into the
relucence of the world. Life is full of detours (*umwegig*) and is, as we have
already noted, "hazy" (*diesig*). In a word, relucent life is *ruinous*. Worse,
the very animatedness of life, what Aristotle called κίνησις and μεταβολή,
is ruinance. From here it is all downhill, and we are always already there.

The entire second chapter of Part Three of Heidegger's lectures on
factical life treats of *Ruinanz*. We shall turn to it in a moment, in order to
confront the mystery of a life that is both fallen in complacency and passionate to know itself, both decrepit and upsurgent, both oblivious and
perspicuous, both vacuous and vigilant. Meanwhile, Heidegger lends a hos-
tage to fortune. If in later years he drops the expression *life* in favor of
Dasein and *Existenz*, if he comes to criticize *Leben* in Nietzsche and other
life-philosophers as balefully ambiguous, in WS 1921–1922 he tells his
students: "It merely corresponds to the complacency of factical life itself
when interpretation rescues itself from the conceptual tendency it is following by saying that life has manifold meaning and that therefore it cannot be readily grasped in an apt manner. However, we reach the acme of

complacency and bankruptcy in philosophy when we enter a plea for the abandonment of this 'expression.' One shakes off a disturbing premonition—and writes a system" (89). Is the abandonment or subordination of life to Dasein—the "neutral" term that Heidegger latches onto in *Being and Time* in an abrupt, elliptical, almost brutal fashion[7]—a form of complacency? Is it the very complacency that forgets being? Is fundamental ontology a system, and is it written in order to suppress a disturbing premonition?

If *process* is the meaning of life-related-to-world, then the sense of that world-relation is one of care, concern, trouble, renunciation, and deprivation (90: *Sorgen, Bekümmerung, Darbung*). Life as such is restive. Such is its very animation, which is an animatedness, a being prodded from the outside, as it were. A fragmentary marginal note to the WS 1921–1922 lecture course gives us some insight into the restless movement or movedness of factical life:

> The animatedness of factical life is provisionally interpretable, describable, as *restiveness* [*die Unruhe*]. The "how" of such restiveness as full phenomenon defines facticity. With regard to life and restiveness, see Pascal, *Pensées*, I–VII; what is valuable here is the description, not the theory and the intention. Above all, [not] soul-body, [not] *le voyage éternel*: to such things existentiell philosophy has no access. Illumination of restiveness, illuminated restiveness, rest-lessness and questionability; the temporalizing powers; restiveness and the wherefore. The restless aspect of restiveness. The unrelieved, undecided "between" of the aspect of factical life: between the surrounding world, sociality, the sphere of the self, ancestry, and posterity [*zwischen Um-, Mit-, Selbst-, Vor-, und Nachwelt*]; something positive. The way in which restiveness trickles through; the configurations and masks of restiveness. Rest—restiveness; phenomenon and movement (cf. the phenomenon of movement in Aristotle). (93)

One can scarcely avoid hearing in *Unruhe* the fundamental Augustinian tone of restlessness and agitation—*inquietum est cor nostrum, donec requiescat in te*—even if Heidegger would insist that the Augustinian "ontology" of body and soul be held at arm's length. For the restiveness of factical life there is no repose.

The animatedness of factical life rises to meet us in the very passivity of the passive voice form, *Bewegtheit*. If Aristotle defines life as self-movement, all κίνησις and μεταβολή are nonetheless moved. All motion is therefore restive, under way on a voyage eternal, quite beyond the categories of soul and body. The problem is how to illuminate such restiveness, how to gain access to it, without falling back into complacency and bankruptcy. Interrogation of restiveness must itself be restless. Questioning must be driven by the wherefore, the *Wozu*, the restless aspect of illumination on the expressive face of factical life. It is the face which Hegel once called "absolute dialectical unrest," and which he thought as a scepticism that would somehow accomplish itself and culminate in the absolute. By contrast, Heidegger's restiveness marks the first appearance of the daimonic, of the powers of process, the might of maturation, and the potency of timely growth. In a word, *die Zeitigungsmächte*. These are the forces of what I am venturing to call *daimon life*. Somewhere beyond the traditional categories of soul and body, animation and movement, ensoulment and auto-motion, somewhere between ancient lineages and succeeding generations, between self and other, between life and its sphere, its environs, and its generations—daimon life disseminates.

Heidegger says that to inquire into factical life is to leap into a boat adrift. Perhaps in saying so he recalls Nietzsche's great sailing ship, gliding along as silent as a daimonic ghost: "Oh, what ghostly beauty! With what enchantment it grips me! Could it be? Has all the tranquillity [*Ruhe*] and silence in the world embarked on this ship? Does my happiness itself have its seat there in that quiet place, my 'happier' 'I,' my second, dearly departed [*verewigtes*] self? To be, not dead, yet no longer alive? As a ghostlike, silent, gazing, gliding, hovering daimon [*Mittelwesen*]?" This is of course the passage from *Die fröhliche Wissenschaft* (StA 3, 424–25, no. 60) in which Nietzsche identifies the ship that skims the sea "like a huge butterfly," identifies it in the most unsettling way—*es sind die Frauen*, it's the women! No wonder Rickert wants to keep his distance from life-philosophy! Ironically, distance itself is attributed to women—"Women and Their Action at a Distance"—as though the "between" were in some way "of woman." From here it would not be far to Diotima's instruction concerning daimonic ἔρως in *Symposium* (202–203), or to the derivation of the heroic-erotic δαιμόνιον or *Cratylus* (397–98), or the location of the site of the daimonic in *Statesman* (271–72) as between earth and sky, the realm of the overpowering as such. Yet daimon life, for all its overpowering ouranian qualities, is as restive as the sea and the eruptive earth, as fecund and as given to mourning as the goddesses of the depths. Heidegger makes no explicit reference or even allusion to such a δαιμόνιον, however; the Mother of the Muses, Dame Memory, *die Gedächtnis*, rather than *das Gedächtnis*, lies much farther down the path.[8] It is high time we reverted to factical life.

Heidegger's analysis of factical life as relationship to the surrounding world (*Umwelt*), the world of others (*Mitwelt*), and the world of my self (*Selbstwelt*), which is by no means the cogitative "I" or intellectual intuition of reflexive philosophy, deserves the most meticulous study (see

David Farrell Krell

GA61 94–100). I shall have to content myself with a brief listing of the four fundamental categories of life's "relational meaning," *Bezugssinn*, the sense of its world-relatedness.

1. *Neigung*, "inclination," "proclivity," or "tendency": life is drawn to things, as though by gravity. Such being drawn into the world is the proper meaning or *sens* of life's temporal unfolding. A curious operation of anagram relates inclination to propriation, *Neigung* to *Eignung*. Life "finds itself properly [*eigentlich*] there where it retains its own inclination [*seine eigene Geneigtheit*]" (101). Factical life lets itself be swept away (*mitgenommen-werden*) by the world. This word is cognate with the words Heidegger will use in his WS 1929–1930 lecture course in order to characterize animal life[9]; yet here, in WS 1921–1922, the power of the world pertains to factical life as such. Thus the relations of care both disperse life and preserve life's vigilance. Scattering or dispersion is here juxtaposed to vigilant inclination, in what will become the principal mystery of the metaphysics of Dasein, and it is no accident that Heidegger at this juncture (101–102) introduces a series of remarks on metaphysics and on the "devilish" difficulty of gaining access to one's own presuppositions about factical life. Inclination, proclivity, being drawn into and swept away by the world, dispersion in the world, and complacency about it are the "categorial keys" that Heidegger believes will unlock radical conceptions of motion—motion as process, stream, flux, life-event, the nexus of process, and temporalization.

2. *Abstand*, "distance"; or, contrariwise, *Abstandstilgung*, "elimination of distance." With equal originality (*gleichursprünglich*), life covers over and obfuscates its own inclination. It is torn away into dispersion, finds itself (for somehow, inexplicably, it does find itself) as dispersed and scattered in its world. Thus life is "in ruinance" (102–103). Life loses its "in the face of," sees itself falsely and in a skewed perspective; as Heidegger will repeat twenty-five years later, in "Poetically Man Dwells . . . ," life measures but misses itself (*vermißt sich*).[10] Life chases after rank, success, and position in the world; dreams of overtaking the others and securing advantage; maneuvers itself so as to close the distance, yet remains forever distant; devotes itself to calculation, busy-ness, noise, and façade. Here Heidegger uses the very word he will employ in *Being and Time* (SZ 126), namely, *Abständigkeit*, to designate the consuming passion to put distance between oneself and the others, either by boosting oneself beyond them or oppressing them beneath oneself. Ironically, in the passion to keep one's distance from the others, one is swept away and becomes precisely like the others, who, presumably, are all trying to do the same thing. One thus winds up without any distance on the others at all.

The others? Who are they? Heidegger would have admired Henry

David Thoreau's description of the They, had he known it. (If the Heidegger of the 1930s bemoans *pragmatic* America, how close to him nevertheless is *puritan* America!)

> When I ask for a garment of a particular form, my tailoress tells me gravely, "They do not make them so now," not emphasizing the "They" at all, as if she quoted an authority as impersonal as the Fates, and I find it difficult to get made what I want, simply because she cannot believe that I mean what I say, that I am so rash. When I hear this sentence, I am for a moment absorbed in thought, emphasizing to myself each word separately that I may come at the meaning of it, that I may find out by what degree of consanguinity They are related to me, and what authority they may have in an affair which affects me so nearly; and, finally, I am inclined to answer her with equal mystery, and without any more emphasis of the "they,"—"It is true, they did not make them so recently, but they do now." Of what use this measuring of me if she does not measure my character, but only the breadth of my shoulders, as it were a peg to hang the coat on? We worship not the Graces, nor the Parcae, but Fashion. She spins and weaves and cuts with full authority. The head monkey at Paris puts on a traveller's cap, and all the monkeys in America do the same. I sometimes despair of getting any thing quite simple and honest done in this world by the help of men.[11]

No doubt the head monkey is headed for a difficult season. Thoreau's prescribed therapy for the "they," a kind of baptism by fire, will be a drastic one, and it will be applied in the name of a "they" without quotation marks, a "they" that follows upon the phrase "by the help of men" so effortlessly that we do not believe that the "they" is being invoked (by one of "them") at all.

> . . . by the help of men. They [sic] would have to be passed through a powerful press first, to squeeze their old notions out of them, so that they would not soon get upon their legs again, and then there would be some one in the company with a maggot in his head, hatched from an egg deposited there nobody knows when, for not even fire kills these things, and you would have lost your labor. Nevertheless, we will not forget that some Egyptian wheat was handed down to us by a mummy.

Yet the effort to isolate maggots from wheat kernels fails. The maggot is hatched of an egg, the living germ from the living ear of wheat. The "they," if they are men, and if men are human beings, and if human beings are for the time being living, are crammed higgledypiggledy with both uncritical "notions" and genuine food for thought. Are matters any differ-

ent for Heidegger? As much as he would like to purge *das Man* of complacent notions, does he not always find the wheat mixed in, so that the
"proper" and the "inappropriate" are inextricably intermixed? Is that not
part of the sense of the exteriority and passivity that mark *Bewegtheit*,
animatedness? Is that not part of the reason why Heidegger will insist over
and over again that the analysis of everydayness in the first division of
Being and Time reveals essentially neutral structures, structures that are
not to be scorned as "merely" quotidian, purely inappropriate?

   3. *Abriegelung*, "bolting" or "locking oneself away," sequestering oneself and thus producing a situation of enforced isolation. Heidegger assures us that this third characteristic of care and concern is even less
perspicuous than the first two, and we believe him. The syntax is odd, as is
the thought: *Mit der Neigung in ihrer abstandsverkümmernden Zerstreuung gerät und ist weiter in Verlust was?* "With inclination, in its
dispersion, a dispersion that deteriorates distance, something else gets lost
and remains lost—what is it?" (105). What gets lost is that which is "before" me, not in a spatial sense, nor even in a temporal sense. When I live
on the basis of something (*ich lebe ausdrücklich von etwas*), my factical
self or self-world is co-experienced, if not intellectually apperceived. Yet
this "before" is never fully appropriated (106: *unterbleibt die Aneignung
des "vor"*), and it relation to things slackens. What gets lost? "In this veiled
quality, 'life' speaks." Life speaks behind the mask of its varied signifi-
cances. Life is *larvant*. (Is it the mask of grammar and logic, the Stoic and
Scholastic mask, that obscures living speech?) What gets lost is life itself,
as taking trouble and being concerned about itself, *das Leben als sor-
gendes*. What gets lost is the simple fact that life comes to the fore as
such—"the temporalizing of life's proper *Vor-kommen*" (106). Such
proper coming to the fore must be appropriated, emphasizes Heidegger
once again (*ist . . . anzueignen!*). In hyperbolic pursuit of significance, life
avoids itself, evades itself, allows itself to get sidetracked (107: *es geht sich
aus dem Wege*). As life closes the distance between itself and other things,
other people, it represses that distance (Heidegger uses the psychoanalytic
word, no doubt unwittingly, attaching it to his own variation on Nietzsche's "pathos of distance": *Abstandsverdrängung*). As a result of repression, life gains an illusory self-assurance. In a kind of evasion (107; cf. SZ
§40), life preoccupies itself with itself in order to forget itself. "In taking
trouble [*Sorgen*], life incarcerates itself from itself [*riegelt sich das Leben
gegen sich selbst ab*]. Yet precisely in this incarceration life does not get
shut of itself. Averting its glance again and again, life seeks itself, encountering itself precisely where it never guessed it would be, for the most part
in masquerade (larvance)."

Frenetic in its search for scraps of meaning, for ever-novel significance, life becomes careless of itself. Its most passionate concerns mask a
lack of concern (*Unbekümmerung*), which nevertheless is troubled. Restive. Life mistakes itself ceaselessly, makes endless errors, and takes such
endlessness to be infinity and the plenitude of eternity. Always more life!
Always more than life! Such infinity is the mask that factical life holds up
to the world. Larvance is the ruse of infinity, as Heidegger will later portray it in the final lines of section 65 of *Being and Time*. He criticizes the
unclarified idea of infinity and eternity that vitiates "modern life-philosophy" as a whole. Although he names no names, he is surely thinking of
Jaspers' *Psychology of Worldviews* (1919), just as we might think of works
in our own time that operate with an uncritical appeal to Eternity and
Infinity: "With this infinity, life blinds itself, enucleates itself. Incarcerat-
ing itself, life lets itself go. It falls short. Factical life lets itself go precisely
by expressly and positively fending off itself. Incarceration therefore proceeds and temporalizes as *elliptical*. Factical life paves its own way for
itself by the way it takes its directives [*Weisungnahme*], inclining, repress-
ing distance, shutting itself off in the direction of life" (108). Which brings
us to the final relational category of factical life.

4. *Das "Leichte,"* the "easy," the "facile." Heidegger cites Aristotle's
Nicomachean Ethics B 5 (1106b 28ff.) on the limitless ways one can err.
The ways of errancy are many, and they are easy to travel, whereas the
good is μοναχῶς, unifold, singular, *einfältig*. One can err by either going
too far or by falling short of the goal: error is either hyperbolic or elliptical. In both cases it is ῥάδιον, "easy," like rolling off a log. Life craves
security, the security of insouciance. Life is inclined to flee, to make
things easy for itself. It swathes its guilt in mists of fog; it tempts itself,
falls, and invariably rescues itself. Life enhances itself, tosses Zarathustra's
golden ball fairly far; yet in so doing it remains elliptical: factical life always falls short of primal decision (109: *Urentscheidung*).

Heidegger now summarizes the categories of relational meaning—
that is to say, the categories of life's relation to the world—and (almost
parenthetically) indicates the ruinous tendency of the whole:

> *Inclination:* proclivity, being swept away, dispersion, self-satisfac-
> tion.
> *Distance* (Elimination of): mistaking, miscalculating, remoteness in
> proclivity (worldly); the hyperbolic.
> *Incarceration:* evading oneself and precisely thereby not being shut
> of oneself, proliferation of ways to go wrong, blinding oneself; the ellipti-
> cal.

(Indication of a unified temporalizing: seeking relief [or: easing up, making things easier, *Erleichterung*]; cf. taking care that one can worry [*Sorge in der Besorgnis*]; appearance, creating masks, so that one "makes life hard" for oneself!) (109–10)

It is intriguing to think that Heidegger is here engaged not so much in a descriptive phenomenology of factical life but in a genealogy of masquerade and ruinous self-deception. We ought to read the WS 1921–1922 lecture course alongside Nietzsche's "What Do Ascetic Ideals Signify?" Then the crucial question would be whether Heidegger can allow the kind of recoil that characterizes Nietzschean genealogy—for genealogy is always genealogy of the genealogist—to take place in his own analysis of factical life. It is true that Heidegger freely concedes the diabolical difficulty of liberating one's point of departure from inherited ideas and ideals; but when he involves the masquerade of pretending to "make life hard" for oneself while fleeing constantly to one's own *securitas*—whether it be security in sanctity or security in a priori phenomenological science—is he really thinking of himself and his own project? As Heidegger nears his own situation, that of a lecturer and researcher in an institution of higher learning, the risk that he will "make discoveries" grows, and so in tandem so the polemic and the vituperation grow. In tandem, precisely, it seems, in order to prevent those discoveries from coming home. Such is the unhappy lesson of Heidegger's "University of Life," of "the spiritual condition" of university life, which is fallen and forever falling farther: "It is not my ambition to make discoveries and to have them patented. Only the belle-lettrists and those corruptors of spiritual life [*Verderber des geistigen Lebens*] who are so sensitive and solicitous about their little treasure chests—only they abuse philosophy today in order to expend their vanities" (117–18).

Amen.

How hard Heidegger's life must be, locked into an institution where belle-lettrists and seducers run free! And yet one might also have to say that Heidegger is here on the verge of a very important discovery, a discovery whose implications embrace the entire project of fundamental ontology. It is a discovery that seems to transcend the very epoch of *Being and Time*, marking that book's limits and soaring beyond them. It is a discovery concerning appropriateness or "authenticity," *Eigentlichkeit*, the axis about which the fundamental ontology of *Being and Time* rotates—albeit not always smoothly. The first chapter of Part Three of the 1921–1922 lecture course, "Factical Life," ends with this discovery of limits, and chapter two is called "Ruinance." It is perhaps the ultimate discovery concerning the categories of motility, the categories that cluster about life's animatedness (*Bewegtheit*). Heidegger's discovery is that—Aristotle to the contrary notwithstanding—factical life is not self-moving; at least, not unambiguously so. "Prestructuring" and "relucence" are inextricably interlaced in factical life. When life takes trouble concerning itself and its world, it becomes embroiled in the very possibilities that such *Sorgen* opens up: life needs the security of possibilities that are already "lived-in," and which it thus tends to fixate. Here is one of the earliest places where Heidegger's understanding of life converges with that of Nietzsche: from 1936 to 1939 Heidegger will focus on Nietzsche's interpretation of life as *Festmachung*.[12] Here, in his own hermeneutics of factical life, Heidegger descries and decries life's tendency "to live by falling into a rut in its world," *sich in seiner Welt festzuleben*. He laments life's self-petrifaction, its congealing in its proper possibilities, *Sichfestleben* (13). The result is an anomalous situation with regard to the appropriateness or propriety of life's proper possibility. Life has its autochthony and its autonomous movement or animatedness, its *Eigenständigkeit* and its *Eigenbewegtheit*, precisely in its living out beyond itself: whatever is life's *own* (*die gerade darin eigene ist*) derives from its living *outside* or *out beyond itself* (*daß das Leben* aus sich hinauslebt). In other words, factical life is properly its own in the very impropriety by which it is always already expropriated by and exposed to the world. Neither relucence nor ruinance is epiphenomenal. Both pertain to life's essential *Praestruktion*. Thus life's "own" animation, an animatedness that is not its own. If anything is contingent here it is the "illumination" that seeks to penetrate ruinous complacency.

Thus the ironic exclamation point within parenthesis in this final paragraph, after the appearance of the word *eigentlich*, "appropriately," "properly." It marks an irony that would have shaken the entire existentialist account of Heideggerian "authenticity," from Sartre to Macquarrie and Robinson, had the 1921–1922 lecture course been available a generation ago. Hans-Georg Gadamer, when he first read and lectured on the 1921–1922 course (at the 1986 Collegium Phaenomenologicum in Perugia), announced his astonishment and perplexity over the lectures—and his intention "to live a few years longer" in order to come to terms with Heidegger's early analysis of factical life. One might speculate that the irony of a property that is never a property (!), a propriety that is always improper (!), is one of the things that amazed Gadamer most. Heidegger writes: "The animatedness is such that, as a motion in itself, it helps itself toward itself [*die als Bewegung in sich selbst sich zu ihr selbst verhilft*]. It is the animatedness of factical life that constitutes life itself; indeed, factical life, living in the world, does not itself properly (!) constitute the movement [*daß das faktische Leben . . . die Bewegung eigentlich (!) nicht selbst macht*]. Rather, factical life lives the world as the in-which, upon-which, and for-which of life [*sondern die Welt als das Worin und Worauf und Wofür des Lebens lebt*]" (130).

Factical life *lives* the world. Or, reading *die Welt* as the subject of the sentence, the *world* lives. Perhaps this is why Nietzsche and the other life-philosophers find themselves forever confusing life and world. Perhaps this is why in 1929–1930 when Heidegger tries to differentiate the world-relation of various forms of life, particularly the forms of life we call *animal* and *human*, his effort is doomed to fail. Factical life lives the world in such a way that the world lives, and not some properly proprietary possibility of ownness. And the world lives and moves factically as *ruina, Sturz, Ruinanz*.

If we continue to fall with Heidegger's 1921–1922 lecture course we will never be able to escape back (or forward) to *Being and Time*. Therefore, only one word more about ruinance. For ruinance will not help us to read *Being and Time*; it can only hinder us and make things harder. Only one word about ruinance: the word is "nothing," *das Nichts*.

Even though ecstatic temporality has not yet emerged as the enrapturing and rupturing horizon of the meaning of being; and even though no analyses of anxiety and being-unto-death appear in the 1921–1922 course; the crucial word for the analysis of *Ruinanz* is nonetheless "nothing." It is as though a continuous line might be traced from WS 1921–1922 to the SS 1928 logic course and the 1929 "What Is Metaphysics?" and "On the Essence of Ground." That line would not circumvent *Being and Time* but pierce it through at one point—the point at which (in section 58, "Understanding the Call, and Guilt") the very being of Dasein is defined as nullity. Guilt is "being the ground of a being that is determined by a not—i.e., *being the ground of a nullity*" (SZ 283). As thrown projection, Dasein is "the (null) being-the-ground of a nullity" (285). The 1921–1922 "Introduction to Phenomenological Research," after an extraordinary itinerary of ruinance—through plunge and masquerade, through kairological time and the instant of a counterruinance that is always gnawing at life's false securities, always boring and burrowing, always subverting life's complacency, through the necessity of a phenomenological destruction of all interpretative seductions (particularly those of an ethico-religious sort)—culminates in an account of the "whither" of ruinance (GA61 143–48).

Where does factical life land when it falls? Nowhere.

When does ruinance strike home? Never.

What rises to break its free fall? Nothing.

The fall is nothing but unobstructed fall, uninterrupted crash (145: *Sturz*). Thus the very animatedness of factical life is nihilation: the nothing of factical life is that which no philosophical dialectic, from Plato's *Sophist* through Hegel's *Phenomenology of Spirit*, has mastered. The nothing contemporalizes (147: *mitzeitigt*) with the fall, so that life is not only animation but also annihilation—not in any "wild metaphysical" sense, but in the sense of a kind of renunciation or doing-without (148: *Darbung*). Life as renunciation, as deprivation, returns to the scene in 1929–1930, when Heidegger tries to think the very essence of animal life as deprivation (*Entbehren*). At which point animal and human life seem very close indeed—in the face of daimon life.

What remains most mysterious in the early Freiburg lecture course is the counterruinance or resistance that enables phenomenological research to struggle against complacency. What *Being and Time* proclaims as its starting-point, namely, the intimacy of *questioning* as an intrinsic mode of being for Dasein, here resists depiction. If life falls but lands nowhere, whence the upsurge and upswing of inquiry? Whence the flourishing of life in the university, whence the university of life?[13] If factical life does without, if *Darbung* is its situation, whence the thrust of phenomenological research?[14] When does genuine questioning gnaw its way to the surface? When does life become sufficiently restive? How do we ever know whether or not it is simply a matter of the phenomenologist's thoroughgoing self-deception and rigorous complacency: "Ah, how hard my science is!"?

Whenever we do return to *Being and Time* we ought to be chastened by the realization that Heidegger's earliest reflections on factical life bring his magnum opus of 1927 to a point of perpetual crisis. The way to prevent Heidegger's "ways" from congealing into "works" is to confront without subterfuge such crisis.

21

The Truth that is not of Knowledge

John Sallis

In the WS 1925–26 lecture course *Logic* (GA21) the bonds are still in place, those that bind truth to knowledge and knowledge to intuition and presence. Indeed, it is precisely in these lectures that these bonds are displayed, not only as governing the phenomenological defense of logic against the assault by psychologism, but also as bonds that have held throughout the history of philosophy, that serve even to mark, if not to define, the unity of that history. And yet, in the very display of these bonds there are signs that Heidegger has begun to loosen them, or rather, that the very movement of the things themselves has made them begin to fray.

Near the beginning of the lectures Heidegger orients philosophical logic to the question of truth. The central question of such a logic would be: What is truth? Yet, before such a logic can commence, before it can take up its question of truth in a positive way, it is necessary to dispel the specter of scepticism that has haunted logic since the ancients, the specter that has challenged the question of logic by attempting to interrupt it with another question, with the question "whether the very idea of truth is not a phantom" (GA21 19). Heidegger resumes the classical responses to the threat of scepticism: for example, that in order to be able to set about determining whether truth really exists or is only a phantom, one must already have some understanding of truth, must already know *what* it is; so that, even if it should eventually turn out that there is no such thing as truth, the very assertion that truth is only a phantom would presuppose some understanding of what truth is, of what it would be if there were truth. Yet, rather than regarding this and the other classical responses as sufficiently meeting and defeating the challenge of scepticism so as to banish its specter and clear the field for the commencement of philosophical logic, Heidegger proceeds to challenge these responses, exposing within them a series of fundamental, unexamined presuppositions. He considers, for example, the response that, calling attention to the sceptical assertion that there is no truth, observes that this very denial itself lays claim to being a true proposition and thus presupposes that there is truth, presupposes precisely what it denies, contradicts itself. But instead of merely confirming, reformulating, or even setting limits to the range of this response, Heidegger exposes within this perhaps most classical response a nest of fundamental presuppositions the force of which cannot but interrupt the response and leave it stammering no less than the scepticism whose challenge it was to have met: in the response it is presupposed that truth means propositional truth; and it is assumed that the issue raised by the sceptical assertion can be settled by appealing to the principle of contradiction, without any questions having been asked about what constitutes and gives force to a principle, without the slightest doubt having been raised about the ultimate status thus accorded the principle of contradiction (GA21 22f.). Because this classical response is integral to Husserl's critique of psychologism, Heidegger insists that the presuppositions he has exposed in that response continue to haunt Husserl's critique, even though the *Logical Investigations* is the one place "where vital questioning is today still to be found in logic" (GA21 24). More precisely, these presuppositions prevent Husserl's critique of psychologism from decisively expelling the specter of the sceptical question. Driving scepticism and psychologism from the field of pure logic is not a task that Husserl's Prolegomena to Pure Logic would already have completed but rather is carried on—and indeed first taken up in a decisive way—in the theoretical developments within the Investigations themselves.

The most germane of these developments is the theory of intentionality. For Heidegger makes it explicit that psychologism is to be rejected, not because it treads upon territory not its own, the domain of pure logic, but rather because it relies on a psychology that does not understand the very theme that would define the discipline. Not that it would be, then, simply a matter of replacing one psychology with another. Heidegger refers to the ambiguity in which the delimitation of psychology has been entangled from the beginning, the ambiguity involved in its being oriented both to *bios* (hence belonging to ethics) and to *zoe* (hence belonging to physics). Heidegger notes that this ambiguity still persists insofar as psychology is regarded "both as a natural science of living beings and as a science of human existence" (GA21 35); in the current phrase *human science* one finds expressed much the same ambiguity. As a result of this ambiguity the delimitation of psychology, the very determination of what it is, remains fundamentally confused: "Thus, when in the sequel we speak of psychology, we must keep quite clearly in mind that fundamentally we do not know what it is" (GA21 36).

Nonetheless, the *Logical Investigations* makes a decisive breakthrough by uncovering intentionality as the fundamental character of the psychic; through this discovery a means is provided for understanding in a positive, descriptive way the distinction on which Husserl's entire critique of psychologism turns, the distinction between real and ideal. Though there are clear signs of Heidegger's reluctance to allow the distinction between real and ideal to govern his own analyses or even his appropriation of the Husserlian analyses (see GA19 98)—no doubt because of his keen awareness of how directly this distinction derives from the Platonic opposition between sensible (*aistheton*) and intelligible (*noeton*) (GA21 52)—he is no less insistent than was Husserl that only a psychology based on an understanding of the psychic as intentional could succeed in rigorously determining the basic concepts of logic and thus preparing the field of pure logic. The question is only whether such a psychology would be sufficiently continuous with what has been called psychology to warrant retaining this designation; even Husserl, who in the first edition of the *Logical Investigations* designated his work as descriptive psychology, soon came to regard the phrase as misleading and to elaborate the increasingly more complex distinction between phenomenology and psychology. Heidegger is still more hesitant about assimiliating to psychology the phenomenological theory of intentionality opened up by the *Logical Investigations*, to say nothing of the more radical guise that the theory will assume in the analysis of Dasein carried out in *Being and Time* but already near completion at the time of the lecture course *Logic*.[1]

In order to take up the phenomenon of truth within the new domain of intentional analysis, Heidegger undertakes an analysis of knowing as such; in effect, though without taking note of it, he thus affirms the bond between truth and knowledge, leaves it intact for the moment, tacitly assuming that the phenomenon of truth is to be found in the act of knowing. Heidegger's analysis retraces in more didactic form the intentional analysis of knowledge developed in the *Logical Investigations*. It is a matter of focusing on the intentional structure of knowing, and this requires, above all, marking the distinction between psychic content and the intentional object of an act. Whatever its specific character, an intentional act is always directed, not at contents within consciousness (such as sensations or images), but rather at the things themselves. In the perceptual act in which (to use Heidegger's example) one perceives a wall, one's act is directed to the wall itself and not to sensations or images within consciousness that would be supposed somehow to resemble the wall itself outside consciousness. The same holds if the act is one in which the thing itself is not actually perceived but only spoken of: if one speaks of the table that is behind one's back, one still intends that table itself and not some mental content that would only represent it; but now, instead of seeing the thing in its bodily presence, one merely intends it, means it in an intention empty of intuitive givenness, represents it (*vorstellen*). In both cases, representation and perception, what is meant is the thing itself; but only the latter type of act, in which the thing is had originarily, in the flesh, is an act of knowing. But, in turn, such having of the thing itself in the flesh is precisely what phenomenology designates as intuition (*Anschauung*). Thus is knowledge bound to intuition, the latter taken in the broadest sense: it includes not only vision but also hearing (as of a musical piece), as well as the intuitive "understanding" involved when one "sees," for example, that two plus two equals four. Hence, intuition is not limited to the sensible, to perception; rather, intuition is involved in every mode of comportment in which the thing meant is present in the flesh (*leibhaftig anwesend*). It is because intuition presents the thing itself, because it is demonstrative, that it is bound to knowledge.

Heidegger interrupts—briefly—the series of phenomenological analyses, as if to insert in parentheses a divergence from the primacy accorded to intuition and presence by those analyses, a divergence that *Being and Time* will release across the entire field, undoing the bonds that the lectures will have left largely intact. The question inserted is whether for the most part things are had in their bodily presence when one has to do with them within one's most proximate surroundings. Heidegger's example: while writing at a table, one feels the resistance of the table, which to that extent is given in the flesh; and yet, in the strict sense it is not the table that is there in the flesh (*leibhaftig da*), present to the writer, but rather the words that he is writing and the meaning of what is being written. Heidegger mentions that the concept of bodily presence, of *Leibhaftigkeit*, is oriented to theoretical knowledge, in distinction from the usual manner of dealing with things in one's most proximate surroundings, where for the most part they are not directly and expressly given in the flesh. Thus does Heidegger broach—in unmarked parentheses—the radical divergence from presence that *Being and Time* will produce through its orientation to the most proximate surrounding world (*die nächste Umwelt*) (GA21 103f.).

Closing the parentheses, Heidegger turns to an analysis of the demonstrative character distinctive of intuition. Intuition is demonstrative because it serves to fulfill those intentions in which something is merely meant; as when, merely speaking of something behind one's back, one then turns toward it and, by seeing it in the flesh, there before one's perceptual gaze, one demonstrates what one has said, demonstrates that it is true. The intuition thus fulfills the empty intention executed in speech, filling it with the intuitive content given in the flesh, also bearing out the expectations that lay in the empty representation; now one *sees* there upon the wall that very picture hanging askew that previously one only *said* was hanging there askew. In demonstration there is a coincidence of what is intuited with what was emptily represented; and yet, such demonstration does not, as it were, live only in the things but involves also a moment of unreflective self-understanding, which phenomenology calls *Evidenz*, the experience of truth.[2] Thus it is that the legitimacy (*Rechtmässigkeit*) of knowledge is not something to be established *nachträglich*, for instance, through some further act of knowledge that would legitimate the first and that, once invoked by a theory of knowledge, would expose that theory to "senseless consequences" such as that of an infinite regress of acts of knowledge, each required to legitimate the one preceding it.

In the intentional fulfillment in which the intuited comes to coincide with the meant, what gets demonstrated and is "known" to be therein demonstrated is the *truth* of what was meant. Thus Heidegger's definition: "Truth is the sameness of the meant and the intuited" (GA21 109). Knowledge occurs when the intuited comes to coincide with the meant, and truth is the sameness of the meant and the intuited, the sameness that is demonstrated through the coincidence. Thus are they bound together: knowledge, truth, intuition. Through the latter they are bound also to presence, even though Heidegger has begun, parenthetically, to loosen the bond.

To truth as thus determined, intuitive truth (*Anschauungswahrheit*), Heidegger traces back the more derivative determination of truth as propositional (*Satzwahrheit*): a proposition can be true, can be a locus of truth, precisely insofar as it can belong to an act of identification in which something intuited comes to coincide with what is meant in the proposition. Focusing on the question of the primacy of intuitive truth, Heidegger proceeds finally to trace out quite succinctly the bonds with which the entire series of analyses has remained deeply involved. First, regarding the bond of truth to knowledge: truth is a determination of knowledge in such a primary way that one can call the expression *true knowledge* a tautology. Only if knowledge is true, is it knowledge; and something apprehended as false is precisely *not known*. In turn, knowledge is bound to intuition: Heidegger says even that knowledge has been, in the analyses, determined as intuition, though he adds that this does not mean that every instance of knowing is an intuiting, only that intuiting is proper knowing (*eigentliches Erkennen*), at which all other knowing aims, to which it is oriented as the ideal (GA21 113).

Then, suddenly, Heidegger opens the phenomenological analysis to the entire history of philosophy: "By radically comprehending the concept of intuition for the first time, Husserl thought the great tradition of Western philosophy through to its end" (GA21 114). There follows a series of brief discussions in which Heidegger indicates how the relevant bond has been affirmed throughout the history that Husserl is said to have brought to its end by finally thinking that bond radically. The bond that has been affirmed is that of knowledge to intuition, which, conjoined with the tautological bond of truth to knowledge, has sustained a determination of truth as essentially intuitive, that determination that Husserl has thought through to its end. The bond of knowledge to intuition is openly expressed in Husserl's so-called principle of all principles, which requires of all principles that they appeal ultimately to intuition; intuition is thus posited as the source from which all knowledge is to be legitimated (*Rechtsquelle der Erkenntnis*). For Kant, too, knowledge proper is intuition; even though thought is set over against intuition in the Kantian conceptuality, it is in the end only a means in service to intuition, a means of compensating for the finitude of human intuition, which Kant contrasts with the *intuitus originarius* of the divine intellect. Heidegger extends the bond, binding together the exemplary moments of the history of philosophy, from Leibniz through Descartes to Scholasticism, in particular to Thomas Aquinas, to Augustine, and eventually back to Aristotle; only at the end of these discussions does Heidegger turn back to enclose Hegel too within this history, referring to the Hegelian concept of knowledge as self-intuition, as *noesis noeseos*.[3] He concludes: "But it is the task of philosophical logic as characterized to question whether in fact this undiscussed predetermination of truth is or is not something final, something grounded in itself, or whether in the end it is not a prejudice" (GA21 124). Having thus displayed the bonds that sustain this predetermination, especially the bond linking knowledge to intuition (knowledge, in turn, being bound tautologically to truth), having shown how these bonds and the predetermination they sustain have the effect of binding together the entire history of Western philosophy, the task is to loosen the bonds, at least sufficiently to examine them more closely even than did Husserl in thinking this history through to its end. The task is also to open the possibility of a "more radical question" of truth, "over against this predetermination of truth" that has held sway since the Greeks—in short, to stretch and twist the bonds, perhaps to break them, perhaps even to venture a truth that is not of knowledge as intuition.

In fact, at the time of the lecture course *Logic* such a venture had already in effect been launched: most thoroughly in the lecture course of the previous semester, *History of the Concept of Time*, but in a sense from the very moment that Heidegger began sketching the project that came to its (limited) fruition in *Being and Time*.[4] For that project vigorously displaces intuition and presence (at least in its determination as *Vorhandenheit*, though implicitly in all its traditional determinations, which depend on the correlation of presence with intuition). By displacing intuition, the project stretches and twists the bond that had, since the ancients, kept truth bound to intuition. When, finally, in *Being and Time* Heidegger turns to a radical redetermination of truth, the bond is broken.

In *History of the Concept of Time* Heidegger begins with phenomenology. He outlines its fundamental discoveries (intentionality, categorial intuition, the original sense of the a priori), traces the developments that these themes underwent in the decade following the *Logical Investigations*, and calls finally for an investigation of what these developments had left undetermined: an investigation of the Being of the intentional, hence, of the Being of that being that is intentional, the being that Husserl had distinguished as consciousness, but without questioning the ontological differentiation on which the distinction of consciousness from reality was dependent. To his initial discussion of phenomenology, Heidegger then adds an elaborate sketch of the investigation called for, an analysis of the being that is intentional, now designated no longer as consciousness but as Dasein, an analysis of Dasein oriented to the question of the meaning of Being. In this sketch almost the entirety of the First Division of *Being and Time* is included in a form only slightly less detailed and precise than in the published work.

The relevant displacement is produced through the analysis of the most proximate surroundings; this is the analysis to which Heidegger also alludes in the *Logic* but in such a way as to keep it distinct from the phenomenological analysis. In *History of the Concept of Time* Heidegger develops this analysis and allows the displacement that it produces, the displacement of intuition and presence, to come into play, even though (and this is one of the instances of less precision) a certain language of presence (in the form of the words *Präsenz* and *Anwesenheit*) remains temporarily intact. The differentiation is clearly marked: what is genuinely given most proximally are not perceived things present in the flesh, in their *Leiblichkeit*, but rather the familiar things of concerned preoccupation (*das im besorgenden Umgang Anwesende*), the things with which one deals concretely in one's proximate surroundings, things that are thus embedded in a referential totality, a world, from which they receive their particular sense, the things that Heidegger calls by the name *das Zuhandene*, displacing eventually even the very word *Ding* because of the predetermination linking it to *das Vorhandene* (GA20 264; regarding *Ding*, see SZ 67f.). The mode of access to the latter, to things as present-at-hand, the mode of access in which one foregoes concernful dealings with things and merely perceives them, is a founded mode that comes to be constituted only through a certain interruption of what is in play in one's concernful dealings, an interruption especially of the operation of the referential totality, of the world in which each thing is linked up referentially with others and the totality oriented to certain tasks to be done, certain possibilities for Dasein (GA20 300). As the table on which one is writing has its place in the room along with the chair on which one sits while writing, along with the lamp that illuminates the top of the table, across from the door that is closed so that the writer will not be disturbed, all of these things display-ing in their mutual references an orientation to certain tasks, certain kinds of dealings in which they serve their purpose, certain of Dasein's possibilities, for instance, of writing.

In *Being and Time* the same displacement is produced through an analysis that is even richer in its concrete descriptive elaboration and that calls attention specifically to the displacement produced. The displacement is linked to what the analysis demonstrates regarding Dasein's sight (*Sicht*): first, that the sight by which Dasein deals concernfully with things and solicitously with others is a matter not of just perceiving but rather of apprehending things and others in their involvements in the world; hence, that sight is grounded in understanding, the moment of comportment in which Dasein projects upon the referential structure of its world in such a way that things and others can show themselves (in their involvement in the world) to Dasein's sight. These determinations of Dasein's sight pro-duce the displacement: "Through the demonstration of how all sight is grounded primarily in understanding . . ., pure intuition is deprived of its priority, which corresponds noetically to the priority of the present-at-hand [*des Vorhandenen*] in traditional ontology" (SZ 147).

What does this displacement of intuition and presence entail with regard to the bond between knowledge and intuition? Heidegger touches upon this question in the course of tracing in *Being and Time* the genesis of the theoretical attitude, specifically, in his discussion of the thematizing that objectifies things as present-at-hand and that thereby carries out the scientific projection of nature. In order to situate such objectifying within the temporal interpretation of Dasein, Heidegger identifies it as a distinc-tive presenting (*Gegenwärtigung*) and then adds in a note: "The thesis that all knowledge has 'intuition' as its goal has the temporal meaning: all knowing is presenting. Whether every science or even philosophical knowledge aims at presenting, need not be decided here" (SZ 363). The thesis that all knowledge has intuition as its goal is of course the one that in *Logic* Heidegger has traced throughout the history of philosophy. The question that Heidegger leaves open is whether all scientific and philo-sophical knowing exhibits such an orientation and, hence, in the terms of the temporal interpretation of Dasein, is a presenting. Yet, if Heidegger leaves this question open, he clearly does not leave open the question as to the founded character of such intuitive presenting, indeed of knowing as such in the sense sustained in the history of Western philosophy.[5] For when Dasein comes to present things so as to objectify and thematize them, it will have done so only by modifying the comportment that it will already have had to them in its circumspective concern, its dealings with them as *zuhanden*. Unless knowledge is to be redetermined in a way that transgresses the previous determinations, knowledge will also be displaced in the displacement of intuition and presence. The field will thus have been cleared for a radical redetermination of truth.

Such a redetermination is provided in section 44 of *Being and Time*, the only major analysis in the First Division that is not to be found virtually intact in *History of the Concept of Time*. And yet, it is remarkable how the analysis of truth evokes the discussions from the lecture courses, especially from *Logic*, situating those discussions within the context in which intuition and presence undergo displacement. Heidegger notes that "according to the general opinion, what is true is knowledge" (SZ 216), his hint of irony beginning to stretch this bond that *Logic* still characterized as tautological, preparing the questioning that will clear the field for the analysis of truth. The statement of another general opinion furthers that questioning: it is said that knowledge is judging, and so it can be said, as has almost always been said in the history of philosophy, that truth has its locus in judgment. Heidegger follows for a moment the train of Husserl's reflections: in judgment one must distinguish between the real psychic process and the ideal content of judgment, the latter (in the case of a true judgment) standing in a relation of correspondence to the real thing judged about. But now Heidegger is more outspoken in his willingness to have recourse to what he now calls "the ontologically unclarified separation of the real and the ideal." Voicing his suspicion that this separation already perverts the question, he even takes—for a moment, in the guise of questioning—the side of psychologism: "Is not psychologism right in opposing this separation . . . ?" (SZ 217).

It is against this background that Heidegger then proposes his analysis, proposes it in the most rigorous phenomenological terms. Adhering still to the general opinion that truth belongs to knowledge, he asks: "When does truth become phenomenally explicit in knowledge itself?" His answer provides the primary direction for the analysis that is to follow: "It does so when knowing demonstrates itself *as true*" (SZ 217). What is required, then, is an analysis of demonstration, since it is precisely in demonstration that truth comes to show itself *as truth*. Yet, such an analysis has already been given in *Logic*, appropriated from Husserl's *Logical Investigations*, and so *Being and Time* has only to orient that analysis more rigorously to the methodological directive and, most significantly, to integrate it into the analysis of Dasein, exposing it to the displacement of intuition and presence that that analysis produces.

It is a matter, then, of an intentional analysis of the demonstration that occurs when, having asserted that "the picture on the wall is hanging askew" while standing with one's back to the wall, one then turns around and perceives the picture hanging askew on the wall. That is, it is a matter of repeating with this example the analysis of intentional fulfillment that Heidegger took over in *Logic* from Husserl's *Logical Investigations*, a matter of showing through that analysis that the truth of the assertion consists in its saying the thing itself just as that thing comes to show itself, in its uncovering that thing just as that thing proves demonstrably to be, in short, in its being-uncovering (*entdeckend-sein*).

Heidegger could have extended the analysis and integrated it more radically into the analysis of Dasein, had he gone on to introduce another example, one in which the self-showing of the thing spoken of would have taken the form, not of perception, but of circumspective concern. For at least to this extent truth would, then, have been detached from knowledge as intuition. That Heidegger does not pause to develop such an example is a measure of the decisiveness that he attaches to the move that he broaches almost immediately upon having established the character of truth as being-uncovered. The move is announced as a regress from truth to its ontological condition of possibility: "Being-true as being-uncovering is, in turn, ontologically possible only on the basis of Being-in-the-world" (SZ 219). The move is a doubling of *truth*, doubling truth as being-uncovering, doubling it with the originary phenomenon of truth, which is the ontological condition of possibility of truth as being-uncovering. Though Heidegger does not elaborate the move descriptively, it is clear how it could be shown concretely that both the assertion and the self-showing of what is spoken of, both the empty intention and its fulfillment, are possible only on the basis of Being-in-the-world, only on the basis of the disclosedness (*Erschlossenheit*) by which Dasein is its "there" ("*Da*"), by which it is there in the world from out of which things can then show themselves in such a way that what has been said of them comes to be demonstrated. Thus doubling *truth*, Heidegger encloses within the unity of the word both truth in the extended phenomenological sense of being-uncovering *and* the condition of the possibility of such truth. Indeed, he declares: "What makes this very uncovering possible must necessarily be called 'true' in a still more originary sense" (SZ 220)—declares it as if it were self-evident, doubly marking ("must necessarily") the necessity of this doubling of *truth*.

It is this doubling that decisively breaks the bond of truth to knowledge in its traditional determination as intuition. For disclosedness is a matter neither *of* intuition nor *for* intuition. The originary phenomenon of truth, truth as disclosedness, is a truth that is not of knowledge.

The consequences of this doubling move to truth as disclosedness are virtually unlimited, and one could take it even as the point of departure for a rigorous narrative on the way forged by Heidegger's thought after *Being and Time*. Along that way such a narrative would be compelled constantly to mark consequences of the doubling.

For instance: the way in which during the 1930s Heidegger's lectures on Nietzsche put into question that tautological bond between truth and knowledge, marking that bond as one that even Nietzsche has in common with Plato, hence as binding even Nietzsche to the unity of the history of Platonism,[6] proposing then over against this history a thinking of a truth, most notably in art, that would be explicitly not of knowledge.

And then: the way in which "The Origin of the Work of Art" determines the truth in art as a truth that happens, that takes place in being set into the work of art, a truth therefore that is not of knowledge, that could be linked to knowledge only if knowledge were to be radically redetermined outside, at least, its bond to intuition, a redetermination that Heidegger broaches in this very text in his discussion of the preservation (*Bewahrung*) of the work of art, which he characterizes as a knowing (*Wissen*) constituted by "the ecstatic engagement of existing man in the unconcealment of Being."[7]

Until finally: in "The End of Philosophy and the Task of Thinking" Heidegger comes to retract the doubling, or, more precisely, the doubling of *truth*, insisting that the double, which he has come to call unconcealment (*Unverborgenheit*), clearing (*Lichtung*), and *aletheia*, is not to be equated with truth, since it is what first grants the possibility of truth, insisting—more disruptively—that the question of unconcealment is not the question of truth, so that it was, says Heidegger, "inadequate [*nicht sachgemäss*] and misleading to call *aletheia* in the sense of clearing, truth" (SD 76f.). Thus, even if he will no longer say that what makes truth possible "must necessarily be called 'true' in a still more originary sense," what remains decisive is the doubling. Even if the double ought not be called truth, ought not be called even the originary phenomenon of truth, still what remains decisive is the turn to that which grants truth; and it is, above all, in order to safeguard the difference, the twofold, that Heidegger retracts truth as a name for that granting, that opening, that can be neither an act nor an object of knowledge. Unless *knowledge* is itself doubled along the lines proposed by "The Origin of the Work of Art," with the same risk no doubt that calling the double *knowledge* will be just as inadequate and misleading as in the case of the double of truth, it will need to be said and to be *thought* how unconcealment, *die Sache des Denkens*, can be, nonetheless, decisively not of knowledge.

22

The First Principle of Hermeneutics

Will McNeill

Das Denken ist das Vorläufigste alles vorläufigen Tuns des Menschen. . . . . Thinking is the most precursory of all precursory activities of man. . . .[1]

Reflecting on the end of philosophy, Heidegger finds himself impelled to recall the extent to which the place of the *question* of Being cannot be severed from its beginning. In his introductory remarks to the lecture first published in 1966, "The End of Philosophy and the Task of Thinking," Heidegger states the following:

> The following text belongs to a wider context. It is the attempt, undertaken repeatedly since 1930, to shape the questioning [*die Fragestellung*] of *Being and Time* in a more primordial fashion. This means to subject the beginning [*Ansatz*] of the question in *Being and Time* to an immanent critique. In this way it must become clear to what extent the *critical* question of what the matter of thinking is necessarily and constantly belongs to thinking. (SD 61/55)

At the end of philosophy, of philosophical questioning, the thinking now at issue is thus directed back to reflect upon its beginning in *Being and Time*. In this way the questioning that belongs to thinking is to become more primordial, to become critical. The working out of the questioning (*Fragestellung*) in *Being and Time* comprises the whole of the analytic of Dasein, that is, the two published divisions of that book. The way in which the questioning unfolds is governed by its beginning (*Ansatz*) and point of departure.

Consider, for a moment, another end: the end of fundamental ontology as it is articulated by Heidegger well before 1930, at the end of the analytic of Dasein in *Being and Time*: "Philosophy is universal phenomenological ontology, taking its point of departure from [*ausgehend von*] the hermeneutic of Dasein which, as analytic of *existence*, has installed the end of the guiding thread of all philosophical questioning at the place from which it *springs* [*entspringt*] and upon which it *recoils* [*zurückschlägt*]" (SZ 436/487, cf. 38/62). Is this second end, the end of the analytic of Dasein, really another? Or do these ends perhaps somehow coincide: the end discerned in 1966 which finds itself compelled to return to the beginning of the question of *Being and Time*, and the end of philosophy that announces itself at the premature close of the analytic of Dasein in 1927? If this were the case, then what in 1966 is referred to as the *critical* question—a question which is itself no longer philosophical—would already be in play in *Being and Time*, in the recoiling movement of the analytic of Dasein.[2] We note that philosophy, conceived by Heidegger in 1927 as "universal phenomenological ontology," is said to take its *point of departure* from the hermeneutic of Dasein. This suggests that the hermeneutic of Dasein is perhaps not—or not yet—philosophy. Indeed, if our records are accurate, Heidegger himself says as much in his SS 1923 course on the "hermeneutics of facticity": "I for my part suspect . . . that hermeneutics is not philosophy at all, but something distinctly precursory [*etwas recht Vorläufiges*] which certainly has a character all of its own: The point is not to be finished with it as quickly as possible, but to hold out in it as long as possible" (GA63 20).

   In any case, whether in 1927 or in 1966, the thinking of the end of philosophy finds itself directed towards the beginning of the question of Being in *Being and Time*. But what is the beginning or *Ansatz* of the question in *Being and Time*? Or, more precisely, where is the place of that beginning? Where is the point of departure from which all philosophical questioning springs? In what way are both the beginning and end of philosophy inscribed in the analytic of Dasein? And why is that analytic, as a hermeneutic, said to be something "distinctly precursory"? In short: What, for Heidegger, is the *arche* or first principle of hermeneutics?

I. The Point of Departure of the Question as an Explication of Dasein

   Heidegger's Marburg lecture course of SS 1925, delivered under the title *History of the Concept of Time*, provides us with an initial answer. The course presents, in a preliminary form, the material which was to become the first division of *Being and Time*. The first chapter of the main part of the course indicates that the question of Being can only arise out of a particular historical (*geschichtliches*) understanding which is already there. Such understanding coincides in an eminent way with Dasein itself, insofar as Dasein is defined as that which discloses possibilities and in doing so is itself disclosed: "The sole ground of the possibility of the question of Being in general is *Dasein itself as possible being, its discovered-*

ness [Entdecktheit] in possibilities (GA20 184–85/136).[3] *Dasein* is thus the name given to the place where the question of Being arises. The next steps of the course (§§15–17) proceed to elaborate a more detailed delimitation of this place in terms of a preliminary explication of Dasein. The working out of the question of Being, that is, of the posing of that question (*die Fragestellung*), as an analytic of Dasein that is *prior* (*vorgängig*) or precursory (*vorläufig*) (201–202/149), is thus by no means the most original, but only the first step towards shaping the way in which the question of Being is posed. Yet before the question can be thematically worked out in even a preliminary way, it must already be given. In what way is it given, and how does Heidegger locate more precisely the place in which it first arises?

§15 of the course identifies the explicit question of Being as arising from a preunderstanding of Being, a preunderstanding which is indeterminate (*unbestimmt*). This preunderstanding belongs to Dasein; it is the place where the working out of the question of Being will *begin* as a preliminary analytic of Dasein. It is not by accident that Dasein's most extreme possibility, that of its death, its *end*, will likewise bear the mark of indeterminacy, *Unbestimmtheit*: an indeterminacy ultimately belonging to time itself.

What is the import of the "pre-" of that preunderstanding whence the question of Being springs, and how does this "pre-" guide the working out of the question? What, in effect, does it mean to say that the question of Being is *already* there? The question as a possibility is already there before being thematically posed (*gestellt*), i.e., before being explicitly raised as a question for investigation. The question in its possibility is presupposed, understood in advance, that is, preunderstood in such a way that this understanding can return to it so as to retrieve and repeat it thematically. This retrieval (*Wiederholung*),[4] as we shall see, constitutes the method of the investigation as hermeneutic interpretation. Yet how does this apparent circularity of the question's already being there in advance (which is, more precisely, the recoil inherent in the question itself) relate to the indeterminacy of the horizon from which it arises? This is the task which the thematic posing and working out of the question is to assume. The explicit posing of the question, as emerging from an indeterminate preunderstanding, is itself as yet indeterminate. To pose explicitly the question of Being therefore first entails working out the question in such a way as to determine "the secure horizon of questioning" (193/143). How is this horizon initially envisaged, that is, what is the initial access of the investigation to this horizon? How is this horizon initially determined?

And why, in the first place, is the question indeterminate? The indeterminacy of the *question* of Being is due to the indeterminacy of the preunderstanding of *Being* lying in the question itself. Not only the question of Being, but an understanding of Being itself is already there. The question 'What is Being?' asks what is meant or understood by Being: it seeks to determine the meaning of Being. Yet even as we ask: What 'is' Being?, we have an understanding, however indeterminate, of what the 'is' means. The questioning itself is thus somehow already determined by what it asks about, namely, Being. In order to pose the question in a transparent way it is necessary to first clarify this relatedness between the questioning and what is questioned. The first step toward determining the question with respect to its horizon is therefore to examine the formal structure of the question.

§16 of the course explicates three structural moments belonging to the question. The question asks what Being *means*: the goal of the question, what is asked after (*das Erfragte*), is the meaning of Being.[5] This first moment is easily identified as a formal structure: it is immediately self-evident from the question itself as a meaningful question, even if its content remains empty at first, i.e., even if we have no clear idea of what we understand by *meaning*. The second moment is not so self-evident; indeed, it seemingly cannot be drawn immediately and directly from the question itself. The question asks what *Being* means: what is asked about (*das Gefragte*) is therefore Being. So far, so good. Yet Heidegger's determination of this second moment—and it is important to note this—does not stop here: "If Being is asked after in this way, then this means: asking concerning the fundamental character [*Grundcharakter*] of beings, that which determines beings as beings. What determines beings as beings is *their Being*. In the meaning of Being lies *what is asked about [das Gefragte]—the Being of beings*" (195/144). The indeterminate understanding of Being has thus here already been given a certain determinacy, and this determinacy will in turn extend to the formal delimitation of the structure of the question. Being means not simply Being itself as such, but the Being *of beings* as that which grounds them: Being is now understood specifically as the *ground* (*Grund*) of beings. Insofar—and only insofar—as this determinate understanding of Being as the (determinative) Being of beings is assumed, access to Being will be via beings themselves. Beings themselves thus constitute the third structural moment of the question, as that which is questioned or interrogated (*das Befragte*).

With what right does Heidegger here delimit the second moment, what is asked about, as the Being *of beings*? May we perhaps detect a certain violence operative here in the very unfolding of the question of Being? To what extent can this determination of Being be said to lie in the question itself? We shall return to these questions in a moment.

Given that beings themselves are what is to be questioned, there immediately arises a further series of *questions*, a further set of issues to be determined. The working out of the question of Being now entails deciding, firstly, *which being* can be experienced in itself in such a way as to provide the meaning of Being; secondly, *how* this being is to be experienced (the manner of access to it); thirdly, the *respect* in which this being is to be questioned so that its Being can be made visible; and fourthly, the *conceptuality* by which the meaning of Being thus made visible is to be articulated—whether, for example, it requires a different kind of conceptuality than that used to describe various regions of beings.

Yet here the determination already given of the second structural moment of the question of Being, the determination of what is asked about as the Being of beings, is again brought into play. For the questions of the choice of being, of access to it, of the respect in which it is to be questioned and of the conceptuality this will require are, as ways of *questioning*, in themselves *beings* (197/146). Deciding these issues therefore first entails determining this questioning itself, as a being. Insofar as questioning itself is a being, and Being is that which determines beings, this means determining the questioning with respect to *its* Being: "The question and the posing of the question of Being will become all the more transparent the more properly we have made visible this being, namely, the Being of the questioning of the questioners themselves. The answering of the question of the Being of beings thus entails the *prior working out of a being with respect to its Being*, of that being which we designate the questioning itself [*das Fragen selbst*]" (197/146). Thus, insofar as the question of Being is itself a being, the determination of the questioning necessitates the determination of the Being of a being.

Yet this step, which parallels Heidegger's determination of the second structural moment, is in itself just as little self-evident. It has not yet justified itself phenomenologically. Questioning, according to Heidegger's analysis, is itself a being. Is there not, once again, a certain violence in this determination? Without pursuing further the remarkable way in which all distinction between the question and questioning seems to be effaced in the analysis (isn't it akin to effacing the very distinction between Being and beings so steadfastly proclaimed . . . ?), isn't it possible to detect a certain *reduction* of questioning here? What if questioning were something *more* than a being? And yet, this reduction does not imply a finality. It is, rather, only a first step toward unfolding the question. The violence, if that is what is involved, will find its response. Any excess of and in questioning will return in the recoil of the determinacy thus imposed: "What is asked after here recoils [*schlägt . . . zurück*], as that which is asked after, upon questioning itself, insofar as the latter is a being" (199/148). With what right, and to what extent, may question and questioning be thus assimilated?

    In §17 Heidegger insists, in keeping with the phenomenological prin-
ciple, that questioning be allowed to determine itself: its relationship of
Being (*Seinsverhältnis*) to itself is to show itself of its own accord (*von
sich aus*). And yet, in the very beginning of the working out of the question, it seems to be a foregone conclusion that whatever questioning *is*, it
is a being: "If the task is to work out this questioning about Being itself,
then we must recall that this questioning is for its part already a being.
Questioning is itself a being, one that is given with the question of the
Being of a being in the course of questioning [*im Vollzug des Fragens*],
whether it is explicitly noted or not. This being is to be secured more
precisely in a precursory way [*vorläufig*] . . ." (199/148). The determination of questioning as a being seems itself to be *unquestioned*. Why, and
by what necessity, should this be so?
    Yet what is it, before any determination of the questioning, that in
accord with the phenomenological principle is absolutely unquestionable?
Nothing other than the pregivenness of the questioning itself. This pregivenness thus forms the initial horizon of questioning, *a horizon whose
meaning must initially be assumed, must remain unquestioned in the
beginning of every question*:

> Yet in questioning about Being we are not posing the question of the
> Being of that being that questioning itself is, but we satisfy the meaning
> of the question of Being if we initially merely uncover [*aufdecken*] ques-
> tioning as a being in that which it is. We cannot yet explicitly ask after its
> meaning, since it is precisely this questioning and posing of questions
> [*Fragenstellen*] that seeks to determine itself more closely as a being in
> what it is pregiven as [*in seinem Was, als was es vorgegeben ist*]. (199/
> 148)

The determination of questioning with respect to its Being can thus only
be preparatory at this stage. It remains eccentric to the question of Being
in general.
    What is the pregivenness in terms of which questioning is to be al-
lowed to determine itself? Nothing other than the preunderstanding of the
question which involves for its part a preunderstanding of Being itself.
This preunderstanding is still an understanding which bears the possibility
of the question within it. The explicit questioning is thereby pregiven *as*
. . . such and such, pregiven in a certain preunderstanding whose horizonal meaning is itself indeterminate. Heidegger now continues: "What is
this being of which we say: questioning, having regard to [*hinsehen auf*],
addressing as, relating [*beziehen*]—pregiven as? It is *that* being which we
ourselves are; this being that I myself in each case am we name *Dasein*"

(199–200/148). To work out the question of Being, to allow that question to work itself out means to allow the particular understanding of the question—an understanding lying in that preunderstanding out of which the question first arose—to show itself, i.e., to show itself in the determinate way in which it is pregiven. In this instance, questioning is pregiven as a possibility of Being that belongs to we ourselves as questioners. However—and this is the decisive point—we, the questioners who are questioning, understand ourselves, i.e., are pregiven—*as beings*.

It is only at this point that (1) the determination of what is asked about (*das Gefragte*) as the Being *of beings* and (2) the consequential and somehow reductive determination of questioning as *a being*, the assimilation of question and questioning, receive their rightful justification. That is, it is only because there lies, within the preunderstanding from which the question arises, a particular understanding of questioning as a function or possibility of a questioner, and of this questioner *as a being*, i.e., with respect to its Being, that (1) Being can be legitimately exposed phenomenologically as the Being of beings, as the ground that determines beings as such, and that (2) questioning as a possibility of Being of a *being*, the questioner, can itself be phenomenologically determined in terms of a being, i.e., understood in its Being from the perspective of a being. This is why the working out of the question of Being thus demands "the prior working out of a being with respect to its Being" (197/146).

Yet it has already become apparent that this particular understanding from which the point of departure of the question is allowed to unfold phenomenologically may not be the most original one. For the relation of Being (*Seinsverhältnis*) of questioning to itself involves an excess of meaning which must, in the beginning, be suspended, for questioning cannot question absolutely its own meaning. The latter is what exceeds the questioning, the unquestionable. This suspension is the reduction of questioning to a being, the point of entry into the circling of the question. It is only now, now that questioning has been determined as and reduced to a being, that questioning itself can question what it, questioning, itself is, and in this very opening, this relation of Being, there is an excess of meaning which is left indeterminate: "We thus have a quite exceptional questioning, insofar as in the content of the question, in what is asked after [*im Erfragten*], what is asked after [*das Erfragte*] is itself what questioning itself is. What is asked after in it, the meaning of Being, is thereby given in complete indeterminacy, as indeterminate as what is sought after can possibly be" (199/147). Questioning, *Fragen*, is itself the opening, the place where the moments of what is asked after (*das Erfragte*), what is asked about (*das Gefragte*), and what is questioned or interrogated (*das Befragte*) meet or gather, a place of emergent opening and recoiling closure.

In this opening it is now not only questioning and question that are mutually assimilated, but the *questioner* too, the questioner who is understood as a being: "The matter itself being asked after, in this case Being, demands the exhibiting of a being—*Dasein*. The phenomenological tendency alone—to elucidate and understand Being as such—contains the inherent task of explicating that being that questioning itself is—the Dasein that we, the questioners, ourselves are" (201/149).

And yet, no sooner has this opening of the working out of the question been determined as the explication of the Being of this being, Dasein, than this beginning is itself somehow at once put in question, in a different kind of question, obliquely dislocated: another caution, we might say, another *Vorsicht*, is immediately brought into play. For the pregivenness of this being, the questioning, is in fact highly problematic, by no means as self-evident or as straightforward as it seems:

> Questioning is that being which is explicitly given with the question, yet at the same time also given in such a way that it in the first place and above all is overlooked [*übersehen*] precisely in the course of questioning [*im Zuge des Fragens*]. Here the attempt is to be made not to overlook precisely this being from the very commencement, not to overlook it precisely with respect to questioning concerning Being itself. (200/148)

It is as though questioning were immediately called upon to take distance from itself, from this very commencement (*Anfang*) of the question of Being.[6] In this other opening, an uncertain play of nearness and distance, another commencement of the question of Being is already intimated. Dasein has at its disposal a particular meaning of Being (*einen bestimmten Sinn von Sein*), a meaning that, strangely enough, is maintained in a kind of "non-understanding" (*Unverständnis*) which is to be "determined." Notice, once more, how determinacy is presupposed: there is given a particular, determinate meaning of Being. We have already indicated the hermeneutic justification of this presupposition: the initial givenness of I myself, Dasein, as a being. This presupposed understanding, its phenomenological givenness, is not in doubt, is not in question. But, in distinct contrast to the *cogito*, it is precisely the meaning of this non-doubt, of this apparent certainty, which is to be put in question, to be thrown into the most radical doubt. For the meaning of the givenness of the indubitable, determinate understanding whose explication governs the beginning of the question of Being is intimately bound up with "a certain non-understanding" or lack of understanding (*einem gewissen Unverständnis*) (202/150), that is, with the indeterminate preunderstanding that is its source. Indeed, it "maintains itself" (*hält sich*) in this non-understanding as though in its very element. It is the latter, a radical uncertainty, which, in the beginning of the question, is the only certainty. How deep does this non-understanding reach? Presumably, at least as far as death, the only "certainty" (*Gewißheit*) in the hermeneutic of Dasein.[7]

Already one must wonder to what extent it will ultimately be possible to determine, to differentiate the meaning of this non-understanding—a non-understanding which may not simply be the perplexity from which the question arose. What is, more precisely, this beginning? It is the beginning of the question of Being in *difference*, in the difference between Being and beings, a difference which is latently already there, prescribed in a particular preunderstanding, and which inscribes itself in the thematic working out of the question. This particular beginning, the understanding of Being as the Being of beings, which is allowed to expose itself phenomenologically, is not transparent to itself with respect to its meaning. The latter is to display itself in the thematic working out of the question. The title of the first half of *Being and Time*—"The Interpretation of Dasein in terms of Temporality, and the Explication of Time as the Transcendental Horizon of the Question of Being"—already indicates that this horizonal meaning of the *question* will somehow prove to be *time*. And yet, already in this determinate beginning of the question in difference we can see that the place of this beginning bears the mark of an indeterminacy, that is to say, of a certain indifference. It is presumably none other than that indifference or undifferentiatedness (*Indifferenz*) which Heidegger elsewhere identifies as constituting the point of departure (*Ausgang*) of the analytic of Dasein.[8]

II. The Point of Departure of the Question as Phenomenological Interpretation

The point of departure of the question thus delimited in fact corresponds quite precisely to the phenomenological method in accordance with which the analytic of Dasein will proceed as hermeneutic interpretation. In order to illustrate this in a preliminary way, I shall now turn to Heidegger's outline of interpretation in *Being and Time* and *The Basic Problems of Phenomenology*.

The phenomenological method of the investigation is not fully unfolded in *Being and Time*. Heidegger there confines himself to elaborating "the preliminary concept of phenomenology" (*Introduction*, §7C). The term *phenomenology* is said to be primarily a methodological concept. The methodological meaning of phenomenological description is, Heidegger tells us, *interpretation*; phenomenology of Dasein is *hermeneutics* as the "business of interpretation" (SZ 37/62).

An outline of interpretation as the "development" (*Ausbildung*) of understanding is provided in Chapter Five of the First Division of *Being and Time*, in Part A of that chapter, which deals with: "The Existential Constitution of the There [*Da*]." What is to become the theme of the phenomenological analysis is in each case pregiven, i.e., shows itself, as such and such. The "as"-structure is constitutive of interpretation (149/189). Interpretation, which Heidegger characterizes as "the *working out* [*Ausarbeitung*] of the possibilities projected in understanding" (148/189, emphasis added), is itself founded by pre-having, pre-sight, and pre-conception (*Vorhabe, Vorsicht,* and *Vorgriff*) (150/191). Somewhat later, at the beginning of the second division, these three moments together—the whole of these "presuppositions" (*Voraussetzungen*)—are said to constitute the *hermeneutic situation* of the analysis (231–32/275). The hermeneutic situation of the interpretation is, in effect, nothing other than the 'place' or point of departure of the explicit beginning of the question of *Being and Time*. The situation will be characterized as the "existential determinacy" of the most original disclosedness, i.e., Being, of the there (*Da*) of Dasein—of the Dasein which marks the beginning of the question (299/345).

How does this structure of interpretation coincide with the beginning of the question of Being? The theme of the working out of the question of Being is the question itself, or what can be designated more precisely as the posing of the question (*Fragestellung*), i.e., *questioning*, insofar as this term unites the moments of question and questioner. At the outset of the analysis questioning is *pre*given as a being: the pre-having (*Vorhabe*) of the interpretation is thus a being, questioning. Insofar as this being is pregiven *as* a being, it is pregiven in a particular respect, namely, with respect to its Being: the *Being* of this being thus constitutes the pre-sight (*Vorsicht*) of the interpretation. Pre-having and pre-sight, the pregivenness of a being in its Being, in themselves entail that the Being of this being is preunderstood in accordance with a certain conceptuality, that is, they entail a prefiguring of the conceptuality via which what is thus understood can be explicitly articulated: they entail a pre-conception (*Vorgriff*). This pre-conception prescribes the conceptuality of the Being of this being.

A more explicit outline of the phenomenological method is provided by Heidegger in condensed form in his introduction to the SS 1927 course entitled *The Basic Problems of Phenomenology*. This brief account was to be elaborated in greater detail in the third part of the course, which did not attain completion. The essential core of the method may nevertheless be gleaned from it. §5 of the Introduction, "The methodological character of ontology," identifies the three basic components of the phenomenological method (GA24 26–32/19–23). In the way in which the theme of the phenomenological analysis is pregiven, i.e., is allowed to show itself so as to constitute the *pre-having* of the interpretation, there lies the first moment of the phenomenological method: the *phenomenological reduction*. The reduction entails directing the investigative gaze of the phenomenologist away from the being itself toward the horizon upon which it is pregiven as such, namely, toward its Being. In the present case, the reduction entails, as we have seen, that questioning be reduced to, i.e., determined as a being, in order for the phenomenological gaze to look toward the horizon of its givenness. This re-directing of the phenomenologist's perspective away from beings thus also requires a positive directive—the perspective is to be directed *toward* Being—and this is provided by the *pre-sighting* of Being inherent in the interpretation. This positive directive corresponds to the methodological moment of *phenomenological construction*. Finally, because the conceptuality of Being prefigured in the *pre-conception* of the interpretation is itself historical, because the starting point of the question of Being is permeated by traditional concepts, the critical working out of this starting point will simultaneously occur as *phenomenological destruction*.

The working out of the question of Being will thus take the form of a reductive, constructive, and destructive interpretation as the development (*Ausbildung*) of the possibility of the question, a possibility projected in a certain preunderstanding. Insofar as the structure of being-possible is termed *Dasein*, the place of this preunderstanding is thereby also designated, and the working out of the question of Being will occur as the interpretation of Dasein. Yet interpretation is itself a possibility of Dasein. Dasein thus names the place where the working out of the question of Being both begins and ends. Yet if this is so, then the structure of interpretation which guides the investigation must be identical to the structure of Dasein itself. In what way do beginning and end of the working out of the question of Being converge?

The question of Being, as we have seen, initially emerges from a certain indeterminate preunderstanding in which, however, there lies a particular understanding of Being. In being pregiven in this way, the question shows itself *as* a being, as that being which we the questioners ourselves are. This "as"-structure is constitutive of interpretation as the working out, development, or explicit appropriation (*Zueignen*) of what is pregiven in understanding (SZ 148/188). The "as"-structure is founded by pre-having, pre-sight, and pre-conception, corresponding in this case to beings, Being, and the conceptual terminology of Being/beings in which a latent meaning is prescribed. The "pre-" of these three moments is a reference to the essential locus of *understanding* which gives beings *as* such in advance upon a particular horizon. This locus of understanding is itself the horizon, in this case Being. Being is thereby given as that which is 'earlier,' namely, earlier than the givenness of beings; the question of Being is the question of what this 'earlier' means: "How are we to grasp the character of this "pre-"? Have we done so by formally stating "apriori"? . . . How does the structure of the "as" pertaining to what is interpreted as such relate to it? . . . do the pre-structure of understanding and the as-structure of interpretation show an existential-ontological connection with the phenomenon of projection?" (150–51/192)

The answer to the latter question is already intimated at this stage of the inquiry, for the structure of *meaning* itself belongs to interpretation that understands: "*Meaning is the upon-which [Woraufhin] of projection, structured by pre-having, pre-sight, and pre-conception, from out of which something becomes understandable as something*" (151/193). To work out the meaning of Being then means to conceptually articulate, i.e., to interpret that horizon upon which beings are understood, and to do so in such a way as to expose the inherent connection between the pre-structure of understanding and the as-structure of interpretation. This entails that the interpretation thematically lay bare the structural, horizonal unity of the "presuppositions" of its own understanding, that is, the horizonal unity of its own pre-having, pre-sight, and pre-conception as a whole, insofar as this interpretation is the interpretation of the question of the meaning of the Being of beings. This exposition of the horizonal unity of the pre-having, pre-sight, and pre-conception of the understanding of the question of Being will thus delimit the *point of departure* from where that question begins out of a preunderstanding of Being, of the "is," and where it ends as the exposition of the meaning of Being.

III. The Beginning of the Question

We have so far displayed the point of departure of the question of Being as the analytic of Dasein, of that being which has an understanding access to Being. With the identification of the point of departure as Dasein in its pregivenness we have determined *which* being is to constitute the theme of the interpretation, and were able to see how the *determination* of this being with respect to its as yet non-perspicuous horizon constitutes a moment of reduction. This reduction, however, proved to be a necessary part of the phenomenological method. We were thus able to explicate the point of departure of the question as phenomenological interpretation which is in itself hermeneutic: The phenomenological method of the investigation always comprises the interaction of reduction, construction, and destruction as a whole, and these methodological moments are *structured* and *guided in advance* in accordance with the pre-having, pre-sight, and pre-conception of hermeneutic interpretation. Yet how is the hermeneutic to proceed concretely?

In his preliminary characterization of the task which the phenomenological method faces in revealing its primary phenomenon (letting it be seen) as that which is at first and for the most part concealed (*verborgen*), namely, the "meaning and ground" of the *Being* of beings, Heidegger in *Being and Time* anticipates three key moments of this method. Insisting that our access to Being is never without presuppositions, he states the following: "The manner in which Being and the structures of Being are encountered in the mode of phenomenon must first of all be *wrested* from the objects of phenomenology. For this reason the *point of departure* [*Ausgang*] of the analysis, as well as the *access* [*Zugang*] to the phenomenon and our *penetrating through* [*Durchgang durch*] the dominant concealments demand their own methodological securing" (36/61). These three moments belonging to interpretation are not equivalent to the tripartite structure of pre-having, pre-sighting, and pre-conception, nor to that of reduction, construction, and destruction. Furthermore, it is important to distinguish between the terms *point of departure* (*Ausgang*) and *beginning* (*Ansatz*). Whereas point of departure refers to the formal pregivenness of the being which is to constitute the theme of the analytic, namely, Dasein, beginning refers to the initial entry of Dasein into and deployment of the entirety of the presuppositions constituting the hermeneutic situation of interpretation (as a hermeneutic of existence).

To work out or interpret the question of Being means to work out the *horizon* upon which the question, as a being, is pregiven. But to work out this horizon, Being, then entails not only the formal construction (projection) of this moment, but also working out the *way* in which Being is pregiven as the Being of a being, Dasein. This being, Dasein, is pregiven with respect to its Being, and the next task is to work out this *respect* (*Hinsicht* or *Hinblick*), i.e., the initial access (*Zugang*) to Being (cf. GA20 §16). This access will be critical for the way in which Dasein enters and engages with the hermeneutic situation.

What this means, then, is that the purely formal identification of the three structural presuppositions of interpretation (pre-having, pre-sight, and pre-conception) is not in itself sufficient to initiate the phenomenological construction of the Being of this being, Dasein. That is, the formal determination of the point of departure of the question of Being is not sufficient to get the investigation underway. The point of departure (*Ausgang*) of the question of Being refers to the *formal pregivenness* of the question, i.e., of Dasein in its Being. This point of departure is not in itself the beginning (*Ansatz*) of that question. The point of departure of the question indeed belongs to its beginning, but is not identical with it. The beginning of the question of Being demands a further deliberation and decision regarding the pre-having, pre-sight, and pre-conception of the interpretation, one that will be utterly decisive, not only for the initiation but also for the entire working out of the investigation, its destructuring and penetrating through (*Durchgang durch*) the dominant concealments.

In what way will this hermeneutic prevent the analytic of Dasein from becoming a purely formal analysis of existence? In his WS 1929–30 course, *The Fundamental Concepts of Metaphysics*, Heidegger argues that the fateful thing (*das Verhängnisvolle*) about formal description is that it does not provide the *essence* of what it seeks to understand (GA29/30 424–25). All philosophical concepts, Heidegger insists, are merely formally indicative (*formal anzeigend*). They merely provide a formal indication or directive (*Anweisung*). Ordinary understanding takes these concepts as though they were describing something that is simply at hand (*vorhanden*), which is why it misunderstands the essence of philosophizing. The nature of these concepts, however, is to stake a claim (*Anspruch*) upon our understanding, namely, that it "transform itself into the Da-sein in it" (428).[9] Formally indicative concepts "point into Dasein. Da-sein, however—as I understand it—is always *mine*. Because in providing this indication they indeed, in accordance with their essence, in each case point into a concretion of the individual Dasein in human being, but never bring this concretion with them in their content, they are *formally indicative*" (429). This transformation (*Verwandlung*) of the formally indicative structures of interpretation into its concrete execution is a critical moment. It is what Heidegger elsewhere refers to as the existentiell involvement (*Einsatz*) of the Dasein that is philosophizing.[10] The ontological structure of mineness (*Jemeinigkeit*) is merely the formal claim or call to such involvement.

This moment of involvement is the moment of *the beginning* of the hermeneutic of Dasein, the moment of access to Dasein, of Dasein's access to itself, of Dasein's taking up and acknowledgement of its own concretion. What happens in such involvement? How does it occur? We have already seen that access to Dasein entails a certain indeterminacy or indifference. However, what is crucial is that such indifference or indeterminacy is not equivalent to the empty or formal indifference that threatens all metaphysical concepts. Rather, it is what Heidegger understands as the "peculiar *neutrality*" of Dasein. Indeed, in the context where he refers most explicitly to this, Heidegger suggests that existentiell involvement is the *condition* of attaining such neutrality (GA26 176/140).

The involvement of Dasein thus occurs as an engagement in the concrete horizon of the hermeneutic itself. This horizon, as we have seen, is not only *formally* pregiven as the point of departure of the hermeneutic. It is *indeterminately pregiven*—given prior to its being formally determined as such. Dasein's involvement in the beginning and execution of this hermeneutic will thus occur as a running ahead into a horizon that is given both indeterminately and earlier than the explicit formulation of any question. This horizon in *Being and Time* receives the preliminary name of 'death.'[11] But Heidegger will argue that this horizon is ultimately *time*, understood as the horizonal unity of temporality (*Zeitlichkeit*) whose threefold structure mirrors the tripartite "pre"-structure of interpretation. Yet is not time as horizon, i.e., as *Temporalität*, precisely on account of this "pre"-structure, somehow *earlier* than the three ekstases of temporality (*Zeitlichkeit*)? And if so, does this not imply a certain confusion between future as inscribed in temporality and a more radical kind of futuricity? Is not Heidegger's later thought perhaps the attempt to say this more radical futuricity?

Already in 1924 Heidegger knows that running ahead (*Vorlaufen*) comprises the very movement of the hermeneutic of Dasein. In his lecture "The Concept of Time"—a lecture that begins with the remarkable claim *not* to be philosophical!—he asserts that "running ahead is the fundamental way in which the interpretation of Dasein is carried through [*der Grundvollzug der Daseinsauslegung*]" (BZ 18/13). Running ahead is nothing less than Dasein's coming toward itself—its radical futuricity in coming toward the indeterminate yet historical preunderstanding out of which the question of Being first emerges. Such running ahead is Dasein's entering into its own historicity, the historicity of its own understanding. It is, Heidegger tells us, the first principle of hermeneutics: "*The possibility of access to history [Geschichte] is grounded in the possibility according to which any specific present understands how to be futural. This is the first principle of all hermeneutics*" (26/20). The "precursiveness" or *Vorläufigkeit* of hermeneutics does not therefore simply mean that this hermeneutics is preliminary. It refers to the very *movement* of this thinking. What may be especially significant is that while Heidegger will later distance himself from using the term 'hermeneutics,' he will continue to insist upon this 'precursiveness' or running ahead as essential to his later thinking.[12] In 1952, unfolding another question—the question "What calls for thinking?"—Heidegger will attempt to let this question run ahead (*vorauslaufen*) into "what is most precursory," *das Vorläufigste*, namely, that from which thinking first receives its determination:

> The question "What calls for thinking?" is an attempt to reach that unavoidable way which leads into what is most precursory. The question even runs ahead of thinking itself, of what is most precursory. Thus it

appears to be a question of the kind to which modern philosophy liked to
lay claim as it went looking for the most radical question—the question
without presuppositions—which was to lay the unshakeable foundations
of the entire edifice of the system of philosophy for all future ages. But
the question "What calls for thinking?" is not without presuppositions.
Far from it: it goes directly toward what would here be called presupposition [*Voraussetzung*], and becomes involved in it. (WhD 161–62/160)[13]

Such a *critical* question, no longer or not yet philosophy in that it runs
ahead to what is pre-supposed in any philosophical question, would no
longer attempt to determine this "pre-" in terms of an apriori horizon. It
would be an attempt, rather, to remain open to an indeterminacy which,
"earlier than every possible earlier" (as an early intimation had it),[14] is, like
time itself, "nothing temporal" (SD 4/4). Yet in its very movement it
would, presumably, continue to adhere to the first principle of hermeneutics.

Abbreviations

In references to Heidegger's texts, a slash separates the pagination of the original German work and that of the published English translation, though individual authors have often either modified the published translation or given their own translation. The following abbreviations are also used: Kriegsnotsemester (KNS), Summer Semester (SS), Winter Semester (WS).

HEIDEGGER'S GESAMTAUSGABE (Frankfurt: Klostermann, 1975ff.)

GA1   Vol. 1: *Frühe Schriften* (1978).

GA2   Vol. 2: *Sein und Zeit* (1977)/*Being and Time*, trans. John Macquarrie and Edward Robinson (New York: Harper & Row, 1962).

GA3   *Kant und das Problem der Metaphysik* (1990)/*Kant and the Problem of Metaphysics*, trans. Richard Taft (Bloomington: Indiana University Press, 1990).

GA9   Vol. 9: *Wegmarken* (1976).

GA13   Vol. 13: *Aus der Erfahrung des Denkens* (1983).

GA19   Vol. 19: *Platon: Sophistes* (1992). Marburg lecture course of WS 1924–25.

GA20   Vol. 20: *Prolegomena zur Geschichte des Zeitbegriffs* (1979; 2nd ed. 1988)/*History of the Concept of Time: Prolegomena*, trans. Theodore Kisiel (Bloomington: Indiana University Press, 1985). Marburg lecture course of SS 1925.

GA21   Vol. 21: *Logik. Die Frage nach der Wahrheit* (1976)/*Logic: The Question of Truth*, trans. Thomas Sheehan and Reginald Lilly (Bloomington: Indiana University Press, forthcoming). Marburg lecture course of WS 1925–26.

GA24   Vol. 24: *Die Grundprobleme der Phänomenologie* (1975; 2nd ed. 1989)/*The Basic Problems of Phenomenology*, trans. Albert Hofstadter (Bloomington: Indiana University Press, 1982). Marburg lecture course of SS 1927.

GA25   Vol. 25: *Phänomenologische Interpretation von Kants Kritik der reinen Vernunft* (1977; 2nd ed. 1987). Marburg lecture course of WS 1927–28.

GA26   Vol. 26: *Metaphysische Anfangsgründe der Logik im Ausgang von Leibniz* (1978; 2nd ed. 1990)/*The Metaphysical Foundations of Logic*, trans. Michael Heim (Bloomington: Indiana University Press, 1984). Marburg lecture course of SS 1928.

GA29/30   Vol. 29/30: *Die Grundbegriffe der Metaphysik. Welt-Endlichkeit-Einsamkeit* (1983)/*The Fundamental Concepts of Metaphysics. World—Finitude—Solitude*, trans. Will McNeill and Nicholas Walker (Bloomington: Indiana University Press, 1994). Freiburg lecture course of WS 1929–30.

GA56/57   Vol. 56/57: *Zur Bestimmung der Philosophie* (1987). Freiburg lecture courses of KNS and SS 1919.

GA58   Vol. 58: *Grundprobleme der Phänomenologie* (1992). Freiburg lecture course of WS 1919–20.

GA61   Vol. 61: *Phänomenologische Interpretationen zu Aristoteles. Einführung in die phänomenologische Forschung* (1985). Freiburg lecture course of WS 1921–22.

GA63   Vol. 63: *Ontologie (Hermeneutik der Faktizität)* (1988)/*Ontology (Hermeneutics of Facticity)*, trans. John van Buren (Bloomington: Indiana University Press, 1995). Freiburg lecture course of SS 1923.

OTHER TEXTS BY HEIDEGGER

BZ   *Der Begriff der Zeit* (Tübingen: Max Niemeyer, 1989)/*The Concept of Time*, trans. Will McNeill (Basil Blackwell, 1992).

FS   *Frühe Schriften* (Frankfurt: Klostermann, 1972).

KPM   *Kant und das Problem der Metaphysik* (Frankfurt: Klostermann, 1927; 4th ed. enlarged, 1974)/*Kant and the Problem of Metaphysics*, trans. Richard Taft (Bloomington: Indiana University Press, 1990).

PIA   "Phänomenologische Interpretationen zu Aristoteles (Anzeige der hermeneutischen Situation)," *Dilthey Jahrbuch für Philosophie und Geschichte der Geisteswissenschaften* 6 (1989): 228–69/"Phenomenological Interpretations with Respect to Aristotle (Indication of the Hermeneutical Situation)," trans. Michael Baur, *Man and World* 25 (1992): 355–93.

SD   *Zur Sache des Denkens* (Tübingen: Niemeyer, 1969; 2nd ed. 1976)/*Time and Being*, trans. Joan Stambaugh (New York: Harper & Row, 1972).

SZ   *Sein und Zeit* (Tübingen: Niemeyer, 1927; 7th ed. reset, 1953;

15th ed. 1979; 16th ed. 1986)/*Being and Time*, trans. John Macquarrie and Edward Robinson (New York: Harper & Row, 1962).

US   *Unterwegs zur Sprache* (Pfullingen: Neske, 1959; 7th ed.
1982)/*On the Way to Language*, trans. Peter D. Hertz (New
York: Harper & Row, 1971).

Notes

Introduction

1. Otto Pöggeler, *Der Denkweg Martin Heideggers* (Pfullingen: Neske, ²1983), p. 351. English translation by Daniel Magurshak and Sigmund Barber, *Martin Heidegger's Path of Thinking* (Atlantic Highlands: Humanities, 1987), p. 285. See note 3 below for Heidegger's letter to Karl Löwith in August 1927, in which he expresses disinterest with regard to his development from the Scotus habilitation of 1915–16 to *Being and Time*, which had just appeared, and nevertheless sketches out the basic lines of that genetic development for Löwith's benefit. See Abbreviations for translations of the shorthand citations of Heidegger's texts, like US, which will be employed in all of the essays in this volume.

2. As my colleague John van Buren points out, the full polysemy of the "start," which we are employing here within Apollinian limits, manifests its full Dionysian glory only with the later Heidegger's search for "the other start," in "startling" forms like the shock of *Erschrecken*, the arousal of *Aufschrecken*, and the sudden displacement of *Entsetzen* (GA65 249, 269, 482–4, §§ 5–6).

3. Dietrich Papenfuss and Otto Pöggeler (eds.), *Zur philosophischen Aktualität Heideggers*, vol. 2, *Im Gespräch der Zeit* (Frankfurt: Klostermann, 1990), p. 36.

4. Heidegger reiterated this story and variants thereof in a series of conversations with Otto Pöggeler from 1959 to 1963. Pöggeler recounted it in a series of articles from 1977 to 1983. See e.g. his *Denkweg*, the 1983 Postscript, p. 351f./285.

5. GA56/57 75. Gadamer's astonishment over the early occurrence of this phrase is recorded in his article, "Wilhelm Dilthey nach 150 Jahren," in *Dilthey und die Philosophie der Gegenwart*, ed. E.W. Orth, Sonderband der *Phänomenologischen Forschungen* (Freiburg and Munich: Alber, 1985), p. 159.

6. I am grateful to my co-editor, John van Buren, for his suggestions toward improving a first draft of this Introduction.

Chapter 1

1. With the exception of the first paragraph the following translation is from H.-G. Gadamer's "Der eine Weg Martin Heideggers" in Gadamer, *Gesammelte Werke*, Band 3 (Tübingen: J.C.B. Mohr, 1987), pp. 417–430. The first paragraph

has been taken from the original presentation of this piece in Messkirch on the tenth anniversary of Heidegger's death [May 26, 1986], published in a *Sonderheft der Martin-Heidegger-Gesellschaft* (Wuppertal, 1986), pp. 7–25 (translator).

2. GA61 182. Remarkably, given that Kierkegaard is criticizing Hegel as much as anyone here, the play on *Verzweifeln and Zweifeln*, despair and doubt, originates in Hegel's *Phanomenologie des Geistes* (Hamburg: Felix Meiner, 1952), p. 67 (translator).

3. I have resorted to the Old English *beon* here to render Heidegger's antiquation, *Seyn*. Though nothing is adequate, *beon* has the advantage of meaning "to come up into being." Thus it renders the Greek *phyein*, to which it is related, and circumvents the static presence (Heidegger: *stete Anwesenheit*) of the Greek *einai* (translator).

4. J. Taminiaux provided a first rate analysis of *poiēsis* in his Oxford lecture of April 1986.

5. Heidegger's *Beiträge zur Philosophie* appeared as Volume 65 of the *Gesamtausgabe* (1989) (translator).

6. *das Seiende im Ganzen*. Heidegger, I submit, is building here upon the original, preconceptual sense of Aristotle's *katholou*, or "taken on the whole," as opposed to *kath' hekaston*, or "each taken individually." The point Gadamer sees here is that generalization must be taken as it is prior to representative thought's abstraction and withdrawal (*aphairesis*) to an eidetic "universal" (translator).

7. Martin Heidegger, *Identität und Differenz* (Pfullingen: Gunther Neske, 1957), p. 33.

Chapter 2

1. GA56/57 8: "The inner struggle with the enigmas of life and the world seeks to come to rest in the establishment of something conclusive about the world and life. Objectively put: every great philosophy completes itself in a worldview—where it arrives at its uninhibited development according to its innermost tendency, every philosophy is a metaphysics." [These footnote citations of Heidegger, left in the original German by the author, have been translated into English by the editors.]

2. In GA61 169 Heidegger speaks of "a contemplation that cuts off any further discussion once it has been understood, but instead is there insofar as it makes itself concretely felt in the factical."

3. GA56/57 110: "Since phenomenology alone can prove itself and can only do this by itself, every standpoint is a sin against its ownmost spirit. And the *mortal sin* would be the opinion that *it itself is a standpoint*" Compare SZ 27/49–50.

4. GA29/30 32: "Is it then so certain that the interpretation of human Dasein

in which we move today—according to which, e.g., philosophy, is a so-called cultural good among others . . . , that this interpretation of Dasein is the ultimate one?" Compare GA56/57 131; GA61 41, 120, 169.

5. GA61 174: "The formal indication of the 'I am' that guides the problem of the sense of being of life becomes methodically effective in the way that it is brought into its genuinely factical enactment [*Vollzug*], i.e., is enacted in the demonstrable *character of questionability* ('unrest') belonging to factical life as the concrete historical question '*Am I?*', whereby the 'I' is to be taken simply in the sense of pointing toward my concrete factic life in its concrete world."

6. GA63 19: "How [*Als was*] . . . Dasein encounters itself in thus being alert [*Wachsein*] and so guided, this character of being cannot be reckoned in advance and is nothing for universal humanity [*Menschheit*], nothing for a public, but is instead the particular and deciding possibility of each concrete facticity."

7. See also *Was heißt Denken?*, 3rd ed. (Tübingen: Niemeyer, 1971), p.164./*What is Called Thinking?*, translated by Fred D. Wieck and J. Glenn Gray (New York: Harper & Row, 1968), p. 169: "No thinker has ever entered into another thinker's solitude [*Einsamkeit*, also 'loneliness']. Yet it is only out of its solitude that any thinking speaks, in hidden fashion, to the thinking that follows or precedes it. What we represent and maintain to be the effects of a thinking are the misunderstandings to which it inevitably falls prey."

8. The reading and writing that is no longer *about* Heidegger (by foregoing the thought that Heidegger's work brings up philosophical contents) and takes the formal character of this thinking seriously (by following the idea that it exists only in the problem of the accessibility to thinking) was inaugurated by Van Dijk and then by Oudemans. See Th.C.W. Oudemans, "Heidegger's logische Untersuchungen," *Heidegger Studies* VI (1990): 85–105; and R.J.A. van Dijk, "Grundbegriffe der Metaphysik," *Heidegger Studies* VII (1991): 89–109.

9. Re-presentation is "a cognitive determining which, in developing the process of ordering, constantly develops its own possibility, orders itself from out of itself such that it can be constant and universal movement" (GA63 62).

10. See PIA 259.

11. GA63 64: ". . . philosophy offers Dasein objective refuge, the prospect of the comforting security of agreement, the glory of the immediacy of life's proximity, coupled with the overcoming that comes with a shortwinded detailed questioning that, slowly inching along, shoves aside great answers. Absolute 'lack of necessity', 'freedom from want', absolute 'needlessness' [*Bedürfnislosigkeit*] (Hegel) is achieved."

12. GA61 33: "Formal indication involves a very definite bond. It implies that I stand at the starting point of a very definite *direction of approach*, that—if it is to come to the proper—the only given is the path [*Weg*] of making the most of and fulfilling what is improperly indicated, of following that indication. Making the

most out of it, drawing out [*Herausheben*] of it. . . . Object 'empty' [i.e. formal] nevertheless means: and yet decisive! Not arbitrary and without an approach, but precisely 'empty' *and* directive, i.e., defining, indicating, binding the direction."

13. GA61 132: "It is not immediately apparent that caring absorption is a motion of life 'against itself', such that life is 'still' something else, a something else that is indeed there and found in ruinance, but in the mode of being pushed away."

14. Inasmuch as life stands clear of itself, it is "*da*" (GA61 107). "In every getting-out-of-the-way of itself, life is factically there for itself" (PIA 244).

15. SZ 86/119: "That *wherein* Dasein understands itself in advance in the mode of self-reference is the *upon-and-towards-which [Worauf]* of letting entities be encountered in advance. *As the upon-and-towards-which of letting entities be encountered in the kind of being that belongs to relevance* [Bewandtnis], *the wherein of self-referring understanding is the phenomenon of world.*"

16. GA61 20: "The idea of definition in 'formal' logic is here revoked, and this only because this idea of definition and 'formal' logic are not at all 'formal', but rather always spring from a 'logical' problematic that essentially takes its orientation from a material region of objects (things, the living, the meaningful) and its particular cognitive way of apprehending (ordering accumulation)."

17. GA63 16: "'Concept' is not a schema, but rather a possibility of being, the possibility of the eye-opening moment, constitutive of the eye-opening moment; a meaning drawn [in advance]. . . . Basic concepts are not afterthoughts, but rather pre-supportive: in their way, they take Dasein into their grasp."

18. Compare GA24 297/208: "It is not the case that there are first words that are coined as signs for meanings, but rather the reverse—it is from the Dasein that understands itself and the world, from an already unveiled texture of meaning, that each word grows towards these meanings. If words are grasped in what they say in accord with their essence, they can never be taken as free-floating things." Compare also GA29/30 445f.

19. GA29/30 398f: ". . . in the *everydayness* of our Dasein we at first for the most part let entities approach us and be present-at-hand in a curious indifference. Not such that for us all things merge indifferently—on the contrary, we are receptive to the manifold content of entities that surround us, we never have enough of variety and are greedy for what is new and different. And yet here the entities that surround us are *equally manifest [offenbar]* as that which is simply *present-at-hand in the widest sense.*"

20. GA29/30 504: "Common sense cannot see the world for all the entities . . . that indifference in which it holds all the entities that move in its way, this indifference in the comportment toward entities is—itself rooted in something deeper—another reason for not seeing the world."

21. GA29/30 211: "Boredom and its emptiness consist here in subjection to being that denies itself as a whole. What is going on here in the fact that being as a whole denies the possibility of acting and leaving undone for a *Da-sein*, a being-there, in the midst of this is possibility? All nay-saying is in itself a saying, i.e., a making manifest, bringing into the open."

22. GA29/30 8: ". . . they are concepts of a unique sort. In each case they include the whole, they are *incepts*. But they are incepts in a second sense which is just as essential and connected with the first sense; in each case they always include the human being that does the including along with its Dasein."

23. GA29/30 214: "This denial is not accidental, but rather is as denial corresponding to its essence—in itself an announcing of the fallow possibilities of the Dasein that finds itself there in such a subjection in the midst of beings. In such announcing of denied possibilities there is something of a hint of something else, of possibilities as such, of fallow possibilities *as* possibilities of Dasein."

24. GA29 216: "Beings that deny themselves as a whole do not announce just any of my possibilities, they do not give a report about these possibilities. Rather, this announcing in the denying is an *appeal*, that which properly enables the *Dasein* in me."

25. GA29/30 215–16: "But what concerns a possibility as such, this is *that which enables* it, what confers pos*sibility* on it itself as this something possible. This outermost and first that enables all possibilities of Dasein as possibilities, that which supports the can-be of Dasein and its possibilities, is affected by beings which deny themselves as a whole."

26. GA20/30 485–86: "*Contemplation of origin* and analytic thus mean questioning back to the ground of inner possibility or, as we also put it briefly, questioning back to this ground in the sense of *fathoming*, plotting a ground [*Ergründen*]. Contemplation of origin is not a grounding in the sense of factic proof, but rather an inquiry into the origin of essence, letting it spring forth out of the ground of essence, fathoming in the sense of showing the ground of the possibility of the structure as a whole."

27. Heidegger speaks of "bringing *Hingehaltenheit* to its extremity, to that which originally enables Dasein in the midst of beings thus manifest as a whole and thus brought into the open" (GA29/30 216).

28. GA29/30 211: "But this *withdrawal* [*Entzug*] of entities that shows itself in entities is only possible when Dasein as such can no longer go on, is spellbound as *Da-sein*, as being-there, and indeed as a whole. Thus that which holds open being as a whole and makes it at all accessible as such, . . . precisely this must simultaneously bind [*binden*] Dasein to itself, spellbind [*bannen*] it."

29. The point is "to break the spell [*Bann*] of that need—the need to stay away [*Not des Ausbleibens*] from distress as a whole—in short, in order to be for once

equal to that deep need and open for it, in order to experience it truly as distressing" (GA29/30 246).

30. GA29/30 252: "Whence and why this necessity of relating breadth and extremity—horizon and eye-opening moment—world and loneliness? What kind of 'and' is this that stands between both. . . . ? Is the essence of the unity and juncture of both ultimately a *breach*? What does this *brokenness of Dasein in itself* mean? We name it the finitude of Dasein and ask: *What is finitude? . . . Is it not the finitude of Dasein that sounds in the basic mood of profound boredom and attunes us to the core?*"

31. GA29/30 306: "*Zur Endlichkeit gehört Un-folge, Grund-losigkeit, Grundverborgenheit.*" ("To finitude belongs in-consequence, ground-lessness, ground-concealment.")

32. GA29/30 428: ". . . this going back [*Zurück*] into the improper is the extinguishing of the eye-opening moment, which extinguishing does not after all just happen by external causes, but rather is grounded essentially in the momentousness [*Augenblicklichkeit*] of the eye-opening moment."

33. Dasein suspects, regarding its source, "that this original springing from the source [*Urspringen*] flows from it, i.e., holds itself, is held in the state of vitality constantly flowing from it [*Entquellen*]" (GA61 194).

34. According to Heidegger, "we have also already together snuck out of the danger zone of Dasein in which we perhaps overtax ourselves when it comes to taking over Dasein. That distress as a whole stays away today is shown perhaps most pointedly in the fact that presumably no one today is any longer overtaxed with Dasein" (GA29/30 247).

Chapter 3

1. The present essay draws upon the following early writings of Heidegger which are concerned importantly with logic in the then-current sense: "Das Realitätsproblem in der modernen Philosophie" (1912), "Neuere Forschungen über Logik" (1912), Review of "Charles Sentroul, *Kant und Aristoteles*" (1914), *Die Lehre vom Urteil im Psychologismus* (1914), and *Die Kategorien- und Bedeutungslehre des Duns Scotus* (1915; with a 1916 conclusion, "Das Kategorienproblem"). I refer to these works in the text according to the pagination in *Frühe Schriften* (GA1). All translations are my own, though I have consulted previous translations where available.

2. This was a *systematic* site of the "modernist/anti-modernist" controversy and was crucial to the neo-Scholastic strategy, made official by the encyclical *aeterni patris* (1879), of showing that "modern" thinkers and issues—including modern science—could be absorbed into a scholastic framework. Thus Wolf-Dieter Gudopp, *Der junge Heidegger* (Frankfurt: Verlag Marxistische Blätter, 1983), 21,

sees in Heidegger's early work a decisive neo-Scholastic "anti-modernism." But in his more nuanced look at Heidegger's early milieu, Hugo Ott, *Martin Heidegger: Unterwegs zu seiner Biographie* (Frankfurt: Campus Verlag, 1988), 74f., provides strong evidence that Heidegger was deeply attracted to "modernist" positions.

3. Since I don't have space to defend it fully here, I now simply note that I will translate *Bedeutung* and its kin as "signification" and *Sinn* and its kin as "meaning." The "preparatory work" Heidegger mentions in the cited passage has affinities with the task of translating natural language into logical form (e.g., symbolic notation). This raises the question of Heidegger's relation to the emergence of symbolic logic, though I shall not discuss that here. In the 1912 logic review Heidegger takes note of Russell and Whitehead, only to argue that "logistics" is unable to reach the "genuine logical problems," i.e., "where the conditions of possibility [for the "mathematical handling of logical problems"] lie" (GA1 42–43).

4. Heidegger's reconstruction is based in part on *De modis significandi*, subsequently shown to have been authored not by Scotus but by the Scotist Thomas of Erfurt. Since this has little bearing on Heidegger's text, given its *problemgeschichtlich* approach (GA1 196, 399), I will continue to refer to "Scotus" in my essay.

5. Thus, as Manfred Brelage has shown in his "Transzendentalphilosophie und konkrete Subjektivität," *Studien zur Transzendentalphilosophie* (Berlin: de Gruyter, 1965), 72–230, Heidegger's project can be seen as one of several efforts, characteristic of late Neo-Kantianism, to complete or go beyond a formal "objective logic" of principles of valid knowledge. Among these efforts to contextualize critical epistemology, in addition to Heidegger's, Brelage discusses Husserl's transcendental phenomenology, the later Natorp's *Denkpsychologie*, R. Hönigswald's "monadology," and N. Hartmann's "gnoseology/ontology."

6. Immanuel Kant, *Critique of Pure Reason*, trans. Norman Kemp Smith (London: Macmillan, 1968), 98 (A59/B84), 100 (A62–63/B87).

7. Ibid., 97 (A58/B82).

8. The term *Wirklichkeitsbereich* (realm of reality) is Heidegger's usual term for the categorial "sort" to which different objects and object domains (*Gegenstandsgebiete*) belong, though he sometimes uses related terms like *Daseinsform*, *Wirklichkeitsform*, *Wirklichkeitsweise*, etc. Given the connection between these concepts and the subsequent ontic/ontological difference, it is noteworthy that here "being" is restricted to the status of a category governing a single realm of reality, viz., that of sensibly existent entities. Heidegger expressly repudiates this usage, "deriving from Lotze," in WS 1925–26 (GA21 64).

9. Such as "being," "causality," "occurrence," etc. The empirical scientist is not concerned with such categories, but with relations in and among the objects of the science. But—and this is how Heidegger understands the "rational" dimension of science—it is evident that, in abstraction from the categorial dimension, the

scientist's "theoretical" approach to objects loses its *meaning*, as will be discussed below.

10. Cf. Brelage, op. cit., 103.

11. It is beyond the scope of this essay to show, not *that* Heidegger's approach is phenomenological in these early writings (which cannot be doubted), but the *sort* of appeals to phenomenology Heidegger makes. I must express the same caveat with respect to Dilthey. For good discussions of both issues see the articles in Frithjof Rodi, ed., *Dilthey-Jahrbuch* 4 (1986–87).

12. In the logic review, and then again verbatim in his Dissertation, Heidegger credits Husserl with having "broken the psychologistic curse," while at the same time approving Natorp's claim that the Neo-Kantians had "little more to learn" from Husserl's anti-psychologistic arguments (GA1 19, 64).

13. Emil Lask, *Die Logik der Philosophie und die Kategorienlehre*, in *Gesammelte Schriften* II, ed., Eugen Herrigel (Tübingen: J.C.B. Mohr, 1923), 6. References to this 1911 work will be given in the text, abbreviated LP. On my use of the term "ontological difference" above, compare the formulations in which Lask directly anticipates those Heidegger will use (e.g., LP 21, 46, 117, 121). For some discussion see Steven Galt Crowell, "Lask, Heidegger, and the Homelessness of Logic," *Journal of the British Society for Phenomenology* 23/3 (1992): 222–39.

14. Neo-Kantians did not, of course, view categories as psychic forms of thought. But they did understand categories to be formal principles of valid knowledge. This reference to knowledge is rejected by Lask, however, for whom "knowledge" implies a knowing subject. The relation between the mode of reality called "validity" and the "subject" of knowledge is one Lask tries to determine, rather than assume definitionally, though it is just here that Heidegger finds him to fail, as will be discussed below. See also Crowell, "Lask, Heidegger," op. cit.

15. A full account of what Lask has in mind here would require entering into his distinction between *Erleben* and *Erkennen*, coupled with an exposition of his "functional form/material" distinction. The aim of the present essay is more limited, but see Steven Galt Crowell, "Husserl, Lask, and the Idea of Transcendental Logic," in *Husserl and the Phenomenological Tradition*, ed., Robert Sokolowski (Washington, D.C.: Catholic University of America Press, 1988), 63–85.

16. Though as early as 1912 Heidegger argues that the question of whether Kant's philosophy was in essence psychologistic or transcendental had already been decided "in favor of the transcendental-logical interpretation" (GA1 19), the very existence of a psychologistic interpretation bespoke an unclarity in Kant's ideas (e.g. of "syntheses"). Lask, in any case, did not absolve Kant fully of psychologism (LP 243–262). Heidegger is known to have taken a renewed interest in Kant around the time of *Sein und Zeit*, primarily because he saw a way to interpret Kant phenomenologically (GA25 6). See Daniel Dahlstrom, "Heidegger's Kantian Turn: Notes to His Commentary on the *Kritik der reinen Vernunft*," *Review of Metaphysics* XLV (1991): 329–361. Dahlstrom does not deal with the Kant interpreta-

tion in Heidegger's earliest work, where Heidegger seems to have found it convenient to share some of Husserl's contemporaneous reservations about Kant.

17. This term—central to the analysis of "worldhood" in *Sein und Zeit*—is translated by MacQuarrie and Robinson as "involvement," though as Ernst Tugendhat points out in *Der Wahrheitsbegriff bei Husserl und Heidegger* (Berlin: de Gruyter, 1970), 290, "there is probably no other language which contains a single word for the two significations" involved in Heidegger's use of it. This issue deserves separate treatment, but it is enough at present to point out that if the *Beziehungsganzes* of logical space is the precursor of *Sein und Zeit*'s *Bewandtnisganzheit*, an important moment in this transformation is Heidegger's adoption of Lask's term, *Bewandtnis*, as an explication of logical form. I mark the problematic novelty of this term by leaving it for the most part untranslated in my text.

18. This forms the theme of Lask's second major treatise, *Die Lehre vom Urteil* (1912), in *Gesammelte Schriften*, op. cit., esp. 413ff. Future references to this treatise are given in the text, abbreviated LU.

19. In Lask's terms, this is a process in which the already *logos*-immanent paradigmatic meaning "becomes immanent" to the subject (LU 414). Though Heidegger praised Lask's judgment book as being "even more significant for the theory of categories than his *Logik der Philosophie*" (GA1 407), and though in his Dissertation he employs Lask's "metagrammatical subject-predicate theory" (GA1 177–181; and in 1912 GA1 32f.), the notion of "transcendence" which contrasts with such "becoming immanent" renders a noetic inquiry into the relation of object and judgment impossible for Lask, and, as will be seen in Section 4 below, it is here that Heidegger turns to phenomenology.

20. The cited phrases are Lask's (LU 425), and he introduces them in explicit opposition to Husserl's concept of *Sinn* in the *Logische Untersuchungen*. For further discussion of Lask's concept of transcendence, see Crowell, "Husserl, Lask," op. cit., 73–78. For Lask, transcendental logic was a logic of an object "untouched by all subjectivity," yet due to the "original sin" of knowledge, this object is a "lost paradise" (LU 426).

21. A phrase anticipating the idea of categories as "formal indicating" concepts which "interpret a phenomenon in a particular way" (GA61 86), that Heidegger introduces in WS 1921/22. Here categories are "at life in life itself," eminent ways "in which life comes to itself" (GA61 88).

22. For some discussion see Roderick M. Stewart, "Signification and Radical Subjectivity in Heidegger's *Habilitationsschrift*," *Man and World* 12 (1979): 360–386; and John Caputo, "Phenomenology, Mysticism, and the *Grammatica Speculativa*: A Study of Heidegger's *Habilitationsschrift*," *Journal of the British Society for Phenomenology* 5 (1974): 101–117. In a forthcoming paper, "Kriegsnotsemester 1919: Heidegger's Hermeneutic Breakthrough," Theodore Kisiel provides an important critical corrective to Stewart's and Caputo's treatment of the *modi*. See

also Theodore Kisiel, *The Genesis of Heidegger's BEING AND TIME* (Berkeley/Los Angeles/London: The University of California Press, 1993), pp. 31, 515f.

23. This is related to Heidegger's observation that medieval thought "exhibits a lack of methodological self-consciousness" in the "modern" sense of "reflecting" on its "problems as *problems*," on the "possibility and manner of solving them." In a word, "medieval man is not *bei sich selbst* in the modern sense" (GA1 199). This is not without its advantages, according to Heidegger, for it precludes the errors of psychologism, but it also leads to the above-mentioned lack of a "precise [i.e., logically adequate] concept of the subject."

24. Heidegger goes into these matters in his 1912 essay on the problem of reality (GA1 1–15, esp. 13–15), which is background for his brief note in the *Schluss*.

25. In the end Heidegger rejects critical—or "scientific"—realism because it collapses the distinction between philosophy and empirical science. On Külpe's "naturalistic" view (e.g., in his 1902 *Die Philosophie der Gegenwart in Deutschland*), problems of knowledge were to be resolved ultimately by an "inductive metaphysics" which projects the results of the sciences of subject (psychology) and object (physics) to their ideal point of intersection. Already in 1912 Heidegger finds the "hypothetical" character of such metaphysics objectionable (GA1 15).

26. In SS 1925, for example, Heidegger identifies categorial intuition as one of the "fundamental discoveries" of phenomenology (GA20 63f.), and the report from the 1973 seminar in Zähringen suggests that Heidegger held the concept of categorial intuition to be the "flashpoint of Husserlian thought." See *Vier Seminare*, translated from the French seminar protocols by Curd Ochwadt (Frankfurt: Klostermann, 1977), 111.

27. In WS 1921–22 Heidegger himself investigates the "value and limits" of the form/material dichotomy, ultimately cautioning that it "is best to keep the concept of form separate from the concept of category" (GA61 86), a conclusion already implied in the idea of categorial form as the *Bewandtnis* of the "material."

28. This problem is addressed ultimately in Heidegger's "hermeneutic of facticity." See Theodore Kisiel, "Das Entstehen des Begriffsfeldes 'Faktizität' im Frühwerk Heideggers," *Dilthey-Jahrbuch*, op. cit., 91–120. I would only add that this hermeneutics is still explicitly conceived as transcendental philosophy. An interpretation of *Sein und Zeit* from this perspective can be found in Carl-Friedrich Gethmann, *Verstehen und Auslegung* (Bonn: Bouvier Verlag, 1974).

29. See John Caputo, *The Mystical Element in Heidegger's Thought* (Athens: Ohio University Press, 1978), esp. 145–152. Caputo correctly sees Heidegger's turn to Eckhart's mysticism as motivated by the desire for a "solution to the problem of truth, where truth is taken to be the correlativity or belonging together of thought and being" (151), and he speculates—again with good reason—that this solution aimed at a "realism in the form of . . . Husserl's *Logical Investigations*" (152), though such realism is far from Scholastic realism and quite close to transcenden-

tal idealism. But mysticism as such becomes an option because of the issue Heidegger specifically mentions: the "principle of the material determination of form" (GA1 402). Again Lask provides part of the background here: he describes the givenness of the ultimately alogical material as a mystical-sounding "*Versunkensein in sinn– und bedeutungsberaubten Impressionen*" (LP 84).

30. This problem preoccupies Heidegger from the beginning. In 1912 he mentions the suspicion that "the sharp separation of logic from psychology may not be achievable"; further, "the fact that the logical is embedded in the psychological" is a "peculiar and perhaps never fully clarifiable problem" (GA1 29–30). Again in 1914 he notes the question of "how the relation between the psychical reality and valid subsistence of the judgment is to be characterized" and wonders "whether a deeper solution of this matter can even become a goal" (GA1 176). In the present context, 1916, he suggests that the problem can be solved by a metaphysics of living spirit. In *Sein und Zeit*, however, he implies that "the separation of the real accomplishment and ideal content of the judgment" is altogether unjustified, that "psychologism" may indeed be "right to hold out against this separation" even if it does not clarify the (ontological) relation (GA2 287). This of course does not mean that Heidegger now accepts psychologism, though Tugendhat argues that he falls victim to a version of it nonetheless. See *Wahrheitsbegriff*, op. cit., 331f.; 340f.

Chapter 4

1. These are the transcripts of WS 1919–20, "Grundprobleme der Phänomenologie" (published meanwhile as GA58); SS 1920, "Phänomenologie der Anschauung und des Ausdrucks (Theorie der philosophischen Begriffsbildung)" (published meanwhile as GA59); WS 1920–21, "Einleitung in die Phänomenologie der Religion"; and the transcript of 10 lectures that Heidegger gave in Kassel in April 1925 under the title, "Wilhelm Dilthey's Forschungsarbeit und der Kampf um eine historische Weltanschauung" (published meanwhile in *Dilthey-Jahrbuch* 8 [1992–93], ed. Frithjof Rodi). These transcripts will be abbreviated hereafter as GP, PhA, PhR, K.

2. See Richard Schaeffler, *Frömmigkeit des Denkens? Martin Heidegger und die katholische Theologie* (Darmstadt: Wissenschaftliche Buchgesellschaft, 1978), p. 5.

3. In SZ this kind of criticism is still present (namely in the thematization of the problem of truth [SZ 216/259]), but is not given as much prominence as in the earlier lecture courses.

4. Heidegger's objection to mathematical logic is that it obscures the *meaning* of propositions (see GA1 42).

5. See also the discussion of "*Sinn*" (GA1 170 ff.). Connected with this is Heidegger's treatment of the problem of "method." His main suggestion is that method and object are not to be separated (see GA1 200f.; GA56/57 126, 181; GA58

135f.; GA61 23, 31, 59, 153, 160f.; GA9 9). It is for this reason that he welcomes phenomenology (as a "method" conforming wholly to the object), and that is why he says that there is no such thing as *the* phenomenology, i.e., understood as a "technique" or "method" (see GA24 467/328). For aspects of the *Habilitations-schrift* that anticipate important later themes, such as "facticity" (exemplified by Heidegger's interest in Scotus' concept of *haecceitas*), see Theodore Kisiel's detailed reconstruction in his paper "Das Kriegsnotsemester 1919: Heideggers Durchbruch zur hermeneutischen Phänomenologie," *Philosophisches Jahrbuch* 99 (1992): 105–122. See also his "The Genesis of *Being and Time*," *Man and World* 25 (1992): 21–37, esp. 22, 27.

6. The letter is quoted by Thomas Sheehan in his "Heidegger's Early Years: Fragments for a Philosophical Biography," in Thomas Sheehan (ed.), *Heidegger: The Man and the Thinker* (Chicago: Precedent, 1981), p. 8.

7. Let me nevertheless indicate the main points in brief. Neo-Kantianism is said to have formed its outlook not so much out of the "things themselves"—on the truly scientific grounds Heidegger thinks it should have been based on—but more by way of an emergency or embarrassment (KPM 246f. [cf. Dilthey, *Gesammelte Schriften*, Vol. 5, p. 357]; further GA20 17f., GA61 4; GA3 304ff.). Husserl is claimed to have fallen victim to Neo-Kantianism (KPM 247); the self-delimitation of phenomenology is said to be carried out not so much out of the "things themselves" as in blindly joining with the tradition. Existence-philosophy cannot seize upon existence itself, for its conceptual apparatus is quite inadequate. Finally, historicism strives for an "objective" knowledge of history (an impossible aim), rather than for an authentic historical "being" of human life, and the first not so much promotes but instead suppresses the second.

8. See GP 10-14-19 on the *"Ursprungsgebiet"* of philosophy: *"Das Schicksal der Philosophie! Tendenz in der Geschichte der Philosophie: immer neu anfangen, um es zu erreichen"*. "The fate of philosophy! Tendency in the history of philosophy to begin ever anew in order to reach the domain of origin."

9. This was the general tendency of the age; see GP 10-10-19; PhA 5-6-20; GA9 14f.

10. Edmund Husserl, "Philosophie als strenge Wissenschaft," *Logos* 1 (1910–11): 289–341, esp. 305, 337, 340.

11. For one of the best descriptions of the claims of phenomenology, embedded in a historical characterization, see H.-G. Gadamer, *Philosophical Hermeneutics*, tr. and ed. by D. E. Linge (Berkeley: University of California Press, 1976), pp. 131ff.

12. Characteristic of Heidegger's understanding of the fusion of philosophy and phenomenology is the following passage from SS 1920: "Phenomenology as a fundamental science is problematic as long as we have not explicated the concept of philosophy in phenomenological radicality" (PhA 5-20-20). See also GA61 18: "As

an object . . . philosophy has its own way of *being-had in a genuine manner*". See further PIA 247; GA20 108/79.

13. On several occasions, Heidegger will later return to Husserl's "principle of all principles." In retrospect, he will say in the sixties that he wanted to rethink exactly this principle and the specific "matter" of phenomenology (SD 69ff./62ff.). With the publication of Heidegger's early lecture courses, we now have a wide textual basis to reenact what we have so far known only from Heidegger's retrospective accounts, namely, that something remained unthought in the phenomenological call "to the things themselves" (see SD 84/77; see also the reference to SD in note 27 below).

14. See GA56/57 16f., 24, 32, 39. On p. 95 Heidegger observes that this circular character is an essential characteristic of all philosophy and an index of potentially genuine philosophical problems. For the purposes of this chapter, it may be of use to note that the circular character of philosophy was clearly stated by Dilthey in his *Das Wesen der Philosophy* (*Gesammelte Schriften*, vol. 5, pp. 343ff.; see esp. the following sentence: "one seems to have to know already what philosophy is when one sets out forming this concept out of facts"). §3 of GA56/57 (esp. p. 21) offers a Diltheyean approach to the problem, when the definition of philosophy is explored through the history of philosophy—an exploration that (just as with Dilthey) proves to be a dead end. For analogous considerations in the young Heidegger, see the last paragraph of Section I of this chapter.

15. GA56/57 131; GA61 187f.; GA63 14ff. The term "phenomemological hermeneutics of facticity" occurs four times in PIA 247–49. "Ontology" is not lagging behind either; for the expressions "ontological phenomenology," "phenomenological ontology," see GA61 60; for "ontology of facticity," see PIA 246.

16. We should realize, writes Heidegger in the Jaspers-review, that "life-philosophy . . . is tending towards the phenomenon of existence." "The pioneering element of Jaspers' work lies . . . in having directed attention to the problem of existence" (GA9 14f.). Heidegger's position on Kierkegaard will manifest a series of reservations in *Being and Time*; for some decisively positive hints in the earlier period, see GA9 41; GA63 5, 30. Characteristic of Heidegger's understanding of facticity, i.e., of opposing it to the "objectivity" pertaining to "theory," are the following assertions: "secure objectivity is indeed an insecure flight from facticity" (GA61 90); "to meditate upon universal validity is to misunderstand the fundamental meaning of facticity" (ibid. 87; see also 99 where facticity is said to be the "main matter in philosophy"). On the origin of the term "facticity," see Theodore Kisiel, "Das Entstehen des Begriffsfeldes 'Faktizität' im Frühwerk Heideggers," *Dilthey-Jahrbuch* 4 (1986/87): 91–120.

Recall also the relation of facticity to the earlier Scotian theme of *haecceitas* (note 5 above). Dilthey's turn to "life" can also be understood as a turn to facticity and individuality. For an interesting occurrence of the term *haecceitas* used very much in the later Heideggerian sense of facticity and *Da-sein*, see Wilhelm Dilthey, *Grundlegung der Wissenschaften vom Menschen, der Gesellschaft und der Ges-*

chichte, Volume 19, *Gesammelte Schriften*, edited by H. Johach and F. Rodi (Göttingen: Vandenhoeck & Ruprecht, 1982), p. 348: "The structure of life expresses itself in an individual facticity [*Tatsächlichkeit*], a *haecceitas*, which can be presented by the intellect as not necessary."

17. See the later explicit refutation of the notion of anthropology in KPM 202ff., 212. On the relation of Heidegger's questioning about the "I" to the status and emergence of the being-question, see my "Identität und Wandlung der Seinsfrage. Eine hermeneutische Annäherung," in *Mesotes. Supplementband Martin Heidegger* (Wien: Braumüller, 1991): 105–119.

18. GA63 15. Heidegger's analogy is the relationship between plants and botany, as if a particular conception of botany effected the being of plants. One way of understanding what Heidegger has in mind is that, if hermeneutics possesses facticity as an "object," it has tacitly changed its relation to it (see in *Being and Time* the characterization of existence as a kind of "business procedure" [SZ 294/340]). If one interprets one's facticity as an "object," one has already adopted a particular attitude to one's facticity, and thereby modified it intrinsically. Analogously, see SZ 8/28 regarding the being-question ("here what is asked about has an essential pertinence to the inquiry itself"), as well as the new concept of philosophy (SZ 38/62).

19. GA20 62ff./46ff. On this point, see Rudolf Bernet, "Husserl and Heidegger on Intentionality and Being," *Journal of the British Society for Phenomenology* 21 (1990): 143.

20. See GA20 147/107. See also the retrospective accounts (SD 84/77) referred to in note 13 above, as well as GA56/57 111. These show that the leading methodological insight of this critique was basically present already in 1919.

21. GA20 159/115, 178/128. The term "*unphänomenologisch*" crops up already in a 1923 remark stating that it is unphenomenological to hold up mathematics as the ideal of scientificity (GA63 72).

22. See GA20 155/112, 157f./113f., 178/128f. For Husserl's distinction, see his *Ideen*, vol. I, §76, *Husserliana*, III/1, ed. K. Schuhmann (The Hague: Nijhoff, 1976), p. 159.

23. See GA20 140/102, 157ff./113ff., 178/128f. The being-question simply cannot be dispensed with; all ontologies presuppose it, and even make use of it (ibid. 124/91). I discussed Heidegger's confrontation with Husserl in more detail in my paper "Zum Denkweg des jungen Heidegger. II. Unterwegs zu 'Sein und Zeit': Die Auseinandersetzung mit Husserl," *Annales Universitatis Scientiarum Budapestinensis, Sectio Philosophica* 22–23 (1990): 127–53.

24. GA20 131f./95f., 155f./113f., 162/117, 172/124; SZ 120/156. On this point, see Thomas Sheehan, "Heidegger's Philosophy of Mind," in G. Fløistad (ed.), *Contemporary Philosophy: A New Survey*, Vol. 4: *Philosophy of Mind* (The Hague: Nijhoff, 1983), p. 294; and John van Buren, "The Young Heidegger and Phenomenology," *Man and World* 23 (1990): 255.

25. The eminently phenomenological character of Heidegger's 1925 criticism of Husserl is emphasized by Walter Biemel in his paper "Heidegger's Stellung zur Phänomenologie in der Marburger Zeit," *Phänomenologische Forschungen* 6/7 (1978): 178f. Heidegger now undermines the very distinction of psychic act and ideal content, of which he was once a fervid supporter; he shows that anti-psychologism abandons the empirical realm to the psychologistic-naturalistic perspective. He shows in particular that, in the "natural" attitude, Husserl tends to "experience" reality, as his own words show, in a naturalistic way. Anti-psychologism is thus shown to be pervaded by naturalism. Rickert takes psychology as a kind of mechanics. The criticism of psychologism is significant and meaningful only as a critique of psychology, and not by opposing it to a realm of pure logic. (See GA20 160/115f., 172/124; GA21 89ff.) Cf. the quotations of GA1 29f. in Section I above.

26. Heidegger speaks of the "intellectualism of the Greeks" as early as GP 10-7-19 and in a note in PhA 6-26-20: *"griechisches Vorurteil der Allherrschaft des Wissenschaftlich-Theoretischen,"* "Greek prejudice of the total domination of the scientific and theoretical" (see further PIA 248f. and, comprehensively, Otto Pöggeler, "Heideggers Begegnung mit Dilthey," *Dilthey-Jahrbuch* 4 [1986/87]: 139f.). This is probably a Laskian influence; see my paper "Lask, Lukács, Heidegger: The Problem of Irrationality and the Theory of Categories" in Christopher Macann (ed.), *Martin Heidegger: Critical Assessments*, Vol. 2 (London: Routledge & Kegan Paul, 1992), pp. 373–405.

27. Phenomenology, which was ahistorical in Husserl (see GA63 75; K 22), and turned away from the history of philosophy, permitted Heidegger a new access to the tradition, one that may be called hermeneutical in that it rejected both mere thoughtless adoration of the past and the similarly self-evident and self-conceited contempt for it in the Enlightenment. The term that expresses this dynamic attitude is: *"Wiederholung"* (see SZ 385/437 and the title of §1; KPM 232; GA20 184ff./136ff.; the hitherto earliest occurrence of the term in its specifically Heideggerian sense known to me is GA61 80; for a detailed discussion, see John D. Caputo, "Hermeneutics As the Recovery of Man," *Man and World* 15 [1982]: 343–67). In the foreword of Heidegger's 1923 course on the hermeneutics of facticity we find significant passages sounding much like an autobiographical intimation: "Companions in my searching were Luther and Aristotle. . . . Kierkegaard gave impulses, and *Husserl gave me my eyes"* (GA63 5; my emphasis). This passage points in the same direction as the memories of the old Heidegger, namely, that while phenomenology meant for Husserl rejecting the authority of tradition and history, it became for him an important device to reappropriate it (see SD 86/78; see also US 95). Another fact hitherto known only from personal records—namely, that Heidegger was reluctant to accept Husserl's transcendental ego, because he regarded the historical ego as more original (see Gerda Walther's letter to Alexander Pfänder on June 20, 1919, quoted by T. Sheehan, "Heidegger's 'Introduction to the Phenomenology of Religion', 1920–21," *The Personalist* 60 [1979]: 312–24)—can now be ascertained in the published text of the 1919 courses (see GA56/57 85, 88f., 206).

On the theme of "destruction" in the early period, see GA9 3f., 6, 34; GA61 67, 96, 141; GA63 48, 75f., 89, 105, 107; PIA 245, 249f., 252; GA24 31f.

28. GA20 173f./125f. This definition was challenged already in 1923 (see GA63 25ff.). The criteria of philosophical criticism are also redefined. The only reasonable phenomenological criterion of critique is posed on motivational grounds; free-floating, purely "conceptual" questions are to be avoided (GA56/57 125ff.; see GA63 71), as are the free-floating "problems" proper to Neo-Kantian *"Problemgeschichte"* (GA63 5; later GA26 197/155; GA45 7f.). See Gadamer, *Wahrheit und Methode* (Tübingen: Mohr, 1975), pp. 358f.

29. See already in 1919: GA56/57 85, 71f. On July 8, 1920, F. J. Brecht noted the following: "Sense data as such are neither seen nor heard." Concerning *"Erfahrung,"* *"Grunderfahrung,"* in a hermeneutical-phenomenological sense, see GA9 6, 29, 32; GA61 21, 24, 38, 42, 91, 176; GA63 110; PIA 249, 253f., 264. The origin of Gadamer's later concept of hermeneutical experience lies clearly in these Heideggerian insights (see *Wahrheit und Methode*, pp. 329ff.).

30. Heidegger, as we now know, developed a "phenomenology of life" in his postwar lecture courses; H. Tanabe reported this in Japan in 1924 under the title: "A New Turn in Phenomenology: Heidegger's Phenomenology of Life" (see O. Pöggeler, "Neue Wege mit Heidegger?" *Philosophische Rundschau* 29 [1982]: 57; see also his "Zeit und Sein bei Heidegger," *Phänomenologische Forschungen* 14 [1983]: 155 and, more generally, his "Heidegger's Neubestimmung des Phänomenbegriffs," *Phänomenologische Forschungen* 9 [1980]: 132ff.).

31. See GA9 31, 32f., 36, 38; GA56/57 85, 88f., 117, 206; GA61 1, 76, 111, 159, 163; GA63, 83, 107; PhR passim. Heidegger frequently spoke of Dilthey's appreciation of Husserl (see GA56/57 165; GA20 30/24; K 7). This may have prompted him to assume the task of uniting the impulses of both thinkers.

32. See the references in note 9 above. That philosophy has life as its subject matter appears clearly from SZ 46/72. Heidegger says here that the expression "philosophy of life" amounts to nothing more than "botany of plants" (a pleonasm), and that in a genuine "philosophy of life" "there lies an unexpressed tendency towards an understanding of Dasein," i.e., existential analytic. An anticipation of this is GA9 14f., as quoted in note 16.

33. See Heidegger's use of *"Begriffssurrogat"* (GA9 10).

34. See, e.g., GA63 45: *"Was heißt irrational? Das bestimmt sich doch nur an einer Idee von Rationalität. Woraus erwächst deren Bestimmung?"* "What does irrational mean? This is still defined in terms of an idea of rationality. Where does this definition come from?" This view of Heidegger's was to be held through four decades up to the sixties (see SD 79). For a fuller discussion of Heidegger's treatment of rationalism and irrationalism, see my paper "Heidegger und Lukács. Eine Hundertjahresbilanz," I. M. Fehér (ed.), *Wege und Irrwege des neueren Umganges mit Heideggers Werk* (Berlin: Duncker & Humblot, 1991), pp. 43–70.

35. GA9 18f. See Christoph Jamme, "Heideggers frühe Begründung der Hermeneutik," *Dilthey-Jahrbuch* 4 (1986/87): 76. The terms "reification" (*Verdinglichung*), "reify," do appear several times in the early lecture courses; and this raises anew the question of parallels with G. Lukács, a thesis first presented by L. Goldmann; see my paper "Heidegger und Lukács. Überlegungen zu L. Goldmanns Untersuchungen aus der Sicht der heutigen Forschung," *Mesotes. Zeitschrift für philosophischen Ost-West-Dialog* 1 (1991): 25–38. In addition to occurrences of the term "*Verdinglichung*" quoted and examined in this paper, see also GA58 127, 187, 232.

36. GA63 42; PhA 6-15-20; GA20 19/17. See also the end of note 7.

37. BZ 26 (emphasis in original). These considerations should be seen against the background of the thesis that philosophy is always that of a particular present (GA63 18; PhA 5-6-20; see K 28f.), that the hermeneutic situation as a repetition-retrieval of the past is always present-centered (PIA 237; GA58 256; GA61 3; GA63 35f.). In the Kassel lectures, historicity has a priority even over the being-question. The being-question, viz., doing philosophy, appears as just one way of being historical. This anticipates a major tension, inherent in SZ, between system and history, ontology and historicity (see O. Pöggeler, "Heidegger's Neubestimmung des Phänomenbegriffs," p. 150, and *Heidegger und die hermeneutische Philosophie* [Freiburg/München: Alber, 1983], pp. 164, 227ff., 286). The "first principle of all hermeneutics" is clearly directed against historicism, which confines itself to "analysing" history as a "*Betrachtungsgegenstand der Methode*," and thus stands in the way of being genuinely historical (the subject of this description being a fantastic ahistorical nowhere man or transcendental ego). As a result, any kind of history-*making* becomes impossible. By contrast, "*Nur wer sich selbst zu verstehen versucht, vermag die gewesene Geschichte zu verstehen, die in ihr liegende 'Kraft des Möglichen' zu wiederholen*" (Pöggeler, *Heidegger und die hermeneutische Philosophie*, p. 273). See also the last sentence of note 7 and the citations of GA61 in note 16 above.

Chapter 5

1. *Einführung in die Metaphysik, Gesamtausgabe*, vol. 40 (hereafter GA40), p. 18. All translations in this study, unless indicated otherwise, are mine.

2. "Wege zur Aussprache" in *Aus der Erfahrung des Denkens (1910–1976), Gesamtausgabe*, vol. 13 (hereafter GA13), p. 18.

3. For an examination of Heidegger's thought and teaching activities prior to 1928, see Theodore Kisiel, *The Genesis of Heidegger's Being and Time* (Berkeley: University of California Press, 1993); and John van Buren, *The Young Heidegger: Rumor of the Hidden King* (Bloomington: Indiana University Press, 1994).

4. *Was ist das—die Philosophie?* 4th ed. (Pfullingen: Neske, 1966), p. 19. See also GA1 193–206. Among other texts, the latter passage in his 1915 "Die Ka-

tegorien- und Bedeutungslehre des Duns Scotus" (written in 1915 as his *Habilitationsschrift* at Freiburg) indicates his early search for a more essential, primordial "idea" of philosophy. Heidegger, however, is not exploring the psychology of worldviews like Karl Jaspers; he is not developing a phenomenology of the acting person like Max Scheler. See, for instance, Karl Jaspers, *Psychologie der Weltanschauungen* (first published in 1919) (Munich-Zürich: Piper, 1985) and Max Scheler, "Vom Wesen der Philosophie und der moralischen Bedingung des philosophischen Erkennens" (first published in 1917), *Vom Ewigen im Menschen, Gesammelte Werke*, vol. 5, 5th ed. (Bern-Munich: Francke, 1968), pp. 63–99. See also Max Scheler, "Philosophische Weltanschauung" (first published in 1928), *Späte Schriften, Gesammelte Werke*, vol. 9 (Bern-Munich: Francke, 1976), pp. 75–84. For Heidegger's review (written sometime between 1919 and 1921) of the abovementioned work of Jaspers, see GA9 1–44.

5. *Beiträge zur Philosophie (Vom Ereignis)*, GA65 45, 436; see also 43, 48.

6. SD 61–80. Heidegger's lectures on Nietzsche, given between 1936 and 1946, are essential for understanding the background and development of his idea of the "end of philosophy."

7. Regarding Fichte as the "forerunner" of the teleological method and the transformation of his thought into a constructive dialectic, see GA56/57 37 and also GA65 200.

8. Edmund Husserl, *Ideas: General Introduction to Pure Phenomenology*, tr. by W. R. Boyce Gibson (New York: Collier Books-Macmillan, 1962), p. 83. When Heidegger reflects on this text, however, he quotes directly only a few words from it in GA56/57 109.

9. For a discussion of the significance of GA61 and GA63 for the development of Heidegger's thought, see Th.C.W. Oudemans, "Heideggers 'logische Untersuchungen'," *Heidegger Studies* 6 (1990): 86–94.

10. Heidegger's break with Rickert becomes quite clear in "Phenomenology and Transcendental Philosophy of Values" (the second course included in GA56/57; the reference indicated in the text is taken from this course). For a brief discussion of this issue, see my review of GA56/57 in *Research in Phenomenology* 19 (1989): 304–310. Hans-Georg Gadamer speaks of Heidegger's early journey of thought as freeing, liberating (*Befreiung*) himself (especially in 1922) from Neo-Kantian philosophy, from pseudo-Hegelianism, and from pseudo-modern Thomism. See Hans-Georg Gadamer, "Die Hermeneutik und die Diltheyschule," *Philosophische Rundschau* 38 (1991): 170. See also Theodore Kisiel, "The Genesis of *Being and Time*," *Man and World* 25 (1992): 22 (Kisiel speaks of Heidegger's "methodological crossroad" in GA56/57). An incisive analysis of the significance of "The Idea of Philosophy and the Problem of Worldview" as Heidegger's breakthrough to the "matter" of thinking can be found in Theodore Kisiel, "Das Kriegsnotsemester 1919: Heideggers Durchbruch zur hermeneutischen Phänomenologie," *Philosophisches Jahrbuch* 99 (1992): 118–21.

11. See especially GA1 198 (surrender, tradition), 199 (transcendence), 406 (theoretical attitude, error), 409 (medieval teleological worldview), 410 (philosophy as worldview).

12. Heidegger's claim, however, that medieval philosophy is characterized by a basic lack of methodology-consciousness may be too general and even questionable, especially in the light of the systematic reflection by the great medieval thinkers (e.g., Aquinas, Bonaventure) on the relationship between philosophy (reason) and theology (faith), as well as on other methodological issues (e.g., *objectum materiale, objectum formale quod, objectum formale quo*).

13. See, for instance, the following works of Heidegger: GA2 21–26 (§5), 36–52 (§7); GA24 26–32 (§5); GA61 11–40. See also Kisiel, *The Genesis of* Being and Time.

14. *Was ist das—die Philosophie?*, p. 28.

15. Martin Heidegger, "Das Wesen der Philosophie," *Jahresgabe der Martin Heidegger Gesellschaft* (1987): 21–30, 27.

16. Ibid., pp. 27, 26, 23.

17. The English text of the poem is from *Poetry, Language, Thought*, tr. Albert Hofstadter (New York: Harper & Row, 1975), p. 6.

Chapter 6

1. The present article represents a reworked version of the first part of an article published in French under the title, "Temps de l'Etre, temps de l'Histoire. Heidegger et son siècle" in *Les Temps Modernes*, Number 552–553 (July/August, 1992): 89–140.

2. Martin Heidegger, "Anmerkungen zu Karl Jaspers 'Psychologie der Weltanschauungen,'" GA9 3–6. See also Karl Löwith's quotations from a letter that Heidegger sent him during this same period in Karl Löwith, "Les implications politiques de la philosophie de l'existence chez Heidegger," *Les Temps Modernes* 2, (1946): 343–360. Unless otherwise indicated, all translations are my own.

3. Hannah Arendt, "Martin Heidegger ist achtzig Jahre alt," *Merkur* 10 (1969): 893–902; Karl Löwith, *Appendix zu Heidegger. Denker in dürftiger Zeit. Zur Stellung der Philosophie im 20. Jahrhundert*, vol. 8 of *Sämtliche Schriften* (Stuttgart: Metzler, 1984), pp. 294–96; H.-G. Gadamer, Introduction to Martin Heidegger, *Der Ursprung des Kunstwerkes* (Stuttgart: Reclam, 1962), pp. 102–107.

4. GA9 40–41; Martin Heidegger, "Methodische Einleitung" in "Einleitung in die Phänomenologie der Religion," unpublished Oskar Becker transcript of Heidegger's WS 1920–21 Freiburg lecture course.

5. See for example Rudolf Bultmann, "Die liberale Theologie und die jüngste

theologische Bewegung" (1924), in *Glauben und Verstehen*, vol. I (Tübingen: Mohr, 1933), pp. 1–25; for the analysis of Heidegger's courses "Einleitung in die Phänomenologie der Religion" and "Augustinus und der Neuplatonismus" in relation to these theological topics see O. Pöggeler, *Der Denkweg Martin Heideggers* (Pfullingen: Neske, 1963); J.A. Barash, *Martin Heidegger and the Problem of Historical Meaning*, Phaenomenologica 102 (Dordrecht: Nijhoff/Kluwer, 1988); GA60.

6. Ernst Cassirer and Martin Heidegger, "Davoser Vorträge. Davoser Disputation," appendix to *Kant und das Problem der Metaphysik*, 4th enlarged edition (Frankfurt: Klostermann, 1973), p. 256.

7. See for example BZ 21; GA24 241; GA2 178, 395 (pagination of the earlier Niemeyer Edition noted in GA).

8. Although Heidegger refers in this quotation to Descartes, its implications for the problem of textual interpretation extend well beyond the limits of Cartesian thought.

9. On the problematic character of some of the implications of Heidegger's thought in this regard, see Frank H. W. Edler, "Philosophy, Language, and Politics: Heidegger's Attempt to Steal the Language of the Revolution in 1933–34," *Social Research* 57 (1990): 197–238; J. A. Barash, "L'image du monde à l'époque moderne: les critères de l'interprétation historique dans la perspective du dernier Heidegger" in *Heidegger: Questions Ouvertes* (Paris: Osiris/Collège International de Philosophie, 1988), pp. 143–157; and J. A. Barash, "Über den geschichtlichen Ort der Wahrheit. Hermeneutische Perspektiven bei Wilhelm Dilthey und Martin Heidegger" in *Martin Heidegger: Innen- und Aussenansichten* (Frankfurt am Main: Suhrkamp, 1989), pp. 58–74. Concerning the continuing debate on contextualism in the contemporary human sciences, see the enlightening discussions in *Meaning and Context: Quentin Skinner and his Critics*, ed. James Tully (Cambridge: Polity Press, 1988).

Chapter 7

1. I am grateful to Ted Kisiel and John Drabinski for their comments on an earlier draft of this paper.

2. A recent but particularly blatant example is Hubert L. Dreyfus, *Being-in-the-World* (Cambridge, Mass.: MIT Press, 1991). Dreyfus acknowledges that "phenomenological critique must be complemented by what Heidegger in *Basic Problems* calls 'deconstruction'" [sic], but that constitutes the sole reference to destructuring in what is presented in the book's subtitle as "A Commentary on Heidegger's *Being and Time*, Division I."

3. A recent example of an interpretation that finds *Being and Time* "inherently destructive of tradition" can be found in Richard Wolin's *The Politics of Being* (New York: Columbia University Press, 1990), p. 32.

4. For Derrida's own account of the word *déconstruction*, see especially "Lettre à un ami japonais," in *Psyché. Inventions de l'autre* (Paris: Galilée, 1987), pp. 387–393; trans. David Wood, "Letter to a Japanese Friend," in David Wood and Robert Bernasconi (eds.), *Derrida and Différance* (Evanston: Northwestern University Press, 1988) pp. 1–5.

5. On Derrida's adoption of Heidegger's term destruction (*Destruktion*), see R. Bernasconi, "Seeing Double: Destruktion and Deconstruction," in Diane P. Michelfelder and Richard E. Palmer (eds.), *Dialogue and Deconstruction* (Albany: State University of New York Press, 1989), pp. 233–250. On Heidegger's own subsequent interpretation of *Being and Time*, see F.-W. von Herrmann, *Die Selbstinterpretation Martin Heideggers* (Meisenheim am Glan: A. Hain, 1964).

6. For a more concrete presentation of these issues as they relate specifically to §§15–18 of *Being and Time*, see R. Bernasconi, "Heidegger's Destruction of *Phronesis*," *The Southern Journal of Philosophy* XXVIII (Supplement): 127–147 and Walter Brogan's "Response," pp. 149–153.

7. See also Samuel Ijsseling, "Heidegger and the Destruction of Ontology," *Man and World* 15 (1982): 3–16.

8. It is worth noting that the focus on primordial experience that is so prominent in *Being and Time* is absent from the account of destructuring to be found in *Basic Problems of Phenomenology*.

9. Already in 1928 Heidegger's remarks about destructuring are mainly directed at dispelling the misunderstandings that the term attracted (GA26 197/155), a task that continued through such texts from the 1950s as *Zur Seinsfrage* (GA9 416–417) and *Was ist das—die Philosophie?* (Pfullingen: Neske, 1956), pp. 33–34, until "Zeit und Sein" in 1962 (SD 9/9).

10. The important question here of whether "the twin tasks of freeing history and of constituting a tradition are . . . incompatible" is posed by Dennis Schmidt in *The Ubiquity of the Finite* (Cambridge, Mass.: MIT Press, 1988), pp. 217–219. One could understand the present essay as an attempt to explore Heidegger's resources for engaging this problem.

11. Yves Charles Zarka, *La décision métaphysique de Hobbes* (Paris: Vrin, 1987), pp. 113–114.

12. In *History of the Concept of Time* Heidegger similarly proposes that the (never completed) investigation of time should proceed from Bergson, through Kant and Newton, to Aristotle (GA20 11/8–9).

13. See Francisco Suarez, *Disputationes Metaphysicae* II (Hildesheim: Georg Olms, 1965), Disputatio XXXI, pp. 224–228; trans. Norman Wells, *On the Essence of Finite Being as such, On the Existence of that Essence and their Distinction* (Wisconsin: Marquette University Press, 1983), pp. 44–51.

14. For an examination of Heidegger's discussion of Suarez, see Carlos G.

Norena, "Heidegger on Suarez: The 1927 Marburg Lectures," *International Philosophical Quarterly* 23 (1983): 407–424. For a reading of Suarez by one of France's leading Heidegger scholars, see Jean-François Courtine, *Suarez et le système de la métaphysique* (Paris: Presses Universitaires de France, 1990).

15. For confirmation, see Pierre Aubenque, "La thèse de Kant sur l'être et ses origines aristotéliciennes," in A. Cazenave and J.-F. Lyotard (eds.), *L'art des confins. Mélanges offerts à Maurice Gondillac* (Paris: PUF, 1985), pp. 513–533. Some reservations can be found in Hans Seigfried, "Kant's Thesis about Being anticipated by Suarez?" in L. W. Beck (ed.), *Proceedings of the Third International Kant Congress* (Dordrecht: Reidel, 1972), pp. 510–520.

16. Aristotle, *Categories* V 2a11–18. Heidegger discusses this passage in *Nietzsche*, Vol. II (Pfullingen: Neske, 1961), pp. 405–407; trans. Joan Stambaugh, *The End of Philosophy* (New York: Harper and Row, 1973), pp. 6–8.

17. See Alain Boutot, *Heidegger et Platon* (Paris: Presses Universitaires de France, 1987), pp. 55–56. Heidegger notes that the German word *Anwesen* also carries the sense of property, albeit in the sense of landed property, premises, or estates rather than of possessions (GA24 153/109; GA31 53). This reliance on the language of property as a source for the language of ontology clearly warrants further investigation.

18. Heidegger does not go as far as Charles Kahn who argues that the concept of existence is not a subject of philosophical reflection until after Aristotle. See "Why Existence does not Emerge as a Distinct Concept in Greek Philosophy," *Archiv für Geschichte der Philosophie* 58 (1976): 323–334.

19. There are important differences, however. "The characteristics of *essentia* developed in reference to what is produced in producing or else to what belongs to producing as producing. The concept of *ousia*, in contrast, lays more stress on the producedness of the produced in the sense of things disposably present at hand" (GA24 153/109).

20. In *Metaphysical Foundations* Heidegger insisted also that the terms "essence" and "existence" had to be understood in terms of their temporal determination (GA26 183–184/145–146).

21. *Nietzsche*, Vol. II, pp. 402–403; *The End of Philosophy*, p. 4. Somewhat surprisingly, Heidegger does not emphasize as much as he might the incongruency between the Latin and the Greek terms.

22. It should be clear from my account of the discussion of essence and existence in *Basic Problems* that I do not understand Heidegger to have said there that "Christian creationism fits hand in glove with the categories of Greek ontology." See J. D. Caputo, *Heidegger and Aquinas* (New York: Fordham University Press, 1982), p. 88. The difference between the account in *Basic Problems* and that found in "Metaphysics as History of Being" is not located at the historiological level.

23. *Nietzsche*, Vol. II, p. 415; *The End of Philosophy*, pp. 14–15.

24. It should be emphasized that §6 of *Being and Time* is not so much a statement of method as an outline of what would have appeared in the Second Part of *Being and Time* had it been completed, just as §5 offers a sketch of Part One.

25. An exception is David Hoy's "History, Historicity, and Historiography in *Being and Time*," Michael Murray (ed.), *Heidegger and Modern Philosophy* (New Haven: Yale University Press, 1978), pp. 329–353, esp. pp. 338, 348. However, Hoy's focus is not on destructuring as such.

26. For further discussion of Heidegger's distinction between *Historie* and *Geschichte*, see R. Bernasconi, *Heidegger in Question* (Atlantic Highlands: Humanities Press, 1993), chap. 9. Although, as I note there, Heidegger's use of these terms in his later thought is somewhat different from that found in *Being and Time*, the sense of *Historie* as a narrative remains important in the context of the present essay.

27. It is, of course, true that the famous sentence from §7, namely, "higher than actuality stands *possibility*" (SZ 38/63), points in the same direction, but because it occurs in the context of a discussion of the phenomenological method, the link with destructuring is not yet clear at that point in the book.

28. Paul Ricoeur indicates the role of this sentence in Heidegger's overall schema, while at the same time acknowledging certain aporias in the account. See *Temps et Récit*, Vol. 3 (Paris: Seuil, 1985), pp. 113–114; trans. Kathleen Blamey and David Pellauer, *Time and Narrative*, Vol. 3 (Chicago: University of Chicago Press, 1988), p. 76.

29. *Der Satz vom Grund* (Pfullingen: Neske, 1971), p. 171; trans. R. Lilly, *The Principle of Ground* (Bloomington: Indiana University Press, 1991), p. 102.

30. "Vom Nutzen und Nachteil der Historie für das Leben," in *Sämtliche Werke, Kritische Studienausgabe*, Vol. 1 (Berlin: de Gruyter, 1980), p. 264; trans. R. J. Hollingdale, "On the Uses and Disadvantages of History for Life," in *Untimely Meditations* (Cambridge: Cambridge University Press, 1983), p. 72.

31. For an extensive discussion of this passage that attempts to find in it, not a philosophy of history, but a rethinking of political judgment, see Peg Birmingham, "The Time of the Political," *Graduate Faculty Philosophy Journal* 14–15 (1991): 25–45.

32. J. Caputo, *Radical Hermeneutics* (Bloomington: Indiana University Press, 1987), p. 91. Caputo actually says "deconstructive." "Deconstruction" is his translation of *Abbau* (p. 64). *Abbau* does not appear in *Being and Time*, but in *Basic Problems* Heidegger refers to *Destruktion* as *ein kritischer Abbau* (GA24 31/22–23).

33. The distinction is not consistently marked across the various editions of *Being and Time*, nor by the English translation. Compare, for example, the

Weltgeschichtliche of GA2 504, line 23, with the *Welt-geschichtliche* of *Sein und Zeit* (Halle: Max Niemeyer, 1927), p. 381, line 28. Two paragraphs later, the English translation (p. 433, line 40) introduces a hyphen not found in the German texts.

34. It has been suggested that the much quoted remark about destiny (*Geschick*) as "the historizing of the community, of the people" (SZ 384/436) also points in the direction of multiplicity and heterogeneity. See Birmingham, "The Time of the Political," p. 30. While I agree both that Heidegger in this context leaves the priority of the individual Dasein over the collective Dasein of the community unchallenged and that he is still far from advocating the politics of National Socialism, nevertheless, this conception of destiny readily allows for certain cultures to be designated "exotic or alien," as I quoted Heidegger as doing above.

35. *Identität und Differenz* (Pfullingen: Neske, 1957), p. 38; trans. J. Stambaugh, *Identity and Difference* (New York: Harper and Row, 1969), p. 48.

36. Ibid., p. 30/41.

37. I have taken up this question in "'We Philosophers': Barbaros m deis eisit" in Rebecca Comay and John McCumber (eds.), *Endings: The Question of Memory in Hegel and Heidegger* (Evanston: Northwestern University Press, forthcoming).

Chapter 8

1. GA29/30 107. Compare *Hölderlins Hymnen "Germanien" und "der Rhein"* (GA39 190); *Nietzsche* (Pfullingen: Neske, 1961), vol. 1, p. 124. For the following, see *Beiträge zur Philosophie*, GA65 204.

2. Compare my essay "West-East Dialogue: Heidegger and Lao-tzu" in G. Parkes (ed.), *Heidegger and Asian Thought* (Honolulu: University of Hawaii Press, 1987), pp. 47–48. Heidegger finally broke off this endeavor concerning Lao-tzu, and sought to discover the other beginning out of the European tradition itself, e.g., in the paintings of Paul Klee. See the remarks on this in my book *Die Frage nach der Kunst* (Freiburg/Munich: Alber, 1984), pp. 26ff.

3. See G. Neske (ed.), *Erinnerung an Martin Heidegger* (Pfullingen: Neske, 1977), p. 215f. The discussion of "illumination" also points to the East-Asian tradition, though Heidegger actually takes it from Humboldt (see US 268). *Identität und Differenz* (Pfullingen: Neske, 1957), p. 65, for example, shows that Heidegger combines the moment from *Sein und Zeit*, the site of the moment in the *Beiträge*, and the sudden of his later works. Around 1960 Heidegger liked to point to notes for his "major work," for which "only" the language had escaped him. These efforts seem to have shattered Heidegger. His way of thinking during the last twenty years of his life still lies completely in the dark. See my comments on this in "Wächst das Rettende Auch? Heideggers Letzte Wege" in the memorial volume for Martin

Heidegger's 100th birthday edited by W. Biemel and F.-W. von Herrmann, *Kunst und Technik* (Frankfurt: Klostermann, 1989).

4. On this topic see my essays "Bergson und die Phänomenologie dur Zeit" in B. Adams et al. (eds.), *Aratro Corona Messoria. Festgabe für Günther Pflug* (Bonn: Bouvier, 1988), pp. 153ff.; "Heideggers Begegnung mit Dilthey," *Dilthey-Jahrbuch* 4 (1987): 121ff. Cf. the lecture "Der Vorbeigang des letzten Gottes" in Otto Pöggeler, *Neue Wege mit Heidegger* (Freiburg/Munich: Alber, 1992), pp. 465ff.

5. In my opinion, this methodological and not the factical aspect of the required atheism—or a philosophy that holds to the differences between atheism, theism, and pantheism—must be emphasized. In comparison, see Theodore Kisiel, "War der frühe Heidegger tatsächlich ein 'christlicher Theologe'?" in A. Gethmann-Siefert (ed.), *Philosophie und Poesie* (Stuttgart: Frommann, 1988), Vol. 2, pp. 59ff.

6. See *Wegmarken* (Frankfurt: Klostermann, 1976), p. 11; and for the following, see pp. 25, 11. Regarding Kierkegaard as the prophet of indirect communication, see Jaspers, *Psychologie der Weltanschauungen* (Berlin: Springer, 1971; 6th ed.), p. 376.

7. *Wegmarken*, p. 40; and, for the following, pp. 29f., 44. Regarding formal indication, see my essay "Heideggers logische Untersuchungen" in "Forum für Philosophie" (ed.), *Martin Heidegger. Innen- und Aussenansichten* (Frankfurt: Suhrkamp, 1989).

8. See SZ 338/388, 190/235. In his vague relationship to Hegel, Kierkegaard did not become clear about the fact that Hegel, when he wrote the *Phenomenology of Spirit*, gave the final form to his philosophy by adopting the dialectic of the later Plato and its Neoplatonic interpretation. See my essay "Geschichte, Philosophie, und Logik bei Hegel" in H.-Ch. Lucas and G. Planty-Bonjour (eds.) *Logik und Geschichte in Hegels System* (Stuttgart: Frommann, 1989), pp. 101ff.

9. SZ 172/216, 165/208, 142/181, 258/302.

10. SZ 299/346. For the following, see 300/346–47, 307f./354f., 326/373–74. Regarding the quotation from Goethe, see Jaspers, *Psychologie der Weltanschauungen*, pp. 55, 274; GA20 441/319; SZ 288/334. Concerning the notion of chance, see SZ 300/346–47.

11. SZ 328/376; for the following, see 349/400, 344/394, 258/302, 302/349, 386/438, 354/405.

12. SZ 371/422; for the following, see 347/398, 385/437, 391/444.

13. While "destruction" determines the character of philosophizing, the "moment" is developed in *Sein und Zeit* for Dasein in the full sense of the word. The unpublished third division would have had to show how temporal interpretation as formally indicative hermeneutics and as schematizing gives philosophy a logic that can do justice to the orientation of time to the moment. Vladimir Vukićević tries to show that Oskar Becker, Carl Friedrich von Weizsäcker, and Ernst Tugendhat are

unable to appreciate the unique quality of Heidegger's "logical investigations"; see his *Logik und Zeit in der phänomenologischen Philosophie Martin Heideggers (1925–1928)* (Hildesheim: Olms, 1988). For the general context here, see my essay "Zeit und Hermeneutik" in G. Abel and J. Salaquarda (eds.) *Festschrift für W. Müller-Lauter* (Berlin: de Gruyter, 1989).

14. SZ 235/278. Kierkegaard refers to the Aristotelian description of the transition from possibility to actuality as *kinesis* and does not present time as a series of now-points; Heidegger's criticism is consequently short-sighted and unjustified. In addition, Kierkegaard proceeds from open Socratic questioning to faith, something which Heidegger does not sufficiently take into account.

15. SZ 427/479; for the following, see 423/475, 338/387–88.

16. "Was ist Metaphysik?," p. 42, in *Wegmarken*, p. 121; see Heidegger's remark in Otto Pöggeler, *Der Denkweg Martin Heideggers* (Pfullingen: Neske, 1983; 2nd ed.), p. 350.

17. *Sophist* 242. On this theme, see Hans-Georg Gadamer, "Der Platonische Parmenides und seine Nachwirkung" and Wilhelm Anz, "Responsio zu H.G. Gadamers Vortrag," *Archivio di Filosofia* LI (1983): 39ff.

18. GA29/30 373ff., 300. For the following see SZ 384/436. For the general theme, compare my essay "Heideggers politisches Selbstverständnis," in A. Gethmann-Siefert and O. Pöggeler (eds.), *Heidegger und die praktische Philosophie* (Frankfurt: Suhrkamp, 1988), pp. 17ff.

19. *Die Psychologie der Weltanschauungen*, p. 256; for this theme, see also Günther Wohlfahrt, *Der Augenblick* (Freiburg/Munich: Alber, 1982).

20. GA39 111. Heidegger's interpretation of Hölderlin is undoubtedly dated and onesided; see my introduction to the anthology Ch. Jamme and O. Pöggeler (eds.), *Jenseits des Idealismus. Hölderlins letzte Homburger Jahre* (Bonn: Bouvier, 1988), pp. 9ff.

21. SD 58. For the following, see Hans Erich Nossack, *Nach dem letzten Aufstand* (Frankfurt: Suhrkamp, 1981), p. 398.

22. See the account of notes by Hermann Mörchen, *Adorno und Heidegger* (Stuttgart: Klett-Cotta, 1981), p. 557f. For what follows, see GA63 24f.; GA20 108f./129f.; GA26 211/165–66; GA29/30 103ff. Regarding *numen* and the numinous, see *Parmenides*, GA54 59.

23. See Emmanuel Levinas, *Die Spur des Anderen* (Freiburg/Munich: Alber, 1983), pp. 209ff., esp. p. 235; Keiji Nishitani, *Was ist Religion?* (Frankfurt: Insel, 1982), p. 310. In contrast to the starting points of Levinas and Nishitani, see the comments in my book *Heidegger und die hermeneutische Philosophie* (Freiburg/Munich: Alber, 1982), pp. 359ff. For the following, see the chapter "Todtnauberg" in my *Spur der Worts. Zur Lyrik Paul Celans* (Freiburg/Munich: Alber, 1986), pp. 259ff.

Chapter 9

1. Karl Jaspers, *Philosophische Autobiographie* (München: R. Piper, 1977), p. 92–93; translated as "On Heidegger," *Graduate Faculty Philosophy Journal* 7 (1978): 108–109.

2. Theodore Kisiel, "The Missing Link in the Early Heidegger," in Joseph J. Kockelmans (ed.), *Hermeneutic Phenomenology: Lectures and Essays* (Washington, D.C.: University Press of America, 1988), p. 25.

3. Julius Ebbinghaus, "Julius Ebbinghaus," in Ludwig J. Pongratz (ed.), *Philosophie in Selbstdarstellungen*, Vol. 3 (Hamburg: Felix Meiner), p. 33.

4. GA56/57 18; GA58 58, 62, 204–205; GA61 7, 182–83; GA63 5, 14, 27, 46, 106. For SS 1920 (GA59), see "Phänomenologie der Anschauung und des Ausdrucks (Theorie der philosophischen Begriffsbildung)," June 17, 1920, transcript by Franz-Josef Brecht, in the *Archiv der Dilthey-Forschungsstelle, Ruhr-Universität*, Bochum, Germany; I am grateful to Professor Friedrich Hogemann for permission to cite from this manuscript. For WS 1920–21, see Thomas Sheehan, "Heidegger's 'Introduction to the Phenomenology of Religion,' 1920–21," *Personalist* 60 (1979): 322 (hereafter abbreviated as "IPR"). For SS 1921 (GA60), see Otto Pöggeler, *Der Denkweg Martin Heideggers*, 2d ed. (Pfullingen: Neske, 1983), pp. 40–43 (hereafter abbreviated as "DMH").

5. Theodore Kisiel, "Why the First Draft of *Being and Time* Was Never Published," *Journal of the British Society for Phenomenology* 20 (1989): 5.

6. William J. Richardson, "Verzeichnis der Vorlesungen und Übungen von Martin Heidegger," in his *Heidegger: Through Phenomenology to Thought* (The Hague: Martinus Nijhoff, 1963), pp. 664.

7. Edmund Schlink, "Weisheit und Torheit," *Kerygma und Dogma* 1 (1955): 6.

8. Otto Pöggeler, "Destruction and Moment" in this volume, p. 155; *Neue Wege mit Heidegger* (Freiburg: Karl Alber, 1992), pp. 466–67.

9. Karl Löwith, *Mein Leben in Deutschland vor und nach 1933: Ein Bericht* (Stuttgart: J.B. Metzlersche Verlagsbuchhandlung, 1986), p. 29.

10. Heinrich Schlier, "Denken in Nachdenken," in Günther Neske (ed.), *Erinnerungen an Heidegger* (Pfullingen: Neske, 1977), p. 219.

11. W.R. Boyce Gibson, "From Husserl to Heidegger: Excerpts from a 1928 Diary," *Journal of the British Society for Phenomenology* 2 (1971): 74.

12. Gerhard Ebeling, *Lutherstudien*, Vol. II, *Disputatio de Homine, 1. Teil, Text und Traditionshintergrund* (Tübingen: J.C.B. Mohr, 1977), p. ix.

13. Johannes Baptist Lotz, "Im Gespräch" and Hartmut Buchner, "Fragmentarisches" in Neske (ed.), *Erinnerungen an Heidegger*, pp. 157, 51.

14. "Contributions to *Der Akademiker*, 1910–1913" (German and English), trans. John Protevi in *Graduate Faculty Philosophy Journal* 14–15 (1991): 486–519; see also Thomas Sheehan, "Heidegger's *Lehrjahre*," in J.C. Sallis, G. Moneta, and J. Taminiaux (eds.), *The Collegium Phaenomenologicum* (Kluwer Academic Publishers, 1988), pp. 77–137.

15. Curd Ochwadt and Erwin Tecklenborg (eds.), *Das Mass des Verborgenen: Heinrich Ochsner (1891–1970) zum Gedächtnis* (Hannover: Charis-Verlag, 1981), p. 92; Martin Heidegger and Elisabeth Blochmann, *Briefwechsel, 1918–1969*, ed. Joachim W. Storck (Marbach am Neckar: Deutsche Schillergesellschaft, 1989), pp. 9–13; GA56/57 134; DMH 326.

16. Hugo Ott, *Martin Heidegger: Unterwegs zu seiner Biographie* (Frankfurt: Campus, 1988), p. 106–108.

17. GA58 205, 61–62. Regarding Heidegger's interest in mysticism at this time, see also GA56/57 5, 18, 211; GA58 107, 212; GA61 7; John van Buren, *The Young Heidegger: Rumor of the Hidden King* (Bloomington: Indiana University Press, 1994), Chaps. 7 and 14; and Theodore Kisiel, *The Genesis of Heidegger's Being and Time* (Berkeley: University of California Press, 1993), Chap. 2.

18. Heidegger and Blochmann, *Briefwechsel*, p. 16.

19. Sheehan, "Heidegger's *Lehrjahre*," p. 94.

20. Martin Luther, *D. Martin Luthers Werke, Briefwechsel*, Vol. I (Weimar: Hermann Böhlaus, 1883ff.), p. 359/*Luther's Works*, Vol. XLVIII (Philadelphia: Fortress Press, 1955f.), p. 112. Hereafter abbreviated as "WA." Unless otherwise indicated the volume numbers given in Roman numerals refer to the volumes in the main body of the German edition of Luther's works.

21. Heidegger and Blochmann, *Briefwechsel*, p. 16.

22. For Heidegger's reading of these phenomena, as well as kairological time, in Augustine, medieval mysticism, Luther, Pascal, and Kierkegaard, see my *The Young Heidegger*, Chaps. 8, 14.

23. DMH 39–42; cf. *Holzwege*, GA5 (Frankfurt: Klostermann, 1977), p. 367/*Early Greek Thinking*, tr. David Farrell Krell and Frank A. Capuzzi (New York: Harper & Row, 1975), p. 53.

24. Cf. *Einführung in die Metaphysik*, GA40 (Frankfurt: Klostermann, 1983), p. 110/*An Introduction to Metaphysics*, tr. Ralph Manheim (New Haven: Yale University Press, 1959), pp. 102–103.

25. Schlink, "Weisheit und Torheit," p. 6; cf. GA58 204.

26. For Luther's critique of Aristotle, cf. Friedrich Nitzsch, *Luther und Aristoteles* (Kiel, 1883); Peter Peterson, *Geschichte der aristotelischen Philosophie im protestantischen Deutschland* (Leipzig: Felix Meiner, 1921), p. 34; and Gerhard Ebeling, *Luther*, trans. R.A. Wilson (Philadelphia: Fortress Press, 1970), pp. 76–92.

27. Helmar Junghans, "Die probationes zu den philosophischen Thesen der Heidelberger Disputation Luthers in Jahre 1518," *Lutherjahrbuch* 46 (1979): 35.

28. Junghans, "Die probationes zu den philosophischen Thesen," p. 35; WA I 363/XXXI 55.

29. Ebeling, *Luther*, pp. 89–92. For Luther's appropriation of Aristotle, cf. Nietzsche, *Luther und Aristoteles*, pp. 25–34.

30. For Kierkegaard's reading of Aristotle, see GA63 42; John D. Caputo, *Radical Hermeneutics: Repetition, Deconstruction, and the Hermeneutic Project* (Bloomington: Indiana University Press, 1987), pp. 11–35; Georg J. Stack, *Kierkegaard's Existential Ethics* (Alabama: University of Alabama Press, 1977).

31. WA LVI 239, 441–42/XXV 225, 433–35; cf. 329–30, 218–19/317, 204.

32. Nitzsch, *Luther und Aristoteles*, pp. 30–31, 39.

33. WA LVI 238–46, 374–80/XXV 223–32, 364–70; WA XLIV 703–705/VIII 171–72; Nitzsch, *Luther und Aristoteles*, pp. 28–29.

34. WA XLII 106–176/I 141–236; GA61 182; GA20 404/292; GA2 253/235.

35. Thomas Sheehan, "Heidegger's Early Years: Fragments for a Philosophical Biography," *Listening* 12 (1977): 11.

36. WA *Deutsche Bibel* VII 23–25/*Reading in Luther*, ed. C.S. Anderson (Minneapolis: Augsburg Publishing, 1967), pp. 211–12.

37. Soren Kierkegaard, *Training in Christianity*, trans. Walter Lowrie (Princeton: Princeton University Press, 1972), p. 83.

38. Soren Kierkegaard, *Either/Or*, Vol. I, tr. Walter Lowrie (Princeton: Princeton University Press, 1971), p. 38.

39. GA61 92, 2–3, 170. For the details of Heidegger's deconstructive repetition of Aristotle, see the essays by Franco Volpi and Walter Brogan in this volume, as well as my *The Young Heidegger*, Chap. 10.

40. Hans-Georg Gadamer, *Heideggers Wege: Studium zum Spätwerk* (Tübingen: J.C.B. Mohr, 1983), p. 142.

41. See my *The Young Heidegger*, Chap. 14.

42. Gadamer, *Heideggers Wege*, p. 29.

43. Heidegger, "Drei Briefe Martin Heideggers an Karl Löwith," in Dietrich Papenfuss and Otto Pöggeler (eds.), *Zur philosophischen Aktualität Heideggers*, Vol. 2: *Im Gespräch der Zeit* (Frankfurt: Vittorio Klostermann, 1990), pp. 28–29.

44. Heidegger and Blochmann, *Briefwechsel*, p. 16.

45. GA9 47–67; "Phenomenology and Theology," in James G. Hart and John

C. Maraldo (eds.), *The Piety of Thinking* (Bloomington: Indiana University Press, 1976), pp. 5–21.

Chapter 10

1. For a more detailed factual and conceptual account of the virtually unknown religious interregnum in Heidegger's career from 1917 to 1919, see Theodore Kisiel, *The Genesis of Heidegger's BEING AND TIME* (Berkeley/Los Angeles/London: The University of California Press, 1993), Chap. 2; on the KNS-Schema, see Chap. 1, and on the two schematisms from the religion courses, see Chap. 4.

2. I am indebted to the late Ada Löwith for access to these letters, and to Klaus Stichweh for assistance in deciphering them.

3. Quotations are from student transcripts of the course of WS 1920–21. The forthcoming GA-edition of this course will also be a composite of four extant transcripts. So much for the "principle" of an *Ausgabe letzter Hand*!

4. This letter dated August 19, 1921, has been published in Dietrich Papenfuss and Otto Pöggeler (eds.), *Zur philosophischen Aktualität Heideggers*, Vol. 2: *Im Gespräch der Zeit* (Frankfurt: Klostermann, 1990), pp. 27–32, esp. p. 29.

5. Theodore Kisiel, "Diagrammatic Approach to Heidegger's Schematism of Existence," *Philosophy Today* 28 (Fall 1984): 229–241. Supplemented by "Professor Seigfried's Misreading of my Diagram and Its Source," *Philosophy Today* 30 (Spring 1986): 72–83.

6. WS 1927–28 (GA25 198, 368); SS 1928 (GA26 52, 73, 266); WS 1929–30 (GA29/30 460); SS 1930 (GA31 25, 61, 68, 76, 126, 131); SS 1931(GA33 17); WS 1931–32 (GA34 313).

Chapter 11

1. See especially Heidegger's lecture courses of WS 1921–22 (GA61), SS 1922 (GA62), SS 1924 (GA18), WS 1924–25 (GA19), WS 1925–26 (GA21), and SS 1926 (GA22), as well as his 1922 essay on Aristotle (PIA).

2. *Aristoteles: Metaphysik IX*, GA33.

3. Hans-Georg Gadamer, *Heideggers Wege: Studium zum Spätwerk* (Tübingen: J.C.B. Mohr, 1983), p. 32.

Chapter 12

1. See PIA. For a full and interesting account of the historical background of this essay and details leading to its discovery, see "The Missing Link in the Early

Heidegger" by Theodore Kisiel in Joseph J. Kockelmans (ed.), *Hermeneutic Phe-nomenology: Lectures and Essays* (Washington, D.C.: University Press of America, 1988), pp. 1–40. See also Rudolf Makkreel, "The Genesis of Heidegger's Phenome-nological Hermeneutics and the Rediscovered 'Aristotle Introduction' of 1922," *Man and World* 23 (1990): 305–320.

2. For example, in WS 1921–22 Heidegger offered the course entitled *Phä-nomenologische Interpretationen zu Aristoteles* (GA61), and that summer he lec-tured again on Aristotle's ontology and logic (GA62). In 1922–23, he also gave seminar exercises on Book VI of the *Nichomachean Ethics*, *De Anima* and *Meta-physics* VII. Heidegger's courses on Aristotle became fewer after the publication of *Being and Time*, but they continued into the 1930s.

3. Among Heidegger's most well-known students of Aristotle were Hannah Arendt, Hans-Georg Gadamer, and Leo Strauss. Other students who were Aristotle scholars were Walter Bröcker, Ernst Tugendhat, Helene Weiss, and Fridolin Wip-linger.

4. See in particular the above-cited article by Theodore Kisiel entitled "The Missing Link in the Early Heidegger."

5. In his essay *"Ousia et Grammè"* in *Marges* (Paris: Les Éditions de Minuit, 1972), pp. 64ff., Jacques Derrida suggests that the entire force of Aristotle's think-ing hinges on the tiny word *hama*.

Chapter 13

1. GA20, 2nd. ed., 30; GA21 114, 88. Double quotation marks signify a cita-tion, single quotation marks mention of a word. I am indebted to my colleagues John McCarthy, Thomas Prufer, and Robert Sokolowski for helpful criticisms and comments on the penultimate draft of this paper.

2. Before Heidegger's critique of Husserl's philosophy is examined, a word should be said, at least parenthetically, about the significance he attaches to what he considers Husserl's "three decisive discoveries": intentionality, categorial intui-tion, and the original sense of the A priori. In a play on the motto "to the things themselves" or "back to basics" (*zur Sache selbst*), Heidegger asserts that, inas-much as it encompasses the complete set of particular beings and ways of relating to them (*die Gesamtheit der Verhaltungen und die Gesamtheit des Seienden*), the first decisive discovery, intentionality, determines the "basic field" (*Sachfeld*) of phenomenological research. The third discovery, the original sense of the A priori, determines the "basic respect" (*Sachhinsicht*) in which things are considered, namely, in regard to what it means, respectively, for them "to be." Husserl's second discovery, the categorial intuition, is decisive, in Heidegger's estimation, because it points to the way of treating things in that basic respect (*Behandlungsart*). The truth of an empirical judgment, for example, is "experienced" in a categorial intu-ition without being grasped as such; accordingly, philosophical method consists in

a self-critical analysis or elaboration of what Dasein unthematically does, understands, experiences, and so on. For Heidegger's complete review of these discoveries, see GA20 34–103; his summary of how they determine the *Sachfeld, Sachhinsicht,* and *Behandlungsart* can be found in GA20 103–108.

3. Paul Natorp, "Kant und die Marburger Schule," *Kantstudien* 17 (1913): 198: "If Kant and then even Cohen in his first writings did not cautiously avoid the language of psychology, still the tremendous divergence of the transcendental viewpoint from the psychological one was continually emphasized. Hence, in this connection there does not remain all that much for us to learn from Husserl's fine elaborations (in volume one of the *Logical Investigations*) which we could only applaud." See also GA20 31; GA21 51; and Hermann Cohen, *Die Logik der reinen Erkenntnis* (Berlin: Cassirer, 1902), p. 56; Heinrich Rickert, "Zwei Wege der Erkenntnistheorie," *Kantstudien* 14 (1909): 196, note.

4. GA21 35: "If we are honest, no one today can say what psychology is." Psychologism is thus not entirely wrong in claiming not to have been refuted, Heidegger notes, adding that his own line of questioning, while seeming to flirt with psychologism, challenges psychology's presuppositions just as much as those of the philosophy of logic and knowing; see GA21 92, 98 and SZ 217.

5. In a very broad sense, GA20 may be said to broach this criticism more from the side of psychology, while GA21 does so more from the side of logic. The focus of the criticism in GA21 is the *Logische Untersuchungen* (and the connection with Lotze), while GA20 traces Husserl's subsequent development.

6. In this regard Heidegger is anything but original; Husserl acknowledges Lotze's "decisive influence" upon him, and Lask proclaims that Lotze's development of the sphere of validity (*Geltung*) "has shown the way to philosophical research in the present." See Edmund Husserl, *Logische Untersuchungen, Erster Band,* 5th ed. (Tübingen: Niemeyer, 1968), p. 219 (hereafter cited as LU I) and *Logische Untersuchungen, Zweiter Band, Erster Teil,* 5th ed. (Tübingen: Niemeyer, 1968), p. 132, note (hereafter cited as LU II/1), as well as Emil Lask, *Die Logik der Philosophie und die Kategorienlehre* (Tübingen: Mohr, 1911), pp. 12, 272–273; ibid., p. 12: "Husserl introduced the Lotzean concept of validating into a completely determined area of Bolzano's thought, leading to a significant revision of the fundamental logical concepts." See Richard Falkenberg, "Hermann Lotze, sein Verhältnis zu Kant und Hegel zu den Problemen der Gegenwart," *Zeitschrift für Philosophie und philosophische Kritik* 150 (1913): 17–25 and Arthur Liebert, *Das Problem der Geltung* (Leipzig: Meiner, 1920²), p. 4.

7. "Things *are*," "events *happen*," "relations *obtain*," but "what we call actually true is a proposition that is *valid*." In this way Lotze differentiates four modes of actuality (*Wirklichkeit: Sein, Geschehen, Bestehen, Gelten*), a differentiation based in part on his influential interpretation of Plato's doctrine of ideas; see Hermann Lotze, *Logik,* ed. Georg Misch (Leipzig: Meiner, 1912) pp. 506–509, 511–512 and Liebert, *Das Problem der Geltung,* 205, n. 1; for Heidegger's critique, see GA21 63–88; Lotze's larger logic was first published in 1874 and re-issued in 1880.

8. Lotze, *Logik*, pp. 510–514. Evidence that the term *Geltung* had become, as Heidegger puts it (GA21 79, 62), a *Zauberwort* among his contemporaries: Leo Ssalagoff's "Vom Begriff des Geltens in der modernen Logik," *Zeitschrift für Philosophie und philosophische Kritik* 143 (1911): 145–190; Fritz Munch's *Erlebnis und Geltung: Eine systematische Untersuchung zur Transzendentalphilosophie als Weltanschauung* (Berlin: Reuther & Richard, 1913); Richard Hebertz, "Ueber Wert- und Geltens-Wirklichkeit," *Zeitschrift für Philosophie und philosophische Kritik* 161 (1916): 161–172; Arthur Buchenau, "Eine Geltungstheorie auf kritische Grundlage," *Zeitschrift für Philosophie und philosophische Kritik* 162 (1917): 112–126; Heinrich Rickert's "Ueber logische und ethische Geltung," *Kantstudien* 19 (1914): 182–221 and *Der Gegenstand der Erkenntnis* (1892[1]) (Tübingen: Mohr, 1921[5], 1928[6]); the already cited works by Lask and Liebert; Bruno Bauch's *Wahrheit, Wert und Wirklichkeit* (Leipzig: Meiner, 1923) I, II, 4 ("*Geltung und Gültigkeit*") and I, III, 1 ("*Wahrheit, Sachverhalt und Geltung*").

9. GA21 109, n. 4; GA20 67–68. Precisely through his clarification of the sense in which knowing is basically an intuition (and not a judgment) or, in other words, by locating *logos* within *nous*, Husserl is said by Heidegger to have thought the tradition to end; see GA21 110, 113–114.

10. *Logische Untersuchungen, Zweiter Band, Zweiter Teil*, 4th ed. (Tübingen: Niemeyer, 1968), pp. 121–22 (hereafter cited as LU II/2); GA20 59, 64–67; Robert Sokolowski, *Husserlian Meditations* (Evanston, Illinois: Northwestern University Press, 1974), p. 22: "Only when we are able to experience the object in its presence and in its absence do we encounter its identity."

11. In LU Husserl identifies three other senses of 'truth': the ideal relation obtaining between acts of intending and intuiting that coincide in knowing, the ideal realization (or fullness: *Fülle*) of something intended, or "the correctness of a judgment." But the primary meaning of truth is the coincidence of what is meant and what is given. See LU II/2 21, 23–35, and 122f.

12. LU II/2 122–124; Husserl identifies the senses of 'truth' in terms of acts and correlates, apart from whether the acts are "relating" (predicating) or "non-relating" (absolutely positing) or whether the correlates are "facts" or "other sorts of objects."

13. GA21 111–112; LU II/2 123: "4. . . . the truth as *correctness of the intention* (especially, e.g., *correctness of a judgment*). . . ."

14. GA21 112; GA20 70–71; see also GA21 111: "Validity in the sense of a proposition's being true is now led back to truth proper in the sense of identity."

15. Although expositing LU, Heidegger frequently employs terminology from *Ideen I*, for example, Husserl's use of "*leibhaftig*"; in regard to the latter, however, see Ernst Tugendhat, *Der Wahrheitsbegriff bei Husserl und Heidegger* (Berlin: de Gruyter, 1970), pp. 67–68, n. 78.

16. But not exclusively, see GA20 73 and GA21 109, n. 4, as well as the text

partially cited by Heidegger here: LU II/2 125. As for "nonrelating intentions,"
Heidegger notes explicitly: "If we emphasize the domain of expressions in particular, judgments as intentions in the form of [empty] assertions or as realizations of
what is asserted [*Urteile als Aussageintentionen oder Aussageerfüllungen*] need not
be considered; even nominal acts can enter into an adequation."

17. SZ 216–217: "How is the relation between some ideal, particular being
and something really present-at-hand [*zwischen ideal Seiendem und real Vorhan-
denem*] supposed to be grasped ontologically? . . . Does not the perverseness of the
question already lie in the point of departure, in the ontologically unclarified separation of the real and ideal?" See also SZ 366. In the summer semester of 1927
Heidegger turns this question on Husserl's notion of intentionality, arguing that
the latter evidences and presupposes, but cannot itself explain, transcendence; see
GA24 89–91, 249.

18. LU II/2 122: "1. If we hold fast to the concept of truth just suggested, then
the *truth* as correlate of an identifying act is a *fact*. . . ." LU II/2 140: "The relating
[sense of] 'to be' that predication brings to expression, for example, 'is,' 'are,' and
the like, is something not self-sufficient; if we fashion it into something fully concrete, then the respective fact emerges, the objective correlate of the complete
judgment." See, however, also LU II/2 125–126 where Husserl notes that 'truth' is
principally used "in relation to judgments and propositions or, better, their objective correlates, facts," while 'being' is spoken of "principally in relation to absolute
objects (nonfacts)." Yet, he also suggests that, in regard to his original breakdown
of the four senses of 'true,' the concepts of truth be related to the two senses
dealing with the acts, the concepts of being to the other two senses dealing with
the objective correlates.

19. GA21 112; Heidegger ignores non-relating intentions here.

20. GA20 70–71: "'To be' [*Sein*] here signifies nothing less than the *obtaining*
[*Bestand*] of the truth, of the *truth-relation* [*Wahrverhaltes*], the obtaining of the
identity."

21. To put it differently, in "'the chair is yellow' is true," "true" is iterative and
superfluous on the reading "the chair *is* yellow," but it is not iterative of the *fact* of
the chair's being yellow.

22. GA21 113; see Emil Lask, *Die Lehre vom Urteil* (Tübingen: Mohr, 1912),
pp. 23–24, 170–171.

23. GA20 73; LU II/2 140: "If under judgments people understand not only the
intentions of significance belonging to the present assertions but also the possible
fillings [of those intentions], fillings perfectly suited to them, then it is certainly
correct *that a being* [*ein Sein*] *can only be grasped in a judgment*. . . ."

24. GA20 130–131, 135–139; although, as explained subsequently, Heidegger
finds fault with the method of reduction in a crucial respect, he also understands it
in a quite positive sense fully in conformity with his own project; see GA20 136:

"This phenomenological turning-off of the transcendent thesis has the sole function of making present the particular being in regard to [the meaning of] its 'to be' [das Seiende hinsichtlich seines Seins]."

25. GA20 124, 140; see 125–129 for Heidegger's review of Husserl's development between LU and *Ideen*; see *Ideen zu einer reinen Phänomenologie und phänomenologischen Philosophie* (Tübingen: Niemeyer, 1980 [reprint of 1922 edition, original edition: 1913]), hereafter cited as *Ideen I*; see GA20 165–174 for a critical review of Husserl's attempts to develop a personalistic psychology after 1914. The key role of the 1910 essay "Philosophie als strenge Wissenschaft" is emphasized at GA20 127–128, 133–134, 164–167.

26. *Ideen I* 86: "Everything thinglike, given in the flesh [*leibhaft*], can also not be, [but] no experience given in the flesh can also not be. . . ."

27. *Ideen I* 77; see also 76: "A basic, essential distinction thus emerges between *being as an experience* and *being as a thing*."

28. GA20 147, 178, 165; in GA20 140–48 Heidegger demonstrates this point by examining four "determinations of the being of pure consciousness" from *Ideen I*, namely, that such being is "immanent," given "as 'absolute,'" "in need of nothing else to exist," and "pure" (see *Ideen I* 80–81, 77–87, 143–45, 121–22).

29. GA20 151: "I do not regard its existence and just by not doing that I do not regard the essence of its existence."

30. GA20 131–34, 153, 155; *Ideen I* 58; see also "Philosophie als strenge Wissenschaft," *Logos* 1 (1910/11): 298.

31. "Philosophie als strenge Wissenschaft," pp. 293–295, 302, esp. 312: "Considered in its own right, everything that we call 'a psychological phenomenon' in the broadest sense of psychology is a phenomenon and *not nature*."

32. "Philosophie als strenge Wissenschaft," pp. 314–15.

33. GA20 167–168; Heidegger even cites a letter from Husserl announcing a new personalistic psychology (published as Book Two of *Ideen zu einer reinen Phänomenologie und phänomenologischen Philosophie* in 1952).

34. I am grateful to Robert Sokolowski for clarification of this point.

35. Probably because it does not serve his immediate expository or pedagogical aims, Heidegger does not mention to his students Husserl's delineation of the components of intentionality (quality, material, content, representing object, and represented object) in LU; he simply introduces Husserl's distinction between noesis and noema in *Ideen I*, without any indication of how this distinction alters (deliberately) the earlier analysis. On the "subtle omissions and emendations" in Heidegger's presentation, see Rudolf Bernet, "Husserl and Heidegger on Intentionality and Being," *Journal of the British Society for Phenomenology* 21 (1990): 136–52.

36. In Husserl's defense, however, see Edmund Husserl, *Zur Phänomenologie des inneren Zeitbewußtseins (1893–1917)*, ed. Rudolf Boehm (Haag: Nijhoff, 1966), p. 127 (hereafter cited as Zb): "The entire phenomenology that I had in view in the *Logical Investigations* was phenomenology in the sense of the givennesses of the inner consciousness and that is, in any event, a self-contained domain."

37. Zb XXV. As discussed below, Bernet gives a quite different reading of Heidegger's foreword as well as of his brief mention of Husserl's investigations.

38. John Brough, "Husserl's Phenomenology of Time-Consciousness," *Husserl's Phenomenology: A Textbook*, ed. J. N. Mohanty and William R. McKenna (Washington, D.C.: The Center for Advanced Research in Phenomenology and University Press of America, 1989), p. 275: "What Husserl, in effect, insists on is the overthrow of the prejudice of the now, the view that one could not possibly be directly and immediately conscious of the past because it is gone, lost, and that one must therefore gain access to the past through present contents, contents really contained in the now of consciousness." In the same context Brough notes that this insistence is a mature view of Husserl, appearing roughly after 1909, and that its difference from an earlier view does not always surface adequately in the 1928 edition.

39. Brough, "Husserl's Phenomenology of Time-Consciousness," p. 276.

40. See also Zb 361–62, 371, and Sokolowski, *Husserlian Meditations*, pp. 138–45.

41. Heidegger's highlighting of '*worinnen*' is an obvious allusion to Kant's depiction of "pure form" (B34); the latter's account of time, while not to be confused with an account of the original, ecstatic temporality, is to be distinguished from "the vulgar concept of time"; see SZ 419–428; Bernet also calls attention to three such levels in "Die Frage nach dem Ursprung der Zeit bei Husserl und Heidegger," *Heidegger Studies* 3/3 (1987/88): 95, 98–99.

42. Zb 75: "They [the time-constituting phenomena] are not individual objects and not even individual events; the predicates of the latter cannot be meaningfully attributed to them. Thus there also cannot be any sense to saying of them (and in the same meaning saying) that they are now and previously have been, that they followed one another temporally or are contemporaneous with one another and so forth." See also Zb 126–27. In this connection Thomas Prufer notes that, insofar as consciousness is identified solely with acts intending objects, internal time-consciousness "is finally neither 'inner' nor 'temporal' nor 'consciousness.'" See his "Heidegger, Early and Late, and Aquinas," in *Edmund Husserl and the Phenomenological Tradition*, ed. Robert Sokolowski (Washington, D. C.: The Catholic University of America Press, 1989), p. 200.

43. Yet both philosophers recognize that they must find their way to the "original" phenomenon of time through what is constituted by it, resulting in the unavoidable but misleading talk of a "flow" (Zb 75) or an "ecstasis" (SZ 326–327, 334, 419–420); see Prufer, "Heidegger, Early and Late, and Aquinas," p. 212.

44. Bernet makes this point in "Zeit bei Husserl und Heidegger," p. 101.

45. GA24 429; see also 379: "Dasein is intentional only because it in its essence is determined by temporality."

46. In addition to the bare mention of the manuscripts in the lectures, Bernet maintains that two facts speak in favor of his claim that Heidegger had not studied them thoroughly and had developed his own analysis of time independently: first, the fact that Heidegger promised to see to the editing of the manuscripts only after SZ had been published and, second, the thin character of Heidegger's preface to the published manuscripts in 1928. All three facts, it seems to me, can be plausibly advanced as indicating the very opposite of Bernet's thesis. See Bernet's introduction to Edmund Husserl, *Texte zur Phänomenologie des inneren Zeitbewußtseins (1893–1917)*, ed. Rudolf Bernet (Hamburg: Meiner, 1985), p. LX and his "Zeit bei Husserl und Heidegger," p. 89.

47. While Husserl, as Rickert's successor, began lecturing in Freiburg in SS 1916, Heidegger began his career as a *Privatdozent* at Freiburg in the preceding semester, remaining there until 1923. After a somewhat shaky start, the relationship between the two men became quite close, especially after 1917. See Hugo Ott, *Martin Heidegger: Unterwegs zu seiner Biographie* (Frankfurt/New York: Campus, 1988), pp. 96–97, 102–105, 114–115. During a spring vacation that they both spent in Todtnauberg, Husserl made the suggestion to Heidegger that some of these investigations, edited by Edith Stein, be published, as they were with a preface by Heidegger in 1928; see Boehm's introduction in Zb XXIII-XXIV.

48. Prufer, "Heidegger, Early and Late, and Aquinas," p. 201.

49. A basic manifestation of this difference: Husserl arrives at the way in which the absolute flow of internal time-consciousness underlies the structure of objectifying acts through an analysis of perception or, more exactly, the adequate perception encompassing a primal impression, retentions, and protentions (see Zb 38); Heidegger, on the other hand, analyzes how temporality makes transcendence possible primarily in a practically engaged being-in-the-world, more basic than perception. See Bernet, "Zeit bei Husserl und Heidegger," pp. 102–103.

50. For Husserl the primal impression (*Urimpression*) as the first and original consciousness of the now enjoys a privileged status; see Zb 67: "The primal impression is the absolutely unmodified, the original source for all further consciousness and being. Primal impression has for its content what the word 'now' says, provided that the latter is taken in the most rigorous sense." See also Zb 14, 35, 325. However, it should also be noted that in lectures on "Fundamental Problems of Logic," lectures that he repeatedly offered since his arrival in Freiburg in 1916, Husserl refers to protentions or, better, a kind of protention in a much more specific and significant sense than that of the protention at the level of internal time-consciousness. These lectures have not been edited as a separate volume, though portions of them can be found in *Analysen zur passiven Synthesis aus Vorlesungs- und Forschungsmanuskripten 1918–1926* (Husserliana XI, 1966) and

in *Formale und transzendentale Logik* (Husserliana XVII, 1974). In these lectures, which Husserl also calls a "transcendental aesthetic," an account is given of the genetic, temporal constitution of passive syntheses prior to the distinction of act and object. The account in these lectures, some of which were offered during the period of Heidegger's tenure (and close contact with Husserl) at Freiburg, both anticipates Heidegger's own account of temporality and considerably neutralizes his criticism of Husserl.

51. Zb 127: "A perceiving does not in turn stand behind this perceiving, as if this flow itself were again a unity in a flow."

Chapter 14

1. Cf. J.-L. Marion, *Réduction et donation. Recherches sur Husserl, Heidegger et la phénoménologie* (Paris: PUF,1989); M. Henry, *Phénoménologie matérielle* (Paris: PUF, 1990); J.-F. Courtine, *Heidegger et la phénoménologie* (Paris: Vrin, 1990), pp. 207–247; M. Henry, "Quatre principes de la phénoménologie," *Revue de Métaphysique et de Morale* 96/1 (1991): 3–26.

2. Cf. M. Henry, "Philosophie et subjectivité" in *Encyclopédie philosophique universelle*, I (Paris: PUF, 1989), p. 46: ". . . the phenomenological reduction that aims precisely at pro-ducing subjectivity as a theme proposed for a comprehensive investigation."

3. Marion, *Réduction et donation*, pp. 305, 295.

4. See "Quatre principes de la phénoménologie," p. 10: "This catastrophic confusion of the world's manifestation together with the universal essence of the manifestation corrupts almost all philosophies making up western thought. . . ."

5. See "Quatre principes de la phénoménologie," especially pp. 3–15.

6. E. Fink, *VI. Cartesianische Meditation. Teil 1: Die Idee einer transzendentalen Methodenlehre* (Husserliana-Dokumente II/1) (Dordrecht/Boston/London: Kluwer, 1989). For a more complete presentation of this text, we refer to R. Bernet, "Différence ontologique et conscience transcendantale. La réponse de la *Sixième Méditation Cartésienne* de Fink" in E. Escoubas and M. Richir (eds.), *Husserl* (Grenoble: Millon, 1989), pp. 89–116.

7. GA20 147/107: "Husserl's primary question is simply not concerned with the character of the being of consciousness." Cf. 157/113–114, 172/124, 177–78/127–29.

8. E. Husserl, *Ideen zu einer reinen Phänomenologie und phänomenologischen Philosophie. Erstes Buch: Allgemeine Einführung in die reine Phänomenologie* (Husserliana III/1) (The Hague: Nijhoff, 1976); *Ideas Towards a Pure Phenomenology and Phenomenological Philosophy*, trans. F. Kersten (The Hague/Boston/London: Nijhoff, 1982). See especially "Zweiter Abschnitt: Die phänomenologische

Fundamentalbetrachtung." The most thorough critique of this presentation of the phenomenological reduction is to be found in Heidegger's lecture course of SS 1925 (GA20 §§10–12). For a first exposition of the main issues of this Heideggerian critique of the first book of the *Ideas* as well as his for more positive appraisal of the *Sixth Logical Investigation*, consult R. Bernet, "Husserl and Heidegger on Intentionality and Being," *The Journal of the British Society for Phenomenology* 21/2 (1990): 136–152.

9. E. Husserl, *Ideen zu einer reinen Phänomenologie und phänomenologischen Philosophie. Zweites Buch: Phänomenologische Untersuchuungen zur Konstitution* (Husserliana IV) (The Hague: Nijhoff, 1952); *Ideas Pertaining to a Pure Phenomenology and to a Phenomenological Philosophy. Second Book: Studies in the Phenomenological Constitution*, trans. R. Rojcewicz and A. Schuwer (Dordrecht/Boston/London: Kluwer, 1989). See especially "Dritter Abschnitt: Die Konstitution der geistigen Welt" and more specifically §50.

10. See R. Bernet, "Husserl's Concept of the World" in A.B. Dallery, C.E. Scott, and P.H. Roberts (eds.) *Crisis in Continental Philosophy* (Albany: State University of New York Press, 1990), especially pp. 7–16.

11. J.-F. Courtine was among the first to show that "in *Being and Time*, it is the analysis of anxiety that constitutes as it were the "repetition" of the Husserlian problematic of the *epoché* and of the phenomenological-transcendental reduction." See *Heidegger et la phénoménologie*, p. 234; and already "L'idée de la phénoménologie et la problématique de la réduction" in J.-L. Marion and G. Planty-Bonjour (eds.), *Phénoménologie et métaphysique* (Paris: PUF, 1984), p. 232.

12. See Marion, *Réduction et donation*, especially pp. 79–104 and already "L'étant et le phénomène" in Marion and Planty-Bonjour (eds.), *Phénoménologie et métaphysique*, pp. 172–196.

13. *Réduction et donation*, p. 93. Marion mentions still a third aspect of the depth of the phenomenon of being that we have not discussed within the compass of our discussion, and that leads Heidegger to examine in a more and more pressing manner not only the being of beings, but also "the sense of being" or "being without beings" (p. 107). By exploring in depth the question of the phenomenon of being understood as the phenomenality of the phenomenon, Heidegger's procedure would thus have ended in disclosing this paradoxical phenomenon which is the manifestation "of nothingness."

Chapter 15

1. Edmund Husserl, *Logische Untersuchungen, Zweiter Band, Erster Teil* (Husserliana XIX/1) (The Hague: Martinus Nijhoff, 1984), p. 32/*Logical Investigations*, Vol. 1, trans. J.N. Findlay (London: Routledge & Kegan Paul, 1970), p. 270.

2. *Logische Untersuchungen*, p. 31/270.

3. *Ideen zu einer reinen Phänomenologie und phänomenologischen Philosophie*, Vol. 1, in *Jahrbuch für Philosphie und phänomenologische Forschung* 1 (1913): 255/*Ideas: General Introduction to Pure Phenomenology*, trans. W.R. Boyce Gibson (New York: Collier, 1962), p. 318.

4. "Ernst Cassirer, *Philosophie der symbolischen Formen. 2. Teil: Das mythische Denken*," *Deutsche Literaturzeitung* 21 (1928): 1000–1012/"Review of Ernst Cassirer's *Mythical Thought*," in *The Piety of Thinking: Essays by Martin Heidegger*, ed. and trans. James G. Hart and John C. Maraldo (Bloomington: Indiana University Press), pp. 32–45.

5. Edmund Husserl, *Die Krisis der Europäischen Wissenschaften und die Transzendentale Phänomenologie* (Husserliana VI) (The Hague: Martinus Nijhoff, 1954), p. 209/*The Crisis of European Sciences and Transcendental Phenomenology*, trans. David Carr (Evanston: Northwestern University Press, 1970), p. 205.

6. Jacques Derrida, *La voix et le phénomène: introduction au problème du signe dans la phénoménologie de Husserl* (Paris: Presses Universitaires de France), pp. 10–13/*Speech and Phenomena and Other Essays on Husserl's Theory of Signs*, trans. David B. Allison (Evanston: Northwestern University Press, 1973), pp. 11–13.

Chapter 16

1. See KPM XIV–XVI. KPM overlaps with GA25 (delivered roughly one year before the publication of KPM) more than with any other lecture course. Yet KPM is in no way a carbon copy of GA25. In contrast to a few pages on the subject in KPM, Heidegger devotes several pages in this course to the "Idea of a Transcendental Logic" (B74–88). His examination of the "transcendental clue" (B91–129) ranges over a hundred pages in GA25, but is pared down to roughly twenty pages in KPM. On the other hand, only three concluding and sketchy pages in GA25 are devoted to the *Schematismuslehre*. Its treatment in KPM 85–109 builds upon the more extensive study in WS 1925–26 (GA21 357–415).

2. For a review of Heidegger's decade of Kant studies, see my "Heideggers Kant-Kommentar, 1925–1936," *Philosophisches Jahrbuch* (1989, 2. Halbband): 343–366.

3. Cf. GA21 220–226; GA24 172–218; GA25 315–316, 375; KPM 150–154; and "Von der Typik der reinen praktischen Urteilskraft" in *Kritik der praktischen Vernunft, Akademie Ausgabe* (Berlin: de Gruyter, 1968), pp. 67–70. For a criticism of Heidegger's interpretation of the categorical imperative in the Freiburg lecture course, see my "Seinsvergessenheit oder moralphilosophische Naivität? Heideggers Interpretation der praktischen Philosophie Kants," in Dietrich Papenfuß and Otto Pöggeler (eds.), *Zur philosophischen Aktualität Heideggers, Band 1: Philosophie und Politik* (Frankfurt: Klostermann, 1991), pp. 167–179.

4. The divisions together with the pages listed here and in the outline of the first Kant-course are only approximations, since there is a considerable overlap between them.

5. It should be noted, however, that, in addition to the brief discussion of the schematism chapter and the Analogies of Experience at the end of GA25, the introduction to this course contains an important discussion of the Architectonic at the end of KrV.

6. GA25 417–418: "The productive imagination is the root of the power [*Vermögen*] of subjectivity, it is the basic, ecstatic constitution of the subject, of Dasein itself. Insofar as out of itself, as has been shown, it releases pure time and thus contains pure time in itself as far as the possibility is concerned, it is *the original temporality* and thus the radical power for ontological knowledge."

7. Dieter Henrich, "Die Einheit der Subjektivität," *Philosophische Rundschau* 3 (1955): 28–69. However, Henrich's attempt to link Heidegger and the idealists is unconvincing.

8. Paul Natorp, "Kant und die Marburger Schule," *Kantstudien* XVII (1913): 204f., 219; Hermann Cohen, *Logik der reinen Erkenntnis* (Berlin: Cassirer, 1922), p. 12.

9. Natorp, "Kant und die Marburger Schule," pp. 199–200; Cohen, *Logik der reinen Erkenntnis*, p. 15.

10. Natorp, "Kant und die Marburger Schule," p. 201.

11. Cohen, *Logik der reinen Erkenntnis*, pp. 58f., 80–83.

12. Paul Natorp, *Die logischen Grundlagen der exakten Wissenschaften*, 3d edition (Leipzig: Teubner, 1923), p. 276f.

13. GA21 271; GA25 77; KPM 48; Natorp, *Die logischen Grundlagen der exakten Wissenschaften*, pp. 266–280.

14. That the synthesis is addressed within the "Transcendental Logic" attests, Heidegger observes, to the hold of an ancient, logical prejudice on Kant. In this tradition logic defines the parameters of ontology, conflating the significance of 'being' and 'truth' with true assertions about the present-at-handness of particular beings. See GA25 167.

15. GA25 365: "Thus only from the standpoint of the doctrine of schematism may the present, at first violent interpretation be justified."

16. Fichte, it should be noted, first puzzled over Kant's assumption of a manifold and, in order to explain it, posited an intellectual intuition that posits its own other (*Nicht-Ich*) and thereby engenders a manifold. Roughly a century later, though from a quite different philosophical perspective, a similar adjustment of critical philosophy is urged by Natorp. See Fichte, *Grundriß des Eigentümlichen der Wissenschaftslehre* (1795) in *Werke 1794–1796, Gesamtausgabe I, Band 3*, ed.

Richart Schottky (Stuttgart-Bad Canstatt: Frommann, 1966), p. 145: "That a manifold be given for a possible experience must be proven"; see also 208; as well as
Versuch einer neuen Darstellung der Wissenschaftslehre, pp. 201, 216–220; Schelling, *Vom Ich als Princip der Philosophie* (1795) in *Sämtliche Werke*, Band I (Stuttgart und Augsburg: Cotta, 1856), p. 189 and *Philosophische Briefe über Dogmatis-
mus und Kriticismus* (1795), *dritter Brief*, pp. 294f., 404f. See Natorp, "Kant und
die Marburger Schule," p. 210f. for an acknowledgment that the Marburg school in
a qualified respect has come closer to the "great idealists, especially Hegel."

17. Natorp, *Die logischen Grundlagen der exakten Wissenschaften*, p. 48.

18. In this connection, see Heidegger's occasional references to "the idealism
that follows" (GA21 283) and to "the romantic idealists" (GA21 310f.).

19. Natorp, *Die logischen Grundlagen der exakten Wissenschaften*, p. 268:
"Meanwhile *Kant* does not fail to recognize that time and space are merely 'representations of relations.' He calls them 'pure' intuitions not in the sense of something intuited, data of the intuition, but rather as ways of intuiting."

20. See, however, Klaus Düsing, "Objektive und subjektive Zeit. Untersuchungen zu Kants Zeittheorie und zu ihrer modernen Rezeption," *Kantstudien*
71 (1980): 1–34.

21. From this fact, moreover, it by no means follows that time (and the same
holds for space) is something subjective; see GA21 290f. and the concluding section
of this chapter.

22. GA21 275: "This towards-which of the view [*Worauf des Hinblicks*], which
is constitutive for each order, is, in relation to the manifold of the senses that is
being confronted, the sheer sequence, pure succession—*time*." GA21 277: "Time is
[the] sheer manifold given immediately to itself." GA21 297: "To repeat it once
again—time is accordingly that towards which a view is taken in the process of
the manifold in general letting itself be encountered, as it is accessible through the
inner sense; [in this way time] is entertained unthematically, but it is an unthematic entertaining that proceeds both in advance of and along with the encounter
of the manifold [*das unthematisch vorgängig, mitgängig vorgestellte Worauf des
Hinblicks im Sichbegegnenlassen des Mannigfaltigen überhaupt*]." See also GA21
280–82, 287, 294.

23. In the first Kant-course Heidegger does not make use of Kant's references
to the involvement of imagination in intuition (e.g., A102, B162, note). This short-
coming is somewhat remedied in the second Kant-course. However, even here
(GA25 264f., 272) he insists on a somewhat wooden distinction between three
syntheses: intuitional ("syndosis"), gnoseological (imagination), and intellectual
(understanding), all of which is out of step with Kant's basically organic ("epige-
netic") model of knowing (B167).

24. The two unthematic and coincident, but not identical structures are the

structures of existentiell-hermeneutical understanding ('taking x as notes') and existential-hermeneutical understanding ('taking x as ready-to-hand').

25. Just as *'zurückweichen'* can connote a mere maneuver or a weakness and lack of resolve (consider the difference between the two translations 'pulls back from' and 'retreats from'), so *'schwanken'* can connote a state of honest uncertainty ('wavering') or an impugnable failure of nerve ('vacillating').

26. GA21 401: "The presenting [*Gegenwärtigen*] is, in the first place, the condition of the possibility for the fact that something like 'now' can become explicit as now that, now this." See also SZ 408.

27. While Heidegger credits Kant with approximating an account of the ecstatic and horizonal character of temporality, it remains that of inauthentic temporality. Thus, Heideger characterizes time in its original sense for Kant as "*Gegenwärtigen*" (and not "*Augenblick*"); see SZ 350.

Chapter 17

1. For Heidegger's earliest treatment of the problem of forming categories, see GA1 193ff. As far back as his 1912 investigation "Neuere Forschungen über Logik," Heidegger had treated the issue of defining the categorial formation of sense as developed by Emil Lask and other Neo-Kantians, as well as the implications that a retrieval of Kant's transcendental philosophy held for understanding logic more primordially (GA1 17–34).

2. Cf. Theodore Kisiel, "The Missing Link in the Early Heidegger," in Joseph J. Kockelmans (ed.), *Hermeneutic Phenomenology* (Washington, D.C.: University Press of America, 1988), pp. 1–40. Also see Kisiel's discussion of the three different drafts of Heidegger's magum opus, "Why the First Draft of *Being and Time* Was Never Published," *Journal of the British Society for Phenomenology* 20 (1989): 18–20.

3. For a more detailed discussion of this topic, see my *The Renewal of the Heidegger-Kant Dialogue: Action, Thought, and Responsibility* (Albany: State University of New York Press, 1992). See particularly Chapter II, "The Rift between Judgment and Truth."

4. GA3 156–160, 279–280/*Kant and the Problem of Metaphysics*, trans. Richard Taft (Bloomington: Indiana University Press, 1991), pp. 107–110, 175. Also see one of Heidegger's earliest references to Kant on the issue of ethics in BZ 18. Cf. John van Buren, "The Young Heidegger and Phenomenology," *Man and World* 23 (1990): 247, 251.

5. See GA9 106–112/"What is Metaphysics?," trans. David Farrell Krell in *Basic Writings* (New York: Harper & Row, 1977), pp. 98–104. Heidegger does not simply abandon logic and replace the discipline of systematic thought with a logic

of experience that draws upon the ensemble of meanings housed in factical life. Also see GA63 65ff., 109.

6. Theodore Kisiel, "The Genesis of *Being and Time*," *Man and World* 25 (1992): 23–25.

7. Cf. Theodore Kisiel, "Why Students of Heidegger Will Have to Read Emil Lask," in Deborah G. Chaffin (ed.), *Emil Lask and the Search for Concreteness* (Athens: Ohio University Press, forthcoming). Also see GA2 46/58.

8. See GA9 1–49 and Theodore Kisiel, "On the Way to *Being and Time*," *Research in Phenomenology* 15 (1985): 193–226.

9. Ernst Cassirer, "Remarks on Martin Heidegger's Interpretation of Kant," in Moltke S. Gram (ed.), *Kant: Disputed Questions* (Chicago: Quadrangle Books, 1967), p. 150.

10. For an excellent analysis of this topic, see Daniel Dahlstrom, "Heidegger's Kantian Turn: Notes to His Commentary on the *Kritik der reinen Vernunft*," *Review of Metaphysics* 45 (1991): 337–40.

11. GA 21 392. Also see Walter Biemel's *Nachwort* to that work, 417–18.

12. For an interesting if not different interpretation of this Kantian question, see Jacques Taminiaux, *Heidegger and the Project of Fundamental Ontology*, trans. Michael Gendre (Albany: State University of New York Press, 1991), pp. 69ff.

13. GA25 56. Cf. my discussion "Re-Opening the Issue of World: Heidegger and Kant," *Man and World* 20 (1987): 195–99.

14. David Farrell Krell, *Intimations of Mortality* (University Park: The Pennsylvania State University Press, 1986), p. 58.

15. GA9 164/*The Essence of Reasons*, trans. Terrence Malick (Evanston: Northwestern University Press, 1969), p. 103.

16. GA24 22–24/17–18. As Heidegger states later in his SS 1928 lecture course *The Metaphysical Foundations of Logic*, "being is different than beings, and only this difference in general, this possibility of distinction, insures an understanding of being" (GA26 193/152).

17. GA3 240–41/165. See my "Time as an Afterthought: Differing Views on Imagination," *Philosophy Today* 36 (1992): 76–86. For a discussion of how the entirety of Heidegger's thought can be developed as an inquiry into imagination, see John Sallis, *Echoes: After Heidegger* (Bloomington: Indiana University Press, 1991), pp. 97–117.

18. For an account of this "aberration" theory, see John van Buren, "The Young Heidegger: Rumor of a Hidden King (1919–1926)," *Philosophy Today* 33 (1989): 103–104.

19. GA31 300. Cf. my discussion of this thesis in "Heidegger on Kant: Fron-

tiers Extended," *Research in Phenomenology* XV (1985): 259–67; also see GA26 199/157. For an account of the relation between the ethical question and the task of retrieving the issue of imagination, see the concluding section in my *The Renewal of the Heidegger-Kant Dialogue*, pp. 383–97.

20. Cf. note 18 above. See Rudolf A. Makkreel, *Imagination and Interpretation in Kant: The Hermeneutic Import of the Third Critique* (Chicago: The University of Chicago Press, 1990), pp. 21–22, 166–67. Also see Makkreel, "The Genesis of Heidegger's Phenomenological Hermeneutics and the Rediscovered 'Aristotle Introduction' of 1922," *Man and World* 23 (1990): 306–16.

Chapter 18

1. Theodore Kisiel, *"Kriegsnotsemester* 1919: Heidegger's Hermeneutic Breakthrough," *Proceedings of the Twenty-fourth Annual Heidegger Conference* (1990, unpublished). See now his *The Genesis of Heidegger's BEING AND TIME* (Berkeley/Los Angeles/London: The University of California Press, 1993), chap. 1.

2. See *The Young Heidegger: Rumor of the Hidden King* (Bloomington: Indiana University Press, 1994). See the article by the same name that sketches van Buren's views in *Philosophy Today* 33 (1989): 99–108; and "The Young Heidegger and Phenomenology," *Man and World* 23 (1990): 239–72.

3. Soren Kierkegaard, *Philosophical Fragments*, trans. H. Hong & E. Hong (Princeton: Princeton University Press, 1985), pp. 107–108; *Repetition*, in *Repetition and Fear and Trembling*, trans. H. Hong & E. Hong (Princeton: Princeton University Press, 1983), pp. 131–33. For a full analysis of this conception of repetition, see my *Radical Hermeneutics: Repetition, Deconstruction and the Hermeneutic Project* (Bloomington: Indiana University Press, 1987).

4. On Heidegger's militarism, see Theodore Kisiel, "Heidegger's Apology: Biography as Philosophy and Ideology," *Graduate Faculty Philosophy Journal* 14–15 (1990–91): 363–404.

5. The commentary on this text is to be found in the forthcoming GA60: *Augustinus und der Neuplatonismus*. See also Kisiel, *The Genesis of BEING AND TIME*, chap. 4.

6. Alasdair MacIntyre, *After Virtue: A Study in Moral Theory* (Notre Dame: University of Notre Dame Press, 1981), pp. 169–74.

7. I Cor. 1: 26–29. See the illuminating exegesis of this text in Jean-Luc Marion, *Dieu sans l'être* (Paris: Fayard, 1982), pp. 124–57.

8. Heidegger, *An Introduction to Metaphysics*, trans. R. Manheim (Yale University Press, 1959), p. 133.

9. See Jacques Derrida, *The Ear of the Other*, trans. Peggy Kamuf (New York: Schocken, 1985), pp. 23–24, note.

10. It should not be lost sight of that the root of *phronesis* is *phren*, the heart, midriff or diaphragm, which in Homer was taken to be the seat of the soul, of both feeling and thinking. But Plato and Aristotle follow a Pythagorean tradition, which located the seat of thought in the brain; for them the word *phronesis* had a more noetic force. Heidegger gave passing notice to Aristotelian *synesis* (understanding what someone else says), which he evidently translated as *"Rücksicht"* ("considerateness") and *syngnome* (forgiveness: *Nicomachean Ethics*, VI, 11), which he translated as *"Nachsicht"* ("forbearance"); see GA2 164/159. But even these Aristotelian virtues were directed at a closed circle of equals and were nothing like the radical biblical virtues of serving the outcast and lowliest.

11. *Summa Theologica*, I–II, Q. 65.

12. "Dasein in Heidegger is never hungry." Emmanuel Levinas, *Totality and Infinity*, trans. A. Lingis (Pittsburgh: Duquesne University Press, 1969), p. 134.

13. See Sander Gilman, *Disease and Representation: Images of Illness from Madness to AIDS* (Ithaca: Cornell University Press, 1988).

14. Elaine Scarry, *The Body in Pain: The Making and Unmaking of the World* (Oxford: Oxford University Press, 1985). See especially Scarry's treatment of torture.

15. Frederick Nietzsche, *Ecce Homo*, trans. R. J. Hollingdale (Baltimore: Penguin Books, 1979), p. 41.

16. See above, n. 2.

17. I can only summarize here certain ideas that I developed more fully in "Heidegger's *Kampf*: The Difficulty of Life," *Graduate Faculty Philosophy Journal* 14–15 (1990–91): 61–83.

18. Michael Zimmerman, *Heidegger's Confrontation with Modernity: Technology, Politics, Art* (Bloomington: Indiana University Press, 1990), chs. 4–5.

19. Ernst Jünger, *Werke*, Bd. 5, *Essays I* (Stuttgart: Klett, n.d.), p. 151.

20. Here I summarize an idea I develop more fully in "Heidegger's Revolution: An Introduction to *An Introduction to Metaphysics*," forthcoming in *Heidegger in the Thirties*, ed. James Risser, (State University of New York Press).

21. On the Trakl reading, see my "Thinking, Poetry and Pain," *The Southern Journal of Philosophy* 27 (Supplement) (1990): 155–82. On essentialization, see my "Incarnation and Essentialism: A Reading of Heidegger," *Philosophy Today* 35 (1991): 32–42. On the "scandals," see my "Heidegger's Scandal," *The Heidegger Case: Philosophy and Politics*, ed. Joseph Margolis and Tom Rockmore (Philadelphia: Temple University Press, 1992), pp. 265–281.

22. See *Kierkegaard's Writings*, VI, *Fear and Trembling and Repetition*, trans. Howard and Edna Hong (Princeton: Princeton University Press, 1983), p. 7.

Chapter 19

1. This text is an updated self-translation of a paper that originally appeared under the title "Das junghegelianische und ethische Motiv in Heideggers Hermeneutik der Faktizität," in I. M. Fehér (ed.), *Wege und Irrwege des neueren Umgangs mit Heideggers Werk* (Berlin: Duncker & Humbolt, 1991).

2. See E. Levinas, "L'ontologie est-elle fondamentale?" *Revue de Métaphysique et de Morale* 56 (1951): 88–98, which formed the starting point of his *Totalité et infini. Essai sur l'extériorité* (The Hague: Martinus Nijhoff, 1961, 4th ed., 1984).

3. Compare the observations (influenced by Levinas) of Robert Bernasconi, "Habermas and Arendt on the Philosopher's 'Error': Tracking the Diabolical in Heidegger," *Graduate Faculty Philosophy Journal* 14–15 (1991): 3–24, especially p. 3: "The scandal arising from Heidegger's political involvement with Nazism and from his postwar silence on the holocaust refuses to go away, but the evident glee of Heidegger's philosophical opponents in the consequent damage to his reputation is misjudged. It is not only Heidegger, both the man and his thought, who is diminished by the whole affair, but also, and perhaps primarily, philosophy itself."

4. *De l'esprit* (Paris: Galilée, 1987).

5. See my "Prolegomena to an Understanding of Heidegger's Turn," *Graduate Faculty Philosophy Journal* 14–15 (1991): 85–108.

6. *Wegmarken* (Frankfurt: Klostermann, 2nd ed., 1978), p. 353.

7. See his letter of August 19, 1921 to Karl Löwith in D. Pappenfuss and O. Pöggeler (eds.), *Zur philosophischen Aktualität Heideggers*, vol. 2 (Frankfurt: Klostermann, 1990), p. 29.

8. GA63. On the anything but accidental combination of ontology and hermeneutics in this programmatic title, see my "Die Hermeneutik der Faktizität als ontologische Destruktion und Ideologiekritik," in Papenfuss and Pöggeler, *Zur philosophischen Aktualität Heideggers*, pp. 163–78.

9. GA31: *Vom Wesen der menschlichen Freiheit. Einleitung in die Philosophie*.

10. See the contributions of C.F. Gethmann and G. Prauss in A. Gethmann-Siefert and O. Pöggeler (eds.), *Heidegger und die praktische Philosophie* (Frankfurt: Suhrkamp, 1988).

11. For this reading of hermeneutics, compare C.F. Gethmann, *Verstehen und Auslegung. Das Methodenproblem in der Philosophie Martin Heideggers* (Bonn:

Bouvier, 1974), p. 117; and R. Thurnher, "Hermeneutik und Verstehen in Heideggers Sein und Zeit," *Salzburger Jahrbuch für Philosophie* 28–29 (1984): 107.

12. Though it was more prevalent in the early lecture courses, the expression *Selbstdurchsichtigkeit* also appears here and there in *Sein und Zeit* (compare 144/183, 146/186). On the importance of this notion in Heidegger's earliest period, see H.-G. Gadamer, "Heideggers 'theologische' Jugendschrift," *Dilthey-Jahrbuch* 6 (1989): 232; and his "Heidegger und die Griechen," in D. Pappenfuss and O. Pöggeler (eds.), *Zur philosophischen Aktualität Heideggers*, vol. 1 (Frankfurt: Klostermann, 1991), p. 62.

13. *Wegmarken*, p. 336.

14. GA21 410; cf. GA63 80. That Heidegger retained this notion of formal indication after *Sein und Zeit* is confirmed by the lecture course of WS 1929–30 (GA29/30 421–35).

15. "Anmerkungen zu Karl Jaspers 'Psychologie der Weltanschauungen,'" in *Wegmarken*, p. 32.

16. See O. Pöggeler, "Heideggers Begegnung mit Dilthey," *Dilthey-Jahrbuch* 4 (1986–87): 134. Compare Gadamer, "Heidegger und die Griechen," p. 70: "What is at issue is really not to repeat Heidegger's language. Heidegger always struggled resolutely against this. He was in the beginning so very conscious of the dangers of such repetition that he called the essence of philosophical expressions precisely 'formal indication.' By this he intended to say: In thinking one can at most point out the direction. But one must open one's eyes on one's own. Only then will one find the language which says what one sees."

17. Here I am following a suggestion of Manfred Riedel in his "Seinsverständnis und Sinn für das Tunliche. Der hermeneutische Weg zur 'Rehabilitierung der praktischen Philosophie,'" in *Hören auf die Sprache. Die akroamatische Dimension der Hermeneutik* (Frankfurt: Suhrkamp, 1990), pp. 131–62.

18. "Grußwort an die Teilnehmer des zehnten Colloquiums vom 14.–16. Mai 1976 in Chicago," *Jahresgabe der Martin-Heidegger-Gesellschaft* (1989): 13.

19. "Anruf an die Deutschen Studenten (3. Nov. 1933)," in B. Martin (ed.), *Martin Heidegger und das 'Dritte Reich'* (Darmstadt: Wissenschaftliche Buchgesellschaft, 1989), p. 177.

20. See I.M. Fehér, "Fundamental Ontology and Political Interlude: Heidegger as Rector of the University of Freiburg," in M. Dascal and O. Gruengard (eds.), *Knowledge and Politics: Case Studies in the Relationship Between Epistemology and Political Philosophy* (San Francisco: Westview Press, 1989), pp. 316–51.

Chapter 20

1. Alois Bernt and Konrad Burdach, eds., *Der Ackermann aus Böhmen* (Berlin: Weidmannsche Buchhandlung, 1917), pp. 3, 45–46. Heidegger refers to lines 19–20 of chap. 20 in SZ 245. For the larger context of the piece, see Part One of my book, *Daimon Life: Heidegger and Life-Philosophy* (Bloomington: Indiana University Press, 1992).

2. See Jacques Derrida, *De l'esprit: Heidegger et la question* (Paris: Galilée, 1987), pp. 38–42, on (at least) three types of such indifference; English translation by Geoffrey Bennington and Rachel Bowlby, *Of Spirit: Heidegger and the Question* (Chicago: University of Chicago Press, 1989), see pp. 19–22.

3. Nietzsche, *Der Wille zur Macht*, no. 582; see the *Kritische Studienausgabe* (Berlin and Munich: Walter de Gruyter and DTV, 1980), *12*, 153 (cited in the body of my text at StA); see Heidegger's *Nietzsche*, 2 vols. (Pfullingen: G. Neske, 1961), I, 518; see the second, revised edition of the English translation of Heidegger's *Nietzsche* (San Francisco: Harper Collins, 1991), *3*, 40. See also Jacques Derrida, "Interpreting Signatures (Nietzsche/Heidegger: Two Questions)," in Diane P. Michelfelder and Richard E. Palmer, eds., *Dialogue and Deconstruction: The Gadamer-Derrida Encounter* (Albany: State University of New York Press, 1989), pp. 58–71.

4. On Dilthey's conception of "life," see the introductory remarks by the editor of the *Gesammelte Schriften*, H. Nohl, remarks that were extremely important for Heidegger; see esp. vol. V, *Die Geistige Welt: Einleitung in die Philosophie des Lebens, Erste Hälfte* (Leipzig: Teubner, 1924), pp. LII–LV. The importance of Dilthey and of *Lebensphilosophie* in general for the gestation of Heidegger's *Being and Time* has recently been underscored by a series of excellent essays by Frithjof Rodi, Otto Pöggeler, Friedrich Hogemann, Christoph Jamme, Carl Friedrich Gethmann, and Theodore Kisiel in the *Dilthey-Jahrbuch für Philosophie und Geschichte der Geisteswissenschaften*, vol. IV, ed. Frithjof Rodi (Göttingen: Vandenhoeck & Ruprecht, 1986–1987), passim. See also the helpful review of this volume by Jacob Owensby in *Research in Phenomenology* XIX (1989): 311–15.

5. Published by J. C. B. Mohr (Paul Siebeck) in Tübingen in 1920. Heidegger refers to the second edition, published in 1922; see esp. p. 194.

6. See SZ 126 on taking-one's-distance, *Abständigkeit*, as the principal existential characterization of everyday being-with.

7. Thus Derrida, in "Geschlecht I: différence sexuelle, différence ontologique," in *Psyché: Inventions de l'autre* (Paris: Galilée, 1987), p. 398; English translation in *Research in Phenomenology* XIII (1983): 68.

8. Martin Heidegger, *Was heißt Denken?* (Tübingen: M. Niemeyer, 1954), pp. 6–7.

9. See GA29/30 §61, esp. 376–78, for *Genommenheit, Hingenommenheit, Eingenommenheit*, and *Benommenheit*.

10. Martin Heidegger, "Dichterisch wohnt der Mensch . . . ," in *Vorträge und Aufsätze* (Pfullingen: G. Neske, 1954), pp. 195–96.

11. Henry David Thoreau, *Walden*, the Variorum Edition, Walter Harding, ed. (New York: Washington Square, 1968), pp. 17–18, for this and the following.

12. See, for example, *Nietzsche*, I, 249–50, 465–66, and 636; Engl. trans., *1*, 216–17; *2*, 200–201; and *3*, 140.

13. See GA61 62–76, the most important pages we have in Heidegger's early writings for his attitudes concerning the university—and his own life in it. I have commented on these themes in Part III of chapter 4 of *Daimon Life*, "You in front of Me, I in front of You: Heidegger in the University of Life."

14. Heidegger continues to use the word *Darbung* through the first draft of *Being and Time*, although it disappears from his magnum opus. See GA20 408/295.

Chapter 21

1. The text of the lecture course *Prolegomena zur Geschichte des Zeitbegriffs* (GA20), presented in the semester just preceding that in which *Logik* was presented, is the penultimate draft of *Sein und Zeit*.

2. "Evidenz ist vielmehr nichts anderes als das 'Erlebnis' der Wahrheit" (Edmund Husserl, *Logische Untersuchungen* [Tübingen: Max Niemeyer, 1968], 1: 190).

3. Heidegger notes that Hegel's logic seems to break through this idea of knowing as intuition, but he insists that this is mere seeming, semblance. No doubt it is because the case of Hegel is less apparent that Heidegger turns to it only after the unity of the history has been established. The very brief remarks to which he limits himself hardly suffice to enclose Hegel decisively within that history. To suggest that there is a moment in Hegel's thought that breaks the bond to presence and to intuition taken as correlate of presence, it suffices to cite the following passage from Hegel's *Wissenschaft der Logik*: "One can easily perceive that in absolute clearness one sees just as much, and as little, as in absolute darkness, that the one seeing is as good as the other, that pure seeing is a seeing of nothing. Pure light and pure darkness are two voids which are the same. Something can be distinguished only in determinate light or darkness . . ." (Volume 21 of *Gesammelte Werke* [Hamburg: Felix Meiner, 1985], 80). In the SS 1923 lecture course *Hermeneutik der Faktizität*, Heidegger is even less receptive to a radical moment in Hegel's thought: "All dialectic really lives always on what it takes from the table of others. The illuminating example: Hegel's *Logic*. . . . The dialectic is bilaterally nonradical, i.e., basically unphilosophical. It has to live from hand to mouth . . ." (GA63 45f.).

4. The project is sketched as a whole as early as July 1924 in the lecture that Heidegger gave to the Marburger *Theologenschaft*: *Der Begriff der Zeit* (BZ).

5. See especially the discussion in which knowing the world is exhibited as a founded mode of Being-in-the-world (SZ §13).

6. *Nietzsche*, Bd. I (Pfullingen: Günther Neske, 1965), pp. 176, 188. It is imperative to note that Heidegger's enclosing of Nietzsche's thought within the very Platonism that Nietzsche sought to overcome is only one moment in Heidegger's interpretation, a moment along with which one ought to mark, with Heidegger and perhaps more extensively than Heidegger, the moment of Nietzsche's twisting free (*Herausdrehung*) of Platonism (see p. 242). I have proposed to mark this latter moment also in Nietzsche's early work (see *Crossings: Nietzsche and the Space of Tragedy* [Chicago: University of Chicago Press, 1991], especially 1–8).

7. *Holzwege*, GA5 55.

Chapter 22

1. *Was heisst Denken?* (Tübingen: Niemeyer, 1954), p. 161/*What is Called Thinking?*, tr. Fred D. Wieck and J. Glenn Gray (New York: Harper & Row, 1972), p. 160. Hereafter cited as WhD. Throughout this chapter, I have used existing translations where possible, modified as necessary to suit the context.

2. For a discussion of the end of philosophy and the end of *Being and Time*, see John Sallis, "End(s)," *Research in Phenomenology* XIII (1983): 85–96.

3. Note that in the SS 1925 lecture course the term *discoveredness* (*Entdecktheit*) corresponds to what is called *disclosedness* (*Erschlossenheit*) in *Being and Time*, and refers to the openness of Dasein as opposed to that of intraworldly beings. Cf. the footnote on GA20 349/253.

4. Cf. SZ §1, "The necessity of an explicit retrieval of the question concerning Being," where Heidegger concludes: "To retrieve the question of Being thus means: first adequately working out the *posing* of the question [*die Fragestellung*]."

5. Note that the first, untitled page of *Being and Time* identifies this goal—a "precursory" (*vorläufiges*) goal!—as "the interpretation of time."

6. Indeed, Heidegger straightaway appeals to a metaphorics of spatiality: "The working out of the posing of the question is the prior experience and explication of the questioning being itself—of the Dasein that we ourselves are. At issue is a being to which we have the exceptional, or in any case remarkable relation of Being that we ourselves are it—a being that is only insofar as I in each case am it. It is therefore a matter of a being that is nearest to us. But is it also what is given as nearest? In this respect it is perhaps what is most distant. . . ." (GA20 201–202/149)

7. It is not by chance, indeed, that this certainty is seen to go hand in hand with a peculiar indeterminacy, an indeterminacy that is *temporal*. See SZ §52, 258/302: "Along with the certainty of death goes the *indeterminacy* of its 'when.'"

8. See SZ §9, 43/69. On the question of indifference, cf. my remarks "On the Concreteness of Heidegger's Thinking," *Philosophy Today* 36 (1992): 83–94.

9. Since this essay was written, two articles have appeared which deal with the question of formally indicative concepts. See Th.C.W. Oudemans, "*Heideggers 'logische Untersuchungen,*'" *Heidegger Studies* VI: 85ff.; and R.J.A. van Dijk, "*Grundbegriffe der Metaphysik. Zur formalanzeigenden Struktur der philosophischen Begriffe bei Heidegger,*" *Heidegger Studies* VII: 89ff..

10. See especially GA26 §10, 175–77/139–41. Note that in the Appendix to this section, Heidegger identifies *Verwandlung* with the retrieval (*Wiederholung*) and destructuring (*Destruktion*) of the tradition.

11. Cf. David Farrell Krell, "Death and Interpretation" in F. Elliston (ed.), *Heidegger's Existential Analytic* (Mouton: New York, 1978), pp. 247–55. The concept of death is merely preliminary because it is intrinsically bound up with the formally indicative structure of mineness ("death is . . . in each case essentially mine" [SZ 240/284]). Yet in the phenomenon of Dasein's being toward death, its 'running ahead,' death will show itself as nothing individual, but rather as the very *horizon* of individuation, in a word: transcendence. It is doubtless significant that precisely in the context of the analysis of death Heidegger is drawn to remark upon the "peculiar *formality* and emptiness of all ontological characterization" (248/292). The issue of *formality* is related to the problem of the regulative nature of the concepts in Kant's critical project. Indeed in *The Fundamental Concepts of Metaphysics* (GA29/30), when discussing the formally indicative nature of metaphysical concepts, Heidegger comments explicitly on Kant's analysis of dialectical illusion in the *Critique of Pure Reason*. Preeminently problematic among these formal concepts is, of course, the concept of freedom. Note that Heidegger also relates the phenomenon of 'running ahead' to the formal nature of Kantian ethics in his 1924 lecture "The Concept of Time" (BZ).

12. Regarding the way in which Heidegger's later thinking may nonetheless be said to preserve a hermeneutic character, see F.-W. von Herrmann, *Weg und Methode. Zur hermeneutischen Phänomenologie des seinsgeschichtlichen Denkens* (Frankfurt: Klostermann, 1990).

13. Cf. "Summary of a Seminar on 'Time and Being,'" which identifies precursiveness with the *step back* and with the finitude of thinking (SD 38/35).

14. See SZ 419/472, as well as GA24 463/325: "*Earlier than every possible earlier* of any kind is *time*, because it is the fundamental condition of any earlier in general." Cf. GA26 184/146: "Earlier than every possible 'earlier than' is, however, time!" Time itself is thereby intimated as what is earlier in the most radical sense: so radical as to make a non-sense—a withdrawal or lack of sense, of meaning, of horizon—of the discourse that would attempt to say it *as* such.

Contributors

JEFFREY ANDREW BARASH teaches as a Maître de Conférences in the Philosophy Department at the Université de Picardie in Amiens, France. He is the author of *Martin Heidegger and the Problem of Historical Meaning* (1988) and *Temps de l'Etre, temps de l'histoire. Heidegger et son siècle* (forthcoming).

ROBERT BERNASCONI is Moss Professor of Philosophy at Memphis State University. He is the author of *The Question of Language in Heidegger's History of Being, Heidegger in Question*, and *Between Derrida and Levinas* (forthcoming). He is editor of *The Relevance of the Beautiful and Other Essays, Derrida and Difference, The Provocation of Levinas*, and *Re-Reading Levinas*.

RUDOLF BERNET is Ordinary Professor of Philosophy at the University of Leuven and a member of the Board of Directors of the Husserl-Archives. He has edited texts by Husserl, translated texts by Derrida, and written numerous articles on Husserl, Heidegger, Merleau-Ponty, Derrida, Freud, and Lacan. He is the author of *Introduction to Husserlian Phenomenology* (1992) in collaboration with I. Kern and E. Marbach.

WALTER BROGAN is Associate Professor at Villanova University. He has written several articles on contemporary Continental interpretations of Greek philosophy and on Nietzsche, Heidegger, and Derrida.

JOHN D. CAPUTO, David R. Cook Professor of Philosophy, Villanova University, is the author of *Against Ethics* (1993), *Demythologizing Heidegger* (1993), *Foucault and the Critique of Institutions* (co-editor, 1993), *Modernity and its Discontents* (co-author, 1992), *Radical Hermeneutics* (1987), *Heidegger and Aquinas* (1982), *The Mystical Element in Heidegger's Thought* (1978). He currently serves as Executive Codirector of the Society for Phenomenology and Existential Philosophy.

STEVEN GALT CROWELL, Associate Professor of Philosophy and Humanities at Rice University, is the author of several articles on figures and issues in the phenomenological tradition. He is currently working on a book-length reassessment of Heidegger's transcendental philosophy.

DANIEL O. DAHLSTROM, Professor of Philosophy at The Catholic University of America, is the author of *Das logische Vorurteil* (1993). He has published widely on a variety of philosophical themes, but with particular focus on the thought of Kant, Hegel, and Heidegger.

ISTVÁN M. FEHÉR is Professor of Philosophy at Budapest University. He is the author of books on Sartre and Heidegger, as well as articles on Lukács, Popper, Croce, phenomenology, hermeneutics, and German Idealism. He is the editor of *Wege und Irrwege des neueren Umganges mit Heideggers Werk* (1991).

HANS-GEORG GADAMER is Professor Emeritus of Philosophy at the University of Heidelberg in Germany. Among his many writings on Heidegger, which are gathered in his *Gesammelte Werke* (1985ff.), is *Heideggers Wege. Studien zum Spätwerk*.

JEAN GRONDIN is Professor of Philosophy at the University of Montréal. His book publications are *Hermeneutische Wahrheit? Zum Wahrheitsbegriff Hans-Georg Gadamers* (1982); *Le tournant dans la pensée de Martin Heidegger* (1987); *Kant et le problème de la philosophie: l'a priori* (1989); *Emmanuel Kant. Avant/Après* (1991); *Einführung in die philosophische Hermeneutik* (1991).

THEODORE KISIEL is Professor of Philosophy at Northern Illinois University. He is the author of *The Genesis of Heidegger's Being and Time* (1993) and (with J. Kockelmans) *Phenomenology and the Natural Sciences* (1970). In addition, he is the author of numerous articles in English and in German on philosophy of science and hermeneutic philosophy.

GEORGE KOVACS is Professor of Philosophy at Florida International University. He is the author of *The Question of God in Heidegger's Phenomenology* (1990), as well as numerous articles on continental philosophy.

DAVID FARRELL KRELL is Professor of Philosophy at DePaul University. He is the author of *Daimon Life: Heidegger and Life-Philosophy* (1992); *Of Memory, Reminiscence, and Writing: On the Verge* (1990); *Intimations of Mortality: Time, Truth, and Finitude in Heidegger's Thinking of Being* (2nd ed., 1991); *Postponements: Woman, Sensuality, and Death in Nietzsche* (1986). He is editor and translator of a wide range of books and articles by Heidegger, including *Basic Writings*, *Nietzsche*, and *Early Greek Thinking*, all now in their second, revised editions.

DANIEL MAGURSHAK teaches at Carthage College. He is co-translator of *Martin Heidegger's Path of Thinking* by Otto Pöggeler.

WILL MCNEILL is Assistant Professor of Philosophy at DePaul University. He has published a number of articles on Heidegger's work, and is the translator of Heidegger's 1924 lecture *The Concept of Time* (1992), as well as co-translator of Heidegger's 1929–30 lecture course *The Fundamental Concepts of Metaphysics: World—Finitude—Solitude* (1994).

TH.C.W. OUDEMANS is Professor Extraordinarius in contemporary philosophy at the Rijks Universiteit Leiden. In 1987 he published, together with A. Lardinois, *Tragic Ambiguity: Anthropology, Philosophy, and Sophocles' Antigone*. He has also published an essay on formal indication in *Heidegger Studies* (1990).

OTTO PÖGGELER is Professor of Philosophy at the Ruhr-Universität Bochum and the Director of the Hegel-Archiv. Among his publications are *Neue Wege mit Heidegger* (1992), *Der Denkweg Martin Heideggers* (3rd ed., 1990), *Die Frage nach der Kunst. Von Hegel zu Heidegger* (1984), *Heidegger und die hermeneutische Philosophie* (1983), and *Philosophie und Politik bei Heidegger* (2nd ed., 1974).

JOHN PROTEVI teaches philosophy at Villanova University. He is the author of several articles on Heidegger, Derrida, and Levinas, as well as the forthcoming *Time and Exteriority: Aristotle, Heidegger, and Derrida*.

FRANÇOIS RENAUD is a doctoral candidate at the University of Tübingen. His work is centered on Gadamer, Heidegger, and Greek thought.

JOHN SALLIS is W. Alton Jones Professor of Philosophy at Vanderbilt University. Among his many books are *Being and Logos: The Way of Platonic Dialogue* (1975, 1986), *The Gathering of Reason* (1980), *Delimitations* (1986), *Spacings—of Reason and Imagination* (1987), *Echoes: After Heidegger* (1990), and *Crossings: Nietzsche and the Space of Tragedy* (1991).

FRANK SCHALOW has served as Associate Professor at Loyola University, New Orleans, and has been Visiting Professor at Tulane University. He is the author of *The Renewal of the Heidegger-Kant Dialogue* (1992) and *Imagination and Existence* (1986), as well as co-author of *Traces of Understanding* (1990).

P. CHRISTOPHER SMITH received his Ph.D. in 1966 after five years of study with H.-G. Gadamer in Heidelberg. He has translated three of Gadamer's books for Yale University Press, and has published numerous articles on Heidegger and on Gadamer. His book *Hermeneutics and Human Finitude: Toward a Theory of Ethical Understanding* appeared in 1991.

JACQUES TAMINIAUX is Professor of Philosophy at Boston College and at the University of Louvain-la-Neuve, where he is the director of the Center for Phenomenological Studies. Among his numerous publications on Heidegger are *Dialectic and Difference* (1985) and *Heidegger and the Project of Fundamental Ontology* (1991).

JOHN VAN BUREN is Assistant Professor at Fordham University. He is the author of *The Young Heidegger: Rumor of the Hidden King* (1994) and translator of Martin Heidegger, *Ontology (Hermeneutics of Facticity)* (1995).

FRANCO VOLPI is Professor of Philosophy at the University of Padua and the University of Witten/Herdecke. His major publications are *Heidegger e Brentano* (1976), *La rinascita della filosofia practica in Germania* (1980), and *Heidegger e Aristotele* (1984). He is Director of the programme for the translation of Heidegger's works at Adelphi Press in Milan.

Name Index

(compiled by Donald A. Ringelestein and Theodore Kisiel)

Subject Index

(compiled by Donald A. Ringelestein and Theodore Kisiel)

Absence, 11, 39, 40, 156, 165, 180, 227, 233, 259, 261, 270, 306, 320

Absorption, 26, 319, 320

aei on (enduring being), 222, 225

Affection, 12, 14, 206, 246, 248, 265, 267, 296, 313, 316

aletheia (truth), 11, 31, 98, 124, 152, 198–199, 217, 227, 337, 391

Analytic of Dasein, 6, 50, 78, 215, 220, 277, 393–395, 401, 404, 406

anamnesis (recollection), 145, 329

Anxiety, 12, 142–144, 146, 147, 163–165, 170, 184, 263–267, 280, 286, 336, 337, 339, 362, 378; as phenomenological reduction, 256, 263–264, 287; dread, 170, 185

Apollinian, 29, 138, 152, 153, 413

Apophantic, 27, 199, 218, 223, 224, 272, 273; "as", 149–150

Apperception, 250, 252, 296, 297, 301, 307, 308

A priori, 58–59, 182, 259, 276–281, 298, 301, 313, 376, 387, 444 n. 2; Kant's sense of, 397–308 *passim*, 310, 313–317

Art, 16, 21, 91, 111, 341, 391

"As" structure, 402, 403

atopia, 260, 264; *a-topos*, 261; no-place, 40, 144, 259, 279

Augenblick, 46, 51, 144, 154, 163, 208. *See also* Moment

Becoming a Christian, 10, 175, 182, 184, 190, 191

Bedeutung (signification of signs), 196, 270, 273, 277, 278, 280, 286

Befindlichkeit (finding oneself disposed), 205–208, 265, 267, 336, 338

Beginning, start: in facticity, 327; first and another, 2, 29–32, 341–343, 393–394, 400–408, 436 n.2; genuine, 171–173; of Heidegger's ways, 1–7, 22, 28; as onset (*Ansatz*), 16, 393–394, 405–406; of philosophy, 127–128, 136, 365–366; of questioning, 401, 404; theological, 2, 9, 159–160

Being: analogy of, 140, 179, 248; as (constant, permanent) presence, 4, 7, 117, 130, 149, 151, 237–239, 244, 321, 328–331, 334, 345; language of, 3, 5; as living, 363–364, 368; and nothing, 149–152, 222; as primal something (*Ur-etwas*), 179–180, 189; is said in many ways, 15, 197; as temporal movement, transition, 142–156, 180–183, 328; and value, 98. *See also* History of being, Question of being

Being-in-the-world, 29, 32, 43, 117, 146, 147, 149, 180, 243, 256, 257, 263, 265, 280, 285, 311, 314, 327, 333–335, 338, 339, 349, 390

Beiträge zur Philosophie (*Contributions to Philosophy*), 19, 26, 27, 29, 138, 150, 153, 350, 366, 414, 430, 436

Bewandtnis (appliance), 421 n.17; conjuncture, 279–280; "how matters stand," 259; as human relevance, 6, 416 n. 4; order, 63–65, 67, 70–71; purposiveness, 264

Bezugssinn (relational sense), 44, 161, 162, 165, 168, 180, 183–184, 187, 372–376. See *Gehaltssinn*

Boredom, 5, 47–52

Can-be (*Seinkönnen*), 147, 206, 208, 256, 280, 281, 286, 287, 289, 314, 334, 349, 354

Time-consciousness, 239–244, 277; absolute
flow of, 12, 231, 241–244, 449 n. 49
To-be (*Zu-sein*), 15, 180, 203–206, 208,
265, 347, 354.*See also* Can-be
Trace (*Spur*), 1, 6, 156, 266, 284
Tradition, 8, 36, 91, 94, 103, 113, 115–120,
123–130, 132–136, 138, 142, 144, 322
Transcendence, 13, 14, 58, 65, 69, 131, 180,
187, 234, 236, 243, 246, 257, 275–277,
284, 308, 310, 313, 316, 318
Transcendental aesthetic, 68, 292–296,
299–302, 305, 450 n.50
Transcendental subject (-ivity, consciousness, ego), 24, 73, 85, 88, 199, 200, 245–
254, 256, 258, 284–286; difference in its
being, 266–267; its solipsism, 254
Transcendentals, 14, 55
Truth, 5–6, 260, 263–267, 273, 295, 445–
446; as adequation, correctness, correspondence, 6, 31, 58–59, 65, 198, 309,
446; across time, 11, 213–214, 216–227,
321–322; as *aletheia*, 11, 31, 124, 198–
199, 217, 391; as constancy of validity,
55–59, 61–72, 97–98, 232–234; doubling
of, 16, 390–391; in human sciences, 116–
119; integral with untruth, 267; as intentional identity, 59, 65, 220, 233–235,
385, 390; intuitive, 198, 220–221, 385–
387; as kind of (ideal) being, 57, 66, 197,
232, 235, 446 n. 18; (not) of knowledge,
16, 381–391; locus of, 11, 197–200, 273,
385, 389; in logic, 55–59, 232–234, 381;
as opening, 46, 51, 103, 163, 187, 263,
399, 400; its origin in disclosedness, 16,
310, 341, 390; propositional (assertional)
truth, 149, 198–201, 214, 220–227, 232–
235, 381, 385, 390; as unconcealment,
11, 216, 226–227, 320
Turning (*Kehre*), 5, 25–29, 341, 346; as circle, 27; as going back, 27

Umgang (going about), 216, 387
Understanding, 286, 349, 363; as can-be
206; equiprimordial, 162, 205–208; ethical, 355; grounds sight, 388; intuitive,
142, 384; practical, 207; as *phronesis*,
162; prereflective, 181, 183, 226, 306;
primitive, 282; as self-determination, 206;
self-referential, 181, 416; self-u., 349–
350; situational, 162, 348–349; as *sophia*,
219; as *Vollzugssinn*, 187; time, 211
Understanding of being, 26, 312, 315–316,
318–321; categorial intuition becomes,
12, 286; which we live, 226, 363; prereflective spiral, 181; pregiven preunderstanding, 395–403; primitive, 282–283;
as transcendence, 276–277
Untruth, 143, 266, 267

Vollzugssinn (actualizing, enactment-, ful-
fillment-sense), 5, 161, 162, 165, 168,
180, 183–184, 187, 372–376. *See also*
Zeitigungssinn

Whole, on the (as a): versus totality, 29,
48–51; evokes astonishment and boredom, 29, 48–51
World, 26, 187, 192; as dispersion, 372; as
openness, 48; as familiar environment
(*Umwelt*), 43–44, 50, 101, 216, 247, 256;
258–263, 278–282, 371, 384, 387–388; as
horizon, 51, 258, 369; life's relation to,
369–378; as nothing, 288, 290; phenomenologically reduced, 245–267; self-, 160,
184, 371, 374 as totality of beings, 43–45
Worldview, 7, 93–95, 112, 142, 365, 375

Zeitigungssinn (temporalizing sense), 161,
181, 187, 370–373. *See also Bezugssinn*